Who Was Who in the

ROMAN WORLD

Contributors

Diana Bowder
Alan Bowman
Andrew Drummond
Jill Harries
Nicholas Horsfall
David Hunt
Cathy King
Oliver Nicholson
Graham Piddock
Nicholas Purcell
Danuta Shanzer
Roger Tomlin

Who Was Who
in the
ROMAN
WORLD

753 BC–AD 476

Edited by
Diana Bowder

A PHAIDON BOOK

Cornell University Press
ITHACA, NEW YORK

© 1980 by Phaidon Press Limited

First published 1980 by Phaidon Press Limited, Oxford
and Cornell University Press, Ithaca, New York

International Standard Book Number 0–8014–1358–3
Library of Congress Catalog Card Number 80–67821

Phototypeset by Tradespools Ltd, Frome, Somerset
Printed in Great Britain by Morrison and Gibb Ltd,
Edinburgh

Frontispiece: The Emperor Trajan with lictors (Rome, Vatican Museum).

The publishers wish to thank all the individuals as
well as museums, libraries, and other institutions
for photographs and permission to reproduce them.
Further acknowledgement is made to the following:
Alinari, Florence: 2–3, 48, 53, 55, 56, 62, 66t, 68,
    75, 80 (jacket), 82, 100t, 104b, 114b, 124, 130,
    133r, 149, 154, 155, 170, 176, 182r.
Ashmolean Museum, Oxford: 19l, 25r, 31, 37b, 44,
    47, 49l, 51, 54, 63, 67b, 72, 74, 81t, 84, 85l, 97b,
    106l, 115, 117, 122r, 129, 131, 133l, 134, 137,
    142, 144, 145, 151, 159, 164, 166, 175l, 177, 179,
    182l, 183b, 191, 197b, 202, 207b, 208b, 211l.
Biblioteca Apostolica Vaticana, Rome: 70, 90, 91,
    97, 208, 228, 229.
Bibliothèque Nationale, Cabinet des Médailles,
    Paris: 89, 167t.
Bildarchiv Preussischer Kulturbesitz, Berlin: 196t.
Diana Bowder: 85b, 207t, 220b.
British Crown Copyright: Department of the
    Environment: 49r, 168.
Peter Clayton: 19r, 25l, 43, 66b, 69tl, 73t, 85b, 102,
    116, 128, 141l, 147, 199t, 227t.
C.N.R.S., Paris: 81.
Pierre Courcelle: 42.
Deutsches Archäologisches Institut, Rome: 18r,
    67t, 99, 104t, 106r, 136r, 148r, 195, 217t.
Fototeca Unione, Rome: 17l, 18, 37, 46l, 61, 69tr,
    73b, 77, 135, 139t, 151r, 173, 206.

Giraudon, Paris: 23l, 109, 118.
Hirmer Fotoarchiv, Munich: 28, 113l, 138l, 140l,
    201, 210.
Israel Department of Antiquities and Museums,
    Jerusalem: 175r.
G. B. D. Jones: 126.
Kunsthistorisches Museum, Vienna: 60.
Mansell Collection, London: 29b, 33, 83, 136l, 158,
    167, 185, 212, 216t.
Ny Carlsberg Glyptotek, Copenhagen: 94, 174.
Osterreichische Nationalbibliothek, Vienna: 78.
Smithsonian Institute, Freer Gallery of Art,
    Washington D.C.: 198.
R. S. O. Tomlin: 21, 29t, 210.
Jocelyn Toynbee: 163.
The Trustees of the British Museum, London: 86,
    115, 113r, 122l, 138r, 178, 180, 220t.
Universitetsbiblioteket Uppsala: 218.
University of London, Warburg Institute: 24, 50,
    59, 87, 230.
Vatican Museum, Rome: 80 (jacket), 164.
Victoria and Albert Museum, London: 103, 204.
Walker Art Gallery, Liverpool: 22.

Many of the photographs in this book are from the
Phaidon archive and include the work of the late
Ilse Schneider-Lengyel.

Contents

Chronological Table

753 BC	Foundation of Rome	
753–715 BC	Romulus first king	
715–673 BC	Numa Pompilius	
673–642 BC	Tullus Hostilius	Regal period (dates
642–617 BC	Ancus Marcius	very unreliable)
616–579 BC	Tarquinius Priscus	
578–535 BC	Servius Tullius	
534–510 BC	Tarquinius Superbus	
509 BC	Establishment of Republic	
496(?) BC	✗ Lake Regillus (victory over Latins)	
451–450 BC	Twelve Tables (law code)	Expansion into
396 BC	Capture of Etruscan town Veii	Italy
390 BC	Sack of Rome by Gauls	
295 BC	✗ Sentinum: Romans defeat Samnites and others	
280–275 BC	War with Pyrrhus	
264–241 BC	First Punic War: Rome becomes a naval power and acquires Sicily	
218–201 BC	Second Punic (Hannibalic) War: definitive defeat of Carthage; Romans acquire Spain (206)	
214–205 BC	First Macedonian War	Defeat of Carthage
200–196 BC	Second Macedonian War: Philip V defeated at ✗ Cynoscephalae (196)	and expansion into
172–168/7 BC	Third Macedonian War: Perseus defeated at ✗ Pydna (168)	east and west
147–146 BC	Annexation of Macedonia and Greece	Mediterranean
149–146 BC	Third Punic War: destruction of Carthage (146)	
133 BC	Rome receives province of Asia	
133 BC	Destruction of Numantia (Spain)	
133 BC	Tribunate of Tiberius Gracchus	
123–122 BC	Tribunate of Gaius Gracchus	
112–105 BC	War with Jugurtha (Africa) ⎱ Marius reforms	
114–101 BC	Invasions of Cimbri and Teutones ⎰ the army	
91–87 BC	Social War (Italy)	
88–63 BC	Wars with Mithridates (Asia Minor)	
82–79 BC	Dictatorship of Sulla	
73–71 BC	Spartacus' slave revolt	
67–62 BC	Pompey in East (pirates and Mithridates); Syria made province	
63 BC	Cicero consul; conspiracy of Catiline	Break-up of the
58–51 BC	Caesar's conquest of Gaul	Republic
53 BC	✗ Carrhae: Crassus defeated by Parthians	
49 BC	Caesar crosses Rubicon	
48 BC	✗ Pharsalus: defeat of Pompey	
46 BC	Death of Cato at Utica (North Africa)	
49–44 BC	Caesar dictator	
44 BC	Murder of Caesar on Ides of March (15th)	
43 BC	Second Triumvirate formed (Antony, Octavian, Lepidus)	
42 BC	✗ Philippi: Brutus and Cassius defeated and killed	
31 BC	✗ Actium: Octavian defeats Antony	

27 BC	Octavian becomes Augustus, first emperor	
AD 14	Death of Augustus	
AD 14–37	Tiberius emperor	Julio-Claudians
AD 37–41	Gaius 'Caligula'	
AD 41–54	Claudius	
AD 54–68	Nero	

AD 68–69	Galba	
AD 69	Year of the Four Emperors: Galba, Otho, Vitellius, Vespasian	
AD 69–79	Vespasian	
AD 79–81	Titus	
AD 81–96	Domitian	
AD 96–8	Nerva	Flavians and
AD 97–117	Trajan	Antonines
AD 117–38	Hadrian	
AD 138–61	Antoninus Pius	
AD 161–80	Marcus Aurelius (with Lucius Verus 161–9)	
AD 177–92	Commodus	

AD 193	Pertinax	
AD 193	Didius Julianus	
AD 193–211	Septimius Severus	
AD 211–17	Caracalla	Severan dynasty
AD 217–18	Macrinus	
AD 218–22	Elagabalus	
AD 222–35	Alexander Severus	

AD 235–8	Maximinus Thrax	
AD 238	Gordian I and II	
AD 238	Balbinus and Pupienus	
AD 238–44	Gordian III	
AD 244–9	Philip the Arab	
AD 249–51	Decius	Invasions,
AD 251–3	Trebonianus Gallus	usurpations, and
AD 253	Aemilianus	chaos; Illyrian
AD 253–60	Valerian (with son Gallienus)	soldier-emperors
AD 253–68	Gallienus	re-establish unity
AD 268–70	Claudius Gothicus	
AD 270–5	Aurelian	
AD 275–6	Tacitus	
AD 276–82	Probus	
AD 282–3	Carus	
AD 283–4	Carinus and Numerian	

WEST		EAST
	Diocletian and First Tetrarchy (284–305)	
Maximian Augustus (285–305)		Diocletian Augustus (284–305)
Constantius I Caesar (293–305)		Galerius Caesar (293–305)
	Second Tetrarchy (305–6)	
Constantius I Augustus (305–6)		Galerius Augustus (305–11)
Severus Caesar (305–6)		Maximin Daia Caesar (305–8/10)
	Disintegration of Tetrarchy (306–13)	

WEST		EAST
Severus Augustus (306–7) Constantine I Caesar (306–8) subsequently Augustus (308–37)	Usurpation of Maxentius in Italy (306–12) Usurpation of Domitius Alexander in Africa (308–9/11) Joint rule of Constantine I and Licinius (313–24)	Galerius Augustus (305–11) Maximin Daia Caesar (305–8/10) subsequently Augustus (308/10–313)
Constantine I (306–37) ──────────┐	Constantine I sole ruler (324–37)	Licinius (308–24)
Constantine II (337–40) Constans (340–50) ←	Constans (337–40)	Constantius II (337–61)
Usurpation of Magnentius (350–3)		
Julian Caesar (355–61)	Constantius II sole ruler (353–61) Julian (361–3) Jovian (363–4)	Gallus Caesar (351–4)
Valentinian I (364–75)		Valens (364–78)
Gratian (375–83) and Valentinian II (375–92)		Theodosius I (379–95)
Usurpation of Magnus Maximus (383–8)		
Valentinian II, ruler of West (388–92)		
Usurpation of Eugenius (392–4)		
	Theodosius sole ruler (394–5) ←	
Honorius (395–423)		Arcadius (395–408)
(Stilicho regent 395–408)		Theodosius II (408–50)
Constantius III (421)		
Usurper John (423–5)		
Valentinian III (425–55)		Marcian (450–7)
Petronius Maximus (March–May 455)		
Avitus (455–6)		
Majorian (457–61)		Leo I (457–74)
Libius Severus (461–5)		
Anthemius (467–72)		
Olybrius (April–November 472)		
Glycerius (473)		
Julius Nepos (473–5)		Zeno (the Isaurian) (474–91)
Romulus Augustulus (475–6)		

Introduction

We have had two aims in compiling this book: firstly, to provide a biographical reference work of scholarly accuracy and reliability that is easily accessible to the student and general reader of Roman history, and, secondly, to unite with it an important collection of pictorial documentation, consisting not only of portrait sculpture and coin portraits, where these exist of the subject, but maps illustrating, for example, a general's campaigns, and photographs of buildings constructed by, and places strongly associated with, a particular person, together with some interesting inscriptions. The chronological limits have been set as wide as possible, so as to include all the major figures of Roman history: the book begins at the legendary date of the foundation of Rome, 753 BC (but including only historical or largely historical persons), and closes with the end of the Empire of the West (AD 476). Within this large span the aim has been to give an even coverage of the various periods in relation to each other, apportioning words to the number and importance of the major personages known, rather than to any preconceived idea of the relative interest of each period. The first centuries BC and AD, when our sources of information are particularly rich, are naturally dealt with in some detail, but there is no neglect of the middle and later Empire, as afflicts some works of reference. Many minor characters have had to be omitted, but every effort has been made to include all historical and cultural figures of importance. A good number of these are, of necessity, not 'Romans' at all, but foreigners with whom the Romans came into contact, such as kings or princes of adjacent States, or Greek historians who wrote about Rome. It must not be forgotten, moreover, that the 'Roman World', for much of the period, comprised the whole of the predominantly Greek-speaking eastern Mediterranean.

The form of each entry is as follows: the heading normally consists of the name (often a short name in the case of a well-known person), a brief identification or description, and one or more dates. The date or dates of a person's birth and/or death almost invariably follow the name, in brackets. Dates of an office held, on the other hand, follow the mention of that office on the right-hand side of the heading, and this is also the case with less precise dates, e.g. 'Philosopher, 2nd century AD'. A date of death following, exceptionally, the office indicates that the person died in office (generally murdered or executed). Inclusive dates, e.g. 'AD 192–8', are indicated by a hyphen, meaning that the person held office (or lived) from one date to the other. The stroke convention shows that the office was held (or the person was born or died) somewhere between the dates indicated, e.g. 'Consul AD 192/8'. In the body of the entry (and elsewhere), cross-references are indicated by an asterisk at the beginning of the name under which a person is classified. Additional cross-references are sometimes given at the bottom of an entry, to supplement incidental ones in the text, and to help a reader in search of further information on a particular topic. At least one bibliographical reference, whether to an ancient source or to a book for further reading, appears at the foot of almost every entry, the only exceptions being in the case of a few writers whose own works can readily be consulted, generally most easily in the Loeb Classical Library series of texts with translation. (The existence of a Loeb of most writers is assumed and is not mentioned specifically in each bibliography.)

The book also contains additional information of various kinds. An index of persons mentioned in other entries, but not important enough to be given their own entry, supplements the main text. A chronological table is also included, comprising major events and dates of the Republic and a list of emperors with the dates of their reigns. Several stemmata (family trees), principally of imperial houses, show the family connections of various groups of entries. In addition to the maps illustrating some individual entries, there are a number of general maps at the end of the book showing the Empire at different stages of development; virtually all geographical names appearing in the text are to be found on the appropriate one of these. The bibliography includes a list of all abbreviations used in the main text, and a few extra general works, not mentioned elsewhere, for further reading. There is also a glossary in which technical terms used in the entries, such as offices held and specialized literary terms, are explained.

The entries are arranged alphabetically, and in most cases a decision has had to be made under which of three or more names to classify a person. Under the Republic and early Empire, Roman citizens normally had three names, the *tria nomina* that are the hallmark of a citizen in the period of the extension of the citizenship from Rome and Italy to increasing numbers of people in the provinces. These names consist of, first, a *praenomen*, such as Marcus or Gaius, which was regularly abbreviated (e.g. M. for Marcus, M'. for Manius, and C. (not G.) for Gaius, which might be spelt Caius but was always pronounced Gaius); a few of these abbreviations appear in cross-references, but the full name is invariably given in the person's own entry. Then comes the *nomen*, or name of the family (the *gens*, hence sometimes called the gentile name), such as Julius, Cornelius, or Tullius. Lastly there is (normally) the *cognomen*, which might be a name frequently used in the family, such as Scipio in a branch of the Cornelii or Caesar in a branch of the Julii, or might be one more particular (originally at least) to the person, e.g. Naso for someone with a large nose; *Pompey had no *cognomen*, being simply Gnaeus Pompeius, and assumed the *cognomen* Magnus, 'the Great'. Sometimes, where a *cognomen* was in frequent use in a family, a 'surname' (*agnomen*) might be added as well, in the course of a person's life, e.g. Africanus or Asiagenus or Aemilianus (an 'adoptive' surname showing that he originated in the Aemilii family) to Scipio. Women's *praenomina* were often dropped, e.g. *Cicero's daughter was just known as Tullia. Freedmen took their patron's *praenomen* and *nomen*, retaining their slave name as *cognomen*, e.g. Marcus Tullius *Tiro. With the passage of time the system grew increasingly complex, and, especially after the *Constitutio Antoniniana* of AD 212 (see *Caracalla) made almost everyone in the Empire a Roman citizen, and the *tria nomina* ceased to be a proudly proclaimed distinguishing mark of new citizens, nomenclature became positively chaotic, particularly in the later Empire.

This compounds the difficulties, caused by the Roman nomenclature system, in adhering to a single principle of alphabetical organization. If one attempts to classify everyone by their family name, the results are highly inconvenient, in that, on the one hand, people who wish to find out about Cicero, for example, would need to look him up under Tullius, and, on the other other hand, persons classified under the commonest *nomina*, such as Flavius or Julius, would quickly run into hundreds (as they do in the *Prosopographia Imperii Romani*, which does follow this system of classification). If, on the other hand, everyone is classified by a *cognomen*, families are frequently split up under different letters of the alphabet. This is, however, the system followed by the *Prosopography of the Later Roman Empire*—being a reasonably satisfactory solution to the chaos that afflicts the nomenclature of that period—and its classification of the late Roman names (from AD 260 to 395, soon to be extended, in the second volume) has generally been adopted in this book. This also makes it less confusing for someone wishing to consult both works. For the same reason, the arrangement in the *Oxford Classical Dictionary* has normally been followed for the Republic and early Empire. This attempts to take a common-sense approach, and in most cases lists people under their best-known name, e.g. Cicero or Caesar (*cognomina*), or the Emperor Gaius (*praenomen*), while some families, notably the Claudii and Valerii, are grouped under the *nomen*. A few Christians appear as arranged in the *Oxford Dictionary of the Christian Church* (e.g. *Sulpicius Severus). Names of people not to be found in any of these works have been treated in much the same way, classified under the name by which they can be referred to by a single name, or, failing that, under the less common name. In borderline cases it is impossible to be sure by which name a person has been classified, but it is a relatively simple matter to look them up under each name to see which has been chosen.

Where more than one person of the same or similar name appears in the book, they are arranged alphabetically as follows: if there is one very famous person of that name, he is listed first, by the well-known name, e.g. *Crassus; his full name (Marcus Licinius Crassus) will then appear in the first sentence of the entry. Next, others of the same name appear in alphabetical order of the names after the comma, e.g. *Crassus, Lucius Licinius and then *Crassus, Marcus Licinius. Then follow any others with surnames or additional *cognomina* appearing after the first name and before the comma, e.g. *Crassus Frugi, Marcus Licinius. Emperors are normally listed first, if there are others of the same name. Numbering of people has been kept to a minimum, and only resorted to where there is more than one person of exactly the same name, and the difficulty cannot be made to disappear, as in the case of the Crassi, by listing one very well-known person by a single name. This avoids leaving the reader wondering, for example, whether 'Crassus (2)' in another entry is the famous

Crassus or quite a different one.

If no entry can be found under either (or any) likely name, the reader should consult the index at the back of the book to see if the person is mentioned in an entry devoted to someone else, as will sometimes be the case. If the name does not appear there, either, the reader is urged to remember that there were, during the 1,200 years of Roman history covered, something of the order of 1,000 million 'Romans', that vast numbers of them are known to the historian through an inscription (note the size of the index of personal names in the index volume of the *Corpus Inscriptionum Latinarum*) or a mention in a literary work, and that the number of those who could be described as 'well-known' runs into thousands, leading to a great many difficult choices over whether to include or exclude a particular person, in the interests of keeping this book down to a reasonable size. I have been helped in the choice by my contributors, whose enthusiasm and helpfulness have been a great source of strength in this herculean task. I owe a special debt to Roger Tomlin, whose advice on numerous matters of policy and organization has been of inestimable value. I should also like to thank my husband for his tireless support and encouragement, and Phaidon for having the original idea, and for their help in carrying it out.

Outline History 753 BC–AD 476
The legendary date of the foundation of Rome, 753 BC, does not represent the earliest period of settlement on the site of Rome, where earlier Bronze Age traces have been found. But from at least the eighth century on there were several Iron Age settlements on the hills and in the Forum, near the Tiber ford and a salt trade-route. By c. 600 these groups of huts had united to form a single city. The sixth century was a period of considerable structural development, with the emergence of some of Rome's earliest institutions, and the drainage of marshes and building of temples, under the influence of the Etruscans from the north. Until the expulsion of *Tarquinius Superbus in 510 BC, Rome had been ruled by kings, later arranged in a neat series, with precise dates, stretching back to *Romulus in 753. Although the seven names may be authentic, the dates (and deeds) assigned to the earliest ones are likely to be badly awry.

The kings had been advised by a senate, or council of elders (nobles), and it was this institution that took over control of the city and its territory from the foundation of the Republic in 509, with the annual pair of chief magistrates, the later consuls, chosen from their number. The next centuries (to 264 BC) were dominated by internal conflicts between the noble patricians and the humbler plebeians, of which the codification of law

in the Twelve Tables (451–450) was a major landmark, and by the establishment of Rome's supremacy over her neighbours in Italy, in which her central position gave her a great advantage. Rome early became the leading city in Latium, and, with the Latin League to support her, was drawn into conflict with peoples further afield, such as the Aequi and Volsci. Meanwhile the Gauls swept down Italy and sacked all but the Capitol of Rome (390 BC), but Rome recovered from this disaster as from so many others throughout her history. New involvements and alliances drew her into Etruria, Samnium, and southern Italy, with its Greek cities, one of which summoned its ally *Pyrrhus, king of Epirus in northern Greece, to its aid (280 BC). He won two 'Pyrrhic' victories, but was later defeated and returned to Greece (275). There was no deliberate policy of conquest, but Rome's genius for organization and discipline, and her superior manpower, expressed in her superb citizen army and in wise diplomacy, had gradually made her mistress of a confederacy extending to all Italy.

The elimination of the Etruscans and the arrival of Romans in south Italy brought Rome into conflict with the chief power in the west Mediterranean, the Phoenician colony Carthage. The First Punic War broke out in 264 BC, and by the end of it (241) Rome had built herself a navy and won Sicily, soon followed by Corsica and Sardinia (238). The Carthaginians turned to the exploitation of Spain, and it was from there that *Hannibal set out, at the beginning of the Second Punic War (218–201), on his famous march to Italy, bringing elephants over the Alps. He destroyed two legions at lake Trasimene (217), and inflicted a terrible defeat at Cannae (216), but Rome's Italian allies remained loyal, and Hannibal was eventually forced to leave Italy (203), and met defeat in Africa at the hands of *Scipio Africanus at the battle of Zama (202). Meanwhile Rome had also won Spain from Carthage (206). She had also, earlier, become embroiled in the Hellenistic East, where her main antagonists were Hannibal's ally *Philip V of Macedon and *Antiochus III (ruling principally in Syria and Asia Minor). After the First Macedonian War (214–205 BC) and the Second (200–196), which ended in *Flamininus' victory at Cynoscephalae, Rome withdrew from Greece, but further disorders, including a Third Macedonian War (172–168/7; see *Perseus), led eventually to the annexation of Macedonia and Greece (Achaea) as provinces (destruction of Corinth by *Mummius in 146). The Romans had also become involved in Asia Minor, where the ruler of Pergamum bequeathed his kingdom to Rome in 133 BC, and it became the province of Asia. Carthage had also been destroyed (see *Cato the Elder, *Scipio Aemilianus) in the same year as Corinth, after the Third Punic War (149–146 BC). The pacification of Spain (see *Viriathus) was partially achieved with the destruction of

Numantia in 133 by Scipio Aemilianus, and southern Gaul became the province of Gallia Narbonensis (121 BC).

The next century (from 133) saw the collapse of the Republic and its replacement by a form of monarchy. The republican constitution, created for a city-state, was unsuitable for the government of a large Empire and the control of increasingly permanent armed forces, and there were a number of other problems, such as unrest among the Italian allies, and the need to return large numbers of landless unemployed from the towns to the countryside, from which they had been ejected by the growth of large estates and cattle-raising. Selfish and short-sighted policies by a hard core of reactionary nobles, the *optimates*, circumvented attempts at solution and aggravated the problems. In 133 Tiberius *Gracchus, and in 123–122 his brother Gaius *Gracchus attempted to pass agrarian reforms, the latter also wishing to give the allies citizenship, but both were bitterly opposed by the *optimates* and met their death in riots. *Marius, hero of the war against *Jugurtha (112–105) and of the invasions of the German Cimbri and Teutones (114–101), was the next to take up *popularis* causes. He had won his victories with the aid of an army which he had reformed, and which was no longer composed only of citizens of property but partly of landless men, who looked to their victorious leader rather than the State for reward in the shape of land on discharge. This set a pattern, and, when in 91–87 BC the Social War, caused entirely by the *optimates'* refusal to share the benefits of Roman citizenship with their Italian allies (*socii*), was fought (and won by Rome, though the allies got their citizenship), several commanders emerged from it, each at the head of a loyal and experienced army: principally *Sulla, *Cinna, Marius, and *Pompey's father *Pompeius Strabo. For the next 50 years these and their successors, especially Pompey and *Caesar, *Antony and Octavian, used their armies in furtherance of their political aims, causing a spate of civil wars that were only ended by Octavian/*Augustus, the final victor, who was able to re-establish ordered government for a war-weary Roman world.

In 88 BC Sulla captured Rome and outlawed his enemies, in 87 Cinna and Marius did the same. Sulla returned from the East in 83 and marched on Rome again, establishing himself as dictator and passing reactionary laws meant to stabilize the republican regime. His new constitution did not long outlast his retirement in 79. The mid-first century BC was dominated by Pompey, *Crassus, and Caesar, who were eventually driven to co-operate ('First Triumvirate', 60 BC) in order to get their often just demands met by the senate. Pompey had held major commands in the East, against pirates and *Mithridates (67–62), and Caesar spent the years 58–50 conquering Gaul to

the Rhine and Channel. *Cicero, who as consul in 63 had put down a minor conspiracy led by *Catiline, tried to get an alliance of all right-minded elements in the State, but was politically ineffectual in the face of increasing violence, with rival gangs led by *Clodius and *Milo dominating the popular assemblies. Meanwhile Crassus, who in 73–71 had put down *Spartacus' slave revolt, secured himself a command against Parthia, but died in the humiliating defeat at Carrhae in 53 BC. With his removal, the rivalry between Caesar and Pompey increased, and Pompey, like Cicero, was pressed into unwilling support of the optimate cause. In 49 BC Caesar crossed the Rubicon from his province into Italy, and open civil war began, with Pompey defeated at Pharsalus in 48, and *Cato dying at Utica in Africa in 46, symbolizing the collapse of senatorial resistance and the republican cause. As dictator (49–44 BC) Caesar promoted important reforms, one of which was the introduction of the Julian calendar (45 BC). But the republican idealist conspirators led by *Cassius and *Brutus prevented Caesar from devising a new constitution by assassinating him on the Ides of March (15th), 44 BC, and plunged the Empire into further civil wars. The Caesarians Antony and Octavian defeated Brutus and Cassius at Philippi (42 BC), but rapidly fell out with each other, and the Second Triumvirate (with *Lepidus) ended in the elimination of Antony (supported by *Cleopatra) by Octavian in the Actium campaign (31 BC). Antony's suicide in Egypt in 30 BC left Octavian master of the Roman world at the age of 32.

A wide-ranging programme of reform, carried out during his reign of over 40 years, brought stabilization and reconstruction on all fronts. Augustus, as he became in 27 BC, was not a king or a dictator, but 'first citizen' (*princeps*). He held all the reins of power himself, but honoured the senate and left it some functions, using the services of individual senators as governors and army commanders in a reformed army and provincial administration. The equestrian class was also brought into the government, to an increasing extent. The frontiers of the Empire began to be defined, with a lot of new territory being taken in, and by the end of his reign, after the failure of the experiment of including Germany to the Elbe (see *Varus), were in approximately the form they were to maintain for the rest of the Roman period. An emperor-cult was established as a focus of loyalty.

The problem of who should succeed to his commanding position became acute for Augustus after the deaths of *Marcellus and Gaius and Lucius *Caesar, but was solved by recourse to his stepson, *Tiberius, who acceded in AD 14 on Augustus' death. Tiberius' relations with the senate were not good; his reign was marred by a series of treason trials and by the sinister power of his praetorian prefect *Sejanus. The basically autocratic nature of the principate stood revealed by the end of his reign, and was emphasized by the ephemeral one of *Gaius 'Caligula' (AD 37–41). Under *Claudius (AD 41–54) the imperial civil service was built up, and several provinces were added (Britain in AD 43). *Nero's reign (AD 54–68) began well but ended in disorder, and was followed by civil war in the Year of the Four Emperors (AD 69), in which the armies concentrated in certain provinces used their power to create and impose emperors. *Vespasian (AD 69–79) emerged victorious and established the Flavian dynasty, devoted to solid and unglamorous ideals of hard work and good government. His second son *Domitian (AD 81–96), however, degenerated into a tyrant whose reign ended in a bloodbath and his own assassination. The aged *Nerva (AD 96–8) adopted the army commander *Trajan (97–117), who as emperor took the boundaries of the Empire to their farthest extent by his conquest of Dacia on the north bank of the Danube; his Parthian campaign was less successful. This 'best emperor' (*optimus princeps*) set the pattern of public order, good relations with the senate, sound administration, and reward for the talented individual, that was to endure throughout the 'Age of the Antonines', comprising much of the second century. This was the time when the Empire reached its peak of unity, peace, and prosperity, under the Emperors *Hadrian (117–38) and *Antoninus Pius (138–61)—the heyday of the *pax romana*, with its benefits of stability, public order, good roads, beautiful public buildings, and beneficent government. The reign of *Marcus Aurelius (161–80), however, saw the first terrible plague, as new strains of bacteria travelled along the trade-routes from China to populations with no immunity, and also the renewal of the barbarian incursions, as tribes moved westwards from the steppes of Russia, building up a pressure on the Rhine and Danube frontiers which was to cause great devastation in the third century, and the eventual collapse of the western Empire. Marcus' son *Commodus (177–92) unwisely made peace with the Germanic tribesmen whom his father was fighting at his death, and his corrupt rule ended in his murder.

Civil war followed, with the main armies again putting up contenders for the throne: *Clodius Albinus in Britain, *Pescennius Niger in Syria, and Septimius *Severus on the Danube. It was Severus (193–211) who succeeded in eliminating his rivals and founding a new dynasty. By now the military basis of the emperor's power was becoming more apparent. Severus' son *Caracalla (211–17) is chiefly remembered for his *Constitutio Antoniniana*, the measure extending Roman citizenship throughout the Empire (212). He was assassinated by his praetorian prefect *Macrinus (217–18), the first of several prefects to usurp the throne during the third century. Offpsring of the Syrian family of

Severus' empress *Julia Domna then continued the Severan dynasty: first *Elagabalus (218–22), who proved highly unsuitable owing to his depravity and extravagant devotion to Syrian cults, and was discarded in favour of his cousin *Severus Alexander (222–35), an amenable boy whose reign, controlled by his mother, was notable for co-operation with the senate. His murder in 235 inaugurated half a century of near-anarchy, with a succession of short-lived emperors, numerous usurpers, invasions on all the frontiers of the Empire, plagues, parts of the Empire splitting off (notably a 'Gallic empire', including Britain and Spain, under *Postumus, *Tetricus, etc. (260–74), and in the East the Palmyrenian 'empire' under *Zenobia (266–73)), and administrative chaos including rampant inflation. (For a full list of emperors, see the preceding Chronological Table.) The Emperor *Decius (249–51) attempted to unify the Empire by means of a general order to sacrifice and a persecution of Christians who failed to do so: the first Empire-wide Christian persecution (previous ones had been local and sporadic). His successor *Valerian (253–60) also persecuted for a time, but was captured by the Persians (see *Shapur I). The sole reign of his son and associate *Gallienus marks the nadir of the third-century anarchy, but he prepared the way for recovery by military reforms, and his Illyrian soldier-emperor successors *Claudius Gothicus (268–70), *Aurelian (270–5), and *Probus (276–82) restored the military situation and re-established the unified Empire.

In 284 *Diocletian became emperor, and this man of administrative genius, in a 20-year reign (284–305), carried out a thorough reorganization of the military and civil administration of the Empire, now made fit for an Empire under siege, and set up a new system of government, the Tetrarchy or Rule of Four, with two emperors proper, the Augusti, and two Caesars under them; only the senior Augustus—Diocletian himself—could legislate, thus the unity of the Empire was preserved. He strove for religious unity through a general persecution of the Christians, the Great Persecution. In 305 he and the other Augustus, *Maximian, abdicated, and their Caesars *Galerius and *Constantius I became the new Augusti, with new Caesars appointed. But Constantius died in 306, his son *Constantine (the Great) entered the foursome of rulers, and in the next seven years the tetrarchic system collapsed owing to the ambitions of Constantine and others. In 312 at the battle of the Milvian Bridge Constantine conquered *Maxentius and became emperor of the West, and in 313 another tetrarch, *Licinius, defeated *Maximin Daia and became emperor of the East. In 324 Constantine eliminated Licinius to become sole emperor, and in 330 inaugurated his new capital, Constantinople. A Christian since winning at the Milvian Bridge under the Christian God's patronage, Constantine made it a Christian city, and his excellent strategic choice enabled this almost impregnable capital to continue until 1453 as the bastion of east Rome and of Christianity. A great reformer like Diocletian, Constantine continued his work of re-laying the foundations of the Empire after the near-collapse of the third century. His three surviving sons *Constantine II, *Constantius II, and *Constans ruled in partnership after his death (337). In the West Constans eliminated Constantine II in 340, and fell victim to the usurper *Magnentius in 350. By 353 Constantius II was sole ruler, and in 354 he executed *Gallus, whom he had created Caesar in 351. He made *Julian Caesar in 355 and sent him to govern Gaul and Britain. Julian usurped in 360, but armed conflict was avoided when Constantius died in 361. The last pagan Roman emperor, Julian died in Persia after a brief reign (361–3), and was replaced by *Jovian (363–4), on whose death the brothers *Valentinian I (364–75) and *Valens (364–78) ruled West and East respectively. Valentinian strengthened the Rhine and Danube defences; Valens had to face the rebellion of *Procopius in 365–6, and died fighting the Visigoths in the terrible disaster of Adrianople (378), from which the Roman army never recovered. Valentinian's sons *Gratian (375–83) and *Valentinian II (375–92) took over in the West, the latter still a boy, while *Theodosius I (379–95) founded a new dynasty in the East. There were two usurpers in the West during these years: Magnus *Maximus (383–8), murderer of Gratian, and *Eugenius (and his patron *Arbogast: 392–4).

On his death Theodosius left his young sons *Arcadius (395–408) and *Honorius (395–423) in charge of East and West respectively, Honorius under the tutelage of the commander-in-chief *Stilicho, who beat off several invasions and dominated affairs till his execution (408). The western Empire now began to break up: the central government lost control of Britain from c. 407; in 406 Vandals and others crossed the Rhine, and went on into Spain (409) and later Africa (429; see *Geiseric); the Visigoths moved west some years after Adrianople, sacked Rome (410; see *Alaric), and from 418 established a federate kingdom in south-west Gaul (see *Athaulf). A succession of powerful quasi-regents—relatives or officials—held sway at both eastern and western courts, not only under Arcadius and Honorius, but under their equally youthful successors *Theodosius II (East, 408–50) and *Valentinian III (West, 425–55). In the West this was generally the commander-in-chief: *Constantius (III) followed Stilicho, and even became emperor briefly (421), marrying Galla *Placidia. In the East the powers behind the throne were usually civil officials or ladies of the imperial house: *Rufinus (praetorian prefect 392–5), the chamberlain *Eutropius ((2) exiled 399), the Empress *Eudoxia (died 404), *Anthemius (prefect 405–15), and then *Pulcheria the sister of Theodosius II (Augusta 414) and her rival, his wife *Eudocia (Augusta 423, banished 443). When *Valentinian III was installed as western emperor by the eastern government (425), his mother Galla Placidia and the commander-in-chief *Aëtius, who had close relations with the Huns, ruled in his name, the latter until his assassination by Valentinian himself in 454. *Attila and his Huns across the Danube were the dominant threat in these years: in the 440s they invaded the Balkans, but were kept in periodic check by the payment of subsidies; then in 451 they invaded Gaul, where Aëtius fought them with some success, and the next year Italy, where Pope *Leo persuaded them to retreat from Rome; Attila's death in 453 removed the threat. The Vandal Geiseric from Africa sacked Rome in 455.

With the end of the House of Theodosius (455), the links between East and West began to weaken. In the East the commander-in-chief *Aspar proceeded to create emperors, first *Marcian (450–57), then *Leo I (457–74). In the West there was a succession of short-lived emperors (see Chronological Table), several of them created by the commander-in-chief *Ricimer (of barbarian origin like Stilicho and Aspar), who deposed *Avitus (456) and held the main power for the next 16 years. *Majorian, his first appointee as emperor, proved too active for Ricimer's liking, and was executed (461) on his return from a disastrous joint East-West expedition against the Vandals in North Africa, the 'granary' region which it was vital for the survival of the western Empire to recover. Ricimer also disposed of his emperor *Anthemius (2), nominee of the eastern emperor, in a civil war (472). On the death of Ricimer later that year, three more ephemeral emperors followed each other, the last—a youth aptly named *Romulus and given the nickname Augustulus ('little Augustus') in derision —being the son of the commander-in-chief *Orestes. By now there were not only Vandals in Africa and Visigoths in Spain and parts of Gaul, but Burgundians and Franks settled in the rest of Gaul, Alamanni in Raetia, and Ostrogoths in Noricum and Pannonia; Brittany and Britain were now independent, and Dalmatia had been so since the death of Aëtius (454) under *Marcellinus and his successor. In 476 Romulus was deposed by a Germanic chief named *Odoacer, who nominated no more emperors, but himself ruled instead as king of Italy: the western Empire was defunct. The East survived; and thus we have the paradox that the Greek East, which Rome had subjugated, survived as the Byzantine Empire, while the Roman West, economically less stable and with her society now largely reduced to feudal lords and serfs with no middle classes, disintegrated into the barbarian kingdoms of the early Middle Ages.

Ablabius Praetorian prefect AD 329–37.

A native of Crete, of humble birth, Flavius Ablabius began with a post in the governor's office in Crete, and rose to be *Constantine's right-hand man, the most powerful official in the Empire —praetorian prefect of the East—and consul for 331. He was a Christian. Jealous of the influence of the philosopher *Sopater over Constantine, he conspired for his downfall. Constantine assigned him as mentor to the young *Constantius II, but after his father's death Constantius dismissed and then executed him. 'Thus was the ''ever-fortunate'' Ablabius paid out for the death of Sopater' (Eunapius). His daughter Olympias was first betrothed to the Emperor *Constans and then married, c. 354, to the king of Armenia.

BIBL. *PLRE* i, Ablabius 4.

Accius (170–c. 85 BC).

Lucius Accius was a native of Pesaro in Umbria and a prolific author: two *praetextae* and some 45 adaptations of Greek tragedies are attested. Accius also wrote in prose and verse on dramatic history and orthography. Anecdotes reveal an aggressive figure and the fragments a contentious and quirky critic, but a dramatist of real and lofty distinction.

BIBL. Fragments: *GRF* 22 ff.; *TRF* 157 ff., 326 ff.; *FPL* 34 ff.

Achilleus Rebel in Egypt AD 297–8.

In the summer of 297 Egypt rose against the Tetrarchy. Achilleus is named in narratives as leader of this revolt, although coins and documents surviving on papyrus name Domitius Domitianus as the rebel emperor. *Diocletian took personal charge of military operations, and recaptured Alexandria after a siege of eight months.

BIBL. T. D. Barnes, *Phoenix* xxx (1976) 180–1; *PLRE* i, Achilleus 1, Domitianus 6.

Adventus, Marcus Oclatinius Urban prefect and consul AD 218.

Born c. 160, Adventus became an army executioner and spy, later serving as imperial financial administrator in Britain under *Severus. His appointment by *Macrinus as urban prefect and consul and his elevation to the senate roused scandalized opposition.

BIBL. PW Supp. viii, Oclatinius; Birley, *Severus*.

Aedesius (AD 280/90–c. 355) Neoplatonist philosopher.

A native of Cappadocia, Aedesius studied Neoplatonic philosophy under *Iamblichus in Syria before settling at Pergamum to teach. His pupils included *Maximus of Ephesus, *Priscus, and the future Emperor *Julian, whom he persuaded, perhaps through fear of imperial displeasure, to go instead to his pupils Eusebius and *Chrysanthius, as his own powers were failing. He died soon after.

BIBL. *PLRE* i, Aedesius 2.

Aegidius Master of the Soldiers in Gaul, c. AD 458.

As *Majorian's Master of the Soldiers, Aegidius defended Arles (458), but after 461 broke with the policy of *Ricimer and established an independent Roman enclave based on Soissons. He cultivated the support of the Salian Franks and sought an alliance with the Vandals against the Goths, but died in 464.

BIBL. Gregory of Tours, *History of the Franks*, II. 11–12, 27; Hydatius, *Chronicle, s.a.* 463; Stroheker, *Adel*, prosop. 1.

Aelian (c. AD 170–235) Writer.

Claudius Aelianus taught rhetoric at Rome and is known to have held a priesthood at Praeneste. His main extant works (in Greek) are the *De Natura Animalium* and the *Varia Historia* (on human life and history). His philosophical ideas are mainly

Portrait bust of Lucius Aelius Caesar.

derived from Stoicism, with great emphasis on the notion of universal reason.

BIBL. Aelian, *On Animals*, trans. A. F. Scholfield (Loeb, 1958–9); Aelian, *Varia Historia*, ed. M. R. Dilts (Teubner, 1974).

Aelius Caesar, Lucius Consul AD 136 and 137.

From a distinguished senatorial family which first rose to prominence in the reign of *Vespasian, Lucius Ceionius Commodus was the son of the consul of 106. In the year of his own first consulship he was adopted by *Hadrian as his son and successor (at the same time his daughter, Fabia, was betrothed to the young *Marcus Aurelius). He took the name Lucius Aelius Caesar, was designated as consul for 137, and given a grant of tribunician power. He was then sent to the Danube with military responsibility, as a training for the imperial power he was to assume. He returned to Rome in the winter of 137, fell ill on New Year's Eve, and died in January 138, perhaps of tuberculosis.

BIBL. Birley, *Marcus*; Syme, *Tacitus*; *PIR* C 605.

Aemilian Emperor AD 253.

Governor of Moesia Inferior in 253, Marcus Aemilius Aemilianus succeeded in ending the Goths' devastation there, and was proclaimed emperor by his troops. He immediately marched on Italy, caught *Trebonianus Gallus unprepared, and killed him in battle. About three months later he

was murdered while marching north to quell *Valerian's uprising.

BIBL. *ANRW* ii. 2; Walser and Pekary, *Krise*.

Aëtius Master of the Soldiers AD 430–2, 433–54.

Flavius Aëtius, a Danubian-born general, was virtual master of the western Empire for most of the reign of *Valentinian III. His career depended on his contacts with the Huns, among whom he had been a hostage in his youth. He arrived too late to help the usurper John (423–5), but secured the command in Gaul from the new regime of Galla *Placidia and Valentinian, before his Huns were sent home. By 430 he was commander-in-chief, and when Galla Placidia tried to replace him with *Boniface, Aëtius recovered his supremacy with the help of the Huns (432–3). He used these allies to restore order in Gaul, where the Visigoths and Burgundians were in revolt (436–9), but his policy foundered when *Attila crossed the Rhine and devastated Gaul (451). Aëtius was forced to call upon the tribes he had defeated (principally the Visigoths) against his old allies, and won a limited victory near Troyes, which did not stop Attila from invading Italy in 452. Aëtius' prestige did not recover from this blow, but only assassination could dislodge him; on 21 September 454 he was accused of treason and stabbed to death by the emperor himself.

BIBL. Oost, *Galla Placidia*, chs. 6–7.

Afer, Gnaeus Domitius Consul AD 39.

The greatest orator of his time, Afer played a part in many of the important cases of the reigns of *Tiberius, *Gaius, and *Claudius. Narrowly escaping death under Gaius he was made consul instead. *Quintilian was his most famous pupil. He died in AD 59.

BIBL. *PIR* D 126.

Agricola (AD 40–93) Governor of Britain AD 78–85.

Born at Fréjus, Gnaeus Julius Agricola was educated at Marseilles. His mother was killed by *Otho's troops, his father by *Gaius for refusing to prosecute Marcus Silanus. He was rapidly promoted by *Vespasian, and as consul in 77 betrothed his daughter to the historian *Tacitus, who later wrote a panegyrical description (still extant) of his life. As governor of Britain he advanced the Romanization of the province and extended its frontiers with a series of vigorous and successful campaigns far into Scotland. *Domitian recalled him before he had completed the conquest, and saw to it that the remainder of his career was less distinguished.

BIBL. Tacitus, *Agricola*; Frere, *Britannia*; *PIR* I 126.

Agrippa (died 12 BC) Lieutenant of Augustus.

Marcus Vipsanius Agrippa was the most

important of the supporters of *Augustus, and a friend of his from childhood. He was his deputy in the Perusine war; he fought the Aquitanii and Ubii, and was the principal director of the naval war against Sextus *Pompey, the Dalmatian war, and the battle of Actium; when Augustus was finally established, Agrippa was deployed against rebellious Gauls and unpacified Cantabrians, and on a ten-year mission in the East, when he solved the problems of the Black Sea area. At home he shared censorial activity, tribunician power, and two consulships with Augustus, while spending his share of the spoils of war on the beautification of Rome with a lavishness rivalling that of Augustus himself. He married first the daughter of the great equestrian Pomponius *Atticus, and his later marriages with Augustus' niece Marcella and, in 21 BC, with *Julia (2) brought him closely into contact with the dynastic network, and involved him and his children in the plans for the succession (see stemma). He had not been entirely sure of his role before the death of *Marcellus, and had indeed been reduced to self-imposed exile on Lesbos before the marriage to Julia restored his position. He died in 12 BC, and his ashes were placed in Augustus' Mausoleum.

His modest refusal of triumphs and pliant obedience to Augustus, which may cause surprise, derived partly from the impossibility of his ever attaining the position of *princeps* because of his humble birth—as it was, he found it expedient to refer to himself as Marcus Agrippa, without reference to his outlandish gentile name. His reward was power and influence on a vast scale, and the knowledge that without his military skills the Augustan settlement would have been impossible.

BIBL. Syme, *Rom. Rev.*

Agrippa, 'Herod' King of Judaea AD 37–44.

Grandson of *Herod the Great, Marcus Julius Agrippa was born in 10 BC, was educated with his contemporaries *Claudius and *Drusus (*Tiberius' son), and was always closely associated with the circle of *Antonia. His activities during Tiberius' reign, known in great detail from *Josephus, form a complex story of prodigality, debt, quarrels with relatives of Roman officials in the East, and eventually suspected treason. *Gaius' accession saved him, and he was given a large kingdom: he

The Pantheon, Rome. Built by *Hadrian to replace Marcus Agrippa's original temple in the Campus Martius (27–25 BC).

also managed to prevent Gaius from insisting that his statue be placed in the Temple at Jerusalem. Claudius much valued his advice about eastern affairs, but he seems to have been more independent in spirit than befitted a client king, and only his death in 44 prevented some confrontation between him and Claudius. He was a devout Jew, and persecuted the nascent Christianity of the later years of his reign.

BIBL. *PIR* I 131.

Agrippa Postumus (12 BC–AD 14).

Son of *Agrippa and *Julia, Marcus Vipsanius Agrippa Postumus was adopted by *Augustus in AD 4. A truculent and uncouth manner seems to have been reinforced by the difficulties and frustrations of playing second fiddle to the other— and much more distinguished—heir, *Tiberius, who enjoyed *Livia's favour. Exile, first to Sorrento and then to Planasia, followed, and in AD 14 *Sallustius Crispus took the precaution of having him killed. The extent of rumour and the episode of a false Agrippa proved that this had been expedient.

BIBL. Bassano, *C. Phil.* 1941.

Agrippina the Elder (died AD 33).

Agrippina was the daughter of *Agrippa and *Julia and wife of *Germanicus, to whom she bore nine children including the Emperor *Gaius (see stemma). She was tireless in her support of her husband, accompanying him to Germany and to the East, whence she brought back his ashes in 21. Her independent bearing annoyed *Tiberius, and *Sejanus played upon this dislike so that she was exiled to the island of Pandateria in 29, where she

later starved herself to death. She was very popular in Rome.

BIBL. Levick, *Tiberius*; Tac. *Ann*. i.69.

Marble statue of Agrippina the Younger (AD 45–50). Naples, Museo Nazionale.

The epitaph of Agrippina the Elder, wife of *Germanicus, mother of Emperor *Gaius, from the Mausoleum of *Augustus, Rome. *CIL* vi, 886.

Agrippina the Younger (AD 15–59).

Daughter of *Germanicus and *Agrippina the Elder, Julia Agrippina was married by *Tiberius in AD 28 to Gnaeus *Domitius Ahenobarbus (2). She shared in her sisters' honours under *Gaius, but was exiled for her part in the conspiracy of *Lentulus Gaetulicus. Restored by *Claudius, and left a widow, she failed to persuade *Galba to marry her, and chose *Sallustius Passienus Crispus instead, whom she is said to have killed so as to inherit his wealth. She was popular in Rome none the less, and with the help of *Pallas and *Vitellius managed to secure marriage with her uncle

Claudius in 49, after which she had enormous power. In 50 she became Augusta and had her son *Nero adopted. Among her acts was the foundation of Colonia Agrippina (Cologne), the removal of *Lollia Paulina, and the appointment of *Burrus as praetorian prefect. Afraid that Claudius might prefer *Britannicus to Nero she poisoned Claudius, and announced Nero's succession. At first her power was little diminished, but Nero soon became more self-assertive, particularly in his private life, and was supported by Burrus and *Seneca. Elaborate plots for killing Agrippina, which proved difficult, were laid, including the famous collapsible boat, and her murder (59) was made an occasion for public rejoicing.

BIBL. Tac. *Ann.* xiv. 1–13 (the murder).

Silver coin (*denarius*) of *Brutus (54 BC) showing his legendary ancestor C. Servilius Ahala.

Ahala, Gaius Servilius 5th century BC

Ahala supposedly killed Spurius *Maelius—an aetiological explanation, in fact, of his *cognomen* (usually interpreted as the 'armpit' where he hid his sword). In early historians (Cincius and *Piso Frugi), Ahala acted as a private citizen, exemplifying the universal obligation to kill prospective tyrants. Others, perhaps building on *Ennius and reacting to the murder of the *Gracchi, made him Master of the Horse to *Cincinnatus, with Maelius' execution a punishment for defying the dictator's summons. *Brutus claimed descent from Ahala through his mother and adoptive father.

BIBL. PW ii A 1768 ff.; Ogilvie, *Livy* 550 f.; Crawford, *RRC* 455 f.

Alaric Leader of the Visigoths c. AD 395–410.

Alaric sacked Rome (August 410), an achievement which shocked the world, but he failed to find a home for his people. After fighting for *Theodosius in 394, he rebelled after the emperor's death and, after eluding *Stilicho in Greece, reached a settlement with the eastern government (397). In 401 he invaded Italy, but was driven out by Stilicho, with whom he later collaborated in a plan to seize eastern Illyricum. When this miscarried, and Stilicho was murdered, Alaric put pressure on the western government by

invading Italy and blockading Rome (408–10). He even proclaimed a rival emperor to *Honorius, Priscus *Attalus. But he was unable to negotiate a settlement, and soon after his sack of Rome died in southern Italy while waiting to invade Sicily.

BIBL. Matthews, *Aristocracies*, 270 ff.

Alexander of Abonuteichos Religious impostor, 2nd century AD.

A Greek-speaking mystic from Paphlagonia, Alexander is known mainly through an attack made on him by his contemporary, *Lucian. Claiming divine aid from Asclepius in the form of a serpent, he gave oracles and conducted mystical rites for which he gained a large following.

BIBL. Bowersock, *Sophists*; Lucian, *Alexander or the False Prophet* (Loeb, Lucian, vol. iv, trans. A. M. Harmon (1925)).

Alexander, Domitius Usurper in Africa AD 308–309/11.

Complicated civil wars followed the abdication of *Diocletian. In 308 *Maxentius, ruling in Rome, tried to consolidate his hold on Africa; the ill-armed African army promptly proclaimed as emperor Domitius Alexander, the elderly and timid governor-general of Africa. Rome, Maxentius' principal support, thus lost its main corn supply; Maxentius sent an army which defeated and strangled Alexander and devastated the finest parts of Africa.

BIBL. Zosimus ii. 12–14 (with Paschoud's notes).

Alexander Peloplaton Sophist, 2nd century AD.

A sophist from Seleucia in Cilicia (the nickname means 'Clay-Plato'), Alexander visited Rome on an official embassy to *Antoninus Pius from his native city. Summoned to Pannonia by *Marcus Aurelius during the Marcomannic wars, he was given the post of secretary for Greek correspondence and died whilst holding this office.

BIBL. Bowersock, *Sophists*; PIR A 503.

Gold medallion showing *Constantius I entering London after defeating Allectus. Arras, museum.

Allectus Usurper in Britain AD 293–6.

Allectus held high office under the usurper *Carausius (287–93), whom he murdered and succeeded. He ruled Britain and north Gaul for three years, until an army of the Caesar *Constantius I killed him in battle in south-east England. The victory was commemorated in a panegyric of Constantius (*Pan. Lat.* iv), and in a gold medallion found at Arras, which depicts Constantius' triumphal entry into London.

BIBL. *PLRE* i, Allectus; P. J. Casey, *Britannia* viii (1977) 283–301.

Alypius Governor-general of Britain AD 358.

Educated at Antioch, Alypius, a former governor-general of Britain, supervised the Emperor *Julian's attempt to rebuild the Temple at Jerusalem (363). The project was abandoned, it is said because flames kept bursting from the foundations.

BIBL. *PLRE* i, Alypius 4.

Amandus Gallic usurper *c.* AD 286.

Amandus was a leader of the Bagaudae in Gaul, together with Aelianus. Both were defeated by *Maximian *c.* 286.

BIBL. *PLRE* i, Amandus 1.

St Ambrose Bishop of Milan AD 374–97.

The son of a praetorian prefect (born *c.* 340), well educated in Latin and Greek, Ambrose in 374 was governor of the province whose capital was Milan, when he was chosen by popular acclamation to be its bishop. He had not been baptized, but his elder sister had been a nun for twenty years (he became a zealous advocate of virginity). After consecration he accumulated more influence than most praetorian prefects; eloquence, force of character, contacts at court, and a mass following made him more successful than any pagan panegyrist in imposing moral standards upon the emperors who resided at Milan. *Gratian removed the altar of Victory from the Roman senate house (382), and in 384 Ambrose defeated his kinsman *Symmachus' plea for its restoration. At the Council of Aquileia (381) he deposed the surviving *Arian bishops; when in 385/6 the Empress *Justina demanded a church for Arian worship, Ambrose occupied it with a congregation keyed up to resist a 'siege', and the court gave way. Amid wild enthusiasm, he discovered the relics of two local martyrs. When in Italy, *Theodosius I, too, yielded to Ambrose's influence, by hardening towards paganism, and by offering public penance for having ordered the massacre at Thessalonica (390).

Despite having been a layman, Ambrose rapidly became an accomplished preacher, winning St *Augustine's professional admiration. By defining the Catholic faith in Latin from his first-hand knowledge of Greek theology and Neoplatonism (see *Plotinus, *Manlius Theodorus), he became, like Augustine and St *Jerome (who disliked him), a 'Doctor' of the western church. The conversion of Augustine occurred within the context of Christian intellectual life at Milan; he was baptized by Ambrose at Easter 387, in which year it was the recollection of a hymn of Ambrose ('Deus, creator omnium') which consoled him when he mourned his mother's death. Ambrose, the archetype of the bullying ecclesiastics who asserted the independence of the western Church, could also speak to men's hearts.

BIBL. P. R. L. Brown, *Augustine of Hippo*, ch. 8; Matthews, *Aristocracies*, ch. 8.

Ambrosius, Aurelius Romano-British leader, mid-5th century AD.

Perhaps legendary but named by Gildas (sixth century), Aurelius Ambrosius is said to have inspired British resistance to the Saxon invasions. His career may have formed the basis for the King Arthur legend.

BIBL. Gildas, *On the Ruin of Britain* (*De Excidio Britanniae*), 25, 3.

Ammianus Marcellinus (*c.* AD 330–c. 395) Historian.

Ammianus, who calls himself 'a former soldier and a Greek', came from Antioch, but wrote his history of the period AD 96–378 in Latin at Rome. The surviving books (353–78) are the main source for the secular history of the reigns of *Constantius II, *Julian, *Valentinian I, and *Valens. Ammianus was an army officer, at first on the staff of *Ursicinus; he saw active service in Gaul (including the assassination of *Silvanus) and Mesopotamia (he was besieged by the Persians in the cliff-top fortress of Amida, and took part in Julian's Persian expedition). After leaving the army in *c.* 363, he lived at Antioch, but continued to travel. Finally he settled at Rome, perhaps by *c.* 383, where we know from a congratulatory letter from *Libanius that he had published part of the *History* by 392.

Ammianus used his own notes and those of others, as well as such written accounts as may have been available (see *Eunapius), for contemporary history. He wrote carefully in a florid, typically late-Roman 'literary' Latin, to appeal to educated circles at Rome; but his satirical descriptions of society there may suggest that he felt himself to be an outsider. He did not share *Symmachus' complacent view of the senatorial class, nor its tastes in history, whether for the potted variety (see *Eutropius and Aurelius *Victor) or for pure biography (see *Augustan History). Instead he wrote a large-scale work in which events at Rome were secondary, describing the Empire's wars and diplomatic relations with foreign peoples, and its internal weaknesses, such as bureaucratic corruption, court intrigue, treason trials, and usurpations.

Amida (modern Diyarbakır in S. E. Turkey): tower of fortress in the eastern wall on basalt cliffs above the river Tigris.

In the manner of Herodotus he digressed into subjects which interested him—descriptions of Roman provinces and foreign peoples, military indiscipline, the dishonesty of lawyers, and popular science (divination, Egyptian hieroglyphs, rainbows, eclipses, earthquakes, and how to make siege-engines). The result is rich and readable, but Ammianus is also outstanding as a historian, remarkably accurate and fair-minded; thus he criticizes his hero Julian, and records actions to the credit of people he disliked. He omits religious history, for safety's sake, or because it was 'unclassical'; he was a pagan, but represses his own beliefs, and limits his criticism of Christianity to lapses by Christians from their own standards of morality. He paid *Tacitus the compliment of continuing where he ended, and is the only later historian writing in Latin who can be compared with him: in style and ordering of material Tacitus is far superior, but Ammianus surpasses him in breadth and impartiality.

BIBL. *PLRE* i, Marcellinus 15; Thompson, *The Historical Work of Ammianus Marcellinus* (1947).

Ammonius Saccas Philosopher, mid-3rd century AD.

Little is known of this Alexandrian thinker, though he was a pioneer in the Late Antique revival of Platonism. He wrote nothing, but his lectures electrified his pupils. It was largely through *Plotinus, who was his disciple for 11 years, that his influence remained live in Neoplatonist circles in the fourth century.

BIBL. A. H. Armstrong, *Cambridge History of Later Greek and Early Medieval Philosophy* (1967) 196–200.

Andriscus King of Macedonia c. 150 BC.

An Asian Greek who claimed to be Philip, son of *Perseus, and heir to the defunct Macedonian throne, Andriscus was arrested in Syria by *Demetrius Soter and sent to Rome; he escaped, however, and easily overran Macedonia with assistance from Thracian dynasts in 150/49 BC. The success of the 'Pseudo-Philip' in actually establishing himself as king of Macedonia was regarded as incomprehensible by contemporaries. He defeated a Roman army under Publius Juventius Thalna before succumbing to *Metellus Macedonicus in 148.

BIBL. Walbank, *HCP* iii.

Anicius Gallus, Lucius Consul 160 BC.

As praetor in 168 BC Anicius conducted a lightning campaign against *Perseus' ally, Genthius of Illyria, who surrendered within a month. *Livy claims that this victory was reported in Rome before the news of the campaign's start. His triumph in 167 was followed by bizarre games (described by *Polybius 30.22.1–12) in which distinguished Greek flute-players were required to fight each other on stage to please the philistine Roman audience. Anicius' consulship was famous as a wine vintage.

BIBL. Walbank, *HCP* iii, esp. 445–7.

Annia Faustina Empress AD 221.

Annia Aurelia Faustina was one of *Elagabalus' three attested wives: he married her both for prestige (both her parents were related to *Marcus Aurelius) and to stabilize a reign endangered by his weakness and degeneracy.

BIBL. *PIR* A 170.

Annius Verus Consul AD 97, 121 and 126.

Of a family of Spanish origin, Marcus Annius Verus was a senator of the second generation, and was the grandfather of *Marcus Aurelius. He was given patrician status by *Vespasian, and his distinction is shown by the remarkable honour of a third consulship in 126. He adopted his grandson Marcus Aurelius after the death of his own son, Marcus' father (also called Marcus Annius Verus), and Marcus in his *Meditations* refers to the

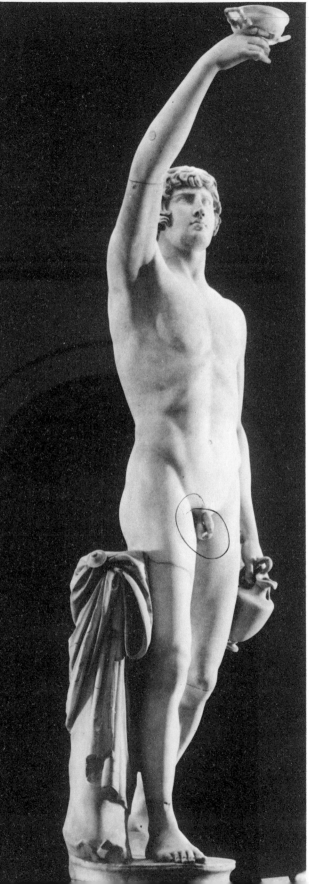

influence of his grandfather. He is said to have been much addicted to a ball-game which was played with a glass ball.

BIBL. Birley, *Marcus*; *PIR* A 695; Syme, *Tacitus*.

Anthemius (1) Praetorian prefect AD 405–15.

Anthemius was the grandson of *Philippus, praetorian prefect under *Constantius II. After other court offices, Anthemius was praetorian prefect of the East for a decade in which he was virtually regent for the boy-emperor *Theodosius II. His prefecture was marked by the construction of the great Land Walls protecting Constantinople.

BIBL. PW i, 2365.

Anthemius (2) Western emperor, AD 467–72.

Grandson of the eastern regent *Anthemius (1) and son-in-law of *Marcian, Anthemius had a distinguished career in the East before his nomination by *Leo as western emperor and proclamation in 467. Despite support from the East, his reign was marked by disasters against the Vandals (468) and Visigoths in Gaul. Relations with his son-in-law, *Ricimer, were always strained and open conflict broke out in 472. Anthemius was besieged in Rome, arrested, so the story goes, disguised as a beggar in a Roman church, and executed by Gundobad of the Burgundians.

BIBL. Sidonius Apollinaris, *Poem* II, *Panegyric on Anthemius* (delivered as urban prefect in 468); Bury, *Later Empire*, x. 4.

Antinous Imperial courtier, reign of Hadrian.

From Claudiopolis in Bithynia, Antinous was *Hadrian's favourite. He died by drowning in the Nile during Hadrian's visit to Egypt (130). Hadrian founded a city named after him (Antinoopolis), had him deified, and established temples for his cult. Numerous statues survive.

BIBL. *PIR* A 737; C. W. Clairmont, *Die Bildnisse des Antinous* (1967).

Antiochus III (the Great) Seleucid king 223–187 BC.

Antiochus' campaigns in the East (212–206 BC) in emulation of Alexander earned him a formidable reputation, the title of 'Great', and extensive but transient conquests. After *Philip V's defeat at Cynoscephalae, territorial ambitions drew Antiochus reluctantly into a conflict with Rome, which broke out in 192/1 after five years of 'cold war'. The Romans massively overestimated Antiochus' strength; in two campaigns (191–190) he was easily defeated by *Glabrio and the *Scipios (Africanus and Asiagenus) and compelled to evacuate Asia Minor.

BIBL. Badian, *Studies*, 112 ff.; Will, *Histoire politique*, index; Toynbee, *Hannibal* i. 59–64.

Antinous as Ganymede. Liverpool, Walker Art Gallery.

Portrait head of Antiochus III (the Great). Paris, Louvre.

Silver coin (tetradrachm) of Antiochus IV Epiphanes.

Antiochus IV Epiphanes Seleucid king 175–164/3 BC.

The younger son of *Antiochus III, Antiochus Epiphanes was a hostage in Rome from 188 until 175, when he succeeded his brother on the Seleucid throne. *Polybius draws attention to his eccentricity (26.1), but he was able in war and had a far-sighted policy of strengthening his kingdom by Hellenization and urbanization. This brought him into contact with minority groups, especially the Jews, and his reputation has suffered accordingly. He tried to maintain good relations with Rome at all costs, but took advantage of Rome's involvement in the Third Macedonian War to annex Ptolemaic Egypt. He was compelled to relinquish this notable prize in 168 by Gaius *Popillius Laenas, who carried out a latent Roman threat of war. After his death, and with Roman encouragement, the Seleucid kingdom sank into permanent decline.

BIBL. Mørkholm, *Antiochus IV of Syria* (1966); Will, *Histoire politique*, index.

Antonia (36 BC–AD 37).

Daughter of *Antony and *Augustus' sister *Octavia, Antonia married the elder *Drusus and bore him many children, including *Germanicus and *Claudius. After Drusus' death in 9 BC she resisted pressure to marry again, and became a model of matronly behaviour, remaining influential throughout *Tiberius' reign. Through her freedmen (who included *Pallas, the minister of *Claudius, and Caenis, the mistress of *Vespasian) she is said to have played a vital part in helping Tiberius thwart the ambitions of *Sejanus. After *Livia's death *Gaius and Drusilla, her grandchildren, were brought up in her household, where several client princes from the East,

including 'Herod' *Agrippa, were often to be found—Antonia inherited much goodwill and many connections (as well as huge amounts of property) in the East from her father. She died in 37; the tradition that Gaius forced her to suicide is without foundation. Posthumous honours were not given her until the reign of her son Claudius.

BIBL. Levick, *Tiberius*, 173–5; Balsdon, *Gaius*, 31–4; *PIR* A 883.

Antoninus Pius Emperor AD 138–61.

Titus Aurelius Fulvus Boionius Antoninus was born at Lanuvium on 19 September 86. His family originated from Nimes in Gallia Narbonensis, but his grandfather and father had both been consuls at Rome. Antoninus himself held the consulship in 130 and was later appointed to a judicial post (*IVvir consularis*) in Etruria and Umbria, before governing Asia at some point between 133 and 136. There is a famous story connected with this governorship; the sophist *Polemo of Smyrna is said to have thrown Antoninus out of his house. On 25 February 138 he was adopted by *Hadrian as his son and successor, given tribunician power and proconsular *imperium*, and when Hadrian died on 10 July 138 Antoninus succeeded him.

One of his first acts was to secure from the senate, which had particularly resented Hadrian in his last years, the deification of his predecessor and ratification of his acts. He did this by promising to abolish the Italian circuit-judges (*IVviri consulares*) instituted by Hadrian. The senate conferred the title of Pius on Antoninus himself, in recognition of his sense of duty towards the memory of Hadrian. In 139 he was also given the title of 'Father of his Country' (*Pater Patriae*). He succeeded in maintaining good relations with the senate throughout his reign. This was largely due to his tact, for the powers and

Bronze bust of Antoninus Pius (95 mm high) from Willingham Fen, Cambridgeshire. Cambridge, Museum of Archaeology and Ethnography.

responsibilities of the senate were not in any way increased. In fact the bureaucracy became more streamlined, and Antoninus reserved decisions on all matters of importance for his privy council.

His reign was largely a period of peace and prosperity. Antoninus was not extravagant (he is said to have left 675 million *denarii* in the treasury at his death), but there was imperial support for continued building, particularly in Italy. Trouble is attested in some provinces. In Britain a defensive wall of turf (the Antonine Wall) was built between the Forth and Clyde estuaries; this was probably begun in 143 after a couple of years of serious fighting. Important developments continued on the Rhine frontier. The African provinces were troubled by brigandage, which escalated to open revolt in Mauretania (c. 145–50). There was a revolt in Dacia and trouble at the eastern end of the Danube frontier. In the later years of the reign a serious war with Parthia threatened, but a peace was patched up.

Antoninus died on 7 March 161 at Lorium and was buried in Hadrian's Mausoleum in Rome. His chief monuments in Rome are the Temple of Antoninus and Faustina, by the Forum, and a commemorative column, originally placed in the Campus Martius.

His character and personality have earned general commendation. His qualities are best described by his heir, *Marcus Aurelius, in the

Meditations: 'gentleness and unshaken resolution in judgements taken after full examination; no vainglory about external honours; love of work and perseverance; readiness to hear those who had anything to contribute to the public advantage; the desire to award to every man according to desert without partiality,' and 'his energy on behalf of what was done in accord with reason, his equability everywhere, his serene expression, his sweetness, his disdain of glory, his ambition to grasp affairs' (trans. A. S. L. Farquharson, 1944).

BIBL. W. Hüttl, *Antoninus Pius* (1933–6); M. Hammond, *The Antonine Monarchy* (1959); *PIR* A 1513.

Antoninus, Arrius Consul AD 69 and possibly under Nerva.

Little is known of Arrius except that he ruled Asia singularly well under *Vespasian, and was the grandfather of *Antoninus Pius; his importance is, however, attested by *Pliny the Younger's elaborate praise of his friendliness and goodness. He was a particular friend of *Nerva.

BIBL. Pliny, *Letters* iv. 3.

Antonius, Iullus Consul 10 BC.

*Augustus attempted to end the differences of the Civil War by allowing *Antony's son Iullus Antonius a full political career, and by marrying him to his niece Marcella. This policy seems to have been successful for a long time, though Antonius eventually became involved in the scandal of the elder *Julia in 2 BC, which may have amounted to a conspiracy, and committed suicide to avoid the consequences.

BIBL. *PIR* A 800.

Antonius, Marcus Consul 99 BC.

A distinguished orator, Antonius apparently rose to political prominence under *Marius. As praetor in 102 BC he was appointed to an important proconsular command against the pirates in Cilicia. Although he achieved little, he was able to triumph on his return in 100 and secure election to the consulship of 99. In his censorship (97) he controversially admitted some Italians to Roman citizenship, an act which was reversed by the consuls of 95 (one of whom was L. *Crassus, his rival in oratory and politics). In the 90s Antonius defended some leading supporters of Marius in the courts, notably *Aquillius (2) and *Norbanus, but later he switched his allegiance: he supported Livius *Drusus (2) in 91, and fell a victim in 87 to Marius' massacre of his political opponents.

BIBL. Badian, *Studies*; Gruen, *Politics*; *ORF* 221 ff.

St Antony (c. AD 251–356).

Antony lived alone with God in the Egyptian desert, wrestling with demons for twenty years before his way of life attracted attention. Earlier

Silver coin (*denarius*) of Mark Antony (41 BC).

Coptic monastery of St Simeon (still in use) in the desert west of Aswan, Egypt. View across lower church with keep behind.

hermits seem to have lived in the villages, but during the Great Persecution many Christians came to the wilderness as Antony's disciples. Later, great men also came for help from this illiterate Coptic farmer's son; among them was *Athanasius, bishop of Alexandria, whose popular and influential *Life of Antony* soon carried monastic ideals all over the Empire.

See also *Pachomius.

BIBL. *Vita di Antonio*, ed. G. J. M. Bartelink (1974); D. Chitty, *The Desert a City* (1966).

Antony, Mark Consul 44 and 34 BC; triumvir 43–38, 37–33 BC.

Grandson of *Antonius (1), Marcus Antonius was born (about 83 BC) into an increasingly prominent noble family, and rose to power as an adherent of *Caesar. He served under him in Gaul (52–51), represented his interests at Rome as tribune (49), and commanded the left wing at Pharsalus (48).

At various periods between 49 and 47 he administered Italy in Caesar's absence. As Caesar's colleague in the consulship of 44 he was very favourably placed after Caesar's assassination to assume the leadership of his powerful faction, and to inherit his dominating position in the State. This he did with the co-operation of *Lepidus (2), forcing *Brutus and *Cassius to leave Rome, but following a generally conciliatory policy towards the senate. His leadership of the Caesarians was then challenged by Caesar's heir, *Octavian, who joined forces with the senate against him early in 43, but entered into a power-sharing agreement with him and Lepidus later in the year. This ('second') triumvirate was backed by a *Lex Titia*, which gave the three Caesarian leaders extensive powers in Rome and over the western provinces for five years. With Octavian, Antony defeated the republican opposition under Brutus and Cassius at Philippi (42) and assumed control of their eastern provinces. With Lepidus fading into obscurity the rivalry between Antony in the East and Octavian in the West became more apparent, particularly when Antony's wife, *Fulvia, and brother stirred up a rebellion against Octavian in Italy (the Perusine War, 41–40). Their differences were patched up at Brindisi (40) when Antony married Octavian's sister, *Octavia (1), and at Tarentum (37), when their triumviral powers were renewed.

Thereafter Antony increasingly identified himself with the Hellenistic East, showing a contempt for Roman traditions and entering into a close political and personal alliance with *Cleopatra. He reorganized the eastern provinces, launched an unsuccessful invasion of Parthia (36), and conquered Armenia (34), for which he celebrated a triumph at Alexandria. Soon afterwards he staged the Donations of Alexandria, which assigned certain eastern provinces and anticipated conquests to Cleopatra and her children. Antony's 'oriental' policy helped to secure him a powerful economic and strategic base, but played into Octavian's hands by alienating Italian opinion and allowing him to declare a national war on behalf of Rome against Cleopatra (32). Defeated by Octavian at Actium (31) and deserted by his troops, he died by suicide at Alexandria (30).

BIBL. Plutarch, *Life of Antonius*; Syme, *Rom. Rev.*

Anullinus

Gaius Annius Anullinus, consul in AD 295, was proconsul of Africa during the *Diocletianic persecution. Twice urban prefect of Rome during the usurpation of *Maxentius, he was retained in office by *Constantine (November 312). His son (?) Anullinus was proconsul of Africa the following year (313), when he received letters from Constantine favouring Christianity.

BIBL. *PLRE* i, Anullinus 3 and 2.

Anullinus, Publius Cornelius Urban prefect AD 196.

From Spain, Anullinus was a long-standing friend of *Severus; he served as proconsul of Africa in 193, and as general against *Pescennius Niger in 194 and in the First Parthian War. He was urban prefect in 196 and *consul ordinarius* in 199.

BIBL. Birley, *Severus*; *PIR* C 1322.

Aper Praetorian prefect, died AD 284.

Aper was praetorian prefect to *Numerian (283-4), who was married to his daughter. Ancient writers accuse him of murdering Numerian in order to become emperor himself. If Aper was guilty, his planning was inept: *Diocletian was promptly proclaimed emperor. At the solemn inaugural parade of the new reign Diocletian affirmed his own innocence; then, turning to Aper standing by his side, in front of the massed and astonished troops, with his sword he slew the praetorian prefect.

BIBL. H. W. Bird, *Latomus* xxxv (1976) 123-32.

Aphra'at Persian ascetic, early 4th century AD.

The first of the Syriac Church writers, Aphra'at lived in the Persian empire and held some Church office, surviving the persecution by *Shapur II. His 23 *Demonstrations* or *Homilies* (written 337-45) form a survey of the Christian faith, and are a valuable source for early Christianity in Persia.

BIBL. *ODCC*, Aphraates.

Apicius

Apicius was a nickname bestowed upon gluttons over a long period, notably upon Marcus Gavius under *Tiberius. The name has come to be attached to a collection of surviving recipes of uncertain title and date (fourth or fifth century AD), whose obscure ingredients and textually corrupted quantities have long represented a challenge to critics and gastronomes.

BIBL. Trans. Flower and Rosenbaum (1958); for textual details the American Teubner edition, for gastronomic information, the French Budé edition should be consulted.

Apollinaris (c. AD 310-c. 390) Heresiarch.

Son of a *grammaticus* of Beirut, Apollinaris was a staunch anti-*Arian who became bishop of Laodicea in Syria c. 360. With his father, also called Apollinaris, he turned the Bible into classical forms (epic, Platonic dialogue, etc.) when *Julian (361-3) forbade the teaching of the pagan classics by Christians. His heretical teaching, inspired by Greek thought, was that the Logos (Word) replaced Christ's spirit; but this made Christ less than fully human, and was rejected at Church councils at Rome and at Constantinople (381). Some works survive.

BIBL. Socrates, *Hist. eccl.* ii. 46, iii. 16; *ODCC*, Apollinarius.

Apollonius of Tyana Philosopher, 1st century AD.

The details of Apollonius' life are known from a biography written by *Philostratus c. 220. He was born early in the first century and died in the reign of *Nerva (96-8). His letters and other writings were known in antiquity but are now lost. He was a neo-Pythagorean who was said to have performed miracles, raising the dead, healing the sick, and finally making a bodily ascent to heaven. He is supposed to have had a vision of the murder of *Domitian, as it happened in Rome, when he himself was in Ephesus. Because there are virtually no references to him before the third century (*Lucian has a brief and uncomplimentary statement), it is impossible to disentangle fact from legend. During the persecution of Christians under *Diocletian a parallelism was first developed between Apollonius and Christ, with pagans attempting to claim Apollonius as Christ's equal. He was thus an important figure in the struggle of paganism against Christianity in the fourth century and even *Augustine, in refuting the comparison, clearly took it seriously.

BIBL. Philostratus, *Life of Apollonius*, trans. and ed. C. P. Jones, G. W. Bowersock (1970); J. Hempel, *Untersuchungen zur Überlieferung von Apollonius von Tyana* (1920); PW ii. 146-8.

Appian Historian, 2nd century AD.

An Alexandrian born in the reign of *Domitian, Appianus perhaps died c. 165. He refers to an experience in the Jewish Revolt in Egypt (115-17). He held an administrative post in Alexandria, went to Rome where he probably held the equestrian post of advocate of the imperial treasury, and then received a procuratorship from *Antoninus Pius through the good offices of *Fronto. His major historical work (in Greek) is in 24 books (of which 9 survive complete, 7 in fragmentary form) and deal with Roman wars and conquests arranged ethnographically. The most valuable part of it, despite its errors, is the section dealing with the 'civil wars' between 146 and 70 BC (books 13–17), for which other narrative sources are lacking.

BIBL. Appian, trans. H. E. White (Loeb, 1912–13); E. Gabba, *Appiano e la storia delle guerre civili* (1956).

Apuleius (born *c.* AD 125) Novelist, controversialist, and philosopher.

A native of Madauros (Numidia), Apuleius studied at Carthage and Athens, travelled in the East, lived in Rome, returned to North Africa, married a rich widow, and in 158/9 was charged with winning her by black arts. Tried at Sabratha, he was apparently acquitted and moved to Carthage, where he enjoyed the respected old age of a philosopher, poet, and rhetorician of distinction; the base of one of several statues erected in his honour has been discovered.

His writings are extremely numerous, and the extant works (many are now lost) show an uncanny mastery of a wide range of styles: (1) *On the Daemon of Socrates* and *On Plato and his Dogma*—inaccurate popular expositions of Platonism. (2) *De Mundo*—a translation of the pseudo-Aristotelian *On the Cosmos*. (3) *Florida* (*Bouquet*)—a selection of 23 speeches from his respectable old age. (4) *Apology*—a vigorous defence against the charge of sorcery. (5) The *Metamorphoses*—a novel in eleven books, of uncertain date. Superficially, the tale is of one Lucius, who, through excessive curiosity, is changed into an ass, but is ultimately restored to human form by Isis; but book xi in particular is partly autobiographical, and reveals a passionate devotion to the goddess. Inset is *Cupid and Psyche*, a closely parallel story filling approximately two books. Whereas the main novel is directly comparable to a Greek romance *Lucius or the Ass*, attributed to *Lucian, *Cupid and Psyche* is in origin a folk-tale, but written up by Apuleius with all the embellishments of sophisticated literary reminiscence. The style of the whole is rich, bizarre, and baroque, closest in character to the Asianic rhetoric criticized by *Cicero and to the Greek rhetoric of Apuleius' own day. The whole novel is fascinating as a religious document and delightful as an adventure story.

BIBL. The Budé edition is recommended; *Cupid and Psyche*, ed. Purser (1910); Walsh, *Roman Novel* (1970); *Apology*, ed. Butler and Owen (1914); see also Nock, *Conversion* (1961) 135 ff.

Aquilia Severa Empress *c.* AD 220, 221–2.

Julia Aquilia Severa was a vestal virgin whom the emperor *Elagabalus first married *c.* 220, causing great scandal at Rome. The emperor claimed the marriage had a religious function, but public opinion was not appeased. After divorcing her to marry *Annia Faustina, he remarried Aquilia late in 221.

BIBL. *PIR* J 648.

Aquillius (1), **Manius** Consul 129 BC.

As consul Aquillius suppressed the last remnants of *Aristonicus' revolt in Asia Minor and organized the former kingdom of Pergamum as a new Roman province (Asia) before returning to a triumph in 126 BC. In Pergamum he received divine status, but in Rome he was accused (unsuccessfully) of extortion.

BIBL. Magie, *Asia Minor*.

Aquillius (2), **Manius** Consul 101 BC.

Aquillius was a leading political associate of C. *Marius, whose colleague he became in the consulship of 101 BC. He had a distinguished war record as a senior officer under Marius in the German wars and as consul in Sicily, where he suppressed a serious slave revolt. But his subsequent fleecing of Sicily earned him a reputation for personal avarice which he was later to regret, although in the short term he survived a prosecution for extortion at Rome. He led an embassy to Asia Minor in 89 to restore Rome's shattered prestige there. He was able to exploit the considerable personal influence established there by his father, *Aquillius (1), and succeeded in forcing *Mithridates to evacuate Bithynia and Cappadocia. But he went too far when he persuaded Nicomedes of Bithynia to invade Pontus, and provoked Mithridates into a war with Rome. Mithridates easily defeated the meagre Roman forces in Asia, and having captured Aquillius made a public example of him as a symbol of Rome's oppressive and extortionate rule in Asia: he was cruelly but ironically put to death by the pouring of molten gold into his throat.

BIBL. Magie, *Asia Minor*; Gruen, *Politics*.

Arbitio Master of the Cavalry AD 351 (?)–61.

From a common soldier, Flavius Arbitio rose to be commander-in-chief, and consul for 355. *Constantius II used the services of his Master of the Cavalry against the usurper *Magnentius, and for a variety of tasks, including the review of *Gallus Caesar's troops in 354, a campaign against the Alamanni in 355, investigating the fall of Amida (see *Ursicinus, *Ammianus) in 360, and to resist *Julian. Julian, on becoming sole emperor, to win Arbitio's support made him president of the Commission of Chalcedon (361), and he and the other generals on it took their revenge on Count *Ursulus. Arbitio then retired, but used his influence with the troops on behalf of the Emperor *Valens during the rebellion of *Procopius in 365–6. Ammianus describes him as unjust and cruel, and an inveterate intriguer against rivals, enriching himself with his victims' property.

BIBL. *PLRE* i, Arbitio 2.

Arbogast Master of the Soldiers, died AD 394.

Like his uncle *Ricomer, Arbogast was one of the Frankish-born generals at the court of *Gratian. He played a leading part in *Theodosius I's defeat of the usurper *Maximus, and was attached to *Valentinian II as his commander-in-chief (388). They quarrelled, and after Valentinian's unexplained death (probably suicide) Arbogast replaced him with *Eugenius. He remained virtual ruler, and with Nicomachus *Flavianus revived pagan cults. After the defeat of their army by Theodosius (September 394), he killed himself.

BIBL. *PLRE* i, Arbogastes.

Arcadius Eastern emperor AD 395–408.

As the elder son of *Theodosius I, Flavius Arcadius was early marked out as his intended successor, receiving the title of Augustus as a boy in 383. His tutor was the philosopher *Themistius. He succeeded to the throne in Constantinople on the news of Theodosius' death in Milan in January 395. Despite his status as the senior Augustus (his younger brother *Honorius ruled in the West), Arcadius never succeeded in breaking away from the dominance of others. On 27 November 395 he looked on as the praetorian prefect *Rufinus was murdered by the troops: an act which facilitated the supremacy of the chamberlain *Eutropius; four years later Eutropius in turn fell victim to the power of the Empress *Eudoxia (whose marriage to

Portrait bust of the Emperor Arcadius. Istanbul, Archaeological Museum.

the emperor, Eutropius had himself arranged). Eudoxia's ascendancy came to an end with her death in 404, and *Anthemius the praetorian prefect emerged as the chief influence on Arcadius' last years; his supremacy at the eastern court outlasted the emperor's death on 1 May 408.

BIBL. *PLRE* i, 99; PW ii, 1137 ff.

Aristides, Aelius (AD 118–*c.* 180) Sophist.

Publius Aelius Aristides Theodorus was born on 27 January 118 into a wealthy landowning family from Mysia; his father Eudaemon may have been a friend of *Hadrian. He was a citizen of Smyrna. His teachers included Alexander the *grammaticus*, *Polemo, Tiberius Claudius Aristocles at Pergamum and *Herodes Atticus at Athens. In the 140s he travelled round the cities and islands of Asia and to Egypt, visiting Rome for the first time in 144 (where he delivered his famous panegyric *To Rome*). Then began the first of a long series of illnesses (aggravated by advanced hypochondria) which led him to spend most of the rest of his life either at his home in Smyrna, writing and lecturing, or in the Asclepieium at Pergamum. He makes much of his services to his native Smyrna, notably his intercession with the emperors for financial assistance when the city was all but destroyed by earthquake in 177. His writings (in Greek) include public and private speeches, declamations on historical themes, polemical essays, and prose hymns. Perhaps the most striking work is the *Sacred Tales* (in 6 books), a long account of revelations made to him by Asclepius in a dream, in effect an intimate account of a personal religious experience. He died in 180 or very shortly after.

BIBL. A. Boulanger, *Aelius Aristide* (1923); Bowersock, *Sophists*; J. H. Oliver, *The Ruling Power* (1953).

Aristobulus Praetorian prefect and consul AD 285.

Tiberius Claudius Aurelius Aristobulus served *Carus and *Carinus (AD 282–4) as praetorian prefect, and *Diocletian kept him in the post despite his original opposition to that emperor's accession (Aurelius *Victor, *Caesars* xxxix. 14). He was later proconsul of Africa (290–4), where he provided public buildings for a number of small cities in the hinterland, and urban prefect at Rome (295–6).

BIBL. *PLRE* i, Aristobulus; *PIR* C 806.

Aristonicus Rebel in Asia Minor *c.* 130 BC.

An illegitimate son of *Eumenes II, Aristonicus raised a revolt in Asia when the last king of Pergamum bequeathed his kingdom to Rome. Apart from his anti-Roman stance Aristonicus adopted an apparently idealistic and socially revolutionary programme. His support was not drawn from the Greek cities in Asia but mainly

from the non-Greek Asiatic population and from slaves, to whom he promised freedom. He was defeated by Marcus Perperna, the consul of 130 BC, and was later executed at Rome.

BIBL. Magie, *Asia Minor*.

Aristophanes Governor under Julian, AD 363.

A member of the local council of Corinth, Aristophanes studied at Athens and, after the seizure of his inheritance by a relation who was a powerful official, fled to Syria, where he became a State agent (*agens in rebus*). In 357 he was sent to Egypt, but in 359 became involved with the governor in the treason and magic trials held at Scythopolis in Palestine; he was exiled for three years and fined. In 362 *Libanius addressed a speech on his behalf to the new emperor *Julian, who reinstated this devout pagan and gave him high office (perhaps governor-general of Macedonia).

BIBL. Libanius, *Or.* xiv (Loeb); *PLRE* i, Aristophanes.

Arius (and **Arianism**) Heresiarch (*c.* AD 260–336).

Probably Libyan by birth, a pupil of *Lucian of Antioch and then a leading priest at Alexandria, Arius was the most important early Christian heretic. In about 319 he began propagating the theory that the Son is a creature and subordinate to the Father, created before Time and superior to the rest of creation, but different in being (Greek *ousia*, Latin *substantia*) from the Father. He wrote popular songs to spread his doctrines. Excommunicated by a council summoned by his bishop at Alexandria, Arius sought support from fellow-disciples of Lucian, especially *Eusebius bishop of Nicomedia. *Constantine the Great, arrived in the East in 324, sent Bishop *Hosius to

North colonnade of the Asclepieium, Pergamum.

mediate, but this failed. The great ecumenical Council of Nicaea assembled in 325 and, through the influence of St *Athanasius (q.v.), then a deacon at Alexandria, condemned Arius and his teachings, and adopted the term *homoousios* (of the same being) to describe the relation of Christ to the Father; Arius was exiled to Illyricum. More favourable to Arianism late in his reign, Constantine recalled him from exile *c.* 334. He died

Baptistery of the Arians, Ravenna: vault mosaics, 5th century AD.

at Constantinople in 336, allegedly of a sudden haemorrhage while on his way to be received back into communion by the reluctant bishop.

Arius' doctrines, espoused in a moderate form by *Constantius II (337–61), became the prevailing orthodoxy under that emperor, but, despite a long series of councils and some persecution, he failed to impose his views on the Church. The eastern emperor *Valens (364–78) was also an Arian, and the Nicene faith was not finally accepted in the East until the Council of Constantinople in 381. But the evangelization of the Goths by *Ulfila, under Constantius, prolonged the life of Arianism by promoting its spread among the northern barbarians; in the fifth century the orthodox were persecuted by Arian Vandals in North Africa and Visigoths in Spain. Arianism gradually died out thereafter.

BIBL. *ODCC*, Arius, Arianism; Chadwick, *The Early Church*, 129–51.

Arminius German leader AD 9.

Arminius was a German nobleman, who was given Roman citizenship and an equestrian career in the army, and who stirred up the movement among the German tribes which led to the destruction of *Varus' legions. Further fighting against Rome and against neighbouring tribes was less spectacularly successful. He died in AD 19, already a popular hero.

BIBL. Velleius Paterculus II. cxviii. 2.

Arnobius Man of letters, floruit *c.* AD 300.

Arnobius, a North African rhetorician, was converted to Christianity as the result of a dream. Afterwards he wrote seven books *Against the Pagans*, which contain little Christian doctrine but vilify the established observances of the cities of Roman Africa with chaotic vigour and much vivid and intriguing detail. Arnobius is said to have been tutor to *Lactantius.

BIBL. Trans. G. E. McCracken, *Arnobius of Sicca: The Case against the Pagans* (1949).

Arria Stoic, 1st century AD.

After the failure of *Scribonianus' conspiracy (AD 42), one of those involved, Caecina Paetus (consul AD 37), was shown the way to die by his wife Arria, who stabbed herself with the words 'It doesn't hurt, Paetus'. Their daughter, also called Arria, was with difficulty restrained from doing the same when her husband *Thrasea Paetus committed suicide in 66. Her child *Fannia married *Helvidius Priscus: the two Arriae were thus at the centre of the dissident tradition of the late first century AD, though Arria the younger lived through exile to see better days under *Nerva.

BIBL. *OCD* (2 entries); Pliny, *Letters* iii. 16; Martial i. 13.

Arrian Philosopher and historian, consul AD 129 (?).

A native of Nicomedia in Bithynia, Flavius Arrianus was a pupil of the Stoic philosopher *Epictetus. After his consulship he was governor of Cappadocia, where he suppressed an invasion of the Alani. It is he who is responsible for the survival of the *Discourses* of his teacher Epictetus (4 of 8 books are preserved as well as a *Manual* summarizing his teaching). An imitator of the style of Xenophon, he wrote various historical works in Greek: on Parthia, on India, an account of the expedition against the Alani, and a history of the successors of Alexander the Great. There is also a work on military tactics, but his major importance as an historian lies in the *Anabasis*, the best extant account of the campaigns of Alexander the Great.

BIBL. Arrian, *Opera*, ed. A. G. Roos (1967–8); Arrian, vol. i, trans. P. A. Brunt (Loeb, 1976).

Arruntius, Lucius Consul AD 6.

Wealthy, eloquent, and uncorrupted, Arruntius was thought by *Augustus to be worthy of imperial power and capable of trying for it. He was too outspoken for *Tiberius, and an enemy of *Sejanus and of *Macro, through whose machinations he was driven to suicide in AD 37. His father (of the same name, consul 22 BC) wrote a history of the Punic Wars in the *Sallustian manner; his adoptive son was Camillus *Scribonianus.

BIBL. Tac. *Ann.* iv. 48.

Artemidorus of Daldis Writer on dreams, 2nd century AD.

Nothing is known of Artemidorus, the author of a major ancient work on *The Interpretation of Dreams*, possibly dedicated to *Maximus of Tyre. He also wrote works on augury and cheiromancy which have perished.

BIBL. Artemidorus, *The Interpretation of Dreams, Oneirocritica*, trans. and comm. R. J. White (1975).

Asclepiodotus Praetorian prefect AD 290–6, consul 292.

Asclepiodotus, a military man, rose to be praetorian prefect in the early years of *Diocletian. In 296 *Constantius I dislodged the usurper *Allectus from Britain, with Asclepiodotus in command of one of the two expeditionary forces. He landed in Hampshire under cover of a Channel fog, and easily defeated Allectus. Constantius, coming from further east, then entered London, thereby securing the Empire's north-west frontier.

BIBL. *PLRE* i, Asclepiodotus 3.

Asconius (9 BC–AD 76) Grammarian.

Of the considerable output of Quintus Asconius Pedianus (who went blind in AD 64) there survive commentaries on five speeches of *Cicero, two being on lost speeches. His work is careful, based upon good sources, and frequently of great value.

Asinius Gallus Consul 8 BC.

Son of the orator and historian C. *Asinius Pollio, Gaius Asinius Gallus was the father of three consuls. He was a competent orator himself, though overshadowed by his father, from whom he inherited an antipathy to *Cicero. He was a friend of Augustus, who characterized him as eager for imperial power but unequal to it. *Tiberius was very ill-disposed towards him, partly because he married Vipsania after her divorce from Tiberius, but also because of his intractable attitude in the senate. He was damaged, too, by his association with *Sejanus and *Agrippina. He was condemned in AD 30, and died in custody in 33, probably by starvation.

BIBL. Tac. *Ann.* ii. 32–6; Levick, *Tiberius*, 77.

Asinius Pollio, Gaius Consul 40 BC.

A partisan of *Caesar and later of *Antony, as governor of Hispania Ulterior after Caesar's death Pollio joined his forces with those of Antony and *Lepidus (3) against the Republic. He tentatively supported Antony in the Perusine War, but as consul in 40 BC he helped to reconcile him with Octavian at Brundisium. In 39 he triumphed as proconsul of Macedonia over the Parthini in Illyria; he then retired from public life to follow literary pursuits. He was of great importance in Roman letters, as the founder of the city's first public library, and as the initiator of the pernicious habit of recitations-by-invitation. His literary career and acquaintance spanned both the generation of *Cicero and *Catullus and that of *Virgil and Cornelius *Gallus. He composed tragedies, of which he wrote to Cicero, and which Virgil and *Horace knew; he was renowned as an orator and later as a declaimer; he delivered memorably pithy comments on literary and stylistic matters, but achieved greatest renown as the composer of a ferociously independent and arguably influential history of the period 60 (or 49) –42 (?) BC (see Horace, *Odes*, ii. 1).

BIBL. Syme, *Rom. Rev.* 4 ff. *et passim*; *ORF* 516 ff.; *HRR* ii. 67 ff.

Aspar Master of the Soldiers, consul AD 434.

One of the ablest generals of the East, Flavius Ardaburius Aspar came to prominence as the ally of Galla *Placidia against the usurper John (425), and was awarded the western consulate after serving for her in Africa (434); a *missorium* with an inscription commemorates this event. Of Alan birth, Aspar's dominant position in Constantinople rested on the Germanic, especially the Ostrogothic, military presence in the city. He engineered the choices of *Marcian and *Leo as

Silver *Missorium* (diameter 42 cm) of Aspar, commemorating his accession to the western consulate in AD 434. Florence, Bargello.

emperors (450 and 457) but from 466 his position was challenged by Leo's promotion of Zeno, and, although his son, Patricius, was made Caesar in 470, Aspar's family's intrigues to safeguard their position led to his assassination by palace eunuchs (470/1).

BIBL. Bury, *Later Empire*, 221–5, 316–20.

Asturius Consul AD 449.

The consular celebrations of Turcius Rufius Asturius (449) at Arles are commemorated by

Consular diptych of Asturius. Ivory. Darmstadt, museum.

*Sidonius Apollinaris and by one of the few surviving and ascribable consular diptychs of the fifth century.

BIBL. Sidonius Apollinaris, *Letters*, VIII. 6.

St Athanasius Bishop of Alexandria AD 328–73.

Born at Alexandria *c.* 296, Athanasius the great defender of the Nicene faith against Arianism, was probably educated at the Christian (Catechetical) school there, before becoming deacon and secretary to the bishop. It was through his influence that *Arius (q.v.) and his doctrines were condemned at the Council of Nicaea in 325. Athanasius was made bishop of Alexandria in 328. A hard and narrow-minded man who made bitter enemies, he fell foul first of the court of *Constantine the Great (where Arius had powerful supporters: see *Eusebius of Nicomedia), being exiled to Trier in 336–7, and then of the moderate Arian *Constantius II (337–61), whose principal religious opponent he was. In 339 he fled to Rome, was restored to his see in 346 at the insistence of of the western emperor *Constans, against Constantius' will, and was again driven out in 356. He was exiled twice more (362–3, 365–6). In 362 he succeeded in reconciling the semi-Arians (homoiousians, who said Christ was 'of like being' to the Father) to the orthodox homoousians who professed full Nicene consubstantiality, and worked for the triumph of orthodoxy in the East that took place in 381. He died in 373.

A man of sufficient rather than good education, who maintained close relations with St *Antony and the peasant monks of Egypt, and opposed the subtle *Origenist theologians who befriended Arius, Athanasius wrote brief theological treatises (notably *On the Incarnation*), and various works attacking the Arians' views and exposing their political manoeuvres. The victory of the doctrine of consubstantiality owes more to him than to anyone. He also introduced the idea of monasticism to the West.

BIBL. *ODCC*, Athanasius.

Athaulf Leader of the Visigoths AD 410–15.

Athaulf inherited from his brother-in-law *Alaric, whom he succeeded, the stalemate in relations with the government of *Honorius which ensued after the Sack of Rome in 410, but he at least had a strong bargaining position: in 412 he broke his alliance with the Gallic usurper Jovinus, and delivered him to the Romans; and he had in his entourage as hostage Honorius' step-sister Galla *Placidia—whom he married at Narbonne in January 414, thereby giving substance to his reported aim of a reconciliation between the Goths and the Roman Empire. But Athaulf encountered strong resistance from Honorius' commander, *Constantius (q.v. III), who blockaded the Mediterranean coast of Gaul and Spain, and

was murdered at Barcelona in 415 at the instigation of a rival chieftain.

BIBL. Oost, *Galla Placidia*, ch. 3; Matthews, *Aristocracies*, ch. 12; E. A. Thompson, *Historia* xii (1963).

Athenaeus Writer, floruit *c.* 200 AD.

From Naucratis in Egypt, Athenaeus was the author of a lost work on the Syrian kings and the *Feasting Scholars*, of which 15 books survive. A large number of guests (philosophers, men of letters, doctors, artists) discuss over several days questions of language, literature, art, philosophy, law, and science, and their discussions are illustrated invaluably and on a huge scale by citations from earlier authors.

BIBL. Kleine Pauly, Athenaios 3.

Athenagoras Christian apologist, 2nd century AD.

Author of a vigorous apology addressed to Marcus Aurelius and *Commodus, Athenagoras was concerned both to rebut anti-Christian slanders and to advance positive expositions of doctrine with some philosophical elaboration.

BIBL. Migne, *PG* vi.

Attalus I King of Pergamum 241–197 BC.

Attalus' reputation was secured by victories over the Galatians in the 230s, which provided the incentive for the great sculptural monuments of the acropolis at Pergamum. His opposition to

Portrait bust of Attalus I. Berlin, Preussischer Kulturbesitz.

*Philip V's ambitions led him to co-operate (via the Aetolians) with the Roman commanders *Laevinus and *Galba (210–207 BC). He confirmed Pergamum's future status as a Roman pawn when in 201 (together with Rhodes) he urged the Romans into a second Macedonian war. He died shortly before Philip's defeat at Cynoscephalae.

BIBL. Hansen, *Attalids of Pergamon* (1971), index.

Attalus II Philadelphus King of Pergamum 159–138 BC.

Attalus made many influential Roman friends through his participation in the campaigns against *Antiochus III and *Perseus. For this reason his brother *Eumenes II sent him on at least four embassies to Rome. On one such occasion in 168/7 BC Attalus was approached by leading senators who offered him part of Eumenes' kingdom. Although he remained loyal to his brother, his power within the kingdom was greatly enhanced by his influence at Rome. When he succeeded Eumenes in 159 his foreign policy was initially adventurous, but a document of c. 156 shows that he soon adopted a policy of strict adherence to Roman wishes.

BIBL. Welles, *Royal Correspondence* (1934) 245 ff.; Hansen, *Attalids of Pergamon* (1971), index.

Attalus, Priscus Usurper AD 409–10, 414–15.

Priscus Attalus was a leading senator at Rome (urban prefect in 409), who had the unique distinction of twice being proclaimed emperor by the Goths—at Rome in 409 and at Bordeaux in 414—in an effort to force their terms on the government of *Honorius at Ravenna. Both his reigns lasted only a matter of months, the first ending with his deposition by *Alaric, the second when he was captured by Honorius' men as he attempted to flee. He was led in triumph by Honorius through the streets of Rome in 416, before ending his days in exile in the Lipari islands.

BIBL. Chastagnol, *Fastes*, 266–8; Matthews, *Aristocracies*, 291–306.

Atticus (110–32 BC).

A very close friend of *Cicero, Titus Pomponius Atticus was the most regular of his correspondents. He withdrew from the strife-torn Italy of the 80s BC to settle first in Athens and then intermittently in Epirus. Although not without influence in Roman politics, he followed the Epicurean ideal of a life sheltered from the traumas and stress of political life. But he was not above the pursuit of financial and commercial activities (from which he amassed a large fortune), and his extensive literary interests involved him in the publication of Cicero's writings. He was the author of a *Liber annalis*, which provided a reliable chronological framework for Roman history and superseded the *Chronica* of *Nepos; he also wrote a number of treatises on the fashionable subject of genealogy, and a collection of portraits on a more modest scale than *Varro's *Imagines*. He should not be considered as having run a publishing house in any modern sense, though his numerous slaves were expert copyists.

BIBL. D. R. Shackleton Bailey, ed., *Cicero's letters to Atticus* i, 3–59; Sommer, *Hermes* 1926, 389 ff.

'Attila the Scourge of God', supposed portrait: Renaissance wooden plaque on the podium of the façade of the Certosa di Pavia.

Attila King of the Hunnic Confederacy, AD 434–53.

Attila the Hun, son of Mundiuch, succeeded his father as leader of the Huns (434) with his brother, Bleda, whom he later murdered (445). His dominant personality held together a federation of subject-tribes, extending from Scythia to east of the Rhine and from the Alps to the Baltic—an empire which disintegrated on his death.

By contemporaries Attila was known as a man who combined love of war with restraint, was wise in counsel, and merciful to those guaranteed his protection. Physically he was short, broad-chested, and with a large head, small eyes, thin beard, flat nose, and swarthy complexion; he inspired fear with his arrogant stride and rolling eyes. He had many wives, the last of whom, Ildico, saw his death (from apoplexy?) on their wedding night (453).

From his base in Pannonia, formally given to the Huns by *Aëtius (433), Attila terrorized both halves of the Empire. Hunnic auxiliaries helped Aëtius in Gaul against Burgundians and Visigoths until Litorius' defeat at Toulouse (439). *Theodosius II's failure to supply the Huns with an indemnity agreed in 435 was then made the excuse for

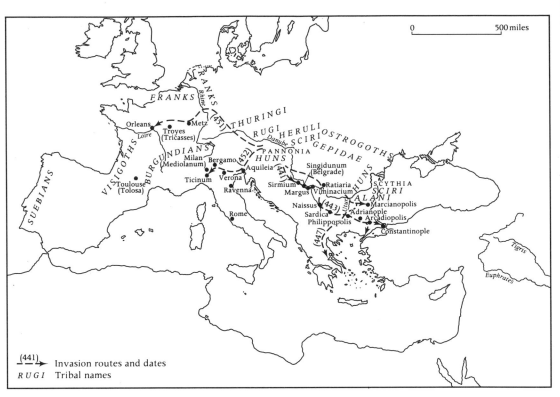

(441) → Invasion routes and dates
RUGI   Tribal names

whirlwind invasions down the Danube, marked by the sack of great imperial cities such as Singidunum and Sirmium (441), and Naissus and Serdica (443). In 447, the fall of Marcianopolis to Attila caused panic in Constantinople, but the Huns stopped short of the hastily reconstructed Walls of *Anthemius. After yet another treaty Attila was free to attack the West, but his invasion of Gaul was halted at Orleans and he was defeated on the Catalaunian Plains by Aëtius and Visigoths (451). The following year, after sacking Aquileia, he was persuaded to withdraw from Italy by Pope *Leo (and perhaps by fears of a threat to his rear in Pannonia). Meanwhile, in the East *Marcian refused to continue the indemnity to the Huns, but the Empire was spared the consequences by the death of Attila before he could retaliate.

Attila's most lasting achievement was his legend. His 'discovery' of the so-called Sword of Mars in Scythia was supposed to herald the resurgence of Hunnic military might. News of his death came to Marcian in a dream in which he saw that Attila's bow was broken, a true omen in that the threat posed by Attila to the Empire did not survive him.
  BIBL. Priscus, *Byzantine History* (fragments); E. A. Thompson, *A History of Attila and the Huns* (1948).

Aufidius Victorinus Consul AD 155 (?) and 183.
  From Pesaro in Umbria, Gaius Aufidius

The Roman Empire and the Invasions of Attila, AD 441–52.

Victorinus was a schoolmate and close associate of *Marcus Aurelius, and a correspondent of *Fronto. Between his consulships he governed the provinces of Germania Superior, Baetica and Tarraconensis (simultaneously), and Africa. After distinguished service in the German wars, he became urban prefect at the end of Marcus' reign. Shortly before 185 he fell into disfavour with *Commodus, and died soon afterwards.
  BIBL. Birley, *Marcus*; *PIR* A 1393; H.-G. Pflaum, *CRAI* 1956.

Augustan History (Scriptores Historiae Augustae).
  Historia Augusta is the modern title of a surviving collection of imperial biographies, Caesars and usurpers included, for the period AD 117–284 (with a gap, 244–59), written in the manner of *Suetonius by—they claim—six authors, in the reigns of *Diocletian and *Constantine. The six authors, who are otherwise unknown, quote over one hundred imperial letters or 'documents' otherwise unattested (and often implausible); they cite many 'writers' who are otherwise unattested, as well as genuine sources like *Herodian and *Marius Maximus. Most scholars now condemn 'documents' and 'writers' as fictitious, like much of their context. Study of the style and language also suggests that the 'six' authors are a fiction, and that

the *History* is the work of one man writing later. No fourth-century source seems to have read it, and its own sources and anachronisms suggest that it may have been composed in the 390s, perhaps at Rome. Unfortunately the *History* is a major source for the ill-documented second and third centuries AD. Much effort has been devoted to deducing its sources, its purpose (if any), and, in general, to disentangling truth from fiction. It also has some intrinsic interest as a kind of historical novel from Late Antiquity.

BIBL. R. Syme, *Ammianus and the Historia Augusta* (1968); T. D. Barnes, *The Sources of the Historia Augusta* (1978).

St Augustine (AD 354–430) Bishop of Hippo AD 395–430.

Aurelius Augustinus, the great philosopher and 'Doctor' of the western Church, was born at the African town of Thagaste, the son of a small landowner and a possessive Christian mother, St Monica. He completed his education in rhetoric at Carthage, but never mastered Greek. His *Confessions* (397/400), a masterpiece of introspective autobiography, analyse his life until the death of his mother (387). At the age of 19 he read *Cicero's (lost) Hortensius*, which inspired him to seek for 'Wisdom'. At first he sought it as a *Manichee, but became disillusioned while teaching rhetoric at Carthage (376–83). He moved to a chair first at Rome (383–4) and then, with a reference from *Symmachus, at the imperial capital of Milan (384). He abandoned scepticism when St *Ambrose's sermons resolved the Old Testament, and the discovery of Neoplatonism (see *Plotinus) gave him a concept of transcendent reality. He was converted (August 386), at first to the ideal of a philosophic life within the Catholic Church, but then to an ascetic withdrawal from a public career and an advantageous marriage (to which he had already sacrificed his common-law wife of fifteen years). After baptism by Ambrose (Easter 387), he returned to Africa where he lived a monastic life at Thagaste (388–91) until he was forcibly ordained priest at Hippo (391).

Ordination (and consecration as bishop in 395) was no less a turning-point than his conversion. Augustine now became a public figure, a pastor, a Christian teacher, the formidable spokesman and agent of Catholic unity in Africa. He wrote and preached against *Donatism, organizing councils and secular intervention which culminated in the hearing at Carthage (411) between the rival hierarchies that condemned the Donatists. Coercion was then used, which Augustine justified by the need to bring schismatics into the universal Church. He began the 'great and arduous work' of the *City of God* (413–26) to rebut the pagan accusation that Rome had fallen in Christian times, but passed from a demolition of paganism to the idea of a Christian community in this world and the next contrasted with the 'Earthly City'. Among the refugees from Rome who visited Africa was *Pelagius, whose teaching on free will had been prompted by a sentence from the *Confessions* (x. 29), 'Give what You command, and command what You will'. In a series of treatises against him and his disciple Julian of Eclanum, Augustine worked out his sombre views of the helplessness of human will and the inscrutability of God's justice: humanity was a 'mass of sin' from the Original Sin of Adam, and souls could only be saved (some of them) by the Grace of God. Towards the end of his life (426/7) Augustine reviewed his enormous literary output: 93 works, most of which survive, in 232 volumes, as well as hundreds of sermons and letters. He died (28 August 430) during the siege of Hippo by the invading Vandals, with the consolation that no great man thinks it a great thing that stone and timber fall, and mortal men die. The thought came from Plotinus.

BIBL. P. R. L. Brown, *Augustine of Hippo* (1967); H. Chadwick, *The Early Church* (1967) 216 ff. The *Confessions* (R. S. Pine-Coffin) and the *City of God* (H. Bettenson) are both translated in Penguin Classics.

Augustus (Octavian) (63 BC–AD 14) Emperor 27 BC–AD 14.

The colossal achievement of Rome's first emperor defies ordinary biographical treatment. Gaius Octavius, born to a senatorial but humble father, became Gaius Julius Caesar Octavianus as the legal (and political) heir of Julius *Caesar; in 27 BC Octavian, securely established as master of the world, became Caesar Augustus. He was then thirty-six years old. Despite the copious information we have on the events of his extraordinary rise to power and remarkable reign, it is almost impossible to isolate the talents and qualities of character which enabled this man, from his late adolescence to his dotage, to gain possession of and rule so diverse a dominion.

Augustus the man—his proud retention of his juvenile grammatical errors, his ventures into Greek drama, his antiquarian interest in fossils, his dicing, joking, tastes, and appetites—is preserved for us by *Suetonius and others, but the emperor remains hidden. Some have therefore tried to present *Agrippa, *Tiberius, *Drusus, *Statilius Taurus and Munatius *Plancus with the credit for Augustus' rise to power, and *Maecenas and *Livia with his retention of it. He was certainly fortunate in his helpers, as he was in the weaknesses of *Antony and the feeble few who thereafter disturbed the Augustan order from within: he was fortunate above all in the war-weariness of the Roman world, the decline in numbers of the senatorial class who could remember the Republic before Caesar, and his own long and (for the most part) healthy life. More explanation is required, and though historians may make all too easy deductions of ruthlessness, intelligence, cynicism, ambition, and shrewdness, a more satisfactory analysis is impossible. It is easier to find his weaknesses: he was only a moderately able commander, he was an over-optimistic strategist, he turned his family from a potential mainstay into a hotbed of disorder. Most importantly he imposed insuperable difficulties on his three successors by creating a system which focused sharply upon the *princeps* within a framework which pretended to allow government by the senate. This structure—no dyarchy, but dependent on the personalities of Augustus and his contemporaries—was responsible for the turmoil that we associate with the Julio-Claudian period. Not that Augustus attempted to impose a monolithic system on the Roman State; in fact, the brilliance of his repeated constitutional and administrative experiments, by which he adapted creatively all the most promising parts of the Republican polity to fit his needs, impresses more than do many of his more vaunted successes. The adoption of the tribunician power as the 'indication of the highest rank' is only the most famous of these expedients; some, like the attempt to revive the censorship in 22 BC, failed, but others, more numerous, for example the urban prefecture, which lasted until the end of the Empire, proved most useful. Like any Roman politician, Augustus also depended on his personal influence; indeed,

Augustus addressing troops: Tiberian copy (from Prima Porta) of late 1st-cent. BC statue. Rome, Vat. Mus.

this alone entitled him to the rank of *princeps* (i.e. *senatus*), which carried no power. The success of his armies and the possession of wealth on the vastest scale guaranteed this informal authority.

It was by a similar combination of influence and actual power that Augustus was able to further so dramatically the process of welding the area of direct Roman rule—the *imperium Romanum*—much of which he supervised personally, with the motley collection of allied cities, client kingdoms, and dependent tribes which filled in the gaps between and surrounded the edges of the Roman provinces. One of his principal tools in this task was the exaltation of the city of Rome, and by the end of his reign the city had become a worthy centre for the Roman Empire in its new form, full of noble buildings, properly administered, and glorified like its ruler in the words of the greatest poets of the time. It is easy to forget that Rome had previously been the capital of the world only in practice: Augustus now made the fact more obvious, as Caesar had intended to do before him. Much of the image of Rome's glory begins only now, and it is for his successes in this field, and for the contributions of the greatest of Roman poets, in particular *Virgil and *Horace, that his reign is best remembered.

Augustus himself wrote the 'Record of his Enterprises' (*Index rerum a se gestarum*, better known as *Res Gestae*), which he directed to be published posthumously. This survives in copies on stone, notably on the so-called *Monumentum Ancyranum*, with a locally-made Greek translation); the style is clear, sober, and formal, in the traditional manner of official record.

The chronological and factual framework of these developments: Octavian's main supporters and opponents became obvious early in the years after Caesar's murder, when the compromise which had created the Second Triumvirate (43 BC) broke down. The years of war which followed saw him married to Antony's relative Scribonia, who bore him his only offspring, *Julia, and later to *Livia, who remained a support to him all his life. The defeat of Sex. *Pompey and the neutralization of *Lepidus gave him the West, and he began his life's work by concentrating on the unification and restoration of Italy. In 31 the campaign of Actium (in which that battle played a minor role) gave him the final mastery. Antony killed himself. The next years were spent in consolidation and the perfecting of his position, reaching a climax in 27 BC with his change of name and the gaining of provincial power. There were further important modifications of the formal position in 23 and in 19; his absence from Rome in Spain (27–25) and the East (22–19) had raised problems in Rome (see *Egnatius Rufus) and his near death of an illness in 23 and the death of his heir *Marcellus had caused a serious breach within the closest circles of his

advisers. Tiberius and Drusus, Livia's children, now became his principal agents, though in 2 BC a grand demonstration of the maturity of the system, centred on the new heirs, Gaius and Lucius, and the opening of his new Forum in Rome, a monument to the dynasty, revealed how affairs had changed; Agrippa, Maecenas, and Drusus were all dead, Tiberius in self-imposed exile on Rhodes. These years were also marked by dramatic conquests, particularly in the Balkans and on the Danube. With the disgrace of Julia, the deaths of Gaius and Lucius, the return of Tiberius and his adoption, the revolt of Pannonia, and the disaster of *Varus in Germany, the last phase of the principate had come; but, although it represented partial failure of a number of projects, the difficulties that faced Tiberius on his accession in AD 14 were personal and the inevitable product of the system, not the result of the senility of the old emperor. For, although delegating much business, Augustus had remained in control to the end.

BIBL. Syme, *Rom. Rev.*; *Res Gestae*, ed. and trans. Brunt and Moore (1973).

Aurelian Emperor AD 270–5.

An Illyrian of humble birth, Aurelian (Lucius Domitius Aurelianus) belongs to the late third-century group of 'soldier emperors' instrumental in restoring the Empire. Noted for his military ability, he possessed great strength of mind and body but lacked subtlety. His empress was Ulpia Severina about whose origins and life little has survived, although she is attested by inscriptions and coins. At the start of his reign Aurelian successfully intercepted the Iuthungi on their return home after invading Italy, and defeated them. Not long after, he decisively defeated the Vandals who had invaded Pannonia. In a second invasion of Italy by the Iuthungi, Aurelian was initially defeated, but later virtually destroyed them. Back at Rome, he put down a revolt of the imperial mint-workers and began to fortify the city with new walls. Reorganization on the Danube

The Walls of Aurelian, Rome. A well-preserved section (some later reconstruction) east of Porta Appia.

Reformed coin of Aurelian: reverse with Sun-God.

frontier led to the withdrawal of troops and civilians from Dacia and the creation of a new Dacia composed of parts of Moesia, Dardania, and Thrace. In 271 he was forced to deal with the Palmyrene problem. *Zenobia (q.v.), its queen, although a nominal ally of Rome, had moved into Egypt and was trying to occupy Asia Minor as far as the Hellespont. Aurelian recovered the Asian territories and Egypt, and then besieged Palmyra successfully. In 272 he went to fight the Carpi on the Danube. A second rebellion in 273 at Palmyra led to the defeat and sack of the city. Aurelian moved against the Gallic empire in 273, and recovered Gaul in 274 after a battle with *Tetricus near Châlons. Aurelian also instituted a reform of the coinage and the city grain supply. On campaign in the East in 275 he was murdered by his generals.

BIBL. *RAC* Aurelianus; Syme, *Emperors and Biography*; *CAH* xii.

Aurelius, Marcus: see **Marcus Aurelius**.

Aureolus Usurper in Italy AD 268.

Of humble birth, Aureolus served in the army under *Valerian, defeated the usurper *Ingenuus in 260, and was probably *Gallienus' cavalry commander in Illyricum *c*. 261–7. In 267 he was sent to northern Italy, where in 268 he assumed the title Augustus. After Gallienus' murder in 268, he surrendered to *Claudius II at Milan, but was himself put to death.

BIBL. *CAH* xii; *PLRE* i, Aureolus; *PIR* A 1672.

Ausonius (c. AD 310–c. 393) Poet and politician.

Decimius Magnus Ausonius, the son of a successful doctor at Bordeaux, taught Latin literature and rhetoric in its university for thirty years, before being summoned to court (c. 367) to tutor the crown prince *Gratian. His uncle, a professor at Toulouse, had made a fortune by teaching at Constantinople and tutoring one of *Constantine I's sons; Ausonius' own career illustrates the opportunities open to a classical education in the Late Empire. When Gratian succeeded his father (November 375), Ausonius became a key figure, securing the praetorian prefecture (378–9) for himself and posts for numerous relatives; he was already a correspondent of leading senators like *Symmachus and (from a respectful distance) Petronius *Probus. In 379 he retired to his estates near Bordeaux with the consulship, for which he thanked Gratian in a prose panegyric of self-congratulation.

Ausonius was a fluent versifier, and many of his works survive. They include scholarly epigrams and catalogues (the days of the week, principal cities of the Empire, etc.), verse obituaries of relatives and university colleagues which collectively are a major source of contemporary social history, and even a wedding ode assembled from snatches of *Virgil to match one by *Valentinian I. One piece has real poetic merit, a description of the river Moselle, on which stood Valentinian's capital of Trier: though full of reminiscences of the *Georgics* and typical lists (fishes, tributaries, etc.), it was inspired by a sense of natural beauty. Ausonius was a nominal Christian, but a one-sided correspondence in prose and verse with his former pupil St *Paulinus pitifully illustrates the growing gulf between the new ascetic ideal of withdrawing from the world, and the tradition of government by eloquent amateurs.

BIBL. *PLRE* i, Ausonius 7: Matthews, *Aristocracies*, ch. 3.

Avidius Cassius Usurper AD 175.

From Cyrrhus in Syria, the son of *Avidius Heliodorus, Gaius Avidius Cassius was born in the reign of *Hadrian. Suffect consul 160/9, he achieved prominence by playing an important part in the Parthian War of the reign of *Marcus Aurelius (162–6). He quelled the revolt of the Boukoloi in Egypt (172–3), and then became governor of Syria (and perhaps virtual regent in the East). In 175, spurred on by false rumours of Marcus' death and perhaps with the complicity of *Faustina I (with whom he is said to have had an affair), he had himself proclaimed emperor. His 'reign' lasted only three months (April–July 175), and he was only recognized in parts of the East. He was assassinated by a centurion as Marcus prepared an expedition to put down the revolt.

BIBL. Birley, *Marcus*; A. K. Bowman, *JRS* lx (1970); *PIR* A 1402.

Avidius Heliodorus Imperial secretary, 2nd century AD.

A Greek rhetorician from Cyrrhus in Syria, Gaius Avidius Heliodorus held the equestrian post of secretary for Greek correspondence to *Hadrian before becoming prefect of Egypt (137–42). He was the father of *Avidius Cassius.

BIBL. *PIR* A 1495; Pflaum, *Carrières*, no. 106.

Avienius, Postumius Rufius Festus Poet, mid- or late 4th century AD.

Born in Volsinii, Avienius (formerly known as Avienus), best known for his Latin translation of Aratus' astronomical work *Phaenomena* (before 387), a *Description of the World*, and a *Maritime Shores*, led a prosperous life attested by his dedicatory poem to Nortia, Etruscan goddess of Destiny (*CIL* vi. 537): he was proconsul of Africa and of Achaea. He was a descendant of *Musonius Rufus, the Stoic philosopher.

BIBL. A. Cameron, *CQ* xvii (1967) 385.

Avienus Poet, floruit 5th century AD.

Avienus, a pagan poet, author of *fables* which enjoyed great popularity in the Middle Ages, was probably born around 380, and dedicated his work to *Macrobius. Presumably in return for the compliment he was cast anachronistically as the youngest interlocutor in the *Saturnalia*.

BIBL. A. Cameron, *CQ* xvii (1967) 385.

Avitus Western emperor AD 455–6.

Eparchius Avitus, father-in-law of *Sidonius Apollinaris, was raised to the purple as the candidate of the Gallo-Roman nobility on the death of *Petronius Maximus. He also relied on the Visigoths, with whom he had negotiated a treaty (439) and whom he enlisted against *Attila in 451. However, he alienated support in Italy and, while his Gothic allies were involved in Spain, he was defeated by *Ricimer and *Majorian at Placentia and forcibly consecrated a bishop. He died on a journey to Clermont, perhaps of natural causes, and was buried at the shrine of St Julien at Brioude.

BIBL. Sidonius Apollinaris, *Poem* VII, *Panegyric of Avitus*; Stroheker, *Adel*, prosop. 58.

Balbinus Emperor AD 238.

Decimus Caelius Calvinus Balbinus (c. 178 (?)–238) was elected joint emperor with *Pupienus by the senate in the confusion which followed the fall of Gordian I and II in Africa, while *Maximinus Thrax was marching against Italy. With Maximinus' defeat and death the power of the two senatorial emperors appeared unchallenged, but the disaffected praetorian guard seized both and murdered them only 99 days after they had assumed power.

BIBL. *CAH* xii; *PIR* C 126; *ANRW* ii. 2.

Balbus, Lucius Cornelius Consul 40 BC.

A Spanish millionaire enfranchised by *Pompey in 72 BC, Balbus attained enormous influence at Rome, especially as an agent of *Caesar in the 50s. When in 56 his citizenship was contested in the courts, it was really the First Triumvirate that was under attack, and Pompey, *Crassus, and *Cicero all spoke in his defence. He survived and, although not a senator, became prominent among Caesar's partisans during and after the Civil War. After 44 he transferred his allegiance to *Octavian, who rewarded him with a brief consulate.

BIBL. Syme, *Rom. Rev.*

Ballista General, praetorian prefect AD 260–1.

A general of *Valerian, under whom he fought the Persians, Ballista persuaded Fulvius *Macrianus to allow his sons to be proclaimed emperor after Valerian's capture by the Persians. He was defeated and killed with *Quietus *c.* 261 by *Odaenath.

BIBL. *PIR* B 41; *PLRE* i, Ballista.

Barbia Orbiana Empress AD 225–6.

Possibly the daughter of Seius Herennius Sallustius Barbius, Gnaea Seia Herennia Sallustia Barbia Orbiana was married to *Severus Alexander *c.* 225. After her father was slain for an attempted revolution *c.* 227 she was sent into exile.

BIBL. *CAH* xii.

Bar-Cochba, Simon (died AD 135) Jewish leader.

'Son of a star', Simon Bar-Cochba was the leader of the Jewish revolt against Rome in 132–5. Under his leadership the Jews mounted prolonged resistance to Roman oppression, which led to a serious and costly war in which *Hadrian had to deploy a large legionary force. Much light has been thrown on this by recent discoveries of letters of Bar-Cochba in a cave in the Judaean Desert. They show that one of the bases of the Jewish insurgents was at Engeddi. In the final phase of the revolt the Jews resorted to guerrilla tactics. Some finally took refuge in the Dead Sea Caves, others made a last stand at Bethar, where Bar-Cochba was killed. Examples of a coinage issued by Bar-Cochba, as 'Shimeon, president of Israel', during the revolt are also known. At the conclusion of the revolt a new province, Syria Palaestina, was created in place of Judaea, and the site of Jerusalem was renamed Aelia Capitolina, thus effectively ending the Jews' occupation of their traditional homeland.

BIBL. P. Benoit, J. T. Milik, R. de Vaux, *Discoveries in the Judaean Desert* II (1961); Y. Yadin, *Bar-Kokhba* (1971).

Bardesanes (Bar Daisan) (AD 154–222) Armenian heresiarch.

Bardesanes of Edessa believed that the body of Christ was a phantom and denied the resurrection of the body. He was a hymnographer and author (?) of the *Book of the Laws of the Nations*, an anti-Gnostic dialogue on fate, sin, and free will, extant in the original Syriac and in dependent Greek and Latin versions.

BIBL. Drijvers, *Bardaisan of Edessa* (1966).

Barea Soranus Consul AD 62.

A friend of *Rubellius Plautus and *Vespasian, and perhaps uncle of *Titus' wife Marcia Furnilla, Barea Soranus was renowned for his goodness—he was unusually conscientious as proconsul of Asia—and wealth, but was not averse to proposing measures popular in high circles. Accused of treason in AD 65 he committed suicide.

BIBL. *PIR* B 55.

St Basil the Great (*c.* AD 330–79) Bishop of Caesarea in Cappadocia AD 370–9.

Basil, his younger brother St *Gregory of Nyssa, and their friend St *Gregory of Nazianzus were the 'Cappadocian Fathers' who achieved the victory of eastern Catholicism over the *Arian heresy. Basil

Bar-Cochba's (Aramaic) letter of the 'four kinds', requesting palm branches, citrons, myrtles, willows for the Feast of Tabernacles. Fragment: Jerusalem, Israel Museum.

came from a rich Christian family of Caesarea and studied at Constantinople and Athens, but under the influence of his elder sister St Macrina he became a hermit (358–64) in Pontus, where he founded monasteries and devised the Rule which is still the basis of monastic life in the Orthodox Church. In 364 he returned to Caesarea, where he was consecrated bishop (370). Despite poor health, he was intensely active as metropolitan bishop of Cappadocia, as well as in Pontus and Armenia. He gained the personal respect of the Emperor *Valens, and mitigated the effects of his *Arianizing persecution by his contacts at court and by persuading semi-Arians to accept the Nicene formula; but he failed to gain significant western support. He founded a complex of charitable institutions outside Caesarea.

BIBL. *ODCC*, Basil.

Basilides Christian theologian, 2nd century AD.

One of the earliest important Christian Gnostics (who believed that it was through the revealed knowledge of God that spiritual redemption could be achieved), Basilides taught at Alexandria c. 125–50. He wrote a biblical commentary (*Exegetica*) in 24 books.

BIBL. E. R. Dodds, *Pagan and Christian in an Age of Anxiety* (1965); W. H. C. Frend, *Religion Popular and Unpopular in the Early Christian Centuries* (1976).

Basiliscus Eastern usurper AD 475–6.

The brother of the Emperor *Leo's wife, Basiliscus commanded the fleet sent against the Vandals in 468, but was deceived by *Geiseric into granting a delay, during which the Vandals mounted a surprise attack with fire-ships. After Leo's death (474) Basiliscus exploited the intrigues of his sister to depose Leo's successor, Zeno, but alienated support in many quarters by his appointments and his condemnation of the decisions of Chalcedon. On Zeno's return, he was exiled to Cappadocia and starved to death.

BIBL. Stein, *Bas-Empire*, i. 359, 363–4..

Bassus, Junius Praetorian prefect AD 318–31, consul 331.

A member of the senatorial aristocracy, Junius Bassus was one of Constantine's praetorian prefects. He built a basilica on the Esquiline hill at Rome, from which survives a marble-inlaid picture of the consul's procession, in a style far removed from the classical. He was possibly a Christian.

BIBL. *PLRE* i, Bassus 14; E. Nash, *Pictorial Dictionary of Ancient Rome* (1961–2) i, 190–5.

Bassus Theotecnius, Junius Urban prefect of Rome AD 359.

Son of Junius *Bassus, born in 317, Junius Bassus Theotecnius held various offices culminating in the prefecture of Rome, but died shortly after taking up office. He was a Christian, baptized, as was the custom, on his deathbed. He was buried in St Peter's, Rome, and his sarcophagus (now in the crypt) is the finest masterpiece of this branch of

Marble intarsio of consul's procession, Basilica of Junius Bassus, Rome. Rome, Palazzo dei Conservatori.

Roman Christian art. A poem inscribed on the sarcophagus lid describes the mourning of the City, and how the people wept and vied with each other to carry his bier.

BIBL. *PLRE* i, Bassus 15; Chastagnol, *Fastes*.

Berenice (born AD 28) Jewish princess.

Julia Berenice was the daughter of ('Herod') *Agrippa I. In Acts (25:13) she is shown sharing the business of the kingdom with her brother Agrippa II, and she continued to do this after a brief marriage to another eastern prince. She became a Flavian sympathizer, and *Titus grew so infatuated with her as to promise marriage: at Rome this proved most embarrassing because of her nationality, and he had to dismiss her.

BIBL. *PIR* B 108.

Bibulus Consul 59 BC.

As *Caesar's colleague in the consulship (59 BC) Marcus Calpurnius Bibulus suffered violence and other indignities from Caesar's supporters when he tried to block his agrarian laws. He withdrew to the safety of his house where he made all Caesar's subsequent legislation technically invalid by watching for omens. His resistance to violent methods won him much sympathetic support. Later he proposed the special sole consulship for *Pompey (52), and after governing Syria was put in charge of Pompey's fleet against Caesar (49).

BIBL. Gruen, *Republic*; Taylor, *Party Politics*.

Blossius (died 129 BC) Philosopher.

Blossius of Cumae was a Stoic philosopher, and a loyal friend and mentor (in an ill-defined manner) to Tiberius *Gracchus. After his death he joined the rising of *Aristonicus, and on its suppression committed suicide.

BIBL. Dudley, *JRS* 1941, 94 ff.

Boethius (*c*. AD 476–524) Poet and philosopher.

Son of Manlius Boethius (consul 487) and great-grandson of *Symmachus, Anicius Manlius Severinus Boethius, a poet-philosopher and statesman, was an accomplished Greek scholar, renowned for his learning (Ennodius, *Ep*. vii. 13) as early as 507. He devoted his youth to the translation and commentary of the works of Aristotle, and had intended to translate all of Aristotle and Plato into Latin and to attempt to reconcile their philosophies, but did not live to complete the task. From this period remain a translation and commentary of Aristotle's *On Interpretation* and an *On the Teaching of Arithmetic*. Boethius was appointed consul for 510 by Theoderic: his fortunes rose, and in 522 he saw his two sons joint consuls for the year, while he himself, as Master of the Offices, delivered a panegyric of Theoderic. By 523 he had fallen from favour, and was imprisoned at Pavia for about a year, during which time he wrote the *On the Consolation of Philosophy*. In 524 he was summarily clubbed to death after hideous tortures.

The nature of his offence is not entirely clear: probably he was over-eager to defend a fellow-

Sarcophagus of Junius Bassus Theotecnius, detail: Job on his dunghill, Adam and Eve. Rome, St Peter's.

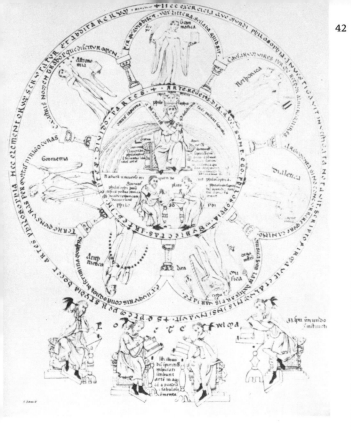

Philosophy and the Seven Liberal Arts. Illustration from the 12th-century manuscript of the *Hortus deliciarum* of Herrade de Landsberg.

senator accused of treacherous correspondence with the Emperor Justin, and was thereby himself implicated in the charge. Contemporary sources (Procopius and the Anonymus Valesianus) consider him innocent, and the impression of a moral and passionate character to be drawn from his own works would confirm this. His most famous work, *On the Consolation of Philosophy*, written in stylized Menippean satire form based on *Martianus Capella, deals with classic philosophical problems on the nature of fate and fortune, and the relationship between evil, free will, and Providence. For a long time Boethius' Christianity was in doubt, since he appeared to have turned to philosophy rather than to theology in his utmost need: four Christian tracts attributed to him were considered spurious. The discovery of the *Anecdoton Holderi* in 1871 put an end to the controversy and established his authorship beyond doubt. The synthesis of Platonism and Christianity found in the *Consolation* made it one of the most influential and popular books of the Middle Ages.

BIBL. P. Courcelle, *La Consolation de Philosophie dans la tradition littéraire*; H. M. Barrett, *Boethius, Some Aspects of his Times and Work* (1940); H. Usener, *Anecdoton Holderi. Ein Beitrag zur Geschichte Roms in ostgothischer Zeit* (1877).

Bolanus, Vettius Governor of Britain AD 69–71.

Marcus Vettius Bolanus fought under *Corbulo in Armenia, and in AD 69 was appointed by *Vitellius as governor of Britain, where he was popular with the troops but inactive in warfare. He was later proconsul of Asia.

BIBL. Tac. *Agricola*, viii. 1.

Bonifatius (Boniface) Master of the Soldiers, AD 432.

A loyal supporter of Galla *Placidia, Boniface had earned a reputation for valour by wounding the Gothic chieftain *Athaulf at Marseilles in 413. As Count of Africa he actively supported the restoration of Placidia and *Valentinian III during the usurpation of John (423–5), but incurred the hostility of Catholics in Africa by marrying an *Arian wife. He refused the demand for his recall and was forced into rebellion (427); it is later alleged that the Vandals first crossed from Spain into Africa at his invitation, but it was Boniface who led the resistance to the invaders—he was besieged in Hippo at the time of *Augustine's death (430). On his recall to court in 432 as Master of the Soldiers he had to fight, and defeat, *Aëtius in a civil war, but died soon after.

BIBL. Oost, *Galla Placidia*, chs. 5–6; PW iii, 698–9.

Bonosus Gallic usurper *c.* AD 276–80.

Known only from the obviously spurious biography in the *Augustan History and a few coins of barbarous fabric, Bonosus' existence is open to doubt.

BIBL. *PLRE* i, Bonosus 1; *RIC* v. 2; A. Chastagnol, *Recherches sur l'histoire Auguste* (1970).

Boudicca British queen, mid-1st century AD.

(Boadicea is a textually unsound variant). Boudicca was wife of Prasutagus king of the Iceni, who had co-operated with Rome. Atrocities committed after his death in AD 61 caused her to lead a revolt. The absence of *Suetonius Paulinus the governor and the disunity of the Roman forces allowed her to burn Colchester, London, and St Albans, but Suetonius returned from his campaign in Anglesey and defeated her in a pitched battle; she committed suicide.

BIBL. Tac. *Ann.* xiv. 29–39.

Brennus

Brennus was the reputed Gallic leader at the Sack of Rome (390 BC). His name has probably been borrowed from the chieftain who led the Gallic raid on Greece in 280–279 BC.

BIBL. PW iii. 830; Ogilvie, *Livy*, 719.

Britannicus (AD 41–55)

Tiberius Claudius Britannicus was the son of *Claudius by *Messallina; after her fall his position of heir was seriously jeopardized. The adoption of *Nero made matters still worse, and, although Claudius was said to have begun to have his doubts about this shortly before his death, nothing was done, and Britannicus did not live far into Nero's reign: his violent death at dinner was attributed to epilepsy.

BIBL. Tac. *Ann.* xiii. 15–17.

Bruttius Praesens Consul AD 118/9 and 139

A friend and correspondent of *Pliny the Younger, Gaius Bruttius Praesens was decorated in *Domitian's Marcomannic War (89) and again in *Trajan's Parthian War when he commanded a legion. He governed Cilicia in 117 and, after his first consulship, Cappadocia, Moesia Inferior, then Africa in 133–4, and Syria at the end of *Hadrian's reign. His distinction is indicated by the fact that he was the first consular colleague of *Antoninus Pius at the beginning of his reign.

BIBL. C. P. Jones, *Phoenix* 22 (1968); R. Syme, *Historia* 9 (1960); id., *Tacitus*.

Brutus Assassin of Caesar 44 BC.

An able and popular aristocrat famed for his moral integrity and patriotism, Marcus Junius Brutus emerged in 44 BC as the leader of *Caesar's assassins, and led the republican resistance to the Second Triumvirate. In 53 he had served in Cilicia as quaestor to Appius *Claudius Pulcher, whose successor, *Cicero, found that 'the honourable Brutus' was extorting 48 per cent interest on a loan to the city of Salamis in Cyprus. Schooled by his mother *Servilia to hate *Pompey (who in 77 had killed his father, Marcus Brutus, in *Lepidus' (2) rebellion), he nevertheless joined him in 49 against Servilia's erstwhile lover Caesar. Here he was perhaps following his republican instincts and the example of *Cato (Uticensis), whose daughter Porcia he later married.

After Pharsalus he was pardoned by Caesar, who gave him a command in Cisalpine Gaul, elevated him to the praetorship (44), and designated him for the consulship of 41. He was induced by his friend and colleague *Cassius to become the figurehead of the conspirators against Caesar, giving ideological respectability to their act of 'tyrannicide'. He was forced out of Italy within a month of the Ides of March by popular resentment and the growing influence of *Antony, but in 43 the senate voted him a major proconsular command over the Balkan provinces. With Cassius he built up a powerful republican presence in the East against the triumvirs, but in 42 he was defeated by Antony and *Octavian at Philippi, where he committed suicide.

BIBL. Plutarch, *Life of Brutus*; Syme, *Rom. Rev.*; Radin, *Marcus Brutus* (1939).

Brutus, Lucius Junius Consul 509 BC (?).

Traditionally Brutus was chiefly responsible for

Denarius of Brutus: portrait (obverse); 'Ides of March' (EID MAR), daggers, and cap of liberty (reverse).

overthowing the Roman monarchy. Later Junii, especially *Brutus the assassin of *Caesar claimed descent from him, but their plebeian status has cast doubts on his authenticity. If he was in fact one of the first consuls, his revolutionary role was probably elaborated from that basis, and although originally the legend of *Lucretia was probably an independent story, Brutus had been incorporated by the early second century BC. As consul he supposedly executed his own sons for treason and concluded the first Carthaginian treaty.

BIBL. PW Supp. v. 356 ff.; Ogilvie, *Livy*, 216 ff., 232; Crawford, *RRC* 455, 517, 741.

Brutus Albinus, Decimus Junius Praetor 45 BC.

Brutus Albinus was originally a leading partisan of *Caesar, whom he served as legate in the Gallic and Civil Wars, and as propraetor in Gaul (48–46 BC). Caesar secured him a proconsular command in Cisalpine Gaul (44), and had designated him for the consulship of 42. But before leaving for his province Brutus joined the conspiracy to assassinate Caesar, and thereafter he was the principal commander of republican forces against *Antony in north Italy (44–43). He withstood a long siege at Modena before being relieved by *Hirtius and *Octavian, but was eventually trapped and killed by *Antony, whom he had pursued into Gaul.

BIBL. Syme, *Rom. Rev.*

Burrus Praetorian prefect AD 51–62.

Member of an equestrian family from Vaison in Provence, Burrus worked his way up through the service of *Livia, *Tiberius, and *Claudius, and was made praetorian prefect through *Agrippina's influence in AD 51. He and *Seneca, relying on each other's support, acted as advisors to *Nero in the first years of his reign, although the emperor became increasingly impatient of restraint. They helped weaken Agrippina's position, but Burrus was unable to help *Octavia. When he died in 62 poison was suspected.

BIBL. Tac. *Ann.* xiii–xiv; *PIR* A 441.

Caecina Alienus, Aulus Consul AD 69.

Caecina joined first *Galba and later *Vitellius, for whom he fought vigorously against *Otho. But he successfully transferred his allegiance to *Vespasian, and only fell foul of the new dynasty in 79, when he joined *Eprius Marcellus in a mysterious but unavailing conspiracy.

BIBL. Tac. *Hist*. i. 53.

Caelius Praetor 48 BC.

A gifted but impetuous young politician and a member of the Roman smart set of the 50s BC, Marcus Caelius Rufus succeeded the poet *Catullus in the line of lovers of *Clodia. He was a friend of *Cicero, who defended him in a celebrated trial for intimidation (*vis*) in 56. From 51 to 50 he kept Cicero informed of events at Rome in a series of letters which combine an accomplished literary style with an evident penchant for political journalism. At the outbreak of Civil War Caelius followed *Caesar, who procured him the praetorship of 48. Disappointed by the dictator's failure to countenance revolutionary legislation, Caelius espoused a radical programme and raised a somewhat desperate rebellion in south Italy, in which he was joined by *Milo. This was easily suppressed by Caesar's troops, and Caelius and Milo killed.

BIBL. R. G. Austin ed., *Cicero, Pro Caelio* (2nd ed., 1952); Cicero, *Fam*. viii.

Caepio, Quintus Servilius Consul 106 BC.

An extreme conservative, Caepio promoted a law during his consulship which restored to the senate the control of the juries in Rome's increasingly frequent political trials. He proceeded to a military command in southern Gaul where he captured Toulouse, the enormous booty from which mysteriously disappeared. As proconsul in 105 BC he refused to co-operate against the Cimbri with his military commander, but social inferior, the consul Gnaeus Mallius Maximus. He thus caused at Arausio (Orange) the worst Roman defeat since Cannae. He was immediately deprived of his *imperium* and expelled from the senate. In 103 he succumbed to prosecution for appropriating the Tolosan treasure.

BIBL. Gruen, *Politics*.

Caesar, Gaius Augustus' heir died AD 4.

Eldest son of *Agrippa and *Julia (2), born in 20 BC, Gaius Julius Caesar was adopted in 17 BC by *Augustus, and clearly designated as successor by a series of honours which culminated in his public presentation by Augustus in 5 BC (there had already been noisy demonstrations in his favour). His training continued with accelerated progress up the *cursus honorum*, attending debates on the Jewish question (4 BC), for example, and making an uneventful visit to the Danube. In 1 BC his first real

job, a mission to the East with extra powers, was given him, and his consulate in AD 1 began while he was still in Syria. His advisers were selected with care (they included *Lollius, *Quirinius, *Domitius Ahenobarbus, and *Sejanus) and the expedition was successful; but Gaius was wounded in fighting the Parthians and died in Lycia on his way home in AD 4, frustrating Augustus' plans for the succession.

BIBL. *PIR* I 216.

Silver coin (*denarius*) showing wreathed head of Caesar.

Caesar, Gaius Julius (100–44 BC) Consul 59, 48 and 46–44 BC; dictator 49–44 BC.

The most famous of all Romans and the embodiment of Roman military and administrative genius, Caesar's most conspicuous achievements were the conquest of Gaul and the permanent dislocation of Rome's republican constitution. His early career was marked by a strict adherence to the *cursus honorum* at a time when a contemporary dynast, *Pompey, was breaking all the constitutional rules. A senator before 70 BC, he took a *popularis* line in the 60s, advertising his anti-Sullan credentials as *Marius' nephew and *Cinna's son-in-law. He was associated in the schemes of *Crassus (from whom he received powerful backing) to supplant Pompey in popular esteem, but he also courted popularity by supporting Pompey's interests against the *optimates*. In 63 he was prominent in *Labienus' prosecution of Gaius Rabirius and in opposing *Cicero's execution of *Catiline's supporters. The same year saw him elected to the prestigious office of *pontifex maximus*, defeating the *optimates* *Catulus (2) and *Servilius Vatia, and to the praetorship of 62, which he followed with a successful military command in Spain.

Returning in 60 Caesar was confronted by *Cato's hostility, and had to waive his claim to a triumph so that he could stand for the consulship of 59. As consul he promoted the interests of Pompey and Crassus, whom he brought together into an informal coalition against the *optimates* (the 'First Triumvirate') receiving for himself a coveted five-year proconsular command in Gaul and Illyricum (through a law of *Vatinius). His radical legislation (notably the agrarian laws) won him widespread popular support, but was carried largely by intimidation in the face of fierce senatorial opposition led by Cato and *Bibulus. The illegalities of his consulship and the powerful enemies he had made rendered him especially vulnerable to prosecution if he should ever relinquish his *imperium*: this decisively influenced his subsequent career. It was thus essential in 56, when Lucius *Domitius Ahenobarbus threatened to supersede Caesar in Gaul, that the Triumvirate be renewed to keep him out of the consulship and to extend Caesar's command for a further five years. Because of the proximity of Caesar's army to Italy, he could use his soldiers to influence politics at Rome, and with the enormous booty from the Gallic campaigns he could buy adherents in the senate. But his influence declined sharply in the late 50s, when Pompey sided with the *optimates* against his now too powerful rival.

Caesar had completed the pacification of Gaul by 56, but was occupied until 51 with token military demonstrations in Britain and Germany and with a series of revolts culminating in that of *Vercingetorix. He had acquired not only a formidable military reputation to match Pompey's, but also a loyally devoted army of experienced veterans who were ready to march against the government in defence of their commander's threatened *dignitas*. When the senate early in 49 refused Caesar permission to stand for the

consulship of 48 *in absentia* and declared him a public enemy, he crossed the Rubicon (from his province into Italy) and quickly overran the peninsula. He secured Spain before taking on the main republican forces under Pompey in the Balkans and defeating them at Pharsalus (48 BC).

Caesar consolidated his mastery of the world by a series of follow-up campaigns: in Egypt, Pontus, Africa, and Spain (48–45). At Rome his position became increasingly monarchical as he held successive consulships (except 47 BC), received progressively longer grants of dictatorial powers (from 49 onwards), and assumed the trappings of royalty and godhead. Among the people and the all-important legions his popularity remained strong, almost idolatrous, especially after the magnificent series of triumphs which he held in 46. But, although he attempted to conciliate the senatorial opposition with his famous *clementia*, his evident intention of permanently superseding the republican regime led to *Cassius' and *Brutus' conspiracy to assassinate him in 44 BC. During his dictatorship he had achieved a partial restructuring of the government, introduced many essential administrative reforms, and extended Roman citizenship to Cisalpine Gaul. The Julian calendar, which survived unaltered until the sixteenth century, was introduced on 1 January 45, thus ending centuries of chaos caused by a lunar

Julius Caesar: The Gallic and Civil Wars.

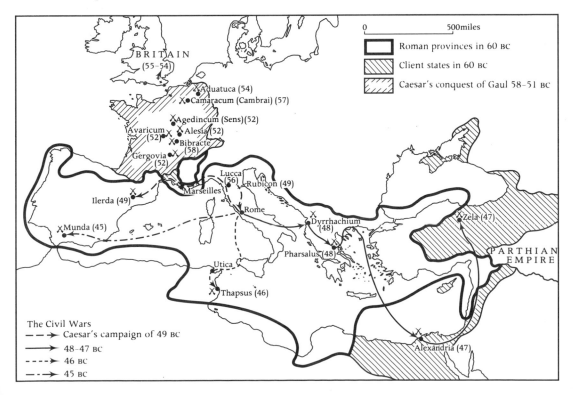

calendar out of phase with the solar year; the year 46 BC was lengthened to 445 days to correct this divergence. Before his death Caesar was planning an invasion of Parthia.

Caesar's decisive influence on the course of Roman history is matched by a formidable intellectual achievement. He was an orator of great distinction (*ORF* 383 ff.), described by Cicero as the most elegant of Roman speakers, a poet (rather unfavourable comments in verse on *Terence survive), grammarian (two books on grammatical analogy, dedicated to Cicero, were written while he was crossing the Alps), a wit (his jokes and sayings were published), a copious pamphleteer and letter writer, and an authority on astronomy. He is especially famed for his *Commentaries*, of which 7 books on the Gallic War (written *c.* 52/1) and 3 on the Civil War (incomplete and evidently written towards the end of his life) survive. The choice of form (*commentarii*) was a matter of exquisite calculation: the genre was that of 'notes', the raw material of the historian, a bald record of events to be written up by the literary stylist. Cicero (*Brutus* 262) declares, in a passage of warm admiration, that there was actually no room for improvement. The cool, sober, chaste, third-person narrative, containing speeches largely in indirect speech and, in the *Gallic Wars*, the occasional ethnographic excursus, is designed to create the illusion of impartial objectivity. In fact, both works are masterpieces of subtle propaganda, intended, in their studied moderation, to counter the numerous charges of aggression (against both Gaul and Pompey) which he incurred. *Hirtius (q.v.) completed and added to Caesar's own commentaries; the African and Spanish wars were written up by other members, now anonymous, of Caesar's staff.

Julius Caesar, portrait bust. Naples, Museo Nazionale.

BIBL. Plutarch, *Life of Caesar*; Suetonius, *Divus Julius*; Gelzer, *Caesar: politician and statesman* (1968); Weinstock, *Divus Julius* (1971); F. E. Adcock, *Caesar as Man of Letters* (1956); Kennedy, *Rhetoric*, 283 ff.

Caesar, Lucius Augustus' heir, died AD 2.

Born in 17 BC, son of *Agrippa and *Julia (2), Lucius Julius Caesar was at once adopted by *Augustus. In 2 BC honorific measures made it quite clear that he and his elder brother Gaius were intended as successors to Augustus, but Lucius died at Marseilles on his way to the armies in Spain.

BIBL. *PIR* I 222.

Calcidius Philosopher, early 4th century AD.

Calcidius, author of an important translation and Middle Platonic commentary on the *Timaeus* (written at the beginning of the fourth century), was probably a Christian and deacon to *Hosius of Cordova.

BIBL. J. Dillon, *The Middle Platonists* (1977); J. H. Waszink, *Timaeus a Calcidio Translatus* (1962).

Caligula: see **Gaius 'Caligula'**.

Callicrates of Leontium Achaean statesman, *c.* 180–149 BC.

Callicrates rose to prominence on an embassy to Rome *c.* 180 BC by departing from his instructions and urging the senate to give unequivocal support to Roman partisans in Greece (of whom he was a

The Maison Carrée at Nimes, France (*c.* 20 BC): temple dedicated to Gaius and Lucius Caesar, the heirs of Augustus.

prime example). His ascendancy supplanted
*Philopoemen's more independent policy towards
Rome, and entailed deference to Roman wishes on
all major issues. Callicrates' position was further
strengthened by the deportation of 1,000 notable
Achaeans (including *Polybius) to Italy from 167
until 151. IIis death in 149/8 allowed a resurgence
of Achaean hostility to Rome which resulted in
L. *Mummius' conquest in 146. Polybius was
bitterly hostile to Callicrates, and represented him
as unpopular in Achaea.

BIBL. Walbank, *HCP* iii, esp. 260–4.

Calpurnius Siculus Bucolic poet, mid-1st
century AD (?).

Titus Calpurnius Siculus was the author of
seven bucolic poems, in manner closely reminiscent
of Virgil (whom he calls 'a sanctified bard' (iv. 65)),
but in matter at times sharply distinct—notably
vii, on the Colosseum. The date is controversial:
Champlin argues forcefully for a date under
*Severus Alexander, but metrical analysis is likely
to vindicate the traditional date of composition
under *Nero.

BIBL. Text: Loeb, *Minor Latin Poets*, 294 ff ·
Champlin, *JRS* 1978, 95 ff.

Calvinus, Gnaeus Domitius Consul 53 and 40 BC.

Calvinus was a prominent opponent of the First
Triumvirate in the 50s, both as a tribune in
*Caesar's consulship and as an anti-triumviral
candidate in the notoriously corrupt consular
elections for 53 BC. He secured election with
conservative backing and by buying the collusion
of the incumbent consuls, L. *Domitius
Ahenobarbus (1) and Appius *Claudius Pulcher.
But in the Civil War he was one of the few
ex-consuls who actively supported Caesar, and
after Caesar's death he transferred his allegiance to
*Octavian. He held a second consulship in 40 and
a series of important military commands. But in
spite of his undoubted prominence, little is
recorded of his achievements.

BIBL. Syme, *Rom. Rev.*; Gruen, *Republic*.

Calvus, Gaius Licinius (born 82 BC) Orator and
poet.

The son of Licinius *Macer, Calvus called *Cicero
'formless and flabby', and Cicero retorted with
'dry and bloodless' (i.e. 'Atticist'). A friend of
*Catullus (poem 96), he was himself admired as a
love poet and notorious as another slanderer of
Caesar and his henchmen.

BIBL. *ORF* 492 ff.; *FPL* 84 ff.

Camillus, Marcus Furius Consular tribune 401,
398, 394, 386, 384, and 381 BC.

After an early censorship (403 BC) Camillus
captured Veii as dictator (396), vowing a temple to
her patron goddess Juno Regina and reputedly

dedicating offerings at Delphi. He made peace
with the Faliscans (394), but was subsequently
exiled (in 391 according to most sources). His
recall after the Gallic Sack (390) is plausible, but
his victories over the Gauls, Etruscans, Volsci, and
Aequi as dictator (390 and 389) are probably
patriotic fictions. Later he reputedly defeated the
Volsci (386 and 381), recovered Sutrium and
Nepete (386), and ensured Tusculum's loyalty
(381). His dictatorships of 368 and 367 and
foundation of a temple of Concord, linked to the
agitation of C. Licinius *Stolo, are highly suspect.

BIBL. PW vii. 324 ff.; A. Momigliano, *CQ* xxxvi
(1942) 111 ff. (= *Secondo Contributo* 89 ff.);
Ogilvie, *Livy*, 626 ff.; J. Hellegouarc'h *REL* xlviii
(1970) 112 ff.

Candidus, Tiberius Claudius Senator, general,
2nd–3rd centuries AD.

Probably of Numidian origin, Candidus had been
an equestrian officer at the end of *Marcus
Aurelius' reign, and was made a senator by
*Commodus. He served as a general under *Severus,
commanding the Illyrian army from 193–7.

BIBL. Birley, *Severus*; *PIR* C 823.

Canuleius, Gaius Tribune 445 BC.

Canuleius reputedly proposed the plebiscite
removing the Twelve Tables' prohibition of inter-
marriage between patricians and plebeians
(although, strictly, early plebiscites had no legal
force). *Dionysius of Halicarnassus omits the
measure entirely.

BIBL. PW iii. 1499 f.; Ogilvie, *Livy*, 527 f.

Capito, Gaius Ateius Lawyer; consul AD 5.

A jurist, Capito was particularly renowned for
his knowledge of pontifical law; a legal
conservative, he was eclipsed by *Labeo and
exercised no lasting importance, except perhaps
on the ritual of the secular games.

Silver coin (*antoninianus*) with emperor wearing radiate
crown, introduced by Caracalla.

Caracalla (Marcus Aurelius (Septimius Bassianus)
Antoninus) Emperor AD 211–17.

The elder son of Septimius *Severus and *Julia
Domna, Caracalla was born in Gaul in 188. In 195,

Above: portrait bust of Caracalla. Naples, Museo Nazionale.

two years after becoming emperor, Severus proclaimed himself son of *Marcus Aurelius and renamed Caracalla after Marcus. Caracalla was created Caesar in 196, emperor designate in 197, and was co-opted into the priestly colleges and named Augustus in 198. In 202 the all-powerful praetorian prefect *Plautianus arranged for him to marry his daughter *Plautilla, but Caracalla so loathed his bride and her father that he refused to have anything to do with her, and after Plautianus' fall in 205 he had her exiled. According to *Dio, Caracalla engineered the plot by which Plautianus met his death, claiming that he had intended to murder the emperors. From 205–8 Caracalla and his younger brother *Geta gained a reputation for loose living, and their intense brotherly rivalry grew into mutual hatred. Both accompanied their father on the British campaigns of 208–11. By this time Caracalla's mental instability was causing concern, and on one occasion it looked as if he were about to stab his father in the back in full view of the army. After Severus' death in 211 Caracalla and Geta abandoned the British campaign and returned to Rome, where their rivalry was so intense that even the palace was physically divided. Caracalla arranged to have Geta stabbed to death late in 211. His strength as emperor lay in his ability to win the soldiers' allegiance by sharing

Below: the Baths of Caracalla, Rome (built AD 212–16).

their burdens. His nickname Caracalla came from the designation of the hooded cloak he so frequently wore. His mental instability, brutal treatment of senators and any who opposed him, and harsh fiscal policies made him bitterly hated. He spent the years 213–17 organizing a Parthian campaign in the East, and was murdered by his praetorian prefect *Macrinus early in 217. Perhaps the most significant event of his reign was the edict granting citizenship to all free inhabitants of the Empire in 212.

BIBL. Millar, *Dio*; Birley, *Severus*; Herodian (Loeb).

Silver coin (*denarius*) of Caratacus.

Above: Britain AD 43–80.
Below: the Saxon Shore fort at Richborough on the Kent coast, held by Carausius. The ditches of the Claudian base are still discernible.

Caratacus British king *c.* AD 41/2–51.

Son of *Cunobellinus, Caratacus gallantly resisted the Roman invasion of AD 43, holding out for several years in the Welsh Marches. Defeated by *Ostorius Scapula, in 51 he was captured through the treachery of Queen *Cartimandua and sent to Rome, where his dignified bearing won him pardon and honours from *Claudius.

BIBL. Tacitus, *Annals* xii. 33–8.

Carausius Usurper in Britain and Gaul *c.* AD 287–93.

Marcus Aurelius Maus. Carausius was a distinguished soldier from the Low Countries, who as a young man had earned his living steering ships. In about 286 the Emperor *Maximian put Carausius in charge of a fleet to clear the North Sea of barbarian pirates. Success led to suspicions that he was not handing over all his booty to public funds, and Maximian sentenced him to death. Carausius accordingly used his forces (paid with copious coin partly struck from the barbarians' booty) to seize Britain and north Gaul and proclaim him emperor. Maximian failed to dislodge him in 290, but in 293 the newly-appointed Caesar *Constantius I was already making inroads into Carausius' territories when the usurper was murdered by *Allectus, one of his own generals.

BIBL. *PLRE* i, Carausius; Shiel, *The Episode of Carausius and Allectus* (B.A.R. xl, 1977).

Carbo, Gnaeus Papirius Consul 85, 84, and 82 BC.

After service in the Social War Carbo became a prominent figure in *Cinna's regime, sharing the consulships of 85 and 84 BC with him. On Cinna's death he abandoned the Dalmatian campaign and concentrated on consolidating the government's strength and popularity in Italy by carrying the long delayed measure to distribute newly enfranchised citizens equally among tribes. But in the face of *Sulla's impending invasion and military superiority, he was unable to retain sufficient loyalty either in Italy or in the senate to allow a successful resistance; nor could he maintain Cinna's control over events at Rome. After the military failures of *Norbanus and his colleague in 83, Carbo held a third consulship in 82 with *Marius' son. But after a series of reverses at the hands of *Metellus Pius, *Pompey, and Sulla he fled from Italy and eventually reached Sicily, where he was captured and killed.

BIBL. Badian, *Studies*, 224 ff.

Carinus Emperor AD 283–5.

Elder son of *Carus and husband of Magnia Urbica, Marcus Aurelius Carinus was proclaimed Caesar by his father in 282 and ruled in the West. He was noted for his vicious and cruel nature. It is not certain whether he or his brother *Numerian was the father of Nigrinianus. Carinus was slain by his own men at the battle of Margus, fought against *Diocletian in 285.

BIBL. *ANRW* ii. 2; *PLRE* i, Nigrinianus 1; *PIR* A 1473.

Cartimandua British client queen, mid-1st century AD.

Queen of the Brigantes in northern Britain, Cartimandua maintained her position with Roman support (forming a buffer state) after the Roman conquest of southern and midland Britain in AD 43. In 51 she handed over the fugitive *Caratacus to the Romans. Her expulsion in 68/9 encouraged the Roman advance into the north under *Vespasian (see Petillius *Cerealis, *Agricola).

BIBL. Frere, *Britannia*.

Carus Emperor AD 282–3.

Marcus Aurelius Carus was acclaimed emperor in 282 before the death of *Probus; the latter's murder by his own troops precluded civil war. Carus was probably born in Gaul, and he held both civil and military offices, serving as praetorian prefect under Probus. Once emperor, he concentrated his attention on the Persian campaign, first quelling an incursion of Quadi and Sarmatians. Carus decisively defeated the Persians and took Seleucia in 283. Continuing the campaign, he was almost certainly killed by a bolt of lightning near Ctesiphon, thus becoming one of the rare third-century emperors to die of natural causes.

BIBL. *PLRE* i, Carus; *ANRW* ii. 2; *PIR* A 1475.

Carvilius Maximus, Spurius Consul 293 and 272 BC.

A *novus homo*, Carvilius captured six Etruscan

Bronze mount with Celtic scroll-decoration of the time (AD 60/70) and from the territory (Elmswell, Yorks.) of *Cartimandua of the Brigantes.

strongholds and forced the Faliscans to sue for
peace after campaigning successfully with his
colleague, Lucius Papirius Cursor (the younger),
in Samnium (293 BC). In 272 he and Papirius finally
subjugated Tarentum and her Italic allies.
  BIBL. PW iii. 1630; Salmon, *Samnium* 270 ff.

Cassian, John (*c.* AD 360–*c.* 433) Monk of
Marseilles.
  Cassian was an important influence in bringing to
the West ideas of monasticism which flourished in
the Egyptian desert. With his friend Germanus he
spent some time at a monastery in Bethlehem, and
moved from there to visit the monks at Scete in
Egypt. Around 400 they were driven from Egypt,
and fled to Constantinople, where they were
welcomed by *John Chrysostom; an embassy on
behalf of the exiled Chrysostom brought them to
Rome. Later Cassian settled at Marseilles, where he
established monasteries for men and women on the
model of those he had witnessed in the East.
Here he wrote his *Institutes*, setting out his
monastic rule, and *Conferences*, the record of his
meetings with Egyptian monks; both these works
were heavily influenced by the monastic thinking
of Evagrius of Pontus.
  BIBL. O. Chadwick, *John Cassian* (2nd ed., 1968).

Cassius Assassin of Caesar 44 BC.
  As quaestor of *Crassus in Syria (53 BC), Gaius
Cassius Longinus survived the débâcle at Carrhae
to take command of the remaining forces. He
achieved outstanding military successes before
being replaced by *Bibulus in 51. He fought on
*Pompey's side in 49, but was pardoned by
*Caesar after Pharsalus. Like *Brutus, whose career
is paralleled closely by Cassius', he rose under
Caesar to be praetor in 44 and consul designate for
41. But he became the leading instigator of the
assassination plot against Caesar, and was forced to
leave Italy in April 44. In the senate's distribution
of provinces in 43 he was allocated Syria, where he
superseded and defeated the Caesarian, *Dolabella.
He joined forces with Brutus to meet the
triumvirs in Greece in 42, and died by suicide
after the defeat at Philippi.
  BIBL. Syme, *Rom. Rev.*

Cassius Chaerea Assassin AD 41.
  As a centurion Chaerea distinguished himself for
his bravery at the time of the mutiny of the Rhine
army in AD 14. He was promoted to the praetorian
guard and rose to the tribunate. *Gaius' taunts
drove him to plan the successful assassination of
24 January 41. *Claudius had him put to death.
  BIBL. *PIR* C 488.

Cassius Longinus, Gaius Consul AD 30.
  Cassius' descent from *Caesar's assassin brought
him into grave danger under *Gaius and *Nero,

but he survived both to die old, blind, wealthy,
and highly respected under *Vespasian. He had
the difficult job of governing Syria after the death
of *Agrippa and was most influential as a jurist.
  BIBL. *PIR* C 501.

Silver coin (*denarius*) of 102 BC recalling Spurius
Cassius Vicellinus' dedication of the temple of Ceres.

Cassius Vicellinus, Spurius Consul 502, 493, and
486 BC.
  Cassius reputedly campaigned against the
Aurunci (certainly fiction) or Sabines (502 BC),
dedicated the temple of Ceres, and concluded a
treaty with the Latins (493). In 486 he allegedly
made peace with the Hernici and proposed a
redistribution of public land. He was accused of
aiming at tyranny, and executed (by his father or
the quaestor(s)); his house, on the site of the later
temple of Tellus, was destroyed, his property
confiscated (485). The narratives of his agitation
are modelled primarily on events of the Gracchan
period. In origin probably only his execution for
tyrannical ambitions was remembered. If genuine,
this may be connected with the Fabian dominance
of 485–479; if fabrication, it is perhaps an
aetiological explanation of a statue in Ceres'
temple inscribed 'given from Cassius' property'.
  BIBL. PW iii. 1749 ff.; Ogilvie, *Livy*, 277 f.;
E. Gabba, *Athenaeum* xlii (1964) 29 ff.; A. W.
Lintott, *Historia* xix (1970) 18 ff.

Catiline Conspirator 63 BC.
  An ambitious and unprincipled aristocrat from
an obscure patrician family, Lucius Sergius Catilina
enriched himself as legate of *Sulla in the
proscriptions of 82 BC, and rose to political
prominence in the 60s. Praetor in 68, he was
prevented by an extended prosecution for
extortion from standing for the consulship until
64, when *Cicero kept him out of office by
capturing the conservative vote. Turning
demagogue, he now proceeded to build a vast
personal *clientela* by exploiting the widespread
agrarian unrest in Italy and proposing
revolutionary reforms. This failed to secure him
the consulship of 62, since conservative elements
once more combined against him. Persecuted by

the consul Cicero, he left Rome late in 63 and proceeded to open rebellion against the senatorial establishment, joining forces (like *Lepidus (2) in 78) with the anti-government uprisings he had provoked throughout Italy. The rebellion was easily crushed by Cicero, who magnified his achievement by presenting it as a gigantic co-ordinated conspiracy against the State, and even invented a so-called 'first Catilinarian conspiracy' in 66/5 which probably never occurred.

BIBL. Syme, *Sallust* (1964); Seager, *Historia* xxii (1973) 240 ff.; Gruen, *Republic*.

Catilius Severus Consul AD 110 and 120.

A distinguished senator, correspondent of *Pliny the Younger, and maternal step-grandfather of *Marcus Aurelius, Lucius Catilius Severus held a number of military and administrative posts under *Trajan, and was decorated for his service in the Parthian War (114–17). On *Hadrian's accession he was made governor of Syria; after his second consulship he was governor of Africa and urban prefect. He was holding the latter post when Hadrian adopted *Antoninus Pius, and is said to have shown displeasure because he had hopes of succeeding Hadrian. He therefore incurred Hadrian's wrath, and was deprived of his post.

BIBL. Syme, *Tacitus*; Sherwin-White, *The Letters of Pliny*; PIR C 558.

Cato the Elder (234–149 BC) Consul 195 BC.

A political personality and orator of immense stature, Marcus Porcius Cato projected himself as a vigorous defender of traditional Roman society and values against the encroachment of dangerous new influences. Born in 234 BC, he obtained political advancement as an able *novus homo* through the patronage of the noble Lucius Valerius Flaccus, and held the consulship of 195 with him. In that year he was assigned to Spain, where his military successes were sufficient to earn a triumph. It is unlikely that *Scipio Africanus tried to succeed him in his command, as some sources state; but the hostility certainly existed in the 180s, when Cato was prominent in the political attacks on Africanus and his brother, *Scipio Asiagenus. He achieved further military distinction in 191, when, as legate of *Glabrio in Greece, he claimed much of the credit for the victory over *Antiochus III at Thermopylae.

These solid achievements and his record of opposition to the Scipios (together with a carefully cultivated public image) probably helped to secure Cato's election as censor (184), again with Flaccus as colleague. This censorship became proverbial for its severity: Cato aggressively asserted the censors' traditional role as moral guardians of the State, and clashed with the *publicani*. He also used the office to press home attacks on political opponents, notably the Scipios and *Flamininus,

whose careers marked a dangerous drift towards autocracy.

He survived for another 35 years as a respected elder statesman, making a conspicuous but largely ineffective stand against the influx of luxury and Greek culture as the principal causes of moral degeneracy at Rome. In foreign affairs he saved Rhodes from the threat of war in 167 and secured the release of Achaean detainees in 151. But after 153 he became increasingly obsessed with the threat from Carthage, and ended each of his pronouncements in the senate with the famous: 'Carthage must be destroyed'. Before his death in 149 he had overcome the opposition of *Scipio Nasica, and war had been declared.

An accomplished *poseur*, Cato successfully distorted his biographical record with his own propaganda. Behind the façade of the sturdy peasant-soldier from Tusculum, a second Curius *Dentatus, lurked a wealthy landowner who also profited from dubious commercial enterprises. Again, the strident anti-Hellenist masks a highly educated man whose learning extended to various branches of Greek culture. 'Keep to the subject, the words will follow' (fr. 15), he proclaimed; nevertheless, his contribution to Latin prose was substantial and sophisticated. Treatises addressed to his son on agriculture, rhetoric, and medicine, works on law and war, and 150 speeches are lost but for fragments, which juxtapose a Latin still crude and simple with Greek learning and rhetoric. Seven books of *Origins* narrated both the foundation legends of Rome and the Italian cities (based on written sources, local legend, and on the spot research) and the history of recent wars. The vigorous and confused *On Agriculture* survives: a terse and engaging medley of prayers, spells, recipes, and precepts. His well-advertised thrift was recognized by *Plutarch as inexcusable meanness, especially his notorious treatment of slaves. But he was consistent in his public stand and correct in his diagnosis of the disruptive effects of new wealth, power, and ideas on Roman society and on the aristocracy itself.

BIBL. Plutarch, *Life of Cato the Elder*; Astin, *Cato the Censor* (1978). Works. Speeches: *ORF* 12 ff.; *Origines*: *HRR* i. 51 ff. There has been no complete edition of the fragments since Jordan's (1860). *De agri cultura*: Loeb edition (with *Varro, *Res Rusticae*). (The *Sayings of Cato*, beloved of medieval Europe, are spurious.)

Cato 'Uticensis' Republican champion, praetor 54 BC.

Spurred on by Stoic principles, by his respect for Roman traditions, and by a desire to emulate his great ancestor, the Elder *Cato, Marcus Porcius Cato 'Uticensis' won fame as a passionately committed defender of the aristocratic republican regime in its dying years. Despite his youth and junior rank he

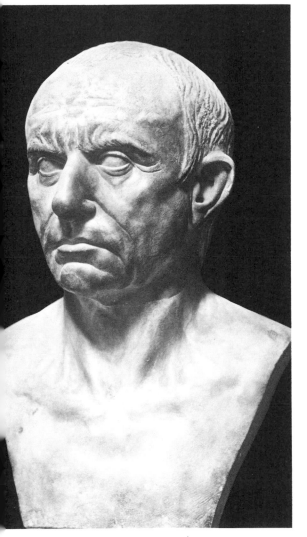

Portrait bust of Cato 'Uticensis'. Rome, Capitoline Museum.

emerged as the leader of the so-called *optimates* (superseding the aged *Catulus (2)) in 63 BC, when he clashed with *Caesar over the execution of *Catiline's supporters. In the late 60s he dominated the senate, especially in its opposition to the demands of the dynasts *Pompey and *Crassus and to Caesar's candidacy for the consulship of 59. Thus, by his uncompromising adherence to constitutional principles, he precipitated the First Triumvirate and hastened the drift towards dictatorship, which he had resolutely opposed. In 59 his opposition to Caesar's legislation was strident but ineffectual, although it helped to turn popular sentiment against the triumvirs. He was removed from Rome in 58 by a law of *Clodius on behalf of the triumvirs, which appointed him to administer the annexation of

Cyprus. On his return he supported his brother-in-law L. *Domitius Ahenobarbus' (1) campaign against Caesar, and was kept out of the praetorship until 54 by the renewed triumvirate. Pompey's sole consulship in 52 meant an abandonment of Cato's principles, and after failing to reach the consulship of 51 he dropped temporarily from prominence, unwilling perhaps to be associated closely with Pompey. But Cato inspired the intransigent attitude towards Caesar which accelerated the onset of civil war, and after Pharsalus he became the figurehead of the continuing republican resistance. Serving under *Metellus Scipio in Africa he held Utica, where he committed suicide after Caesar's victory at Thapsus.

BIBL. Plutarch, *Life of Cato the Younger*; Syme, *Rom. Rev.*; Taylor, *Party Politics*.

Catullus Poet, floruit 60–55 BC.

A native of Verona, Gaius Valerius Catullus was the son of a citizen of substance acquainted with Julius *Caesar. He was active in Roman literary circles, as poems such as those to *Cicero (49), Cornelius *Nepos (1), *Hortensius (65), Helvius *Cinna (95), and *Calvus (14) bear witness. Only a visit to Bithynia in the entourage of the governor Gaius *Memmius (2) (see *Lucretius), probably in 57–56 (poems 4, 10) stands as solid and datable biographical fact. His famous love-affair with Lesbia, a cover-name, possibly for *Clodia, conceivably the wife of Quintus Metellus Celer (praetor 63) cannot be charted in detail (51: the first poem; 11 the last?), nor can an alleged rivalry with *Caelius for her favours (poems 58, 77, 100). In public, he spared neither Caesar (29, 93, etc.) nor his chief engineer, Mamurra (29, 94, etc.; often under the nickname of Mentula, i.e. 'O'Toole').

The surviving collection of poems is itself an enigma: it consists of (i) a *libellus* ('little book') of short poems in a wide variety of lyric metres (1–51a, 51b–60), largely if not wholly collected by the author and showing strong traces of careful arrangement; (ii) 61–4, a sequence of long poems, (including the extraordinary metrical *tour de force* 63, in 'galliambics', on the ecstatic worship of Attis), rising to the 'Peleus and Thetis' epyllion in 408 hexameters; and (iii) 65–8 (longer elegiac poems) and 69–116 (a sequence of epigrams in elegiacs). (ii) and (iii) appear to have been collected by an editor. Though the subject matter of (i) and (iii) contain many common elements (e.g. love poems, poems of erotic disillusion, attacks on Caesar, literary squibs), it has become clear that the three elements in the collection do differ significantly: in (i) and (ii), as in 65–8, we see bold literary experiments, fluent and often erudite, under the strong influence of Alexandrian poetry, whereas the poems in (iii) develop along simpler lines and express powerful emotions in traditional

Roman terms (the application of 'the vocabulary of political alliance' to the poetry of love is the clearest example).

BIBL. D. O. Ross, *Style and Tradition in Catullus* (1969). The commentary by W. Kroll (1922, 1959, etc.) is still to be preferred to those of Fordyce (1961, expurgated) and Quinn (1970); Clausen, *C. Phil.* (1976) 37 ff; T. P. Wiseman, *JRS* 1979, 161.

Catulus, Gaius Lutatius Consul 242 BC.

As consul Catulus renewed Rome's naval effort and won the decisive naval victory at Aegates Insulae as proconsul on 10 March 241 BC. This ended the 24-year struggle with Carthage for control of Sicily (First Punic War). He negotiated a treaty with *Hamilcar which took his name.

BIBL. Walbank, *HCP* i. 124–6.

Catulus (1), Quintus Lutatius Consul 102 BC.

Catulus was a conservative senator noted for his cultural interests and literary patronage. His consulship as *Marius' colleague (102 BC) and their joint triumph in 101 reflect the solidarity of the senatorial establishment behind Marius in the crisis of the German wars. Resentful of Marius' greater reputation, Catulus became a bitter political opponent of his in the 90s. In 87 he was a prominent victim of Marius' reign of terror.

BIBL. Badian, *Studies*; Gruen, *Politics*.

Catulus (2), Quintus Lutatius Consul 78 BC.

Catulus inherited the strong conservative instincts of his father *Catulus (1), and after joining *Sulla in 83 BC became a respected pillar of the post-Sullan establishment, which he defended as consul (78) against the attempted *coup d'état* of his colleague *Lepidus (2). As proconsul in 77 he crushed Lepidus but could not make *Pompey disband his private army. He accepted the restoration of tribunes' powers in 70, but strongly opposed their use to grant extraordinary commands to Pompey in 67 and 66. As censor in 65 he clashed with his colleague *Crassus, but his reactionary influence was effectively broken in 63 when *Caesar was elected *pontifex maximus* at Catulus' expense.

BIBL. Gruen, *Republic*.

C(a)eionii Late-Roman aristocratic family.

This prolific late-Roman family, with origins in the third century and earlier, during the fourth and fifth centuries produced many consuls and urban prefects, as well as governors of Italian and African provinces. A central figure is Gaius Ceionius Rufinus Volusianus (consul 314), who recovered Africa for the usurper *Maxentius, became urban prefect (310), and repeated the post under *Constantine (313–5). His son Ceionius Rufius Albinus (consul 335) was also urban prefect (335–7), like *his* son Gaius Ceionius Rufius

Volusianus Lampadius, who in 365 advertised his own name while repairing 13 Tiber bridges and numerous public buildings. Meanwhile (364/7) Lampadius' son Publilius Caeionius Caecina Albinus was an unusually active governor of Numidia, where 18 inscriptions still attest his repairs to public buildings including temples: the family was stubbornly pagan, but had a penchant for marrying Christian heiresses. Albinus, the father of St *Jerome's patron Laeta (see *Eustochium), and his brother Ceionius Rufius Albinus (urban prefect 389–91), grandfather of St *Melania the Younger, are two of the learned pagan

Ivory diptych: the Ceionian (?) Lampadius and his sons presiding at the Circus Maximus. Brescia.

aristocrats in *Macrobius' *Saturnalia*. Rufius' son Rufius Antonius Agrypnius Volusianus (urban prefect 417–8), however, corresponded amicably with St *Augustine about the difficulties of accepting the Christian faith, and was baptized on his deathbed. The family's fifth-century consuls (down to Caecina Decius Faustus Albinus in 493) may include the 'Lampadius' depicted on an ivory diptych of c. 425, presiding over the traditional, and very expensive, Circus games: he may be the urban prefect Rufius Caecina Felix Lampadius who repaired the Colosseum (426/50).

BIBL. *PLRE* i. s.v. *Ceionii* and stemma 13; A. Chastagnol, *Le Sénat romain sous le règne d'Odoacre*.

Celsus Philosopher, 2nd century AD.

A Greek-speaking Platonist, Celsus wrote a polemic against Christianity (now lost) towards the end of the reign of *Marcus Aurelius. Its content is known through *Origen's refutation and was an important influence on later Neoplatonist anti-Christian thought.

BIBL. H. Chadwick, *The Early Church*; id., *Origen, contra Celsum* (1965); M. Borret, *Origène, contra Celse* (1967–9).

Celsus, Aulus Cornelius Encyclopedist (floruit under Tiberius).

In the tradition of *Cato the Elder and *Varro (*Disciplinae*), Celsus composed an encyclopedia (*Artes*) under *Tiberius, of which eight books (vi–xiii of the whole) survive, on medicine. Deeply revered in the Renaissance, Celsus presents an admirable conspectus of medicine as the science was understood at Rome.

BIBL. Scarborough, *Roman Medicine* (1969) 59 ff.

Celsus, Publius Juventius Jurist, floruit c. AD 100.

Head of the Proculian school of jurists in succession to *Pegasus, Celsus was a prominent lawyer of *Domitian's reign. He is said to have

conspired against this emperor but escaped by means of a trick.

BIBL. Dio LXVII. xiii. 3. 4.

Cerealis, Naeratius Consul AD 358.

Cerealis, a Roman aristocrat like his half-brother *Rufinus (Vulcacius), was trusted by *Constantius II, who made him urban prefect of Rome (352–3) immediately after the defeat of the usurper *Magnentius. In old age he asked the saintly Marcella to marry him, but she refused: 'If I wished to marry, I would marry a husband not an inheritance.'

BIBL. *PLRE* i, Cerealis 2.

Cerealis, Petillius Consul AD 70, 74 (?), and 83.

Probably the adopted son of a *Tiberian informer, of Umbrian origin, Quintus Petillius Cerealis Caesius Rufus was commander of IX Hispana when it was routed by *Boudicca in AD 60–1, and was not much more successful as commander of the Flavian cavalry during the march on Rome, a position he won through family connections with the Flavians; nor was his conduct of the war against *Civilis entirely successful. Two consulships followed, and the governorship of Britain in between: it is almost certain that during his three years there (71–3) he not only conquered the Brigantes (see *Cartimandua), but laid the foundations for *Agricola's success by expeditions further north. *Tacitus was hostile to Petillius, who may have been favoured by *Domitian with a third consulship in 83, as a snub to Agricola. He remains one of the most important figures of the early Flavian period.

BIBL. Birley, *Britannia* (1973); Tac. *Hist.* iii–v; *Ann.* xiv 32.

Cestius Epulo, Gaius.

Nothing is known of Cestius, a senator of the age

The Pyramid of Cestius Epulo, Rome, incorporated into the *Porta Ostiensis* (now the Porta S. Paolo).

of *Augustus, except that he was tribune, *septemvir epulonum* (a member of a minor priesthood), and left part of his property to *Agrippa: this information derives from the inscription on the huge pyramidal tomb on the road to Ostia, later incorporated in the *Porta Ostiensis* and so preserved.

BIBL. *PIR* C 686; Nash, *Pict Dic.*, ii. 321 ff.

Charops Epirote dynast *c.* 170–160 BC.
One of the first eastern dynasts to be educated at Rome, Charops took advantage of the Third Macedonian War and his Roman contacts to establish an almost tyrannical position for himself in Epirus (characterized by *Polybius as a reign of terror). As a notorious pro-Roman, it was probably his left-wing policies that aroused Polybius' intense hatred and which led to his being refused entry to the houses of *Lepidus (1) and *Paullus (2) while on an embassy to Rome *c.* 160 BC. He may have been implicated in the massacre of a rival Epirote tribe by Paullus (2) in 167.

BIBL. H. H. Scullard, *JRS* xxxv (1945) 55 ff.; Walbank, *HCP* iii. 313 f., 522 ff.

Chrysanthius Neoplatonist philosopher, 4th century AD.
Member of a leading family of Sardis, Chrysanthius studied philosophy under *Aedesius at Pergamum, and helped his fellow-pupil *Maximus of Ephesus to initiate the young *Julian into the pagan mystery-cults. Unlike Maximus and *Priscus, he refused Julian's later invitations to court (361–2), pleading contrary omens, and he and his wife were appointed high priest and priestess of Lydia, in which office he also showed caution. Teacher of *Eunapius, who wrote his biography, he died aged 80.

BIBL. Eunapius, *Lives of the Philosophers* (Loeb (with Philostratus), pp. 431–5, 539–64).

Chrysanthus *Vicarius* of Britain, after (?) AD 395.
Chrysanthus was one of the last governors-general (*vicarii*) of Britain. His father was a priest of the rigorist sect of *Novatianists (later its bishop) whom the Emperor *Valens chose to tutor his daughters. Chrysanthus served at court, before governing an Italian province under *Theodosius I, and then Britain. He retired to Constantinople, where he hoped to become urban prefect, but instead he was forcibly consecrated bishop of the Novatianists (died 419).

BIBL. *PLRE* i, Chrysanthus.

Cicero (106–43 BC) Orator, consul 63 BC.
The greatest of Roman orators and an articulate but self-opinionated politician, Marcus Tullius Cicero is the most intimately known of all republican personalities, chiefly from his own voluminous writings, in which, however, his

Portrait bust of Cicero. Rome, Capitoline Museum.

political importance is overstated. A *novus homo*, he secured political advancement as a successful advocate in political trials, notably by his prosecution of *Verres in 70 BC, when he eclipsed the legal reputation of Q. *Hortensius. He followed a moderately *popularis* line and attached himself particularly to the cause of his hero, *Pompey, speaking as praetor in favour of the unlimited powers conferred on him by the *Lex Manilia* in 66. In 64 he profited from suspicions against *Catiline to secure election to the consulship of 63 as the 'safe' candidate. This was the turning-point in his career: having made his way into the exalted and exclusive clique of the nobility (where he was not rapturously welcomed), he proceeded to identify with the interests of the *optimates*, killing the radical agrarian bill of Rullus and taking a solid conservative stand against Catiline's revolutionary posturing. Cicero's relentless persecution drove Catiline into open rebellion, which Cicero then suppressed, posing as the man who saved the State from a violent *coup d'état*; and by exaggerating the scope of the 'conspiracy' he was able to magnify his own achievement.

The Catilinarian scare induced a momentary solidarity of upper-class, propertied interests (senatorial and non-senatorial), the perpetuation of which now became Cicero's political ideal (*concordia ordinum*). But he could not prevent the extreme *optimates* led by *Cato (Uticensis) from precipitating the First Triumvirate (59 BC: see *Caesar), after which he was prevented by the military dynasts from exercising the authority and influence due to his rank. His continual boasting about his suppression of the Catilinarians seriously backfired in 58, when he was exiled by a special law of *Clodius for executing Roman citizens without trial. His recall in 57 was instigated by Pompey, for whom he retained his admiration and whom he sought to attach to the *optimates*.

After 56 Cicero's political independence was humiliatingly broken by the Triumvirate, whose tool he became, defending his former enemies in the courts. By a law of Pompey (52) he received a proconsular command in Cilicia, where he attempted with mixed success to put his theoretical principles on good government into practice. Returning to Italy in 49 to the outbreak of civil war, Cicero retained his *imperium* as proconsul until 47. But he played little part in the war, rejecting further resistance to Caesar after Pharsalus (48) and accepting his pardon.

Welcoming Caesar's assassination in 44 and emerging from a long political obscurity, Cicero attacked *Antony's autocratic aspirations in a series of hysterical speeches (the *Philippics*) and sought (with success initially) to attach *Octavian to the republican cause. His failure was announced in 43 by the formation of the Second Triumvirate: he became an early and prominent victim of their proscriptions.

WORKS. 1. Poems. Cicero was far more than an occasional dabbler in verse; he experimented copiously with Hellenistic forms in his youth and translated the astronomical poem of Aratus from the Greek; 40 fragments and one sequence of 480 lines survive. Later he wrote an epic of three books *On His Consulship*, of which there are many fragments, and another, also in three books, *On His Own Times*, of which nothing survives. Furthermore, his philosophical works contain numerous translations of Greek epic and tragedy. The occasional infelicities of his uninspired and bombastic epics have tended to blind critics to the fluency and technical skill of his compositions, especially the version of Aratus.

2. Letters. They are collected into: *Letters to *Atticus* (the present collection—not the first—in 16 books was probably made in *Nero's reign), *Letters to his Friends* (also in 16 books, including some letters to Cicero), *Letters to his brother Quintus* in three books, and two books of the correspondence between Cicero and *Brutus (43 BC, including 8 letters from Brutus). It is likely that the three latter collections (and others now lost) were published by *Tiro. A total of 931 letters are preserved, the vast majority by Cicero himself. Most, though not all, were written without any thought of publication, in a lively, allusive, colloquial style, liberally sprinkled with Greek; they present an invaluable and exceptionally vivid picture of the history and society of the period 61–43 BC (only a handful of letters are earlier).

3. Speeches. 58 survive, some incompletely; the earliest is from 81 BC (*Pro Quinctio*), the latest (*Fourteenth Philippic*) was delivered on 21 April 43. Over that period, style and manner remain fairly consistent for the last 30 years, after Cicero has abandoned some of the attention to formal structure and the 'Asianic' exuberances of his youthful style, and has begun to speak with the authority of his public position.

The circumstances of his speeches vary widely: not all were delivered (the last five *Verrines*, the *Pro *Milone*, and the 'divine' *Second Philippic*), and many were not published as delivered. Some were composed for the senate (and the *Catilinarians* and *Philippics* for times of extreme national crisis), some for the popular assembly, some for the courts (and not all for clients as attractive as *Caelius, 56 BC), some to defend (notably the *Pro Milone*) and some to attack (spectacularly, the *In Pisonem*). It is therefore hard to isolate general characteristics: there was no room for wit in the *First Catilinarian*, no place for dramatic rhetorical splendour in the *Pro Caelio*. Only an ample (indeed often pompous) manner and a regular, rhythmical sentence structure (see glossary, s.v. *clausula*) remain consistent.

4. Rhetorical works. Cicero's earliest treatise on rhetoric, the *Rhetorica*, in two books, was probably written while he was still in his teens, the latest, the *Topica*, belongs, like much of his writing on this subject, to 44 BC. Certain themes of abiding importance may be distinguished: (1) the history of oratory at Rome (notably in the *Brutus*, which contains generous tributes to Cicero's masters and to the great orators of his youth); (2) the characteristics and education of the perfect orator (*De oratore, Orator*), who must also be philosopher, historian, and lawyer; (3) the controversy between the florid Asianists and dry Atticists, in which Cicero remained an aggressive neutral, insisting on his adherence to a middle way; and (4) the formal classifications and divisions of classical rhetorical theory.

5. Philosophy. Cicero's philosophical education was excellent and his interest in philosophy lifelong (note his view on the philosophical training of the orator, above). Two political dialogues, *On the State* and *On the Laws* belong to the 50s BC, a Roman's answers to Plato in the light of Hellenistic theory, Roman history, and reaction against current events. The rest of his huge philosophical output belongs to a period of intense activity in 46–44, during which he synthesized eclectically vast areas of Greek ethical thought (e.g. *On Duties, On Ends*—i.e. good and evil aimed at—*On Old Age, Tusculan Disputations*, especially on grief and death) and religious thought (*On Divination, On the Nature of the Gods, On Fate* (and free will)), both classical and Hellenistic, in often attractive dialogue form, creating a successful and

notably long-lasting Latin philosophical vocabulary, rendering accessible (as a conscious mission) Greek thought to the Greekless, and transmitting to later ages much of what they knew of Greek ethics.

BIBL. Plutarch, *Life of Cicero*; Stockton, *Cicero: a political biography* (1971); Rawson, *Cicero: a Portrait* (1975); *Cicero*, ed. T. A. Dorey (1964) (especially articles by Townend, Nisbet, Douglas); Soubiran's Budé edition of the poems; Shackleton Bailey's editions of the *Letters to Atticus* and *To his Friends*; Clarke, *Rhetoric at Rome* (1953) 50 ff.; Kennedy, *Rhetoric*, 103 ff.

Cicero, Quintus Tullius Praetor 62 BC.

The younger brother of *Cicero, Quintus Cicero is the alleged author of the *Commentariolum petitionis*, a treatise in epistolary form advising his brother on the technique of canvassing for the consulship. After his praetorship he governed Asia as proconsul, and later served as legate of *Caesar in Gaul and Britain, and of his brother in Cilicia. He quarrelled with his brother over relations with Caesar after Pharsalus, but shared his fate in the proscriptions of 43 BC.

BIBL. Rawson, *Cicero: a Portrait* (1975).

Cilo, Lucius Fabius Consul AD 193 and 203.

A senator from Iluro in Baetica, Cilo was a close friend of the Emperor *Severus and was favoured by him. He was consul suffect in 193, governor of Bithynia-Pontus and Moesia Superior (195–6), governor of Pannonia, urban prefect, and, in 203, *consul ordinarius*.

BIBL. *PIR* F 27; Birley, *Severus*.

Cincinnatus, Lucius Quinctius [Dictator 458 BC].

Cincinnatus was a legendary hero who left his plough to save Rome from a military crisis. The story, linked aetiologically to the 'Quinctian Meadows', was usually dated to 458 BC, with Cincinnatus rescuing the beleaguered L. *Minucius Esquilinus Augurinus (a fiction modelled on the action of Q. *Fabius Maximus 'Cunctator' in 217 BC). He was then credited with a suffect consulship (460) or, according to *Diodorus, with membership of an additional consular college (457/6); his poverty was attributed to his forfeiture of bail for his son (461), and he was resurrected as dictator to suppress Sp. *Maelius (439).

BIBL. PW xxiv. 1020 ff.; Ogilvie, *Livy*, 416 f., etc.; O. Skutsch, *Ennius* (Entretiens sur l'antiquité classique xvii, 1971) 26 ff.

Cinna Consul 87, 86, 85, and 84 BC.

Lucius Cornelius Cinna served in the Social War, probably as a legate of *Pompeius Strabo, until 88 BC, and was elected consul for 87. He disregarded an oath to observe the conservative legislation that Sulla had recently passed by force, and proposed a liberal law on Italian citizenship and the recall of Sulla's exiled opponents. He was violently attacked and deposed by his conservative colleague, Gnaeus Octavius; he escaped from Rome, however, and reoccupied the city by force late in 87, at the head of a large army of disaffected Italians, undisbanded legionaries, and exiles (including *Marius). He failed to curb Marius' massacre of political opponents, but restored order after Marius' death early in 86. The period of his last three consulships (86–84) is often called the *Cinnae dominatio*, but his terms of office seem to have been marked by political moderation and conciliation. The historical tradition on Cinna has been tainted with Sullan propaganda. He was killed in a mutiny of newly-levied troops at Ancona in 84, by which time the threat from the absent Sulla was beginning to be taken seriously.

BIBL. Bulst, *Historia* xiii (1964) 307 ff.; Badian, *Studies*, esp. 206 ff.

Cinna, Gaius Helvius (died 44 BC) Poet.

Conceivably tribune of the plebs in 44 BC, 'Cinna the poet' was killed by the mob after *Caesar's murder, by mistake for the conspirator Lucius Helvius Cinna. A friend of *Catullus (poem 95), he was the author of a poem addressed to *Pollio, love-poems, epigrams, and the *Zmyrna*—a short work on unnatural love, of the deepest Alexandrian learning, which took him nine years to complete.

BIBL. *FPL* 87 ff.

Civilis Rebel leader AD 69–70.

A Batavian noble of royal blood, Gaius (?) Julius Civilis served with the Roman army's auxiliaries—a not uncommon practice (see *Arminius)—but was suspected of fomenting rebellion. The maltreatment which followed, although he was acquitted by *Galba, turned him against Rome, and he raised a revolt in earnest in north-east Gaul which was with difficulty suppressed by Petillius *Cerealis. *Tacitus remarks on his intelligence; being blind in one eye he was compared with such notorious enemies of Rome as *Sertorius and *Hannibal.

BIBL. Tac. *Hist.* iv–v; P. A. Brunt, *Latomus* (1960) 494.

Claudian (c. AD 370–c. 404) Poet.

Claudius Claudianus, the most talented poet of the Late Roman Empire, was born in Egypt c. 370. He wrote both in Greek and Latin composing epigrams, *Patria* on Berytus, Tarsus, Anazarbus, and Nicaea, as well as a *Gigantomachy* before he came to Rome in 394. There he first appears in 395 composing a panegyric for the consulship of Probinus and Olybrius, who were sons of Petronius *Probus (q.v.) and thus members of the powerful Christian Anicii. By January 396 he had

already begun his most important poetic
commissions, propaganda for *Stilicho, in his
poem on the third consulship of *Honorius. From
this period till 404 it is possible to study political
controversies at the western court in Claudian's
poetry. He makes notable use of invective in his
Against Rufinus, written in two parts, and probably
recited in 397 after the murder of *Rufinus. *On the
Gildonic War*, a historical epic on the revolt of
*Gildo, Count of Africa, came next, followed in
399 by *Against Eutropius*, an attack on the
eunuch *Eutropius, *Arcadius' chief minister and
one of the most savage invectives ever written.
The year 400 saw the recitation of *On the
Consulate of Stilicho* (i–iii), and 402 that of *On the
Getic War*, both political works, tendentious
accounts of Stilicho's campaigns against *Alaric.
Claudian probably died in 404, four years before
the fall of his master. In addition to his political
and panegyric works, *On the Rape of Proserpina*, a
mythological epic, survives. Claudian disproves all
theories that late authors are bad authors. He writes
in the best classical tradition, and is an exceedingly
accomplished poet, master of the rhetorical
description and the well-turned hexameter.

BIBL. A. Cameron, *Claudian, Poetry and
Propaganda at the Court of Honorius* (1970).

Claudius (10 BC–AD 54) Emperor AD 41–54.
Son of the elder *Drusus by *Antonia, Tiberius
Claudius Drusus was the younger brother of
*Germanicus and a patrician Claudian. He was
born at Lyons in Gaul, shortly before the death of
his father. Serious ill-health, which rendered him
incapable of maintaining the dignity required of
the imperial family on public occasions, deprived
him of any career, and he devoted himself to
scholarship, with some success: he wrote histories
of Etruria and Carthage, as well as a continuation
of *Livy. He was, however, occasionally entrusted
with some task—under *Gaius he was made
consul—and *Suetonius preserves letters from
*Augustus to *Livia in which he expresses surprise
at the young Claudius' astuteness. Moreover, in the
household of Antonia he was not far removed from
the councils of state, and his inexperience in
government revealed itself during his reign only
in his obsession with points of detail, and in an
astonishing devotion to the exercise of the
jurisdiction he had so long been denied.

The coincidence of his retiring way of life, the
general belief in his stupidity, and the vicissitudes
of the dynasty in general spared him from
suspicion and either exile or death under
*Tiberius and Gaius, and he was the only adult
male survivor of the Julii or Claudii when the
murder of Gaius brought him to the attention of
the praetorian guard. This military support
provided him with a firm base from which to
crush the group of senators who were, in an

Head of bronze portrait statue of Claudius, found in
a river near Colchester. London, British Museum.

inefficient, contentious, and grandiloquent way,
attempting to manage without a *princeps*. A more
serious revolt came from Dalmatia, under
*Scribonianus, when military support was again
vital to Claudius, and he took the opportunity
of weeding out some dissident elements. Although
he came to have a bad record for the execution of
senators, this was not so much because he tried to
rule without senatorial help, or failed to recognize
the status of many senators, but rather because
they found his manner and style of rule offensive.
In fact, the reign of Claudius is another chapter in
the story of the incompatibility of the two
institutions, a story whose first chapter had been
written under Tiberius. Unaccustomed to
senatorial deputies, and without a large group of
senatorial friends, Claudius was forced to rely on
freedmen and equestrians, particularly the former,
and on such friends as he did have, notably
Lucius *Vitellius, who acquired great power and
responsibility.

The greatest upheaval of the reign was Claudius'
discovery of the treasons and adulteries of his
wife *Messallina; the repercussions included
Claudius' new marriage to his niece *Agrippina,
and his decision to adopt her son Domitius (later

Onyx cameo: Claudius, Agrippina the Younger, Tiberius (?), and Livia. Vienna, Kunsthistorisches Museum.

*Nero) rather than leave the succession clear for his son by Messallina, *Britannicus.

Claudius was impetuous, absent-minded, and cruel, and not the ideal controller of the system of government he had created; the hatred of him found among senators, and best expressed in Seneca's *Pumpkinification* (*Apocolocyntosis*), was therefore partly justified. However, the system was in many ways the precursor of the one which was to work so well under the Flavians (from AD 69 onwards) and their successors, and Claudius' surviving edicts demonstrate amply that he was a thoughtful and careful, if pedantic and idiosyncratic, legislator and administrator. The mixture of the apologetic and the bullying, learned allusions and irrelevant digressions found in these documents evokes vividly the character described by Suetonius: but it is clear that the Empire benefited despite the disgust of the senatorial class at the petty and donnish buffoon who ruled them so strictly.

Not the least important step taken by Claudius was the annexation of Britain in AD 43; his reign was also distinguished by military successes in

other areas (including Germany and Mauretania). He realized that he derived much *cachet* from being the brother of Germanicus and son of Drusus, and sought to exploit this while keeping the army usefully employed. In AD 54 Agrippina, who had shared the machinery of government for some time, felt the time had come to make an end, and Claudius was poisoned with a dish of mushrooms.

BIBL. A. Momigliano, *The Emperor Claudius and his Achievement*; B. Levick, *Latomus* 1978.

Claudius II Gothicus Emperor AD 268–70.

An Illyrian, Marcus Aurelius Valerius Claudius was probably born *c.* 214. He had a distinguished military career, the details of which are somewhat uncertain owing to the unreliability of the *Augustan History*. He may have been military tribune under *Decius, and became supreme commander of the Balkan legions under *Valerian. Claudius was proclaimed emperor after *Gallienus' death, which had been engineered by him together with other leading generals. He continued the siege of Gallienus' mutinous general *Aureolus at Milan, and had him put to death after he surrendered. Claudius then conducted a successful campaign against the Alamanni. He was unable, however, to deal either with *Postumus or *Victorinus in Gaul, and in the East the Palmyrenians were extending their empire by absorbing Roman territory (see *Odaenath, *Zenobia). Claudius found his energies fully occupied in his great campaign against the Goths, and he routed them at the battle of Naissus (Nish) which earned him the title 'Gothicus Maximus'. He died, possibly at Sirmium, in 270, of the plague which was ravaging the area.

BIBL. *PLRE* i, Claudius II; P. Damerau, *Klio*, Beiheft xxxiii (1934).

Claudius Caecus, Appius Consul 307 and 296 BC.

As censor (312 BC (310 BC: *Diodorus)) Appius constructed the Appian Way and Aqua Appia (Rome's first aqueduct), perhaps removed restrictions on membership of the rural tribes, and conducted the first known censorial adlections to the senate, allegedly admitting freedmen's sons (see also Cn. *Flavius). His first consulship was undistinguished, his second variously narrated, with possible campaigns in Samnium, Sabinum, and Etruria (where he vowed a temple to Bellona). As praetor (295) he defeated the Samnites in Campania, and in 280/279 successfully opposed peace with *Pyrrhus. Clearly an individualistic and innovative censor, the interpretation of his career is bedevilled by the sources' schematic depiction of him as either populist or reactionary, and by the supposed contrast and enmity between him and Q.*Fabius Maximus Rullianus.

BIBL. PW iii. 2681 ff.; E. Ferenczy, *From the Patrician State to the Patricio-Plebeian State* (1976).

Consecratio (deification) coin of Claudius II.

Claudius Caudex, Appius Consul 264 BC.

As consul with military ambitions Appius persuaded the people, against the advice of the senate, to intervene in Sicily on behalf of Messina. He crossed to Sicily and declared war on Carthage, thus committing Rome to centuries of wars and expansion outside Italy.

BIBL. Errington, *Dawn of Empire*, 15 ff.

Claudius Crassus Inrigillensis Sabinus, Appius Decemvir 451–449 BC.

Elected consul for 451 BC, Appius became instead a member of the First Decemvirate, established to compile the Twelve Tables. The fabrication of the Second Decemvirate, which he supposedly headed, and his introduction into the legend of *Verginia encouraged his depiction as a potential tyrant whose conduct provoked the overthrow of the Decemvirate (449). The Capitoline Fasti, perhaps correctly, identify him apparently with the consul of 471, to whom the historians attribute a stereotyped Claudian hostility towards the plebs and a similar ignominious end (470).

BIBL. PW iii. 2698; Ogilvie, *Livy* 461 f., 476 ff., 503 f.

Claudius Etruscus

An equestrian who enjoyed *Domitian's favour, Claudius Etruscus is remarkable for the career of his father (whose name is lost), who raised the family's status from servile to equestrian: a slave from Smyrna freed by *Tiberius, he accompanied *Gaius to the north and rose to be secretary for finance under *Nero. *Vespasian continued to promote him, but he fell from favour under Domitian.

BIBL. Martial vii. 40; Statius, *Silvae* iii. 3; *PIR* C 673 (the father).

Claudius Fronto, Marcus Consul AD 165 or 166.

One of the leading generals in the reign of *Marcus Aurelius, Claudius Fronto won decorations in the Parthian War (162–6) and went on to hold governorships of several Balkan provinces. The senate voted him a statue at the public expense in *Trajan's Forum.

BIBL. Birley, *Marcus*; *PIR* C 894.

Claudius Pompeianus Consul before AD 167 (?) and in 173.

A senator of fairly humble origin from Antioch, Tiberius Claudius Pompeianus married *Marcus Aurelius' daughter *Lucilla after the death of Lucius *Verus in 169. He was Marcus' leading general in the German Wars, and after Marcus' death he tried to persuade *Commodus to pursue the war, but without success. When his nephew was involved in a conspiracy against Commodus (182) he retired from public life, alleging ill-health and poor eyesight, but he was back in Rome when Commodus was murdered in 192. *Pertinax, whose commanding officer and patron he had been, made the formal gesture of offering him the throne,

The Appian Way, near Rome. A stretch of the road built by Appius Claudius Caecus from Rome to Brindisi.

which he wisely refused. After the murder of Pertinax he was again offered a share of imperial power by *Didius Julianus, but he again refused.

BIBL. Grosso, *Lotta*; Birley, *Marcus*; *PIR* C 973.

Claudius Pulcher, Appius Consul 54 BC.

The eldest brother of P. *Clodius, Appius reached the consulship in 54 BC and was *Cicero's predecessor as governor of Cilicia (53–51). Cicero, who corresponded with him, recognized his degeneracy but courted him for his influence in the senatorial establishment. But their relations were frequently embarrassed—by the link with Clodius, by *Dolabella's prosecution of Claudius for misconduct in Cilicia (50), and by Cicero's own attempts to remedy his abuses there. As censor in 50 he used his office as a partisan tool against *Caesar's supporters. He died in 48 as republican governor of Achaea.

BIBL. Gruen, *Republic*.

Claudius Pulcher, Publius Consul 249 BC.

An impetuous commander in Sicily, Claudius unsuccessfully attacked Drepana by sea in 249 BC. Legend held that he had drowned the sacred chickens which had refused to provide an auspicious omen. His disastrous defeat and that of his colleague ended Rome's naval effort until Gaius Lutatius *Catulus' campaign of 242.

BIBL. Errington, *Dawn of Empire*, 25.

Claudius Severus Consul before AD 163 and in 173.

Son of Gnaeus Claudius Severus Arabianus (consul AD 146), Gnaeus Claudius Severus was a devotee of philosophy (particularly Aristotle), a follower and patron of *Galen, and friend and son-in-law of *Marcus Aurelius (perhaps married to Annia Galeria Aurelia Faustina). He accompanied Marcus on his visit to Athens in 176.

BIBL. Birley, *Marcus*; *PIR* C 1024.

Cleander, Marcus Aurelius Praetorian prefect AD 187–9.

A Phrygian slave brought up in the imperial household as a childhood companion of *Commodus, Cleander was freed by *Marcus Aurelius and eventually became the chamberlain of Commodus on the death of *Saoterus. He was one of the emperor's closest associates and wielded very great power. He was responsible for the removal of Tigidius *Perennis from the praetorian prefecture and for the murder of a subsequent prefect Aebutianus, whereupon he himself took the office with two colleagues. He was killed on Commodus' orders in 189, after the prefect of the corn supply inflamed the mob against him by aggravating a corn shortage.

BIBL. Grosso, *Lotta*; *PIR* A 1481; Howe, *The Pretorian Prefect*.

Clemens, Flavius Consul AD 95.

A nephew of *Vespasian, Clemens married his

Mithraeum beneath the Church of San Clemente, Rome.

relative Flavia Domitilla. *Domitian intended their
children to be possible successors. In AD 95
Clemens was killed and Domitilla exiled; the charge
was impiety, connected in some way with
Judaism. It has often been claimed that they were
converts to Christianity, but it seems more likely
that they were proselytes to Judaism proper. (See
stemma.)
BIBL. *PIR* F 240.

Clement of Alexandria (*c.* AD 150–215)
Christian writer.

Probably an Athenian by birth, Titus Flavius
Clemens was a pupil of *Pantaenus at Alexandria
and succeeded him as head of the Catechetical
School in 190. One of the most important Christian
writers and thinkers of his age, he fled Alexandria
in the persecution of 202 and took refuge with a
pupil, Alexander, Bishop of Cappadocia. He was
much influenced by Gnostic ideas, and brought a
training in Greek philosophy and literature to bear
on Christian theology. His works are: the
Protrepticus (*Exhortation to the Greeks*) in which he
asserts the superiority of Christianity to pagan
religion and philosophy; the *Paidagogus*, an
examination of Christ's moral teaching; the
Stromateis, a miscellaneous comparison of Greek
and Christian philosophical ideas.
BIBL. H. Chadwick, *The Early Church*; id., *Early
Christianity and the Classical Tradition* (1966);
S. R. C. Lilla, *Clement of Alexandria* (1971);
Clement of Alexandria, trans. G. W. Butterworth
(Loeb, 1919).

St Clement of Rome Theologian, floruit *c.* AD 96.

Clement followed St *Peter, Linus, and Anacletus
as bishop of Rome, and was the author of a letter
to the Corinthians exhorting them to order and
obedience. The document is valuable evidence of
the early development of both hierarchy and the
Eucharist by about AD 96. Several spurious
writings and a number of legends, especially
concerning an exile under *Trajan, are attached to
him.
BIBL. Loeb, *Apostolic Fathers*.

Cleopatra Queen of Egypt 51–30 BC.

The last of the Macedonian rulers of Egypt,
Cleopatra succeeded her father *Ptolemy Auletes as
joint ruler in 51 BC. Her position was strengthened
by liaisons with *Caesar (48/47) and *Antony
(41/40), to both of whom she bore children. From
37 onwards she became increasingly closely
associated with Antony, providing him with
money and supplies and serving as a useful focus of
loyalty in the Greek East. In the West, however,
she was the focus of *Octavian's hostile
propaganda, which represented her as an oriental
threat to Roman ascendancy. After Octavian's
victory at Actium she committed suicide with

Silver coin (*denarius*) of Antony with portrait of
Cleopatra, 34 BC. Reverse.

Antony, choosing to die from the poisonous bite
of the royal asp (30 BC).
BIBL. Syme, *Rom Rev.*; Will, *Histoire politique*.

Clodia Society beauty, mid-1st century BC.

A sister of the aristocratic demagogue *Clodius,
Clodia 'slept around' to achieve temporary
political influence. Two very different views of her
have survived: the idealized portrait of 'Lesbia' in
the poems of her sometime lover *Catullus; and the
abusive scandal in the letters of her bitter enemy
*Cicero, who accused her of poisoning her husband
and having incestuous relations with her brother.
BIBL. Gruen, *Republic* 307 ff.

Clodius Aedile 56 BC.

Publius Clodius Pulcher was a brilliant but
unorthodox aristocrat whose demagogic methods
established him as a powerful independent force in
Rome in the 50s. His volatile political opportunism
had become apparent in 68 BC, when he stirred up
mutiny in the army of his brother-in-law *Lucullus.
In 61 he survived prosecution for sacrilege after
profaning a religious ceremony forbidden to men,
but he harboured a grudge against *Cicero, who
had destroyed his alibi. Clodius, who used the
popular form of his patrician gentile name
Claudius, had long courted popularity. He now
sought adoption into a plebeian family so that he
could legitimately hold the tribunate, an office in
which he could massively extend his popular
clientela. Cicero, a victim of his tribunate,
egocentrically assumed that the whole manoeuvre
was an act of vengeance against himself. *Caesar
and *Pompey assisted in Clodius' controversial
adoption in 59, and probably helped him obtain
the tribunate of 58, in which he secured the
removal from Rome of the triumvirs' most
influential opponents, Cicero and *Cato (Uticensis).

But Clodius was not long, if at all, an agent of
the triumvirs, his legislation being designed to
increase his own personal authority and influence,
especially among the urban plebs: to this end he
often found it useful to fill the vacuum he had
created and attack the unpopular Triumvirate. He
consolidated his control of the popular assemblies

by organizing armed gangs and intimidating his opponents. His political and physical attacks on Pompey prompted the latter in 57 to sponsor *Milo as a largely negative agent to copy Clodius' methods and break his influence. Cicero's recall from exile marked the end of his temporary domination, but he remained a powerful, if no longer independent, figure. Standing for the praetorship of 52, he tried to prevent Milo becoming consul, but early in 52 he was killed in a violent clash with Milo's gang. In an ensuing demonstration Clodius' supporters burnt the senate house, and the escalating violence led to Pompey's sole consulship.

BIBL. Gruen, *Phoenix* xx (1966) 120 ff.; Lintott, *Violence*; Gruen, *Republic*.

Clodius Albinus Caesar and usurper, AD 193–7.

An African from Hadrumetum, Decimus Clodius Albinus won distinction early in the reign of *Commodus in a campaign against the Dacians. He may have been governor of Germania Inferior before proceeding to the governorship of Britain late in Commodus' reign (probably in 192). After Septimius *Severus was proclaimed emperor in the summer of 193 he offered Clodius Albinus the title of Caesar, implying collegiality as a junior, to forestall open enmity. Albinus held the consulship with Severus in 194. In the course of that year he began more openly to assume the airs of an emperor, and issued coinage proclaiming himself Augustus. Whilst Severus was occupied against *Pescennius Niger in the East, Albinus gained control of Gaul which he maintained through 195 and into 196, but in 196 Severus was able to turn against him. The decisive battle between the two rivals took place at Lyons on 19 February 197. Albinus was defeated and committed suicide. Severus is said to have ridden his horse over the corpse.

BIBL. Birley, *Severus*; id., *Fasti* (forthcoming); *PIR* C 1186.

Cloelia Legendary heroine, 6th century BC.

Cloelia was among the hostages given by Rome to *Porsenna, but boldly engineered their escape. An equestrian statue on the Via Sacra, reputedly set up in her honour but originally perhaps representing Venus Equestris, may have suggested the legend.

BIBL. PW iv. 110 f.; Ogilvie, *Livy*, 267 f.

Cogidubnus, Tiberius Claudius British client king, mid-1st century AD.

When *Ostorius Scapula was governor of Britain, Cogidubnus was rewarded with extra territory. At Chichester there is an inscription which may refer to him as a 'great king', and it is almost certain that the nearby palace at Fishbourne was also part of his reward. His services may well have been connected with the strategic importance of the harbours of the Solent.

BIBL. Frere, *Britannia*; Barrett, *Britannia* x (1979).

Columella Agronomist, mid-1st century AD.

A contemporary of *Celsus (A. Cornelius), the Elder *Pliny and *Seneca, and a native of Cadiz, Lucius Junius Moderatus Columella held lands in Italy as did his family in Baetica. After some military service, he turned to treatises on agriculture. Of the first, in two books, we have the second book, *On Trees*. The second, *On Agriculture*, survives intact in twelve well-organized and lucidly-written books, which are indebted not only to earlier authorities (*Varro, Celsus, *Virgil), but to personal experience. In x, he takes up Virgil's bequest to 'others' (*Georgics*, iv.

Inscription from temple of Neptune and Minerva, Chichester, naming Cogidubnus as 'great king in Britain'.

147)—an exhaustive treatment of horticulture, which he undertakes in a solemn hexameter pastiche of the *Georgics*; xi and xii (in prose, once more) on the duties of the bailiff and his wife were added in old age by way of afterthought.

BIBL. K. D. White, *Roman Farming* (1970) 26 f.

Commius

A Gallic chieftain installed by *Caesar as king of the Belgic Atrebates, Commius was sent by him as envoy to Britain before the invasion of 55 BC. He later joined the revolt of *Vercingetorix against Caesar, and then withdrew finally to Britain, where he established a powerful dynasty as ruler of the British Atrebates.

BIBL. Frere, *Britannia* (2nd ed., 1978).

Commodian Christian poet, 3rd century AD.

Born a pagan in Gaza, and converted to Christianity by reading the Scriptures, Commodianus, author of the *Instructiones*, an acrostically structured Christian polemic, and of a *Carmen Apologeticum*, a verse account of basic Christian doctrine, writes a very idiosyncratic hexameter, dependent on ictus rather than on quantity. His date is uncertain: possibly around 250 AD.

BIBL. J. Martin, *Traditio* xiii (1957) 1–71.

Commodus (Marcus Aurelius Commodus Antoninus) Emperor AD 177–92.

Son of *Marcus Aurelius, Lucius Aurelius Commodus was born on 31 August 161, one of a pair of twins (the other was dead by 165 or 166). His status as Marcus' heir was consolidated in a number of stages. In 166 he was given the title of Caesar, in 176 that of *Imperator*. He held his first consulship in 177 and in that year became joint emperor with his father, with whom he spent the last three years of the reign fighting against the Marcomanni. When Marcus died at Vienna on 17 March 180, Commodus became sole emperor. The verdict of posterity on his reign harmonizes with the notion that he was idle, vicious, and dissolute, though a contemporary historian was more inclined to see his failing as simply a vulnerability to evil influence. For Edward Gibbon the inception of his sole reign marked the turning point in the history of the Empire.

At the beginning of his reign he retained the services of his father's best advisers, though he went against their advice in concluding an almost immediate peace with the Sarmatian and German tribes, which involved paying them large subsidies and evacuating Roman garrisons from territories occupied by Marcus. He returned to Rome to a rapturous welcome, but things soon began to go wrong. In 182 there was an alleged plot (abortive, anyway, if genuine) to murder him, in which his sister *Lucilla and other prominent people were

Commodus and Crispina as Mars and Venus. Rome, Museo delle Terme.

involved. From that point on he showed increasingly overt hostility to the senate and ruled much more through his personal favourites, first Tigidius *Perennis (until 185), then *Cleander (until 189), then Aemilius *Laetus.

There was only one serious military problem during his reign after the conclusion of peace on the German frontier. In 184 the Caledonians in Britain broke through the Antonine Wall and overran southern Scotland. It took the governor Ulpius *Marcellus three campaigns to deal with this.

His last years were marked by personal excesses. The city of Rome is said to have been renamed 'colonia Commodiana'. In 190 a mockery was made of the consulship by the nomination of 25 consuls for the year. Commodus exhibited a particular devotion to the cult of Hercules; he adopted the dress and weapons of the hero, and had himself venerated as the living incarnation of Hercules. It was his fondness for gladiatorial combat, both as spectator and participant, which led to the most spectacular excesses. In 192 he mounted an extravagant series of games which lasted for two weeks, and in which he personally took part. The final straw seems to have been his plan to appear as consul on 1 January 193 in gladiatorial dress. A

Portrait bust of Commodus as Hercules. Rome, Palazzo dei Conservatori.

plot to murder him was formed by *Marcia, *Eclectus and Aemilius *Laetus. On New Year's Eve they attempted to poison him and, when this plan failed, they got an athlete named Narcissus to strangle him. He was buried in *Hadrian's Mausoleum in Rome. The news of his death stimulated the senate to displays of joy and vindictiveness; his memory was erased (*damnatio memoriae*) but was soon to be restored by Septimius *Severus, who had him deified (a necessary consequence of Severus' own fictitious claim to be the 'son' of Marcus Aurelius).

BIBL. Birley, *Severus*; Grosso, *Lotta*; *PIR* A 1482.

Bronze coin (enlarged) of the Emperor Constans.

Constans Western emperor AD 337–50.
Youngest son of *Constantine I and *Fausta,

Flavius Julius Constans was born *c*. 320 and proclaimed Caesar on 25 December 333. After his father's death in May 337, he ruled Italy, Africa, and Illyricum under the supervision of his eldest brother *Constantine II (q.v.), whom he defeated and killed when he invaded Italy in 340, and took over the whole of the West. He visited Britain in 342/3, the last reigning emperor to do so. A baptized Christian, fanatically orthodox, in 346 he threatened war on the eastern emperor, his second brother *Constantius II, if he would not let *Athanasius return to Alexandria. In January 350 he was killed in Gaul after the usurpation of *Magnentius.

BIBL. Piganiol, *Emp. chr.*

Constantia Empress AD 313–24.
Daughter of *Constantius I and Theodora, Constantia was one of *Constantine's six half-brothers and sisters (see stemma). He married her to his co-emperor *Licinius at Milan in 313, to strengthen their alliance. Her son, also named Licinius, was executed in 326, after the defeat and death in 324 of her husband, for whose life she pleaded with her brother. She was a Christian of Arian sympathies, allegedly responsible for Constantine's reconciliation with *Arius, after her dying wish had led Constantine to take over her Arian confessor.

BIBL. *PLRE* i, Constantia 1.

Constantina Wife of Gallus Caesar AD 351–4.
Elder daughter of *Constantine I and *Fausta, Constantina was married first to her cousin *Hannibalianus (335–7), and later, also for dynastic reasons, to another cousin, *Gallus (Caesar 351–4). In 350, on the usurpation of *Magnentius in Gaul, she persuaded *Vetranio to rebel and block Magnentius' progress eastward. Magnentius wished to marry her, but her brother *Constantius II gave her to Gallus instead. *Ammianus described her as a 'mortal Fury', who encouraged Gallus' cruelty. She died in Bithynia on her way to put Gallus' case to Constantius, and was buried at Rome in a beautiful porphyry sarcophagus in a mausoleum attached to the basilica of St Agnes which she founded. Now known as S. Costanza, the mausoleum and its mosaic decoration, uniting Christian and purified pagan motifs, still survives.

BIBL. *PLRE* i, Constantina 2; W. F. Volbach, *Early Christian Art* (1961), pl. 29–35.

Constantine I ('the Great') Emperor AD 306–37.
Flavius Valerius Constantinus, first Christian emperor, was the son of the tetrarch *Constantius I and of *Helena, born *c*. 285 at Naissus in Serbia. He spent his youth at the eastern court of *Diocletian, head of the Tetrarchy, as a hostage for his father's good behaviour, and served as an army

Santa Costanza, Rome: the Mausoleum of Constantina (AD 325–50), interior.

officer. In 306 he escaped from the court of *Galerius, Diocletian's successor, and joined his father in the West shortly before his death at York (25 July). There Constantine was immediately proclaimed emperor by the troops, and with Galerius' consent became ruler of Britain and Gaul with the title of Caesar.

The usurpation of *Maxentius in Rome on 28 October 306 gave Constantine further opportunities. First they became allies, and Constantine married *Fausta, daughter of the retired emperor *Maximian, who was supporting his son Maxentius. Then Maximian quarrelled with his son and took refuge with Constantine. In 309/10 he rebelled against Constantine, who

disposed of him. To replace this discredited connection, a descent from *Claudius Gothicus was 'discovered' for Constantine, who had by now acquired Spain and the title of Augustus. In May 311 Galerius died, and the four remaining *de facto* rulers formed rival alliances, Constantine with *Licinius and Maxentius with *Maximin Daia. Thus fortified, Constantine turned on Maxentius in 312, marching down through Italy to a final victory at the Milvian Bridge (28 October). He was now Emperor of the West, adding Italy and Africa to his dominions. Next year, Licinius eliminated Maximin Daia and became Emperor of the East, with Constantine's sister *Constantia as his wife. After a war—won by Constantine—fought to settle the ownership of the Balkans (316), the two emperors ruled in uneasy partnership until 324, when Constantine finally defeated (and later executed) Licinius, becoming sole emperor of a reunified Empire.

Already in 312 Constantine had taken the first steps towards Christianity, as a result of a dream-vision exhorting him to entrust his army and fortunes in the campaign against Maxentius to the Christian God. The victory at the Milvian Bridge, decisive for the fortunes of Christianity, convinced him of the necessity of putting the Empire under

Left: gold coin (*solidus*) of Constantine I.
Right: reverse of silver coin with personification of Constantinople commemorating the city's dedication on 11 May 330. Milan, Museo del Castello Sforzesco.

the protection of his own new patron-deity. First
he ended the Great Persecution of the Christians,
begun under Diocletian, by means of the Edict of
Milan, agreed with Licinius in February 313.
Major patronage for the Church ensued, and
Constantine expended much effort throughout his
reign in attempts to unify it, the main problems
being the *Donatist schism in Africa and, after 324,
the *Arian heresy in the East. A succession of
Church councils was summoned, including the
famous Council of Nicaea in 325, at which an
illusory unanimity over Arianism was achieved.
Constantine encouraged Christianity in the still-
pagan governing classes and army, and promoted it
by example and the granting of favours. He was
baptized on his deathbed, as was the custom.

Because of his conversion, the great new capital,
Constantinople, was founded (in 324–30) as a
Christian city, resplendent with new churches.
Strategic considerations dictated the permanent
establishment of the main capital nearer the
threatened frontiers of the Empire, and Byzantium
was better than Diocletian's Nicomedia. A 'New
Rome', though technically lesser in status,
Constantinople had a senate and a corn dole for
the populace. It was inaugurated with magnificent
ceremonies in May 330. A domestic tragedy
during a visit to Rome itself in 326, when he
executed his eldest son *Crispus, then his wife
Fausta, hastened Constantine's cutting of links
with the old capital.

A great reformer, who throughout his long reign
spent many summers campaigning on the Rhine
and Danube frontiers, and was preparing for a
Persian war at his death, Constantine created a
central reserve force of crack troops, able quickly
to reinforce beleaguered frontier armies, fulfilling a
vital need for the survival of the Empire. He also
completed the separation of military and civil
powers begun by Diocletian, appointing two
supreme commanders—the Master of the Infantry
and the Master of the Cavalry—answerable directly
to the emperor. The civil administration was also
reorganized, and the office of praetorian prefect
began to be divided up. A reformed coinage
comprised new gold and silver currencies, and
went far towards the re-establishment of a
monetary economy; but the bronze coinage was
debased. Compulsory heredity of calling was
extended from agriculture to soldiers, bakers, civil
servants, and others, in a kind of caste system
devised to cope with the shortage of manpower
caused by the epidemics and wars of the third
century.

Constantine had three surviving sons—
*Constantine II, *Constantius II, and *Constans—
and two nephews (Fl. Julius *Dalmatius and
*Hannibalianus) of an age for governing, the sons
of his eldest half-brother (see stemma), causing a
major succession problem. He tried valiantly to lay
down a system in which each would play his
part in ruling the Empire, but after his death (22
May 337) it was destroyed by mutual suspicion
between sons and nephews, leading to a massacre
in which the sons triumphed.

Hot-tempered and generous, a man of action
impatient with theological niceties or outraged by
some flagrant example of oppression, superstitious
like all his contemporaries but endowed with a
grandiose sense of being God's vice-gerent on
earth, the founder of the Christian Empire is for
us a vivid personality readily perceptible through
the medium of his surviving letters and laws and
accounts of his actions. A strong and effective
ruler and reformer, he shares with Diocletian the
main credit for the very existence of the later
Roman Empire, and the long years of stable
government in his reign made possible a genuine
renaissance of civilian life and the fine arts.

BIBL. A. H. M. Jones, *Constantine and the
Conversion of Europe* (2nd ed., 1972); R. MacMullen,
Constantine (1969); N. H. Baynes, *Constantine the
Great and the Christian Church* (2nd ed., 1972);
D. R. Bowder, *The Age of Constantine and Julian*
(1978).

Constantine I: colossal head of portrait statue (now
in fragments). Rome, Palazzo dei Conservatori.

Gold medallion of the Emperor Constantine II.

Constantius I sacrificing (left, with spiked helmet). Decennalia Base of jubilee monument. Rome, Forum.

Constantine II Western emperor AD 337–40.

Son of *Constantine and *Fausta, Flavius Claudius Constantinus was born at Arles in 317 and proclaimed Caesar shortly after. Installed at Trier in 333, he ruled Britain, Gaul, and Spain after his father's death in 337, and supervised his youngest brother *Constans who was ruling Italy, Africa, and Illyricum, while *Constantius II governed the East. He quarrelled with Constans in 340 and invaded Italy, where he was defeated and killed. He was an orthodox Christian, and protected *Athanasius.

BIBL. Piganiol, *Empire chr.*

Constantine III Usurper AD 407–11.

Constantine, a common soldier with a distinguished name, was the third in a series of usurpers promoted in the last years of Roman rule in Britain (406–7). He invaded Gaul and established his court at Arles, from where he gained control of Spain, and even temporary recognition (409) by *Honorius. But he soon lost Spain to his own general Gerontius, and in 411 was besieged in Arles by Honorius' generalissimo *Constantius (q.v. III). He was surrendered to the besiegers, and executed.

BIBL. Matthews, *Aristocracies*, 307 ff.

Constantius I Western emperor AD 293–306.

Constantius had been governor of the key province of Dalmatia at the time of *Diocletian's accession; in 293 he and *Galerius were chosen as Caesars in the newly-formed Tetrarchy. Constantius was given charge of all provinces north of the Alps, and, helped by *Asclepiodotus, overthrew *Allectus (q.v., illustration p. 19), usurper in Britain. *Lactantius says that the Great Persecution in Constantius' domain went no further than the destruction of Christian buildings. Even if true this is not innocuous; a pious pagan naturally thought temples essential to religious observance. Constantius was much occupied in guarding the Rhine frontier; his base at Trier was given public buildings worthy of an imperial city. He became an Augustus in 305 when Diocletian and *Maximian abdicated, but died the following year at York. His troops promptly acclaimed his soldier son *Constantine as emperor.

BIBL. *PLRE* i, Constantius 12; Frere, *Britannia*.

Constantius II Emperor AD 337–61.

Son of *Constantine and *Fausta, Flavius Julius Constantius was the most effective ruler of the sons of Constantine. He was born on 7 August 317, and created Caesar by his father in 324. In 333 he was installed at Antioch, and in 335 he married the daughter of his uncle Julius *Constantius. (He later married *Eusebia, and Faustina, by whom a posthumous daughter was born.) When Constantine died in May 337, by his will Constantius (still only 19) was to rule the rich Eastern part of the Empire, his elder brother *Constantine II was to have

Constantius II: colossal bronze head. Rome, Palazzo dei Conservatori.

Constantius II as consul, distributing largesse, from *Calendar of 354* (see *Filocalus). Rome, Vatican Library.

Britain, Gaul, and Spain, and his younger brother *Constans Italy, Africa, and Pannonia. Constantine's nephews Fl. Julius *Dalmatius and *Hannibalianus were to have the Balkans and eastern Asia Minor respectively. Mutual suspicion between sons and nephews rendered government impossible, and it was probably Constantius, strong man of the new regime, who instigated the massacre at Constantinople of virtually the entire faction of uncles (Fl. *Dalmatius and Julius *Constantius) and cousins. After the elimination of Constantine II in 340, Constantius continued to rule the East and Constans the West, until the usurpation of *Magnentius and death of Constans in 350. He spent much of these years campaigning against Persia, with varying success. In 353 he finally defeated Magnentius, and became sole emperor. In 351 he had nominated as Caesar his cousin *Gallus, *Julian's elder brother, only to depose and execute him in 354. Barbarian invasions of Gaul in 355 led him to create Julian Caesar to take charge there, while he himself returned east after a magnificent triumph in Rome in 357 (an obelisk was erected there in commemoration). Campaigns on the Danube and in Mesopotamia occupied his last years. In 361, while on his way to deal with Julian's usurpation, he died suddenly of a fever near Tarsus (5 October).

A man of mediocre intellect but unswerving devotion to duty, Constantius gave the Empire 24 years of stable government, and made the Constantinian system work. His main faults were an exaggerated suspiciousness, which made him harsh and cruel and meant that his reign was marred by a series of treason trials on flimsy evidence, and over-generosity to his favourites, in which he was even worse than his father. He also increased unduly the size of the bureaucracy and palace staff. Brought up a Christian, he early became a moderate *Arian, opposed *Athanasius, and made constant efforts to obtain Church unity around a moderate Arian creed; but he was statesmanlike enough to give way when his brother Constans, fanatically orthodox, threatened war. After Constans' death he persecuted the orthodox to gain control of leading sees. Highly superstitious, he also passed harsh laws against magic and paganism, and some temples were destroyed; but his elevation of Julian and alleged deathbed nomination of him as successor inadvertently paved the way for the pagan revival.

BIBL. Bowder, *Constantine and Julian*, 42–53, 66–96; Piganiol, *Empire chr.*

Constantius III Emperor in the West, AD 421.

Of Danubian origins, Constantius by 411 had become Master of the Soldiers at the court of *Honorius, and the most dominant influence to emerge since the fall of *Stilicho in 408. He suppressed the usurpation of *Constantine III, and achieved the settlement with the Visigoths which had eluded Stilicho. His vigorous blockade of the Mediterranean coast of Gaul and Spain forced the downfall of the regime of *Athaulf and *Attalus, and secured the restoration of Galla *Placidia. She married Constantius in a political union (417), and their son, the future Emperor *Valentinian III, was born in 419. Constantius was recognized by Honorius as fellow-Augustus on 8 February 421, but died after only seven months of rule.

BIBL. Oost, *Galla Placidia*, ch. 4.

Constantius, Julius Consul AD 335.

Son of *Constantius I by his second wife Theodora, Julius Constantius was *Constantine's second half-brother, and leader of the faction formed by his own full brothers and sisters and nephews (see stemma of Constantine). He married first Galla, who bore him *Gallus (Caesar) and another son, and then the noble Christian lady Basilina, who bore him the future Emperor *Julian. His youth and early manhood were spent in semi-exile in Toulouse and Corinth, because of the jealousy of Constantine's mother *Helena. Then, brought out of obscurity with the rest of his family, he was made patrician and consul for 335. He and his eldest son perished in the family massacre of 337 after Constantine's death (see *Constantius II).

BIBL. *PLRE* i, Constantius 7; Piganiol, *Empire chr.*

Corbulo (died AD 67) General.

Brilliant campaigns as governor in Germania Inferior in AD 47—which, according to *Tacitus, made him long for the days when Roman generals were less subject to orders from above—gave Gnaeus Domitius Corbulo a reputation which he increased when he was sent to the East with special powers to settle the Armenian question. (Connections with the circle of L. *Vitellius will have helped as well.) He was there from AD 54–64, and his campaigns are described in detail by Tacitus, who admired him greatly, as did others, as a model of otherwise extinct independence, rectitude, and firmness. Some have seen in his family connections evidence to connect him with various dissidents, but the suspicion which led *Nero to summon him to Greece in 67 and order him to commit suicide seems to have been based only on jealousy of his popularity and success, particularly in the East (where we know he was worshipped as a hero). In fact his bearing and manner seem to have been as much responsible for his image as his military success, which was limited by the difficulties of the terrain and local politics, disagreements with his subordinates, and others' incompetence (for example that of Caesennius *Paetus).

BIBL. Syme, *JRS* 1970 = *RP* 58.

Coriolanus

After distinguishing himself in military campaigns, notably at Corioli (hence his *cognomen*), Gnaeus Marcius Coriolanus alienated the plebs and was driven into exile (491 BC). He then (489/8) led the Volsci through Latium and was dissuaded from attacking Rome itself only by the entreaties of his mother Veturia (an aetiology of the shrine of Fortuna Muliebris). The source of this legend (originally probably timeless) is uncertain: it may have been a family story of the plebeian Marcii, some of whom perhaps derived from Corioli.

BIBL. PW Supp. v. 653 ff.; Ogilvie, *Livy*, 314 ff.; M. Bonjour, *REL* liii (1975) 157 ff.

Cornelia (born c. 190 BC) Mother of the Gracchi.

The younger daughter of *Scipio Africanus, Cornelia married Ti. Sempronius *Gracchus and became famous as the mother of the Gracchi. She survived at least 11 of her 12 children as well as her husband, but maintained the severe dignity of an aristocratic Roman matron. As a widow she rejected the marriage proposal of a reigning monarch, *Ptolemy VIII. She was ambitious for her children, but probably did not influence their political activities.

BIBL. Bernstein, *Gracchus*.

Cornificius, Lucius Consul 35 BC.

An early adherent of *Octavian who sought prominence by prosecuting *Brutus for *Caesar's murder, Cornificius served under Octavian in the Sicilian war against Sextus *Pompey. His military exploits were rewarded by the consulship of 35 BC

and commemorated by his somewhat unusual habit of riding an elephant when dining away from home.

BIBL. Syme, *Rom. Rev.*

Cornutus, Lucius Annaeus (born AD 20) Philosopher.

A native of Lepcis and a freedman of one of the *Senecas, Cornutus taught both *Lucan and *Persius (who addressed poem v to him). He was exiled probably because of his involvement in the *Pisonian conspiracy of AD 65. He wrote on both literature and philosophy in both Greek and Latin. Apart from fragments, a treatise on mythology explained along Stoic lines survives.

Coruncanius, Tiberius Consul 280 BC.

A *novus homo* from Tusculum, Coruncanius campaigned in Etruria, and then reinforced his colleague Publius Valerius Laevinus after *Pyrrhus' victory at Heracleia (280 BC). He was appointed dictator to hold elections in 246, and was the first plebeian *pontifex maximus* (c. 254 to his death in 243 (?)). According to the second-century AD jurist Pomponius, he first (regularly?) admitted outsiders to his legal consultations, thus contributing ultimately to breaking the priestly monopoly of legal expertise.

BIBL. PW iv. 1663 ff.; F. Schulz, *History of Roman Legal Science* (1946) 10 f.; F. D'Ippolito, *Labeo* xxiii (1977) 131 ff.

Cossus, Aulus Cornelius Consul 428 BC; consular tribune and Master of the Horse 426.

Cossus won *spolia opima* ('spoils of honour') by killing the Veientan king, Lars Tolumnius. The exploit was usually dated to 437 BC when Cossus was military tribune, but that campaign is suspect and if, as was usually believed, only a general could win *spolia opima*, Cossus' achievement must belong in 428 or 426. However, an inscription on Cossus' spoils which, according to *Augustus, named him as consul is probably fabrication, belatedly justifying the rejection of the claims of M.Licinius *Crassus (consul 30 BC) to *spolia opima*.

BIBL. PW iv. 1289 ff.; Ogilvie, *Livy*, 557 ff.; E. Mensching, *Museum Helveticum* xxiv (1967) 12 ff.

Crassus Consul 70 and 55 BC.

Marcus Licinius Crassus was a highly influential aristocrat noted for his great wealth and for his continuous struggle with *Pompey for a position of primacy in the State. He was born in about 115 BC into a distinguished noble family. His father having died in *Marius' massacre (87), he fled to Spain before 85 where he raised a sizeable private army from his family's clients, and in 83 joined *Sulla in overthrowing the Marian government. His famous wealth derived largely from property acquired in Sulla's proscriptions, and helped to establish his political influence in the

70s. He rose in the Sullan establishment, by an orthodox route, to the praetorship (probably in 73), at the same time watching with jealous apprehension the meteoric rise of the upstart Pompey. In 72 he received a proconsular command with six legions against *Spartacus in south Italy, superseding the two defeated consuls. He finished the war in six months and received a minor triumph (*ovatio*) in 71; but he was incensed by the behaviour of Pompey, who, returning from Spain, had defeated a small remnant of Spartacus' army in the north and claimed the credit for finishing the war. He proceeded to the consulship of 70 with Pompey as an uneasy colleague, but co-operated with him in the restoration of tribunician powers to prevent him taking all the credit.

After 67 he became increasingly concerned to match the excessive influence of Pompey (now in the East with unlimited powers) with schemes intended to usurp his popular constituency and to establish vast popular support for himself. His *popularis* methods and his association with *Caesar, *Catiline, and Rullus estranged him from the *optimates*: his attempt as censor in 65 to extend Roman citizenship to Transpadane Gaul was frustrated by his colleague *Catulus (2). He joined the *optimates* led by *Cato in opposing Pompey's demands, but was thwarted by them in his own demands on behalf of the Asian *publicani*. He was thus drawn by Caesar in 59 into a temporary pact of co-operation with Pompey (the 'First Triumvirate'), which he was forced to renegotiate in 56 to prevent a possible coalition between Pompey and the *optimates*. He obtained for himself a second consulship (55) and a large military command against the Parthians, which he now realized was essential for achieving the political prominence he desired. Seeking military glory he invaded the Parthian empire in 53, but within months he had been defeated and killed at Carrhae.

BIBL. Plutarch, *Life of Crassus*; Adcock, *Marcus Crassus, Millionaire* (1966); Ward, *Marcus Crassus and the Late Roman Republic* (1977).

Crassus, Lucius Licinius Consul 95 BC.

A shadowy but influential member of the senatorial establishment in the age of *Marius, Crassus ranked in *Cicero's estimation as the greatest of Roman orators to date. Coming from a long-established noble family, he scarcely needed his rhetorical abilities to achieve political advancement; and, indeed, as censor in 92 BC he discouraged such advancement by outsiders by banning the teaching of rhetoric in Latin. As consul with *Scaevola in 95 he deprived recently enfranchised Italians of their citizenship. He supported his protégé, Livius *Drusus (2), in 91 with a famous speech against L. *Philippus, but died in that year before the crisis developed.

BIBL. *ORF* 237 ff.; Gruen, *Politics*.

Crassus, Marcus Licinius Consul 30 BC.

Crassus was a follower of Sex. *Pompey and then of *Antony before joining *Octavian. When fighting in Moesia in 29 BC he killed the enemy leader himself, and won a triumph; Octavian denied him the *spolia opima*, however, to which this feat had made him the fourth Roman commander ever to be entitled.

BIBL. Dio, li. 23–7; Syme, *Rom. Rev.* 308 ff.

Crassus Frugi, Marcus Licinius Consul AD 27.

Crassus was killed at *Messallina's instigation in AD 46 because his birth and military success in Macedonia and Britain made him a threat to *Britannicus. *Seneca thought him 'as like to *Claudius as one egg to another' and therefore that 'he was so stupid that he could even have been emperor'.

BIBL. Seneca, *Apocolocyntosis*, xi. 3–5.

Crinagoras (*c.* 70 BC–AD 15) Epigrammatist.

Author of 51 epigrams in the Greek Anthology, Crinagoras acted as ambassador to Rome for his native Mitylene, and came to frequent imperial circles; he commemorates equally the gift of a toothpick to Lucius *Caesar and Rome's victories over the northern barbarians. He may have been influenced by the Latin poets of his day, notably *Horace.

BIBL. *Garland of Philip*, ed. Gow and Page, 1773 ff; G. W. Williams, *Change and Decline* (1978) 129 ff.

Bronze coin (*follis*) of Flavius Julius Crispus with spear and shield.

Crispus Caesar AD 317–26.

Born *c.* 305, Flavius Julius Crispus was the eldest son of *Constantine, by his first wife Minervina. He was educated in Gaul by *Lactantius, and proclaimed Caesar in 317, together with his half-brother *Constantine II. After distinguishing himself as an admiral in the war against *Licinius in 324, he accompanied Constantine and his stepmother *Fausta (q.v.) to Italy in 326, but was executed for reasons unknown at Pola.

BIBL. *PLRE* i, Crispus 4; Jones, *Constantine*, 243–6; MacMullen, *Constantine*.

Celtic bronze coin (enlarged) with portrait of
Cunobellinus, British client king.

Cunobellinus (died c. AD 41/2) British client king.

Son of Tasciovanus of the Catuvellauni,
Cunobellinus, in the course of a reign of about 40
years, established a powerful kingdom in south-
east Britain with a new capital and mint at
Colchester. Trade with the Romans flourished, and
his coins show Roman influence. He died before the
Roman invasion of AD 43 (which was resisted by
his son *Caratacus), and passed into medieval fable
and Shakespeare as 'Cymbeline'.

BIBL. Frere, *Britannia*.

Curtius, Mettius

Mettius Curtius was invented to explain the
name of the Curtian Lake in the Forum Romanum,
into which he supposedly rode while fighting for
Titus *Tatius against *Romulus. Other explanations
were that here a Marcus Curtius sacrificed himself
to satisfy an oracle in 362 BC or that Gaius Curtius
(consul 445 BC) fenced in an area struck by
lightning.

BIBL. PW iv. 1865; Ogilvie, *Livy*, 75 ff.; E. Nash,
Pictorial Dictionary of Ancient Rome I (2nd ed.
1968), s.v. Lacus Curtius.

Cynegius Praetorian prefect AD 384–8.

Maternus Cynegius was a leading member of the
coterie of pious Spaniards which surrounded

Relief of Mettius Curtius. Copy of 2nd-century BC
original in Capitoline Museum, Rome.

*Theodosius I, whose kinsman he may have been.
After holding lower offices at court, he became
praetorian prefect in 384 and inspired a series of
laws against Jews, heretics, and pagans. During an
official tour of inspection in Egypt and Syria he
encouraged the destruction of pagan temples by
bands of monks, despite the orator *Libanius'
protests at the illegal behaviour of 'men dressed in
black who eat more than elephants'. Consul in 388,
he died in office.

BIBL. Matthews, *Western Aristocracies*.

St Cyprian Bishop of Carthage c. AD 248–58.

Born early in the third century at Carthage,
Thascius Caecilius Cyprianus had a formal training
in rhetoric. He was converted to Christianity
c. 246, and by 248 had become bishop of Carthage.
During the following ten years he suffered official
harassment and prosecution during the Christian
persecutions of *Decius, *Trebonianus Gallus, and
*Valerian, and in the last he lost his life. He was a
prolific writer on many subjects and actively
involved in the dispute as to whether apostates
should be allowed to re-enter the Church and on
what terms. His great moral authority made
possible a compromise on this issue, which eluded
the African Church after the Great Persecution of
c. 300 (see *Donatus).

BIBL. *RAC* Cyprian; Kleine Pauly, Cyprian;
ODCC Cyprian.

St Cyril of Alexandria Bishop AD 412–44.

In political influence and theological acumen
Cyril was a dominant figure of his time. In
Alexandria he pursued vigorous opposition to
Judaism, heresy, and paganism (and may not have
been innocent of the death of *Hypatia), while in
the Church at large he was the principal defender
of 'Alexandrian' Christology, the union of God and
Man in Christ. This brought him into conflict
with *Nestorius, bishop of Constantinople, whom
he accused of denying the divinity of Christ. By
exploiting his influence with the Pope and the
court at Constantinople (particularly the Empress
*Pulcheria) Cyril was able to secure the
condemnation of Nestorius at the Council of
Ephesus in 431 (although not without having to
expend huge bribes at court in order to overturn
his own deposition by a rival synod of Nestorius'
supporters). In 433 Cyril consented to a reconciling
formula, and the controversy subsided for the rest
of his life. He was the author of numerous works,
including a defence of the Church against the
attacks of the Emperor *Julian.

BIBL. J. Quasten, *Patrology* iii. 116–42; L.
Duchesne, *Early History of the Christian Church*, iii
(1924).

St Cyril of Jerusalem Bishop c. AD 349–86.

Cyril was banished from his see in 357 for

opposition to *Arianism, and reinstated by the
Council of Seleucia in 359; he was subsequently
banished twice more. Doubts about his doctrinal
position led to a mission by *Gregory of Nyssa in
379. In 381 he may have recited the present
version of the Nicene Creed at the Council of
Constantinople. The 24 *Catecheses*, his main
surviving work, were composed c. 350 for the
preparation of candidates for baptism. In 351/3 he
witnessed a celestial cross phenomenon, and wrote
to *Constantius II with the news.
    BIBL. *ODCC*; *PG* xxxiii. 1165–76.

Cyrus Praetorian prefect AD 439–41.
    Flavius Cyrus, an Egyptian, was one of the early
Byzantine 'wandering poets'. His talent brought
him to the notice of the Empress *Eudocia, who
made him urban prefect of Constantinople (439)
and praetorian prefect (439–41). He was the first
prefect to use Greek officially instead of Latin, and
made himself popular in Constantinople by
completing *Anthemius' walls and providing
street lighting. But when Eudocia fell from power
(late 441 ?), Cyrus was accused of pagan sympathies
and removed to an obscure bishopric in Phrygia—
where his first sermon was celebrated for its
brevity.
    BIBL. A. Cameron, *Historia* xiv (1965); D. J.
Constantelos, *GRBS* xii (1971).

Dalmatius, Flavius Consul AD 333.
    Son of *Constantius I and Theodora, Flavius
Dalmatius was the eldest of *Constantine's six half-
brothers and sisters (see stemma of Constantine,
Julius *Constantius). In 333 he was made consul
and 'censor', and held a command in the East,
where he suppressed a usurper in Cyprus, and
coped with troubles concerning *Athanasius. In 337
he apparently fell victim to the family massacre
instigated by the sons of Constantine.
    BIBL. *PLRE* i, Dalmatius 6.

Left: bronze coin (*follis*) of Fl. Julius Dalmatius.

Right: GLORIA EXERCITUS reverse of *follis* of Fl. Julius
Dalmatius with soldiers and standard.

Dalmatius, Flavius Julius Caesar AD 335–7.
    Flavius Julius Dalmatius was the elder son of Fl.
*Dalmatius, and a nephew of *Constantine.
Educated at Toulouse in semi-exile, he was later
included in Constantine's succession arrangements,
being made Caesar in 335. His domain was to be
the lower Danube countries. In 337 he was a
victim of the same massacre as his father, brother
*Hannibalianus, uncle Julius *Constantius (q.v.),
and four cousins.
    BIBL. *PLRE* i, Dalmatius 7; Piganiol, *Empire chr.*

St Damasus Bishop of Rome, AD 366–84.
    The Pope whose magnificence shocked the pagan
aristocrat *Praetextatus, Damasus only succeeded
*Liberius (died September 366) after bloody
fighting between his followers and those of
another deacon, who called him 'the ladies' ear-
tickler'. To his secretary, St *Jerome, he was 'the
virgin teacher of the virgin Church'. He promoted
the cult of martyrs by restoring their shrines and
embellishing them with his own poems beautifully
engraved by *Filocalus. He organized a petition by
Christian senators against the altar of Victory (see
*Symmachus). He did not respond to St *Basil's
appeals for help against *Arian persecution.
    BIBL. *ODCC* Damasus.

Datianus Consul AD 358.
    Éminence grise at the court of *Constantius II,
Datianus was the son of a bath-attendant. Learning
shorthand, he became a 'notary' in the imperial
civil service, and rose to be a senator of
Constantinople, a count, consul, and patrician. He
was a Christian. Unlike *Ablabius and Fl. *Philippus
he wielded great influence without holding office.
    BIBL. *PLRE* i, Datianus 1.

Decius, Trajan Emperor AD 249–51.
    Born in Illyricum c. 190/200, Gaius Messius
Quintus Decius was entrusted by *Philip I with the
task of restoring order on the Danube. His success
led the troops to declare him emperor in June 249,
and Philip was defeated and slain in a battle near
Verona. The Roman senate honoured Decius with
the name Traianus. In 249–50 he initiated a severe
Christian persecution, which lessened late in 250
owing to the Gothic War. Decius' elder son
*Herennius was made Augustus and was sent to
Moesia to fight the Goths. Decius himself followed,
and both died at the disastrous battle of Abritta in
June 251.
    BIBL. *CAH* xii; Kleine Pauly, Decius; (PW
Messius 9).

Decius Mus (1), **Publius** Consul 340 BC.
    After allegedly extricating a trapped consular
army as military tribune (343 BC), Decius
supposedly 'devoted' himself in battle against the
Latins near Capua (340 BC) (see Manlius

Bust of the Emperor Decius. Rome, Capitoline Museum.

*Torquatus). Decius' participation in the engagement and his self-sacrifice have been rejected as an anticipation of the action of P.*Decius Mus (2); but he may at least have died on the battlefield.

BIBL. PW iv. 2279 ff.; J. Heurgon, *Recherches sur . . . Capoue Préromaine* (1942) 260 ff.; Salmon, *Samnium* 196 ff.

Decius Mus (2), **Publius** Consul 312, 308, 297, and 295 BC.

Reputedly ill in 312 BC, Decius nevertheless campaigned successfully against Volsinii (308), was among the first plebeian *pontifices* (300), and operated against the Samnites (297–296). In 295 he and Q.*Fabius Maximus Rullianus (his colleague in his last three consulships and his censorship (304)) defeated the Gauls and their allies at Sentinum, after Decius had performed a ritual self-sacrifice (*devotio*). This *devotio* is probably historical (Duris of Samos, a contemporary, possibly recorded it); those of his father, P.*Decius Mus (1), and son, P.*Decius Mus (3), are more dubious.

BIBL. PW iv. 2281 ff.; Salmon, *Samnium* 243, etc.; Harris, *REU* 49 ff., 69 ff.

Decius Mus (3), **Publius** Consul 279 BC.

Decius and Publius Sulpicius Saverrio were defeated by *Pyrrhus at Ausculum (279 BC). *Ennius and *Cicero believed that he, like P.*Decius Mus (2), 'devoted' himself in the Roman cause;

other sources (*Dio and *De viris illustribus*) suggest that he survived the battle.

BIBL. PW iv. 2284 ff.; O.Skutsch, *Studia Enniana* (1968) 54 ff.

Deiotarus Galatian king died 40 BC.

A Galatian client prince, Deiotarus was rewarded with an enlarged kingdom by *Pompey for his loyalty to Rome in the *Mithridatic wars. In the civil wars he frequently shifted his allegiance between the dynasts, and had to call on *Cicero, his personal friend, to intercede on his behalf with *Caesar in 45 BC.

BIBL. Magie, *Asia Minor*.

Demetrius (died 180 BC) Macedonian prince.

In 197 BC Demetrius' father *Philip V sent him as a hostage to Rome, where he remained until 190, becoming personally popular and acquiring pro-Roman attitudes. When Philip sent him to Rome as special envoy in 183, his personal appearance in the senate did much to restore rapidly deteriorating relations between Rome and Macedon. His ambitions were encouraged by leading Romans, but they brought on him the hostility of his elder brother *Perseus and the suspicion of his father, who had him executed for treason in 180.

BIBL. Walbank, *Philip V of Macedon* (1940).

Demetrius the Cynic Philosopher, 1st century AD.

Demetrius rejected 200,000 sesterces offered him by *Gaius; was highly praised by *Seneca; objected to luxury under *Nero; was a friend of *Thrasea Paetus; was expelled from Rome by *Tigellinus and again, at *Mucianus' suggestion, by *Vespasian; and was a friend and associate of the wise man *Apollonius of Tyana. He was a key figure behind the anti-monarchical and dissident groups in high circles at Rome in the late first century.

BIBL. *PIR* D 39.

Demetrius of Pharos Illyrian client king c. 230–219 BC.

An Illyrian subordinate of Teuta, Demetrius became a Roman client dynast by his betrayal of Corcyra in 229 BC, and eventually succeeded to Teuta's regency. His expanding power and un-client-like behaviour in the 220s led to the senate dispatching *Paullus (1) and *Salinator to eject him in 219. He fled to Macedon and incited *Philip V to war with Rome.

BIBL. Errington, *Dawn of Empire*, 38 ff., 102 ff.

Demetrius Soter Seleucid king 162–150 BC.

Demetrius replaced his uncle *Antiochus Epiphanes as hostage at Rome in 175 BC. When Epiphanes died in 164/3, Demetrius petitioned the senate for his release, intending to claim the throne. When this was refused and news reached Rome of

*Octavius' murder, he made a dramatic escape from Italy in 162 with the connivance of his friend and fellow-detainee, *Polybius (Pol. xxxi. 11 ff.). In Syria he displaced Epiphanes' son, a minor, and seized the throne. Although he had supporters at Rome, the senate as a whole never properly recognized him but gave its support to rival claimants, a policy which enraged Polybius. Demetrius was thus unable to arrest Seleucid decline; he was killed fighting a pretender in 150. Polybius mentions his alcoholic tendencies more than once.

BIBL. Will, *Hist. pol.*; Walbank, *HCP* iii.

Dentatus, Manius Curius Consul 290, 284 (?), 275, and 274 BC.

A *novus homo*, he and Publius Cornelius Rufinus victoriously concluded the Third Samnite War; Curius then subjugated the Sabines and distributed part of their territory (290 BC). According to *Polybius he was suffect consul (?) in 284 (?), defeated the Senones, confiscated their territory, and established the colony at Sena (dated in *Livy c.·290). In 275 he effectively defeated *Pyrrhus, and from the booty began an aqueduct (the Anio Vetus) in his censorship (272). His integrity and frugality, assiduously advertised by the Elder *Cato, became legendary.

BIBL. PW iv. 1841 ff.; G. Forni, *Athenaeum* xxxi (1953) 170 ff.; Salmon, *Samnium*, 276, etc.; M. G. Morgan, *CQ*, N.S. xxii (1972) 309 ff.

Dexippus (*c.* AD 200–270) Historian.

Publius Herennius Dexippus was born *c.* 200/205 into an intellectual non-senatorial Athenian family. He held the chief magistracy at Athens, became a member of an Eleusinian priesthood, and gave the Great Panathenaic games. Only three of his works survive in fragments: the unoriginal *Concerning Alexander*, probably written earliest, followed by an annalistic history in 12 books, and the *Scythica* relating the mid-third century wars in the Greek East in Thucydidean style.

Already over 60, Dexippus led a successful counter-attack against the Heruli after their capture and devastation of Athens *c.* 267–8.

BIBL. F. Millar, *JRS* lix (1969) 12 ff; PW Dexippus.

Diadumenian Caesar AD 217–8, Augustus 218.

Marcus Opellius Antoninus Diadumenianus was the son of the Emperor *Macrinus. His father made him Caesar in 217, and later Augustus, but the administrative and military incompetence of Macrinus resulted in both being slain in 218 by rebellious troops.

BIBL. Millar, *Dio.*

Didius Gallus Governor of Britain *c.* AD 52–8.

Aulus Didius Gallus' finest hour was when he expelled King Mithridates from the Bosporan kingdom and settled its affairs (AD 45–6). He later governed Britain. *Tacitus notes his dignity, and *Quintilian an example of his perversity.

BIBL. Tac. *Ann.* xii. 15.

Gold coin (*aureus*), enlarged, of the Emperor Didius Julianus.

Didius Julianus Emperor AD 193.

From Milan, Marcus Didius Severus Julianus was born into a senatorial family late in the reign of *Hadrian. He was consul with Helvius *Pertinax in 174 or 175, and governed a number of important military provinces. He was acquitted of involvement in a plot against *Commodus, and went on to govern Africa in the early 190s. When Pertinax was murdered (28 March 193), he was on his way to a senate meeting, and was waylaid by two tribunes of the praetorian guard who urged him to seize power and took him to the camp. There he found Flavius *Sulpicianus attempting to have himself proclaimed emperor, and the two bid for power by offering donatives to the guard. Julianus won at 25,000 sesterces per man, was proclaimed, and promised to restore the good name of *Commodus. His reign lasted only 66 days. As Septimius *Severus advanced on Rome, Julianus was forced to defend the city, but, acting on messages from Severus, the senate deposed him and condemned him to death. He was murdered in the palace on 1 or 2 June by a common soldier.

BIBL. Birley, *Severus*; *PIR* D 77; Grosso, *Lotta*.

Dio, Cassius Historian; consul AD 205/6 and 229.

From the city of Nicaea in Bithynia, Cassius Dio was perhaps related, through his mother's family, to *Dio Chrysostom. He was born *c.* 163/4, came to Rome about 180, and began a senatorial career, perhaps in the late 180s. In 193, when Septimius *Severus arrived in Rome, Dio sent him a pamphlet he had written on dreams and portents which foretold Severus' rise to power. He became a friend of the emperor, and was a member of his advisory council. He was later appointed by the Emperor *Macrinus as curator of Pergamum and Smyrna. He went on to govern Africa (perhaps 223), Dalmatia (224–6), and Pannonia Superior (226–8). His second tenure of the consulship was particularly distinguished, since his colleague was the Emperor *Severus Alexander. After this he returned to Nicaea. As well as the pamphlet on dreams he wrote a history of the Civil Wars of 193–7 (both works are lost), but his major work is a history (in Greek) of Rome from its foundation to the death of Severus Alexander. This was perhaps mainly written *c.* 207–19, except for the latter part, and contains a great deal of important material, particularly for the period of Dio's own lifetime. The original text is preserved fully in Books 36–54 (68–10 BC), substantially in Books 55–60 (9 BC–AD 46) and partially in Books 79–80 (AD 217–20). The remainder of the work has to be supplied from summary versions made by Byzantine scholars in the tenth twelfth centuries.

BIBL. F. Millar, *A Study of Cassius Dio* (1964); E. Cary, *Dio's Roman History* (Loeb, 1914–27); *PIR* C 492.

Dio Cocceianus, called **Dio Chrysostom** ('golden-mouth') or **Dio of Prusa** (in Bithynia) (*c.* AD 40–after 112) Man of letters.

A philosopher and orator of distinction (which justifies his inclusion in *Philostratus' Lives of the Sophists*) Dio reached Rome under *Vespasian and was turned to philosophy by *Musonius Rufus. Banished under *Domitian, he experienced prolonged Balkan *Wanderjahre*, then returned to Rome and enjoyed imperial favour there and in his native Prusa. Of the 80 surviving speeches, two are in fact by his pupil *Favorinus; he wrote on politics, giving counsel to his fellow citizens, to the Romans, and to the emperors; on trivialities,

sophistically (On Hair), on literature, and on popular Stoic-Cynic moral philosophy.

BIBL. Bowersock, *Sophists*, 110 f.; Pliny, *Letters*, x. lxxxi. 1, with Sherwin-White's note; MacMullen, *Enemies*, 46 ff.

Diocletian Emperor AD 284–305.

Gaius Aurelius Valerius Diocletianus, commander of the imperial guard, became emperor on the assassination of the short-lived emperor *Numerian. He was to be the first emperor for over a century to celebrate 20 years' continuous rule. Such stability was not to occur again until the consolidation of the dynasty of *Constantine.

Diocletian chose Jupiter as his divine protector. Jupiter had Hercules to do his heavy work: in 286 Diocletian made his old friend *Maximian joint Augustus. In 293 *Constantius I and *Galerius were invested as Caesars and married into the families of the Augusti. Much emphasis was placed on the *concordia* of the resultant Tetrarchy. Constantius was to support Maximian in the West, Galerius was to operate with Diocletian in the East. In 305 the Augusti abdicated and the Caesars succeeded them.

Jupiter gives victory. Much of the tetrarchs' time was spent fighting, both rebels like *Carausius and *Achilleus, and foreign enemies. The Rhine, the Danube, and the Persian frontier were organized as lines of defence in depth. Strategically

The Baths of Diocletian, Rome (begun AD 297/8, dedicated 305/6): reconstruction.

situated cities were transformed into imperial
residences; in particular Nicomedia, half-way
between Syria and the Danube, was refounded as
a Second Rome.

Jupiter also brings plenty and stability. A
leitmotif of Diocletian's publicity is his intention to
bring back the Golden Age 'which flourished long
ago in the reign of Saturn'. Public buildings form
an integral part and an apt symbol of this policy.
Their style was traditional but more massive:
tetrarchic monuments and government were both
meant to last. Diocletian's evocation of
traditional Roman values was deliberate. Latin,
moribund as a literary language for a century, was
revived at schools in Gaul and by *Lactantius'
teaching at Nicomedia. The reformed bronze
coinage was inscribed 'To the Genius of the
Roman People'. The tetrarchs thought themselves
'protectors of the human race who are able to see
ahead'. They extended the administration:
provinces were subdivided and grouped into
twelve units called dioceses, each under a
governor-general. They also attempted to fix
maximum prices for commodities by an edict of
301.

By 303, Galerius had persuaded Diocletian to
persecute the Christians; by May 305, he had
persuaded him to abdicate. Diocletian retired to
Salona (Split in Yugoslavia) and was so content
with the vegetables he grew there that, in the
troubled times which ensued, nothing could tempt
him to resume the purple.

BIBL. Jones, *LRE* ch. 2; G. Costa in *Diz. Epigr.*
s.v. Diocletianus; H. P. L'Orange, *Likeness and
Icon* (1973).

Diodorus called Siculus Historian, floruit late
1st century BC.

A native of Agyrium (near modern Enna, in
Sicily) 'of moderate intelligence and immense
industry' (Bowersock), Diodorus spent thirty
years (roughly 60–30 BC) in travel (e.g. to Egypt),
and in research (in Rome, for the sake of the
outstanding facilities; his Latin remained shakier
than he acknowledged) for the 40 books of his
Historical Library, which narrated events from the
beginnings of time to 59 BC. Fifteen books are
preserved intact, the rest in excerpts and
fragments. This dogged, derivative, disagreeable
work invaluably preserves—amid some confusion
—the judgements and accounts of better men, in
matters both of myth and of history (including the
rise of Rome).

Diogenes Laertius Historian of Philosophy, early
(?) 3rd century AD.

Diogenes Laertius was the author of a history of
Greek philosophy, which took the form of
biographies of the philosophers together with a
summary of their doctrines. His work is confused

but conscientious, and preserves valuable information, notably on Epicurus.

BIBL. Kleine Pauly, Diogenes 11.

Dionysius of Halicarnassus Critic and historian, late 1st century BC.

Dionysius was active in Rome 30–8 BC, both as a teacher of rhetoric to the Roman aristocracy, whose taste he admired, and as an indefatigable research worker. A careful and intelligent Atticist critic of classical Greek literature, with a notably sophisticated ear, he wrote especially on Thucydides and the Greek orators. He left, as the chief 'memorial of his own soul', the massive *Roman Archaeology* (often called *Roman Antiquities*). It originally contained 20 books and came down to the First Punic War (i.e. to where *Polybius began). Only the first half survives intact (plus numerous excerpts and fragments). It is not a work to be read for pleasure—the humour is unconscious—but it serves as an essential and fascinating guide to the research methods of the historian in the ancient world, and stands as a memorial to wide reading, vast erudition, and slender judgement.

BIBL. E. Gabba, Sather Lectures (forthcoming); Kennedy, *Rhetoric*, 342 ff.; Russell and Winterbottom. *Lit. Crit.*, 305 ff.

Dioscorides Pharmacologist, mid-1st century AD.

An army doctor from Anazarbus (Cilicia), Dioscorides compiled a *Materia medica* of high quality and lasting influence, preserved in manuscripts of spectacular beauty.

Dolabella Consul 44 BC.

An ambitious and dissolute young aristocrat, Publius Cornelius Dolabella married *Cicero's daughter, Tullia, against her father's wishes (50 BC), and gained political advancement as a legate of *Caesar in the Civil War. As a radical and disruptive tribune in 47 he clashed with *Antony, but in spite of his youth and Antony's opposition, Caesar nominated Dolabella as suffect consul to replace him in Rome when he assumed his intended Parthian command (44). After Caesar's death Dolabella secured the vacant consulship and the province of Syria by flirting briefly with the republican leaders. But in Asia he turned on the republican governor and killed him, whereupon he was outlawed and succeeded in his command by *Cassius. Defeated by Cassius in Syria, he committed suicide.

BIBL. Syme, *Rom. Rev.*

Domitia Longina Empress AD 81–96.

Daughter of *Corbulo, Domitia was forced to divorce Aelius Lamia and marry *Domitian, to whom she bore a short-lived son in AD 73. She did not escape the normal gossip about imperial

Dioscorides, *De materia medica*: an illustration of the wild blackberry with a description of its properties. A page from the manuscript of AD 513 written and illustrated for Juliana Anicia, the daughter of the Emperor Anicius *Olybrius. Vienna, Österreichische Nationalbibliothek.

Portrait bust of Domitia Longina, wife of *Domitian. Rome, Villa Albani-Torlonia.

women, and was involved in the assassination of Domitian, but lived well into the second century, honoured for her father's reputation rather than tainted by that of her second husband.

BIBL. *PIR* D 181!

Domitian Emperor AD 81–96.

While Titus Flavius Domitianus was a boy, his father *Vespasian was poor and unimportant; his brother *Titus, on the other hand, had been educated at court. Deprived of any position of responsibility, Domitian came to desire power, though, as his father perceived, he was unsuited for it. Shocked by Domitian's reckless actions in Rome in 69, Vespasian (who joked that his son would be appointing the next emperor, so keen was he to exercise his patronage) gave him only the ornaments of power during his reign. The history of Domitian's own reign, however, makes it clear that during this time he learned the principles of sound administration which characterized the Flavian reigns. But a suspicious and irascible temperament—it is eloquent of his character that he was deeply interested in the personality and principate of *Tiberius—combined with his enthusiasm for power to compound a tyrannical and unhappy reign. It became quickly apparent that there would be no dissembling—Domitian was 'Master and God', and the carefully preserved fictions which cloaked the absolutism of the principate were quite disregarded. Senators and theorists were equally offended; attempted uprisings followed (most notably that of *Saturninus (L. Antonius)), and a dreary and terrible spiral of suspicion and repression, until in 96 Domitian was killed by members of his own household, including his wife *Domitia Longina.

The high moral tone of the reigns which succeeded was set by the survivors of Domitian's final reign of terror, loud in their admiration of *Helvidius Priscus the younger, or Arulenus Rusticus. Influential members of the group who opposed the extremes of autonomy in the

The *profectio* of Domitian: the emperor setting out from Rome. Cancelleria relief: Rome, Vatican Museum.

Coin type of the Emperor Domitian.

principate, they execrated the informers and prosecutors, and Domitian himself, who is therefore condemned by tradition as an emperor comparable with *Gaius and *Nero. Yet in his choice of statesman—including *Pliny and *Tacitus who so roundly condemned him—and his government, in the energy with which he devoted himself to the urgent military problems of the Danube, and in his financial arrangements, which allowed him an extensive building policy, he was not a disastrous emperor at all. Indeed he was a man of real culture, and the author of some measures, such as controls on the castration of slaves, which were manifestly humane. While he remains an unattractive man—grim, morbid, egocentric, cruel—he does not deserve comparison as a ruler with the wild and quirky Gaius or the criminally foolish Nero.

BIBL. *CAH* xi. 1; B. V. Jones, *Domitian and the Senatorial Order* (1979).

Domitianus Usurper *c*. AD 270/5 (?).

Gaius Domitianus is known only from a single reference in Zosimus and one coin of apparently Gallic style but doubtful authenticity.

BIBL. *PIR* D 114; *PLRE* i, Domitianus 1; *RIC* v. 2.

Domitius Ahenobarbus (1), Gnaeus Consul 122 BC.

During a command (122–120 BC) as consul and proconsul, Domitius played a leading role in the pacification of southern Gaul, with victories over the Allobroges and Arverni. He supervised the settlement of the area as a Roman province (subsequently known as Gallia Narbonensis), and improved its communications by building the Via Domitia. His extensive influence and personal connections in the province were maintained by his son, a founder of the citizen colony at Narbonne (118 BC), and exploited by his grandson, L. *Domitius Ahenobarbus (1).

BIBL. Benedict, *AJP* lxiii (1942) 38 ff.

Domitius Ahenobarbus (2), Gnaeus Consul AD 32.

The record of Domitius' disgraces began when he was dismissed from the entourage of Gaius *Caesar in the East. He was married to the younger *Agrippina in 28, but only avoided charges of treason, adultery, and incest because of *Tiberius' death. He died when his son, later the Emperor *Nero, was three, and is described by *Suetonius as 'loathsome in every aspect of his life'.

BIBL. Suetonius, *Nero* 5.

Domitius Ahenobarbus (1), Lucius Consul 54 BC.

A prominent noble whose vast inherited wealth, influence, and popularity enabled him, like *Pompey, to raise private armies, Domitius stood with his brother-in-law *Cato (Uticensis) in firm opposition to the First Triumvirate which robbed him of his natural primacy in the traditional constitution. He especially resented *Caesar's tenure of Transalpine Gaul which, as it had been conquered by his grandfather Cn. *Domitius Ahenobarbus (1), he regarded as his family's private domain. When as a consular candidate for 55 BC he threatened to have the province transferred, he precipitated the renewal of the Triumvirate at Lucca, which kept him out of the consulship until 54. He received Caesar's province at the outbreak of war in 49, and engaged him at Corfinium against Pompey's instructions. Defeated but spared by Caesar, he died in 48 commanding Pompey's left wing at Pharsalus.

BIBL. Taylor, *Party Politics*.

Domitius Ahenobarbus (2), Lucius Consul 16 BC.

*Suetonius finds many of *Nero's faults in his grandfather, especially arrogance. *Velleius finds only his straightforwardness to praise. Domitius' military exploits included campaigns in Thrace in 15 BC and the vigorous organization of Germany, in the course of which he led an army further beyond the Elbe than any had previously been. He married *Antony's elder daughter and died in AD 25.

BIBL. *PIR* D 128.

Inscription on milestone of Cn. Domitius Ahenobarbus (1).

Donatus (and **Donatism**) African schismatic (died *c*. AD 355).

In 311 the Church of Carthage elected as bishop

the Archdeacon Caecilian. Many African bishops objected, because one of Caecilian's consecrators was tainted with handing over Scriptures to the authorities during the recent persecution. In Caecilian's place the bishops chose Donatus, formerly bishop of a small town in the olive-growing outback, who shared his electors' enthusiasm for the martyrs. The bishop of Rome, the Council of Arles (314), and the Emperor *Constantine all failed to heal the ensuing schism and, despite imperial condemnation, Donatism remained the dominant religion of Roman Africa until weakened by coercion in the early fifth century.

BIBL. W. H. C. Frend, *The Donatist Church* (1952); Peter Brown, *Religion and Society*, Part iii; A. H. M. Jones, *Constantine*.

Donatus, Aelius Grammarian, 4th century AD.

Donatus, a grammarian and rhetorician, contemporary of Marius *Victorinus and teacher of St *Jerome, lived in Rome around 353. He wrote an *Art of Grammar* and an intelligent and important commentary on *Terence which are still extant. His commentary on *Virgil, known through excerpts in *Servius, is unfortunately lost.

BIBL. G. Goold, *HSCP* lxxiv (1970).

Drusus (1), **Marcus Livius** Consul 112 BC.

As tribune in 122 BC Drusus was the main architect of Gaius *Gracchus' (3) downfall, outflanking him politically with grand—and in the event unfulfilled—schemes of colonization, and leading the opposition to the enfranchisement of Italians. These services to the senatorial establishment were duly rewarded with a successful public career, culminating in the censorship in 109.

BIBL. Gruen, *Politics*.

Drusus (2), **Marcus Livius** Tribune of the plebs 91 BC.

An ambitious and talented young noble, Drusus became tribune in 91 BC, seeking to emulate his father, Livius *Drusus (1), in using that office to advance simultaneously his own career and the interests of the senatorial establishment. He was backed by a powerful faction in the senate, including *Scaurus and L. Licinius *Crassus, whose principal object was reform of the criminal juries after the recent scandal over *Rutilius (Drusus' uncle). To secure this reform Drusus tried to establish wide personal support by proposing a programme of popular legislation. Faced with opposition from the equestrians (backed by *Marius) and the consul L. Marcius *Philippus, Drusus became increasingly arrogant and demagogic. It is not clear at what point he espoused the revolutionary cause of Italian enfranchisement, or whether he intended to use Italian supporters

to overawe his opponents by violence. But this alienated his conservative support in the senate and, increasingly isolated, he was killed in a violent clash in the Forum. His legislation was repealed, but the Italian issue immediately erupted into the Social War.

BIBL. Gruen, *Politics*; Gabba, *Republican Rome, the Army and the Allies* (1976).

Drusus, Nero Claudius (the elder Drusus) WIFE ANTONIA
(38–9 BC) Consul 9 BC.

Son of *Livia, born after his mother's remarriage to Octavian, Drusus was favoured because of his close connections with the ruling family, like his brother *Tiberius, with whom he fought the Raetians in 15 BC. In 13 BC he began a series of expeditions in Germany, and in 12 dedicated the great altar of Augustus at Lyons. The campaign which followed, around the Rhine delta, was particularly successful, and the beginning of a series of victories which took him as far as the Elbe. Divine admonitions forced him to turn back, and he died after a fall from his horse; deep public mourning followed. The tradition of his disagreements with *Augustus and wish to restore the Republic probably derives more from the ambition of a successful Claudian to achieve personal eminence than from political idealism.

BIBL. Dio, liv. 32–4, lv. 1–2; Levick, *Tiberius*, 32–5.

Drusus Julius Caesar (the younger Drusus) Consul AD 15 and 21.

Vipsania Agrippina bore Drusus to *Tiberius in 13 BC; he married Livia Julia (Livilla: see stemma).

Drusus Julius Caesar. Naples, Museo Nazionale.

After his father's adoption his career was accelerated by *Augustus. In AD 14 he was sent to Pannonia to calm the mutinous legions and in 17 to Illyricum to settle the *Maroboduus affair. After receiving the tribunician power (22) he was virtually co-ruler. His death in 23 was rumoured to be the result of a plot between his wife and *Sejanus.

BIBL. *PIR* I 219.

Drusus Julius Caesar (son of Germanicus): see **Nero Julius Caesar**

Dryantilla Augusta *c*. AD 260.

Sulpicia Dryantilla was the wife of the usurper *Regalianus, and possibly the daughter of either Sulpicius Justus or Sulpicius Pollo from Asia. Little is known of her, although she is well attested on the coinage.

BIBL. Göbl, *Regalianus und Dryantilla* (1970).

Duilius, Gaius Consul 260 BC.

Duilius gained the first recorded naval triumph

Imperial period copy of the *columna rostrata* of C. Duilius: column adorned with the prows of captured ships. Rome, Capitoline Museum.

for his victory over the Carthaginian fleet at Mylae (260 BC), for which his introduction of boarding bridges (*corvi*) was largely responsible. His achievements were recorded on the *columna rostrata* in the Roman Forum.

BIBL. Thiel, *History of Roman Sea-power* (1954); Walbank, *HCP* i. 76 f.; Degrassi, *Inscr. Ital.* 13. 3. 69.

Eclectus Imperial courtier, late 2nd century AD.

An Egyptian freedman of the Emperor Lucius *Verus, Eclectus became chamberlain of *Commodus and was a close associate of the emperor after the death of *Cleander (189), taking part in gladiatorial shows with him. Along with *Marcia (to whom he was married) and Aemilius *Laetus, he conspired to kill Commodus in 192 and to elevate *Pertinax. He died along with Pertinax on 28 March 193.

BIBL. Grosso, *Lotta*; *PIR* E 3.

Egeria Holy Land pilgrim AD 381–4.

Originating probably from north-western Spain, Egeria travelled via Constantinople on a pilgrimage to the Holy Land and Egypt; she was based in Jerusalem for three years (381–4?). She wrote a detailed description of her journey (only a portion survives), including the holy places she visited and an important account of the Church liturgy that she witnessed in Jerusalem. This record is our most significant evidence of the growth of Christian pilgrimage to the Holy Land from the era of *Constantine.

BIBL. J. Wilkinson, *Egeria's Travels* (1971).

Egnatius, Gellius Samnite general 295 BC.

General of the Samnites Gellius was defeated, with his Etruscan and Gallic allies, and killed at Sentinum (295 BC). That his name is invention, suggested by Marius Egnatius, an Italic leader in the Social War, is an unnecessary conjecture.

BIBL. PW v. 1994 f.; K. J. Beloch, *Röm. Geschichte* (1926) 128, 432 ff.; Salmon, *Samnium* 263 ff.

Egnatius Rufus, Marcus Praetor 20 BC (?).

Egnatius attempted to direct popular enthusiasm in Rome from *Augustus to himself, especially by the formation of a fire brigade. When checked, he seems to have turned to conspiracy, and was executed.

BIBL. Velleius Paterculus, II. 91–2; *PIR* E 32.

Elagabalus (Varius Avitus Bassianus Marcus Aurelius Antoninus) Emperor AD 218–22.

A Syrian and the son of *Julia Soaemias (a niece of *Julia Domna) and Sextus Varius Marcellus, Elagabalus was proclaimed emperor in 218 by rebellious eastern troops resentful of *Macrinus' rule. As he resembled *Caracalla he was passed off as his bastard son, and Macrinus was defeated and

Bronze coin struck at Emesa (Syria), showing the black stone (Elagabalus' god Baal) *in situ*.

killed about a month later. His name was derived from the Emesene god whose priest he was, and he was to prove one of the most extraordinary emperors Rome ever had. A fanatical devotee of the cult, he actually brought his god (the black stone of Emesa) with him to Rome. There his behaviour scandalized both the senate and the soldiers. Sexually inverted with a tendency to transvestism, he was sufficiently bi-sexual to marry three wives (*Julia Paula, *Aquilia Severa, and *Annia Faustina), including a vestal virgin whom he divorced and later remarried. Actors, dancers, charioteers, and athletes reached prestigious positions based on their sexual excesses, and unfortunately neither his mother nor his grandmother could control his public behaviour. The soldiers became so disgusted at his conduct that it was clear by 221 that he would soon be murdered. His grandmother, *Julia Maesa, who had been instrumental in bringing Elagabalus to the throne, persuaded him to adopt his cousin *Severus Alexander as his son and Caesar in 221. Elagabalus soon became jealous of the boy, who was popular with the troops, and tried to have him killed. The outraged soldiers murdered Elagabalus and his mother in March 222.

BIBL. Birley, *Severus*; *ANRW* ii. 2.

Ennius (239–(?)169 BC) Epic and dramatic poet.

A native of Rudiae (near Lecce) in Calabria, Quintus Ennius claimed three hearts, Roman, Greek, and Oscan. A teacher in Rome, he later followed M. Fulvius *Nobilior's Aetolian campaign, which he narrated in *praetexta* and *Annales*, and received Roman citizenship. His literary output was very large and varied (including the philosophical *Euhemerus* and gastronomical *Hedyphagetica* 'Of Sweet Eating'); most important were twenty-odd tragedies and the *Annales*, which narrated in hexameters Roman history from Aeneas to 171 BC, concentrating on the Second Punic War. Substantial fragments survive; they attest the work's enduring popularity and reveal a majestic command of metre and language.

BIBL. Ed. Vahlen (1928, 1967). *Ennius, Entretiens Fond. Hardt* 1972.

Ephr(a)em Syrus (c. AD 306–373) Syriac Christian poet.

Ephrem was born at Nisibis on the Empire's Eastern frontier and lived through several Persian sieges of the city. After *Julian's death Nisibis became Persian; Ephrem moved to Edessa, 140 miles to the west, where he taught and also continued to compose hymns which employ profuse poetic imagery to adumbrate a distinctive theology.

BIBL. trans. S. P. Brock, *The Harp of the Spirit* (1975); Murray, *Symbols of Church and Kingdom* (1975).

Epictetus (c. AD 55–135) Philosopher.

A Stoic philosopher from Hierapolis in Phrygia, Epictetus was a slave of *Nero's freedman Epaphroditus and a friend and disciple of *Musonius Rufus. He taught philosophy in Rome until forced to leave when *Domitian banished philosophers (92/3). He then went to Nicopolis in Epirus where he taught until his death. His teachings, which probably influenced *Marcus Aurelius, emphasized the unity and order of the world as a manifestation of divine providence. His works survive in a collection made by his pupil *Arrian of 8 books of *Discourses* (of which 4 survive) and a *Manual*.

BIBL. J. M. Rist, *Stoic Philosophy* (1969); F. Millar, *JRS* lv (1965); Epictetus, *Discourses*, trans. W. A. Oldfather (Loeb, 1925–8).

St Epiphanius Bishop of Salamis, AD 367–403.

Born in Palestine (310/20), Epiphanius became a monk, and in 367 bishop of Salamis in Cyprus. He spent his long life fighting heresies, of which 80 (a quarter of them pre-Christian) are catalogued in the *Medicine Chest* (374/7). He was fanatically hostile to Greek philosophy and to *Origen (as the alleged inspiration of *Arianism).

BIBL. *ODCC* Epiphanius.

Eprius Marcellus Consul AD 60/8 and 74.

Despite mean and squalid origins, Titus Clodius Eprius Marcellus was a noted forensic orator whose talents were employed by *Nero against *Thrasea Paetus in AD 66. This, and his establishment position in general, brought him into frequent conflict with *Helvidius Priscus; but he was as useful to *Vespasian as he had been to Nero, and obtained much power and wealth. None the less in 79 he conspired against Vespasian in obscure circumstances, and committed suicide.

BIBL. *OCD*; *PIR* E 84.

Erucius Clarus Consul AD 117(?) and 146.

A nephew of Septicius Clarus, who was praetorian prefect early in the reign of *Hadrian, Sextus Erucius Clarus' early career owed something to the friendship and patronage of

*Pliny the Younger. He held a legateship in *Trajan's Parthian War (114–17) and captured Seleucia on the Tigris. He was urban prefect between his consulships. He is said by *Fronto to have been among the most distinguished senators, and by Aulus *Gellius to have been a devotee of literature.

BIBL. Syme, *Tacitus*; Sherwin-White, *The Letters of Pliny*; PIR E 96.

Eudocia (died 460) Eastern empress AD 421–441/2.

Aelia Eudocia, the wife of the eastern emperor *Theodosius II (7 June 421), blended Christian piety with classical learning. She was the daughter of an Athenian man of letters, with some talent of her own (some verses survive). After becoming Augusta in 423, she acquired equal status with her dominant sister-in-law *Pulcheria, with whom her relations were often strained. Eudocia made a pilgrimage to the Holy Land in 438–9, and returned with relics of St Stephen; but before long she was excluded from court life (441/2(?)) and went into exile, tradition alleges for adultery. She spent the rest of her life in Jerusalem, where she died on 20 October 460, and was buried in the basilica of St Stephen, which she herself had founded.

BIBL. Ch. Diehl, *Byzantine Portraits* (1927) ch. 2.

the eunuch *Eutropius (2) induced *Arcadius to marry (27 April 395). Forceful and quick-tempered, she soon dominated her torpid husband (becoming 'Augusta', 9 January 400) and undermined Eutropius' influence. She was a pious Catholic, and promoted the destruction of paganism at Gaza by allowing Bishop Porphyry to submit a petition to her infant son *Theodosius II (born April 401) at his christening. Her admiration of St *John Chrysostom turned to resentment at his denunciation of luxury, which she took personally, and she allowed him to be deposed and exiled (404). Her death shortly afterwards (9 October 404) was due to a miscarriage.

BIBL. Bury, *Later Empire*, i, esp. 138 ff.

Gold coin (*solidus*) of the usurper Eugenius (enlarged).

Eugenius Western usurper AD 392–4.

Flavius Eugenius was proclaimed emperor by *Arbogast to replace *Valentinian II because he was respectable but unimportant: he was a middle-ranking court official, formerly a professor of rhetoric, whom *Symmachus had commended to Arbogast's uncle *Ricomer. He tolerated a revival of paganism at Rome, although he was himself a Christian. When *Theodosius I invaded Italy, he was taken prisoner and executed (6 September 394).

BIBL. PLRE i, Eugenius 6.

Gold coin (*solidus*) of the Empress Eudoxia.

Eudoxia Eastern empress AD 395–404.

Aelia Eudoxia was the beautiful daughter of the Frankish-born general Bauto (consul 385), whom

4th-century AD cathedral of St Epiphanius at Salamis, Cyprus.

Silver coin (tetradrachm) of Eumenes II (enlarged).

Eumenes II King of Pergamum 197–159 BC.

Eumenes succeeded his father *Attalus I in 197 BC and continued his pro-Roman policy. In the 190s he helped to push Rome into hostilities with *Antiochus III, and benefited from the post-war settlement by a massive extension of Pergamene territory. Eumenes thus made his kingdom a great power in the Hellenistic world, but his position remained very much that of a Roman puppet. In the 170s he jealously watched the growing influence of his rival *Perseus in the Greek world, and in 172 made a special journey to Rome to denounce his activities. He was rapturously received by the senate (with the exception of *Cato the Elder), and seems to have directly influenced the Roman war decision by his intervention. In 169, while the result of the war still hung in the balance, Eumenes mysteriously and foolishly entered into secret correspondence with Perseus, and forfeited Rome's goodwill as a consequence. After the war the senate humiliated Eumenes by refusing him permission to enter Italy, and transferred its favour to his brother *Attalus (II). Attalus remained loyal to Eumenes, but the new situation meant that he effectively became co-ruler until Eumenes' death in 159. *Polybius remarks that Eumenes' standing in the Greek world rose as his standing at Rome declined. He encouraged the development of Pergamum as a cultural centre.

BIBL. Hansen, *Attalids of Pergamon* (2nd ed., 1971); Will, *Hist. pol.*, ii.

Eunapius (AD 345/6–c. 414) Historian.

Author of (apparently) the standard Greek account of fourth-century AD history, which survives only in citations and as used by later historians (notably Zosimus in c. 500), Eunapius studied literature at Sardis (his native town) and Athens, before returning to Sardis to teach rhetoric. His *History* continued *Dexippus (AD 270) until the time of writing, apparently c. 380, and its sources included an account of its hero *Julian by his doctor *Oribasius; *Ammianus seems to have checked his own account against it. Eunapius' treatment is outspokenly anti-Christian, and rhetorical, like his surviving *Lives of the Sophists* (after 396), which are 'saints' lives' of Neoplatonist intellectuals and littérateurs. In c. 414 Eunapius published a milder version of the *History* which took the narrative to 404.

BIBL. *PLRE* i, Eunapius 2.

Euric King of the Visigoths, AD 466–84.

Euric became king of the Goths in Aquitaine by murdering his brother, Theoderic II, in 466, and promptly initiated a more aggressive policy towards the Romans in Gaul, perhaps through fear of the Franks to the north and Burgundians to the east. In 469, he pushed north, taking Bourges and Tours (470), then turned south-east. Auvergne was formally ceded in 475, despite the heroic resistance of Clermont under its bishop, *Sidonius Apollinaris, and Provence was lost to Rome in 476. Meanwhile, Euric had also expanded into north-east Spain (c. 473).

Although Euric, as an *Arian, persecuted orthodox clergy and left some sees without bishops for many years, he also encouraged Roman officials in his administration, some of whom were behind his law-code, drawn up in or after 476. His name was known as far away as Persia, and, by his death in 484, he had not only delivered the *coup de grâce* to Roman power in Gaul but had also established the foundations for the sixth-century Visigothic kingdom in Spain.

BIBL. Sidonius Apollinaris, *Letters*, esp. VII. 6 and 7; *Codex Eurici*; K. F. Stroheker, *Eurich* (1937).

Eusebia Empress c. AD 353–60.

Second wife of *Constantius II and patroness of *Julian, Eusebia, from Thessalonica, was probably the daughter of a consul of 347. Gentle and well educated, she was a good influence on Constantius, and persuaded him to allow Julian to go to Athens in 354. She also supported Julian's appointment as Caesar (355); he wrote a panegyric of her. Her brothers Eusebius and Hypatius were the consuls for 359.

BIBL. *PLRE* i, Eusebia; Julian, *Or.* iii.

Eusebius of Caesarea (c. AD 260–c. 340) Church historian.

Eusebius, the 'Father of Church History', studied at Caesarea in Palestine under the *Origenist scholar Pamphilus, martyred in 309/10. Eusebius then fled to Tyre and Egypt, where he was imprisoned for a time. He was made bishop of Caesarea c. 314, and, when the Arian controversy broke out c. 319, sympathized with his fellow-Origenist *Arius and became a leading moderate Arian, like *Eusebius of Nicomedia. At the Council of Nicaea in 325 he made an unsuccessful stand for compromise, and was finally persuaded to join the majority who condemned Arius. In 335 he was at the Council of Tyre which condemned *Athanasius.

He was a friend of *Constantine, whom he praised in a jubilee speech the same year. After Constantine's death (337) he wrote a panegyric, the *Life of Constantine*, an important—if not always trustworthy—source for his reign. His most famous work is the *Church History*, from the Church's earliest times to contemporary events, continued to 324. In it he made full, if uncritical, use of many documents, which he preserves. The first Christian emperor appears as the fulfilment of history. *Rufinus of Aquileia translated it into Latin and continued it to 395. Other works include the *Preparation for the Gospel*, rejecting Greek philosophy, and *Demonstration of the Gospel* from the Old Testament, biblical commentaries, *Against *Hierocles*, and a *Chronicle* (translated into Latin and continued by *Jerome).

BIBL. Penguin translation of *Church History*; D. S. Wallace-Hadrill, *Eusebius of Caesarea* (1960); *OCD*; *ODCC*.

Eusebius of Nicomedia Bishop, died *c.* AD 341.

Ecclesiastical politician and leader of the moderate Arian party, Eusebius studied with *Arius under *Lucian of Antioch before becoming bishop of the imperial capital Nicomedia in 323. When Arius appealed to him, Eusebius was able to turn the Arian controversy into a wider Church struggle, backed by imperial sanctions. Outmanoeuvred at and exiled after the Council of Nicaea (325), he was recalled in 327/8 and continued to work on Arius' behalf against *Athanasius and his party. He became very influential with *Constantine, whom he baptized on his deathbed in 337, and then with *Constantius II, becoming bishop of Constantinople (337) and mentor of the young emperor till his own death.

BIBL. *ODCC*.

Eusebius Grand Chamberlain AD 337–61.

One of the eunuchs whose power and wealth, derived from access to the emperor, was resented by the rest of the governing class, but who fulfilled a useful function in the Late Empire by linking the isolated god-emperor to court and government, Eusebius was one of *Constantius II's most influential courtiers, often at the centre of intrigues, notably concerning *Ursicinus, and *Gallus Caesar, one of whose judges he was. He was pro-*Arian, and opposed *Athanasius. Present at Constantius' deathbed in 361, he then fell victim to the purge that began *Julian's reign, being executed by the Commission of Chalcedon. See also *Eutherius, *Eutropius (2).

BIBL. *PLRE* i, Eusebius 11; K. Hopkins, *Conquerors and Slaves* (1978), ch. 4.

Eustathius (*c.* AD 300–*c.* 377) Bishop of Sebaste.

A one-time pupil of *Arius, of moderate Arian views, and later a heretic who disputed the

divinity of the Holy Ghost, Eustathius became bishop of Sebaste in Pontus *c.* 357. The pioneer of the monastic movement in Asia Minor (but of extreme views, e.g. the condemnation of marriage and married priests, denounced by the Council of Gangra *c.* 345), he was a major influence on St *Basil.

BIBL. *ODCC* Eustathius, Gangra.

Eustochium, St Julia Nun (AD 370–418/9).

Eustochium, whose parents claimed descent from Aeneas and the *Scipios, was a central figure among the aristocratic patrons of St *Jerome. She and her sister-in-law Laeta both received important treatises on the duties and education of a nun, St Pammachius, the senator who became a monk, was her brother-in-law—and the pagan leader *Praetextatus was even an uncle by marriage. The death of her sister Blesilla under Jerome's ascetic regime led indirectly to Jerome's forced departure from Rome (385), followed by Eustochium and her mother St Paula. Paula founded Jerome's monastery at Bethlehem, and a convent which Eustochium directed after her mother's death (404).

BIBL. J. N. D. Kelly, *Jerome* (1975).

Eutherius Grand Chamberlain AD 356–60.

An Armenian captured and castrated as a boy and sold to Roman merchants, Eutherius served at the courts of *Constantine and *Constans before being appointed Grand Chamberlain of *Julian Caesar in Gaul. Julian used him as a confidential envoy. A pagan of conspicuous uprightness and intelligence, Eutherius is an example of a 'good' eunuch (contrast *Eusebius). Two silver dishes from

Mildenhall Treasure: one of a pair of silver platters, each with Satyr and dancing Maenad and the name Eutherius on the back (4th century AD), probably forming a set with the Great Dish. London, British Museum.

the Mildenhall Treasure bear the name Eutherius, and may have belonged to him.

BIBL. *PLRE* i, Eutherius 1.

Eutropius (1) Historian, consul AD 387.

Author of a surviving *Digest* of Roman history (to AD 364), whose clear, simple style made it for centuries a textbook for Latin beginners, Eutropius was a Gaul, probably from Bordeaux, who worked in the East. He wrote the *Digest* while *magister memoriae* at the court of *Valens; in 371/2 he governed Asia, but was forced into retirement by his successor *Festus. Soon after the accession of *Theodosius I, he became his praetorian prefect of Illyricum (380–1).

BIBL. *PLRE* i, Eutropius 2.

Eutropius (2) Grand Chamberlain AD 395–9.

Eutropius was the first (and only) eunuch to become consul (399). This is almost the only charge of substance brought by *Claudian in 'the cruellest invective in all ancient literature'. Eutropius was a castrated Armenian (?) slave who became one of *Theodosius I's chamberlains; he outmanoeuvred *Rufinus by inducing *Arcadius to marry *Eudoxia (April 395), and after Rufinus' murder (November 395) dominated Arcadius 'like a sheep'. After personally defeating the Huns on the eastern frontier, he took the consulship for 399, which caused ill-feeling exploited by *Stilicho. That summer, because Eudoxia had already undermined his influence with Arcadius, Eutropius fell from power when a rebel general demanded his dismissal. He was exiled, but soon recalled and executed.

BIBL. A. Cameron, *Claudian*, ch. 6.

Eutychianus Actor, early 3rd century AD.

Publius (Marcus?) Valerius Comazon Eutychianus was the author of the plot in 218 in which *Elagabalus was dressed in borrowed robes and passed off as the bastard son of *Caracalla. The Syrian troops, discontented with *Macrinus' rule, proclaimed the boy emperor.

BIBL. Birley, *Severus*.

Fabian Bishop of Rome AD 326–50.

An enterprising bishop, Fabian is credited with dividing Rome into seven districts for administrative purposes and reorganizing the charitable activity of the clergy. He was martyred in 250 during the *Decian persecution.

BIBL. Kleine Pauly, Fabianus 2; *CAH* xii.

Fabius Buteo, Marcus Consul 245, censor 241 BC.

In 218 BC, as the most senior surviving senator, Fabius led an embassy to the Carthaginian senate to demand *Hannibal's extradition. The rejection of this ultimatum led to Fabius' dramatic declaration

of war by seizing the fold of his toga and announcing that it held peace and war (*Polybius 3.33.1 ff.). *Livy wrongly ascribes this episode to Q. *Fabius Maximus ('Cunctator').

BIBL. Scullard, *Politics*, 274.

Fabius Maximus Rullianus, Quintus Consul 322, 310, 308, 297, and 295 BC.

Famous for allegedly defeating the Samnites as Master of the Horse in defiance of L. *Papirius Cursor (325 BC), Fabius fought in Etruria or Samnium in all five of his consulships. The Samnites heavily defeated him as dictator at Lautulae (315: *Diodorus ascribes him a further dictatorship in 313); his most important victory (with P. *Decius Mus (2), his colleague in his last three consulships) was over the Gauls and their allies at Sentinum (295). As censors (304) he and Decius imposed restrictions on membership of the rural tribes. His portrait has been unreliably elaborated, often on the model of Q. *Fabius Maximus 'Cunctator' (see also Ap. *Claudius Caecus). Esquiline tomb paintings may depict episodes from his career.

BIBL. PW vi. 1800 ff.; Salmon, *Samnium* 220 ff.; Harris, *REU* 49 ff., etc.; *Roma Medio-Repubblicana* (1973) 200 ff.

Fabius Maximus Verrucosus, Quintus ('Cunctator') Consul 233 BC etc.

The last of the great Fabii, Fabius Maximus only came to prominence in 217 BC when, in his late 50s, he was elected dictator to meet a military emergency, following the defeat and death of C. *Flaminius in Etruria. Much earlier, as consul in 233, he had won a triumph for his campaign against the Ligurians; and recently, as a distinguished elder of the Roman aristocracy, he had opposed Flaminius' aggressive reaction to *Hannibal's invasion, counselling instead a defensive strategy of avoiding pitched battles. His advice was vindicated by Flaminius' defeat, and as dictator for the rest of 217 he was able to put it into effect. He realized that Rome's strength lay in its superior manpower and the loyalty of its Italian allies, and that Hannibal's comparatively small army could be worn out and neutralized without risking a major battle. This strategy earned him the nickname *Cunctator* (the delayer), and ultimately enabled Rome to survive Hannibal's invasion. Initially Fabius' strategy was unpopular, and there was a reaction which led to the defeat of *Varro and *Paullus (1) at Cannae. But thereafter Fabius was elected to three consulships, his principal achievement being the capture of Tarentum in 209, for which he gained another triumph. However, the improvement in Rome's fortunes by the year 206 was such that Fabius' policy became eclipsed, and he came to be regarded as over-cautious. He led the opposition to *Scipio Africanus' African expedition in 205, and tried unsuccessfully to have him recalled or replaced until his own death in 203.

BIBL. Plutarch, *Life of Fabius Maximus*; Scullard, *Politics*; Lazenby, *Hannibal*.

Fabricius Luscinus, Gaius Consul 282 and 278 BC.

A *novus homo*, Fabricius assisted Thurii against her Italic neighbours and campaigned against the Samnites (282 BC), negotiated with *Pyrrhus (280 or 279), and fought against his Italic allies (278). He was a reputedly moralistic censor (275), and was attributed legendary rectitude and incorruptibility.

BIBL. PW vi. 1931 ff.; M. R. Lefkowitz, *HSCP* lxiv (1959) 147 ff.

Faenius Rufus Praetorian prefect AD 62–5.

Lucius Faenius Rufus' term as Commissioner for the Corn Supply (AD 55–62) was distinguished by the fact that he did not make a profit from it. In 62 he became praetorian prefect with *Tigellinus, but his friendship with *Agrippina stood him in bad stead. He joined Gaius Calpurnius *Piso's conspiracy, and was executed.

BIBL. Tac. *Ann.* xiv. 51.

Fannia mid-first century AD.

As daughter of *Thrasea Paetus and the younger *Arria, granddaughter of Caecina Paetus, wife of *Helvidius Priscus the elder and stepmother of his homonymous son, Fannia was at the heart of that like-minded and dissident group, with appropriate attitudes, which led her into repeated exile. She,

like Arria, returned to Rome after *Domitian's death.

BIBL. Pliny, *Letters*, ix. 13.

Fausta Empress AD 307–26.

Flavia Maxima Fausta, daughter of the Emperor *Maximian and Eutropia, was born and brought up in Rome like her brother *Maxentius. In 307 she was married to *Constantine to cement an alliance, and later revealed Maximian's conspiracy to him. She was the mother of *Constantine II, *Constantius II, and *Constans, and stepmother of *Crispus (q.v.). In 326, shortly after the execution of Crispus, she was put to death at Rome, allegedly by suffocation in an overheated bath, on a charge of adultery with a palace official.

BIBL. *PLRE* i, Fausta; Jones, *Constantine*, 244.

Faustina I Empress AD 138–140/1.

The daughter of Marcus *Annius Verus and Rupilia Faustina, Annia Galeria Faustina was the wife of *Antoninus Pius whom she probably married *c*. 110. She bore him four children, of whom three had died by the time Antoninus became emperor (the fourth, *Faustina II, married *Marcus Aurelius). After Antoninus' accession she received the title Augusta but died early in the reign (140 or 141). Antoninus is said to have been devoted to her, and after her death a temple was built for her by the Forum which, on Antoninus' death, became the Temple of Antoninus and Faustina. Little is known of her personality except for her frankness and *joie de vivre*.

BIBL. *PIR* A 715; Birley, *Marcus*.

Portrait of Faustina I: impression from a lapis lazuli intaglio.

Portrait of Faustina II: impression from a cornelian intaglio.

Faustina II Empress AD 161–76.

The daughter of *Antoninus Pius and *Faustina I, Annia Galeria Faustina was betrothed to Lucius *Verus at the end of *Hadrian's reign, but after *Hadrian's death the arrangements were changed and she was betrothed to *Marcus Aurelius instead. She and Marcus were married in 145 and she bore him twelve (or possibly thirteen) children. She was with Marcus in the East when she died at about the age of 40 (176) in a small village in the foothills of the Taurus Mountains, which was renamed Faustinopolis in her honour. She was deified on the vote of the senate. Ancient sources have a good deal of gossip about her supposed infidelities. She is said to have had a liking for gladiators, and there are hints of an affair with the usurper *Avidius Cassius.

BIBL. Birley, *Marcus*; *PIR* A 716; A. S. L. Farquharson, *Marcus Aurelius, his Life and his World* (2nd ed., 1952).

Favonius Eulogius Rhetorician, 4th to 5th century AD.

Favonius Eulogius studied rhetoric under St *Augustine in Carthage between 375 and 383, subsequently became municipal professor of rhetoric at Carthage (384/7), and wrote a short treatise, the *Disputation on the Dream of Scipio* (388/426), which discusses arithmological questions and celestial harmony, and exercised some influence on the later work of *Macrobius and *Martianus Capella.

BIBL. R.-E. van Weddingen, *Favonii Eulogii Disputatio de Somnio Scipionis* (1957).

Favorinus (*c*. AD 80–*c*. 150) Sophist.

Born at Arles in the early 80s, a congenital eunuch, Favorinus received a Greek education at Marseilles and became one of the leading sophists and rhetoricians of the first half of the second century. He operated mainly in Greek, spoke in Athens, Corinth, the cities of Asia (he had a particular connection with Ephesus) and taught *Herodes Atticus, Aulus *Gellius and *Fronto. He was a member of *Hadrian's circle and gained equestrian rank, but fell into disfavour *c*. 130 and was exiled to Chios. *Antoninus Pius allowed him to return to Rome, and he died there in his reign. He was involved in a famous rivalry with *Polemo of Smyrna. The titles of almost 30 of his works are known, comprising speeches with some philosophical content and two miscellanies. Two speeches survive in the corpus of *Dio Chrysostom (37, 64) and a third on papyrus.

BIBL. E. Mensching, *Favorin von Arelate* (1963); A. Barigazzi, *Favorino, Opere* (1966); Bowersock, *Sophists*.

Felix Governor of Judaea AD 52–55/60.

A freedman of *Antonia, Marcus Antonius Felix owed his influence—and his immunity from punishment for oppression—to his brother *Pallas. His tactless, corrupt, and severe rule in Judaea was notorious; he was known for his liaisons with eastern royalty. St *Paul was brought to trial before him (Acts 23. 24). The date of his recall and prosecution for corruption is uncertain; there are arguments for both 55/6 and 60.

BIBL. Tac. *Ann.* xii. 54; *PIR* A 88; Griffin, *Seneca*, 449 (date of recall).

Festus Governor of Judaea *c*. AD 60–2.

Porcius Festus was the successor of *Felix, who left him with the difficult case of St *Paul (Acts 24). *Josephus records his vigorous action against brigands.

See under Felix for dating.

Calendar of 354 (or *Calendar of Filocalus*):
Left: title page with dedication to Valentinus and name of scribe Filocalus. His characteristic style of lettering, with fish-tail serifs, is to be seen in his engraving of the epigrams of Pope *Damasus.

Centre: personification of the city of Trier in the Rhineland.
Right: Saturday, Trier's patron god, and its astrological properties.

Festus (died AD 380) Historian.

Festus was the author of a surviving *Digest* of Roman history published *c.* 369, when he was *magister memoriae* at the court of *Valens. It gives a brief account of the conquest of the various provinces, and of wars between Rome and Parthia/Persia. He was a barrister from Trent, who worked in the East; during 372–8 he governed Asia, where he persecuted pagan intellectuals like *Maximus of Ephesus, and his predecessor *Eutropius.

BIBL. *PLRE* i, Festus 3; J. W. Eadie, *The Breviarium of Festus* (1967).

Filocalus Scribe and engraver, mid–late 4th century AD.

Furius Dionysius Filocalus is principally famous as the scribe of the *Calendar of 354*, a lavishly illustrated 'diary' of pagan festivals, official events, and important Christian dates at Rome, with various lists and chronicles appended. This was created as a New Year present to a Christian notable named Valentinus. Filocalus later engraved numerous epigrams written by Pope *Damasus in honour of martyrs.

BIBL. H. Stern, *Le Calendrier de 354* (1953).

Fimbria, Gaius Flavius General 86–85 BC.

A leading supporter of *Cinna and legate of the consul Lucius Valerius Flaccus in Asia in 86 BC, Fimbria usurped his command and achieved rapid military successes against *Mithridates, though these were foiled by *Sulla's rival army. Sulla made a quick peace with Mithridates and then turned against Fimbria, who committed suicide. The two 'Fimbrian' legions remained in the East until 67 BC.

BIBL. Magie, *Asia Minor*; Badian, *Studies*.

Firmicus Maternus Astrologer and Christian polemicist floruit *c.* AD 334.

The author of the *Mathesis*, an inferior Latin astrological handbook, and the *On the Error of the Profane Religions*, a violent anti-pagan polemic, Julius Firmicus Maternus was formerly considered two people. He was born in Sicily, lived there, practised as a lawyer, and then retired. The *Mathesis* was written in 334/7 and the *On the Error* in 343/8, after the author's conversion to Christianity.

BIBL. *De errore*, ed. and trans. Heuten (Budé 1938).

Flaccus, Marcus Fulvius Consul 125 BC.

A prominent supporter of the Gracchi, Flaccus became in 130 BC a member of the agrarian commission set up by Tiberius *Gracchus. When the commission's activities conflicted with the interests of Italian landowners, Flaccus proposed as a political bribe the extension of Roman citizenship, a cause to which he subsequently became passionately committed. As consul in 125 he was unable to promote any controversial legislation because of his appointment to a military command in Gaul. After a triumph for his victories there, he became probably the only ex-consul ever to stand for the junior office of tribune. Thus, as a colleague of Gaius *Gracchus in 122 he supported the latter's programme, which included his cherished enfranchisement of Italians. He died in 121 in the attack by the consul L. *Opimius on Gracchus and his supporters.

BIBL. Badian, *Clientelae*; Stockton, *The Gracchi* (1979).

Flaccus, Verrius Grammarian and lexicographer, Augustan era.

Marcus Verrius Flaccus was appointed by *Augustus as tutor to Gaius and Lucius *Caesar. Much of his *On the Meaning of Words* survives in the intermittently invaluable lexicon (second century AD) of Festus, and where Festus is missing, in the excerpts (eighth century AD) of Paul the Deacon.

BIBL. *GRF* 509 ff.

Calendar of 354 (*Calendar of Filocalus*): Personification of months: (left to right) February, March, and October. Rome, Vatican Library.

Flamininus Consul 198 BC.

Titus Quinctius Flamininus was a charismatic figure and gifted diplomatist who dominated Rome's eastern policy in the 190s. A combination of his personal qualities and substantial but unidentifiable senatorial backing carried him to the consulship of 198 BC at the age of 30, and gave him the command against *Philip V. He took to Greece a new Roman policy (with which he personally became closely identified), which was 'philhellenic' and involved the championing of local Greek autonomy. With this diplomatic advantage Flamininus was able to inflict a military defeat on Philip at Cynoscephalae (197), for which he later celebrated a triumph. More impressive, however, was his ability as an inexperienced Roman to hold his own in negotiations with Hellenistic powers. At the Isthmian Games of 196 Flamininus staged a melodramatic announcement of the senate's decree that all Greeks should be free, and as the Roman proconsul in Greece he became the personal focus of their enthusiastic gratitude. Among the extravagant honours heaped upon him were cult worship and the issue of contemporary coins bearing his portrait.

Flamininus' command was prolonged for the third time in 195 amid fears that *Antiochus III would invade Greece. He justified the continued presence of Roman troops by leading an allied campaign against the unpopular *Nabis of Sparta. But in 194 he secured the complete evacuation of Roman forces against considerable senatorial opposition. His apparent idealism masked a shrewd appreciation of Rome's strategic interests; and behind the philhellenism stood a proud Roman aristocrat who expected the nominally free Greeks to recognize their obligations to their Roman benefactors.

Flamininus scored a notable diplomatic success over Antiochus' envoys at a conference in Rome in 193, but as ambassador in Greece in 192 he discovered that his personal authority was insufficient to prevent the defection of Aetolia or to curb Achaean expansion in the Peloponnese. The war with Antiochus and the Aetolians (191–189) wrecked Flamininus' settlement of Greece, but vindicated his stand on Greek autonomy. He was elected censor in 189, but thereafter his political influence at Rome declined, perhaps through jealousy of his rapid advancement and his vast Greek *clientela*. *Polybius gives an unfavourable picture of Flamininus, drawing attention to his devious and underhand dealings.

BIBL. Plutarch, *Life of Titus*; Badian, *Titus Quinctius Flamininus: Philhellenism and Realpolitik* (1970); Briscoe, *Livy*, esp. 22–35.

Flaminius Consul 223 and 217 BC.

A leading proponent of Roman expansion in north Italy, Gaius Flaminius stands out as the only serious challenge to the authority of the senatorial establishment in the 150 years before 133 BC. Widely based popular support enabled him to overcome continual senatorial opposition throughout his career, and achieve a position of predominance at Rome. The historical tradition subsequently branded him as an irresponsible demagogue and belittled his achievements. The origin of the hostility and of his popular support was the land bill which he sponsored as tribune in 232 BC. The bill distributed technically unoccupied Roman public land near Rimini to large numbers of Roman citizens. It was fiercely opposed by the senate and blamed unjustly for provoking the Gallic invasion of 225. As consul in 223 Flaminius carried the counter-attack on the Gauls across the Po and, despite obstruction by the senate throughout the campaign, won a triumph for his successes.

In his censorship (220) he commissioned the building of the Circus Flaminius in Rome and the important Via Flaminia, which ran from Rome to Rimini, thus consolidating his earlier settlements and extending his own considerable influence in that area. Flaminius had acquired another large *clientela* in Sicily, where in 227 he had been the first praetor to govern the province. His military reputation ensured his election to a second consulship in 217 to meet the emergency of *Hannibal's invasion; but he died fighting at Lake Trasimene, having led his army into a massive ambush prepared by Hannibal.

BIBL. Walbank, *HCP* i, esp. 192 f.; Errington, *Dawn of Empire*, esp. 41–5.

Flavianus, Nicomachus Praetorian prefect AD 390–4.

Virius Nicomachus Flavianus (AD 334–94), like his close friend *Symmachus a prominent senator and a pagan, unlike him resorted to violence to oppose Christianity and further his own career. He attracted the notice of *Theodosius I when he came to Italy in 388, first becoming quaestor and then (390) praetorian prefect of Italy; he dedicated a (lost) work of history, the *Annals*, to Theodosius. He collaborated with *Arbogast after the usurpation of *Eugenius, and remained in office (consul 394). After publicly celebrating pagan rites at Rome, where his son was now urban prefect, he committed the western army to fighting under (pagan) divine protection. When it was defeated by Theodosius, he killed himself.

BIBL. *PLRE* i, Flavianus 15.

Flavius, Gnaeus Aedile 304 BC (?).

Allegedly a freedman's son (in some sources a protégé of Ap. *Claudius Caecus), Flavius published the early legal procedural formulae and calendar (including perhaps a list of consuls). As curule aedile, reputedly in 304 BC, he dedicated a shrine to

Concord '204 (?) years after the dedication of the Capitoline temple'.

BIBL. PW vi. 2526 ff.; T. Pekáry, *Röm. Mitt.* lxxvi (1969) 307 ff.; E. Ferenczy, *Studi Grosso* v (1972) 183 ff.

Florus, ? Publius Annius/? Julius Man/Men of letters, (1st-) 2nd century AD.

Florus was the author (under *Hadrian) of a highly rhetorical, wholly derivative and thoroughly imperialistic epitome of Roman history, drawing chiefly upon *Livy. This Florus is perhaps to be identified with P. Annius Florus, an African who visited Rome under *Domitian, withdrew to Tarragona, and composed the dialogue *Is Virgil an Orator or a Poet?* which in part survives. He is probably also to be identified with the Annius Florus who bandied diverting verses with Hadrian.

BIBL. *FPL* 136.

Frontinus Technical author and general, consul AD 73, 98 and 100.

Sextus Julius Frontinus made his mark first in fighting *Civilis in AD 70 and in subjugating the Silures in Britain in 74–8. The climax of his career was only reached in the reigns of *Nerva and *Trajan, to which his spotless record lent respectability. He then sat on the Commission for Public Economy, and supervised Rome's aqueducts. He was a friend of *Pliny, who greatly admired him.

Frontinus was the author of (1) a manual on land-surveying, which survives in fragments (2) a book on warfare (*De re militari*) which is lost, but *Strategemata* survive, officers for the use of (i praef. 1. before the battle ii: the battle iii: sieges iv: of doubtful authenticity) (3) *De aquae ductu* (*On the Conveyance of Water*—this is the correct title). A remarkable survey, administrative, historical, and topographical, of the aqueducts of Rome, it was intended to be used by his successors, to free them from permanent dependence on their professional assistants.

BIBL. Pliny, *Letters*, ix. 19; *PIR* I 322.

Fronto (c. AD 100–after (?) 167) Man of letters.

A native of Cirta (Numidia), Marcus Cornelius Fronto rose to be suffect consul in AD 143. A famed orator (*Minucius Felix ix. 6–7 preserves a fragment against the Christians) according to Cassius *Dio (lxix. 18), he is widely described as the *magister* (master, teacher) of *Marcus Aurelius and *Verus. He was a copious author, but only fragments, chiefly from *Gellius, were known until 1815. Then and in 1823 Cardinal Mai published the two parts of a mangled and incomplete palimpsest, in which the leaves are jumbled and Fronto is sandwiched between two other texts. The palimpsest contains his correspondence with Marcus as heir and as emperor (including letters from Marcus), letters to and from both Verus and *Antoninus Pius, and letters to his friends. The collection was evidently not Fronto's own, but appeared posthumously.

Regular correspondence apart, the palimpsest also held traces of a wide range of other works, a correspondence with Marcus on rhetoric, a preface to a history of Verus' deeds in the Parthian War, *Praises of Smoke and Dust*, *On the Loss of a Grandson*, *Arion*, etc. A sentimental hypochondriac (pains from eyes via groin to toes are attested), he had as little time for philosophy as had Marcus for language (Loeb ed., ii. p.67), yet the tone of cordiality in their correspondence is unmistakable. The letters are of limited historical importance, but, with their taste for the language of the Elder *Cato and Gaius *Gracchus, for example, they constitute a major document of the 'archaizing' movement at Rome.

BIBL. For the complex question of dating, see Champlin, *JRS* 1974, 136 ff.; Brock, *Studies in Fronto* (1911).

Fulvia (died 40 BC).

An ambitious aristocratic lady, Fulvia counted among her husbands *Clodius and *Antony. While Antony was in the East in 41 BC, she attempted to promote his interests by opposing *Octavian's veteran settlements in Italy, and thus precipitated the Perusine War. Octavian's hostile propaganda successfully blackened her reputation, and may account for her being cast as a principal villain of the proscriptions of 43 BC.

BIBL. Syme, *Rom. Rev.*

Furius Philus Consul 136 BC.

A close associate of *Scipio Aemilianus and a member of the Scipionic circle, Lucius Furius Philus was an able orator with interests in religious antiquarianism. As consul he investigated the *Mancinus affair and personally supervised his extradition to Numantia by an antiquated fetial procedure.

BIBL. Astin, *Scipio*; Rawson, *JRS* lxiii (1973) 161 ff.

Gabinius Consul 58 BC

A protégé of *Pompey, Aulus Gabinius as tribune in 67 BC carried a law conferring on Pompey an unlimited command against the Mediterranean pirates. Probably in the same year he passed legislation minimizing the scope for corruption in diplomacy at Rome. From 66 to 63 he served as Pompey's legate in the East, and reached the consulship in 58. With his colleague L. Calpurnius *Piso he co-operated with *Clodius in procuring the exile of *Cicero, and secured for himself the province of Syria. As governor from 57 to 54 he acted vigorously to check the worst

excesses of the *publicani*, even handing some of
them over to local justice. He suppressed uprisings
in Judaea, and intervened in Egypt to restore
*Ptolemy Auletes to his throne in 55. His treatment
of the *publicani* was good for the province but
aroused powerful hostility at Rome, where he
faced among other charges a cynical prosecution for
extortion. He was defended, at the insistence of
the triumvirs, by his enemy Cicero, but was
convicted and exiled (54). Before his death in 47 he
was reinstated by *Caesar, who sent him as legate to
Illyricum.

BIBL. Syme, *Rom Rev.*; Seager, *Pompey.*

Gaius Jurist, 2nd century AD.

Probably born in the early part of the second
century, Gaius appears to have lived and written
at Rome, though his origin was probably in the
Greek-speaking East. His full importance as a
classical Roman lawyer was not established until
the fifth century, when his authority was put on a
par with that of *Paul, *Ulpian, Herennius and
*Papinian. He wrote major works on the Provincial
Edict, the Urban Praetor's Edict, and the Law of the
Twelve Tables, sections of which are transmitted to
us in later legal compilations. His most important
work is the *Institutes*, probably completed soon
after 161, in 4 books, one on the law of persons,
two on the law of things, and one on the law of
actions. The discovery of a manuscript of this work
in the nineteenth century provided us with the
only classical legal work we have in its substantially
original form. The great influence of Gaius'
Institutes is particularly to be seen in the *Institutes*
of Justinian.

BIBL. Jolowicz, *Roman Law*; A. M. Honoré,
Gaius: a Biography (1962); F. de Zulueta, *The
Institutes of Gaius* (1946–53).

Gaius 'Caligula' (AD 12–41) Emperor AD 37–41.

Gaius Julius Caesar Germanicus was the son of
*Germanicus and *Agrippina (the Elder), whose
greatest legacy was their enormous popularity.
When still an infant he had helped foster this
adulation by being paraded as a mascot before the
Rhine armies in AD 14, at the time of their mutiny.
It was here that he acquired the nickname of
'Bootlet'. The violent death of his father at Antioch,
the supervision first of *Livia and then of *Antonia
(in her household of eastern rulers' offspring), and
several years on Capri with *Tiberius all no doubt
influenced his character. He only just escaped the
machinations of *Sejanus, and cultivated his
successor *Macro. By this time he was the obvious
successor to Tiberius, though he was unable to
begin the education appropriate to such a position
in public affairs before being left in charge by the
death of Tiberius (which there is no reason to
believe he precipitated).

Gaius' actions, which have no doubt been

Gaius 'Caligula'. Copenhagen, Ny Carlsberg Glyptotek.

embroidered by tradition and the imaginative
historians of Antiquity, did none the less range
from the bizarre and ostentatious to the verge of
the demented; scholars are divided on the vital
question of 'mad, bad, or ill?' but the results were
similar in any case. An emphasis on autocracy,
eastern fashion, and disregard for the constitutional
behaviour of his two predecessors lapsed into
tyranny and arbitrary proscription. Military
expeditions to remove internal threats—
particularly from *Lentulus Gaetulicus and his
noble following—and perhaps to ensure peace in
the north while confirming the loyalty of the
Rhine armies, provided an excuse for horseplay
and whimsy on the largest scale. Public
expenditure rapidly became mere extravagance.
His administrative actions were ill-judged at their
best—his relations with the Jews were particularly
unprofitable (see *Petronius, Publius). It is not
enough to explain, for example, his divine
aspirations by comparing his practice to the
conventions of eastern ruler-worship: to have
indulged this taste as freely as he did in Rome was
a lack of judgement so extreme as to constitute
madness. Contempt, fear, and hatred followed the
rejoicing of the beginning of his reign, and
dissatisfied praetorians and anti-monarchical
senators combined to assassinate him. By that
time his victims were numerous and the State
bankrupt.

BIBL. J. Balsdon, *The Emperor Gaius* (1934).

Portrait bust of the Emperor Galba. Paris, Louvre.

Galba (3 BC–AD 69) Emperor AD 68–9.

The Sulpicii were an enormously old and distinguished family. Servius Sulpicius Galba's career was worthy of them, and was assisted also by the favour of *Augustus, *Tiberius, and *Livia, as well as *Gaius and *Claudius. Among various provincial commands, Germania Superior, where he was sent by Gaius to enforce discipline after the revolt of *Lentulus Gaetulicus, and Hispania Tarraconensis, where he spent eight years under *Nero, were particularly important. He seems to have been honest, but severe to the point of cruelty. In 68 *Vindex persuaded him to try for power, and the action of the praetorian guard under *Nymphidius Sabinus made the task easy. Galba was considered an excellent choice until he began to rule—his measures and pettiness soon made him unpopular, especially with the praetorians, who formed a conspiracy, murdered Galba, and put *Otho on the throne.

T. *Vinius, Laco the new praetorian prefect, and Icelus the freedman were Galba's chief helpers; their arrogance and stupidity also did much to damage him. Feeling insecure he had adopted a retiring and shy young man, Lucius Calpurnius Piso Licinianus, who proved ineffectual and weak. Galba seems to have been a man well-suited to subordinate positions and provincial commands, but either too old or too weak-willed to adapt to supreme power.

BIBL. Tacitus, *Histories*, I.

Galba, Publius Sulpicius Consul 211 and 200 BC.

One of Rome's first eastern experts, Galba replaced *Laevinus in the Balkan command, where he fought a desultory naval war against *Philip V (210–206 BC). He achieved little but a reputation for cruelty, and was unable to prevent the defection of the Aetolians in 206. His election to a second consulship late in 201 signifies the senate's commitment to another Macedonian war; but he was at first unable to have his war motion passed by the centuriate assembly. He reached his Macedonian province late in 200, but conducted the 199 campaign with some success. His experience ensured him a senior place on the decemviral commission (196), on which he opposed *Flamininus' policy of military withdrawal from Greece. He played a leading role in the abortive negotiations with *Antiochus III both at Rome and in Asia in 193.

BIBL. Errington, *Dawn of Empire*.

Galen (AD 129–99) Doctor and writer.

Galen was born in Pergamum, where his father, an architect named Aelius Nico, had a dream which directed him to urge his son to take up medicine. He began his studies at Pergamum (where he was acquainted with Aelius *Aristides) and then went on to Smyrna, Corinth, and Alexandria, returning home at the age of 28. In 162 he went to Rome, where he put on public displays of his anatomical skill which attracted the attention of leading senators and of *Marcus Aurelius himself. When the plague reached Italy (166–7) he left, but was recalled by Marcus and Lucius *Verus from Pergamum. He was asked by Marcus to accompany him to the north, but obtained permission to stay in Rome as doctor to *Commodus, and he remained there as court physician (eventually to Septimius *Severus as well) until his death in 199. His connections with the imperial court and with leading senators and sophists earned him immense prestige. He was a prolific writer. His earlier works are philosophical (he had a profound knowledge of Plato and Aristotle), his later ones medical. The latter were enormously influential and display a wide range of skill and profundity of knowledge in diagnosis, prognosis, the teaching of anatomy and physiology, methods of dissection, analysis of the blood system, and methods of treatment by diet and drugs.

BIBL. Bowersock, *Sophists*; G. Sarton, *Galen of Pergamum* (1954); Galen, *Opera omnia* (ed. C. G. Kuhn, 1821–3).

Galerius Maximianus Emperor AD 293–311.

Galerius is also called Maximianus and Armentarius in the sources. He was created Caesar with *Constantius I in 293 to make up the newly-formed Tetrarchy, and had to put away his wife to marry *Diocletian's daughter *Valeria. In 296

Galerius and Diocletian together failed to repulse the army of *Narses, King of Persia, but a counter-attack by Galerius alone in 298 was a resounding success. The cautious Diocletian took charge of the peace negotiations, and the Caesar was sent to command the frontier in the northern Balkans, the homeland of all the tetrarchs. Thessalonica was transformed into an imperial city with an arch commemorating the Caesar's Persian triumph. Galerius' victory disturbed the balance of power, the *concordia*, within the Tetrarchy. Encouraged by his mother Romula, he persuaded Diocletian that it was in the public interest to abolish Christianity. It seems that little difficulty was anticipated; from February 303 onwards, buildings and books were destroyed; the death penalty was generally applied only in the following year.

Galerius next pressed Diocletian into the unprecedented act of abdication; on 1 May 305 he and Constantius I solemnly succeeded Diocletian and *Maximian as the Augusti, and two nominees of Galerius, *Maximin Daia and *Severus, became the new Caesars. In the turmoil of the ensuing wars Galerius tried both to hold the ring and to advance the interests of his friends; at one time there were seven imperial claimants, each backed by an army. Meanwhile Christians continued to be persecuted all over the East. It was therefore with vengeful expectation that they learned in 310 that Galerius lay malodorously and mortally ill. He died at Eastertide 311, after issuing an edict which accorded toleration to the Church. This last act failed to save him from vilification by Christian writers like *Eusebius and *Lactantius, who compared him in size and ferocity to his own pet bears.

Small arch from Galerius' Palace in Thessalonica, showing Galerius and the city's goddess carried to heaven by Persians. Thessalonica, Archaeological Mus.

BIBL. Frend, *Martyrdom and Persecution*; G. S. R. Thomas, *Latomus* xxviii (1969) 658–60; T. D. Barnes, *Phoenix* xxx (1976) 174–93.

Gallienus (c. 218–268) Emperor AD 253–68.
Publius Licinius Egnatius Gallienus was created Caesar in 253, after the senate had confirmed his father *Valerian as Augustus. Shortly thereafter Valerian raised him to the rank of Augustus and entrusted him with the defence of the West, while Valerian himself concentrated on the East. Gallienus spent the years 254–6 campaigning against the Germans on the Rhine, while his generals combated the Goths, Marcomanni, Quadi, and other barbarians on the Danube. During these years Gallienus undertook a number of important military reforms, among them the creation of an independent, highly mobile cavalry corps which was used as a striking-force whenever invasion threatened. By 257 the Balkans were overrun by barbarians, against whom the Roman forces were largely ineffective, and this resulted in the usurpation in Pannonia of *Ingenuus, who was defeated and killed by Gallienus and his chief cavalry commander, *Aureolus. In 258 Gallienus reached an agreement with the Marcomanni and took the chief's daughter Pipa as his concubine. Worse was to come. In 259–60 Valerian was defeated, captured, and killed by the Persians led by *Shapur I. Within the following year Gallienus faced three usurpations: that of *Macrianus and his sons, *Regalianus, and

Aemilianus. All were of brief duration. The uprising of *Postumus in Gaul in 260 resulted in the siege of Cologne, the murder of *Saloninus, and the establishment of the Gallic empire which lasted from 260–74. From 261–7 there were no further barbarian invasions except in Dacia Inferior, which was virtually lost. An alliance in the East with Palmyra led by *Odaenath significantly reduced the Persian threat. Gallienus moved against Postumus in 265, but despite winning battles was unable to remove him, probably because of the dilatoriness of Aureolus.

The reign of Gallienus was one of almost unmitigated military, political, and economic disaster. Invasion, banditry, piracy, and barbarian infiltration led to virtual anarchy. During the years 260–8, the silver coinage was continually debased, dropping from about 15 per cent silver to below 2 per cent. It is hardly surprising that later Roman historians viewed Gallienus as weak, effeminate, and cowardly, but, although it can fairly be said that he was beset by problems beyond his ability to remedy, he was none the less resolute in the face of danger, and campaigned incessantly. His major difficulty was the multiplicity of enemies, internal and external. He earned the enmity of the senate by excluding senators from their traditional legionary commands, and all posts as tribunes were restricted to the equestrians. Gallienus and his wife *Salonina were also deeply involved in the cultural life of their times, and were acquainted with *Plotinus and other leading intellectuals. They may also have influenced a neo-classical trend in sculpture. In 260 Gallienus ended the religious persecution begun by his father. In 267 the Goths again overran the Empire, and Gallienus set out on campaign. In the same year Aureolus, who had been left in charge of the cavalry at Milan, rebelled. Gallienus returned to deal with the problem personally, but during the siege of Milan he was murdered by a group of his leading generals including *Claudius II, the next emperor.

BIBL. L. de Blois, *The Policy of the Emperor Gallienus* (1976); *PIR* L 197.

Gallienus in armour (left: silver medallion) and his series of coins honouring individual legions (right: LEG. XXX ULP., silver *antoninianus*) reflect the military crisis of his reign.

Gallus Caesar as consul, wearing *toga picta* and holding statuette of Victory, from the *Calendar of 354* (*Calendar of *Filocalus*). Rome, Vatican Library.

Gallio Annaeanus, Lucius Junius Governor of Achaea AD 51.

*Seneca's brother Annaeus Novatus was adopted by their father's friend Junius Gallio, the orator and associate of *Sejanus. As governor of Achaea he dismissed the charges brought against St *Paul by the Corinthian Jews (Acts 18:12). He did not long survive the fall and death of Seneca.

BIBL. *PIR* I 757.

Gallus Caesar AD 351–4.

Son of Julius *Constantius and Galla, nephew of *Constantine and elder brother of *Julian, Flavius Claudius Constantius Gallus was born in 325/6. He escaped the massacre of his relations in 337 (see *Constantius II) because he was ill and expected to die. With Julian he was interned for six years at Macellum in Cappadocia, but was then created Caesar by his cousin, Constantius II, married to Constantius' sister *Constantina (an *Arian Christian like Gallus), and sent to Antioch to keep the Persians under surveillance while Constantius moved west against the usurper *Magnentius. Gallus' rule was not a success: brutalized by the experiences of his youth, he suppressed conspiracies and a Jewish rising with ruthlessness. He was brought down by a palace plot led by the chamberlain *Eusebius, was summoned to Constantius, who suspected him (wrongly) of treason, and summarily tried and executed at Pola.

BIBL. *PLRE* i, Constantius 4; Thompson, *Ammianus*, ch. 4.

Gallus, Cornelius Prefect of Egypt 30–26 BC.

One of *Augustus' chief equestrian helpers, of Gallic origin, Gaius Cornelius Gallus was a member of the social milieu and cultural group that also included *Maecenas and Vedius *Pollio. He overreached himself as first Roman governor of Egypt—his arrogance led him, we are told, to write his name on the Pyramids—and he was driven to suicide in 26 BC. Gallus' love-poems in elegiacs were addressed to Lycoris (i.e. Cytheris, mistress also of Mark *Antony), and drew some at least of their mythological learning from *Parthenius. They were widely admired, including by *Virgil (see Eclogue 10), an intimate friend, and were influential upon (e.g.) *Propertius. Eight and a half lines, almost certainly by Gallus, have now been added, from a papyrus discovered in Nubia, to the one line that survived. They come from a sequence of related short poems on love, war, and literature. The quality is perhaps less exalted than might have been expected.

BIBL. Ehrenberg and Jones, *Documents* 21; *PIR* C 1369; Anderson, Parsons, Nisbet, *JRS* lxix (1979) 125 ff.

Gallus, Gaius Sulpicius Consul 166 BC, astronomer.

Gallus was one of the leading Roman proponents of Greek culture and learning in the second century BC. As legate in Macedonia (168 BC) he allayed the superstitious fears of the army by scientific explanation of a lunar eclipse. His behaviour as ambassador in Greece and Asia in 163 attracted *Polybius' criticism, particularly his encouragement of accusations against *Eumenes.

BIBL. PW ii. R. iv. 808 ff.; *ORF* 102 f.

Gannys Politician, early 3rd century AD.

The tutor of *Elagabalus, after the latter was proclaimed emperor, Gannys led the army which defeated *Macrinus in 218. He was killed by Elagabalus in 219 because he openly objected to the emperor's public performance of the Baal ritual.

BIBL. *PIR* G 74.

Gavius Maximus Praetorian prefect *c*. AD 139–58.

An Italian of equestrian rank from Picenum, Marcus Gavius Maximus was procurator in Mauretania Tingitana (perhaps in 129) and then in Asia before becoming praetorian prefect, at first with a colleague, until 143, and then on his own. He was probably *Antoninus Pius' leading military adviser, and his high favour is indicated by the long tenure of the prefecture and by the grant of consular insignia which he received.

BIBL. W. Hüttl, *Antoninus Pius* (1933–6); *PIR* G 104; Pflaum, *Carrières*, no. 105bis.

Geiseric King of the Vandals, AD 428–77.

As sole ruler of the Vandals after his half-brother's death, Geiseric, the son of a slave woman, proved the ablest opponent of Roman power in the Mediterranean. Taciturn, hot-tempered, avaricious, and a shrewd diplomat, he built up a Vandal power-base in North Africa and from it played off his enemies, Goths, Romans, and Huns, against each other.

Invited to Africa from Spain in 429 by *Boniface, then at war with Roman political enemies, Geiseric moved eastwards until, in violation of a treaty of 435, he took Carthage (439). From there he had virtual control of the Roman corn supply and of a fleet with which he threatened all the coastal towns of the Mediterranean, a danger acknowledged at once in Italy (*Nov. Val.* 9 of 440). In 455, allegedly in response to appeals for help against *Petronius Maximus from the Empress *Eudoxia, Geiseric plundered and sacked Rome itself and took Eudoxia and her two daughters back to Carthage, where one of them was married to Geiseric's son, Huneric (whose previous, Gothic, wife had been mutilated and sent back to her father). A series of Roman expeditions against him proved humiliating failures, culminating in the disastrous defeat of *Leo's and *Anthemius' fleet at Mercurium near Carthage (468) due to unfavourable winds, Vandal fire-ships, and the incompetence of the admiral, *Basiliscus: a defeat which bankrupted the eastern treasury.

Within his African kingdom, Geiseric followed a policy of evicting Roman landowners in order to reward his Vandal followers, and, as a fervent Arian, he persecuted the Catholic clergy. He also reorganized the Vandal army and razed the walls of cities to disarm potential centres of resistance. Such was his authority that he could ensure peaceful succession for his descendants down to the time of Justinian, whose historian, Procopius, recorded the king's confident designation of his enemies as 'those with whom God is angry'.

BIBL. Jordanes, *Gothic History*, 167–9, 184; Procopius, *Vandalic Wars*, III. 3–5; F. Martroye, *Genséric* (1907).

Gellius, Aulus (born *c*. AD 130 (?)) Dilettante grammarian.

Gellius studied in Rome and was much influenced by *Favorinus and perhaps by *Fronto. He then worked in Athens for at least a year, in contact with *Herodes Atticus and the Cynic philosopher Peregrinus Proteus. He began collecting philological material there during the winter nights (hence the title of his work, *Attic Nights*), and persevered over a long period, assembling, in deliberately disordered fashion, 20 books of miscellaneous erudition for his children (*praef., passim*); 19 survive. The settings for his disquisitions often offer delightful vignettes of student life in Athens; the disquisitions themselves range bewilderingly over literature, law, grammar, language, religion, philosophy, and science, displaying great learning, not always at first hand, and preserving invaluable quantities of earlier Roman literature.

BIBL. R. Marache, *La critique littéraire . . .* (1952); Marshall, *C. Phil.* 1963, 143 ff.

Genucius, Lucius Tribune 342 BC.

One or more of *Livy's sources attributed to Genucius a plebiscite prohibiting usury, and also, probably, others which forbade the tenure of two magistracies in one year or the same magistracy within ten years, and opened both consulships to plebeians. In their transmitted form these measures are highly suspect.

BIBL. PW vii. 1207; J.-C. Richard, *Historia* xxviii (1979) 65 ff.

George of Cappadocia Bishop of Alexandria AD 357–61.

Overbearing and violent, George, an extreme *Arian, was installed in 357 in the see of Alexandria, left vacant by *Athanasius' flight. He alienated both orthodox Christians and pagans, and in 361, after the death of the Arian *Constantius II, was lynched in a riot provoked by his words before an important temple, 'How long shall this sepulchre stand?' The pagan emperor *Julian merely wrote to the Alexandrians mildly reproving their action.

BIBL. Julian, *Ep.* 21 (Loeb); Ammianus XXII. xi.

Germanicus (15 BC–AD 19) Consul AD 12 and 18.

Germanicus Julius Caesar was the eldest son of *Drusus (the elder) and *Antonia. He received a good education, which enabled him to make a new translation of the astronomical poem of Aratus, showing real interest in the subject-matter (unlike *Cicero), and striving to elucidate factual obscurities; he also excelled at oratory. He only became prominent, however, when the deaths of Gaius and Lucius *Caesar shifted *Augustus' succession plans to the Claudian side of the family. When *Tiberius was adopted by Augustus in AD 4, he adopted his nephew Germanicus in turn. He began the senatorial career, but the Pannonian and German crises took him away from Rome for long periods, and it was at this time that he began to show military promise and to win the affection of the armies. In AD 14 he was able to rely on this affection to quell the mutiny of the Rhine army; in 17 he was brought back to Rome by Tiberius for a triumph after the most spectacular campaign yet—along the North Sea coast, against the Chatti and Cherusci; the extent of his success and the delirious devotion of the people naturally worried the emperor.

At the end of 17 he set out on a mission to settle eastern affairs, and made a triumphal progress from city to city, arranging the conversion of Cappadocia into a province (through the legate

*Veranius), relieving famine at Alexandria, and visiting Troy and the sights of the Nile as a tourist. Returning to Antioch, he was afflicted with an illness which rapidly proved fatal. The governor of Syria, Calpurnius *Piso (q.v.), who had been on bad terms with Germanicus, was suspected of poisoning or cursing the dead man, whose ashes were taken home by his widow *Agrippina (the Elder), to extraordinary scenes of mourning everywhere. If the tradition is to be believed, he was an outstandingly handsome, generous, congenial, and talented man, and it is to be regretted that he died so young. Some called him proud, on the other hand; and the character of his children who reached their prime, the Emperor *Gaius, *Agrippina the Younger, and Drusilla, is not a good advertisement either.

BIBL. Tac. *Ann.* i–iv; Translation of Aratus' *Phaenomena*, ed. Gain (1976) (the attribution to Tiberius is implausible).

Geta Caesar AD 198–209, Augustus 209–11.

Younger son of the Emperor *Severus, Publius Lucius Septimius Geta was born in 189 and made Caesar in 198, when his elder brother *Caracalla became Augustus. From 205–8 Geta and Caracalla caused scandal by their loose living, and the rivalry between the two brothers grew into an intense mutual hatred. During the campaigns in the north of Britain in 208–11, Geta remained behind to administer the southern regions. Late in 209 he was made Augustus, and after Severus' death in 211 he and Caracalla quickly returned to Rome, where their mutual dislike was so great that even the palace had to be physically divided. Geta, who was said to resemble his father closely, apparently never married. Caracalla, however, could brook no rival, and in December 211 on the pretext of an arranged reconciliation, he had Geta stabbed to

Concordia: Geta with *Severus and *Caracalla.
Arch of Septimius Severus, Lepcis: Tripoli, museum.

death in his mother's arms. Caracalla then tried to obliterate Geta's name permanently by having his portraits defaced and his name removed from inscriptions.

BIBL. Birley, *Severus*; Millar, *Dio*; Herodian (Loeb).

Gildo Army commander in Africa AD 385-98.

Gildo's family was the key to the complex tribal politics through which the Romans held Mauretania, the western march of Africa, in the late fourth century AD. His father Nubel, who may be the Roman cavalry officer of that name who built a church in one of the coastal towns, was also a powerful native chieftain. When he died (*c.* 371), his sons fell out over the inheritance, one of them, Firmus, first murdering his pro-Roman brother Sammac, and then rebelling with the help of his sister Cyria and three more brothers. Gildo, however, fought on the Roman side with Count *Theodosius, and in 385 *Theodosius I made him commander-in-chief of the army in Africa; his daughter Salvina married a kinsman of Theodosius at Constantinople. In the 'cold war' after Theodosius' death (395), Gildo sided with the eastern court, and in 397 withheld African grain from Rome. *Stilicho encouraged the senate to declare Gildo a public enemy, and sent an expedition commanded by Gildo's estranged brother Mascezel (a former supporter of Firmus), which defeated and killed him (July 398). Mascezel met an opportune accident on his return to Italy, but his niece Salvina and her children became prominent members of Christian society at Constantinople.

BIBL. *PLRE* i, Gildo, Firmus 3, etc.

Glabrio, Manius Acilius Consul 191 BC.

A supporter of *Scipio Africanus and a *novus homo*, Glabrio received the coveted consular command against *Antiochus III in 191 BC. His victory at Thermopylae forced Antiochus to withdraw from Greece, whereupon he turned against Antiochus' allies, the Aetolians, forcing them to sue for peace and alarming them by his interpretation of the word 'surrender'. His campaign released Delphi from Aetolian control, and he was honoured there with a statue, on whose base an important epigraphical dossier was inscribed. At Rome Glabrio celebrated a triumph, but his further career was blighted by the Elder *Cato's accusation that he had misappropriated booty.

BIBL. Sherk, *Roman Documents from the Greek East* (1969) 221 ff.; Scullard, *Politics*.

Glaucia, Gaius Servilius Praetor 100 BC.

A popular leader, Glaucia was closely associated with L. *Saturninus as tribune (101 BC) and praetor (100). His judiciary law reversed the recent

Portrait bust of the Emperor Gordian I. Florence, Uffizi.

measure of Q. *Caepio by restoring control of criminal courts to the equestrians. But his hostility to the senatorial establishment must have been regarded as serious before 102, when the censor *Metellus Numidicus unsuccessfully attempted to expel him and Saturninus from the senate. He broke the constitutional rules by standing for the consulship of 99, and he probably instigated the violent death of a rival

Portrait bust of the Emperor Gordian III as a boy. Berlin, Preussischer Kulturbesitz.

candidate, C. *Memmius. This was the signal for the senate to authorize the consul *Marius' suppression of Saturninus, Glaucia, and many of their supporters.

BIBL. Gruen, *Politics*.

Glycerius Western emperor AD 473.

Proclaimed emperor by the Burgundian Gundobad, army commander in Italy, at Ravenna in March 473, Glycerius, formerly a mere Count of the Domestics (*comes domesticorum*), had barely time to divert an Ostrogothic invasion from Italy to Gaul before he was deposed by Julius *Nepos and, while still on Italian soil, consecrated bishop of Salonae.

BIBL. *Anonymus Valesianus*, VII. 36; Marcellinus, *Chronicle*, s.a. 473; Stein, *Bas-Empire*, i. 395.

Gordian I Emperor AD 238.

Born c. 159, Marcus Antonius Gordianus Sempronianus had a distinguished public career: consul in 222, he became proconsul of Africa under *Severus Alexander. In 238 young African nobles rebelled against harsh and unjust tax exactions and forced the purple on Gordian who was then over 80 years old. The Roman senate supported Gordian and voted to condemn *Maximinus I's memory. The Numidian governor, however, remained loyal to Maximinus, and his seasoned troops easily defeated the poorly armed militia led by *Gordian II, who died in battle, whereupon Gordian I committed suicide.

BIBL. PW Antonius 61; Herodian (Loeb); *PIR* A 833.

Gordian II Emperor AD 238.

Marcus Antonius Gordianus Sempronianus Romanus Africanus was born c. 192 and was consul under *Severus Alexander. He became emperor with his father, *Gordian I, in Africa in 238, after a rebellion of young nobles. His reign lasted about 21 days before he died in battle against Capellianus, governor of Numidia, a supporter of *Maximinus.

BIBL. Herodian (Loeb); Syme, *Emperors and Biography*; *PIR* A 834.

Gordian III Emperor AD 238–44.

Born in 224, Marcus Antonius Gordianus, grandson of *Gordian I, became Caesar and then emperor at the age of 13 following *Maximinus' death and the murder of *Balbinus and *Pupienus by the praetorian guard. From 238–41 he and his advisers carried out Gordian I's policies. Gordian appointed *Timesitheus praetorian prefect in 241, and married his daughter *Tranquillina. In 242 Gordian went on campaign against the Persians with Timesitheus, and after a stunning series of victories Timesitheus succumbed to illness in 243. His successor, *Philip the Arab, desired imperial

power for himself, and Gordian was murdered by the soldiers early in 244.

BIBL. *CAH* xii; Herodian (Loeb); *PIR* A 835; PW Antonius 60.

Gracchus, Gaius Tribune 123 and 122 BC.

One of the few truly statesmanlike figures in republican history, Gaius Sempronius Gracchus set about a comprehensive reform of Rome's outdated social and political structure; and for a while before his death at the age of about 32 he was unquestionably the most powerful man in Rome. The younger brother of Tiberius *Gracchus, his brief career was motivated by a desire to avenge Tiberius and to sustain his political achievements. But the agrarian issue was only one element in Gaius' more wide-ranging programme, which involved administrative reforms and the crucial question of enfranchising the non-Roman population of Italy. As tribune in 123 BC Gracchus was able to rely on former supporters of his brother, but he had learnt from Tiberius' error the need to build up extensive electoral support. Thus a number of Gracchus' proposals were designed specifically to win the backing of the urban proletariat and the wealthy equestrians. He hoped to attain a position of pre-eminence in which his personal authority would be sufficient to secure necessary but unpopular reforms such as the enfranchisement of Italians.

Gracchus presented a direct challenge to the senatorial establishment, and, when he secured re-election as tribune for 122, it counter-attacked by sponsoring a rival tribune, M. Livius *Drusus (1), who undermined the popular support which Gracchus had carefully built up, by proposing attractive alternative schemes. As a result Gracchus failed to secure citizenship for the Italians and re-election for 121. Deprived of a tribune's inviolability he surrounded himself with a bodyguard, but after several violent incidents the consul L. *Opimius was instructed to suppress the ex-tribune and his followers as enemies of the State. His impassioned, demagogic form of oratory and ostentatious display of influence and *clientela* had prompted the familiar apprehension of tyranny. The precise content and chronology of C. Gracchus' extensive legislation is a matter of dispute. His programme remained incomplete, although many of its features survived him.

BIBL. Gruen, *Politics*, esp. 79 ff.; Stockton, *The Gracchi* (1979).

Gracchus, Tiberius Tribune 133 BC.

Tiberius Sempronius Gracchus (the younger) was a controversial and somewhat tragic figure whose tribunate marks a clear turning-point in Roman history. It closed a comparatively harmonious but reactionary era under the virtually unchallenged supremacy of the senate, and ushered in a century of violent dissension and revolution. Gracchus was no romantic reformer: the son of Ti. Sempronius *Gracchus and *Cornelia, and thus at the heart of the senatorial aristocracy, he was a proud and ambitious young noble seeking the political advancement regarded as his birthright, by largely traditional means. His pride was badly scarred by the senate's repudiation of the treaty he negotiated as quaestor in Spain for *Mancinus (137 BC). When he reached the tribunate in 133 he introduced an agrarian bill which was designed to solve the Roman commonwealth's long-standing demographic problem, thus winning for himself an extensive *clientela* throughout Italy which would serve him in his later career. It was said that Gracchus observed the abandonment of peasant holdings and their replacement by slave labour while travelling to Spain in 137, and deplored the decline of Rome's manpower. But the problem had been identified long before Gracchus, and his bill had the backing of a powerful minority in the senate. However, the proposed redistribution of land seemed too radical for the senate majority, who opposed the bill through the veto of another tribune, M. Octavius. Gracchus had Octavius unconstitutionally deposed, and proceeded to usurp the senate's authority further by proposing to the popular assembly that the bequest of Attalus III of Pergamum be accepted to finance the new smallholdings in Italy. The land allotments were supervised by a powerful commission (initially manned by himself, his brother and his father-in-law), and they succeeded in temporarily arresting the decline of the Roman peasantry. However, at Rome the conservative opposition intensified, provoking Gracchus to seek re-election to safeguard his legislation. This final breach of constitutional practice confirmed the worst fears of his enemies that he was seeking an unacceptable degree of personal power for himself. This, at least, was the justification of the party, led by *Scipio Nasica, that lynched him on the Capitol.

BIBL. Earl, *Tiberius Gracchus* (1963); Bernstein, *Gracchus*; Stockton, *The Gracchi* (1979).

Gracchus, Tiberius Sempronius Consul 177 and 163 BC.

Gracchus was a leading Roman statesman of the mid-second century BC, but is better known as 'the father of the Gracchi'. He seems to have begun his public career as a protégé of the Scipios, although he may have disagreed with them at some point. In 190 he was sent as personal envoy by the consul *Scipio Asiagenus to secure *Philip V's assistance in the passage of the Roman army to Asia Minor; it was probably the same Scipio whom Gracchus rescued from prosecution by using his veto as tribune in the 180s; and shortly afterwards he married *Cornelia, the daughter of *Scipio Africanus.

In 180-179 Gracchus held a particularly distinguished command as praetor and propraetor in Hispania Citerior, which was memorable both for the termination of the war against the Celtiberians and for the establishment of a statesmanlike peace settlement which lasted for 25 years. After a triumph for these successes Gracchus proceeded to the consulship and a second triumph for crushing an insurrection in Sardinia (177-176). His censorship (169) was notable for its severity and also for a bitter clash between the censors and the businessmen to whom they farmed the public contracts (the *publicani*).

Gracchus reached a rare second consulship (163), and died (probably before 150) one of the most powerful men in Rome. His power rested not only on his seniority in the senate but also on the vast range of his personal clients throughout Italy and the provinces. These he acquired through his achievements in Spain and Sardinia, through colonizing activity in Italy, and through two important embassies to the East (166-165 and 162-160 BC) on which he reported favourably on the client states and dynasts in his brief, and adopted a conciliatory attitude markedly different from the abrasive, bullying approach of other Romans in the East.

BIBL. Carcopino, *Autour des Gracques* (1928); Geer, *TAPA* lxix (1938) 381; Bernstein, *Gracchus*, 26-42.

Gold medallion of the Emperor Gratian (enlarged).

Gratian Emperor AD 367-83.

Elder son (born 359) and successor of *Valentinian I, who proclaimed him (titular) emperor in August 367, Flavius Gratianus was handsome and athletic, but over-pious and lacking his father's forceful personality. He was only sixteen when he succeeded (17 November 375), and remained under the influence of others, notably his former tutor *Ausonius (until 379) and the commander-in-chief *Merobaudes. In 378, on his way to help *Valens against the Goths, he was the last emperor to cross the Rhine when he chastised the Alamanni; but the loss of two-thirds of the eastern army at Adrianople posed an insoluble military problem. He recalled *Theodosius I and made him eastern emperor (January 379); between them they tried to contain the Goths. In 383 Gratian had to march against the usurper *Maximus, but, abandoned by *Merobaudes, he fled and was killed at Lyons (25 August). Under the influence of St *Ambrose, Gratian ended his father's policy of religious toleration, by repudiating the title of *pontifex maximus* and removing the altar of Victory from the senate house (see *Damasus, *Symmachus).

BIBL. Matthews, *Aristocracies*.

Grattius Didactic poet (late Augustan).

Possibly a native of Falerii, Grattius was an acquaintance of *Ovid and the author of a poem on hunting, of which 540 hexameters survive.

BIBL. Text: Loeb, *Minor Latin Poets*, ed. Verdière (1964).

Gregory the Illuminator (c. AD 240–332) 'Apostle of the Armenians'.

Gregory was an Armenian noble, but was brought up a Christian in Roman territory. His mission at first met with persecution, but his miracles at court (which in Armenian tradition included the transformation of his monarch into a wild boar) convinced *Tiridates III that Armenia should become Christian (traditionally c. 301). Tiridates invited Gregory to become first Catholicos (primate) of the Armenian Church, an office which became hereditary in his family.

BIBL. Grousset, *Histoire de l'Arménie* (1947).

St Gregory of Nazianzus Bishop of Constantinople AD 381.

Gregory (AD c. 329–89) was the son of the bishop

Bronze triptych (11th–12th century) with Gregory of Nazianzus (left). London, Victoria and Albert Museum.

of Nazianzus in Cappadocia, and a fellow-student of St *Basil at Athens. Here he saw (and disliked) the future Emperor *Julian; his own skill at expressing Catholic theology in 'classical' verse and prose made him resent Julian's identification of their common Greek literary culture with paganism. Like Basil he adopted a monastic life, but returned to Nazianzus to help his father (died 374) and was unwillingly consecrated bishop of an obscure road-station. After another monastic retreat (375–8), he came to Constantinople (379) as chaplain to the orthodox community, and despite *Arian opposition became a successful preacher. He was elected bishop by the Council of Constantinople (381), but soon quarrelled with this 'flock of geese', and resigned. He retired to Cappadocia, where he composed a verse autobiography of self-justification.

BIBL. *ODCC* Gregory of Nazianzus.

St Gregory of Nyssa Bishop c. AD 371–c. 395.

Gregory was the younger brother of St *Basil; they and their friend St *Gregory of Nazianzus were the 'Cappadocian Fathers' who achieved the victory of eastern orthodoxy over the *Arian heresy. Without studying at Athens like the other two, Gregory gained an intimate knowledge of Plato and Neoplatonism (see *Plotinus) which he applied to Christian mysticism. He was a greater theologian than his brother, but lacked his forcefulness and administrative ability. After living as a hermit, he was consecrated bishop of Nyssa in Cappadocia, against his will, by his brother. He played an important part in the Council of Constantinople (381) which affirmed the Nicene Creed: St *Jerome heard him refute the extreme Arian position; but, unlike Jerome, his visit to Jerusalem (c. 380) convinced him that pilgrimage was unnecessary for belief, and even harmful.

BIBL. *ODCC* Gregory of Nyssa.

Gregory the Wonder-worker (Thaumaturgus) (c. AD 210–c. 270) Convert and bishop.

Gregory and his brother, members of a noble family of Pontus, were planning to study law at the famous schools of Beirut until side-tracked by the Christian thinker *Origen. They lived with him five happy years acquiring wisdom; Gregory's farewell address on returning to Pontus is a moving testimonial to the warm relationship between a sage and his spiritual sons. Back home, Gregory became bishop of Neocaesarea, his native city, and his power to stop floods and expel demons was still recalled a century later in the secluded countryside he had converted to Christianity.

BIBL. Grégoire le Thaumaturge: *Remerciement à Origène*, ed. H. Crouzel (SC cxlviii, 1969); *Life*, by *Gregory of Nyssa (Migne, *PG* xlvi. 893–958).

Hadrian Emperor AD 117–38.

Publius Aelius Hadrianus was born in AD 76, probably at Rome, though his family's home-town was Italica in Spain. He was the son of Publius Aelius Hadrianus Afer and Domitia Paulina (from Gades), but when his father died in 85 he became the ward of the future Emperor *Trajan. He saw military service in the Dacian Wars (102–3 and 105–6), governed Pannonia Inferior in 107, held a consulship in 108, and governed Syria in 114. He was designated for the consulship of 118. Throughout his earlier career he had been favoured by the Empress *Plotina, but when Trajan died in Cilicia on 8 August 117 it was not clear that Hadrian would succeed him. The news of Trajan's death was concealed until it could be announced simultaneously with the fact that Hadrian (who was then at Antioch) had been adopted as his successor (11 August).

The year 118 saw a Parthian triumph for Hadrian, the suppression of trouble from the Sarmatians and Roxolani in Moesia, the execution, on the authority of the senate, of four ex-consuls for 'conspiring' against Hadrian, and a series of generous financial measures intended to establish the popularity of the new regime. Hadrian's reign was a very important period in the history of the Empire. Perhaps his greatest contribution was in the area of frontier policy. He abandoned Trajan's conquests in the East and turned instead to a policy of consolidation. He travelled the Empire more extensively than any previous emperor, visiting Gaul and the Rhine (120/1), Britain (121/2),

Hadrian, portrait bust. Rome, Museo delle Terme.

Hadrian's Villa, Tivoli (c. AD 130): view of the Canopus, c. AD 130.

Spain (122), Asia (123), Greece (125), returning to
Rome via Sicily (127), then going to Africa (128),
Athens (winter, 128), Caria, Cilicia, Cappadocia and
Syria (129), and Egypt (130). He returned to Rome
in 131 and spent the remainder of his reign in
Italy.

He put into operation a thoroughgoing overhaul
of the military establishment, and consolidated
the development of linear frontiers which had
begun in the Flavian period. The results can most
clearly be seen in the Rhine and Danube provinces,
in Africa, and in Britain (where Hadrian's Wall was
built between 122 and 125). His reign saw one
major war, in Judaea, where the Jews revolted
under the leadership of Simon *Bar-Cochba; the
suppression of this revolt effectively ended the
existence of Judaea as the Jewish homeland.

A number of administrative changes were also
introduced. More extensive use was made of
equestrians in the bureaucracy, and they were able
henceforth to gain advancement through holding
purely civil posts. He formalized the composition
of the emperor's advisory council, introducing the
presence of legal experts. He introduced a board
of judges (IVviri consulares) to deal with cases in
Italy, thus weakening the authority of the senate.
Hadrian was personally active in almost all areas of
legislation and jurisdiction, and his reign saw a
number of very important developments in Roman
Law, including the codification of the Praetor's
Edict (by Salvius *Julianus).

Hadrian was a great lover of Greek culture and
was particularly attached to Athens, which gained
many new buildings and much imperial
munificence. In Italy he was responsible for the
building of the Pantheon, the Temple of Venus
and Rome, his own Mausoleum, and a magnificent
villa at Tivoli. His tastes and attitudes did not
endear him to the senatorial class. His reign was
marked, particularly at the beginning and end, by
the deaths of a number of leading senators, some
of whom were clearly executed or forced to
commit suicide. His first adopted heir, *Aelius
Caesar, died in January 138, and Hadrian turned to
*Antoninus Pius, a senator of Gallic origin, who
succeeded when Hadrian died at Baiae on 10 July
138. He was buried in his Mausoleum in Rome.

BIBL. Syme, Tacitus; PIR A 184; B. d'Orgeval,
L'Empéreur Hadrien, oeuvre législative et
administrative (1950).

Hamilcar 'Barca' (died 229/8 BC) Carthaginian
general.

As Carthage's land commander in Sicily
Hamilcar was undefeated in 241 BC, when he
negotiated a peace with C. Lutatius *Catulus. He
crushed the mercenary revolt in Africa by 238, and
from 237 until his death he established a new
Carthaginian empire in Spain. Roman demonology
represents him as harbouring an obsessive hatred

Hamilcar on Carthaginian silver coin, minted in
Spain (enlarged).

of Rome, which he inculcated into his son
*Hannibal.

BIBL. Errington, Latomus xxix (1970) 25 ff.;
Walbank, HCP i.

Hannibal (247–183 BC) Carthaginian general.

One of the greatest military geniuses of
Antiquity, Hannibal was regarded by Romans as
the most formidable opponent in their history. The
son of *Hamilcar, he took over the command of
Carthaginian forces in Spain in 221 BC. His attack
on Rome's ally Saguntum in 219 led to the
outbreak of the second Punic War, which later
historians tried to present as a personal war of
revenge gratuitously begun by Hannibal in
fulfilment of an oath to his father. He pre-empted
Rome's planned two-pronged offensive on Spain
and Africa by an overland invasion of Italy in 218.
His epic march over the Alps lost him thousands
of men and most of his war elephants, but he
secured military support from many tribes in
Cisalpine Gaul and was able to inflict successive
defeats on the Romans, culminating in the
destruction of two consular armies at Cannae
(216 BC). Some of Rome's Italian allies now
defected to Hannibal, but his overall strategy of
dissolving the Italian confederation failed,
because most of it remained loyal and assured
Rome of a continuing manpower advantage.

After Cannae, Rome avoided further direct
confrontations with Hannibal, and allowed him to

Carthaginian silver coin from Spain with portrait
of Hannibal (enlarged).

retain control of much of southern Italy. But his
position became hopeless after *Hasdrubal's
failure to bring reinforcements from Spain in 207,
and he was pushed more and more on to the
defensive until he was recalled to Africa in 203 to
resist *Scipio Africanus' invasion. He met defeat
at Zama in 202 BC at Scipio's hands, and thereupon
advised Carthage to accept peace. He was hounded
from Carthage by political enemies in 195, and
found refuge at *Antiochus III's court, where his
presence excited fears at Rome of another
invasion of Italy. After Antiochus' defeat he fled
to Prusias I of Bithynia, and committed suicide in
183 when Rome sent *Flamininus to demand his
surrender.

BIBL. Charles-Picard, *Hannibal* (1967); Proctor,
Hannibal's March in History (1971); Lazenby,
Hannibal's War (1978).

Hannibalianus (died AD 337) Nephew of
Constantine.

Younger son of Fl. *Dalmatius, educated with his
brother Fl. Julius *Dalmatius at Toulouse,
Hannibalianus was included, like him, in
*Constantine's plans for the succession. In 335 he
was given the title *nobilissimus*, married to
*Constantina, and made ruler of Armenia and
Pontus, with the Armenian title 'King of kings'.
He was killed with his father, brother, and other
relations in 337.

BIBL. *PLRE* i, Hannibalianus 1; Piganiol,
Empire chr.

Helena, head of portrait statue. Rome, Capit. Mus.

Hasdrubal (?): Carthaginian silver coin (enlarged).

Hasdrubal (died 207 BC) Carthaginian general.

The younger brother of *Hannibal, by whom he
was left in command of Carthaginian forces in
Spain (218 BC), Hasdrubal was prevented from
joining Hannibal in Italy after Cannae by P. and Cn.
*Scipio. When he eventually reached Italy in 207,
he was defeated by C. Claudius *Nero and
*Salinator at the Metaurus, where he died
fighting. His severed head was thrown into
Hannibal's camp.

BIBL. Lazenby, *Hannibal's War* (1978).

Haterius, Quintus Orator, consul 5 BC.

Quintus Haterius was the most famous orator of
his time, more because of delivery than
composition. *Tacitus criticizes his 'disgusting
toadying', which did less in any case to protect him
from *Tiberius' suspicion than his friendship with
*Livia. He died, much respected, in AD 26, at the
age of 90.

BIBL. Tacitus, *Annals*, iii. 57, iv. 61.

St Helena Augusta *c*. AD 325–*c*. 330.

Born in Bithynia, Flavia Julia Helena, mother of
the Emperor *Constantine, began her career as a
barmaid. She became wife or mistress of
*Constantius I before he was made Caesar, and
bore him the one child before being separated in
favour of Theodora, whose children she later
persecuted. When Constantine, emperor from 306,
was converted to Christianity, she followed his
lead. Perhaps implicated in the death of her
daughter-in-law *Fausta in 326, Helena left Rome on
a pilgrimage to the Holy Places, and supervised
the building of magnificent churches at imperial
expense in Jerusalem and Bethlehem, including the
Churches of the Nativity and Holy Sepulchre. The
legend of her finding of the True Cross appears in
the late fourth century. She died aged about 80
on her return to Rome in 330, and was buried in a
mausoleum beside the Basilica of SS. Pietro e
Marcellino on the Via Labicana.

BIBL. *PLRE* i, Helena 3; *ODCC*.

Heliodorus Writer, 3rd century AD.

Born at Emesa, Heliodorus was the author of the novel *Aethiopica*, which has been ascribed to the fourth century by some. His style is rhetorical, and he is well acquainted with classical Greek literature.

BIBL. *PLRE* i, Heliodorus 3.

Helvidius Priscus Stoic dissenter, praetor AD 70.

The condemnation of his father-in-law *Thrasea Paetus cut short Gaius Helvidius Priscus' promising senatorial career, and he retired to Apollonia. Under *Galba he returned, hoping that he would now be able to attack Thrasea's accuser *Eprius Marcellus: he was not. As praetor he took a dangerously provocative attitude to *Vespasian, who was eventually driven to banish him; he was killed in exile—against Vespasian's will, it was said. As a figurehead of dissent from the character of the principate of his time he was second only to Thrasea, and had very great influence. His attitudes were maintained by his son (of the same name), who was a friend of the Younger *Pliny and killed under *Domitian.

BIBL. *PIR* H 59.

Hengist King of the Jutes in Britain, mid-5th century AD.

Hengist, and Horsa his brother, arrived in Britain in 446, initially with three warships, to help the British against northern tribes. Although settled in Kent as federate allies—legend gave Hengist's daughter, Rowena, in marriage to the British king, Vortigern—the peace did not last. Horsa died in battle and his monument in east Kent was known to Bede. Hengist won several victories, but may not have lived to see the great British victory over the invaders at Mount Badon, c. 500.

BIBL. Bede, *Ecclesiastical History*, I. 14–16; *Anglo-Saxon Chronicle*.

Heraclianus, Aurelius Praetorian prefect AD 267–8.

Heraclianus engineered the plot by which *Gallienus was murdered in 268 with the consent of his leading generals, including the future emperors *Claudius II and *Aurelian.

BIBL. *CAH* xii; *PLRE* i, Heraclianus 6.

Herennia Etruscilla Empress AD 249–51.

Of Etruscan origin, Herennia Cupressenia Etruscilla was the wife of Trajan *Decius and mother of *Herennius Etruscus, and is known chiefly from coins and a few inscriptions.

BIBL. PW Herennius 53.

Herennius Etruscus Caesar c. AD 250, Augustus 250–1.

Elder son of Trajan *Decius, Quintus Herennius Etruscus Messius Decius was created Caesar and later Augustus while still very young. He and his father died fighting the Goths in 251, at the battle of Abritta.

BIBL. PW Messius 10; Walser and Pekary, *Krise*.

Herod the Great King of Judaea 37–4 BC.

Herod's father received Roman citizenship from *Caesar. Herod played a significant role in the troubled history of Palestine in the first century BC, and was for a time an integral part of *Augustus' eastern arrangements. He was on the best of terms with Rome until the perpetual disorder of his family affairs made him a liability, and he lost the emperor's favour. *Josephus also records trouble stirred up by him in Greece.

BIBL. A. H. M. Jones, *The Herods of Judaea* (1938).

Herod Antipas Jewish king 4 BC–AD 39.

As the youngest and ablest son of *Herod the Great he succeeded to part of his father's kingdom, including Galilee. His rule was not unpopular, though he was responsible for the death of John the Baptist. *Pontius Pilate tried to have *Jesus, as a Galilean subject, tried by him, but Antipas would not be involved.

BIBL. A. H. M. Jones, *The Herods of Judaea*; Schürer, *A History of the Jewish People* (revised Vermes and Millar), i. 340–53.

Herodes, Tiberius Claudius Atticus Consul AD 104 (?).

A wealthy Athenian who gained his fortune by a windfall, Atticus Herodes was the father of *Herodes Atticus (below). He was governor of

Fort of Herodium near Bethlehem, built by Herod the Great.

Portrait bust of Herodes Atticus, Athenian orator and public benefactor.

Judaea at the beginning of the second century, and was particularly honoured in his native Athens where he was priest of the imperial cult (97–102).

BIBL. *PIR* C 801; Philostratus, *Lives of the Sophists*, trans. W. C. Wright (Loeb, 1922); P. Graindor, *Un milliardaire antique, Hérode Atticus et sa famille* (1930).

Herodes Atticus Greek sophist, consul AD 143.

Lucius Vibullius Hipparchus Tiberius Claudius Atticus Herodes was born *c.* 101 into a wealthy Athenian family, his father being Tiberius Claudius Atticus *Herodes. The son became a sophist and rhetorician, and is the subject of one of the best-known of *Philostratus' biographies. His eminence as a man of letters won him a wide circle of powerful friends and pupils at Rome, including the emperors *Hadrian, *Antoninus Pius, *Marcus Aurelius, and Lucius *Verus. He became a senator and held the consulship with *Fronto in 143 (they were apparently by then reconciled after an earlier quarrel). His wealth and philanthropy were legendary. He spent enormous sums on public buildings at Athens (notably the Stadium and the Odeum, or Theatre of Herodes Atticus) and at other cities in Greece and Asia

Minor, including Delphi, Eleusis, and Olympia. In spite of (or perhaps because of) his prestige at Athens he made many enemies there, and was involved in a famous legal dispute with a certain Demostratus which culminated in an appeal, in the early 170's, heard by Marcus Aurelius himself at Sirmium. Herodes died in or about 177.

BIBL. Philostratus, *Vitae Sophistarum*, ii, 1; P. Graindor, *Un milliardaire antique, Hérode Atticus et sa famille* (1930); Bowersock, *Sophists*; J. H. Oliver, *Marcus Aurelius: Aspects of Civic and Cultural Policy in the East* (*Hesperia*, Supplement 13, 1971); E. L. Bowie in *Studies in Ancient Society*, ed. Finley (1974) 195 ff.

Herodian (*c.* AD 180–250) Historian.

Herodian was a younger contemporary of Cassius *Dio and probably wrote his history about the time of *Philip the Arab. His origins, early life, and career are obscure. His history extends from the death of *Marcus Aurelius to the accession of *Gordian III, and most of the events related he claims took place in his lifetime. The weakness of his writing lies in his lack of chronological precision, his geographical inaccuracies, errors of historical fact, and significant omissions. In style his work is a product of its time, laden with rhetorical devices, clichés, and stereotypes. His purpose in writing seems in part to have been a desire to depict the ideal ruler by means of the contrast with the undesirable behaviour of contemporary emperors, and he tended to select facts to conform with his theories. He should be read together with Dio where the two overlap, since despite his faults he at times amplifies or corrects Dio's account.

BIBL. History, ed. Whittaker (Loeb); Millar, *Dio*.

Hiero II Tyrant of Syracuse *c.* 270–215 BC.

Hiero initially opposed Rome's intervention in Sicily (264 BC), but in 263 peace was made, and he became Rome's faithful ally in both wars against Carthage until his death in 215. From 241 his kingdom was autonomous within the Roman province of Sicily, but after his death it again turned against Rome, and was incorporated into the province. Hiero's taxation system survived within the Roman provincial structure.

BIBL. Berve, *König Hieron II* (1959).

Hierocles Governor and pagan pamphleteer *c.* AD 300.

As governor of Bithynia (303–7) and subsequently of Egypt during the Great Persecution, Sossianus Hierocles had ample and congenial opportunity to harry Christians, though he preferred them to recant and sacrifice rather than be killed. He tried also to persuade them with a pamphlet, *The Lover of Truth*: *Jesus, he urged, had been a holy man, but his fraudulent followers had exploited his reputation; his signs of power had no significance beyond their own time. *Eusebius of Caesarea wrote a waspish answer, and *Lactantius, who had seen his own friends tried by Hierocles, mentions him angrily as the author of the persecutions (*Mort.* xvi. 4).

BIBL. T. D. Barnes, *HSCP* 80 (1976) 239–52; Loeb ed. of Philostratus, *Life of Apollonius of Tyana* ii, contains Eusebius' *Adversus Hieroclem*.

St Hilary of Poitiers (*c.* AD 315–67) Bishop and theologian.

Given a pagan education, Hilary was converted from Neoplatonism to Christianity by the study of the Scriptures. Made bishop of Poitiers *c.* 353, he became the principal opponent of *Arianism in the West. He was condemned at the Council of Béziers (356) for his obstinate defence of orthodoxy, and exiled to Phrygia by *Constantius II. In 359 he put the orthodox case at the Council of Seleucia before returning to the West. He was the leading Latin theologian of the period, his chief work being *On the Trinity*. Other works include biblical commentaries, the first known Latin hymns, and an account of contemporary Church history, *On the Councils* (synods).
See also St Martin.

BIBL. *ODCC*.

Himerius Sophist, 4th century AD.

Born at Prusa in Bithynia, Himerius was a professional rhetorician under *Constantius II and *Julian, who in 362 summoned him to Antioch from Athens, where he had competed with Prohaeresius and taught St *Basil and *Gregory of Nazianzus. Twenty-four non-political speeches of his are extant as well as rhetorical exercises, all written in a remarkably self-conscious poetic style.

BIBL. PW viii. 2. 1622.

Hippolytus (*c.* AD 170–236) Christian saint and theologian.

Possibly a pupil of *Irenaeus, Hippolytus was active at Rome and may have established himself as antipope. A contentious and unsympathetic figure, he was exiled to Sardinia under *Maximinus Thrax, and died there.

BIBL. Considerable fragments of his polemic works survive: Migne, *PG* x, and ed. de Lagarde (1858).

Hirtius Consul 43 BC.

A partisan of *Caesar, under whom he served as an officer in Gaul and in the Civil Wars, Aulus Hirtius reached the praetorship in 46 BC, and before Caesar's death was designated consul for 43. In that year he joined forces with *Octavian to fight *Antony on behalf of the Republic. He defeated Antony at Modena, but was killed in the victory after being acclaimed *imperator*; at Rome he

received a public funeral in the Campus Martius. He was renowned as a gourmet, and in the literary field he completed Caesar's Gallic Commentaries and appended a *Bellum Alexandrinum*.

BIBL. Syme, *Rom. Rev.*

Honoria Augusta from AD 425.

The sister of *Valentinian III, Justa Grata Honoria caused two palace scandals within two years, first by having an affair with her steward, *Eugenius, who was executed, and then, on her betrothal to a safe man, she is said to have sent her ring to *Attila, promising her hand in return for his help. Attila exploited this in invading Italy (452) and demanding her 'marriage portion' Honoria is not heard of again.

BIBL. Jordanes, *Gothic History*, 223–4.

Honorius Western emperor AD 395–423.

Flavius Honorius was proclaimed Augustus at the age of eight by his father *Theodosius I, whom he succeeded as western emperor in January 395. Effective power lay with the general *Stilicho, whose daughter he married. Stilicho's claim to be the guardian of Honorius' elder brother *Arcadius as well led to a 'cold war' with the eastern Empire. The western Empire fell apart when barbarian invaders swept across Gaul and Spain, and the usurper *Constantine III established himself at Arles (407–11); in 410 Britain was abandoned to its own devices. *Alaric's invasions of Italy led Honorius to seek refuge with his court behind the marshes of Ravenna (402), which remained his capital. Thanks to the efforts of a new commander-in-chief, *Constantius (q.v. III), Honorius recovered much of Gaul and Spain, and reached a settlement

Honorius and Maria: sardonyx cameo (13th-century setting). Paris, Collection E. de Rothschild.

with the Visigoths which led to the establishment of their kingdom in Aquitania (418). Later in his reign (421) he quarrelled with Constantius' widow, his half-sister Galla *Placidia, who was forced to flee to Constantinople. Honorius died childless on 15 August 423.

BIBL. *PLRE* i, Honorius 3; Matthews, *Aristocracies*.

Horace (65–8 BC) Poet.

Thanks to a biography by *Suetonius and to a number of autobiographical poems we are exceptionally well-informed as to the outward circumstances of the life of Quintus Horatius Flaccus. A native of Venusia (modern Venosa), he was the son of a freedman auctioneer, at whose expense he received an excellent education (see *Orbilius; *Satires*, I. vi. 71 ff.). Further studies in Athens followed; in 44–42 he served in *Brutus' army, reached the remarkably high rank of military tribune, and fought at Philippi. On the losers' side, and stripped of his family property (*Epistles*, II. ii. 47 ff.), he became, briefly, a secretary in the treasury, but early in 38 (?) was introduced to *Maecenas by *Varius and *Virgil, and shortly afterwards was embraced by his patronage (*Satires*, I. vi. 54 ff.). From Maecenas he received a villa in the Sabine hills beyond Tivoli, dearly loved and often celebrated; from *Augustus the offer of a post as private secretary, which he was able to refuse. Continued imperial favour is reflected in the commission to write a long ode for the Secular Games of 17 BC (*Carmen Saeculare*). Maecenas in his will requested Augustus to be 'as mindful of Horace as of himself', and the poet was buried at his patron's side. Horace's dazzlingly successful rise attracted criticism, and he was also the target of prolonged literary feuding, but his poems suggest a genius for friendship and a profoundly agreeable personality is projected. He was a fat little man.

WORKS. (1) *Epodes* (*Iambi*: written in the 30s). Seventeen poems, formally and unprecedentedly modelled on Archilochus: 1, 9, and 16 are the earliest serious political poems at Rome. The 'biting' tone of *iambi* is not sustained throughout, and this early collection already displays a prodigious talent for exploitation of Greek forms and themes. (2) *Satires* (*Sermones*: two books, containing 18 poems in all, perhaps published together *c.* 30 BC). Horace's intention is (I. i. 24) 'laughing to tell the truth', in the manner of Greek popular philosophical discourses (*diatribe*), and the poems are best considered as 'conversations' (*sermones*) upon, for example, success and envy (i. 6), town and country (ii. 6), the purpose and nature of the *sermones* (i. 4, 10; ii. 1), sex (i. 2), and legacy-hunting (ii. 5): brisk slander of minor living persons is tempered by richly humorous and mildly circuitous discussion. (3) *Odes* (*Carmina*:

books i–iii (?) issued together, 23 BC (?), iv, 13 BC (?)): 103 poems, demonstrating unsurpassed mastery of widely varied metres, memorably and untranslatably compressed use of language, prodigiously wide reading of earlier poetry of all periods, and vast miscellaneous learning in geography, mythology, and religion. Behind this technical mastery, the life, love, politics, and philosophical opinions of 'Horace the man' remain securely and permanently hidden. (4) *Epistles* i and ii (i probably written between 23 and 19 BC): twenty poems in hexameters, some superficially epistolary in form. The subjects are often slighter than those of the *Satires*, but the treatment is consistently wise, genial, and relaxed; the commonplaces of Hellenistic ethics and the realities of Roman life are perfectly combined. *Ep.* ii. 1 (to Augustus, *c.* 16 BC) is concerned with the place of the poet in society, and ii. 2 (to Florus, 19/18 BC) with themes literary, philosophical, and autobiographical. (5) *Ars Poetica*, sometimes called *Epistula ad Pisones*, *c.* 18 BC or *c.* 10 BC: Horace's longest poem, chiefly on the criticism of drama, enlivened by a brilliant choice of examples and the use of parody.

BIBL. Williams, *GRNSC* vi (1972); E. Fraenkel, *Horace* (1957); N. Rudd, *The Satires of Horace* (1966); *Odes i*, ed. Nisbet and Hubbard (1970), *ii* (1978); *Ars Poetica*, ed. C. O. Brink (1963, 1971).

Horatius Cocles

A legendary one-eyed ('Cocles') hero, Horatius resisted *Porsenna's advance until the Romans could destroy the Tiber bridge. In *Polybius, Cocles then drowned, but in later sources survived, lame, a version perhaps inspired by his identification with a statue in the Area Vulcani.

BIBL. PW viii. 2331 ff.; Ogilvie, *Livy*, 258 f.; E. Gjerstad, *Opuscula Romana* vii (1969) 149 ff.

Horatius Pulvillus, Marcus Consul 509 (?), 507 (?) BC.

Horatius reputedly dedicated the Capitoline temple either in his alleged first consulship or, in one version (*Varro's ?), in his second (omitted by some sources), or as *pontifex*. Whether his name was recorded on the temple (perhaps rededicated after the expulsion of the kings) is uncertain. Alföldi suggests that the temple was in fact rebuilt after the Gallic Sack and its (re)dedication belongs to M. Horatius, consular tribune 378 BC.

BIBL. A. Alföldi, *Early Rome and the Latins* (1963) 323 ff.; PW viii. 2401 ff.; K. Hanell, *Les Origines de la République romaine* (1966/7) 40; H. Riemann, *Röm. Mitt.* lxxvi (1969) 110 ff.

Hormisdas Renegade Persian prince, 4th century AD.

Brother of *Shapur II, Hormisdas fled to the Romans in 324. He served as a cavalry commander under *Constantius II, and accompanied him to Rome in 357. He was a general on *Julian's Persian expedition (363), and Julian may have intended, if successful, to place him on the Persian throne.

BIBL. *PLRE* i, Hormisdas 2; Ammianus XVI. x. 16.

Hortensius (114–50 BC) Orator, consul 69 BC.

Quintus Hortensius Hortalus was already Rome's leading orator when *Cicero's career began. They often clashed, notably in the case of *Verres, but later often worked in tandem and became personal friends. Hortensius was Rome's leading exponent of the florid Asianic style, reinforced by extravagant gestures.

BILB. *ORF* 310 ff.; Kennedy, *Rhetoric*, 96 ff.

Hortensius, Quintus Dictator *c.* 287 BC.

Hortensius ended a plebeian secession by legislation which made plebiscites binding on the Roman State. He also made alterations to the calendar, perhaps introducing *dies comitiales* (prescribed days on which assemblies might be held).

BIBL. PW viii. 2467 f.; A. K. Michels, *The Calendar of the Roman Republic* (1967) 103 ff.; J. Bleicken, *Das Volkstribunat der klassischen Republik* (2nd ed., 1968).

Hosius (Ossius) (*c.* AD 257–357) Bishop of Cordova.

Made bishop of Cordova *c.* 296, Hosius suffered in the Great Persecution and took part in the Council of Elvira (*c.* 306), before becoming *Constantine's Christian adviser, from about 313. Constantine, in an attempt to settle the *Arian controversy, sent him on a mission to Alexandria, and it may have been he who, at the Council of Nicaea in 325, suggested the notorious term *homoousios*. Under the Arian *Constantius II he presided at the Council of Sardica in 343, but in 355 was banished to Sirmium for supporting *Athanasius. From exile he wrote to Constantius asserting the Church's independence from secular control. In 357, aged nearly 100, he ceded to pressure to sign an Arian document, but repudiated it before his death.

BIBL. *ODCC* Hosius.

Hostilian Caesar *c.* AD 250–1, Augustus 251.

Younger son of Trajan *Decius, Gaius Valens Hostilianus Messius Quintus was made Augustus by *Trebonianus Gallus after his father's death, but himself died of plague after a very short reign.

BIBL. PW Messius 11.

Hydatius Spanish bishop and chronicler *c.* AD 400–470.

The career of Hydatius, bishop of Aquae Flaviae (north-west Spain) from 427, reflects the problems of Roman officials living under barbarian

domination. In 431 he appealed to *Aëtius against the Suevi, to some effect, and, in 460, he was imprisoned by the Suevi for suspected conspiracy but released after three months. His *Chronicle*, a continuation of *Jerome down to 469, is a major source for Spanish affairs during this period.

BIBL. Hydace, *Chronique*, SC 218–19 (1974).

Hyginus, Gaius Julius (*c.* 64 BC–AD 17) Scholar.

A Spanish (?) freedman of *Augustus, Hyginus was Palatine librarian from 28 (?) BC, friend of *Ovid, and commentator upon *Virgil; he was also a prolific antiquarian and agricultural writer. The works on mythology, astronomy, and land-surveying which go under the name of 'Hyginus' are not the Augustan scholar's work.

Hypatia (died AD 415) Pagan philosopher.

Despite the violence against paganism in Alexandria fostered by Bishop *Theophilus, Hypatia flourished there as the *doyenne* of the Neoplatonic school of philosophy; the Christian Platonist *Synesius was among her pupils. She became one of the rare pagan 'martyrs' when she was lynched by a Christian mob in 415, an act which appalled many Christians, including the historian *Socrates.

BIBL. *PW* ix. 242–9.

Iamblichus (before AD 250–after 319) Neoplatonist philosopher.

Iamblichus came of an old family in Syria, where he spent much of his life, surrounded by pupils from all over the Near East. He wrote commentaries on Plato and Aristotle, and works on the mathematical basis of reality which probably formed part of a complete course in Pythagorean science. Iamblichus was admired both as a philosopher and as one 'skilled in praying to the gods'. His prayer did not lack warmth, but he found that to sustain divine sympathy he required theurgical techniques considered demeaning by more contemplative Neoplatonists, like *Porphyry, with whom he had studied philosophy. Theurgical technology was not narrowly Hellenic: Iamblichus drew on what he thought were ancient and well-tried traditions from Egypt and Assyria for methods of influencing the myriads of gods and demons that affect life on earth, and to prepare the soul for union with the divine. The 'godlike Iamblichus' was devoted to his disciples, some of whom were to influence the Emperor *Julian.

BIBL. Jamblique: *Les Mystères d'Égypte*, ed. E. des Places (Budé, 1966); *Iamblichii in Platonis Dialogos Commentariorum Fragmenta*, ed. J. M. Dillon (1973).

Icilius, Lucius Tribune 456, 455, and 449 BC.

Icilius supposedly sponsored a plebiscite which opened the Aventine for settlement (456 BC) (according to *Dionysius of Halicarnassus it was publicly displayed in Diana's Aventine temple). Later he was depicted as the fiancé of *Verginia and plebeian leader against the Second Decemvirate.

BIBL. PW ix. 851 ff.; Ogilvie, *Livy*, 446 f.

St Ignatius (*c*. AD 35–107) Martyr-bishop of Antioch.

Author of seven letters of encouragement to the Christian churches (composed *en route* to martyrdom at Rome, perhaps in the Colosseum) Ignatius was a man passionately devoted to the ideal of martyrdom and a staunch supporter of episcopal authority—a fact which lent fire to the prolonged controversy over the authenticity of his works.

BIBL. Text: Loeb, *Apostolic Fathers*.

Ingenuus Ursurper in Pannonia AD 260.

Governor of Pannonia, Ingenuus was proclaimed emperor by the Moesian legions after the capture of *Valerian in 260, but was defeated by *Gallienus at Mursa that same year.

BIBL. *PIR* 123; *PLRE* i, Ingenuus 1.

St Irenaeus (*c*. AD 130–200) Bishop of Lyons.

Probably a native of Smyrna, Irenaeus sat at the feet of *Polycarp, studied at Rome, and eventually became a presbyter at Lyons. He was on a mission to Rome when the persecution occurred at Lyons in 177, and on his return he succeeded to the see, left vacant by the death of his predecessor in the persecution. He was a ferocious defender of orthodox Christian thought; his major work, *Against all Heresies*, is an important attack on Gnosticism, written in Greek.

BIBL. H. Chadwick, *The Early Church*; J. Lawson, *The Biblical Theology of St Irenaeus* (1948).

Javolenus Priscus Jurist, consul AD 86.

Gaius Octavius Tidius Tossianus Lucius Javolenus Priscus was a famous jurist, head of the Sabinian school. This is why, among other provincial commands, he was made one of the first two *iuridici* (governor's legal deputy) of Britain (with Salvius Liberalis), perhaps to help in welding the former client kingdom of *Cogidubnus to the province.

BIBL. *OCD*; Pliny, *Letters*, vi. 15 (amusing anecdote); *PIR* I 14.

St Jerome (*c*. AD 345–420) Christian scholar and controversialist.

Eusebius Hieronymus (Jerome) was born near Aquileia and educated in Latin literature and rhetoric at Rome, where he was baptized. He lived in a monastic community with his fellow-student *Rufinus and others, before going to Antioch (*c*. 374). Here he dreamed that Christ condemned him for his devotion to classical literature ('You are a

Ciceronian, not a Christian'), and he withdrew to the desert, where he learnt Hebrew. Quarrels with the other hermits ('worse than the wild beasts') forced him to return to Antioch (*c*. 377) and then to Constantinople (*c*. 379), where he translated *Eusebius' *Chronicle* and continued it to 378. In 382 he returned to Rome, where he became secretary to Pope *Damasus, at whose request he began his major work: the revision or replacement of existing Latin translations of the Bible, which, after criticism at the time, was gradually accepted as the 'Vulgate'. He also became spiritual adviser to aristocratic ladies, notably St Paula and her daughter St *Eustochium, but his growing unpopularity after Damasus' death forced him to leave 'Babylon' (385).

With Paula and Eustochium Jerome toured the Holy Land (385/6) and in 386 settled at Bethlehem, where Paula built a monastery and convent. Here they remained for the rest of their lives, Jerome's being spent in intense scholarly activity, translating the Bible and writing commentaries, and engaging with relish in controversies. Thus he demolished two critics of his own brand of ascetic Christianity, *Jovinian (*c*. 393) and *Vigilantius (406), the latter in a coarse lampoon composed overnight. His allegorical interpretation of Scripture drew on *Origen, but he criticized St *Ambrose, who did likewise, for 'decking himself out, like an ugly crow, with borrowed plumes', and refused him an entry in *Famous Men* (392/3): this was a collection of biographies of Christian writers which cites only one work of St *John Chrysostom, and concludes with a long list of Jerome's own to date. Origen is described as an 'immortal genius', but in 393 Jerome accepted him as a heretic on the authority of St *Epiphanius; a bitter quarrel followed with the bishop of Jerusalem (who excommunicated him) and his oldest friend, Rufinus. After a reconciliation in 397, the quarrel was renewed by Rufinus' pointed reminder of Jerome's former admiration for Origen (398). Jerome also supported *Theophilus of Alexandria when he deposed John Chrysostom for his alleged sympathy with Origenist refugees from Egypt; when Pope Innocent came to John's support, Jerome translated Theophilus' denunciation of John as a 'murderer' (404).

The fall of Rome (410), 'when the whole world perished in one city', stunned Jerome, but he was able to resume work on Ezekiel with the thought that the 'scorpion' (Rufinus) was now dead. Refugees poured into Palestine, among them *Pelagius, whose teaching provoked some of Jerome's last writings. He died at Bethlehem, 30 September 420. He had been the most learned scholar of his time, master of three languages, and above all a brilliant Latin stylist who excelled in fiction and satire. He was a good hater. He was not an original thinker like St *Augustine, but he was a

Rossano Gospels, 6th century AD: Christ before Pilate, Death of Judas. Rossano, Archiepiscopal Museum.

Christ with pomegranates (divine symbol): 4th-century AD mosaic, Hinton St Mary (Dorset). London, Brit. Mus.

supremely articulate champion of western Catholicism and ascetic practice.

BIBL. J. N. D. Kelly, *Jerome* (1975).

Jesus Christ

This account is concerned mainly with the common ground between the versions of the Evangelists and other sources for the history of the time.

The Evangelists give two dates for the birth of Christ, both remarkably precise but contradictory. It is unlikely that Sulpicius *Quirinius was governor of Syria, or that he could have conducted a census (Lk. 2:2) in Judaea, before AD 6; while the death of *Herod the Great (Mt. 2:1) occurred in 4 BC. No entirely satisfactory way of explaining the mistake, let alone establishing the truth, has ever been found. The preaching of John the Baptist, which is associated with the beginning of the three years of Christ's public ministry, is dated between 27 and 29.

Christ's own teaching, while founded securely on Judaism, in emphasizing the coming of the Kingdom of God and his personal role in Messianic terms, rapidly proved uncongenial to and incompatible with the religious establishment; the Jewish leaders were therefore able to play on Roman fears for public order and persuade the governor *Pontius Pilatus to condemn him to be crucified, after a trial of which the Evangelists preserve a historically convincing account. His chosen followers became convinced of his

Resurrection on the third day after this, and it is undoubted that they were sufficiently inspired to spread and interpret the teachings of their master with a fervour and a success for which it is hard to find a parallel. The Acts of the Apostles (whose veracity may be estimated from its detailed knowledge of contemporary Roman administrative procedures) testifies to this. The new sect was causing trouble at Rome itself under *Claudius (if *Suetonius' words 'at the instigation of Chrestus' are to be so interpreted) and *Nero (Tac. *Ann.* xv); these second-century accounts derive from earlier hostile Roman sources. *Pliny the Younger, describing the well-established Church of Bithynia in the last years of *Trajan, is a more important if only partially informed witness.

See St *Peter, St *Paul.

BIBL. Sherwin-White, *Roman Society and Roman Law in the New Testament* (1963).

St John Chrysostom Bishop of Constantinople AD 398–404.

John 'the Golden-mouthed', an officer's son born at Antioch *c.* 347, was one of the pagan orator *Libanius' best pupils, and his brilliance as a preacher has made him a classic of the Orthodox Church. After his health failed as a monk (*c.* 373–*c.* 381), he returned to Antioch as deacon and (386) priest; hundreds of sermons survive, among them 'socialist' tracts denouncing rich men without conscience. He was arrested by order of *Eutropius and forcibly consecrated bishop of Constantinople

St John Chrysostom: tympanum mosaic (early 10th century) in the nave of Haghia Sophia, Istanbul.

(26 February 398), to the annoyance of the bishop of Alexandria, *Theophilus. John's eloquence, austerity, and reforming zeal won him an enormous following, but made him unpopular with his clergy and at court. When the Empress *Eudoxia arranged a council to hear Egyptian monks' complaints against Theophilus, Theophilus packed it with his own supporters, and deposed John instead (July 403). He was soon recalled, but his outspokenness

alienated Eudoxia again, and he was exiled (June 404) to the Taurus mountains. Here he wrote hundreds of letters, and won Pope Innocent's support, but in 407, while he was being moved to harsher conditions, his death was hastened by deliberate maltreatment (14 September).

BIBL. H. Chadwick, *The Early Church*, ch. 13.

Josephus (born AD 37/8) Jewish historian and polemicist.

A native of Jerusalem, Josephus was a supporter of Rome, but nevertheless defended Jotapata during the Jewish War till its fall in 67. Pardoned by *Vespasian, he was favourably treated, assisted *Titus at the siege of Jerusalem, moved to Rome, and remained securely in favour under Vespasian, Titus, and *Domitian. The *Jewish War* he wrote first in Aramaic (*c.* 73), then (75/6) in Greek, covering the period 175 BC–AD 66 in outline and the Jewish War in great detail. The *Jewish Antiquities* (finished 93/4) in 20 books cover the whole of Jewish history down to AD 66. He also wrote, late in life, a polemical autobiography in answer to frequent accusations, and two books *Against Apion*, in reply to current anti-Semitic slanders.

BIBL. See Schürer, *History of the Jewish People* (revised Vermes and Millar), i (1973) 43 ff.

Procession with spoils from the siege of Jerusalem (described by Josephus): Arch of *Titus, *c.* AD 90.

Jotapianus Usurper *c.* AD 248–9.

Jotapianus came to power either in Cappadocia or Syria as a result of the severe fiscal policies of Gaius Julius Priscus, brother of *Philip I, but was soon killed by his troops.

BIBL. PW Jotapianus.

Gold coin (*solidus*) of the Emperor Jovian, wearing pearl diadem with rosettes.

Jovian Emperor AD 363–4.

A general's son born at Belgrade (331), Flavius Jovianus served on *Julian's Persian expedition as a staff officer. When Julian was killed, the generals disagreed and Jovian was proclaimed by a faction. He extricated the army at the cost of a humiliating treaty, but soon after (17 February 364), *en route* for Constantinople, he was accidentally poisoned by charcoal fumes.

BIBL. *PLRE* i, Iovianus 3.

Jovinian Unorthodox monk (floruit AD 390s).

Jovinianus was a monk at Rome whose view of baptismal regeneration made him reject contemporary asceticism: all Christians who had not lapsed would receive the same reward; there was no superior virtue in being celibate rather than married, or in fasting rather than eating with thankfulness. He was excommunicated by Pope Siricius and St *Ambrose, and deported to an island for holding illicit services. His teaching is chiefly known from St *Jerome's venomous treatise of refutation (*c.* 393).

BIBL. J. N. D. Kelly, *Jerome* (1975).

Juba II King of Mauretania 25 BC *c.* AD 23.

As a child Juba featured in *Caesar's triumph, and was brought up in Italy. He fought with Octavian, was restored to his kingdom in 25 BC, and married the daughter of *Antony and *Cleopatra. He was an intimate of *Augustus and one of the more important client-rulers; but the Elder *Pliny records that he was even more famous for his scholarship than for his government.

BIBL. *FGH* 275.

Jugurtha King of Numidia 118–105 BC.

An ambitious but illegitimate descendant of

*Masinissa, Jugurtha attained royal status through the patronage of *Scipio Aemilianus, under whom he served at Numantia (133 BC). His diligent cultivation of an extensive range of senatorial connections allowed him to pursue his further ambitions with the minimum of Roman interference. Thus by 112 he had united the whole Numidian kingdom under his rule by eliminating his legitimate brothers, but his massacre of Italian residents at Cirta in that year prompted Rome to declare war. He put up a long resistance, and in 109 a scandal arose at Rome over the corrupt and incompetent conduct of the war. At the instigation of *Mamilius many prominent senators were prosecuted for receiving bribes from Jugurtha both before and during the war. These bribes were really the traditional gifts of a client to his Roman patrons, who caused offence by putting their client's interests before their patriotic duty. After military successes by *Metellus Numidicus, the war was eventually finished by *Marius in 105, and Jugurtha was executed at Rome the following year.

BIBL. Allen, *C. Phil.* xxxiii (1938) 90 ff.; Syme, *Sallust*.

Julia (1) (died 54 BC) Daughter of Caesar.

The daughter of *Caesar by Cornelia, daughter of *Cinna, Julia was given in marriage to *Pompey in 59 BC. Her personality seems genuinely to have preserved the political alliance between the two dynasts, since both were devoted to her. Her death in childbirth in 54 brought the Civil War appreciably nearer. She received extravagant funeral honours from the people, being buried in the sacred Campus Martius.

BIBL. Gelzer, *Caesar: Politician and Statesman* (1968).

Julia (2) (39 BC–AD 14) Daughter of Augustus.

Only child of *Augustus, by his first wife Scribonia, Julia was brought up in the traditional way and married first *Marcellus, then *Agrippa, to whom she bore Gaius and Lucius *Caesar, *Julia (3), *Agrippina (the Elder), and *Agrippa Postumus. In 11 BC she married *Tiberius, with whom she soon quarrelled. A scandal of enormous proportions involving Iullus *Antonius and others led to her exile for adultery in 2 BC. She died, still in exile, in AD 14. She was famous for her kindness and sense of humour.

BIBL. Suetonius, *Augustus* 63; Syme, *Rom. Rev.,* 425–7; Levick, *Latomus* (1972) 779.

Julia (3) (*c.* 19 BC–AD 28) Granddaughter of Augustus.

Daughter of *Agrippa and *Julia (2), and wife of Lucius Aemilius Paullus, Julia was condemned to perpetual exile in AD 8 for adultery. Support from *Livia kept her alive until AD 28.

BIBL. Tac. *Ann.* iv. 71.

Portrait bust of the Empress Julia Domna. Munich, Glyptothek.

Julia Domna Empress AD 193–211.

Born in Syria into a family of priestly rulers of Emesa, Julia Domna became the wife of Septimius *Severus in 187 and had two children: *Caracalla in 188 and *Geta in 189. She became empress in 193, and was renowned for her beauty and intelligence. She suffered from the hatred and contempt of *Plautianus, praetorian prefect 202–5, and retreated to the study of philosophy. She gathered round her a group of literary figures which may have included *Philostratus and *Ulpian. In 208 she accompanied Severus on his British campaign. After Severus' death in 211 his two sons, bitter rivals, became co-emperors, but Caracalla, having persuaded Julia to summon them for a reconciliation, stabbed Geta to death in her arms. Julia committed suicide in 217, after Caracalla's death and *Macrinus' proclamation as emperor.
BIBL. *PIR* I 663; Birley, *Severus*.

Julia Maesa Augusta AD 218–c. 224/5.

Sister of the Empress *Julia Domna, Julia Maesa married the consular Julius Avitus and had two daughters: *Julia Soaemias, the mother of the Emperor *Elagabalus, and *Julia Mammaea, the mother of *Severus Alexander. In 218 she engineered a plot whereby the troops in Syria proclaimed Elagabalus emperor and *Macrinus was overthrown. The real power behind the throne from 218 to 224/5, she was instrumental in making

Severus Alexander emperor after his adoption by Elagabalus, but did not survive long into the reign.
BIBL. *PIR* I 678; Birley, *Severus*; Herodian (Loeb).

Julia Mammaea Augusta AD 222–35.

Niece of the Empress *Julia Domna and sister of *Julia Soaemias, Julia Avita Mammaea married Gessius Marcianus and was the mother of the Emperor *Severus Alexander. After the death of her mother Julia Maesa, and later those of *Elagabalus and his mother *Julia Soaemias, she emerged as the real power behind the throne and totally dominated her son. She was notorious for her avarice, even Alexander deplored some of the property confiscations she engineered. Her power and influence are manifest in the honorific titles she was awarded by the young ruler: 'Mother of the emperor, of the army, of the senate, and of the nation'. She was slain with her son while on campaign, after his troops had abandoned him as a result of *Maximinus' mutiny.
BIBL. *PIR* I 649; Herodian (Loeb); Birley, *Severus*.

Julia Paula Empress AD 219–220/1.

The first of *Elagabalus' three wives, Julia Cornelia Paula married him in 219 and was divorced in 220/1.
BIBL. *PIR* I 660.

Coin type of Julia Soaemias, mother of the Emperor Elagabalus.

Julia Soaemias Augusta AD 218–222.

Elder daughter of *Julia Maesa and (Julius) Bassianus, Julia Soaemias Bassiana was born in Syria, became the wife of Sextus Varius and mother of the Emperor *Elagabalus. She and her son were murdered by the soldiers in 222, in reaction against his excesses and his jealousy of *Severus Alexander.
BIBL. Birley, *Severus*; *PIR* I 704; Herodian (Loeb).

Julian (the Apostate) Emperor AD 355–63.

Born at Constantinople in 331/2, Flavius Claudius Julianus, last pagan emperor, was nephew of *Constantine (see stemma), son of his half-brother Julius *Constantius and Basilina (who died soon after his birth). After Constantine's death in 337, Julian's father and several other relations fell

Gold coin of the Emperor Julian, wearing pearl diadem.

victim to a massacre instigated by *Constantius II (q.v.). Julian and his half-brother *Gallus were spared because of their youth. He grew up in the shadow of the Emperor Constantius' suspicion, being interned for six years (342–8?) with Gallus in the remote villa of Macellum in Cappadocia; he became a 'reader' in the Church, but continued avidly reading the pagan classics. Returning to Constantinople and Nicomedia, he studied under leading Neoplatonist philosophers, notably *Maximus of Ephesus, who completed his conversion to a mystical form of paganism associated with magic, though he concealed it for ten years.

Late in 355, after further studies in Athens, he was summoned to Milan, created Caesar (6 November), married to Constantius' sister Helena, and sent to Gaul to cope with disastrous invasions by the Franks and Alamanni. In annual campaigns, crowned by the outstanding victory over the Alamanni at Strasbourg in 357, he restored the Rhine frontier. In 360 Constantius attempted to withdraw some of Julian's best troops for the Persian wars, but on the march through Paris, where Julian was wintering, they mutinied and acclaimed him Augustus. Constantius refused to confirm this, and, late in 361, Julian marched east against him. Constantius left Antioch to counter his offensive, but died of a fever in Asia Minor.

Julian entered Constantinople (December 361), and embarked on a programme of reform and purge. The Commission of Chalcedon disposed of Constantius' most hated servants—and others (see *Ursulus). Julian proclaimed freedom of worship for pagans and Christians, and recalled banished clergy. The palace staff was greatly reduced, as were the State secretaries and agents, virtually secret police. He diminished some taxes and arrears of debts to the treasury, and tightened imperial control of finance. Many reforms benefited the cities and their governing councils, which were in a state of decline.

Portrait statue of Julia Mammaea, mother of the Emperor *Severus Alexander.

The restored city councils were to be the social base for Julian's pagan revival. The reopened and refurbished temples were served by a priesthood remodelled as a pagan 'Church', with a high priest heading each provincial hierarchy under the *pontifex maximus*, the emperor. Julian contributed the *Hymn to the King Sun* and other writings

Portrait statue of the pagan Emperor Julian the Apostate. Paris, Louvre.

towards a unified pagan theology of Neoplatonic and solar monotheism. He sought to include the whole of Greek pagan culture in his religion of 'Hellenism', giving back to pagan literature its religious content by excluding Christians from teaching it. This was bitterly resented by educated Christians like *Gregory of Nazianzus. The army was wooed with sacrificial banquets and bribes, and had to offer incense on pay-day. Pagans were given systematic preferment, and anti-Christian actions, including lynchings (see *George), were lukewarmly condemned. Despite his refusal to create martyrs, Julian's attitude to the Christians verged on persecution, and he attacked Christianity bitterly in *Against the Galilaeans*.

In 362–3 he stayed at Antioch to prepare for a great expedition against Persia. A famine, caused by drought and the presence of the army, was exacerbated by Julian's import of corn and clumsy fixing of prices. The city council's failures over this and other things set it and the emperor at loggerheads, and its failure to celebrate (being largely Christian) the festival of Apollo at Daphne, and the burning of the temple there, made matters worse. Julian's ostentatious asceticism and scorn for the popular pleasures of theatre and race-course irritated the Christian populace. Taunted in popular verses, he wrote the *Misopogon* (*Beard-Hater*), in which he began by mocking himself and then castigated the people of Antioch.

The Persian expedition (363) was at first a brilliant success, as the huge army moved down the Euphrates and across to the Tigris. Several fortresses and cities were taken, and a major battle won. But the failure to take Ctesiphon forced the Romans to retreat up the Tigris and Julian was killed in a skirmish. *Jovian made peace with the Persians, and brought Julian's body back to Tarsus.

Julian was an accomplished writer of Greek, and his works are a rich source of information about the man and his policies. In addition to those mentioned, they include panegyrics, letters, and a satire on previous emperors (*The Caesars*). Though tainted by narrow fanaticism, his lofty spirituality made him a pagan saint; and the intelligence, idealism, and energy which he devoted to a doomed revival of past glories have made him a romantic figure for posterity.

BIBL. J. Bidez, *Vie de l'empereur Julien* (2nd ed., 1965); R. Browning, *The Emperor Julian* (1975); G. W. Bowersock, *Julian the Apostate* (1978) (but see reviews); Bowder, *Age of Constantine and Julian* (1978).

Julian the Theurgist 2nd century AD.
Julian, the son of Julian the Chaldaean, and contemporary of *Marcus Aurelius, was considered co-author with his father of the *Chaldaean Oracles*,

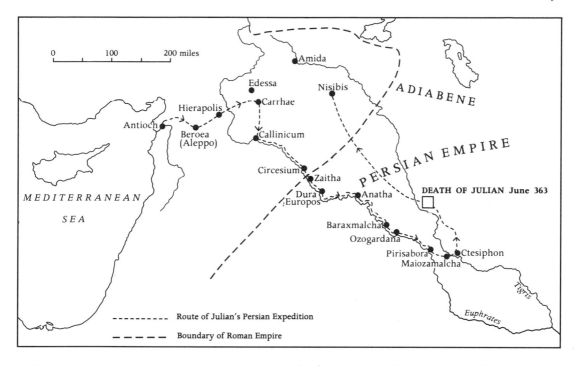

Julian's Persian Expedition, AD 363.

a very important collection of theosophical dicta
inspiring commentaries by *Porphyry, *Iamblichus,
and *Proclus, and influencing the work of writers
such as *Arnobius, *Victorinus, *Synesius,
and *Martianus.
  BIBL. H. Lewy, *Chaldaean Oracles and Theurgy*
(1956); E. R. Dodds, *JRS* xxxvii (1947) 55.

Julianus, Marcus Aurelius Sabinus Usurper
AD 283–5 (?).
  Confusion exists over his exact name, whether
there was one Julianus or two, and the date of his
usurpation, but he is attested by Aurelius *Victor,
Zosimus, and coins.
  BIBL. *PLRE* i, Iulianus 24; *PIR* A 1538; *RIC* v. 2.

Julianus, Salvius Jurist, consul AD 148.
  Perhaps from Hadrumetum in Africa, Publius
Salvius Julianus was a distinguished lawyer, a
pupil of *Javolenus Priscus and the last recorded
head of the Sabinian School of jurists. He held a
number of important posts, including
governorships of Germania Inferior, Hispania
Citerior, and Africa. He was an imperial counsellor
to *Hadrian and *Antoninus Pius and was entrusted
by the former with the important task of revising
and codifying the Praetor's Edict. He was the
author of a *Digest* in 90 books which exercised a
great formative influence on the development of
classical Roman law.
  BIBL. A. Guarino, *Salvius Julianus* (1946);

Jolowicz, *Roman Law*; W. Kunkel, *Herkunft und
soziale Stellung der römischen Juristen* (2nd ed.,
1969).

Julius Bishop of Rome AD 337–52.
  A strong supporter of orthodoxy who helped to
rally the West against *Arianism, Pope Julius
welcomed and championed *Athanasius, *Marcellus
of Ancyra, and other expelled eastern bishops, and
convoked the Council of Sardica (343). He worked
for the right of appeal to the see of Rome. His
church foundations included the predecessor of S.
Maria in Trastevere.
See also *Liberius
  BIBL. *ODCC* Julius I.

Julius Verus Consul *c.* AD 151.
  Of Dalmatian origin, Gnaeus Julius Verus was a
distinguished general and intimate of *Marcus
Aurelius and Lucius *Verus. He perhaps served as a
junior officer in Judaea in 134 under his uncle
Sextus Julius Severus. After his consulship he
governed Germania Inferior, then Britain (*c.* 155–8),
and finally Syria during the crucial period of the
Parthian War (162/6). He was appointed to a second
consulship for 180, but died before entering office.
  BIBL. Birley, *Marcus*; id., *Fasti* (forthcoming);
PIR I 618.

Justin Martyr (*c.* AD 100–65) Christian theologian.
  One of the earliest of the great Christian
apologists, Justin was born in Samaria, studied
philosophy, and became a Christian at about the
age of 30. He first taught at Ephesus, then moved
to Rome and opened a Christian school there

(*Tatian was a pupil). His first *Apology* (c. 155) was addressed to *Antoninus Pius, *Marcus Aurelius and Lucius *Verus, his second (c. 161) to the senate. He also wrote a *Dialogue with Trypho the Jew*. Denounced as a Christian c. 165, he refused to recant, and was scourged and beheaded (an account of his martyrdom is preserved). His works represent an early attempt to explain Christianity in terms acceptable to a philosophically educated audience.

BIBL. H. Chadwick, *Early Christian Thought and the Classical Tradition* (1966); L. W. Barnard, *Justin Martyr: His Life and Thought* (1967); H. Musurillo, *Acts of the Christian Martyrs* (1972).

Justina Empress c. AD 370–88.

Second wife of *Valentinian I, to whom she bore a son (*Valentinian II) and three daughters, Justina was of aristocratic birth and had been married to the usurper *Magnentius. After Valentinian's death she dominated her son's court, but when it moved to Milan (c. 383) her *Arian beliefs forced her into a humiliating struggle with St *Ambrose, who called her 'Jezebel'. When *Maximus invaded Italy (387), she was forced to flee with her son; she persuaded *Theodosius I to restore them, but died during the war (388).

BIBL. *PLRE* i, Iustina.

Juvenal Satirist, floruit early 2nd century AD.

Decimus Junius Juvenalis, a native of Aquinum, is the most famous satirist of Antiquity. Fifteen poems survive, the first nine of which present a vivid picture of life in Rome at the end of the first century AD. The later satires are more in the nature of moral essays on topics such as the desire for revenge. Dr Johnson's famous poem 'London' was in imitation of Juvenal's third satire, considered by some to be his masterpiece, on the many tribulations of living in Rome. The sixth satire is a scathing attack on women. Juvenal's biography cannot be written, and attempts to do so, from the biographies compiled in late Antiquity (deriving from that printed in the O.C.T.) to more modern works, are seriously misleading. *Martial addressed to him three epigrams (vii. 24, 91; xii. 18), and two inscriptions from Aquinum, now lost, *may* have referred to him. We are left with scant indications in the poems (notably xv, showing clear knowledge of Egypt) of this very private individual, and with internal evidence for his having written them between c. 110 and shortly after 127. The undue prominence given to satire i. 79, *facit indignatio versum* ('an intolerance of circumstances prompts my verse') has given rise to a highly-coloured picture of Juvenal as a passionate critic of contemporary Roman society. Falsely: many of the specific individuals he condemns were 'ancient history' by the time he wrote, and recently resuscitated in the pages of *Tacitus; a large

number of his most brilliant vignettes are reworkings of Martial; his first poem opens with an elaborate piece not of social condemnation but of literary in-fighting. It is best to view Juvenal as a superb rhetorician and a skilled declaimer, a master of parody, epigram, and allusion.

BIBL. Coffey, *Satire* 119 ff.; note an excellent Penguin translation (Green). A commentary by Courtney is eagerly awaited.

Juvenal of Jerusalem Bishop AD 422–58.

A leading participant in the Christological controversies of the fifth century, though largely for political reasons, Juvenal's purpose was to raise his see to the level of a 'patriarchate'. By favouring *Cyril of Alexandria at Ephesus in 431 he secured recognition of his aims, and continued to support Cyril's successor Dioscurus at the Second Council of Ephesus in 449. When the decisions of this council were overturned at Chalcedon (451), Juvenal changed sides; he retained his patriarchate, but was forced to overcome a rebellion among the monks in his diocese, who resented his *volte-face*.

BIBL. E. Honigmann, *Dumbarton Oaks Papers* v (1950).

Juvencus Christian poet, floruit c. AD 330.

Gaius Vettius Aquilinus Juvencus, a noble Spanish priest, wrote a fine hexameter version of the New Testament (based primarily on Matthew) during the reign of *Constantine.

BIBL. *Juvenci Opera*, ed. Huemer (CSEL xxiv (1891)).

Labeo, Marcus Antistius (born c. 48 BC) Jurist.

A pupil of *Cicero's and *Horace's friend Gaius Trebatius Testa, Labeo was offered a suffect consulship by Augustus c. AD 5, but refused it. He was a political conservative with a genius for embarrassing the imperial establishment, but was a bold and innovative lawyer.

See *Capito, C. Ateius

BIBL. Horsfall, *Historia*, 1974, 252 ff.

Laberius, Decimus (c. 106–43 BC) Mimographer.

A Roman knight and openly disrespectful towards Julius *Caesar, by whom he was publicly humiliated in July 46 (?), Laberius was a coarse, colourful, and vigorous writer for the stage.

See *Publilius Syrus (and mime)

BIBL. Fragments: *Mimi Romani* ed. Bonaria (1965) 38 ff.

Labienus Tribune 63 BC.

As a popular tribune in 63 BC, Titus Labienus co-operated closely with *Caesar and conducted the notorious prosecution of Gaius Rabirius for his part in the violent suppression of *Saturninus, 37 years previously. As legate he was Caesar's most senior and most trusted officer throughout the campaigns

in Gaul; but on the outbreak of civil war he joined
*Pompey, and fought on the republican side against
Caesar until his death at Munda in Spain in 45.
BIBL. Syme, *Rom. Rev.*; *RP* 7; Gruen, *Republic*.

Lactantius (AD 245/50–325) Christian man of letters.
Lucius Caecilius Firmianus Lactantius was
summoned from his native Africa by *Diocletian
(284–305) to teach Latin rhetoric at his New Rome
at Nicomedia in Asia Minor. As a Christian
Lactantius lost his job in the Great Persecution
(303–313), but wrote, in elegant Ciceronian prose,
two tracts and the seven books of the *Divine
Institutes*. Intended as permanent encyclopedia of
Christian apologetic, the *Institutes* also illuminates
the sufferings, the controversial issues, and,
especially in the apocalypse which ends the work,
the vivid expectations of Lactantius' hectic times. A
later pamphlet, the blood-curdling broadside *On
the Deaths of the Persecutors*, gives a first-hand
account of God's vengeance on the tyrants of the
Great Persecution. In old age Lactantius was tutor
to *Constantine's son *Crispus, and his last known
act was to dedicate an edition of the *Institutes* to
Constantine.
BIBL. Works, ed. Brandt and Laubmann (CSEL xix
& xxvii (1890–7)); Wlosok, *Laktanz und die
philosophische Gnosis* (1960).

Laelianus Gallic usurper AD 268.
Ulpius Cornelius Laelianus rebelled at Mainz
against the Gallic emperor *Postumus, who quickly
defeated and killed him.
BIBL. *PLRE* i, Laelianus.

Laelius ('the Wise') Consul 140 BC.
Gaius Laelius was closely associated with *Scipio
Aemilianus, serving with him at Carthage in 146 BC
and sharing his interests and attitudes. He was a
prominent member of the intellectual 'Scipionic
circle'. *Cicero considered him the outstanding
orator of his day (*Brutus* 82 f.), and used him as a
character in his dialogues. His learning and wide
cultural interests probably account for his
nickname 'Sapiens'. But *Plutarch ascribes this to
his wisdom in dropping his agrarian proposal in the
face of senatorial opposition: the most likely date
for this being his consulship (140). Laelius thus
anticipated Tiberius *Gracchus in tackling the
agrarian problem, but did not resort to Gracchus'
unconstitutional methods. He was in fact involved
in the persecution of Gracchus' supporters by the
consuls of 132.
BIBL. *ORF* 115 ff.; Astin, *Scipio Aemilianus*;
Rawson, *JRS* lxiii (1973) 161 ff.

Laetus, Aemilius Praetorian prefect AD 191 (?)–3.
A very important and influential adviser to
*Commodus in the last three years of his reign,
Quintus Aemilius Laetus was responsible for

recommending Septimius *Severus for the
governorship of Pannonia Superior in 191. He is
said to have taken part in gladiatorial combat with
Commodus. He was the mainspring of the plot in
192 to murder Commodus, to whose memory he
was particularly hostile, and was probably
responsible for the succession of *Pertinax. He may
finally have turned against Pertinax but was
probably not implicated in his murder. He was put
to death by *Didius Julianus in 193.
BIBL. Grosso, *Lotta*; Howe, *Pretorian Prefect*.

Laetus, (Julius) Senator 2nd–3rd century AD.
The identity of this Laetus is difficult to
establish, but he must be distinguished from
Quintus Aemilius *Laetus, *Commodus' murderer.
He may have been the general who saved the day
for *Severus at Lyons and later fought the
Parthians, but was finally put to death by Severus
because he was too popular with the soldiers; it is
generally thought, however, that there was more
than one Laetus.
BIBL. *PIR* I 373; Birley, *Severus*.

Laevinus, Marcus Valerius Consul 210 BC.
When *Hannibal's treaty with *Philip V was
discovered in 215 BC, Laevinus, as praetor, was
given the naval command in the Adriatic against
Philip, which he held until 210. He negotiated a
treaty with the Aetolian League which shocked
Greek opinion by its terms, but which was useful
to Rome, and drew *Attalus I of Pergamum into
Roman friendship. Because of this connection he
led an embassy to Attalus in 205 to acquire the
Magna Mater, an important cult-object which the
Romans wished to import from Anatolia to Italy. It
is unlikely that Laevinus had a second Macedonian
command before his death in 200.
BIBL. Errington, *Dawn of Empire*, esp. 111–14;
Briscoe, *Livy*, 60 f.

Lappius Maximus Consul AD 86 and 95.
Aulus Bucius Lappius Maximus suppressed the
revolt of L. Antonius *Saturninus against *Domitian
in AD 86, and brought the German War to a
successful close in 88–9. The reward for these
services might have been greater had he not caused
suspicion by the public-spirited destruction of
documents belonging to Saturninus, which could
have incriminated others.
BIBL. *PIR* L 84.

Lentulus, Gnaeus Cornelius Consul 14 BC.
Lentulus was certainly a figure of great
importance, but our knowledge of him is patchy.
Fighting the Getae he won triumphal insignia; this
campaign, like those against the Dacians and
Sarmatians, is probably to be dated to *Augustus'
middle years. It was probably he (not a relative)
who joined the younger *Drusus in quelling the

Illyricum mutiny of AD 14, although it appeared that he was not popular with the army (Tac. *Ann*. i. 27). In 24 *Tiberius was shocked to find that men of Lentulus' rank and distinction were not safe from accusations of treason; the charges were dropped, but Lentulus died a year later. *Tacitus praises his patience in poverty and moderation in prosperity (Augustus had endowed him with means befitting his patrician ancestry); but *Seneca calls him tongue-tied, stupid, and greedy.

BIBL. Tac. *Ann*. iv. 29, 44; *PIR* C 1379; Syme, *Danubian Papers* 3.

Lentulus Gaeticulus, Gnaeus Cornelius Consul AD 26.

Gaeticulus had the distinction of being the only important friend of *Sejanus to survive his fall. As governor of Germania Superior he won the army's affection by his mild discipline. In AD 39 he was killed by *Gaius, against whom he was probably conspiring.

BIBL. Balsdon, *Gaius*.

Leo Eastern emperor AD 457–74.

Raised by *Aspar from obscurity to succeed *Marcian in 457, Leo took ten years to assert his authority over his original patron. In 466 he began to promote the Isaurian Zeno, making him his son-in-law in 467. He took an active interest in western affairs, as shown in his appointments of *Anthemius in 467 and later of Julius *Nepos (473) as emperors and his refusal to recognize candidates of local western interests. However, his expedition against the Vandals in Africa (468) came to grief owing to the incompetence of his admiral, *Basiliscus, and bankrupted the treasury. Although freed from Aspar by the latter's assassination, with his son, in 470, Leo continued to have trouble with Aspar's Gothic federates. His main achievement, perhaps, was to survive for so long, despite military disaster, and hand on his power to a successor of his choice.

BIBL. Bury, *Later Empire*, I. x.; Stein, *Bas-Empire*, i. 353–61.

Pope Leo the Great Bishop of Rome AD 440–61.

As a consistent promoter of the authority of the Roman see, Leo is widely regarded as a founder of the modern papacy. Born in Rome, he was, even while a deacon, widely respected. He was elected bishop of Rome *in absentia* and consecrated on 29 September 440.

His most famous diplomatic achievement was the halting of *Attila's invasion of Italy (452) through negotiations at the River Mincius (some versions import a miraculous rejoining of the broken chains of St *Peter), but he also treated with *Geiseric after the sack of Rome (455). Laws of *Valentinian III against *Manichaeism in Rome (445) and in support of papal authority in Gaul (448), and the imperial family's endorsement of Leo's doctrinal stances against the East demonstrate the Pope's high standing at the imperial court.

Leo's opposition to heretics in Rome (445) and Spain (447) culminated in his dispatch of the famous 'Tome of Leo' to the Council of Ephesus (449), where he took issue with Nestorius and Eutyches on the nature of Christ. His Tome was suppressed at Ephesus but endorsed a year later by *Marcian and *Pulcheria and by the Council of Chalcedon in 451.

Through his many letters and sermons, Leo gave guidance to congregations and bishops on matters of doctrine, liturgy, and church discipline, down to his death in 461. He was buried, appropriately, in St Peter's.

BIBL. Leo, *Sermons* and *Letters*, Migne, PL 54–6; the *Sermons* also in SC 22 (1947), 49 (1957), 74 (1961), 200 (1973).

Left: Basilica Aemilia (interior): coin of *c*. 65 BC.
Right: silver *denarius* of Lepidus (3), *c*. 40 BC.

Lepidus (1), Marcus Aemilius Consul 187 and 175 BC.

One of the most distinguished senators of the second century BC, Lepidus was *princeps senatus* from his censorship (179 BC) until his death (152). As a junior member of C. Claudius *Nero's embassy in 200 he delivered the Roman ultimatum to *Philip V at Abydus; he may not have been a senator at this time. Lepidus' patronage of the Ptolemaic dynasty probably dates from this embassy, which also visited Egypt. The Egyptian connection, which was commemorated in the coinage of his descendants, is a matter of dispute.

Lepidus was particularly important in the conquest of Cisalpine Gaul, where he spent both his consulships and was responsible for settling large numbers of Roman citizens. The eponymous Via Aemilia, which ran from Rimini to Piacenza, dates from his first consulship. By these activities Lepidus acquired immense influence in north Italy, which his first-century descendants inherited and exploited. As censor in 179 with his ex-enemy M. *Nobilior he reformed the centuriate assembly and built the Basilica Aemilia.

BIBL. Ewins, *PBSR* (1952) 54 ff.; Scullard, *Politics*; Rich, *Collection Latomus* cxlix (1976) 73 ff., 82 ff., 128 ff.; Heinen, *ANRW* 1. i (1972) 647 ff.

Lepidus (2), Marcus Aemilius Consul 78 BC.

An ambitious noble, Lepidus supported *Cinna's regime in the 80s, but opportunely switched his allegiance to *Sulla and profited from the proscriptions. Sulla distrusted him, but Lepidus reached the consulship of 78 BC with help from the rising *Pompey and by his own considerable popularity. As consul on Sulla's death he made a bid for personal domination by proposing a popular programme of legislation which undermined the Sullan settlement and appealed to its many opponents. He was opposed by his conservative colleague *Catulus (2), but both consuls were sent to suppress a revolt in Etruria which had been provoked by Lepidus' propaganda. At this point Lepidus broke with the government, and sided with the rebels. He posed a considerable threat to the regime because of his substantial military support in Cisalpine Gaul (his province), where he had extensive family connections inherited from his grandfather, *Lepidus (1). But after the passing of the senate's emergency decree Lepidus was crushed in 77 by the forces of Catulus and Pompey.

BIBL. Badian, *Clientelae*, 275 ff.; Gruen, *Republic*, 12–17.

Lepidus (3), Marcus Aemilius Consul 46 and 42 BC; triumvir 43–36 BC.

An influential noble who reached the consulship of 46 BC as a Caesarian partisan, Lepidus emerged after Caesar's death as the most powerful of his supporters after *Antony. His control of the provinces of Gallia Narbonensis and Hispania Citerior (assigned by Caesar) and his inherited influence in Cisalpine Gaul placed him in a particularly strong position in 43 BC, when he joined with Antony against the republican forces, and subsequently entered into the Second Triumvirate with Antony and *Octavian. From this he secured not only far-reaching triumviral powers but also a second Spanish province, and in 42 he held a second consulship. But his influence in the triumvirate rapidly waned when Antony and Octavian assumed control of *Brutus' and *Cassius' eastern provinces. He was deprived of Spain and Gaul and retained only Africa, but in 36 he was able to bring 14 legions to Sicily to help Octavian against Sextus *Pompey. After receiving the surrender of most of Pompey's legions, Lepidus considered himself strong enough to challenge Octavian as an independent force. But his soldiers deserted *en masse* to Octavian, and he was summarily stripped of both triumviral powers and proconsular authority. He retired into private life, but retained the honorific office of *pontifex maximus* (assumed in 44) until his death in 12 BC.

BIBL. Syme, *Rom. Rev.*

Lepidus (4), Marcus Aemilius Consul AD 6.

Aemilius won triumphal insignia for brilliant campaigns in Pannonia with *Tiberius (AD 8–9). He was later successful as governor of Hispania Citerior, though less so as proconsul of Asia. His daughter Aemilia Lepida married *Drusus, son of *Germanicus—her father's influence with Tiberius protected her while he lived, but in AD 36 she was accused of adultery with a slave and killed herself.

BIBL. Tac. *Ann.* vi. 40; *PIR* A 369.

Libanius (AD 314–93) Orator and professor of rhetoric.

A member of an important family of Antioch in Syria, Libanius was the leading man of letters of his time in the Greek-speaking East. Educated at Antioch, then Athens (336–40), he taught briefly at Athens before establishing himself at Constantinople. A conspiracy of rivals forced him to leave (342/3), and he taught at Nicomedia (c. 343–8) until *Constantius II recalled him to Constantinople. A panegyric of Constantius and *Constans (*Or.* lix (348/9)) was well received, a succession of governors honoured him, and he was given property by the emperor. Refusing a post at Athens, he returned to Antioch (353) and became the city's official professor of rhetoric. In 360 he composed a panegyric of Antioch for the Olympic Games there (*Or.* xi).

When *Julian was in Antioch (362–3), Libanius became a friend and addressed speeches to him (see *Aristophanes). Although a zealous pagan, who later (385/6) wrote an eloquent defence of the temples (*Or.* xxx), he was never an intimate of Julian. His own paganism was more rational and cultural, and he wrote letters on behalf of Christians in difficulties under Julian, and gave asylum to one in his own house. He had Christians among his pupils, including St *John Chrysostom and probably St *Basil and St *Gregory of Nazianzus. He mourned Julian greatly, and composed a moving *Funeral Speech* (*Or.* xviii (365)).

The reign of *Valens (364–78) brought personal insecurity, but under *Theodosius I (378–95) he produced most of his extant speeches and was granted an honorary praetorian prefecture. He was spokesman for Antioch after the Riot of the Statues (387). His closing years were soured by disappointments and saddened by the deaths of his slave concubine—he never married—and their son.

Although Libanius' character was flawed by vanity, he was a tireless champion of rhetorical culture, attacked injustice and misuse of authority, and had a noble conception of the role of the orator. His voluminous works—over 1,500 letters (famous for their style) and numerous rhetorical exercises, in addition to the speeches—illuminate many aspects of contemporary life and government in the eastern Empire.

BIBL. *Libanius' Autobiography*, ed. and trans.

A. F. Norman (1965); Loeb of *Selected Works* (Norman) i–ii appeared (1969, 1977); Liebeschuetz, *Antioch* (1972).

Liberius Bishop of Rome AD 352–66.

Elected Pope in succession to *Julius, Liberius also took a firm stand in favour of *Athanasius and Nicene orthodoxy, and in 355 was exiled by the *Arian emperor *Constantius II. In 357 he finally agreed to sign an Arian creed, and was reinstated (358). He built the Basilica Liberiana on the Esquiline, reconstructed in the 430s and now S. Maria Maggiore.

BIBL. *ODCC* Liberius, Santa Maria Maggiore.

Licinius Emperor AD 308–324.

Three years of usurpations and internal wars followed *Diocletian's abdication in 305. In 308 *Galerius, the senior reigning Augustus, convoked a conference which tried, and failed, to settle the differences. At this conference Valerius Licinianus Licinius, an old comrade-in-arms who had served with Galerius against the Persians, was appointed an Augustus with responsibility for the Danube area. Galerius had hoped that he could abdicate after 20 years' rule in favour of his old friend, and when he died in 311 Licinius was at his bedside. In the ensuing scramble for Galerius' territories, Asia Minor fell to *Maximin Daia, who already

controlled Egypt and Syria. But in 313 Licinius made a marriage alliance with *Constantine, by then ruling in Rome; and, with an army fortified by prayer to the Most High God, he defeated Daia and tortured to death his enemy's anti-Christian advisers. The resulting partition of the Empire between Constantine and Licinius was not, however, to last. In 316 Constantine, attacking on the pretext that his colleague had restarted persecution of the Christians, won nearly all of Licinius' European possessions. In 324 Constantine again advanced through the Balkans and Byzantium. His fleet forced the passage of the Dardanelles, Licinius was decisively defeated, and Nicomedia, his capital, captured. Constantine granted him his life and gave him dinner, but killed him within a year. *Eusebius (of Caesarea) promptly excised all complimentary allusions to Licinius from the latest edition of his *Church History*. He had ruled well, keeping finances on a tight rein to encourage prosperity.

BIBL. *RIC* vi. 29–36 and vii. 64–70; T. D. Barnes, *JRS* lxiii (1973).

Livia (Julia Augusta) (58 BC–AD 29) Wife of Augustus.

Santa Maria Maggiore, Rome: interior. 5th-century AD reconstruction of Basilica of Liberius.

The father of Livia Drusilla, Marcus Livius Drusus Claudianus, was a man of excellent family connections, and in 43/2 BC Livia made a good marriage to Tiberius Claudius Nero, to whom she bore *Tiberius. With him she shared various dangers in the Civil War, and she was pregnant with the elder *Drusus when *Octavian arranged that she divorce her husband and marry him. The new match was a great success, except that there were no children. Livia played a very important role as wife of the *princeps*: she was able to demonstrate the matronly virtues which *Augustus was trying to foster in the State, since she was a woman of great dignity and legendary chastity. She also took a great interest in affairs of State, particularly in the various dynastic problems which occurred during her husband's long rule. Her son Tiberius was the object of most of her efforts, and the exile of *Agrippa Postumus, if not the deaths of *Marcellus and Gaius and Lucius *Caesar, are probably to be attributed to her. Her influence continued undiminished in Tiberius' reign—*Sejanus could only hope to succeed in his schemes after her death, and she seemed almost Tiberius' partner in power—they were worshipped together in the East. The most notable result of her influence

Gilded bronze portrait statue of Livia from Cartoceto, early 1st century AD. Ancona, Museo Nazionale.

at this time was the increasing danger in which *Agrippina (the Elder) and the rest of *Germanicus' family found themselves, and which derived in part from her hostility. She died in AD 29; in 42 she was formally deified by *Claudius. Perhaps the best comment on her is that of her great-grandson *Gaius, who no doubt saw beneath the austere public image—he called her 'a petticoat Odysseus'.

BIBL. Syme, *Rom. Rev.*, 340; Levick, *Tiberius*.

Livius Andronicus (died *c.* 200 BC) Founder of Latin literature.

Lucius Livius Andronicus a ((?) half-) Greek from Tarentum came to Rome as a captive and took his patron's name. His plays, in which he acted himself, were first produced in 240 BC, the year after the First Punic War ended; they were chiefly mythological tragedies, after Greek models, but included comedies. A translation of the *Odyssey* into Saturnian metre he used to assist his teaching of Greek at Rome. Both *Odissia* (?) and tragedies long remained popular. His hymn to Juno (207 BC) earned the earliest official recognition of the profession of author at Rome.

BIBL. Fragments: *TRF* 1 ff.; *CRF* 3 ff.; *FPL* 7 ff.

Livy 64 (?) BC–AD 12 (?) Historian.

Titus Livius was a native of Patavium (Padua), and indeed, was notoriously and obscurely accused of *Patavinitas* (Paduanism) by *Asinius Pollio. He was a man of evidently limited horizons: nothing suggests that he read or travelled widely, or that he frequented the 'best literary circles' in Augustan Rome. He began the *Ab urbe condita* (*From the Foundation of the City*) probably not before 29, and the first five books were completed 27/5. The work contained 142 books in all, down to the death of *Drusus (the elder) in 9 BC, and its very bulk, resented as early as *Martial (xiv. 190) ensured both eventual loss (35 books survive) and the production of epitomes. Livy's ideal, as stylist and as representative of good republican principles, was *Cicero (see Seneca, *Suasoriae* 7 for a remarkable obituary); the Augustan age he viewed coolly, declining to bend the evidence when requested to provide convenient historical precedents (LV. xx. 7), and earning a jibe at the expense of his fashionable opposition from *Augustus himself (Tacitus, *Annals* iv. 34); his account of Roman history after 42 BC, moreover, was only published in *Tiberius' reign.

Livy wrote from distress at the present (*praef.* 5), in a spirit of conscious escapism (XLIII. xiii. 12), with the explicit intention of using history as a means of moral education (*praef.*, *passim*); unscholarly and sentimental, he was called harshly and fairly 'verbose and careless' by the Emperor *Gaius. His casual attitude to documents, complete neglect of *Varro's antiquarian researches, often haphazard use of annalistic sources, poor command of Greek, and scant understanding of war and of geography may on occasion arouse our annoyance. However, though the Livian version of early Roman history has been rejected virtually wholesale, he does preserve much material (e.g. lists of magistrates) which is still of great value to historians. Still more important, Livy is a dramatist, orator, and narrator of genius. The characters of his great heroes (*Scipio Africanus, *Camillus) are massively developed, and turning-points of Rome's history are built up to brilliantly staged climaxes (notably Camillus' intervention in 390 BC), sometimes over several books (as in the case of the Second Punic War). His style was characterized rather unfairly by *Quintilian (X. i. 32) as 'milky richness'; his narrative (e.g. the fall of Alba, the Gallic sack of Rome, the aftermath of Cannae) can be tense, dramatic, and superbly imaginative in its capacity to awaken in the reader a strong sense of immediacy of place and of emotional involvement in events.

BIBL. Walsh, *Livy* and Williams, *GRNSC* viii (1974); Luce, *Livy* (1977), bks. i–v ed. Ogilvie (1965).

Locusta: see Lucusta

Lollia Paulina Empress AD 38–9.

Daughter of M. *Lollius, Lollia was married to Memmius Regulus, from whom *Gaius took her as his wife for a short while because of her outstanding beauty. Callistus the freedman suggested that she might be a suitable bride for *Claudius, following the death of *Messallina in 48: *Agrippina's jealousy led to her exile and death.

BIBL. Tac. *Ann.* xii. 1–2, 22; *PIR* L 328.

Lollianus Mavortius Consul AD 355.

Quintus Flavius Maesius Egnatius Lollianus Mavortius, a member of the great Roman family of the *Ceionii, received the dedication of *Firmicus Maternus' treatise on astrology, the *Mathesis*. After holding earlier offices he was urban prefect in 342, consul (355), and praetorian prefect of Illyricum (355–6).

BIBL. *PLRE* i, Lollianus 5.

Lollius, Marcus Consul 21 BC.

A loyal and useful supporter of *Augustus, to whom he owed everything, Lollius supervised the transformation of the kingdom of Galatia into a province, in 24 BC. In Gaul, about 17 BC, he suffered a defeat comparable with that of *Varus. In AD 1 he was C. *Caesar's companion and mentor in the East, and incurred the long-lasting enmity of *Tiberius, then on Rhodes. This eventually led to his downfall, and explains the hostility of the pro-Tiberian *Velleius, who tells us that Lollius was 'keener on money than morality'. This wealth he passed on to his dazzling daughter *Lollia Paulina.

BIBL. *PIR* L 311; Syme, *Rom. Rev.*, 398.

Fort on the Antonine Wall (Rough Castle at Bonnybridge) built by Lollius Urbicus.

Lollius Urbicus Consul by AD 138.

An African, Quintus Lollius Urbicus served in the Second Jewish War and governed Britain (139–42), where he won a victory over barbarian invaders from Scotland, and built a defensive wall of turf (the Antonine Wall) between the Forth and the Clyde. He later held the office of urban prefect.

BIBL. Birley, *Fasti* (forthcoming); *PIR* L 327.

Longinus

Longinus was the name given to the author (a Jew or with Jewish connections) of a treatise *On the Sublime*, dedicated to an unknown Roman, Postumius Terentius. He was a brilliant analyst of what constitutes literary greatness.

BIBL. Ed. Russell (1964); Russell and Winterbottom, *Lit. Crit.*, 460 ff.

Longinus, Cassius Teacher of rhetoric and philosophy c. AD 250–67.

Longinus, a Syrian, was born c. 213 and studied under *Ammonius and *Origen. He taught philosophy, literature, and rhetoric at Athens, where he counted *Porphyry among his students, and continued to correspond with him after Porphyry left for Rome in 262. Literati from all round the Levant came to his dinners in honour of Plato's birthday. Renowned for his learning, Longinus was called to Palmyra by *Zenobia to act as official teacher of Greek and adviser (267/8), and was executed by *Aurelian for his part in the Palmyrene revolt of 273. Only fragments of his writings survive.

BIBL. *PLRE* i, Longinus 2.

Lucan (AD 39–65) Epic poet.

Marcus Annaeus Lucanus was a native of Cordova and nephew of the younger *Seneca; he was therefore raised in the heart of Rome's Stoic aristocracy: a pupil of *Cornutus, alongside *Persius. He early secured *Nero's favour, and was appointed quaestor honorifically young. At about this point (62/3) the first 3 books of the *Civil War* (NOT *Pharsalia*) were published, and relations with Nero began to worsen. It should be stressed that the differences were personal, not political. Tacitus (*Ann.* xv. 49) talks of 'blazing hatreds' and 'private causes'; literary rivalries and personal discourtesies were involved. Lucan became a participant in the *Pisonian conspiracy—not to re-establish the Republic but to change the Empire—was forced to commit suicide, and did so, betraying family and confederates and spouting his own verse. Of his prodigious output (he died aged 25) only fragments survive, alongside ten books (the poem is clearly unfinished and was perhaps meant to go down to 44 BC) of the *Civil War*.

His opening panegyric of Nero is the product not of irony but of a youthful courtier's goodwill, carried away by ingenious fluency. Thereafter the poem substantially ignores Nero, and becomes more and more bitterly hostile towards Julius *Caesar. Even *Pompey does not escape criticism; the two heroes of the beloved cause of *libertas* (liberty) are *Brutus and above all the younger *Cato, as witness the famous epigram, *victrix causa deis placuit sed victa Catoni* ('the gods favoured the conquering cause, Cato the conquered', i. 128). As a historian of the Civil War, he follows chiefly *Livy and also Caesar; he knew intimately, moreover, *Virgil and the verse of his uncle. He made many historical errors. Lucan represents a major break in the history of Latin epic: the historical theme is not new, but the treatment is that of an orator and declaimer; departing from the 'stately measures' and divine machinery of the *Aeneid*, Lucan is all fire and epigram. A superbly skilled rhetorician, he is perhaps not always in full control of his material, as the meteorological and herpetological excursus on North Africa bears witness.

BIBL. Macmullen, *Enemies*, i; Ahl, *Lucan* (1976); Dilke in *Neronians and Flavians* (ed. Dorey) (1972) 62 ff.; *OCD*.

Lucian Greek satirical writer, 2nd century AD.

As a native of Samosata in Commagene, Lucian's mother tongue was probably Aramaic, though he was educated in Greek to a high level. After an apprenticeship to his uncle, a sculptor, he took up a career in forensic rhetoric, which he appears to have abandoned at the age of 42. It is uncertain whether he ever used his rhetorical skill as a travelling lecturer or practising sophist, though some scholars believe this. His only other known employment is as a minor official in the office of the prefect of Egypt. His major importance is as a writer of satirical pieces in dialogue or epistolary form, which were essentially his innovation; over 80 of these survive but the attribution of some of them to Lucian is disputed. He pokes fun at many aspects of second-century society: religion, philosophy, human vanity, chicanery in bureaucracy and the law, and the linguistic foibles of the age. His barbed remarks about philosophers can be connected with his own conversion to philosophy, which took place at Athens in his middle age, but there is little positive evidence for his beliefs. Also notable is the *True History*, a narrative work of the 'Gulliver's Travels' genre.

BIBL. Bowersock, *Sophists*; J. Schwartz, *Biographie de Lucien de Samosate* (1965); Lucian, trans. A. M. Harmon *et al.* (Loeb, 1921–67).

Lucian of Antioch (died AD 311/12) Christian priest and scholar.

Little of Lucian's writing survives, though his elegant edition of the Greek Bible was long standard in the Levant. He founded an important theological school, and his pupils included the heretic *Arius, as well as some of the most influential churchmen of the age of *Constantine. Lucian's martyrdom caused a sensation; in the reign of Constantine a shrine was built, where one of his pupils baptized the emperor on his deathbed —a postponement common at this time.

BIBL. G. Bardy, *Recherches sur Lucien d'Antioche et son école* (1936).

Lucilius (168/7 (?)–103/2 BC) Satirist.

A native of Suessa Aurunca (Roccamonfina), Gaius Lucilius was a great-uncle of *Pompey and a friend of *Scipio Aemilianus. He was the first Roman of good family to turn poet. Wealth and status saved him from retaliation to his savage, specific, and explicit hexameter attacks. Some 1,400 rich and varied lines survive, covering (for example) politics, poets, pederasty, philosophy, and personal revelations. He was also much concerned with questions of grammar and literary criticism. *Horace and *Juvenal were fascinated and heavily influenced by him.

BIBL. The editions by Marx (1904) and Krenkel (1970) are recommended in preference to the Loeb edition; Coffey, *Satire*, 35 ff.

Bronze coin (*sestertius*) of Lucilla (enlarged).

Lucilla Empress *c*. AD 164–9.

A daughter of *Marcus Aurelius and *Faustina II, Annia Aurelia Galeria Lucilla was born *c*. 148 and married Marcus' co-emperor Lucius *Verus in about 164, receiving the title of Augusta. After Lucius' death (169) she married *Claudius Pompeianus. She was involved in a plot against *Commodus in 182, and was exiled to Capri before being executed.

BIBL. Birley, *Marcus*; Grosso, *Lotta*; *PIR* A 707.

Lucretia

According to legend Lucretia was forcibly seduced by *Tarquinius Superbus' son Sextus, and committed suicide after informing her father (Spurius Lucretius Tricipitinus, allegedly suffect consul 509 BC) and husband (Lucius Tarquinius Collatinus, also allegedly consul 509). In revenge they, with L. Junius *Brutus, initiated the overthrow of the monarchy.

BIBL. PW xiii. 1692 ff.; Ogilvie, *Livy*, 218 ff.

Lucretius (*c*. 95–*c*. 55 BC) Poet.

Titus Lucretius was of completely unknown origin. His six books of hexameters *De rerum natura* (On the Nature of Things, with *sous-entendu* 'On the coming-to-birth of things') are evidently unfinished, as may be deduced from repeated passages and from unfulfilled promises of future discussion of topics elsewhere, but the story (in St *Jerome) that *Cicero edited the work is implausible. The poem is addressed to Gaius *Memmius (2), probably the friend and patron of *Catullus, but Lucretius stands alone: we know of no literary or personal friendships, and from contemporary developments in poetic technique he stands apart. Though he is a deeply learned (*doctus*) poet, well-acquainted with the Alexandrian techniques of literary allusion, his hexameters are often rugged and inelegant. That is a matter not of incompetence but of choice: copious imitations by *Virgil and *Ovid (for example) testify to his peers' admiration.

His theme is Epicureanism and his inspiration a passionate conviction of Epicurus' rightness and of the importance of the Epicurean message for the happiness of mankind. Nor is Lucretius much concerned with the more superficially attractive ethical side of Epicureanism, but above all with the physics. His passionately-held materialist convictions of the nature of man and of the universe lead him to a famous and passionate attack upon the fear of death (iii). Epicurus shed light upon the darkness of human ignorance, and it is likewise Lucretius' determination, often expressed with magnificent satirical vehemence, to shatter fundamental popular misconceptions. The poetic form of his treatise, which flies in the face of conventional Epicurean hostility to poetry, owes much, notably, to the Greek philosopher-poet Empedocles; it is the 'honey on the rim of the cup' which contains a draught of hard and bitter doctrine. But the work is no arid treatise enlivened by purple passages; the brilliance of Lucretius' imagery and the dazzling perspicuity of his observations from nature inspire the whole.

BIBL. Kenney, *GRNSC* xi (1977); D. West *The Imagery and Poetry of Lucretius* (1969); P. Boyancé, *Lucrèce et l'épicurisme* (1963).

Lucullus Consul 74 BC.

Lucius Licinius Lucullus came to prominence as an officer of *Sulla in the 80s. As quaestor in 88 BC he was the only officer in Sulla's army to march on Rome. In the East he engaged in important diplomatic activity on Sulla's behalf, and issued an extensive coinage in Greece. On his death in 78 Sulla entrusted Lucullus with his son's education and the publication of his memoirs. As a central figure of the Sullan establishment, Lucullus duly reached the consulship in 74, and by a process of intrigue secured for himself the attractive command against *Mithridates. An able general, he achieved rapid successes in the war, dislodging Mithridates from Bithynia and then driving him from his own kingdom of Pontus. He carried the war into Armenia, where Mithridates received aid and refuge from his son-in-law *Tigranes, and occupied Tigranocerta in 69.

But thereafter Lucullus became incapacitated by mutinies in his army, which rebelled against his strict discipline. At Rome his Asian settlement had offended business interests, and there was pressure from his enemies to terminate his command. In 66 he was replaced by *Pompey and returned to Rome, but political opposition denied him a triumph until 63. He then led the senate's opposition to ratification of his rival Pompey's eastern settlement. Always an Epicurean, he now degenerated into a cultivated hedonism, and his luxury became proverbial.

BIBL. Ooteghem, *Lucius Licinius Lucullus* (1959); Gruen, *Republic*.

Lucusta Poisoner, mid-1st century AD.

Lucusta was a notorious poisoner, said to be of Gallic origin. *Agrippina used her services against

*Claudius, and *Nero against *Britannicus; she also gave Nero a supply of poison in a golden casket for his personal use. She was richly rewarded with estates, but put to death by *Galba.

BIBL. Tacitus, *Annals* xii. 66, xiii. 15.

Lupicinus Master of the Cavalry, AD 360s.

Flavius Lupicinus was attached to the Caesar *Julian in Gaul as his commander-in-chief, when he commanded an expedition to Britain (360). Julian did not trust him, but under the Emperors *Jovian and *Valens he returned to office as commander-in-chief in the East (consul 367).

BIBL. *PLRE* i, Lupicinus 6.

Luscius Lanuvinus Comic dramatist, 2nd century BC.

Called a 'spiteful old poet', Luscius was accused of being a mere literal translator by *Terence, who occupied much of his prologues with rebutting Luscius's charges of 'contamination' ('spoiling' a play by the addition of elements extraneous to its Greek original), plagiarism, unfair aristocratic support, and feebleness, both stylistic and dramatic.

BIBL. *CRF*, 96 ff.

Lusius Quietus Consul AD 117.

A Moorish chieftain who achieved prominence as leader of a native cavalry contingent, Lusius Quietus captured Nisibis and sacked Edessa during *Trajan's Parthian War. He was put in charge of crushing the revolt of the Jews of Mesopotamia, and was then made governor of Judaea by Trajan in 117. He was removed from this post and executed in 118 along with three other ex-consuls, on a charge of plotting against *Hadrian.

BIBL. Syme, *Tacitus*; *PIR* L 439.

Lycophron (born *c.* 320 BC) Poet.

From Euboean Chalcis, Lycophron was the author, notably, of the *Alexandra* (probably, though this has been disputed hotly, *c.* 270 BC): a poem of famed obscurity and colossal erudition, in iambic metre, in the form of a prophecy by Cassandra, reflecting early Greek awareness of Rome's growing importance.

BIBL. Loeb edition with Callimachus, *Hymns* and Aratus; Momigliano, *Essays in Ancient and Modern Historiography* (1977) 55 ff.

Lygdamus Poet.

Lygdamus was the unknown author of six mediocre elegies addressed to one Neaera in book iii of the corpus of *Tibullus.

Macer, Gaius Licinius Historian, praetor 68 BC.

Macer was a *popularis* aristocrat and a follower of *Marius; his account of early Roman history was consequently biased; interestingly, it claimed to be based on the 'linen books' of the archive in the temple of Juno Moneta.

BIBL. *HRR* i. 298 ff.; Ogilvie, Livy, i–v. 7 ff.

Silvered bronze coin of the Emperor Macrianus.

Macrianus Emperor AD 260–1.

Titus Fulvius Junius Macrianus and his brother *Quietus were proclaimed emperor in 260–1 after the defeat and capture of *Valerian by the Persians (their father, Fulvius *Macrianus, having refused the title because of his age). Macrianus and his father marched to Illyricum in 261, where they were defeated and killed by *Aureolus.

BIBL. *PIR* F 546.

Macrianus, Fulvius General, mid-3rd century AD.

Father of the two emperors *Macrianus and *Quietus, Fulvius Macrianus served as *Valerian's general. After the latter's capture by the Persians in 260, he refused to be proclaimed emperor, arguing that he was too old. His sons were acclaimed instead, and the Macriani were defeated and killed in 261 by Gallienus' general, *Aureolus.

BIBL. *PIR* F 549.

Macrinus Emperor AD 217–8.

Obscurely born *c.* 166 in Caesarea in Mauretania, Marcus Opellius Macrinus was *Plautianus' financial agent and later *Caracalla's praetorian prefect. After engineering Caracalla's death, Macrinus became emperor and created his son *Diadumenian, Caesar. His irregular appointments roused senatorial hostility. After a disastrous Parthian campaign, rebellious troops proclaimed *Elagabalus emperor, and Macrinus was defeated, captured, and slain, as was his son.

BIBL. Millar, *Dio*; Herodian (Loeb).

Macro Praetorian prefect AD 31–8.

As successor to *Sejanus as praetorian prefect, Quintus Naevius Cordus Sutorius Macro was supposed to have had a similarly baleful influence: some said he and *Gaius murdered the aged *Tiberius. He gave strong support to Gaius—*Philo represents him as a wise mentor to the young emperor—but was disposed of while being promoted to the prefecture of Egypt.

BIBL. Tacitus, *Annals* vi. 45–6.

Macrobius Writer, praetorian prefect AD 430.

Probably born in Africa at the end of the fourth century, Macrobius Ambrosius Theodosius (known to his contemporaries as Theodosius) is best known as the author of the *Commentary on the Dream of Scipio* and the *Saturnalia*. His date and identity have caused much confusion, but it is now generally agreed that he was praetorian prefect of Italy in 430. The *Saturnalia*, a literary symposium, probably written after 416 and not published until 430, describes a fictional banquet given by *Praetextatus on 17–19 December 384. Discussion of *Virgil occupies most of the work, but there is also much antiquarian religious information, notably in Praetextatus' discourse on the Sun. The interlocutors comprise many of the most important literati of the time, among them *Symmachus, Nicomachus *Flavianus, Praetextatus, *Servius, and *Avienus, and gives a slightly tendentious portrait of the end of the fourth century. The highly influential *Commentary* is the earlier work, and treats of arithmology, the soul, and celestial harmony, and reveals its author to have been well read in Neoplatonic philosophy, and capable of a certain amount of intelligent and original synthesis.

BIBL. A. Cameron, *JRS* lvi, 1966; J. Flamant, *Macrobe et le néoplatonisme latin à la fin du 4ème siècle* (1977).

Maecenas (died 8 BC) Literary patron.

Descendant of Etruscan kings, Gaius Maecenas proved himself a loyal and useful helper to the young *Octavian from 43 BC onwards. He acted as a go-between on several occasions, and was entrusted with the management of Rome and Italy, since his talents were diplomatic and domestic rather than martial; in many ways he was the civilian counterpart of *Agrippa, and no less important. An equestrian by birth, he never aspired to senatorial rank or higher office. His is a name now proverbial for any great literary patron, and justifiably so. Yet it is arguable whether he 'organized opinion' or could fairly be called *Augustus' 'minister of propaganda'.

Maecenas was associated with numerous poets: *Virgil, *Horace, *Propertius, *Varius. The rewards were great for some: witness the sums named in Virgil's will, the profits made by Varius from his *Thyestes*, and the gift to Horace of his Sabine farm. Though Maecenas in some sense directed the composition of Virgil's *Georgics* (iii.41), pressure upon poets could be and was resisted (see Propertius, iii.9): pleas of inability (Horace, *Satires* II. i. 10 ff.) or suggestions of alternative authors (Horace, *Odes*, iv.2) did duty for the actual composition of panegyrics. Only Varius is known to have obliged, while Propertius' patriotism could turn embarrassingly heterodox: the historical themes proposed in iii.9 were intensely

Portrait bust of Maecenas. Paris, Louvre.

compromising. No mailed fist, then; but leisure and security enough were offered to men who had known the civil wars: intelligent authors did not fail to realize that some literary return was expected. Variously, and with elaborate protestations of literary independence, they obliged.

After the conspiracy of his brother-in-law Varro Murena in 23, Maecenas, who had in some way been compromised, lost his influence with Augustus and his position in the councils of state and was encouraged to retire, although it was not until 8 BC that he died. The intervening years were devoted to the cultivated and comfortable life-style for which he became famous.

BIBL. J.-M. André, *Mécène* (1966).

Maecianus, Volusius Jurist, 2nd century AD.

An equestrian, Lucius Volusius Maecianus was a distinguished lawyer and administrator. He was probably a pupil of Salvius *Julianus, and was tutor in law to the young *Marcus Aurelius. He was appointed secretary for petitions to *Antoninus Pius immediately after the latter's adoption as *Hadrian's heir, and held a number of administrative posts in the reign of Antoninus culminating in the prefecture of Egypt (160–1). He was the author of several technical legal works.

BIBL. Pflaum, *Carrières*, no. 141; Jolowicz, *Roman Law*.

Maelius, Spurius

Maelius won popularity by corn distributions,

was denounced as aiming at tyranny by L. *Minucius Esquilinus Augurinus, and killed by C. Servilius *Ahala (439 BC). This story, originally timeless (Sp. Maelius, tribune of the plebs in 436 BC, is an obvious duplicate), probably originated as an aetiology of the Aequimaelium (usually interpreted as the 'level of Maelius' where his house was destroyed after his death). It was elaborated with other aetiologies (see Minucius and Ahala), stock theories of tyranny, and political and constitutional arguments, especially of the Gracchan period.

BIBL. PW xiv.239 f.; Ogilvie, *Livy*, 550 ff.; A. W. Lintott, *Historia* xix (1970) 13 ff.

Left: gold coin (*solidus*) of Magnentius (obverse). Right: bronze coin (*follis*) of Magnentius with chi-rho monogram (reverse).

Magnentius Western usurper AD 350–3.

Probably born c. 303 at Amiens of a British father and Frankish mother, Flavius Magnus Magnentius served as a senior army officer. On 18 January 350 Marcellinus, Count of the Sacred Largesses to *Constans, held a birthday party for his son at Autun, at which Magnentius appeared in purple and was acclaimed emperor. The army deserted to him, and Constans was killed. When the eastern emperor *Constantius II rejected Magnentius' overtures, he left his brother Decentius as Caesar in Gaul and marched into Illyricum, where Constantius defeated him at the bloody battle of Mursa (28 September 351). He fell back on Italy and then Gaul, but was encircled and committed suicide at Lyons (10 August 353). A Christian (though he bid for pagan support), he was the first to issue an unequivocally Christian coinage, large bronzes with the chi-rho monogram.

BIBL. Piganiol, *Empire chr.*; P. Bastien, *Le monnayage de Magnence* (1964).

Magnus of Carrhae Historian AD 363.

Magnus went on *Julian's Persian expedition, and wrote a (lost) account of it. He may be the tribune Magnus who entered the fort of Maiozamalcha through a mine, and won a crown for bravery.

BIBL. *PLRE* i, Magnus 2–3; Thompson, *Ammianus*, 28–32.

Majorian Western emperor AD 457–61.

Proclaimed emperor on 1 April 457, Julius Valerius Majorianus, with the support of *Ricimer (who had helped him to dispose of his predecessor, *Avitus) tried to set the Empire on a firm footing again by a mass of legislation (458) and a programme of conciliating the nobility, including the supporters of Avitus. However, his position was undermined by the capture of his fleet in Spain by the Vandals before it could be sent against them, and he was arrested and executed by Ricimer in northern Italy (2 August 461).

BIBL. 11 *Novellae* of Majorian; Stein, *Bas-Empire*, i.374–80.

Mamertinus, Claudius Praetorian prefect AD 361–5.

A cultivated elderly pagan, Claudius Mamertinus was made Count of the Sacred Largesses in 361 by *Julian, and then praetorian prefect of Italy, Africa, and Illyricum. Consul for 362 with *Nevitta, he pronounced an extant panegyric at Constantinople thanking Julian for the office, and gave the customary circus games. In 365 he was accused of peculation and dismissed from the prefecture.

BIBL. *Panegyrici Latini* xi (iii); *PLRE* i, Mamertinus 2; Ammianus XXII. vii. 1–2.

Mamilius Limetanus, Gaius Tribune 109 BC.

As tribune in 109 BC Mamilius followed up the attack launched by *Memmius on the senate's handling of the war against *Jugurtha. Under his law a commission was set up (the *quaestio Mamiliana*) to investigate corruption in recent dealings with Jugurtha. Several leading nobles were convicted, and the senate's prestige was badly damaged.

BIBL. Syme, *Sallust*.

Silver coin (*denarius*) of C. Hostilius Mancinus, showing ritual oath-taking scene.

Mancinus, Gaius Hostilius Consul 137 BC.

As consul in Spain, Mancinus allowed his army to be surrounded by a smaller Numantine force. He extricated the army through a treaty negotiated by his quaestor, Tiberius *Gracchus. On his return to Rome the senate repudiated the treaty as shameful; but rather than break faith publicly with the

Numantines (for which there were numerous recent precedents) it was decided to surrender Mancinus in expiation as the man personally responsible for the treaty. Mancinus' surrender (he was left outside the gates of Numantia, bound and naked) was supervised by his successor, *Furius, with attention to ceremonial detail; but Rome's ostentatious piety did not deceive the Numantines, who rejected the offer in disgust. Mancinus returned to Rome and regained the status he had forfeited.

BIBL. Bernstein, *Gracchus*, 57–69.

Mani and **Manicheism** Religious leader (c. AD 216–76 (?)).

Mani was a Persian, born near Seleucia-Ctesiphon. Little is known of his personal life, but after a visit to India in 242 he began publicly preaching his heretical doctrines, initially arousing Persian opposition and later that of the Christians. *Shapur I, who extended toleration to all forms of religion, did not persecute him, but his second successor Vahram I imprisoned Mani in 272 and put him to death. Mani's doctrines were based on the conflict of light and darkness and the need to free the particles of light imprisoned in men's brains. To achieve this severe asceticism was required, including vegetarianism. The Manicheans were influenced by Christianity to the extent that they believed *Jesus was the Son of God, but they held that he had come to save his own soul, which had been lost in Adam. The elect were forbidden to work or own goods, and were destined to be freed from the transmigration of the soul. Although Mani wrote extensively, his work survives largely in fragments, which have been found in Egypt and as far East as Chinese Turkestan. Manicheism continued to flourish after Mani's death and, although banned by the Roman Empire in 297, it spread rapidly in the West. *Augustine was a member of the sect for nine years before his conversion to Christianity. The coming of Islam to the eastern half of the Empire drove the sect across central Asia, and it survived in China until the fourteenth century.

BIBL. C. J. R. Ort, *Mani* (1967).

Manilius, Marcus Didactic poet, floruit early 1st century AD.

Possibly of Greek origin, Manilius composed books i and ii of his *Astronomica* in *Augustus' lifetime, iv and v after his death. His five books of hexameters on the 'science' of astrology, influenced by *Virgil and *Lucretius, are enthusiastic, compressed, rhetorical, highly ingenious, and exceptionally difficult; nor is the poem, probably complete, an accurate guide to the subject. He exercised minimal influence on later poets, but has stimulated Latin scholars since the Renaissance to prodigious efforts.

BIBL. Important new Loeb edition by Goold.

Manlius Capitolinus, Marcus

Identified by some sources with the consul of 392 BC, Manlius supposedly saved the Capitol from the Gauls (390) (probably an aetiological explanation of his *cognomen*), but was subsequently executed for aiming at tyranny. Originally his death was probably dated to 385, and may have been an extra-judicial act. Later, Manlius was depicted as championing the indebted plebs; his execution was moved to 384 (perhaps to provide a confrontation with M. Furius *Camillus), and was preceded by a trial conducted by tribunes of the plebs or the *duoviri* (*perduellionis*).

BIBL. PW xiv.1167 ff.; Lintott, *Historia* xix (1970) 22 ff.; Wiseman, *Historia* xxviii (1979) 32 ff.

Manlius Theodorus Praetorian prefect c. AD 382, 397–9.

Flavius Manlius Theodorus was a successful bureaucrat whose career is recorded by the pagan poet *Claudian, but he also influenced St *Augustine. His rapid rise under *Gratian culminated in the prefecture of Gaul (c. 382), after which he retired to near Milan. Here he was the leader of the Christian circle adapting Neoplatonism (see *Plotinus) for Latin-speakers, an important factor in the conversion of Augustine, who dedicated his *On the Happy Life* (386) to Theodorus with a warmth he later regretted, even though it was 'to a scholar and a Christian'. This regret may have been due to Theodorus' return to public life (397) as a senior supporter of *Stilicho, becoming praetorian prefect of Italy, Africa, and Illyricum, and consul (399).

BIBL. Matthews, *Western Aristocracies*.

Marcellinus of Dalmatia Master of the Soldiers (?) 460s AD.

A former friend of *Aëtius, Marcellinus defended Sicily from the Vandals (461) with Hunnic help, but quarrelled with *Ricimer and withdrew to Dalmatia, where he ruled with the support of the eastern court. A Patrician by 468, he joined the attack on the Vandals as commander in Sicily, but was assassinated, perhaps at the instigation of Ricimer. He was succeeded in Dalmatia by his nephew, Julius *Nepos.

BIBL. Stein, *Bas Empire*, i.379 ff.

Marcellus (42–23 BC) Heir of Augustus.

As the child of *Augustus' sister *Octavia (by the homonymous consul of 50 BC), Marcus Claudius Marcellus was the most obvious heir to the Augustan system. He was therefore educated with care, taken to Spain by Augustus, married to his daughter *Julia—in vain: in 23 BC his sudden death caused serious problems within the family of Augustus as well as considerable public grief, reflected in contemporary poetry.

BIBL. Virgil, *Aeneid* vi.860–86.

Marcellus, Lucius Ulpius Consul by AD 184.

A general with a reputation for stern discipline, Ulpius Marcellus is known to have been governor of Britain in 184 when the Caledonians broke through the Antonine Wall and overran southern Scotland. He put down the revolt in three military campaigns. He is said to have kept his soldiers on their toes by distributing (through an aide) pre-written orders at intervals throughout the night, in order to create the impression that he was constantly awake.

BIBL. Grosso, *Lotta*; Birley, *Fasti* (forthcoming).

Silver coin (*denarius*) minted by descendant (50 BC) showing M. Claudius Marcellus and Sicilian symbol.

Marcellus, Marcus Claudius Consul 222, 215, 214, 210 and 208 BC.

In his late fifties Marcellus became a major hero of the Roman war effort against *Hannibal, sharing a dominant role in its conduct with *Fabius Cunctator. He diverged from Fabius' cautious strategy, being of a more reckless and aggressive disposition, and sought confrontation with Hannibal on equal terms. He was less a brilliant general than a dogged fighter of the old Roman tradition. But his limited successes and his vigorous, charismatic personality boosted Rome's flagging morale and won him a large following: to contemporaries he was the Sword of Rome, while the less glamorous Fabius was its Shield.

Earlier, he had established his military reputation in a distinguished first consulship (222 BC) by winning a triumph for victories in Cisalpine Gaul, and becoming the third Roman to dedicate the *spolia opima*. He attained the latter honour by defeating an enemy chieftain in single combat. He held the consular *imperium* continuously from 215 to 208 in Italy and Sicily, his greatest achievement being the capture of Syracuse in 212. The accidental killing of the famous scientist Archimedes unfortunately marred this success. He then celebrated a minor triumph (*ovatio*), in which he brought many Greek works of art to Rome. In his fourth consulship he was accused of misconduct by a Syracusan embassy, and defended himself

Theatre of Marcellus, heir of Augustus (13 BC).

before the senate as a private citizen. The Syracusans thereafter made him their special patron and instituted a cult to him, making Marcellus the first Roman to be so worshipped. For the last three years of his life he held the command against Hannibal in south Italy, being obsessed with the ambition of fighting him in a straightforward pitched battle. This ambition was never realized, and in 208 he lost his life (needlessly, according to *Polybius) when he rode into an ambush with a small party of men.

BIBL. Plutarch, *Life of Marcellus*; Scullard, *Politics*; Lazenby, *Hannibal*.

Marcellus of Ancyra (died *c.* AD 374) Heretical bishop.

Friend and supporter of *Athanasius, Marcellus so strongly affirmed the unity of the Godhead as effectively to deny the separateness of Christ. Pope *Julius took up Marcellus' cause on his expulsion *c.* 339, but later found it embarrassing. The words 'whose Kingdom shall have no end' were added to the Nicene Creed to attack his heresy.

BIBL. *ODCC*; Chadwick, *The Early Church*, 135–41.

Marcia Imperial concubine, late 2nd century AD.

Marcia became the concubine of *Commodus after the banishment of the Empress Bruttia Crispina (who died in or shortly after 185). She is said to have been a Christian. Her influence increased after the death of *Cleander (189) and she played a leading part in the plot to murder Commodus in 192.

BIBL. Grosso, *Lotta*.

Marcian Eastern emperor AD 450–57.

Although only an obscure military tribune, Marcian was appointed to succeed *Theodosius II, perhaps through *Aspar, and his position was legitimized by his marriage with *Pulcheria. In many fields his policy differed from that of his predecessor, notably in his execution of the former favourite, Chrysaphius, his refusal of tribute to the Huns (whose retaliation was luckily prevented by *Attila's death), and his reversal of the decisions of the Council of Ephesus at Chalcedon (451), which conciliated Pope *Leo and thus the western court. His main positive achievement was his reform of imperial finances, in which he was helped by the absence of military threats during his reign. He died of natural causes in 457.

BIBL. 5 *Novellae* of Marcian and laws preserved in *Codex Justinianus*; *Acts* of Council of Chalcedon.

Marcianus Jurist, early 3rd century AD.

A late classical jurist who was active after the reign of *Caracalla, Aelius Marcianus wrote a number of legal manuals and monographs mainly on criminal procedure. His knowledge of rescripts

of the Severan period has led to the notion that he might have held an office in the imperial chancery.

BIBL. Jolowicz, *Roman Law*.

Marcion (died *c.* AD 160).

A wealthy shipowner from Sinope, Marcion was the son of a bishop who excommunicated him for immorality. He went to Rome *c.* 140 where he rejoined the Church, but he became a separatist and was excommunicated again in 144. He stimulated the spread of unorthodox communities, and held views which excited much opposition (e.g., in *Tertullian's *Against Marcion*). He laid much emphasis on the notion that Jesus represented the God of Love, and attempted to exclude the Old Testament from his theology, relying mainly on St Paul's Epistles and the Gospel of Luke.

BIBL. H. Chadwick, *The Early Church*; E. C. Blackman, *Marcion and his Influence* (1948); Tertullian, *Adversus Marcionem*, ed. E. Evans (1972).

Silver coin (*denarius*) of alleged descendant (56 BC), showing Ancus Marcius.

Marcius, Ancus King of Rome 7th century BC (?).

The fourth king of Rome (conventional dates: 640–617 BC), Ancus Marcius remained a shadowy figure of whom virtually nothing was known. His later portrait is modelled partly on *Numa, whose religious rituals he reputedly revived. He is also attributed military successes against neighbouring states, the bridging of the Tiber, and fortification of the Janiculum. His supposed settlement at Ostia (to exploit the salt-beds) has not yet received archaeological confirmation.

BIBL. A. Schwegler, *Römische Geschichte* I (2nd ed., 1869), 598 ff.; Ogilvie, *Livy*, 125 f.

Marcius Rutilus, Gaius Consul 357, 352, 344, and 342 BC.

After defeating Privernum (357 BC) Marcius became the first plebeian dictator (356), repelling an Etruscan force near the mouth of the Tiber. Consul again in 352, he attempted to relieve a debt crisis and was appointed the first plebeian censor (351). In 342 he prevented his troops' attempted seizure of Campanian land, and in some sources both consuls, not M. *Valerius Corvus, reconciled the mutinous troops near Rome by military reforms. Despite *Livy's contrary claims, his career may have owed much to patrician support.

BIBL. PW xiv. 1588 f.; E. Gabba, *Le Rivolte militari romane dal IV sec. a. C.* (1975).

Marcus Aurelius (Marcus Aurelius Antoninus) Emperor AD 161–80.

Born in 121, the son of Marcus Annius Verus and Domitia Lucilla, he was brought up by his grandfather (also called Marcus *Annius Verus) after the death of his father. He won early favour from *Hadrian (who called him 'Verissimus', meaning 'very truthful', a pun on the surname Verus) and when Hadrian adopted *Antoninus Pius as his successor in 138 he, in turn, was made to adopt Marcus (along with Lucius *Verus). After Hadrian's death Marcus was betrothed to Antoninus' daughter, *Faustina II, whom he married in 145. He received an excellent education from many distinguished tutors, his principal teachers in literature being *Fronto (Latin) and *Herodes Atticus (Greek). His correspondence with Fronto, preserved in the *Letters*, provides a valuable insight into the intellectual development of Marcus and the atmosphere of the imperial court in the middle of the second century. From the age of 18, when he was consul for the first time, he began to attend meetings of the emperor's council and to learn the responsibilities of being emperor. In 146 he was given a grant of tribunician power and proconsular *imperium* which clearly marked him out as Antoninus' preferred successor. When Antoninus died on 7 March 161, Marcus was holding his third consulship (and Lucius Verus his second). On Marcus' insistence, the senate granted to Lucius Verus tribunician power, proconsular *imperium*, and the title of Augustus, thereby raising him to the same level as Marcus (though he was younger). Thus the principle of collegiate power was introduced.

Marcus was, in the eyes of posterity at least, almost the perfect emperor, a judgement heavily influenced by knowledge of his personal qualities. He is criticized for having persecuted the Christians and for having allowed his degenerate son, *Commodus, to succeed him; but it must be remembered, with regard to the first, that he was really only following a policy laid down by *Trajan and reaffirmed by Hadrian, and, with regard to the second, that the transmission of imperial power had always been effectively dynastic—he could not have ignored his only surviving son.

Despite Marcus' personal qualities, his reign was very difficult. It saw a long succession of military crises, marking the beginning of a long period during which the Empire was threatened by invasion on all its major frontiers. In 162 the Parthians seized Armenia and precipitated a crisis,

which was dealt with by Lucius Verus and several of Marcus' best generals. The successful conclusion achieved by 166 was tempered by the fact that the soldiers who returned from the East brought a plague back with them which cost millions of lives, and probably had a serious effect on the population of the Empire. About 166–7 German tribes crossed the Danube and pushed as far as northern Italy. Two new legions had to be raised to meet this threat and Marcus was not in a position to come to terms with the invaders until 168. In 169 (the year in which Lucius Verus died) Marcus was forced to auction imperial property in order to raise money to fight the northern barbarians, and the last ten years of his reign were almost fully occupied on the frontiers (except for the brief internal threat offered by the revolt of *Avidius Cassius in 175). From 170–4 he fought the Marcomanni and Quadi, in 175 the Sarmatian Iazyges, In 176 he visited Egypt and returned to Rome for a triumph. But trouble erupted again in Pannonia in 177. Marcus made his son Commodus co-emperor in this year and they spent the last three years of the reign fighting the Marcomanni.

Marcus died at Vienna on 17 March 180. His most conspicuous monuments in Rome are the Column of Marcus Aurelius, depicting scenes from the northern wars, and his equestrian statue which was later incorporated into the design of the Capitol by Michelangelo. As a personality, Marcus is far better known than any other leading statesman of classical antiquity. Apart from the information in the *Letters* of Fronto, Marcus' inner self is revealed in the 12 books of *Meditations* (in Greek) which were written in the last decade of his reign during the northern wars. He had been introduced to Stoicism by one of his tutors, Apollonius of Chalcedon, and turned to it seriously in the mid-

Column of Marcus Aurelius, Rome.

Gilded bronze equestrian statue of Marcus Aurelius. Rome, Capitol.

Marcus Aurelius receiving surrender of barbarian enemies. Detail from Column.

140s. The *Meditations*, which are really a series of personal and psychological diaries written in circumstances of great personal hardship, reveal his preoccupation with his own responsibilities as emperor, with the relationship between man and God, and the nature of world-order. They add little that is new to traditional Stoic doctrines but reveal the intense religious and moral feeling of a sensitive, intelligent, and highly-educated emperor.

BIBL. Birley, *Marcus*; P. A. Brunt, *JRS* lxiv (1974); Marcus Aurelius, *Meditations*, ed. A. S. L. Farquharson (1944); A. S. L. Farquharson, *Marcus Aurelius, his Life and his World* (2nd ed., 1952).

Marius Consul 107, 104–100, and 86 BC.

The principal architect of the Roman professional army, Gaius Marius was a wealthy *novus homo* whose military ability and political ambitions had found advancement under the patronage of the Metelli. After serving as legate of *Metellus Numidicus in Africa for two years (109–108 BC), Marius was nearly fifty years old, and as an ex-praetor had a solid but unspectacular public career behind him. But, returning to Rome, he attacked Metellus' handling of the war, and skilfully exploited the political situation to secure for himself the consulship of 107 and a special mandate to succeed Metellus in Africa. This was

achieved by mobilizing the discontent in business circles (the equestrians) at the senate's inability to end the war, and combining it with the popular agitation initiated by *Memmius and *Mamilius against the conduct of the war. Thus Marius reached the consulship with a powerful anti-nobility coalition behind him; but thereafter he was a member of the nobility, and his conservative instincts led him to seek acceptance in that exalted circle. Of the military reforms associated with his name, by far the most important was the enlistment of *proletarii* (i.e. landless citizens) for his African campaign. Marius thus bypassed the chronic manpower shortage which Tiberius *Gracchus had tried to solve, but thereby created a new kind of army with revolutionary political consequences, as his younger contemporaries, *Sulla and *Pompeius Strabo, demonstrated in his lifetime.

By 105 Marius had ended the long war against *Jugurtha and triumphed at Rome; in the emergency following the disastrous defeat of *Caepio and Mallius at Orange, Marius was elected to a second consulship (104) to face the threat from the Cimbri and Teutones. For the duration of the crisis he held consecutive consulships in defiance of all constitutional precedent but apparently with the sanction of the senate, with whom his relations were at this time harmonious. This is shown by his assisting *Catulus (1) to the consulship of 102 and sharing a joint triumph with him after their final victory over the Cimbri at Vercellae (101). Moreover, he was elected without significant opposition to a sixth, 'unnecessary' consulship (100) and universally recognized as the saviour of the State.

But Marius' prestige required that his landless veterans be rewarded with land allotments. Conservative antipathy to such a measure in the senate was stirred up by Marius' ex-patron and arch-enemy, Metellus Numidicus. Thus Marius was forced to turn to the anti-senatorial politicians, *Saturninus and *Glaucia, and allow his veterans to be used to promote popular legislation by violent intimidation. When the senate passed its emergency decree (*senatus consultum ultimum*) and called upon Marius as consul to save the State, he was happy to follow the precedent of L. *Opimius in 121 and ruthlessly suppress Saturninus and Glaucia as the champion of the senatorial establishment. But Marius did not receive from the nobility the recognition he desired for his services. Increasingly isolated and ineffective, he regarded the return from exile of his enemy Metellus (98) as a personal humiliation, and undertook an embassy to Asia (97) as a self-imposed exile. However, the conviction of *Rutilius Rufus (92) and the failure of Livius *Drusus (2) (91) reflect the political strength of an independent faction surrounding Marius, and as legate in 90 he was one of the more successful commanders in the Social War. But when the coveted command against *Mithridates was allocated to Sulla in 88, Marius again looked to a popular leader, the tribune P. *Sulpicius Rufus, to achieve his ends. Sulla's unexpected march on Rome caused Marius to flee for his life before eventually finding refuge among his old veterans in Africa. When he returned to Rome with *Cinna in 87, he instigated a ruthless massacre of political opponents. He died early in 86 aged 70, shortly after entering his seventh consulship.

BIBL. Plutarch, *Life of Marius*; Carney, *A Biography of C. Marius* (1961); Ooteghem, *Caius Marius* (1964).

Silvered bronze coin of Marius (2).

Marius (2) Gallic usurper AD 268.

Marcus Aurelius Marius was proclaimed emperor after *Postumus' death in 268. The exact length of his reign is unknown, but was probably longer than the few days attested by the sources.

BIBL. *PLRE* i, Marius 4; A. Chastagnol, *HAC* 1971 (1974); *PIR* A 1555.

Marius Maximus (born *c.* AD 158) Historian.

Lucius Marius Maximus Perpetuus Aurelianus had a long and distinguished public career. He wrote a second *Twelve Caesars* modelled on *Suetonius' style but covering the reigns of *Nerva to *Elagabalus. These have perished, but are generally accepted as the main source for these emperors' biographies in the *Augustan History*.

BIBL. Birley, *Severus*.

Maroboduus German king, deposed AD 18.

Of high birth, Maroboduus was educated at Rome. On becoming king of his people, the Marcomanni, he greatly increased their influence and settled them in later Bohemia. His relations with Rome fluctuated violently. In AD 6 a concerted attack on his kingdom by Roman forces was thwarted by the Pannonian revolt, and it was not until 18 that he was finally expelled. *Tiberius allowed him to retire to Ravenna.

BIBL. Tacitus, *Annals*, ii.

Martial (*c.* AD 40–103/4) Epigrammatist.

Born at Bilbilis in Hispania Tarraconensis, Marcus Valerius Martialis came to Rome in AD 64 and enjoyed some support from his compatriot, *Seneca. Some real talent and an insatiable capacity to flatter brought him a number of minor honours and a wide circle of literary acquaintances (e.g. *Juvenal and the Younger *Pliny), but no real financial independence. With the accession of *Nerva in 96, his assiduously obsequious cultivation of *Domitian appeared likely to harm his further prospects, and he withdrew to Spain with some help from Pliny (*Ep.* iii. 21). A total of 1,561 poems are preserved, mostly in elegiacs:
(1) *Liber spectaculorum* (*Book of Combats*), published in AD 80, on the opening of the Colosseum. (2) *Xenia*, mottoes to accompany tokens of friendship (= *Epigrammata* xiii), written AD 84–5. (3) *Apophoreta*: mottoes to accompany presents to take home (= *Epigrammata* xiv), written AD 84–5. (4) 12 books of epigrams, published separately or in pairs between 85/6 and 102/3.

The subject-matter is extremely varied: elegant court-poetry, consolatory and funeral epigrams, descriptions of villas and the foibles of mankind, in and out of bed. Martial is a writer of great technical skill and a master of the sting in the tail; his influence was wide and lasting, not least upon his contemporary and acquaintance Juvenal, who consistently improved upon him.

Martianus Capella Encyclopedist, 5th century AD.

Martianus Minneus Felix Capella was a

The three Hebrews in the fiery furnace (Book of Daniel):
a popular theme in art as an example of martyrdom.
Early 4th-century fresco. Catacomb of Priscilla,
Rome.

Carthaginian rhetorician or lawyer (mid to late 5th
century), author of *On the Marriage of Philology and
Mercury*, an unusual textbook of the seven liberal
arts in prosimetrum form. The work, notable for its
preservation of Neoplatonic and Chaldaean
theology, its abstruse and exuberant style, and its
elaborate allegorical fable, exercised considerable
influence on the art and intellectual life of the
Middle Ages.
   BIBL. W. H. Stahl, *Martianus Capella and the
Seven Liberal Arts* i (1971), ii (1977).

St Martin of Tours Bishop *c.* AD 371–97.
   The late-Roman soldier who became patron
saint of France, Martinus was an officer's son born
in Pannonia (probably in 316), whose father made
him join up; but, after sharing his cloak with a
beggar, he dreamed of Christ, and left the army. He
became a disciple of St *Hilary and founded a
monastery near Poitiers, from which he was taken
to become bishop of Tours. He promoted
monasticism and evangelized the countryside. He
impressed *Maximus, who justified his usurpation
to him, but he failed to save *Priscillian from a
secular court. His *Life* was written by his disciple
*Sulpicius Severus.
   BIBL. Matthews, *Western Aristocracies*.

Martyrs
   Christians were persecuted from the first. Local
communities resented private convictions which
impaired public duty to the indigenous gods.
Especially 'if there is plague, famine or earthquake,
immediately "the Christians to the lion" becomes
their slogan' (*Tertullian). Early action against
Christians was piecemeal: only under *Decius
(249–51) and during the Great Persecution (303–13)
was all the Empire ordered to sacrifice. Christians'
responses to pressure varied: some fled, others
lapsed. But wild enthusiasm greeted the deaths of
the martyrs, who were the heroes of the Christian
faith, rivalled only by ascetics like St *Antony.
When *Constantine stopped the persecutions, this
spirit crystallized into legend. Relatively few
simple early accounts survive.
   The earliest describes the burning of *Polycarp.
Pagan strategy often selected Christian leaders, like
St *Cyprian of Carthage, PAMPHILUS (*c.* 240–309),
learned and beloved teacher of *Eusebius, who
described his agonies in the *Martyrs of Palestine*, or
*Lucian of Antioch. However, judges often
especially encouraged educated Christians to
recant, as in the case of PHILEAS, bishop of Thmuis
in Egypt (executed 304/7). Some repudiated
compromise violently. AEDESIUS was executed
after assaulting *Hierocles, prefect of Egypt, in 307.
The *Acts* of PERPETUA, a young mother eaten by
beasts in the arena at Carthage in 203, vividly
evoke the ecstatic vision which impelled such
martyrs. The sufferings of ALBAN (perhaps *c.* 209)
are obscured by accretions of later cult. His shrine
at St Albans was still active in the Anglo-Saxon
period. Details of GEORGE, a martyr in Palestine
popular in prayer from the sixth century onwards,
are buried irretrievably in myth.
   BIBL. ed. H. Musurillo, *The Acts of the Christian
Martyrs* (1972); Frend, *Martyrdom and
Persecution*; T. D. Barnes, *JRS* lviii (1968) 32 ff.
Perpetua: J. Armitage Robinson, *The Passion of
Perpetua* (1891). Alban: J. Morris, *Hertfordshire
Archaeology* i (1968) 1–8.

Masinissa Numidian king, died 148 BC.
   Masinissa originally served Carthage but was
befriended by *Scipio Africanus in 206 BC; he was
Rome's principal local ally in the African campaign
of 204–202. After Zama and the elimination of his

Numidian bronze coin of Masinissa.

Basilica of Maxentius (AD 306–15), beside Forum Romanum.

rival, *Syphax (whose wife he is said to have loved), he acquired a greatly enlarged dominion and the title of king. Until his death 50 years later he remained the personal client of the Scipio family and the faithful ally of Rome, which tolerated his continual attempts to expand territorially at the expense of a weakened Carthage.

BIBL. Badian, *Clientelae*; P. G. Walsh, *JRS* lv (1965) 149 ff.

Matidia Niece of Trajan.

The niece of *Trajan and mother of the Empress *Sabina, Matidia was present when Trajan died in AD 117. She died in 119 and was deified. *Hadrian delivered her funeral oration.

BIBL. *PW* xiv. 2199–2202.

Mavia Arab queen, AD 370s.

Until the rise of Islam in the seventh century, the scattered Bedouin tribes were not much more than an irritant on Rome's eastern frontier, 'not worth

Sardonyx intaglio: *Trajan, *Plotina, Marciana, Matidia.

having either as friends or enemies', according to *Ammianus. Mavia, who succeeded her husband as 'queen of the Saracens', organized raids in which a Roman army was defeated—and only made peace on condition that a hermit called Moses was forcibly consecrated as bishop of her tribe. Her daughter was married to the Roman commander-in-chief *Victor. In 378 an Arab contingent helped defend Constantinople, its literally bloodthirsty mode of fighting intimidating even the Goths.

BIBL *PLRE* i, Mavia.

Maxentius Western usurper AD 306–12.

When *Diocletian and *Maximian abdicated in 305, Maxentius, Maximian's son, was among the disappointed aspirants for the vacated positions of Caesar. The following year the people of Rome, incensed by the attempts made by *Galerius, now senior Augustus, and *Severus his Caesar to set aside the city's ancient tax immunities, proclaimed Maxentius emperor. The new ruler brought his father out of retirement, so that when Severus marched on Rome with troops who had previously served under Maximian they promptly deserted to their old commander and his son. An attempt by Galerius to dislodge Maxentius met with equally small success. Maximian also arranged an alliance with *Constantine, sealed by the marriage of his daughter *Fausta. When in 308 he quarrelled with Maxentius, it was to Constantine's court that he

moved. At about the same time Maxentius
temporarily lost Africa by the usurpation of
Domitius *Alexander, but he held on to Italy and
formed a close relationship with the grandees of
the senate. At least at first he was also kind to the
Christians: it is to justify Constantine's surprise
attack on him in 312 that Christian historians like
*Eusebius condemn Maxentius as a tyrant.
Constantine advanced remarkably easily down Italy
and, just north of Rome (strengthened, so
*Lactantius and Eusebius aver, by the power of the
Christian God), he defeated definitively Maxentius'
larger forces. Maxentius was drowned in the Tiber
during the chaos of the retreat, a scene which
reminded Eusebius of Pharaoh and his forces
overwhelmed by the Red Sea. It also inspired the
sculptor of an arch dedicated to Constantine by the
senate, whose members in many cases retained the
offices they had held under Maxentius.

BIBL. Jones, *Constantine*; Frazer, *Art Bulletin*
xlviii (1966) 385–92; T. D. Barnes, *JRS* lxiii (1973).

Maximian Western emperor AD 285/6–305.

Like other members of the Tetrarchy, Maximian

Diocletian to celebrate their twentieth anniversary.
The city had seen nothing like it since the triumph
of Aurelian fifty years before; the Baths of
Diocletian and a magnificent monument outside
the senate house commemorated the occasion. The
following May Diocletian and Maximian abdicated;
events were to prove that Maximian was not keen
to stand down.

In 306 *Maxentius, Maximian's son, usurped the
purple at Rome and called his father out of
retirement to support his claim. The old man made
an alliance with *Constantine in Gaul, by giving
him his daughter *Fausta in marriage. After the
failure of a conference called by Galerius in 308 to
unravel the imperial tangles, Maximian returned to
Gaul and proclaimed himself Augustus. Constantine
made a lightning march from the Rhine to
Marseilles, and crushed his father-in-law. The old
man was allowed to select a method of committing
suicide: he chose hanging.

BIBL. W. Seston, *Dioclétien et la Tetrarchie* (1946),
only vol. i. appeared (it has not yet been
superseded); T. D. Barnes, *Phoenix* xxx (1976)
174–93.

Gold medallion (multiple *aureus*) of *Diocletian and
Maximian, AD 287. Berlin, Staatliche Museen.

Coin type of Maximin Daia (enlarged).

was drawn from that reservoir of talent trained in
the army of *Aurelian and *Probus. Soon after his
accession *Diocletian appointed his old comrade-in-
arms Caesar and sent him to Gaul to suppress
insurgents. In 286 he was created joint Augustus,
and continued to guard the Rhine frontier. Two
surviving panegyrics emphasize how closely he
worked with Diocletian: indeed he was Hercules to
Diocletian's Jupiter. In 293 *Constantius I and
*Galerius were appointed Caesars. Maximian
moved to the western Mediterranean, leaving the
North to Constantius. In 296–8 he put down
rebellions in Spain and Africa and made a grand
visit to Rome. He was in Rome again in 304 with

Maximin Daia Eastern emperor AD 305–13.

Daia, a nephew of *Galerius and an officer in the
imperial guard, was made Caesar when *Diocletian
abdicated in 305. All through the ensuing tortuous
internal wars he administered Egypt and Syria, and
in 310 was recognized as an Augustus. After
Galerius' death a year later he forestalled *Licinius,
now ruling in the Balkans, by annexing Asia
Minor, but in the summer of 313 Licinius, now
backed by *Constantine in Rome, defeated him and
he died. Daia was disgusted that Christians
should ignore their public duty to honour the
gods. With the encouragement of petitions from
many parts of the East and oracles from his
adviser *Theotecnus, he sustained the efforts of the

Great Persecution to turn them from what he thought an ephemeral and damaging novelty.

BIBL. *PLRE* i, Maximinus 12; R. M. Grant in *Christianity, Judaism and other Graeco-Roman Cults* iv, ed. J. Neusner (1975) 143–66.

Maximinus Praetorian prefect AD 371–6.

Maximinus was a fellow-Pannonian of *Valentinian I, and chief minister for half the reign. After governing a series of Italian provinces, he ruthlessly pursued cases of magic and adultery among the aristocracy at Rome, first as prefect of the corn supply (c. 369) and then as *vicarius* (370). Promoted to the court as praetorian prefect of Gaul, he maintained his reputation for harshness. When Valentinian died (375), Maximinus fell from power and was executed.

BIBL. *PLRE* i, Maximinus 7.

Maximinus I Thrax Emperor AD 235–8.

Born in Thrace c. 172/3 possibly of barbarian parentage, Gaius Julius Verus Maximinus was renowned for his gigantic stature (over 8 feet), tremendous physical strength, and the brutality of his reign. After enlisting in the cavalry he became a personal guard of the emperor, and later served as tribune under *Elagabalus and as chief military commander under *Severus Alexander. In 235 he was proclaimed emperor by his mutinous troops, and created his son *Maximus, Caesar. He waged a successful German campaign for about 18 months. The insurrection by the *Gordians in Africa in 238 led him to march against Rome, but both he and his son were slain by their own praetorian guard at Aquileia. He married Caecilia Paulina and is alleged (falsely) to have murdered her.

BIBL. *PIR* I 619; Herodian (Loeb); Syme, *Emperors and Biography*.

Maximus, Gaius Julius Verus Caesar AD 235–8.

Son of *Maximinus Thrax, Maximus was created Caesar by his father in 235 and remained with him on the Danube until the uprising of *Gordian I and II in 238, after which Maximinus marched on Italy. Both were killed by their rebellious troops at Aquileia.

BIBL. *PIR* I 620; *ANRW* ii. 2.

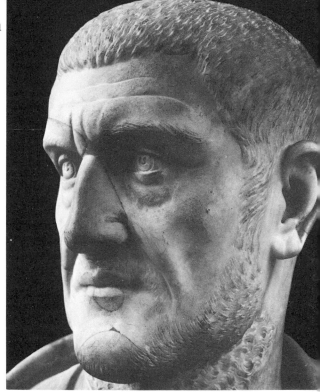

Portrait bust of the soldier-emperor Maximinus I Thrax.

Gold coin (*solidus*) of Magnus Maximus (enlarged).

Maximus, Magnus Western emperor AD 383–8.

Maximus, the 'Macsen Wledig' of Welsh legend, was a Spanish kinsman of Count *Theodosius, with whom he served in Britain and Africa, before being promoted to command the army in Britain. Here he was proclaimed emperor and invaded Gaul, the legitimate emperor *Gratian being deserted by his troops and killed (August 383). Maximus now controlled Spain and Gaul, and was recognized *de facto* by *Theodosius I until he invaded Italy (387); then the eastern army swept through the Balkans and caught Maximus at Aquileia, where he was killed (28 August 388). Maximus, whose earliest (London) coinage imitated coins of *Valentinian I, claimed to be a worthier successor than the two sons he displaced. He emphasized his Catholic orthodoxy by executing the Spanish heretic *Priscillian.

BIBL. Matthews, *Western Aristocracies*.

Maximus of Ephesus (died AD 371) Neoplatonist philosopher.

Member of a rich family of Ephesus, Maximus was a pupil of *Aedesius and became the teacher and intimate adviser of *Julian. *Eunapius describes his long grey beard and keen glances, his hieratic dignity and charm. More magician than true philosopher, he practised 'theurgy', the miracle-working appended by *Iamblichus to Neoplatonic philosophy, and in the early 350s with *Priscus and *Chrysanthius completed the young

Julian's conversion to paganism, initiating him into various mystery cults. When Julian became sole emperor (361), he summoned Maximus and other philosophers to his court and honoured him greatly, despite his un-philosophical arrogance and rapacity. He influenced policy through divination, and remained close to Julian, accompanying him to Persia (363) and attending his deathbed. He fell foul of the regime of *Valens and was tortured and heavily fined, and later executed for complicity in the *Theodorus conspiracy (371).

BIBL. *PLRE* i, Maximus 21; Eunapius, *Lives of the Philosophers* (Loeb with Philostratus).

Maximus of Tyre (*c.* AD 125–85) Sophist.

An itinerant lecturer and sophist, Maximus performed at Athens and Rome. There are 41 extant speeches, which were delivered in Rome in the reign of *Commodus. He was a follower of Plato, but his philosophical thought is generally considered superficial and unoriginal.

BIBL. *Philosophumena* (text), ed. H. Hobein (Teubner, 1910); E. R. Dodds, *Pagan and Christian in an Age of Anxiety* (1965).

Mela, Pomponius Geographer, early 1st century AD.

From Tingentera near Gibraltar, Mela was the author, under *Gaius or *Claudius, of a *Book of Places* in three books. After a general survey of world geography, the form of the work is that of mariners' directions; it may indeed have originated as a commentary upon a map. Lists of names are interspersed with highly-coloured rhetorical digressions on historical and geographical details. The work is a bizarre mixture, from a medley of sources, but contains important information and is the earliest surviving Latin geographical text.

St Melania the Younger (AD 383–439) Abbess.

Of distinguished Roman ancestry, Melania (following the example of her like-named grandmother) abandoned her senatorial heritage to adopt the ascetic life. With her husband Pinianus, she overcame the resistance of her family and liquidated her estates. Fleeing before the ravages of *Alaric's Goths in Italy, the couple crossed first to North Africa, and ultimately settled in Jerusalem, on the Mount of Olives (417), where she founded and presided over monasteries for men and women —and led a life of exemplary piety. Her *Life*, which survives in Greek and Latin versions, was written by her disciple Gerontius, who succeeded her as head of the monasteries.

BIBL. D. Gorce, *Vie de Sainte Mélanie* SC 90 (1962).

Melitius (died AD 325/8) Egyptian schismatic.

During the Great Persecution (303–13) many Christians gave way to pagan pressure. Melitius, of Lycopolis, found them pusillanimous, and rejected the regulations made by *Peter, bishop of Alexandria, for their readmission to the Church. He set himself up as leader of the Church in Egypt; the popular dockland priest *Arius of Alexandria was among his followers. Melitius' 'Church of the Martyrs' persisted after the persecution: like the African 'pure Church' named after *Donatus, it lingered on until the Muslim invasion.

BIBL. H. I. Bell, *Jews and Christians in Egypt* (1924).

Melito (died *c.* AD 190) Bishop and writer.

Melito was bishop of Sardis *c.* 160–70. Little of his work survives. A papyrus has preserved a treatise *On the Pasch* and there are fragments of an *Apology* addressed to *Marcus Aurelius and a work on baptism. Some important later Christian thinkers, notably *Irenaeus and *Tertullian, may have been influenced by his writings.

BIBL. O. Perler, SC 123 (1966).

Memmius (1), **Gaius** Praetor 104 BC.

As tribune in 111 BC Memmius reopened the challenge to the senatorial establishment which had been suppressed with Gaius *Gracchus in 121. He confined himself to denouncing the corrupt handling of relations with *Jugurtha by leading senators, and in 109 he was prominent in securing convictions under the law of *Mamilius. He met his death as a consular candidate in 100, probably at the instigation of *Saturninus—an act which prompted the senate to declare a state of emergency.

BIBL. Gruen, *Politics*.

Papyrus page of Melito's *On the Pasch* (end 3rd cent.): Moses, prophet of Christ. Bibl. Bodmer, Cologny-Genève.

Memmius (2), Gaius Praetor 58 BC.

Undistinguished in politics, Memmius is known chiefly for his patronage of the poets *Catullus and *Lucretius: the latter dedicated the *De rerum natura* to him. He governed Bithynia as propraetor in 57 BC, but as a consular candidate for 53 he was the principal casualty of the notoriously corrupt election of that year, and was exiled for bribery.

BIBL. Gruen, *Republic*.

Merobaudes (1) Master of the Infantry AD 375–88.

The first of the marshals who effectively ruled the western Empire during its last century, Flavius Merobaudes was by birth a Frank. He served in *Valentinian I's last campaign (375) as commander-in-chief, and at his death proclaimed his small son emperor (*Valentinian II). He dominated *Gratian's court (consul 377 and 383), but abandoned him for the usurper *Maximus, under whom he seems to have retained his office. In his almost unprecedented third consulship (388, compare *Aëtius), he was forced to commit suicide in obscure circumstances.

BIBL. *PLRE* i, Merobaudes.

Merobaudes (2) Poet, 5th century AD.

Flavius Merobaudes, a competent but mediocre poet, was probably a Romanized Frank who lived in Spain, but went to Rome to serve at the court of *Valentinian III some time before 435, when he was honoured with a statue in the Forum of *Trajan. He was a man 'of words as well as deeds' (*CIL* vi. 1724) who was commander-in-chief in 443 and died some time before the 460s. Six fragmentary secular poems (mostly panegyric), and one Christian one survive in a single mutilated manuscript.

BIBL. F. M. Clover, *Flavius Merobaudes, a Translation and Historical Commentary* (1971).

Messalina, Statilia Empress AD 66–8.

*Nero's third and last wife, Statilia Messalina was of very high birth and also wealthy, intelligent, and beautiful. She survived him, and was prevented from marrying *Otho in AD 69 only by his fall; she seems to have survived the Civil War as well.

BIBL. *PIR* S 625.

Messalla Corvinus Consul 31 BC.

A patrician, Marcus Valerius Messalla Corvinus was one of the most important figures of the Augustan principate, though he had been influential in the camp of *Brutus and *Cassius and continued to be so with *Antony, until he began to resent *Cleopatra. He fought for Octavian against Sex. *Pompeius in Illyricum, at Actium, and in Gaul (where he won a triumph). *Augustus also employed him in a number of his administrative experiments, particularly the abortive attempt to create the urban prefecture in 26 BC and the setting

Portrait statue of Statilia Messalina (?).

up of the water board in 11 BC. *Ovid wrote a dirge for him, probably before his exile: all his life Messalla was a great patron of poets, most notably of *Tibullus and Ovid, but was also regarded, with *Asinius Pollio, as the greatest orator of his generation, and was noted for his grammatical knowledge and latinity. Notable expenditure on public works also added to this great man's contribution to the Augustan age.

BIBL. *Panegyricus Messallae*; Syme, *Rom. Rev.*

Messalla Messallinus Consul 3 BC.

Son of *Messalla Corvinus, Marcus Valerius Messalla Messallinus as governor of Illyricum in AD 6 was proceeding against *Maroboduus with *Tiberius when he had to return to crush the Pannonian revolt; in doing so he won triumphal insignia. He played an important role—if an adulatory one—in the senate at the beginning of Tiberius' reign.

BIBL. Tacitus, *Annals*, iii. 34.

Messallina Empress AD 41–8.

The patrician Valeria Messallina, *Claudius' third wife, bore him *Britannicus and *Octavia. She made use of her position to destroy many influential figures, including *Valerius Asiaticus and Vinicius, and became notorious for her promiscuity, of which Claudius seems to have been unaware until she took the astonishing step of marrying Gaius Silius, the consul designate, in AD 48: her execution and the official blackening of her memory followed swiftly.

BIBL. Tacitus, *Annals*, xi. 26–38.

Silver coin (*denarius*) of Metellus Pius (81 BC) showing an elephant, the family emblem.

Metellus, Lucius Caecilius Consul 251 and 247 BC.

Defending Palermo in Sicily against Carthaginian attack in 250 BC, Metellus won a notable victory by neutralizing the effect of the reputedly invincible Punic war elephants. He captured many of these for slaughter at Rome. The elephant symbol was adopted on coin issues by later generations of Metelli.

BIBL. Crawford, *RRC* i. 287.

Metellus, Quintus Caecilius Consul 206 BC.

Metellus delivered the funeral oration of his father Lucius Caecilius *Metellus in 221 BC. Sent to Rome by *Salinator in 207 to announce the victory at the Metaurus, he was elected consul. He was a leading supporter of *Scipio Africanus during the *Pleminius scandal. His conduct of an embassy to investigate charges against *Philip V in 185 initiated the deterioration of relations which led to the Third Macedonian War. In the same year he visited Achaea in an apparently unofficial capacity, and was therefore refused access to the Achaean assembly. This snub caused a minor crisis in Roman-Achaean relations, but in 183 he was regarded as an expert on Peloponnesian affairs.

BIBL. Walbank, *Philip V of Macedon* (1940) 227–234; Errington, *Philopoemen* (1969); *ORF* 9 f.

Metellus Macedonicus Consul 143 BC.

As praetor in Macedonia in 148 BC Quintus Caecilius Metellus Macedonicus crushed the revolt of *Andriscus (the so-called Fourth Macedonian War) and supervised the creation of the province of Macedonia. Being nearby he intervened, at first diplomatically and then militarily, in Achaea (147–146), until he was relieved by *Mummius. At Rome he obtained a triumph and built the *Porticus Metelli*. As consul in Spain he suppressed much of the Celtiberian revolt. He acquired a reputation as a moral and political reactionary, and was a prominent opponent of the *Gracchi.

BIBL. Astin, *Scipio Aemil.*

Metellus Numidicus Consul 109 BC.

A prominent member of the powerful Metellan family, Quintus Caecilius Metellus Numidicus took over the command as consul against *Jugurtha, at a time when the conduct of the war was under heavy attack. He achieved immediate and decisive military successes, thus earning the surname Numidicus. But he failed to finish the war, and in 107 BC was superseded by his former subordinate officer, *Marius, whom he henceforth regarded with intense hatred. After initial opposition at Rome, Metellus was able to triumph in 106. A vigorous opponent of the popular demagogues, he attempted as censor in 102 to expel *Saturninus and *Glaucia from the senate, but was compelled by violent intimidation to back down. In 100 he was the only senator not to swear to observe an agrarian law of Saturninus, and went into exile. His recall (probably in 98) was a great triumph for the senatorial establishment.

BIBL. Gruen, *Politics*.

Metellus Pius Consul 80 BC.

Quintus Caecilius Metellus Pius earned his surname for filial piety in 99 BC, when he pleaded for the recall from exile of his father, *Metellus Numidicus. After his praetorship in 89 he fought successfully in southern Italy in the later stages of the Social War, and was still in command of an army in 87. Unable to oppose *Cinna's advance on Rome, he established himself as an independent force in Africa until 84. He was expelled by the praetor C. Fabius Hadrianus, and eventually joined forces with *Sulla in Italy (83). He held the consulship with Sulla in 80, and proceeded to a proconsular command in Hispania Ulterior against *Sertorius. He was initially unsuccessful, but from 76 onwards, with the co-operation of *Pompey, he turned the tide against Sertorius. He returned to a triumph in 71, but sank into political obscurity.

BIBL. Badian, *Clientelae*; Gruen, *Republic*.

Metellus Scipio Consul 52 BC.

An unattractive figure of little ability, Quintus Caecilius Metellus Scipio nevertheless stood at the centre of the old aristocracy, being a Scipio by birth and the adopted son of *Metellus Pius. *Pompey therefore found him a valuable ally in 52 BC, when he sought to enlist the support of the senatorial establishment against the potential challenge from *Caesar. He married Metellus' daughter, and as sole consul elevated him to the consulship he had been unable to secure by election. Metellus supported the uncompromising attitude of the senate towards Caesar which hastened the Civil War in 49. He held a proconsular command in the East and joined forces with Pompey at Pharsalus, whence he escaped to Africa. He assumed command of the Pompeian forces there, and committed suicide after Caesar's victory at Thapsus in 46.

BIBL. Taylor, *Party Politics*; Gruen, *Republic*; Seager, *Pompey*.

Milo Praetor 55 BC.

As tribune in 57 BC Titus Annius Milo was sponsored by *Pompey to counteract the influence of the increasingly independent *Clodius, and in particular to assist in the recall of *Cicero from exile. For the next five years he contested Clodius' organized street violence with rival gangs. His services endeared him to conservative opinion in the senate, but contributed to the breakdown of law and order. He aspired to the consulship of 52, turning against Pompey who refused assistance; but by killing Clodius early in 52 he precipitated a crisis which led to Pompey's sole consulship. Milo was brought to trial by Pompey, and condemned: Cicero was prevented by Pompey's intimidation from conducting Milo's defence. He left his comfortable exile to perish in an abortive rebellion against *Caesar in south Italy (48).

BIBL. Lintott, *Violence*; Gruen, *Republic*.

Silver coin (*denarius*), 135 BC, showing statue-column erected for Minucius Augurinus.

Minucius Esquilinus Augurinus, Lucius Consul (suffect?) 458 BC.

Minucius was allegedly rescued by *Cincinnatus in 458 BC, and appears in the fictitious Second Decemvirate. In 440–439 as corn commissioner he supposedly denounced Sp. *Maelius. Probably family legend originally claimed simply that he relieved a famine (second-century BC coins issued by two Minucii show a statue-column, almost certainly regarded as his, with corn ears below), and that he was co-opted as eleventh tribune (thus explaining their transition to plebeian status). His involvement with Sp. Maelius, though early, may then be secondary and influenced by etymological play on his name (the Greek *menutes* means 'informer').

BIBL. PW xv. 1950 ff.; A. Momigliano, *Quarto Contributo* 331 ff.; Crawford, *RRC* i. 273 ff. (nos. 242–3).

Minucius Felix Christian apologist, 3rd century AD.

Marcus Minucius Felix, probably a North African lawyer, wrote the *Octavius*, the first Christian apologetic dialogue, some time between 200 and 245. The work, transmitted in a single manuscript as the eighth book of *Arnobius' *Against the Pagans*, is largely a compilation of material from *Seneca and from *Tertullian's *Apology*, but still possesses astonishing grace, style, and passion.

Mithridates King of Pontus 120–63 BC.

A vigorous king, Mithridates built up the strength of his Black Sea kingdom until he could seriously challenge Rome's supremacy in the East. In 88 BC he took advantage of the warfare in Italy to invade the Roman province of Asia. For a while he became the focus of anti-Roman sentiment: his propaganda dwelt on the themes of Roman greed and misrule. In Asia 80,000 Italian residents were massacred on his orders, and he publicly executed the ambassador, M'. *Aquillius. His army was welcomed into Greece in 87, but he was defeated there by *Sulla, who drove him back into his kingdom and forced him to relinquish his recent conquests in a treaty of 85 BC.

When in 74 Nicomedes IV of Bithynia bequeathed his kingdom to Rome, Mithridates provoked another major conflict with Rome by invading Bithynia. He was ejected by the consul L. *Lucullus, who also overran Pontus. But Mithridates received assistance from his son-in-law, *Tigranes of Armenia, and continued to resist until Lucullus was succeeded by *Pompey in 66. Further defeats led to an internal revolt in his kingdom, and Mithridates took his life in 63, using a sword since his body had become immune to poison.

BIBL. Reinach, *Mithridate Eupator, roi de Pont* (1890); Will, *Hist. pol.*, 386–423.

Portrait head of Mithridates wearing a lion mask. Paris, Louvre.

Modestus Praetorian prefect AD 369–77.

Chief minister of *Valens for much of his reign, the only civilian to become consul (372), Domitius Modestus was an Arabian who held important offices under *Constantius II and *Julian, when, although described by *Ammianus as uncultured, he received many letters from *Libanius. As prefect (369–77) he is said to have corruptly diverted Valens from personal administration of justice; Christian sources represent him as an agent of the persecution of Catholics. He served both Constantius and Valens as an interrogator in treason trials, but also deserves credit for Valens' success in reducing taxation.

BIBL. *PLRE* i, Modestus 2.

Montanus Christian prophet, 2nd century AD.

A Phrygian prophet, Montanus' preaching (which is dated to either 156–7 or 172 AD) predicted the descent of a heavenly Jerusalem in Phrygia and aroused the opposition of Asian bishops. The ascetic practices which he advocated became a prominent feature of African Montanism, of which the most famous adherent was *Tertullian.

BIBL. W. H. C. Frend, *Martyrdom and Persecution in the Early Church*; T. D. Barnes, *Tertullian* (1971).

Mucianus Consul AD 64/7, 70, and 72.

Overzealous cultivation of the wrong people forced Gaius Licinius Mucianus to live in Asia Minor under *Claudius, but *Nero advanced his career and sent him to Syria; there he became *Vespasian's right-hand man and most loyal supporter in the crucial early stages of the Flavian involvement in the Civil War of AD 69. He proceeded to Rome with *Domitian to prepare the way for Vespasian, but appears in the next years reaping the benefits of his loyalty rather than being given the chance of demonstrating it afresh. He had literary, luxurious, and lascivious interests.

BIBL. Tac. *Hist.* i. 10; *PIR* L 216.

Mummius Consul 146 BC.

A successful general, Lucius Mummius won two triumphs for campaigns in Spain (153 BC) and Greece (146). In his consulship he crushed the revolt of the Achaean League, which thereafter ceased to exist. He followed up his victory by the systematic looting of Corinth (prior to its total destruction by senatorial decree), and shipped vast amounts of booty to Italy. His indiscriminate treatment of valuable works of art among this booty won him a reputation for barbarism.

BIBL. Colin, *Rome et la Grèce* (1905) 628 ff.; Walbank, *HCP* iii. 728 ff.

Musonianus, Strategius Praetorian prefect AD 354–8.

A Christian fluent in Greek and Latin, Strategius made himself useful to *Constantine in ecclesiastical affairs, and won his favour and the name Musonianus honouring his devotion to the Muses and learning. Under *Constantius II he was (probably) proconsul of Constantinople, then of Achaea (353), and then praetorian prefect of the East (354–8). He was dismissed after initiating imprudent negotiations with a Persian general which played into the hands of *Shapur II. He was a good administrator, but venal (*Ammianus).

BIBL. *PLRE* i, Musonianus.

Musonius Rufus (*c.* AD 30–101) Philosopher.

An equestrian from Volsinii (Bolsena) and a Stoic, Gaius Musonius Rufus wrote in Greek and was the teacher of *Epictetus and *Dio Chrysostom. He followed his pupil *Rubellius Plautus into exile, was involved in the *Pisonian conspiracy in AD 65 and suffered banishment, and was exiled afresh under *Vespasian. A number of his sayings and discourses survive.

BIBL. Macmullen, *Enemies, passim.*

Nabis King of Sparta 207–192 BC.

Nabis' revolutionary policy at home and vigorous foreign policy in the Peloponnese incurred the intense hostility of the conservative Achaean, *Polybius, and led to the attack on him by *Flamininus and the other Greek allies (195 BC), although he had joined the Roman side before Cynoscephalae. He joined the Aetolians against Rome in 193, but was defeated by *Philopoemen and assassinated the next year.

BIBL. Briscoe, *Livy*, esp. 122 f.

Naevius Dramatic and epic poet, late 3rd century BC.

A native of Campania, Gnaeus Naevius wrote numerous comedies, tragedies after Greek models, and important *praetextae*. His first dramatic production was in 235 BC. But his epic in Saturnians, the *Bellum Punicum* (on the First Punic War, in which he had served, with an excursus on Rome's legendary origins), was of wider and lasting influence, not least on *Virgil's *Aeneid*, through its combination of history and myth.

BIBL. *CRF* 6 ff.; *TRF* 7 ff.; on the *Bellum Punicum*, no edition earlier than Strzelecki's masterly study (1935) should be consulted; Wigodsky, *Vergil and Early Latin Poetry* (1972) 22 ff.

Namatianus, Rutilius Poet, late 4th to early 5th century AD.

All knowledge of Rutilius Claudius Namatianus rests on the text of his long elegiac poem *On his Return*, discovered in Bobbio in 1493. He was a Gaul, probably born in Toulouse, the son of Lachanius, governor of Tuscany and Umbria, and he held at least two important posts at Rome during the reign of *Honorius: Master of the Offices (412–13), and the urban prefecture, for a short term, between 13 January and 16 September 414. *On his Return*, a description of the author's voyage from Rome to Gaul around 13 October 417, is important for its historical revelations, and for some extremely interesting polemic against the monks, Jews, and against *Stilicho, the 'betrayer of the secret of the Empire' and burner of the Sibylline Books. Rutilius' prayer to Dea Roma and interest in a festival of Osiris may indicate that he was a pagan. The poem's literary merit is considerable, and the well-turned elegiac couplets reveal the engaging character of the author.

BIBL. A. Cameron, *JRS* lvii (1967) 36.

Narcissus (died AD 54) Freedman of Claudius.

Most influential among the imperial freedmen, Narcissus held the post of secretary for correspondence. He was employed on important missions such as the quelling of a mutiny before the British expedition of AD 43, and his power and wealth were enormous, though not always well used. He was opposed to *Agrippina and a supporter of *Britannicus, so he was driven to suicide within hours of *Claudius' death.

BIBL. *PIR* N 18.

Narses King of Persia AD 293–302.

Narses succeeded his great-nephew Bahram III, who reigned four months. He sent two expeditions against Rome. In 296, in Syria, he won; in 298 he was ambushed in Armenia by *Galerius. The Roman army marched on Ctesiphon and the disconsolate Narses had to sue for peace and the return of his family. The diplomatic consequences of this débâcle remained basic to relations between the two great powers for several generations.

BIBL. J. Gagé, *La Montée des Sassanides* (1964); E. Herzfeld, *Païkuli* (1924).

Nemesianus Poet, floruit *c.* AD 284.

Marcus Aurelius Nemesianus Olympius, a North African poet whose work is attested by the *Augustan History*, wrote highly derivative *Bucolics*, and an interesting versified hunting manual, the *Cynegetics*. Two other attested works, the *On Fishing* and the *Nautica* are lost.

BIBL. R. Verdière, *Prolégomènes à Nemesianus* (1974).

Nepos, Cornelius (born *c.* 110 BC) Biographer.

Nepos was a native of Cisalpine Gaul, like *Catullus, who dedicated his 'little book' to him, with no small irony at Nepos' expense. *Cicero and *Atticus were likewise disrespectful of this moderately talented (at best) compiler of moral examples (*Exempla*), chronological synchronisms (*Annales*, establishing, for example, that the Greek poet Archilochus and King *Tullus Hostilius were

contemporaries, and especially of biographies. Of his *On Famous Men*, in at least sixteen books (first edition, 35/2, second, with additions, 29/7), one, on foreign generals, survives; others covered Roman generals, Roman and Greek historians, and perhaps also Roman poets. The extant book, whose authorship is intermittently challenged, is characterized by ungainly style, frequent error, and extreme *naïveté*; it presupposes, mysteriously, readers both tirelessly patient and boundlessly ignorant of foreign history. (However, the life of his friend Atticus and that of the Elder *Cato, which have also survived, reveal traces of a finer talent.) The work as a whole will have been consciously popularizing in character, and was designed to contrast the great men of Greece and Rome (see *Plutarch).

BIBL. E. Jenkinson in *Latin Biography*, ed T. A. Dorey (1967) 1 ff.; A. Momigliano, *The Development of Greek Biography* (1971) 96 ff.

Nepos, Julius Western emperor AD 473–5.

After succeeding his uncle, *Marcellinus, as Master of the Soldiers in Dalmatia, Julius Nepos was appointed emperor in the West by the Emperor *Leo in 473. Although he tried to reassert Roman authority in Gaul against *Euric, to little avail, he was in turn deposed by his Patrician, *Orestes. The East continued to recognize him, officially, but provided no practical support. He was killed near Salonae in 480.

BIBL. *Anonymus Valesianus*, VII. 36; Stein, *Bas-Empire*, i. 395–6.

Bronze coin of Nepotianus (enlarged).

Nepotianus Usurper AD 350.

Son of *Constantine's half-sister Eutropia, Julius Nepotianus was an ephemeral usurper proclaimed at Rome by the opponents of the usurper *Magnentius (q.v.), but killed after a month by Magnentius' troops. A coin of his depicts him holding an orb surmounted by a chi-rho monogram instead of the usual figure of Victory.

BIBL. *PLRE* i, Nepotianus 5; *RIC* viii (forthcoming).

Neratius Priscus Jurist, consul AD 97.

There is much doubt surrounding the family of
the Neratii, who certainly rose under *Domitian.
Their most famous member, Lucius Neratius
Priscus, was an acute and influential jurist, last
head of the Proculian school, and, in one anecdote,
considered as a possible successor by *Trajan.

BIBL. Syme, *Hermes*, lxxxv (1957) = *RP* 27;
Tacitus, 233–4.

Nero (AD 37–68) Emperor AD 54–68.

Lucius Domitius Ahenobarbus, the son of
*Agrippina the Younger and Cn. *Domitius
Ahenobarbus, was brought up by his mother alone
from the age of three, and played the part normal
for children closely connected with the imperial
family. When his mother became *Claudius' last
wife, he took on the more onerous role of Claudius'
son, and was preferred to his adoptive brother
*Britannicus on grounds of age and because of his
mother's influence. When Agrippina had the old
emperor poisoned, Nero—as he had been called
since his adoption—quickly became emperor, and
soon after disposed of Britannicus and his principal
ally, the freedman *Narcissus. He was still young
and in need of guidance, which was amply
provided by his mother, his old tutor *Seneca, and
the praetorian prefect *Burrus. However, Nero
preferred to devote himself to singing, acting, and

Portrait head of the young Nero, *c.* AD 54. Rome,
Museo delle Terme.

Nero's Domus Aurea (Golden House), AD 64–8: part of
interior, with frescoes. Rome, near Colosseum.

chariot racing, and, although he participated in the
affairs of state, he showed the lack of judgement
which derived from his having had no training in
office by making foolish, if generous, suggestions
such as the abolition of all the lesser taxes. At the
beginning of his reign he had been told to avoid the
worst trespasses against senatorial autonomy which
had marked Claudius' reign, especially trials *in
camera*, and at first these principles were adhered
to; indeed, even after Nero had murdered his
mother and asserted his independence of his
advisers, the tone they had given the reign
remained and made it quite different from the
preceding one. The functions of government
proceeded quite smoothly under Nero, and the
successes of *Corbulo and the emperor's
philhellenism (demonstrated especially on his
emotional and spectacular tour of Greece in 67)
ensured that in the East at least he was popular.

Provincial government was not always
successful, however, and the revolt of *Boudicca in
Britain in AD 61 was caused in part by the abuses
of provincial rule. Among the armies of the Empire
too, unemployment (at least in the West) and
growing distaste for the antics of so abandoned and
un-Roman an emperor grew steadily throughout
the reign. For Nero indulged his curious tastes in
many ways, and even the great conspiracy of
senators and officers of the guard in AD 65, with
*Piso as figurehead, which was destroyed with such
bloodshed by Nero's minion and praetorian prefect
*Tigellinus, partner of his excesses, failed to make
him realize how dangerous his behaviour was. In
the end, the revolt of *Vindex in Gaul and *Galba in
Spain, supported by the praetorians under
*Nymphidius Sabinus, drove him to despair and
suicide just before the news of the victory of
*Verginius Rufus for his cause at Besançon. By that
time he had added to the list of his victims two
wives (*Octavia (2), murdered on her island of
exile, and *Poppaea, kicked to death when
pregnant), his former tutor Seneca (told to commit

suicide), and figures of prominence in the senate, such as *Thrasea Paetus, who had the courage to register their disapproval of his ways.

Nero's reign was also marked by the disastrous fire of Rome in AD 64, which he exploited for the building of his vast whimsy of a palace, the Domus Aurea (though it was probably not started on his orders); the way in which the Christians were made scapegoats for this disaster is not the least notorious or disgusting episode of this depressing reign.

BIBL. B. H. Warmington, *Nero* (1969).

Nero, Gaius Claudius Consul 207 BC.

Nero briefly held the command against *Hasdrubal in Spain before the arrival of *Scipio Africanus in 210 BC. As consul in 207 he commanded against *Hannibal in south Italy, while his colleague *Salinator met Hasdrubal's threatened invasion in the north. In this, Rome's last great crisis of the Second Punic War, it was essential to prevent a junction of the two Carthaginian armies. In a move of sudden daring Nero divided his army and, slipping away from Hannibal unnoticed, marched rapidly northwards to join Salinator with 7,000 men. Hasdrubal, realizing that he was now outnumbered, tried to escape but was utterly defeated and killed at the river Metaurus. Nero then undertook another forced march southwards to rejoin his army before Hannibal could discover its weakened state. He announced the news to Hannibal by throwing Hasdrubal's severed head into his camp. Nero allowed his colleague the position of precedence at their joint triumph (the first of the war). He was the senior member of the embassy which delivered Rome's ultimatum to *Philip V in 200 BC.

BIBL. Scullard, *Politics*; Lazenby, *Hannibal*.

Nero Julius Caesar; Drusus Julius Caesar (died AD 31, 33).

Nero and Drusus were sons of *Germanicus and *Agrippina the Elder. Nero was at first given outstanding honours, but *Sejanus poisoned *Tiberius' mind against him, and when Livia's death opened the way for such actions he was accused and exiled, to die in 31. Out of jealousy of Nero, Drusus, who had also been distinguished with honours and a good marriage, turned to Sejanus, but suffered a similar fate to his brother, and died in captivity in Rome in 33.

BIBL. *PIR* I 223, 220.

Nerva Emperor AD 96–8.

Both Nerva's grandfather and father, also named Marcus Cocceius *Nerva, were known for their legal talents. Nerva himself seems not to have shared this ability, and indeed the only intellectual trait that is recorded of him is that he composed verse. It remains a mystery, therefore, what he did to earn honours equal to those of *Tigellinus after

the crushing of *Piso's conspiracy in AD 65, and why *Vespasian chose him—an outstanding honour —as his colleague in the consulship of 71. *Domitian, too, took him as colleague in AD 90: his reliability had perhaps been shown in the crisis of *Saturninus' rebellion. We know of no military experience and no provincial governorships in his career, but he was clearly stalwartly loyal to the Establishment. The story that he was exiled under Domitian seems to be a desirable fiction: Nerva was not so respectable.

In 96 Nerva's age, dignity, and lack of children recommended him as a stop-gap candidate for emperor: also, there was no danger of his founding a dynasty or adopting the autocratic methods of which so many senators disapproved. The exiles returned and *libertas* was proclaimed. Nerva selected venerable and distinguished advisers such as *Frontinus and *Verginius Rufus—but more controversial figures such as Fabricius *Veiento retained all their former influence. Domitian's building projects were completed, and administrative changes and financial reforms contemplated.

In 97 there were two revolts: the lesser one by the ambitious Calpurnius Crassus, repeatedly persuaded by his high birth to attempt a *coup*, but never successful enough even to warrant execution as a punishment; and a serious disturbance by the

Portrait statue of Nerva with oak wreath: detail. Rome, Vatican Museum.

praetorian guard under Casperius Aelianus, in the aftermath of which Nerva was driven to adopt *Trajan. Shortly afterwards Nerva died. He cannot be described as an effective or admirable emperor, and the character of his reign, which saw the beginning of the improved relations between emperor and senate which continued under Trajan, was not the product of any initiative on his part.

BIBL. Syme, *Tacitus*, 1–18; 'Life of Nerva' in Penguin *Historia Augusta*, (Birley).

Nerva, Marcus Cocceius

There were three important men of this name: a supporter of *Antony who changed sides successfully; his grandson, water-commissioner and close personal friend of *Tiberius, who accompanied the emperor to Capri and starved himself to death in AD 33 (he was a remarkable jurist of similar views to those of *Labeo), and *his* grandson who became emperor (q.v.).

BIBL. *PIR* C 1225 (the jurist).

Nestorius Bishop of Constantinople AD 428–31.

Nestorius was a celebrated preacher of Antioch, nominated by *Theodosius II to the see of Constantinople. He aroused theological controversy over the person of Christ by his rejection of the term 'mother of God'; and a campaign against him was led by *Cyril of Alexandria, motivated as much by the political rivalry between his own see and that of Constantinople as by theological belief. Condemned by the Synod of Ephesus in 431, Nestorius withdrew first to Antioch, and then to exile in the Egyptian desert.

BIBL. L. Duchesne, *Early History of the Christian Church*, iii (1924).

Nevitta Master of the Cavalry AD 361–363/4.

Flavius Nevitta was the first known German to be consul. A cavalry leader under *Constantius II, he was appointed Master of the Cavalry by *Julian for the march against Constantius, and, although boorish and cruel, was rewarded by the consulship for 362, with Cl. *Mamertinus. He sat on the Commission of Chalcedon (see *Arbitio), and commanded the right wing on Julian's Persian expedition (363). He voiced the wishes of the Gallic army in the debate over choosing a successor to Julian (see *Jovian), and must then have retired or been dismissed.

BIBL. *PLRE* i, Nevitta.

Nicolaus of Damascus (born *c.* 64 BC) Man of letters.

A man of distinguished antecedents and wide education, Nicolaus followed an important career as a diplomat (including three visits to Italy, shuttling between *Herod the Great and *Augustus) in addition to his literary work, which was most prolific. His writings include (1) a biography of

Augustus' early years, of which substantial fragments survive, of exceptional interest; (2) a collection of ethnographical data; (3) a universal history in 144 books, carried down to 4 BC and of great importance for the recent history of the Near East; and (4) an autobiography, justifying his remarkable career to Greek readers.

BIBL. Trans. and commentary of biography of Augustus, by Hall (1923); *FGH* 90; Bowersock, *Augustus and the Greek World* (1965) 134 ff.; Wacholder, *Nicolaus of Damascus* (1962).

Nigidius Figulus (*c.* 100–45 BC) Polymath.

Possibly of a family of Etruscan origin, Nigidius was praetor in 58, an active supporter of *Pompey, exiled under *Caesar, and supposedly an active follower of Pythagoras. He wrote copiously on grammar, astronomy, astrology and the occult, zoology, and especially on religion; a good deal of his work on omens and portents, under strong Etruscan influence, survives.

BIBL. Works, ed. Swoboda (1889).

Nobilior, Marcus Fulvius Consul 189 BC.

As consul in Greece, Nobilior brought the Aetolian War to a speedy conclusion, the decisive event being the surrender of Ambracia; but he offended against the Roman rules of war by looting Ambracia of its art treasures after its surrender. This became a minor scandal at Rome in 187 owing mainly to the personal hostility of M. *Lepidus (1), who had a decree of the senate passed in favour of Ambracia, but did not prevent Nobilior obtaining a triumph when he returned laden with booty in that year. Lepidus and Nobilior were reconciled when they were both elected to the censorship of 179. Nobilior was also noted for his patronage of the poet *Ennius and his general enthusiasm for Greek culture.

BIBL. Toynbee, *Hannibal's Legacy*, 624 ff.; Scullard, *Politics*.

Nonnus Poet, mid-5th century AD.

Other than his birthplace, Panopolis in Upper Egypt, nothing is known of the life of Nonnus, author of two extant works: the monumental pagan *Dionysiaca*, an epic account of the deeds of Dionysus, and a metrical paraphrase of the Fourth Gospel. His style and vocabulary are remarkable, and he was to exert a lasting influence on the Greek hexameter.

BIBL. G. d'Ippolito, *Studi Nonniani* (1964).

Norbanus, Gaius Consul 83 BC.

As a popular tribune in 103 BC Norbanus assisted the anti-senatorial programme of his colleague, *Saturninus, by successfully prosecuting Q. *Caepio for peculation. He remained attached to *Marius' party and rose under *Cinna's regime to the consulship of 83. He thus led the government's resistance to the invading *Sulla, but after a series of defeats he fled to Rhodes and committed suicide.

BIBL. Badian, *Studies*, esp. 34–70.

Novatian Leader of schism, mid-3rd century AD.

Possibly Phrygian by birth, Novatian was a philosopher before his conversion to Christianity. He became a leading presbyter of the Church in Rome and wrote an influential work on the Trinity. Although orthodox doctrinally, he became the leader of a schism arising from the *Decian persecution (249–50), by opposing the re-admission of lapsed Christians into the Church. Although the Novatianists were excommunicated and Novatian is said to have been martyred under *Valerian (257/8), the sect survived until the fifth century and in some places later.

BIBL. *CAH* xii.

Left: bronze coin, Numa Pompilius and Ancus Marcius (88 BC). Right: *denarius*, Numa Pompilius sacrificing ((?) 97 BC).

Numa Pompilius King of Rome *c.* 700 BC (?).

Numa, from Cures, was the second king of Rome (conventional dates: 715–673 BC). The name may be authentic but his portrait is a (priestly?) stereotype. Through his establishment of priesthoods, cults, and rituals he represents the scrupulous (and simple) observance of public religious obligations. Stories accumulated of his debt to Pythagoras (fiercely contested on chronological grounds), liaison with the nymph Egeria, and various miracles. Alleged writings by Numa were 'discovered' in 181 BC: they were promptly suppressed.

BIBL. PW xvii. 1242 ff.; Ogilvie, *Livy*, 88 ff.

Numerian Emperor AD 283–4.

Younger son of *Carus, Marcus Aurelius Numerius Numerianus was proclaimed Caesar in 282 and became emperor in 283, with his brother *Carinus, following the death of their father. He was murdered by his praetorian prefect *Aper in 284.

BIBL. *CAH* xii; *PLRE* i, Numerianus; *PIR* A 1564.

Nymphidius Sabinus Praetorian prefect AD 65–8.

The mother of Gaius Nymphidius Sabinus was the daughter of Callistus the imperial freedman,

and he used to claim that he had been fathered by *Gaius. Of his early career only military service in Pannonia is known. As praetorian prefect of *Nero from AD 65 he was less notorious than his colleague *Tigellinus but equally powerful. In 68 he brought the praetorian guard over to *Galba, but was later killed while trying for imperial power himself.

BIBL. Tac. *Ann.* xv. 72; *Hist* i. 5–6.

Octavia (1) (died 11 BC) Sister of Augustus.

Elder sister of *Augustus, Octavia was married first to Marcus Claudius Marcellus, to whom she bore *Marcellus, and in 40 BC, for political reasons, to *Antony. Rejected and divorced by Antony, she remained loyal and, after his death in 30, brought up all his children, including *Cleopatra's. She is a shadowy figure, although she played an important part in fostering literature and beautifying Rome. The death of Marcellus in 23 affected her cruelly, and darkened the years until her own demise in 11 BC.

BIBL. Syme, *Rom. Rev.*

Octavia (2) Empress AD 54–62.

Daughter of *Claudius and *Messallina, Claudia Octavia was betrothed to L. Junius *Silanus but married to *Nero, to cement his adoption. Nero's entanglement with Acte and his wish to marry *Poppaea doomed Octavia to divorce (it was claimed that she was sterile), exile, and death at the age of 20 on the barren island of Pandateria, despite much popular sympathy.

BIBL. The tragedy *Octavia* attributed to *Seneca.

Octavian: see **Augustus**

Octavius, Gnaeus Consul 165 BC.

In 169 BC Octavius went with Gaius *Popillius Laenas on a conciliatory embassy to Rome's major Greek allies in the war against *Perseus. The embassy was to publicize a decree recently passed

Portico of Octavia (1), 27 BC. Rome.

by the senate in response to allied complaints about Rome's commanders. In 168 as praetor he commanded the fleet aginst Perseus, whom he captured at Samothrace. His knowledge of Greek qualified him to deliver a Greek translation of *Paullus' (2) speech at Amphipolis on the settlement of Macedonia (167). He celebrated a triumph on his return and built the *Porticus Octavia* (since disappeared). In 163 he led a major embassy to many eastern states, the main purpose of which was to take advantage of the Seleucid kingdom's weakness after *Antiochus IV's death to enforcë the disarmament clauses of the 188 BC treaty. The popular fury aroused by the killing of war elephants and burning of ships led to Octavius' assassination at Laodicea. The assassin was later sent to Rome by *Demetrius Soter, but the senate refused to accept him. At Rome Octavius was honoured with a statue on the Rostra, referred to by *Cicero (*Philippics* ix. 4 f.).

BIBL. Briscoe, *Historia* xviii (1969) 63 ff.; Walbank, *HCP* iii. esp. 330.

Odaenath King of Palmyra *c.* AD 260–6.

Septimius Odaenath was instrumental in checking the Persian advance into the eastern Roman Empire after the capture of *Valerian by *Shapur I in 260. Within a few months he inflicted a stinging defeat on the retreating Persian army, eliminated the usurper *Quietus, and was rewarded with the titles 'corrector totius orientis' and 'dux Romanorum'. He continued to attack the Persians until peace was signed in 264, leaving Odaenath a nominal vassal but in fact the real ruler of Syro-Palestine, Mesopotamia and eastern Asia Minor. A family quarrel led to his murder in 266. (See also *Zenobia.)

BIBL. L. de Blois, *Talanta* 1975; *PLRE* i, Odaenath; Walser and Pekary, *Krise*.

Odoacer King of Italy AD 476–93.

A leader of the Sciri (probably), Odoacer took advantage of discontent with the regime of *Orestes to depose his figure-head, *Romulus Augustulus, and take power himself over Italy and parts of Raetia and Noricum, later expanding into Sicily and, on *Nepos' death, Dalmatia. Acknowledged Patrician by the East, he called himself by the barbarian title of 'king' (*rex*), signalling a break with the past, although Roman officials continued prominent in his administration. In 489 Italy was invaded by Ostrogoths under Theoderic. Despite three defeats, Odoacer held out in Ravenna for three years, but was finally tricked into surrender and killed (493).

BIBL. A. Chastagnol. *Le Sénat romain sous le règne d'Odoacre* (1966).

Ogulnius Gallus, Quintus Consul 269 BC.

As tribunes of the plebs (300 BC) Quintus and

Gnaeus Ogulnius Gallus opened the pontificate and augurate to plebeians, and as curule aediles (296) established a statue group of *Romulus and Remus at the *ficus Ruminalis* (the fig-tree, usually located just below the Palatine Hill, where they were reputedly suckled by the she-wolf). Quintus headed the commission which brought Asclepius from Epidaurus (292), campaigned in Bruttium (269), and celebrated the Latin festival as dictator (257).

BIBL. PW xvii. 2064 ff.; Crawford, *RRC* 35 ff., 137 (n.20), 714.

Olybrius Western emperor AD 472.

A member of the Anicii and also of the Theodosian house through his marriage with Placidia, daughter of *Valentinian III, Olybrius was also related to the house of *Geiseric through Huneric's marriage to his wife's sister. Consul in 464 and Geiseric's nominee for the western throne, Olybrius was finally chosen emperor by *Ricimer (July 472) but died the following November of dropsy.

BIBL. Bury, *Later Empire*, i. 340.

Olybrius, Quintus Clodius Hermogenianus Praetorian prefect AD 378–9.

Olybrius belonged to the Anicii, and like his son-in-law Petronius *Probus typifies that family's happy combination of public office and private gain. After governing Campania and Africa (361), he became urban prefect (368–70), delegating to *Maximinus a criminal investigation which was to implicate his own brother Alypius. In the critical year 378 he became praetorian prefect of Illyricum, the post recently vacated by *Probus; when *Valens died (August 378), he was transferred to the eastern prefecture (consul 379). He was a voluptuary, according to *Ammianus. A letter of *Symmachus (384) exposes him as a ruthless land-grabber who used agents of senatorial rank to evict the rightful owner and kidnap witnesses when the case came to trial. His mother Faltonia Betitia Proba compiled the surviving poem *In Praise of Christ* entirely from lines and half-lines of *Virgil.

BIBL. *PLRE* i, Olybrius 3.

Olympiodorus of Thebes Diplomat and historian, early 5th century AD.

An Egyptian by origin, Olympiodorus is found serving the court of Constantinople on a diplomatic mission to the Huns *c.* 412. He was widely travelled, and came to the West, probably in association with the establishment of *Valentinian III in 425. Our knowledge of him derives entirely from the surviving fragments of his *History*—a narrative devoted predominantly to western events between 407 and 425, which was employed by *Philostorgius, *Sozomen, and later by Zosimus (see *Eunapius). Olympiodorus was an exceptionally able historian of his own times, having access to well-informed sources of information and writing with a high degree of accuracy and independence of judgement.

BIBL. J. F. Matthews, *JRS* lx (1970).

Opimius, Lucius Consul 121 BC.

Opimius became an object of popular hatred for his ruthless suppression, as consul, of Gaius *Gracchus and his partisans. He escaped conviction for the murder of Roman citizens, thus establishing the validity of the senate's emergency decree (*senatus consultum ultimum*), on whose authority he had acted. But in 109 BC he was a prime target of the attack on the nobility by the *popularis* *Mamilius, and he succumbed to a prosecution for receiving bribes from *Jugurtha on an embassy c. 116.

BIBL. Gruen, *Politics*.

Oppian Poet, 2nd–3rd century AD.

There is much confusion over the authorship of two Greek hexameter poems transmitted under the name of Oppian. The *Halieutica*, on fishing, may be the work of a late second-century poet from Cilicia. The *Cynegetica*, on hunting, is dedicated to the Emperor *Caracalla (the author is said to have received a gold coin from the emperor for each verse) and may be the work of a Syrian imitator.

BIBL. Oppian, Colluthus, Tryphiodorus, trans. A. W. Mair (Locb, 1928).

Optatianus Porfyrius (AD 260/270–after 333) Poet and senator.

Publius Optatianus Porfyrius, a former governor in Greece and perhaps a supporter of *Maxentius, was exiled by *Constantine but was permitted to return after presenting him with verses. These poems blend praise of Constantine and of *Jesus and Apollo, Constantine's divine patrons, with reminiscences of Greek Muses. Their acrostic subtleties reveal how late Roman literary men looked for levels of meaning hidden beneath the plain surface of a text. In later life Optatian was twice urban prefect of Rome (autumn 329 and spring 333).

BIBL. *Carmina*, ed. J. Polara (2 vols. *Corp. Parav.* 1973); T. D. Barnes, *AJP* (1975) 173–186.

Orbilius (c. 114–14 BC) Schoolteacher.

After army service, Lucius Orbilius Pupillus taught first at Beneventum, then (from 65 BC on) in Rome. A bitter and abusive man, he was *Horace's master, and famous as 'the flogger' (*plagosus*).

Orestes the Patrician Master of the Soldiers AD 475–6.

A Pannonian and former secretary to *Attila, Orestes became Julius *Nepos' Patrician (475) but rebelled and replaced him with his own son,

*Romulus Augustulus, as a puppet. On his failure to agree to the demands of barbarian federates for one-third of the land of Italy, he was attacked and killed by *Odoacer at Placentia.

BIBL. *Anonymus Valesianus*, VII. 36–8; Jordanes, *Gothic History*, 241–3; Procopius, *Gothic War*, I. i. 1–8.

Oribasius (c. AD 320–c. 400) Doctor.

A native of Pergamum and pupil of Zeno of Cyprus, Oribasius was a famous doctor and teacher of medicine, a pagan who became intimate friend and doctor to the future Emperor *Julian. Julian took Oribasius with him to Gaul (355), where he encouraged the acclamation of Julian as Augustus at Paris in 360. He accompanied him to Persia in 363 and attended him on his deathbed, afterwards writing a memoir of the campaign for his friend the historian *Eunapius. He was later banished from the Empire, but recalled and his property restored. At Julian's request he wrote valuable compilations of excerpts from Greek and Roman medical authors, and parts of these were later translated into Syriac and Arabic.

BIBL. *PLRE* i, Oribasius; *OCD*; Corpus Medicorum Graecorum, vi.

Origen (c. AD 185–254) Christian theologian.

Origen was born in Egypt, probably at

Papyrus page of Origen's *Contra Celsum* (early 7th century). Cairo Museum, Papyrus 88747.

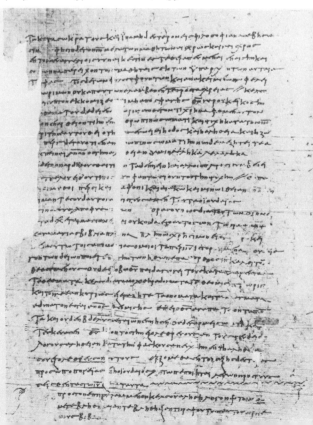

Alexandria, and educated as a Christian. His father
was killed in the persecution of 202. When
*Clement of Alexandria fled, Origen was appointed
head of the Catechetical School by Bishop
Demetrius. He is known to have visited Rome and
Arabia. In 215 when riots broke out in Alexandria
on the visit of the Emperor *Caracalla, he went to
Palestine and preached there. He was recalled to
Alexandria by Demetrius. He again went to
Palestine in 230 and was ordained there, as a result
of which he was deprived of his chair at
Alexandria and exiled. He took refuge in Caesarea
and established a new school there. He was
severely tortured during the *Decian persecution
(250–1) and died not many years later.

Origen was a strict ascetic who castrated himself
in order to be able to teach women without
incurring suspicion. He had a profound knowledge
of Greek philosophy and literature, and wrote a
great deal of very important exegetical work on the
Scriptures. There is also an important treatise on
doctrinal matters, *De principiis*, which survives
virtually only in Latin translations by *Rufinus and
*Jerome.

BIBL. H. Chadwick, *Early Christian Thought and
the Classical Tradition* (1966); J. Daniélou, *Origen*
(Eng. trans. 1955); Migne, *PG* xi–xvii.

Orosius Christian historian, early 5th century AD.

Paulus Orosius, a native of Spain, took refuge
from the barbarian invaders of his homeland, with
*Augustine in Africa (*c.* 410). He visited the Holy
Land on Augustine's behalf to gain *Jerome's
help against the views of *Pelagius. On his return,
he wrote at Augustine's behest a *History against
the Pagans* (417) as a riposte to the pagan view
that recent disasters were the result of the victory
of Christianity. Only in its final chapters, covering
Orosius' own time, does the work have independent
historical value.

BIBL. B. Lacroix, *Orose et ses idées* (1965).

Ossius of Cordova: see **Hosius**.

Ostorius Scapula Governor of Britain, AD 47–52.

Publius Ostorius Scapula (consul before AD 47),
second governor of Britain (47–52), has been
credited with the building of the Fosse Way. He
won triumphal insignia for receiving the surrender
of *Caratacus in AD 51, and died in the province.
His son Marcus Ostorius Scapula, who was
decorated for service under his father, was killed
by *Nero in AD 66 for writing libellous poetry
about him.

BIBL. Tac. *Ann.* xii. 31–9 (P.); xvi. 14–15 (M.).

Otho (AD 32–69) Emperor AD 69.

Marcus Salvius Otho's family was distinguished,
though not particularly old or noble—his father
had won high praise and promotion from *Claudius

Otho, portrait bust. Rome, Capitoline Museum.

for uncovering a plot. He became a close personal
friend of *Nero and shared his wild pursuits; he
was *Poppaea's husband before Nero married her
(whereupon Otho was sent to govern Lusitania). He
became a supporter of *Galba, but organized the
plot which ended in his murder when Galba
appointed Piso Licinianus as his heir, in preference
to him. Once emperor, Otho seemed determined to
emulate Nero, but the advance of the Rhine armies
on Italy under *Vitellius left him little time; he
marched north, was defeated at Bedriacum in the
Lombard plain, and proceeded to commit suicide
with a dignity and courage astonishing in one so
profligate.

BIBL. Tacitus, *Histories*.

Ovid (43 BC–AD 17 (?)) Poet.

A native of Sulmo (Sulmona in the Apennines)
and of equestrian family, Publius Ovidius Naso
received the conventional training in rhetoric,
which remained, he knew, a mixed blessing
(*Seneca. *Controv.* II. ii. 8 ff.); sophisticated
technical perfection now reinforced native fluency
(*Tr.* IV. x. 25). Ovid began writing early, and, after
holding some minor magistracies, abandoned

Ovid, portrait bust. Florence, Uffizi.

sacrifice the ideals of serious elegy upon the altar of contemporary Roman materialism. (3) *Epistulae Heroidum* (*Letters of the Heroines, c.* 1 BC): 15 letters from deserted heroines of mythology to their former lovers; three pairs of doubtful authenticity (lover to heroine; her reply) follow: an exercise in barren and elegant rhetoric. (4) *Remedia amoris* (*Remedies for Love, c.* AD 1): a sequel to (2) on how to fall out of love; by now the vein is running dry. (5) *Fasti* (*The Calendar, c.* AD 4): only six months survive. An extremely ingenious versification of the Roman calendar, enlivened by mythological explanations of festivals and rituals. (6) *Metamorphoses*: 15 books of hexameters, substantially complete by AD 8. An epic on the theme of mythological transformations, from the Creation to Caesar's deification, elegantly varied in scale and narrative treatment: often witty and irreverent, but wide-ranging in its exploration of the extremes of human emotion. (7) *Tristia* (*Sorrows*, 5 books written between AD 8 and 12), and (8) *Epistulae ex Ponto* (*Letters from the Black Sea*, 4 books, AD 13/4): *Tristia* ii is a single long poem, a powerful rhetorical plea to the emperor for justice. The remainder, not without tedium, beg for friends' support and lament minutely the beastliness of life in Rumania.

BIBL. Barsby, *GRNSC* xii (1978); Kenney, *Encyclopaedia Britannica* (ed. 15); Wilkinson, *Ovid Recalled* (1955); Syme, *History in Ovid* (1978) (dating).

Pacatianus Usurper *c.* AD 248–9.

A general under *Philip I, Titus Claudius Marinus Pacatianus was proclaimed emperor by Pannonian and Moesian troops, but was murdered by them shortly afterwards.

BIBL. *CAH* xii; *PIR* C 939.

Pachomius (*c.* AD 290–346) First abbot.

Son of pagans of Upper Egypt, Pachomius was conscripted into *Maximin Daia's army and discharged in 313, whereupon he sought baptism and became a disciple of a hermit. About 320 he founded the first proper monastery, at Tabennisi near the Nile, thus fulfilling the need for organization produced by the large numbers of would-be ascetics—mainly peasants discontented with their earthly lot and seeking a new life of spiritual discipline—attempting to emulate St *Antony and other hermits. At his death Pachomius was superintending nine monasteries for men and two for women. From Egypt monasticism spread to Asia Minor (see *Eustathius and St *Basil), Palestine (see *Jerome), and Syria (see *Theodoret), and, later, to the West (see *Augustine, *John Cassian). Pachomius' Rule (preserved in Latin) was very influential.

BIBL. D. Chitty, *The Desert a City* (1966).

thoughts of a public career and turned wholly to literature. He has left a remarkable account of his literary acquaintances in Rome (*Tr.* IV. x. 40 ff.) including Cornelius *Gallus and *Propertius. However, thanks to a *carmen*, that is, the poem *Ars Amatoria* (2) below and an *error*, a slip-up (*Tr.* ii. 207), he was exiled (AD 8(?)) to Tomi, now Constanza in Rumania, and was not recalled either by *Augustus or indeed by *Tiberius. The nature of his *error* remains elusive.

Ovid's output was rapid, varied, and copious, all in elegiacs apart from (6) below. (1) *Amores* (*Loves*, in 5 books, serially issued down to *c.* 20 BC, reduced to the surviving 3 *c.* 1 BC): love-poems, many explicitly commemorating a relationship with an unknown and perhaps imaginary Corinna; essentially light-hearted in spirit, they reduce to absurdity the poetic conventions employed by Propertius and *Tibullus. (2) *Ars Amatoria* (*Art of Love*, in 3 books: i–ii, *c.* 2 BC, perhaps a second edition; iii, *c.* AD 1): i and ii are instructions on how to find, win, and keep a girl. Brilliant and impudent in their exploitation of didactic conventions, these books parody (for example) *Lucretius and *Virgil's *Georgics*, and cheerfully

Pacuvius, Marcus (*c.* 220–*c.* 130 BC) Tragedian.

A native of Brindisi and *Ennius' nephew, Pacuvius apparently wrote little (only 13 titles are known). He devised unfamiliar plots and baroque stylistic effects; the numerous fragments reveal pedantry, inventiveness, and rhetorical vigour.

BIBL. Fragments: *TRF* 86 ff.

Paetus, Caesennius Consul AD 61.

In AD 61 and 62 Lucius Caesennius Paetus led unsuccessful campaigns against the Parthians and had to be rescued by *Corbulo. *Nero only reacted with jokes, and he was put in charge of Syria by *Vespasian, for whom he reduced the former kingdom of Commagene to provincial status.

BIBL. Tac. *Ann.* xv. 6–17; *PIR* C 173.

Palaemon, Remmius Teacher, 1st century AD.

Quintus Remmius Palaemon was rich and hugely successful, despite *Tiberius' and *Claudius' disapproval of his morals, a luxurious life-style, and outrageous arrogance. He taught *Persius and possibly *Quintilian, composed an important (lost) handbook on Latin grammar, and is famous for including modern (notably *Virgil) as well as ancient poets in the syllabus. He provides a rare example of agricultural investment in ancient times: a vineyard which he bought near Rome was resold, after ten years' improvement by his agent, to *Seneca for four times the price.

BIBL. R. Duncan-Jones, *Economy of the Roman Empire* (1974) 46–7.

Palladas Pagan epigrammatist, 4th century AD.

A pagan official grammarian in Alexandria, Palladas was 72 years old when retired from teaching in 391, as a result of *Theophilus' attempts to eradicate paganism. He is the author of numerous excellent epigrams, which betray a pessimistic and bitter temperament.

BIBL. A. Cameron, *JRS* lv (1965) 17.

Palladius Bishop of Helenopolis from AD 400.

Born *c.* 364 in Galatia, Palladius became a monk in Palestine and Egypt (*c.* 385–400). He fled from Egypt (with other monks driven out by *Theophilus of Alexandria in 400) to Constantinople, where he was welcomed by *John Chrysostom, whose loyal supporter he became, travelling to Italy on an embassy on his behalf (405), and suffering exile to upper Egypt for adherence to his cause (406–12). While in exile he composed a defence of his champion, the *Dialogue on the Life of John Chrysostom*. His other work, the *Lausiac History*, is a compendium of lives and anecdotes of eastern monks, taken mostly from his own experience; it is named after the imperial chamberlain Lausus to whom the work was dedicated (*c.* 420).

BIBL. C. Butler, *The Lausiac History of Palladius* (Texts and Studies vi, 1898–1904).

Palladius, Rutilius Taurus Aemilianus Writer on husbandry, late 4th–early 5th century AD.

Virtually nothing is known about Palladius, possibly a Gallic landowner of high birth, who wrote an *Opus agriculturae* or textbook of farming with a section on remedies for livestock, largely compiled from *Columella. He may have been a friend and relation of Rutilius *Namatianus.

BIBL. J. Svennung, *Untersuchungen zu Palladius und zur lateinischen Fach- und Volkssprache* (1935).

Pallas (died AD 62) Imperial freedman.

A freedman of *Antonia, Marcus Antonius Pallas was, as secretary for finance, one of the most influential members of *Claudius' household, especially after he had recommended *Agrippina as *Messallina's successor. His power and accompanying honours lasted well into *Nero's reign, but he was eventually killed for his enormous wealth in AD 62.

BIBL. Pliny, *Letters*, vii. 29; viii. 6; Tac. *Ann.* xiv. 65; *PIR* A 858.

Palma Frontonianus, Cornelius Consul AD 99 and 109.

The reduction and organization of Arabia Petraea in AD 104–6 was the main achievement of Aulus Cornelius Palma Frontonianus; for it he was granted triumphal insignia. His popularity with *Trajan ensured him great power, but he was an enemy of *Hadrian—though when he was murdered at Tarraco in 118 it was supposed to have been against Hadrian's will.

BIBL. *PIR* C 1412; Syme, *Tacitus*, p. 53 and ch. xix.

Panaetius (*c.* 185–109 BC) Stoic philosopher.

Panaetius went to Rome in 144, and was associated with *Scipio Aemilianus and his friends. In 140/39 he accompanied Scipio on an embassy to the eastern Mediterranean, but, though the two men were associated long and closely, there is no proof of philosophical influence on Scipio's policy.

BIBL. Strasburger, *JRS* 1965, 44 ff.; Astin, *Scipio Aemil.* 296 ff.

Panegyrists, Latin

Public speeches addressed to emperors were important opportunities in the later Empire for publicizing imperial 'successes' and policy; they often make heavy reading, but must have been magnificent to listen to. A collection survives of 11 panegyrics from the years 289–389 in the style of the Younger *Pliny's panegyric of *Trajan (which is preserved with them), by Gallic orators who include:

1. EUMENIUS, teacher of rhetoric. He gave up a post as private secretary to the Caesar *Constantius I (293–7/8) to return to academic life as professor at the newly-restored schools of his native Autun. His surviving speech (*Pan. Lat.* iv), delivered in

the spring of 298, inaugurated the schools.

2. MAMERTINUS. Two speeches survive, both addressed to the Emperor *Maximian at court in Gaul. That delivered on the birthday of Rome in 289 (*Pan. Lat.* ii) describes recent campaigns; that on the fifth anniversary of Maximian's accession in 291 (*Pan. Lat.* v) outlines the character of his rule.

3. LATINUS PACATUS DREPANIUS, who may be the editor of the collection, congratulated the Emperor *Theodosius I on his recent defeat of the usurper *Maximus, when he visited Rome in 389 (*Pan. Lat.* xii). Pacatus was immediately made proconsul of Africa, a promotion reflecting the value set on rhetoric in the later Empire.

See also Claudius *Mamertinus

BIBL. *Panégyriques latins,* ed. E. Galletier (3 vols., 1949), whose numbering is used here; S. MacCormack, *Revue des Études Augustiniennes,* xxii (1976) 29–77.

Pantaenus (died *c.* AD 190) Christian theologian.

A native of Sicily and a convert to Christianity, Pantaenus taught at Alexandria and was the first head of the Catechetical School. During the last ten years of his life he was the teacher of *Clement of Alexandria.

BIBL. H. Chadwick, *Early Christian Thought and the Classical Tradition* (1966).

Papinian (*c.* AD 148/153–211) Jurist.

Born in Syria *c.* 148/153 and possibly related to *Julia Domna, Aemilius Papinianus had been legal adviser to the praetorian prefects of *Marcus Aurelius, but reached eminence under *Severus, who appointed him praetorian prefect in 205. His legal writings include judgments spanning the entire range of private and public law. He accompanied Severus on his British campaign 208–11, and was slain by order of *Caracalla in 211 in the blood-bath that followed *Geta's murder.

BIBL. Birley, *Severus*; *PIR* A 388; *ANRW* 15.

Papirius Cursor, Lucius Consul 326, 320, 319, 315, and 313 BC.

After preliminary operations against the Samnites (326 BC), Papirius became dictator (325/4) and, although his notorious clash with Q. *Fabius Maximus Rullianus is suspect, may well have defeated them. After the Caudine Forks agreement he probably consolidated Rome's position (320–319), but his capture of Luceria and Satricum should be dated later, to 315. He was reputedly dictator in 310/9, again defeating the Samnites decisively. A distinguished general, his portrayal has been heavily influenced by comparisons with Alexander the Great.

BIBL. PW xviii. 1039 ff.; G. Nenci, *Introduzione alle Guerre Persiane e altri Saggi* (1958) 247 ff.; Salmon, *Samnium* 214 ff.

Papirius Dionysius, Aurelius Prefect of the corn supply AD 189.

An equestrian, lawyer, and an imperial counsellor, Marcus Aurelius Papirius Dionysius was secretary for petitions and legal suits under *Commodus, then prefect of Egypt. He was removed from this post by *Cleander and demoted to prefect of the corn-supply. In vengeance, he aggravated a corn shortage in order to inflame the mob against Cleander. In 189 he was put to death on the orders of Commodus.

BIBL. *PIR* A 1567; Grosso, *Lotta*; Pflaum, *Carrières*, no. 181.

Parthenius Man of letters, 1st century BC.

A Greek from Nicaea, Parthenius reached Rome in 73 BC, taught *Virgil, and dedicated to Cornelius *Gallus the *Sufferings in Love*, an epitome of fringe mythology.

BIBL. Loeb ed. with Longus, *Daphnis and Chloe*; Clausen, *GRBS* 1964, 187 ff. (on Parthenius' influence).

St Patrick *c.* AD 390–*c.* 460 'Apostle' of Ireland.

Patrick originated from a Romanized (but still native-speaking) British background; his father was a town-councillor and Christian deacon. Captured by pirates at the age of 16, Patrick was carried off to Ireland, and it was while he was there that he was converted to a life of Christian piety. On escaping to Britain after six years, he was ordained and devoted himself to the study of the Latin Bible; later, he was sent back to Ireland as bishop. Patrick's task was overwhelmingly missionary: the conversion of Ireland to Christianity. His evangelism was itinerant, but it was probably from Armagh that he directed his mission. All that we know of his historical life has to be ascertained from his own writings, the *Letter* to a British chieftain Coroticus (who had led a raid against Ireland), and his *Confession*, a spiritual apologia against attacks on his ministry; later *Lives* of Patrick are contaminated by legendary material.

BIBL. R. P. C. Hanson, *St. Patrick: his origins and career* (1968).

St Paul (died *c.* AD 66) 'Apostle of the Gentiles'.

Born a Roman citizen, at Tarsus in Cilicia, Saul (later Paul) was a Jew of the Diaspora with an education which combined (Pharisaic) Judaism with Hellenic culture (in which mixture he much resembles *Philo). At first violently opposed to nascent Christianity, but later converted, he played a vital part in spreading the new religion by his three journeys among the cities of Asia, Macedonia, and Achaea. These activities brought him into conflict with local and provincial authorities, and the accuracy of the Acts of the Apostles is demonstrated by the circumstantial detail with which it narrates these occasions. Paul was

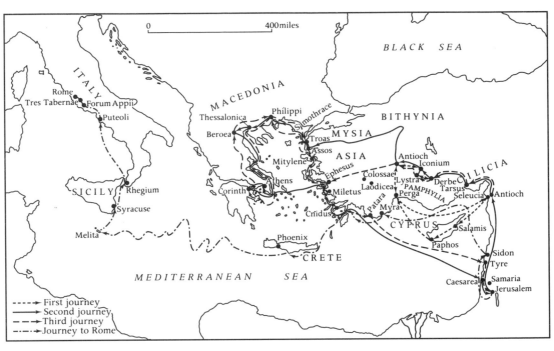

The Journeys of St Paul

St Paul's Without the Walls, Rome: late 4th-century basilica (restored after fire of 1823) over Saint's tomb.

eventually sent to Rome by *Festus, governor of
Judaea, an action which reflects how seriously his
activities were taken by the authorities and also the
natural rights of appeal of a Roman citizen. After
two or more years at Rome and perhaps further
travels in the West, he was executed and buried on
the road to Ostia. His writings, the Epistles,
enjoyed much influence and inspired imitations
from a very early period.

BIBL. Sherwin-White, *Roman Society and Roman
Law in the New Testament.*

Paul of Samosata Bishop of Antioch *c.* AD 260–70.

A monarchian heresiarch, Paul was deposed and
excommunicated for heresy *c.* 269, but remained in
power through *Zenobia's influence until 272. His
orthodox opponents depicted him as avaricious,
rapacious, self-indulgent, and possibly immoral.
Paul upheld the pure humanity of Christ and
affirmed the unity of God and the Word.

BIBL. Kleine Pauly, Paulus 6; F. Millar, *JRS* lxi,
1971.

St Paulinus of Nola AD 353/4–431 Poet and
bishop.

Born in 353/4 in Bordeaux of a Christian
senatorial family, Pontius Meropius Anicius
Paulinus was a student of *Ausonius, became consul
suffect of Rome (378), and governor of Campania
in 381. He was converted to Christianity by
*Ambrose in 390, and shocked the senate by
becoming a priest in 394, selling his goods, and
retiring to a life of poverty as bishop of Nola in
Campania (409), where he remained until his death
in 431. A correspondent of *Jerome, *Augustine,
*Sulpicius Severus, and Ausonius, he left many
fine poems, mostly devotional ones in honour of
his local martyr Felix.

BIBL. P. Fabre, *Chronologie de l'oeuvre de St.
Paulin de Nole* (1948).

Paullus (1), Lucius Aemilius Consul 219, 216 BC.

Aemilius won an easy triumph for the short
campaign of 219 BC which broke the power of
*Demetrius of Pharos (the Second Illyrian War). In
218 he served on *Fabius Buteo's embassy to
Carthage. In his second consulship he shared the
command against *Hannibal with his colleague
*Varro, and fell at Cannae.

BIBL. Scullard, *Politics.*

Paullus (2), Lucius Aemilius Consul 182 and
168 BC.

Aemilius Paullus was the son of *Paullus (1) and a
political ally of *Scipio Africanus. He held a
moderately successful command as praetor in
Hispania Ulterior (191–189 BC). He was appointed

Artist's reconstruction of equestrian statue of L.
Aemilius Paullus (2) at Delphi, (*c.* 167 BC).

Denarius of 62 BC depicting Perseus and his family
taken prisoner by L. Aemilius Paullus (2) (reverse).

to the decemviral commission for the settlement of
Asia (189), and led the opposition at Rome to
Manlius *Vulso's triumph in 187. Owing to Scipio's
political eclipse Paullus did not reach the
consulship until 182, but he won a decisive victory
in Liguria in 181 which earned him a triumph.
Another long period of relative obscurity followed,
until Paullus was suddenly elevated to a second
consulship in 168 at the age of 60. This was part of
a reaction to the disappointing record of previous
commanders in the war against *Perseus. Paullus
restored discipline to the army in Macedonia, and
proceeded within weeks to inflict the final defeat
on Perseus at Pydna.

He combined old-fashioned Roman austerity with
an appreciation of Greek culture. As proconsul in
167 he toured the sights of Greece and had Perseus'
library shipped to Italy. At Delphi he used the
victory monument commissioned by Perseus to
carry his own equestrian statue. It is claimed that
Paullus disagreed with the harsher aspects of the
senate's policy which he executed in 167: these
included the enslavement of 150,000 Epirotes and
the detention of prominent Greek politicians in
Italy. But the consistently favourable historical
tradition about him must partly reflect the bias of
*Polybius, who was closely attached to his family.

Paullus returned to Italy to celebrate a
magnificent triumph in which Perseus was led in
chains. He encountered political opposition for his
failure to distribute booty generously to his army;
but the huge quantity which he brought into the
treasury facilitated the indefinite suspension of
tribute payments by Roman citizens. His career
culminated in a moderate censorship (164), and
when he died in 160 his comparative poverty
surprised contemporaries, as it showed that he had
kept none of the Macedonian booty for himself.
   BIBL. Plutarch, *Life of Aemilius Paullus*; Walbank,
HCP iii.

Paulus, Julius Jurist, late 2nd-early 3rd century
AD.
   The date and place of Paulus' birth are unknown.
He was a member of the emperor's privy council

under *Severus and *Caracalla, but was probably
not a praetorian prefect or *magister memoriae*. The
period in which his works were produced perhaps
began as early as *Commodus' reign, and may have
extended into *Severus Alexander's rule. His
decisions on legal matters spanned a wide range of
topics, and Paulus, with his contemporaries
*Papinian and *Ulpian, was responsible for a
broader and more humanitarian interpretation of
Roman law.
   BIBL. *PIR* I 453; *ANRW* 15; ii. 2; Syme, *HAC*
1968-9 (1970).

Paulus 'Catena' State secretary AD 353-61.
   A Spaniard, Paulus entered the body of State
secretaries known as 'notaries', and became a
notorious confidential agent of *Constantius II, who
used his ruthlessness and cunning for treason
investigations, notably in Britain in 353 after the
suppression of *Magnentius, and in the East in
359 (the Scythopolis trials for treason and magic).
He earned his nickname 'Catena' ('the Chain')
because of his artful interrogation and its results.
He was condemned and burnt alive by the
Commission of Chalcedon in 361/2 (see *Julian).
   BIBL. *PLRE* i, Paulus 4.

Pausanias Writer, floruit *c.* AD 150.
   A Greek traveller and geographer from Lydia,
Pausanias wrote a description of Greece in 10 books
containing much detailed information on the
topography of regions and cities, local religious
foundations, customs and beliefs, historical remains
and artistic monuments.
   BIBL. J. G. Frazer, *Pausanias' Description of
Greece*, text, translation and commentary (1898);
Guide to Greece, trans. P. C. T. Levi (1971).

Pedanius Fuscus Salinator, Gnaeus Consul AD
118.
   The father of Lucius *Pedanius (below) and son-
in-law of Julius *Servianus, he was a friend and
pupil of *Pliny the Younger. He held the
governorship of Moesia soon after his consulship.
   BIBL. Sherwin-White, *The Letters of Pliny*; Syme,
Tacitus.

Pedanius Fuscus Salinator, Lucius Senator under
Hadrian.
   Son of the consul of AD 118 (above), grandson of
Julius *Servianus and great-nephew of *Hadrian, he
was perhaps groomed as Hadrian's potential
successor from an early age, granted special
privileges and a place among the imperial
counsellors. It became clear in 136 that Hadrian
had changed his plans for succession and he was
forced to commit suicide on the pretext of a plot
against the emperor.
   BIBL. E. Champlin, *Zeitschrift für Papyrologie und
Epigraphik* xxi (1976); Syme, *Tacitus*.

Pegasus Jurist, consul *c.* AD 73.

The mythological name of ——tius Pegasus (his first name is lost) was that of the ship of the Roman navy commanded by his father. His legal erudition was such that he was known later just as 'the Book'. He rose—unusually for a man of such an origin—to be urban prefect, and *Juvenal—still more unusually—praises his justice in that office, which he held at the beginning of *Domitian's reign.

BIBL. E. Champlin, *ZPE* xxxii (1978) 269–78 (suggesting Plotius as his *nomen*).

Pelagius Heresiarch, early 5th century AD.

Pelagius was a British-born monk who settled in Rome towards the end of the fourth century, where he acquired a reputation as a spiritual guide and was befriended by aristocratic families. He left Rome at the time of the Visigothic sack (410), and fled to North Africa and Palestine. He put forward controversial views which denied that man was irrevocably committed to sin, emphasizing man's own responsibility for his actions and reducing the necessity of divine grace. *Augustine and *Jerome both wrote works in refutation of his doctrine. Although cleared by a synod in Palestine in 415, Pelagius was condemned by successive Church councils in Africa and ultimately by the verdict of Pope Zosimus (418), but theological controversy over his views continued.

BIBL. Peter Brown, *Religion and Society*, 183–226; R. F. Evans, *Pelagius: Inquiries and Reappraisals* (1968).

Perennis, Tigidius Praetorian prefect AD 180–5.

An Italian with a great military reputation, Sextus Tigidius Perennis was appointed praetorian prefect by *Commodus and was sole prefect and virtual ruler of the Empire from 182 until his death in 185. As such, he made some attempt to check the emperor's extravagance but was very unpopular with the senate. His downfall was brought about by *Cleander, who induced some Illyrian soldiers in Rome to denounce him to the emperor and demand his surrender. He was executed on Commodus' orders.

BIBL. Grosso, *Lotta*; Howe, *Pretorian Prefect*; Birley, *Severus*.

Perseus King of Macedon 179–168 BC.

The elder son of *Philip V whose expansionary policies he inherited, Perseus was distrusted at Rome after plotting the elimination of his pro-Roman brother and rival, *Demetrius, in 180 BC. His relations with Rome steadily worsened after his accession (179), as he built up Macedonian power and prestige by economic regeneration and political intervention in Greece, often in support of left-wing causes. Eventually Rome was persuaded to declare war by a jealously apprehensive *Eumenes II, whose complaints against Perseus were echoed in the Roman propaganda of the war period. But Perseus himself never wanted war with Rome, as

The Hellenistic World at the Accession of Perseus of Macedon, 179 BC

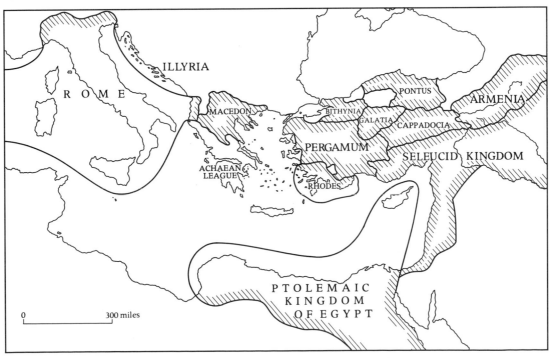

ILLYRIA

R O M E

MACEDON

PONTUS

ARMENIA

BITHYNIA
GALATIA
CAPPADOCIA

PERGAMUM

SELEUCID KINGDOM

ACHAEAN
LEAGUE

RHODES

0   300 miles

P T O L E M A I C
K I N G D O M
O F E G Y P T

Coin type of Perseus King of Macedon (179–168 BC).

Impression of cornelian intaglio with portrait of Pertinax. Athens, National Museum.

his easy deception by Q. *Philippus in 172/1 demonstrates. He successfully resisted Rome's attacks until 169, and was finally defeated by *Paullus (2) at Pydna in 168, after which the Macedonian monarchy ceased to exist. Perseus was captured at Samothrace, paraded in Paullus' triumph, and died in internment in Italy in 165.

BIBL. Meloni, *Perseo* (1953); Walbank, *HCP* iii, esp. 274 ff.

Persius (AD 34–62) Satirist.

A native of Volterra, of good family and excellent education, as a pupil of *Palaemon and *Cornutus, Persius remained independent of literary circles and devoted himself to Stoicism and the composition of six short satiric poems. Persius writes on (1) bad poetry, (2) improper prayers, (3) the consequences of bad living, (4) the importance of self-examination, (5) true liberty, and (6) the comfortable life. He writes outside the real world, but with a philosopher's passion and a savagery born of extreme concision. A close and subtle imitator of *Horace, he writes colloquially and often crudely, with an entirely idiosyncratic, tormented, angular brevity, in a series of bizarre and rough images.

BIBL. Bramble, *Persius and the Programmatic Satire* (1974).

Pertinax Emperor AD 193.

The son of a freedman from Liguria, Publius Helvius Pertinax became a teacher before making a late beginning on a career in the imperial service. As prefect of a cohort in Syria he is said to have used government transport without an official pass, and to have been forced by the governor to walk back from Antioch to his unit's station. After various military and administrative posts in the 160s he was promoted into the senate, and went on to a legionary command and the governorship of Moesia Superior. He held a consulship in 174 or 175, was with *Marcus Aurelius in the East after the revolt of *Avidius Cassius, then governed Moesia Inferior, Dacia, and Syria (to which he was appointed before 180). He had retired from public life by 182 because of connections with alleged

conspirators against *Commodus, but he was appointed governor of Britain in 185–7. In summer 188 he went to govern Africa, and on his return a year later was appointed urban prefect. He may have been involved in (or at least privy to) the plot against Commodus, for immediately after the murder (31 December 192) he went secretly to the praetorian camp, promised the guard a donative, and was proclaimed emperor. His proclamation was enthusiastically approved by the senate, and he initiated a number of popular measures as a reaction against the excesses of Commodus. But on 28 March 193 a detachment of the praetorian guard initiated another *coup*, murdered him, and put his head on a stake.

BIBL. Birley, *Severus*; *PIR* H 73; Grosso, *Lotta*; Pflaum, *Carrières*, no. 179.

Impression of red jasper intaglio with portrait of Pescennius Niger and dedication to Asclepius.

Pescennius Niger Emperor AD 193–4.

An Italian of equestrian background, Gaius Pescennius Niger Justus won military renown early in the reign of *Commodus in a campaign against the Dacians. After a consulship in 191 he was made governor of Syria late in the reign of Commodus, probably because he was not considered a potential threat. In May 193 he was proclaimed emperor by his troops as a rival claimant to *Didius Julianus. His power base was in the eastern provinces, with Byzantium as its centre. In the summer of 193 Septimius *Severus turned against him, after having him declared a public enemy by the senate. Pescennius was defeated after a campaign of three major battles, at Cyzicus, Nicaea, and Issus, which was completed by April or May 194. After the last battle, Pescennius fled to Antioch. The city was captured by Severus' general *Anullinus, and Pescennius was captured on the outskirts of the city as he tried to escape. His head was cut off and sent to Severus at Byzantium.

BIBL. Birley, *Severus*; PW xix. 1086–1102.

St Peter (died AD 64 (?)) Apostle and Bishop of Rome.

The Evangelists are at pains to demonstrate the selection of Peter by Christ as chief apostle, and his acts in this capacity—as well as his conspicuous failures. John (1:35–44) makes him, like his brother Andrew, a fisherman and native of Bethsaida near Lake Tiberias. Many reliable sources, from St *Clement on, connect Peter with Rome, and his death probably took place in the *Neronian persecution. Thorough archaeological research in the Vatican necropolis seems to corroborate the tradition that he was buried there.

BIBL. *ODCC*; Toynbee and Ward Perkins, *The Shrine of St. Peter and the Vatican Excavations* (1956).

Peter of Alexandria Bishop AD 300–311/12.

The Great Persecution (303–13) partially achieved its aims in Egypt by fragmenting the Church. Peter had the hard task of reconciling those who had succumbed to pagan pressure without alienating those who had admired and helped the martyrs. Many, especially *Melitius, thought his pastoral letter of 305/6 erred towards leniency for the lapsed; Peter tried to heal the resulting schism from hidden headquarters in the Western Desert, until a lull brought him back to Alexandria, where he was martyred in the final terror of the persecution.

BIBL. T. D. Barnes, *Tertullian* (1971) 168–71, 184–5; Barns and H. Chadwick, *JTS* xxiv (1973) 443–55.

Petronius Mid-1st century AD.

It is uncertain whether the Petronius, author of the *Satyricon*, was the notorious roué of the same

Street of tombs (mainly 2nd century AD) under St Peter's, Rome. *Constantine built his church over 2nd-century shrine above St Peter's grave in Vatican cemetery.

name of the *Neronian court, who won the sobriquet 'arbiter of elegance' by his style of living, and was driven to commit suicide as frivolously as he had lived, after the *Pisonian conspiracy of AD 65.

Satyricon (probably written AD 63–6) stands for *Satyricon libri*, books of the deeds of satyrs, lecherous half-human mythological beings, who may be thought to symbolize the outrageous and unorthodox behaviour of the participants in the novel; the notion of 'satire' is probably also present in the title, but only as a *sous-entendu*. Originally perhaps in at least sixteen books, the one book we apparently possess *in toto* (xv) may have been as long as 60 modern printed pages. Until 1650 the work was known only from two sets of excerpts and from citations in grammarians; then a manuscript was discovered at modern Trogir, near Split in Dalmatia, containing the *Cena Trimalchionis* (*Banquet of Trimalchio*).

Petronius' place in the traditions of ancient literature is endlessly disputed: for a lecherous and parodic narrative, interspersed with verse, our closest parallel is a recently published papyrus scrap; but analogies are also to be drawn with Greek novels, with Milesian tales (improper short stories; Petr. 111 f. is a superb example; see *Sisenna), with mimes, with Menippean satire (see *Varro), and with epic, which Petronius at times parodies. The novel is picaresque in character, containing the adventures (in south Italy) of Encolpius, Giton his boy-friend, and a varying gallery of motley vagabonds. Outside the *Cena*, our notion of the narrative structure is at times hazy, and indeed there may not have been a strong plot-line. The *Cena* is the unchallenged masterpiece of ancient comic and satiric writing, at the expense of Trimalchio, a parvenu millionaire of immense wealth and no taste: an easy target, yet portrayed with superb inventiveness, attention to detail, and even a certain sympathy, in delightfully crisp narrative, interspersed with engrossing speeches by Trimalchio and his cronies in 'vulgar Latin', revealing and immortalizing the tastes, attitudes, and malapropisms of a class and an era.

BIBL. Coffey, *Satire*, 178 ff.; Walsh, *Roman Novel*; *Cena*, ed. Smith (1975). View with caution, J. P. Sullivan, *Satyricon of Petronius* (1968). Papyrus: Parsons, *BICS* 1971, 53 ff.; Tac. *Ann.* xvi. 16–20.

Petronius, Publius Governor of Syria AD 39–42.

*Philo and *Josephus record the agonizing dilemma faced by Petronius (consul in 19) as governor of Syria, when *Gaius demanded that his statue be set up in the Temple at Jerusalem. He was only saved from forced suicide by Gaius' death early in 41. His daughter married *Vitellius, and he was an old friend of *Claudius: 'he was a fluent speaker of Claudian', says *Seneca.

BIBL. Philo 576–84.

Petronius Maximus Western emperor AD 455.

One of the greatest of Italian office-holders, Petronius Maximus crowned his career with his accession as emperor, although his reign lasted barely eleven weeks. Urban prefect twice, (420–1 and before 433), praetorian prefect of Italy twice (435 and 439–41) and twice *consul ordinarius*, the first time with *Theodosius II as colleague, Maximus may have been an accessory to the assassination of *Valentinian III (455). His claim as Valentinian's successor was based on his offices and wealth and his forced marriage with Valentinian's widow, Eudoxia, who is said to have summoned *Geiseric to her aid. On hearing of the Vandals' approach, Maximus fled but was caught and lynched by a Roman mob.

BIBL. Sidonius Apollinaris, *Letters*, II. 13 (for a contemporary reaction); Chastagnol, *Fastes*, no. 127, pp. 281–6.

Petronius Turpilianus Consul AD 61.

Publius Petronius Turpilianus was governor of Britain briefly AD 61–2. The triumphal insignia were given him by *Nero after the suppression of the *Pisonian conspiracy, but we do not know what form his loyalty had taken. Nero relied on it again in 68 when Petronius was sent against *Galba: there were rumours that the two came to an arrangement, but Galba put him to death anyway.

BIBL. Tacitus, *Histories*, i. 6.

Phaedrus Fabulist, Augustan era.

Phaedrus was a freedman of *Augustus, perhaps from Macedonia. He was prosecuted by *Sejanus (iii. *prol.* 41 ff.)—therefore before AD 31— perhaps because of the perilous implications of some fables (i. *prol.* 5 ff.), but survived. He was also subject to literary criticism of his fables' light-weight triviality (iv. 7.1 ff.). Five incomplete books of fables in iambic senarii survive, terse, amusing, sometimes obscure, and also satiric.

BIBL. Important Loeb edition (with Babrius) by Perry.

Silver coin of Philip the Arab commemorating Games.

Philip (I) the Arab Emperor AD 244–9.

Marcus Julius Philippus was Arabian by birth, but his early life is obscure. He became praetorian prefect on *Timesitheus' death, and emperor after *Gordian III's murder early in 244. Shortly thereafter he appointed his son, *Philip II, Caesar. Abandoning the Persian campaign he hastened to Rome, and in 246 waged successful Danubian

Philip the Arab, portrait bust. Rome, Vatican Museum.

campaigns. In 247 he created Philip II Augustus, and in 248 celebrated the last Secular Games held in Rome. A rash of usurpations shook his confidence, and *Decius was appointed to deal with the Danubian situation. In 249 the troops proclaimed Decius emperor, and Philip fell in battle against him, after which the praetorian guard at Rome murdered his son.

BIBL. *CAH* xii; *ANRW* ii. 2.

Philip II Caesar AD 244, Augustus 247.

Julius Severus Philippus was nominated Caesar by his father *Philip I in 244, aged about seven years, and was created Augustus in 247. The praetorian guard murdered him after his father's defeat by *Decius.

BIBL. *CAH* xii.

Philip V King of Macedon 221–179 BC.

As an ambitious young monarch, Philip was persuaded by *Demetrius of Pharos to take advantage of *Hannibal's successes in Italy, and attack the Roman protectorate in Illyria. His secret treaty of mutual assistance negotiated with Hannibal in 215 BC became known to the Romans, who later remembered it as a stab in the back. The senate dispatched *Laevinus and later Sulpicius *Galba, but relied mainly on their Aetolian allies to neutralize Philip until 205, when the Peace of Phoenice was signed on terms favourable to Philip. In 203/2 Philip seems to have made an ineffectual agreement with *Antiochus III to partition Ptolemaic possessions; at the same time he embarked on a programme of aggressive expansion in the Aegean. By late 201 the senate had been convinced that Philip posed a threat, and went to war. In the Second Macedonian War (200–197) Philip was defeated by *Flamininus at Cynoscephalae, had his territory reduced, and became a Roman ally. He co-operated with *Glabrio and other Roman commanders against Antiochus III (191–189), and regained some lost territory. His subsequent attempts to strengthen the northern frontier of Macedon, and to achieve economic and demographic regeneration within the kingdom, provoked complaints from weaker neighbouring states, and hostile suspicion at Rome. Relations deteriorated throughout the 180s, exacerbated by Roman attempts to subvert the loyalty of Philip's younger son, *Demetrius. Philip was believed to be planning another war with Rome when he died in 179.

BIBL. Walbank, *Philip V of Macedon* (1940).

Philippus, Flavius Praetorian prefect AD 344–51.

Son of a sausage-maker, Philippus learned shorthand and became a 'notary' in the imperial service, rising to be praetorian prefect of the East (344–51) and consul for 348. Like *Ablabius, his career illustrates the role of the bureaucracy in the social mobility of talented men. *Constantius II used him to enforce his pro-*Arian policies: he installed an Arian bishop, Macedonius, at Constantinople, and deported and later executed the orthodox bishop, Paul. In 351 he went as envoy to the usurper *Magnentius, whose troops he addressed, accusing them of disloyalty to the dynasty of *Constantine. Magnentius detained him, and he died soon after.

BIBL. *PLRE* i, Philippus 7; A. H. M. Jones, *Historia* iv (1955) 229–33.

Philippus, Lucius Marcius Consul 91 BC.

An outstanding political figure throughout the first three decades of the first century BC, Philippus' survival and complex political career are best explained by characterizing him as 'pliable'. As consul in 91 he led the opposition to the tribune *Drusus (2), and repealed much of his legislation. His strongly conservative instincts did not prevent him from taking up a leading role in *Cinna's popular regime: he was censor in 86. But he switched his allegiance to *Sulla at the right moment in 83, and defeated the Marian forces in Sardinia. Thereafter he became a respected elder statesman of the restored senatorial establishment in the 70s.

BIBL. Ooteghem, *L. Marcius Philippus et sa famille* (1961).

Philippus, Quintus Marcius Consul 186 and 169 BC, censor 164.

A leading exponent of Rome's eastern diplomacy, Philippus' handling of it earned him a reputation for deviousness and duplicity. On his first embassy (183 BC) he managed to intensify *Philip V's suspicions of *Demetrius and undermine the Achaean League's position in the Peloponnese. His second embassy to Greece (172/1) was intended to secure Rome's diplomatic position on the eve of the Third Macedonian War; a letter (probably of his) survives containing anti-*Perseus propaganda. But his master-stroke was the conference at Tempe, at which he convinced Perseus that war could be averted by further negotiation, and thus bought time for Rome to prepare for war. The

Coin type of Philip V of Macedon.

Silver coin (*denarius*) of 129 BC commemorating Q.
Marcius Philippus' Macedonian connection.

traditionalists in the senate disapproved of
Philippus' 'nova sapientia', but they were a
minority.

In his second consulship (169) he conducted the
first successful campaign of the war against
Perseus, but the final victory eluded him. His
diplomatic contacts in this year with Rhodes and
Achaea betray the familiar deviousness, one of its
victims being *Polybius himself, whose treatment
of Philippus is thus consistently hostile.

BIBL. Briscoe, *JRS* liv (1964) 66 ff.; Scullard,
Politics; Walbank, *HCP* iii; Toynbee, *Hannibal's
Legacy*, ii. 387 ff.

Philo (Judaeus) (*c.* 30 BC–AD 45) Controversialist.
Philo, called Judaeus (the Jew), was born into a
distinguished family of Alexandria, and was the
uncle of *Tiberius Alexander. He represents the
intellectual heights of Alexandrian Judaism; Greek
was his mother tongue, and Hebrew he appears not
to have known. In AD 39–40 he was sent to Rome
on an embassy which was concerned with the
persecution of the Jews by Flaccus, prefect of
Egypt, and with Jewish inability to participate in
emperor-worship. He was a very copious author:
we possess the bulk of his output, but in some
cases in Latin or Armenian versions. He was of
exceptional importance both as a philosophical
expositor of Judaism to the Hellenistic world, and
as a model of discussions on loyalty and
persecution for Christian apologists, particularly in
his works *Against Flaccus* and *The Embassy to
Gaius, written under *Claudius.

BIBL. *In Flaccum*, ed. Box (1939); *Legatio ad
Gaium*, ed. Smallwood (1961); Goodenough, *The
Politics of Philo* (1938), and *An Introduction to Philo*
(1939); Rokeah, *JTS* 1968, 81.

Philodemus of Gadara (*c.* 110–*c.* 40 BC)
Epicurean philosopher-poet.
Philodemus became a client of *Piso (1) (*c.* 70 BC),
and was extremely successful and much imitated as
the author of erotic epigrams, of which some 30
survive; *Cicero acknowledged this to be an
unorthodox skill for an Epicurean philosopher (*In
Pisonem*, 70). Of his philosophical works, numerous

and wide-ranging, yet arid and dully written,
copious and as yet only partly-deciphered papyrus
fragments survive, from the 'Villa dei Papiri' near
Herculaneum, which possibly belonged to Piso and
probably did not belong to Philodemus himself.

BIBL. *Garland of Philip*, ed. Gow and Page, 3160
ff.; Murray, *JRS* 1965, 161 ff.; Cicero, *In Pisonem*,
ed. Nisbet, 183 ff., 186 ff.

Philopoemen (died 182 BC) Achaean general and
statesman.
The outstanding Achaean of his generation,
Philopoemen was the hero and political mentor of
*Polybius, who admired his conservatism and
patriotism, and rather overestimated his
achievements. He had a distinguished military
record, and extended the Achaean League to
include the whole Peloponnese by the
incorporation of Sparta, Messene, and Elis (192–
191). These achievements were only possible in the
power vacuum left by Rome's defeat of Macedon
(197), but Philopoemen never accepted Rome's
right to intervene in Peloponnesian affairs.
Shunning the role of Rome's client, he insisted on
Achaea's complete independence of action as an
equal ally. This unrealistic policy generated
considerable friction with Rome and trouble in the
Peloponnese, but it also earned him the title of 'the
last of the Greeks'.

BIBL. Errington, *Philopoemen* (1969).

Philostorgius (born *c.* AD 368) Church historian.
The earliest of the Church historians at
Constantinople who continued the work of
*Eusebius of Caesarea, Philostorgius was an
admirer of the extreme *Arian Eunomius. His
'heretical' sympathies coloured his *History* (which
went down to *c.* 425), and meant that it survived
only in fragments. He seems to have used
excellent sources, and is of particular interest for
his presentation of Arian views and personalities.

BIBL. J. Quasten, *Patrology* iii, 530–2.

Philostratus Sophist, writer 3rd century AD.
Born into a family of sophists from Lemnos,
Flavius Philostratus was a member of the so-called
circle of *Julia Domna. His most famous work is the
Life of Apollonius of Tyana (*c.* 210–20), but he also
wrote *The Lives of the Sophists c.* 238.

BIBL. Kleine Pauly, Philostratos 5; *PIR* F 332.

Phraates IV King of Parthia *c.* 37–17 BC.
Phraates was a successful ruler from the
Parthian point of view, and was able to rule the
kingdom after the murder of most of his thirty
brothers. He was not a vigorous opponent of the
Romans, and was the king responsible for the
return of the standards captured at Carrhae (see
*Crassus) to *Augustus in 20 BC.

BIBL. Tacitus, *Annals*, vi. 31–2.

Piso, Gaius Calpurnius Conspirator AD 65.

Piso had an ordinary but successful career. His birth recommended him as figurehead for a conspiracy against *Nero which attracted the support of members of many different classes at Rome. In AD 65 the plot, which seems not to have been efficiently organized, was betrayed, and a very extensive purge followed: these events cast a shadow over the last years of Nero's reign.

BIBL. Tac. *Ann.* xv. 48–74; Warmington, *Nero*, xi.

Piso, Gnaeus Calpurnius Consul 7 BC.

Piso was a close friend of *Augustus—who thought him a possible candidate for emperor—and *Tiberius. As governor of Syria (AD 18–19) he quarrelled violently with *Germanicus (q.v.), whom he had perhaps been sent to observe. In the fracas which followed Germanicus' supposed poisoning, Tiberius had to abandon him and he committed suicide.

BIBL. Tacitus, *Annals*, iii. 8–18.

Piso (1), Lucius Calpurnius Consul 58 BC.

An influential and patriotic aristocrat, Piso's friendship with the First Triumvirate secured him the consulate of 58 BC, at which time his daughter Calpurnia became *Caesar's third and last wife. His proconsular command in Macedonia was vociferously attacked by *Cicero whom, as consul, he had failed to save from exile. As censor in 50 he moderated his colleague *Claudius Pulcher's fierce hostility to Caesar. He was neutral in the Civil War and strove to achieve conciliation in both 49 and 43.

BIBL. Cicero, *In Pisonem*, ed. Nisbet, 183 ff., 186 ff.

Piso (2), Lucius Calpurnius ('the *pontifex*') Consul 15 BC.

One of the most distinguished helpers of *Augustus, Piso was probably in Gaul in 16 BC and in Thrace (probably) 12–10 BC, where he won triumphal insignia. From AD 13 until his death in 32 he was urban prefect, earning the highest praise for

Gold medallion of Galla Placidia in ornamental setting.

his moderation and great devotion to duty.

BIBL. Tac. *Ann.* vi. 10–11; *PIR* C 289.

Piso Frugi, Lucius Calpurnius Historian, consul 133 BC.

Piso was jejune and old-fashioned in his manner, and, perhaps in reaction against the contemporary political crisis (see *Gracchus, Tiberius), was particularly concerned to draw moral lessons from the past. He was also strikingly interested in monuments, inscriptions, and works of art.

BIBL. *HRR* i. 110 ff.; Rawson, *Latomus* 1976, 702.

Placidia, Galla Augusta AD 421–50.

Galla Placidia was the half-sister of the Emperor *Honorius and grand-daughter of *Valentinian I.

Mausoleum (originally chapel) of Galla Placidia, Ravenna: Christ the Good Shepherd, 5th-century mosaic.

She was taken hostage by *Alaric, and married his successor *Athaulf (414), but after Athaulf's death the Visigoths were forced to return her. In 417 she reluctantly married Honorius' generalissimo *Constantius (q.v. III), to whom she bore the future Emperor *Valentinian III. After quarrelling with Honorius, she was forced to flee to Constantinople (423); she was restored by the eastern army, which suppressed the usurper John when her six-year old son was installed as emperor at Rome (23 October 425). At first her influence was dominant, but she failed to check the ascendancy of *Aëtius, which was unchallenged after 433. Placidia resorted instead to pious works, especially at the court-city of Ravenna, where her 'Mausoleum' may have been part of one of the churches she founded there. She died in Rome on 27 November 450.

BIBL. S. I. Oost, *Galla Placidia Augusta* (1968).

Plancus, Munatius Consul 41 BC.

Legate of *Caesar in Gaul in the Civil War, Lucius Munatius Plancus was proconsul of Gaul after the dictator's death, and founded the colonies at Lyons and Augst; in 42 BC he triumphed. He became a supporter of *Antony, but in the end was no less zealous in *Augustus' cause, and prominent

Hadrian's Wall: section near Haltwhistle, Northumberland. The construction of the Wall was organized by Platorius Nepos during his governorship (120s AD).

during the 20s. He was one of the censors of 22. His expenditure on buildings at Rome and associations with poets, including *Horace, were notable. His tomb survives, the nucleus of the castle high above the sea at Gaeta.

BIBL. Syme, *Rom. Rev.*

Platorius Nepos Consul AD 119.

A senator, probably from Spain, Aulus Platorius Nepos was a friend of *Hadrian and governor of several important provinces, including Britain (122–4 and possibly as late as 126 or 127). He was responsible for the construction of Hadrian's Wall.

BIBL. Syme, *Tacitus*; Birley, *Fasti* (forthcoming).

Plautianus Consul AD 203, praetorian prefect (?–205).

An African fellow-townsman of the Emperor *Severus and possibly related to him, Gaius Fulvius Plautianus initially served Severus faithfully and became prefect of the Watch and praetorian prefect. His lust for power was unbounded, and in

202 he arranged his daughter *Plautilla's marriage
to *Caracalla. Plautianus was slain in 205 for
allegedly plotting to assassinate Severus and
Caracalla.
   BIBL. Birley, *Severus*; *PIR* F 554.

Plautilla Wife of Caracalla, Augusta AD 202–5.
   Publia Flavia Plautilla, daughter of the praetorian
prefect *Plautianus, married *Caracalla in 202.
Caracalla loathed both his wife and her father, and
she was banished to Lipara after Plautianus' death
and was eventually put to death in 212. Her
reputation for sexual excess is probably unmerited.
   BIBL. Birley, *Severus*; *PIR* F 564.

Plautius, Aulus General in Britain, AD 43.
   Plautius' fame derives solely from his successful
generalship in *Claudius' British invasion of AD 43,
which won him an *ovatio* on his return to Rome in
47; by this time the province had probably been
pacified as far as the line of the Fosse Way. In 57
we find him exercising his husband's judicial rights
when his wife was accused of dabbling in foreign
cults (which may have been Judaism or—possibly
—Christianity).
   BIBL. Frere, *Britannia*; Tac. *Ann*. xiii. 32.

Plautius Silvanus Consul 2 BC, general.
   Marcus Plautius Silvanus brought reinforcements
against the Pannonian rebels in AD 6, and won
important victories in Illyricum over the next three
years, for which he won triumphal insignia. His son
killed himself in AD 24 rather than face trial for
throwing his wife from a window. His daughter
Plautia Urgulanilla was married to *Claudius for a
time, and bore him two children.
   BIBL. Tacitus, *Annals*, iv. 22.

Plautius Silvanus Aelianus Consul AD 45 and 74.
   Tiberius Plautius Silvanus Aelianus played an
important part in *Claudius' British expedition.
Under *Nero he made a brilliant settlement of the
lower Danube as governor of Moesia, making
tributary 100,000 new subjects, receiving the
submission of several kings, and opening a new
source of corn supply. For this—and for his
neutrality in the Civil War of AD 69, perhaps—he
was awarded a second consulship, the urban
prefecture, triumphal insignia, and lavish praise
from *Vespasian.
   BIBL. Smallwood, *Documents*, no. 228.

Plautus (died 184 BC) Comic dramatist.
   Titus Maccius Plautus was probably a *nom de
plume*. The 'facts' of his biography (apart from his
birth at Sarsina in Umbria) are romantic
speculations and worthless deductions from the
text of the plays. Only the dates of the *Stichus* (200
BC) and *Pseudolus* (191 BC) are secure. *Varro
acknowledged 21 plays of Plautus as genuine, and

21 in fact survive, in alphabetical order, of widely
differing character and quality. Though the element
of slapstick and comic 'business' is strong in
Plautus, the plays can rise above farce: *Menaechmi*
is a superbly constructed 'comedy of errors',
Amphitruo a mythological tragi-comedy, and
Rudens occasionally verges upon moral seriousness.
Plautus has altered his Greek originals drastically,
contributing unprecedentedly gross pimps,
outrageously impertinent slaves, torrents of puns,
glorious extravagance of language, deliberately
grotesque blending of Greek and Roman elements,
and metrically complex *cantica* (comic arias).
See also *Terence.
   BIBL. G. Duckworth, *Nature of Roman Comedy*
(1952); W. Beare, *Roman Stage* (3rd edition, 1964);
W. G. Arnott, *Menander, Plautus, Terence*, GRNSC
ix (1975).

Pleminius, Quintus Legate 205 BC.
   In 205 BC *Scipio Africanus left Pleminius in
command of the Roman garrison at Locri, as *legatus
pro praetore*. He was responsible for the looting of
the temple of Persephone and of certain private
property. This led to fighting within the garrison
in which Pleminius' nose, ears, and lips were
mutilated by his subordinates. In an investigation
Scipio vindicated him and confirmed his command.
Pleminius then committed further atrocities which
prompted a Locrian embassy to Rome in 204. The
ensuing scandal nearly deprived Scipio of his
command, but a commission of inquiry exonerated
him. Pleminius was arrested and returned to a long
imprisonment at Rome.
   BIBL. Toynbee, *Hannibal's Legacy*, ii. 613 ff.

Pliny the Elder (AD 23/4–79) Polymath.
   The equestrian career of Gaius Plinius Secundus
involved him in many interesting occasions—a
banquet given for *Gaius, the building of *Claudius'
Ostian harbour, the draining of the Fucine Lake;
it also took him to Germany for a long period under
*Nero, and culminated in the command of the
Misenum fleet. Here his curiosity led to his death
in the eruption of Vesuvius (AD 79) recorded by his
nephew and adopted son, the Younger *Pliny (*Ep.*
vi. 16).
   Like *Varro, he contrived to find time for
authorship on a prodigious scale in the interstices
of an active public life: works on cavalry tactics,
the life of his friend *Pomponius Secundus, the
history of the German wars (in 20 books), grammar,
rhetoric, and contemporary history (*From Where
Aufidius Bassus Left Off* (Bassus being a lost
source for the early first century AD)), in 31 books,
possibly criticized by *Tacitus (at, e.g., *Hist.* ii.
101), are all lost. Not so the *Natural History*, in 37
books, dedicated to *Titus in 77 and more or less
completed by then. He claims engagingly (*praef.*
17) to have read 2,000 volumes by 100 authors and

thence to have culled 20,000 facts: a remarkable underestimate; in the catalogues of book i he lists over 4,000 authors, and his own book-by-book total of facts is nearly 35,000. He is not writing an encyclopedia in the manner of Varro's *Disciplinae* (*pace* his claim at *praef.* 14); his subject is the natural world (xxxvii. 205), and upon it he concentrates, despite excursuses upon human achievements (e.g. the invaluable account of the history of art to be gained from xxxiii–vii). He acknowledges that his theme is barren, but he is concerned for the pleasure and profit of the reader, and therefore makes considerable efforts to write agreeably. But his great achievement is as organizer of his material: 'it must be mentioned because it has been mentioned' (ii. 85). His nephew gives (Pliny, *Ep.* iii. 5) a remarkable picture of the great compiler at work, at wakeful intervals in the night and in the sun after lunch, surrounded by slaves taking notes. The nephew was indeed bequeathed a huge set of such notes (ibid.); better, the uncle had notes made as he watched Vesuvius erupt (Pliny, *Ep.* vi. 16). Despite copious error, Pliny assembled and preserved a vast and invaluable mass of ancient scientific writing.

BIBL. *RP* 52.

Pliny the Younger (*c.* AD 61–*c.* 112) Man of letters, consul AD 100.

Forum of Pompeii with view of Vesuvius: Pliny the Elder met his death investigating the eruption of AD 79.

A member of the municipal aristocracy of Como, Gaius Plinius Caecilius Secundus was adopted by the Elder *Pliny (probably in his will). This relationship, family connections of consular rank, and a good education enabled him to embark on a senatorial career and to begin legal practice. His career proceeded smoothly—embarrassingly so, in that his first prosecution and praetorship both fell in 93 when *Domitian's reign of terror began. He rose steadily and unremarkably to be consul (suffect) in AD 100, and an augur. In 110 he began a special appointment in Bithynia to reduce the various tensions, especially financial ones, which were threatening security in the cities of the area; he probably died in the province which his particular specialities and good relationship with *Trajan had given him. His interest derives from the quantity of information we obtain from his letters rather than from any great personal importance.

Pliny was an occasional and incompetent poet, and a distinguished and successful orator in the courts, but we are left with: (1) the so-called *Panegyric*; rather, *A Rendering of Thanks* (*Gratiarum actio*), a formal thanksgiving for his consulship, delivered before an invited audience.

(2) Nine books of letters to friends. In all, 247 letters, datable between 96 and 108; the dates of publication of individual books are highly controversial. (3) One book of correspondence with Trajan; 14 letters prior to the governorship of Bithynia, 107 (from Pliny to the emperor and some replics) from his time in the East. *Ep*. i. 1 is in answer to a request that Pliny publish those letters he wrote 'rather more carefully'; this he says he has done, not in chronological order but 'as they came to hand'. Hardly so: the books (ix is a rag-bag) are each a rough chronological unity, and each book is itself structured with artifice, containing a careful selection of letters on a number of themes (historical events, court activities, nature, literature, etc.). The letters are occasionally revised with a view to publication, and are never, in contrast to *Cicero's, written without an idea of future literary immortality. Brevity, unity of theme, and consistency of literary style (fluent and extremely elegant, admittedly) are characteristic. Pliny is at his best when busy, whether in the courts or in Bithynia. He has the soul of a *fonctionnaire d'état*, and appears almost admirable when doing his bit towards maintaining the Roman Empire in working order. His evidently limited reading and lack of wider intellectual tastes make some of his other correspondence slightly trying to the modern reader. But the two letters on his uncle (q.v.), for example, or his letter to Valerius Maximus on how to govern Greece (viii. 24) reveal a writer of force and a man of feeling.

BIBL. Sherwin-White, *The Letters of Pliny* (1966); see Radice, Penguin trans. and in *Empire and Aftermath*, ed. Dorey (1975).

Plotina Empress AD 98–117.

'I wish to be the same sort of woman when I leave as I am on entering,' said Pompeia Plotina, wife of *Trajan when she first entered the Palace. She was noted for her modesty, refusing to be made Augusta until 105, and was a supporter of *Hadrian, who paid her outstanding honours on her death in 122.

BIBL. Syme, *Tacitus*.

Plotinus (AD 204/5–270) Neoplatonist philosopher.

All that we have of Plotinus is the finished wisdom of his old age. His 54 surviving essays were edited after his death as the *Enneads* by *Porphyry, his biographer and pupil. They are less the continuous exposition of a philosophical system than a series of 'raids on the inarticulate', carried out in an idiosyncratic style and mobilizing both a lifetime's spiritual experience and the resources of the Greek philosophical tradition, particularly Aristotelian logic, Stoic cosmology, and Platonic metaphysics.

Plotinus was a Greek from Egypt. He was converted to philosophy at the age of 27 and chose *Ammonius Saccas as his master. In 244 he moved to Rome, but before doing so accompanied the Persian expedition of the Emperor *Gordian III to investigate oriental thought. His writings also betray a familiarity with Gnostic sects, but such exotica have little place in his mature thought.

Central to Plotinus' philosophy was the practice of the Return of the soul. By inward contemplation a serious man could ascend to the One, the source of all things. This mysticism was the corollary of a distinctive cosmology. Unlike his Middle Platonist predecessors, Plotinus saw the universe as proceeding from a single and utterly transcendent principle. The One did not create *ex nihilo*: reality continually overflows from it, like water from a fountain. The principal emanations are Intellect and Soul. The physical world is not actively evil: it is simply inferior, furthest from the One, but soaked in Soul like an intricate unbroken net spread like the sea.

Men should strive upwards: Plotinus' last words probably were 'I am trying to give back the Divine in myself to the Divine in the All'. He was heeded: over a hundred years later *Augustine went to his deathbed quoting a saying of the pagan Greek sage.

BIBL. *The Enneads*, trans. S. MacKenna (4th ed., 1969); E. R. Dodds *JRS* l (1960) 1–7; P. Hadot, *Plotin ou la simplicité du regard* (1963).

Portrait of Plotina. Rome, Capitoline Museum.

Plutarch (before AD 50–after 120) Writer.

Born at Chaeronea at the beginning of the reign of *Claudius, Lucius (?) Mestrius Plutarchus studied at Athens and Smyrna, where he came into contact with the latest intellectual trends. Although he visited Rome and lectured there, perhaps under *Domitian, to whom he is hostile, most of his career was devoted to public office in Boeotia and at the shrine of Apollo at Delphi. Under *Trajan and *Hadrian he became famous for his learning and had many friends in high places, including *Sosius Senecio, and among philosophers such as *Favorinus of Arles. In this way he stands on the threshold of the great fusion of Greek and Roman which took place in the second century.

WORKS. Plutarch has left 23 pairs of *Lives*, each dealing with a notable figure from Greek and from Roman history; and four single biographies of a similar nature. These works, optimistic in tone and concerned with moral more than historical analysis, are written in accordance with a general pattern but are not identical in format. Sensible use of (predominantly Greek) sources and a talent for vivid anecdote make them congenial as well as useful reading, and he provides a vast amount of vital historical information. In his Roman lives he shows himself a typical Greek of his time in welcoming Rome's expansion in the Mediterranean, deprecating the moral decline of the late Republic (to which he devotes half the Roman lives) and regarding the Empire as the best solution to the civil commotion which resulted from it. Here, however, as throughout the work, he retains his ability to criticize, and is not slavish in his respect for the conquering power.

Moralia: this collection contains some 78 works, covering a very wide range, from popular moral philosophy (*On Garrulity*, *On the Education of Children*, *Advice on Marriage*), through rhetorical and declamatory works to serious Academic (Platonist) discourses, dialogues (*On the Intelligence of Animals* (terrestrial versus aquatic)) and antiquarian treatises, reflecting a serious interest in religious minutiae, especially those connected with Delphi, where he held a priesthood. Of particular interest to students of the Roman world are: *Advice on Public Life* (798A ff.) on the limits and nature of public life in a provincial city (Sardis), *On the Fortune of the Romans* (316B ff.), on the contributions of fortune and virtue to Rome's greatness, and *Roman Questions* (263D ff.), a work of curious antiquarian learning.

BIBL. C. P. Jones, *Plutarch and Rome* (1971); D. A. Russell, *Plutarch* (1973); A. Wardman, *Plutarch's Lives* (1974); *Roman Questions*, ed. H. J. Rose (1924).

Polemo (*c.* AD 88–144) Greek sophist.

Born at Laodicea in Lycia into a distinguished family which had earlier provided kings in Pontus

and Thrace, Marcus Antonius Polemo was also a citizen of Smyrna. One of the leading sophists of his generation, he was an intimate of *Hadrian and travelled with him on his journey in Ionia and Greece in 123. He is said to have ejected the future Emperor *Antoninus Pius from his house, when the latter was governor of Asia (133/6). His distinction as an orator led to his being invited to speak at the inauguration of the Olympieion in Athens (130). He was involved in a bitter rivalry and quarrel with *Favorinus (as much a manifestation of rivalry between the cities they represented, Smyrna and Ephesus respectively, as between the men

Stele of a warrior thought to be one of a series set up in honour of Polybius. Cast (formerly Berlin).

themselves), which began in Ionia and was carried on in Rome. Apart from his speeches (two are extant, 'set pieces' on a historical theme), he also wrote on history and physiognomy.

BIBL. H. Jüttner, *De Polemonis Rhetoris Vita Operibus Arte* (1898); Bowersock, *Sophists*; *PIR* A 862.

Polybius Greek historian *c.* 200–120 BC.

A prominent Achaean politician, Polybius is best known as the definitive historian of Rome's rise to world power—a remarkably sudden process which he regarded as unparalleled, and which he sought to explain to a primarily Greek audience. In Achaea, as a young man he followed the policies of his hero, *Philopoemen, which involved an independence of approach towards Rome and led ultimately to his deportation to Italy by *Paullus (2) with 1,000 other political prisoners (167 BC). He was fortunate to befriend Paullus' son, *Scipio Aemilianus, and was able to reside in Rome with this powerful family without effective confinement until 151, when the surviving detainees were released. From this vantage point Polybius could observe events at Rome, and question visiting dignitaries and ambassadors on recent history. This greatly helped him with his historical task, as did his extensive travels after 151. He accompanied Scipio to Carthage in 147, and was an important adviser on Rome's settlement of Greece after *Mummius' conquest (146).

Polybius' narrative is extremely reliable by ancient standards because of his use of eye-witnesses and his 'pragmatic' approach, which obliged him to present historical truth as a didactic tool for the aspiring statesman or general reader. Against this must be set his strong pro-Achaean and right-wing bias, distortions incorporated (often uncritically) from other sources, his inability as a Greek to understand Roman institutions, and a propensity for pedantry and moralizing.

BIBL. von Fritz, *The Theory of the Mixed Constitution in Antiquity* (1954); Walbank, *HCP* i–iii; Walbank, *Polybius* (1972).

Polycarp (*c.* AD 69–155/6 or 167/8) Martyr-bishop.

Bishop of Smyrna and the leading Christian figure in Roman Asia in the mid-second century, Polycarp was arrested during a festival at Smyrna on his return from a visit to Rome. Aged 86, he refused to recant his faith and was burned to death. An account of his martyrdom is preserved; the traditional date is 23 February 155/6, but *Eusebius places it in the reign of *Marcus Aurelius (167/8). He was a strong opponent of various heresies and author of a *Letter to the Philippians*.

BIBL. W. H. C. Frend, *Martyrdom and Persecution in the Early Church* (1965); H. Musurillo, *Acts of the Christian Martyrs* (1972); Text: Loeb, *Apostolic Fathers*.

Head of Pompey, early imperial copy. Copenhagen, Ny Carlsberg Glyptotek.

Pompeius Falco, Quintus Consul AD 108.

A distinguished soldier and administrator, Quintus Pompeius Falco was decorated for his service in the first Dacian War (102–3). He governed Lycia-Pamphylia before his consulship and later Moesia Inferior, Britain (before 122), and Asia. He died not before 140.

BIBL. Sherwin-White, *The Letters of Pliny*; Birley, *Fasti* (forthcoming); Syme, *Tacitus*.

Pompeius Strabo Consul 89 BC.

Gnaeus Pompeius Strabo, father of *Pompey, distinguished himself in the Social War first as legate (90 BC) and then as consul in 89, when he effectively ended Italian resistance in the north by the capture of Asculum, and secured the only triumph of the war. At Rome he carried a *Lex Pompeia* conferring Latin rights on Cisalpine Gaul, thus establishing a large personal *clientela* in that region. He emerged from the war at the head of a devoted army, which had been recruited largely through his enormous personal influence in Picenum, where he owned estates. For a further two years he did not disband his army, but maintained a powerful independent presence at Picenum, preparing to intervene decisively in the struggles at Rome. He refused to obey orders from the government at Rome, and allowed his soldiers to murder the consul of 88 who was sent to take over his army. He was probably negotiating with *Cinna when he died in 87. With *Sulla, he was the first of the military dynasts, and left a reputation for unprincipled ruthlessness.

BIBL. Badian, *Clientelae*; Seager, *Pompey*, 1 ff.

Pompey (106–48 BC) Consul 70, 55, and 52 BC.

Gnaeus Pompeius Magnus was an outstanding military leader whose complex political

Pompey's Settlement of the East, 67–63 BC

Theatre of Pompey (begun 55 BC): plan on the
2nd-century Forma Urbis.

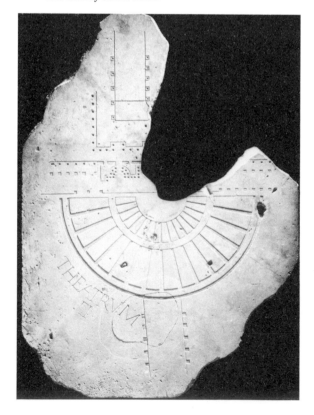

personality dominated the last three decades of the
Republic. His unorthodox public career began in 83
BC when, profiting from the example and vast
clientela of his father, *Pompeius Strabo, he raised a
private army in Picenum and joined forces with
*Sulla to overthrow the government. Retaining
control of his army, he was sent as propraetor to
suppress the anti-Sullan forces in Sicily and Africa,
where he acquired a reputation for ruthlessness and
butchery. Returning victorious to Italy, probably in
81, he extorted a triumph from an unwilling
Sulla, who added the honorific *cognomen* Magnus:
he was still only 25 years old. In 78/7 he received
another special command to assist *Catulus (2) in
suppressing *Lepidus (2), whom he had supported
before his open rebellion. But he refused Catulus'
demand to disband his army until the senate
granted him a proconsular command against
*Sertorius in Spain. There he co-operated with the
equal-ranking *Metellus Pius, but made little
headway before receiving urgently needed
reinforcements in 74. He eclipsed Metellus in the
closing stages of the war, defeating Sertorius'
assassin and successor, M. Perperna, and burning
Sertorius' potentially incriminating correspondence.
His grants of citizenship in Spain were confirmed
by the consuls of 72, and in 71 he returned to
celebrate a triumph; unlike Metellus, who also
triumphed, he did not disband his army
beforehand. For his military successes against the
enemies of the Sullan establishment he was
rewarded with the consulship of 70: this was
technically as illegal as his two triumphs since he
was still a non-senator, but he was clearly an
exceptional case. Owing to his inexperience *Varro
had to write him a handbook on senatorial
procedure. As consul he had as his colleague a
jealous rival, *Crassus, with whom little
co-operation was possible; but both presided over
modifications to the Sullan constitution (notably
the restoration of tribunician powers) which were
generally acceptable to the conservative senatorial
establishment (the *optimates*).

Pompey now enjoyed the status and prestige of a
consularis, but the *optimates* were not prepared to
allow him further advancement. He thus had to
resort to popular legislation to obtain his next
major commands: almost unlimited powers in the
Mediterranean against piracy (67) and over the
eastern provinces against *Mithridates (66). After
rapid military successes Pompey undertook, on his
personal authority (bypassing the customary
commission of senatorial advisers), an extensive
settlement of Rome's eastern provinces and client
states, which trebled the treasury's revenue. His
vast *clientelae* now embraced most parts of the
Roman world: in the East, where he paraded
himself like a Hellenistic monarch, his influence
was immense, and he acquired enormous personal
wealth which dwarfed even Crassus' notoriously

large fortune. At Rome the *optimates* were now distrustful both of his methods and of his excessive power; and, although he disbanded his army in Italy before celebrating his third and most magnificent triumph (61), the senate (led by *Cato 'Uticensis' and *Lucullus) opposed his demands for veteran allotments and ratification of his eastern settlement. Thus he was drawn in 59 into an anti-*optimates* coalition with his rival Crassus and the consul *Caesar, whose daughter *Julia (1) he married.

In the early 50s Pompey's influence at Rome was seriously undermined by the activities of *Clodius and by Caesar's succession of victories in Gaul. But he was strengthened by the renewal of the Triumvirate at Lucca (56): he obtained another consulship (55) and the command of armies in Spain (which he in fact commanded from Rome through legates). The deaths of Julia (54) and Crassus (53) brought his rivalry with Caesar into sharper focus. The *optimates* increasingly courted Pompey as a tool to use against Caesar; Pompey, who above all desired their recognition, disrupted ordered government so that he could then pose as its restorer. The *optimates* met his desire for a dictatorship half-way by allowing him to be sole consul (52): the unholy alliance was sealed by his marriage to Cornelia, daughter of *Metellus Scipio.

In 49 Pompey commanded the government's forces in the Civil War against Caesar. He was obliged to evacuate Italy, which he prepared to blockade from a powerful military position in Greece. When Caesar crossed the Adriatic, Pompey was reluctantly persuaded by the *optimates* on his staff to fight him at Pharsalus (48). Defeated, he fled to Egypt, where he was murdered on the orders of an embarrassed government.

BIBL. Plutarch, *Life of Pompey*; Badian, *Clientelae*; Seager, *Pompey: a Political Biography* (1979).

Denarius: Sextus Pompey as 'son of Neptune'.

Pompey, Sextus (died 36/5 BC).

Inheriting his father *Pompey's vast influence and personal following, Sextus Pompeius was able to figure as a powerful dynast after *Caesar's death, and to continue the republican struggle against the Second Triumvirate until 36 BC. He came to prominence as the successful leader of anti-

Caesarian forces in Spain (44 BC), and after Caesar's death the senate appointed him to an extensive naval command (43). Shortly afterwards the Triumvirate was formed and Pompeius was proscribed, but with his fleet and army he was able to establish a powerful independent base in Sicily to act as a refuge for the proscribed and from which to blockade Italy. He remained popular in Rome, and in 39 the triumvirs were obliged to neutralize his potent strategic threat by including him in their power-sharing treaty of Misenum. *Octavian reopened hostilities in 38, but suffered numerous setbacks before finally eliminating Pompeius at Naulochus (36). Octavian's propaganda represented him as a pirate chief, but Pompeius celebrated his long mastery of the seas by styling himself 'son of Neptune', a title advertised on his coinage.

BIBL. Hadas, *Sextus Pompey* (1930).

Pomponius Secundus, Publius Consul AD 44.

A man of good taste and a competent poet, Pomponius spent the end of *Tiberius' reign in prison. Under *Claudius he was not damaged by the republican tastes and rebellious activities of his brother Quintus (consul AD 41), and as governor of Germania Superior (50–1) won triumphal insignia fighting the Chatti. He was a friend of *Thrasea Paetus and the Elder *Pliny, who wrote his biography.

BIBL. *OCD*, Pomponius (3).

Pontius Pilatus Governor of Judaea AD 26–36.

*Philo and *Josephus give a more unfavourable

Dedication by Pontius Pilate, governor of Judaea.

picture than do the Evangelists of the governor, appointed by *Tiberius, who condemned *Jesus to death. An inscription records a temple of Tiberius built by him at Caesarea. His harshness and intractably provocative attitude to the Jews exceeded any instructions he may have received even from *Sejanus, who seems to have been anti-Semitic. In the end L. *Vitellius, the governor of Syria, had to remove him from office.

BIBL. Smallwood, *Latomus* 1956; Josephus, *Jewish Antiquities*, iii–iv; Philo, *Legatio*, 589–90.

Popillius Laenas, Gaius Consul 172 and 158 BC.

In his first consulship Laenas created a notable constitutional crisis by his successful opposition to the senate's attempts to reverse the actions of his brother and predecessor, M. *Popillius Laenas. There was a virtual cessation of public business, and the senate postponed the imminent war against *Perseus until 171 BC rather than allocate its command to Laenas or his colleague. In 168 he was sent as ambassador to demand *Antiochus IV's withdrawal from Egypt. In a famous scene at Eleusis, Laenas handed the senate's decree to Antiochus, drew a circle around him in the sand, and insisted on his answer before he stepped out of it. Antiochus meekly submitted to this dramatic gesture of Roman superiority; only then did Laenas, who was personally acquainted with Antiochus, greet him as a friend.

BIBL. Mørkholm, *Antiochus IV of Syria* (1966) 93–96; Scullard, *Politics*; Walbank, *HCP* iii. 330, 403 ff.

Popillius Laenas, Marcus Consul 173 BC.

Laenas' conduct in Liguria during his consulship provoked a scandal that provides a familiar example of Rome's unprincipled brutality in foreign affairs, and a much rarer example (for this period) of the senate's powerlessness over insubordinate magistrates. Laenas made a gratuitous attack on a non-hostile Ligurian tribe, the Statielli, who surrendered to him only to be enslaved and to have their land seized for distribution to Roman settlers. Shocked by such immorality and fearful of the international consequences, the senate ordered Laenas to free the enslaved Statielli and restore their property. But, with the collusion of other senior magistrates, Laenas defied the senate and his arrangements stood. His attempted 'solution' to the politically sensitive agrarian problem won him extensive popular support, which secured his brother the consulship of 172 BC and the censorship of 159 for himself.

BIBL.Toynbee, *Hannibal's Legacy*, 206 ff., 632 ff.; Scullard, *Politics*.

Poppaea Empress AD 62–5.

Poppaea Sabina, daughter of a homonymous

Portrait of the Empress Poppaea, AD 65. Rome, Capitoline Museum.

mother and granddaughter of *Poppaeus Sabinus (q.v.), was wife of the future Emperor *Otho when her beauty attracted *Nero's attention. She became first his mistress then his wife, after the divorce of *Octavia. The empress 'had everything she could want—except goodness' (*Tacitus). She encouraged the murder of *Agrippina (the Younger), and died in pregnancy after being kicked by her husband. She was deified.

BIBL. Tacitus, *Annals*, xiii. 45.

Poppaeus Sabinus Consul AD 9.

Governor of Moesia for 24 years until his death in AD 35, Gaius Poppaeus Sabinus won triumphal insignia in Thrace in AD 26: 'a friend of emperors' (*Tacitus). His (very beautiful) daughter Poppaea Sabina was thought to have been *Valerius Asiaticus' mistress—she killed herself in 47. Her daughter was the Empress *Poppaea.

BIBL. Tacitus, *Annals*, vi. 39.

Porphyry (AD 233–after 300) Neoplatonist philosopher.

Porphyry studied in Athens under Cassius *Longinus and then, after 263, with the great philosopher *Plotinus in Rome. Here he encountered the practice of the inward ascent of the soul to the One which he was to advocate in *Aphorisms leading to the Intelligibles*, a skeleton of Neoplatonic principles. After Plotinus' death Porphyry edited his beloved master's works and wrote his *Life*. His own scholarly writings were voluminous but self-effacing. In all, 77 titles are known; little survives. His works included introductions to music, geometry, and astrology; the *Isagoge* (introduction) to logic was, in a Latin translation, a textbook in the medieval schools. Porphyry was concerned with the full range of religious resources available in classical polytheism. He explained how the gods make the crops grow, and interpreted what they had said through oracles; he wrote biographies of ancient sages, and explored deeper meanings in the myths of Homer. One of his most popular works, *On the Return of the Soul*, survives, typically, only in tiny citations by *Augustine. Christian pretensions disturbed Porphyry: he mobilized impressive erudition for *Against the Christians*, an encyclopedic work which survived condemnation by *Constantine to be officially burnt once more in 448.

BIBL. A. Smith, *Porphyry's Place in the Neoplatonic Tradition* (1976); J. Bidez, *Vie de Porphyre* (1913, 1964); T. D. Barnes, *JTS*, N.S. xxiv (1973) 424–42.

Porsenna, Lars Etruscan king, late 6th century BC.

Porsenna, king of Clusium, subjugated Rome *c.* 507 BC, although Roman historians usually acknowledge only a desperate siege. The Latins, supported by Cumae (which doubtless feared renewed Etruscan aggression), defeated his forces at Aricia. Presumably Rome recovered her independence in consequence.

BIBL. A. Alföldi, *Early Rome and the Latins*, 47 ff.; E. Gjerstad, *Opuscula Romana* vii (1969) 149 ff.; G. A. Mansuelli, *Mélanges J. Heurgon* (1976) 619 ff.

Posidonius (*c.* 135–51 BC) Polymath.

A native of Apamea in Syria, Posidonius was a pupil of *Panaetius. He settled in Rhodes, visited Rome, travelled the western provinces, hated *Marius, taught *Cicero, deeply admired *Pompey, and recorded his deeds, as did *Theophanes. Copious fragments of his numerous historical works survive, as do fragments scientific and philosophical, and his influence on historical narrative and geographical excursuses in, for example, *Caesar, *Sallust, *Tacitus, and *Plutarch was profound. Romans could turn to him not merely for a narrative of events from 136 to *c.* 85 BC (severely critical at times of Roman degeneration and brutality but with an aristocratic tinge), but for the means towards a philosophical justification of the existence of their Empire.

BIBL. Strasburger, *JRS* 1965, 40 ff.; Fragments: ed. Edelstein and Kidd (1972); *FGH* 87.

Postumius Albinus Historian, consul 151 BC.

Aulus Postumius Albinus was one of a number of second-century BC senators who wrote histories in Greek. *Cicero appreciated his literary qualities, but his enthusiasm for Greek culture (philhellenism) was excessive and provoked the hostility of the anti-hellenist *Cato the Elder. Cato ridiculed the apology for bad Greek in the preface to Postumius' history.

Postumius also incurred the hostility of *Polybius for his conduct as praetor in 155, when he presided at the audience of an Achaean embassy and sabotaged its mission by a procedural manoeuvre (Pol. XXXIII. i. 3 ff.). In the same year he gave a kinder reception to the famous embassy of Athenian philosophers (Cic., *Acad.* ii. 137). As consul in 151 he ran into serious trouble levying troops, and with his colleague was imprisoned by a tribune. He served on several important embassies to Greece and the East, including the commission for the settlement of Greece (146).

BIBL. *HRR* i. CXXIV. f., 53 f.; Walbank, *HCP* iii, esp. 726 ff.

Postumius Tubertus, Aulus Dictator 431 BC (?).

Allegedly Master of the Horse to the (suspect) dictator Mamercus Aemilius Mamercinus in 434 BC, Postumius defeated the Aequi at Mount Algidus as dictator in 432 (*Diodorus) or 431 (*Livy). If genuine, the victory heralds an apparently more vigorous and successful external policy of Rome and the Latins, and an early death might explain Postumius' subsequent failure to hold a regular magistracy; but the dating and other details of the engagement (including Postumius' execution of his son for leaving his post against orders) are suspect.

BIBL. PW xxii. 945 ff.; Ogilvie, *Livy*, 576 f.

Gold coin (*aureus*) of Postumus, first of the 3rd-century AD Gallic usurpers.

Postumus Emperor in Gaul AD 260–8.

Of humble origin, Marcus Cassianus Latinius Postumus was a military commander in Gaul under *Valerian, and probably governor of one of the Germanies. Together with Silvanus, he was entrusted with the direction of policy in Gaul, ostensibly under the control of *Gallienus' young son *Saloninus. After a quarrel with Silvanus, Postumus successfully besieged Cologne and put Silvanus and Saloninus to death. In 265 Gallienus fought a battle with Postumus, but the outcome was indecisive. Postumus consolidated his authority in the West, and the territory under his control included Britain and extended into northern Spain. He did not move against Gallienus, since he was forced to wage virtually continuous war against the Germans. An uprising by *Laelianus in 268 was put down after a few months, but it prevented Postumus from benefiting from the defection of Gallienus' general *Aureolus. Postumus was killed by his troops in 268, and was succeeded by *Victorinus.

BIBL. *CAH* xii; *ANRW* ii. 2.

Praetextatus Praetorian prefect AD 384.

Vettius Agorius Praetextatus, who died as consul-designate for 385, was the leading pagan intellectual of his time among the Roman aristocracy. 'The Age of Praetextatus' is idealized by *Macrobius in the *Saturnalia*. *Boethius knew his translation of *Themistius on Aristotle. After three provincial governorships, including Greece (326–4), Praetextatus became urban prefect (367–8), when he intervened in favour of Pope *Damasus, to whom he said (St *Jerome alleges): 'Make *me* Pope, and I will be Christian at once.' He was official delegate of the senate seven times, 'always for difficult requests', and in 384 became praetorian prefect of Italy, Africa, and Illyricum, when his friend *Symmachus was urban prefect. His equally aristocratic wife, Aconia Paulina, who lived with him for 40 years and fully shared his beliefs, commemorated her 'learned worshipper of the gods' manifold divinity' (he saw them all as aspects of the Sun God) by listing his public offices only after his numerous pagan priesthoods. He was widely mourned, but Jerome consigns him to outer darkness, not 'the heavenly palace of her imagination'.

BIBL. *PLRE* i, Praetextatus 1.

Primus, Antonius Partisan of Vespasian AD 69.

Marcus Antonius Primus was a vigorous partisan of *Galba (who restored him to the senate after *Nero had expelled him) and *Vespasian. His hour of glory—supervision of Flavian interests in Rome after the fall of *Vitellius—was curtailed by the arrival of *Mucianus; suspected of flirting with the *Othonian and Vitellian causes, he was encouraged to retire to his native town (Toulouse), where he spent the remainder of his life.

BIBL. Tacitus, *Histories*, ii. 86, iii–iv *passim*.

Priscillian (died AD 385) Christian heretic.

During the later 370s Priscillian, a well-born Spanish layman, preached an ascetic, eccentric view of Christian observance which gained many followers in Spain and south-west Gaul. It was condemned by a council in 380, but Priscillian's supporters consecrated him bishop of Avila and gained recognition from the court of *Gratian. The

usurper *Maximus, however, was a Catholic anxious to conciliate orthodox opinion by persecuting '*Manichees'; he allowed Priscillian's enemies to gain first his condemnation by a council at Bordeaux (384) and then, when he appealed to the emperor, despite protest from St *Martin, his execution by a secular court. There was a revulsion of feeling against his accusers, and in Spain, where he was regarded as a martyr, Priscillianism survived until the sixth century.

BIBL. H. Chadwick, *Priscillian of Avila* (1976).

Priscus (*c*. AD 305–*c*. 396) Neoplatonist philosopher.

A pupil of *Aedesius like his associates *Maximus of Ephesus and *Chrysanthius, Priscus taught Neoplatonic philosophy at Athens, and was an influence on the young *Julian, whose intimate adviser he became, attending at court throughout his sole reign (361–3), and accompanying him to Persia (363). Arrested with Maximus under *Valens, he was released and resumed teaching in Greece.

BIBL. *PLRE* i, Priscus 5.

Gold coin (*aureus*) of the Emperor Probus (enlarged).

Probus Emperor AD 276–82.

Born at Sirmium in 232, Marcus Aurelius Probus, like many later third-century emperors, came to power after a distinguished military career, the details of which are unknown. His antecedents are also unclear, and, although his father is said to have been a certain Dalmatius, described as a rustic gardener, this is probably a fiction. The *Augustan History* states that he served as a tribune under *Valerian, and was under *Aurelian's command for a time in Egypt. Although both statements are plausible, the unreliability of the *Augustan History* precludes their unreserved acceptance. Probus was

proclaimed Augustus in 276 after the death of
*Tacitus, and became undisputed emperor when
Florian was betrayed by his troops a few months
later. The East being temporarily peaceful, Probus
concentrated on the West, defeating the Goths in
Illyricum. He then led his army to Gaul, where he
drove the Franks, Longiones, and Alamanni back
across the Rhine frontier. He then pacified Raetia
and repelled a Vandal invasion in Illyricum. His
reign was troubled by provincial unrest but he
dealt successfully with several usurpers. Current
scholarship casts doubt on his reputation for
enjoying good relations with the senate and
increasing their power. His works of physical
restoration in the provinces, notably the repairing
of irrigation channels and attempts to stimulate
viticulture, were soundly based economically. He
celebrated a triumph in Rome c. 282 and then
departed for the Danube. He was killed by his
discontented soldiers in 282.
  BIBL. *ANRW* ii. 2; *PLRE* i, Probus 3.

Probus, Marcus Valerius Grammarian, floruit
1st–2nd centuries AD.
  Probus was a native of Berytus (Beirut).
Numerous works in the corpus of Latin
grammarians attributed to him are not authentic,
and indeed he published little and had followers
rather than pupils (*Suetonius, *Gramm.* 24). But his
work, critical rather than editorial, on the texts of
*Terence, *Lucretius, *Horace, and *Virgil is
recognized as having been of lasting importance.
  BIBL. Büchner, *Geschichte der Textüberlieferung*
(1961) 335 ff.

Probus, Petronius Praetorian prefect AD 368–75
(etc.).
  Sextus Claudius Petronius Probus (c. 328–c. 388),
the great aristocrat who married into the Anicii,
like his father-in-law *Olybrius identified his
private profit with the public good. After
governing Africa (358), he was made praetorian
prefect by *Valentinian I, and administered Italy,
Africa, and Illyricum (368–75) for much of his
reign, the only civilian to become consul (371).
Despite the abrupt revelation of his ruthless over-
taxation in 375, he retained office, and held it once
more in 383. He received obsequious letters from
*Symmachus and *Ambrose, and a posthumous
panegyric from *Claudian; numerous inscriptions
confirm that his splendour and munificence were
widely admired (two tourists are said to have come
from Persia to look at him), but according to St
*Jerome his unfair taxation wiped out his provinces
'before the barbarians did'. The verdict is
confirmed by *Ammianus, who gives a brilliant
portrait (XXVII. xi) of this formidable patron and
landowner. He was buried behind the altar of St
Peter's in a gold-embroidered shroud; his
sarcophagus survives, and a verse epitaph which

congratulates his family on having acquired a
potent protector at the court of Christ.
  BIBL. *PLRE* i, Probus 5.

Proclus (AD 410–85) Scholarch of Athens and
philosopher.
  Born in Constantinople in 410, Proclus studied
first at Alexandria and later in Athens under
Plutarch and Syrianus; he eventually became head
of the School at Athens and remained there till his
death in 485. Imbued in Orphic and Chaldaean
theology, Proclus adhered strictly to ascetic
theurgical practice. He is the most important late
Neoplatonic philosopher upholding radically
realist views, and left a huge corpus including
monumental commentaries on the *Republic* and the
Timaeus of Plato.
  BIBL. L. J. Rosán, *The Philosophy of Proclus*
(1949).

Procopius Eastern usurper AD 365–6.
  Procopius was a kinsman of the Emperor *Julian
from Cilicia, where he was born c. 326. He rose in

Gold coin of the usurper Procopius.

the court secretariat of *Constantius II, and
commanded an army in Julian's invasion of Persia
(363). He later claimed to have been Julian's
intended successor, but after the accession of
*Valens he went into hiding, to emerge at
Constantinople, where he was proclaimed emperor
by disaffected troops (28 September 365). After
initial successes, he lost military support to Valens,
and was defeated and killed (27 May 366).
  BIBL. *PLRE* i, Procopius 4.

Proculus Jurist, 1st century AD.
  One of the elusive but important first-century

legal experts, Proculus flourished in the reign of *Nero and gave his name to the legal tradition which looked back to Antistius *Labeo. He may be Sempronius Proculus, according to one interpretation.

BIBL. *R. Hist. Droit* xxx. 472 (Honoré).

Prohaeresius (c. AD 276–c. 367) Christian rhetorician.

Of Armenian descent, Prohaeresius, the only celebrated Christian professor in the East in the fourth century, studied at Antioch and Athens before gaining a chair at Athens. His pupils came from Asia Minor and Egypt, and included St *Basil, St *Gregory of Nazianzus, and the pagan *Eunapius. He was invited to Gaul by *Constans, and granted an honorary praetorian prefecture. A bronze statue of him was erected by 'Rome, the queen of cities, to the king of eloquence'. He temporarily resigned his post in 362 as a result of *Julian's law forbidding Christians to teach rhetoric, although an exception was made for him. No works survive.

BIBL. *PLRE* i, Proaeresius; Eunapius, *Lives of the Philosophers* (Loeb with Philostratus).

Projecta Christian heiress, late 4th century AD.

Projecta's marriage to one of the Turcii, a great late-Roman family, was commemorated by the magnificent silver casket and other plate in the Esquiline Treasure. She seems to have died soon after, at the age of sixteen.

BIBL. *PLRE* i, Projecta.

Propertius (54 or 47—after 16 and before 2 BC) Elegiac poet.

A proud Umbrian, son of a well-established family of Assisi, Sextus Propertius writes with exceptional force of the horrors of civil war, from which his family probably suffered. Avoiding a public career, he lived in Rome and produced four books of elegies (28, 26, 23, 16 BC (or later)). Though he addressed poems (ii. 1, iii. 9) to *Maecenas, he seems not to have been an active member of the circles in which *Horace and *Virgil moved, and certainly he is deeply unenthusiastic towards many of the Augustan age's ideals, such as moral legislation, military service, and the glories of the victory over Mark *Antony and *Cleopatra at Actium. At least 13 and perhaps as many as 19 elegies in the first book are devoted to his love for the pseudonymous Cynthia, who remains a central theme of his *opus*, though the complex and intense treatment in book i gives way to a grimly brilliant wit in book iv. Non-erotic themes become steadily more important through his work (note the tribute to Callimachus, the founding father of learned and antiquarian poetry, iii. 1); book iv. is a collection of notable force and brilliance on Roman and antiquarian themes, on love, on Cynthia (both comic and tragic), and, in the 'queen of elegies', iv. 11, a posthumous tribute, deeply moving but not wholly comprehensible, to the great, but not certainly identified, aristocratic lady Cornelia. Our understanding of Propertius has not been helped by the corruptions and transpositions perpetrated by medieval scribes; his manner, however, can never have been other than nervy and allusive.

BIBL. J.-P. Boucher, *Études sur Properce* (1965); M. E. Hubbard, *Propertius* (1974).

Silver bridal casket (28 × 56 cm) of Projecta: above, Venus with tritons; below, bride at her toilet flanked by attendants. London, British Museum.

Prosper of Aquitaine Gallic chronicler, 5th century AD.

Born in Aquitaine, Prosper moved to be a monk at Marseilles and later secretary to Pope *Leo I. A correspondent of *Augustine, he wrote works against the *Pelagians, but his most important work is his continuation of *Jerome's *Chronicle* down to the mid-fifth century.

BIBL. E. Valentin, *Prosper d'Aquitaine* (1900); Migne, PL 51.

Prudentius *c.* AD 348–410 Christian poet.

Most information about Aurelius Prudentius Clemens, the finest fourth-century Christian poet, comes from the autobiographical poetic introduction to his collected works. He was probably born in Saragossa in 348, had a rhetorical education, and served first as a lawyer, and then twice as provincial governor. Finally he held a post of honour at the palace at Rome. His works include the *Daily Round* of twelve exceptionally beautiful devotional hymns in Horatian metres, the *Against Symmachus*, a hexameter polemic against the famous speech of *Symmachus for the restoration of the Altar of Victory (written long after the actual controversy), the *Peristefanon*, the first extended poetic celebration of the Christian martyrs, two anti-heretical polemics, *The Origin of Sin* and the *Apotheosis*, and the *Psychomachy*, an allegorical battle of the Virtues and Vices staged within the human soul, which was to exert great influence on the development of medieval allegory.

BIBL. M. Smith, *Prudentius' Psychomachia: A Re-examination* (1976).

Prusias II King of Bithynia *c.* 182–149 BC.

When in 167 BC Prusias brought his son

Coin type of Prusias II of Bithynia.

Nicomedes to Rome to be educated, his servile behaviour in the senate earned *Polybius' contempt (xxx. xviii. 1 f.). He exploited *Eumenes II's fall from Roman favour, but Rome objected strongly to his attacks on *Attalus II in the 150s. When Nicomedes revolted with Pergamene support in 150, Prusias received no effective assistance from Rome, and was killed.

BIBL. PW xxiii. 1107 ff.; Will, *Hist. pol.* ii.

Ptolemy Geographer and mathematician, 2nd century AD.

An Egyptian who wrote in the reigns of *Hadrian and *Antoninus Pius, Claudius Ptolemaeus was a leading authority in various scientific fields. He wrote several important astronomical works of which the most important is the *Almagest*, a complete textbook in 13 books which remained canonical for over a thousand years. In it he developed a new theory of the moon and the five planets. He was also the author of the most accurate and comprehensive geographical work of Antiquity, although it contains serious errors which are due to his having underrated the earth's circumference. In addition, he wrote important works on astrology, music, optics, and philosophy.

BIBL. P. J. Fischer, *Cl. Ptolemaei Geographiae Codex Urbinas Graecus 82* (1932); O. Cuntz, *Die Geographie des Ptolemaeus* (1923); O. Neugebaur, *The Exact Sciences in Antiquity* (2nd ed., 1957).

Ptolemy VI Philometor King of Egypt 180–145 BC.

Ousted from Egypt by his younger brother *Ptolemy Physcon in 164 BC, Ptolemy fled to Rome, allegedly in rags, but he recovered his kingdom the following year, confining Physcon to Cyrene and securing the ratification of this division by Roman envoys. His refusal to accept the senate's decision to amend the division in Physcon's favour led to Rome breaking off its alliance in 161. But Philometor retained his kingdom intact until his death in 145.

BIBL. Walbank, *HCP* iii.; Badian, *Clientelae*, 108 ff.

Ptolemy VIII 'Physcon' King of Egypt/Cyrene 170–116 BC.

Ptolemy's appeals against the 163 BC partition of the Ptolemaic kingdom were upheld by the senate but successfully resisted by *Ptolemy VI Philometor. His close relations with Rome will have been enhanced by the publication of his will (*c.* 155) in which he bequeathed his kingdom to Rome in the event of his dying childless. Although he had children subsequently, the will provided an example to later dynasts. He seized his brother's part of the kingdom in 145 and reigned until his death. At some time he offered marriage to the widowed *Cornelia. He was grossly overweight: hence his nickname 'Physcon' (i.e. pot-bellied).

BIBL. Will, *Hist. pol.*; *SEG* ix. 7 (for the will).

Ptolemy XII Auletes King of Egypt 80–51 BC.

Fearing annexation of his kingdom by Rome, Ptolemy obtained formal recognition in 59 BC by means of a huge bribe to the triumvirs (see *Caesar). Expelled by his subjects a little later, he paid an even larger sum (10,000 talents) to secure his restoration by *Gabinius in 55. This was financed through loans from *Rabirius Postumus, whom he subsequently appointed as finance minister. His activities created a scandal at Rome.

BIBL. Will, *Hist. pol.* ii. 437–47.

Publilius Philo, Quintus Consul 339, 327, 320, and 315 BC.

A highly influential plebeian statesman, Publilius is attributed in 339 BC a triumph over the Latins, a dubious dictatorship, and pro-plebeian legislation: this reputedly made plebiscites binding on the Roman State (at best a misrepresentation), required patrician approval in advance for legislation presented to the centuriate assembly, and reserved one censorship for plebeians. He was himself the first plebeian praetor (336), and was censor in 332. In 327 he besieged Naples, and was the first magistrate to have his command prolonged. His Campanian campaign of 320 BC should be dated to 315.

BIBL. PW xxiii. 1912 ff.; Salmon, *Samnium* 214 ff.; F. De Martino, *Storia della Constituzione Romana*, i–ii (2nd ed., 1972–3).

Publilius Syrus Mimographer, floruit *c.* 43 BC.

Publilius was probably a native of Antioch, and the freedman of a freedman. Popular as an actor throughout Italy, he wrote soberly and with unexpected moral seriousness. A large collection of maxims often falsely attributed to him survives. See *Laberius

BIBL. *Mimi Romani,* ed. Bonaria (1965) 78; *Sententiae,* Loeb, *Minor Latin Poets,* 3 ff.

Gold coin (*tremissis*) of Pulcheria.

Pulcheria Augusta AD 414–53.

The elder sister of *Theodosius II, Pulcheria was proclaimed Augusta on 4 July 414, and after the departure from office of the praetorian prefect *Anthemius she dominated the court. Although only two years his senior, she took in hand the education of her brother; to her influence is attributed the atmosphere of monastic piety which is said to have pervaded Theodosius II's court. Her ascendancy over her brother waned first in the face of her rival Augusta, the emperor's wife *Eudocia, and then gave way to the powerful

Portrait bust of the Emperor Pupienus. Florence, Uffizi.

eunuch-chamberlain Chrysaphius who dominated the court in the 440s. Pulcheria had recovered the initiative by the time of Theodosius' death (450), when she secured the succession to the throne— and became the wife—of a retired soldier, *Marcian. She died in 453.

BIBL. PW xxiii. 1954–63.

Pupienus (174(?)–238) Emperor AD 238.

Elected emperor together with *Balbinus by the senate after the deaths of *Gordian I and II in 238, Marcus Clodius Pupienus Maximus was of humble origin but had had a distinguished career, serving as proconsul of Asia and urban prefect. The joint reign lasted only 99 days, during which *Gordian III was made Caesar and *Maximinus Thrax was killed by his troops. Balbinus and Pupienus were assassinated by the disaffected praetorian guard.

BIBL. *PIR* C 1179; *CAH* xii; *ANRW* ii. 2.

Pyrrhus King of Epirus 319/18–272(?) BC.

Pyrrhus was Molossian king and head of the Epirote League (306–302; 297–272(?) BC). After attempts to secure and expand his position in northern Greece, he responded to Tarentum's request for assistance against Rome, and defeated Publius Valerius Laevinus near Heracleia in 280. Subsequent peace negotiations, variously recorded, foundered (see C. *Fabricius Luscinus and Ap. *Claudius Caecus), and Pyrrhus won a dour struggle at Ausculum (279). He then turned to supporting the Sicilian Greeks against Rome's ally, Carthage (278–277), but, after early victories, stiffening Carthaginian resistance and renewed

Portrait bust of Pyrrhus (?) from Herculaneum. Naples, Museo Nazionale.

Roman pressure on his Italic allies brought him back to Italy. An unsuccessful encounter with M'. Curius *Dentatus near Beneventum or in Lucania (275) induced him to return to Epirus to rebuild his resources. Initially victorious against Antigonus in Macedon, he was killed intervening at Argos.

BIBL. P. Lévêque, *Pyrrhos* (1957); PW xxiv. 108 ff.

Silver coin (*antoninianus*) of the Emperor Quietus.

Quietus Emperor AD 260–1.

Younger brother of *Macrianus, Titus Fulvius Junius Quietus was proclaimed Augustus with his brother in the East, after the capture of *Valerian by the Persians. He was besieged and killed by *Odaenath in Emesa in 261, after the defeat and death of Macrianus in Illyricum.

BIBL. *PLRE* i, Quietus 1; *PIR* F 547.

Quintilian (AD 33/5–before 100) Writer on education.

A native of Calagurris (Calahorra) on the Ebro,

Marcus Fabius Quintilianus probably began pleading in the Roman courts *c.* AD 53 and studying under the orator Domitius *Afer. About ten years later he returned to Spain, but *Galba brought him back to Rome, and in 88 he became the first holder of a public chair of Latin rhetoric at a suitably elevated salary. His pupils included the Younger *Pliny and *Domitian's great-nephews.

Quintilian was the author of *On the Causes of the Corruption of Eloquence*, of speeches, and of two books on the art of rhetoric, but most notably of *The Education of the Orator* (*Institutio Oratoria*), which survives in twelve books (written in just over two years, probably before AD 96). This immeasurably influential work, by a practising teacher and orator, covers education from infancy to the level of the fully-fledged speaker, the 'good man experienced in speaking' which Quintilian had hoped his young son (died aged five) would become. Quintilian is critical of the practice of declamation and of the formal teaching of the rhetoricians, and he thinks the oratory of his day misbegotten; he is an enthusiastic and intelligent admirer of *Cicero. Not all his precepts are realistic, not all his literary judgements (see, above all, x. 1) remain acceptable, but his discussions are lucid, humane (no *Orbilius he!), sensibly patriotic, emotionally committed, occasionally amusing, unwaveringly moral, and regularly and variously illuminating.

BIBL. Kennedy, *Rhetoric*, 487 ff., and *Quintilian* (1969); Bonner, *Education in Ancient Rome* (1977); Russell and Winterbottom, *Lit. Crit.*, 372 ff.

Quintillus Emperor AD 270.

Brother of *Claudius II (Gothicus), Marcus Aurelius Claudius Quintillus was proclaimed emperor in 270 on the former's death, having previously been in command of troops in Italy. His reign was brief: its actual length is uncertain, but it was only a matter of a few months. He then either committed suicide or was killed by his troops.

BIBL. *PLRE* i, Quintillus 1; *PIR* A 1480.

Quintus of Smyrna Poet, 4th century AD.

Quintus, who probably wrote in the fourth century, produced an epic sequel to Homer's *Iliad*, in 14 books, which is particularly important for the tradition of various non-Homeric myths related to Troy.

BIBL. F. Vian, *Recherches sur les Posthomerica de Quintus de Smyrne* (1959).

Quirinius Governor of Syria AD 6.

Publius Sulpicius Quirinius (consul 12 BC) overcame his undistinguished origins by his untiring zeal as a commander; in the last decade BC successful campaigns in Cilicia won him triumphal insignia and probably recommended him as adviser to Gaius *Caesar in the East as successor to *Lollius, whose mistake of not cultivating *Tiberius on Rhodes he did not repeat. In AD 6 as governor of Syria he conducted the census which is referred to in Luke 2. 2: it is not clear how the resulting conflict with Matthew's date for the Nativity is to be resolved. He died in AD 21 wealthy, powerful and disliked (Tac. *Ann.* iii. 48).

BIBL. Syme, *Rom. Rev.*, 399.

Quodvultdeus (died AD 453) Bishop of Carthage.

A deacon, friend, and correspondent of *Augustine (428), Quodvultdeus was bishop of Carthage at the time of the Vandal invasion. He was banished by *Geiseric in 439 and fled to Naples, where he died in 453. He is the author of twelve sermons which have survived as part of the Augustinian corpus, and of *On the Promises and Predictions of God*, formerly attributed to *Prosper of Aquitaine.

BIBL. Quodvultdeus, *Livre des Promesses et Prédictions de Dieu*, ed. R. Braun (1964).

Rabirius Postumus Praetor 48 BC, banker.

A wealthy banker, Gaius Rabirius Postumus attached himself in the 50s to the triumvirs and then to *Caesar, with whose assistance he became a senator and probably reached the praetorship (48 BC). In 55 after arranging loans for *Ptolemy XII Auletes he became finance minister at his court, and proceeded to recover the royal debts by fleecing the Egyptian populace. He was thrown into prison by Auletes, but escaped to Rome, where he faced prosecution for extortion (54). He was defended by *Cicero and acquitted.

BIBL. Dessau, *Hermes* xlvi (1911) 613 ff.

Regalianus Usurper c. AD 260.

Cornelius Publius Regalianus was a general of *Gallienus serving in Illyricum, and was declared emperor c. 260 by the troops who, however, shortly thereafter murdered him.

BIBL. Göbl, *Regalianus und Dryantilla* (1970).

Regulus Consul 267 and 256 BC.

In his second consulship Marcus Atilius Regulus took advantage of his naval victory at Ecnomus to invade Africa, becoming the first Roman to do so. After some initial success his army was annihilated by *Xanthippus in 255 BC, and he was captured. An unhistorical Roman legend relates that he was subsequently sent to Rome by Carthage to argue for peace, under an oath to return; that he in fact urged the senate to reject peace terms, but still kept his oath; and that the Carthaginians tortured him to death.

BIBL. Walbank, *HCP* i. 88–94.

Regulus, Marcus Aquilius Informer, 1st century AD.

Regulus was one of those who gained wealth and position from prosecuting political dissidents— openly under *Nero, and more circumspectly under *Domitian. The vituperative account of him in the Younger *Pliny's letters reflects the unpopularity which his activities caused him: 'the most evil thing that walks on two legs' (*Ep.* I. v. 14).

BIBL. *OCD*; *PIR* A 1005.

Ricimer Master of the Soldiers and Patrician AD 456–72.

Although debarred from the imperial throne himself by his barbarian birth and his *Arianism, Flavius Ricimer directed Roman policy in the West for sixteen years through a series of emperors more or less under his domination. He was the son of Suevian and Gothic royalty, brother-in-law and uncle to Burgundian princes and, for four years, husband of *Anthemius' daughter. His position established by a naval victory over the Vandals (456), he deposed his patron, *Avitus, in favour of *Majorian, whom he also later executed (461). His most amenable puppet, the shadowy Libius Severus (emperor 461–5), acquiesced in concessions to the Goths and Suevi, but Ricimer found his position challenged from within the Roman aristocracy and by *Geiseric. In 467, he agreed reluctantly to the Eastern nomination of Anthemius and married his daughter, but kept aloof from the expedition against the Vandals (468). Political and personal incompatibility led to an open break, and Ricimer replaced Anthemius with *Olybrius (472), but died six weeks later. His period of power had preserved some form of continuity in the administration, but his concessions of Roman territory to Germanic tribes had further weakened the Empire.

BIBL. Stein, *Bas-Empire*, i. 371–95; Bury, *Later Empire*, i. 10.

Ricomer Commander-in-chief AD 388–93.

Like his superior *Merobaudes (1), Ricomer was one of the Frankish-born generals at the court of *Gratian, who sent him to help *Valens against the Goths. In 383 Ricomer was commander-in-chief on the eastern frontier, where he won *Libanius' approval for being a pagan admirer of Libanius. Consul in 384, he was joint commander of the army which overthrew the usurper *Maximus (388), and remained one of *Theodosius I's two commanders-in chief until his death in 393. He introduced his nephew *Arbogast to his future puppet-emperor *Eugenius.

BIBL. *PLRE* i, Richomeres.

Romanus Army commander in Africa c. AD 363– c. 373.

Romanus, who is severely criticized by *Ammianus, commanded the African army for most of *Valentinian I's reign. He failed to protect the towns of Tripolitania from nomad raids (*c.* 363/6) and corruptly suppressed their complaints. His intervention provoked the uprising in Mauretania (see *Gildo) which was crushed by Count *Theodosius. Romanus was dismissed, but escaped further punishment.

BIBL. *PLRE* i, Romanus 3.

Romulus

Romulus was the legendary eponymous founder and first king of Rome (conventional dates: 753–717/16 BC). The story of the twins Romulus and Remus suckled by a she-wolf, established at Rome by the third century BC (see Q. *Ogulnius Gallus), may be native, although Greek motifs heavily influenced its development. To Romulus were attributed Rome's early political and military institutions, and victories over neighbouring peoples, including the Caeninenses, whose king he slew in single combat. His seizure of Sabine women as wives for his men resulted in conflict and then co-rule with Titus *Tatius. He was sometimes identified with the god Quirinus.

BIBL. PW iA. 1074 ff.; Ogilvie, *Livy*, 32 f., etc.; T. J. Cornell, *PCPS* cci (1975) 1 ff.

Romulus Augustulus Last western emperor AD 475–6.

Romulus, the 'little Augustus', was set up as a figurehead emperor by his father, *Orestes. A few months later, after Orestes' murder by *Odoacer, Romulus was deposed, but spared because of his youth and allowed to live on in exile near Naples, supported by a generous pension.

BIBL. Stein, *Bas-Empire*, i. 396; Bury, *Later Empire*, i. 405–6.

Rubellius Plautus (died AD 62).

As son of Julia, granddaughter of *Tiberius, Rubellius Plautus was no further removed from *Augustus than *Nero himself (see stemma). His quiet disposition (he had stoic leanings) probably saved him in 55 when he was accused of revolutionary designs. He was forced to retire to Asia Minor in 60, and was killed there in 62.

BIBL. Tacitus, *Annals*, xiv. 57–9.

Rufinus Praetorian prefect AD 392 5.

The Gaul Flavius Rufinus, a ruthless politician who patronized Christian ascetics, dominated the court of *Theodosius I after *Cynegius' death (388). As Master of the Offices (388) he accompanied Theodosius to Italy, meeting *Symmachus and acquiring relics at Rome for which he built a shrine at his palace near Constantinople, where he also founded a monastery. When the court returned to the East, he became consul (392) and supplanted *Tatianus (q.v.) as praetorian prefect. After being baptized, he inspired anti-pagan legislation. When Theodosius left for the West again (394), Rufinus

Altar from Ostia depicting the legend of Romulus and Remus, the legendary founders of Rome. Rome, Museo delle Terme.

remained as virtual regent for his son *Arcadius, but when the army returned, he was murdered (27 November 395) at *Stilicho's instigation. The charges of corruption and murderous intrigue voiced by Stilicho's propagandist *Claudian are found in other sources.

BIBL. J. F. Matthews, *Western Aristocracies*.

Rufinus of Aquileia Christian scholar (*c.* AD 345–410).

Turranius Rufinus came from a rich north-Italian family; he studied at Rome, where St *Jerome was his fellow-student and friend. After living a monastic life at Aquileia, he left for Egypt in *c.* 372, where he visited monks and studied at Alexandria. In *c.* 380 he founded a monastery at Jerusalem in association with St *Mclania's convent. He and Melania returned to Italy in 397, perhaps because of his bitter quarrel with Jerome over *Origen's alleged heresy. In Italy he translated Greek theology, including Origen; by recalling Jerome's past admiration for Origen (398), he renewed the quarrel and brought down on himself a torrent of abuse. He lived mostly at Aquileia, where he made a free translation of *Eusebius' *History*, which he continued to 395. The Gothic invasions forced him to move south, and he died in Sicily soon after the Sack of Rome.

BIBL. J. N. D. Kelly, *Jerome* (1975).

Rufinus, Vulcacius Consul AD 347.

Rufinus was a Roman aristocrat whose sister married into the Constantinian dynasty (her son was the Caesar *Gallus). Rufinus served his imperial kinsmen as praetorian prefect, and was recalled to office by *Valentinian I in 365–8, when he is described as 'an old man of almost all the virtues, but who never missed a chance of profit if he thought he could conceal it' (*Ammianus).

BIBL. *PLRE* i, Rufinus 25.

Rufus, Cluvius Consul AD 66/8, historian.

Cluvius Rufus was favoured by *Nero, but inoffensive. In the Civil War of 69 he played an important role in Spain, which he left to join *Vitellius. His history was an important source for *Tacitus.

BIBL. Tac. *Hist.*, iv. 43; Syme, *Tacitus*, 178–9.

Rufus, Quintus Curtius Romantic historian.

Dated as early as *Augustus and as late as *Commodus/Septimius *Severus, Curtius Rufus was the author of *Histories of Alexander the Great* in 10 books; i and ii are missing and there are gaps later. His style is basically *Livian, his manner rhetorical, his moral preoccupations Peripatetic (i.e. influenced ultimately by Aristotle), and his historical reliability very variable.

BIBL. Tarn, *Alexander*, ii (1948); McQueen, in *Latin Biography*, ed. Dorey (1967) 17 ff.

Rutilius Gallicus Consul AD 72/3 and *c.* 90.

Quintus Julius Cordinus Gaius Rutilius Gallicus had a reasonably distinguished career including the governorship of Galatia under *Corbulo; *Vespasian gave him the important task of boundary-commissioner in Africa. As governor of Germania Inferior he was notably successful, and returning to Rome, he was made prefect by *Domitian. Illness and death followed his second consulship, in about AD 92.

BIBL. Statius, *Silvae* i. 4.

Rutilius Rufus Consul 105 BC.

Publius Rutilius Rufus was an eminent figure whose wide intellectual learning, political conservatism, and moral integrity put him in the same mould as *Scipio Aemilianus, under whom he served at Numantia (133 BC). Like *Marius he obtained political advancement under the Metelli and served under *Metellus Numidicus in Africa. But Rutilius maintained the connection, and, after reaching the consulship of 105 as a *novus homo*, remained a bastion of the senatorial establishment. As *Scaevola's legate in Asia (*c.* 95) he helped to rectify the financial abuses in the province, thus antagonizing the *publicani*. At Rome the *publicani* dominated the equestrian juries in the criminal courts, and their counter-attack was directed against Rutilius, who was politically more

vulnerable than Scaevola. In a notorious trial (92 BC) he was condemned by an equestrian jury for 'extortion': the scandal caused a clamour for jury reform, which the tribune *Drusus (2) exploited the following year. Rutilius retired to exile in Asia, the scene of his 'extortions', where he received high honours and wrote his political memoirs. As a writer he was an important influence on *Sallust and *Plutarch.

BIBL. Badian, *Studies*; Gruen, *Roman Politics and the Criminal Courts*; *HRR* i. 187 ff.

Portrait statue of the Empress Sabina as Ceres, *c.* 130 AD. Ostia, Museum.

Sabina Empress AD 117–36 (?)

Vibia Sabina was the grand-niece of *Trajan and the wife of *Hadrian, whom she married in AD 100 —a marriage perhaps engineered by the Empress *Plotina, who consistently favoured Hadrian in his earlier career. She bore no children. Hadrian's praetorian prefect, Septicius Clarus, and secretary, *Suetonius, are said to have lost their positions in 121 or 122 through indiscreet behaviour with the empress. She received the title Augusta in 128, and was granted divine honours after her death (probably 136). Rumours that she was poisoned or forced to commit suicide by Hadrian are probably fictions associated with the deaths of other prominent people at this time.

BIBL. Syme, *Tacitus*.

Sabinus, Flavius (died AD 69) Brother of Vespasian.

Elder brother of *Vespasian, Titus Flavius Sabinus fought in Britain after AD 43, governed Moesia, was prefect of Rome from at least 61 and then again under *Otho, and was killed in the siege of the Capitol by the forces of *Vitellius in 69. He was a fair-minded and decent man, but long-winded.

BIBL. *PIR* F 352.

Salinator, Marcus Livius Consul 219 and 207 BC.

Salinator won a triumph in the war against *Demetrius of Pharos in 219 BC, although *Polybius suppresses his role. He was convicted of misappropriation of booty, and retired from public life until 210. In 207 he was reconciled with his ex-surbordinate, C. Claudius *Nero (who had testified against him), and elected to a second consulship as his colleague. He was in overall command at the battle of the Metaurus, which turned the course of the *Hannibalic War in Italy in Rome's favour.

BIBL. Scullard, *Politics*; Walbank, *HCP* i. 327, 331.

Sallust (probably 86 35 BC) Historian.

Gaius Sallustius Crispus achieved greatness as a historian after a failed career in politics. He entered the political scene a partisan of *Clodius, and as tribune reacted to the latter's death in 52 BC with attacks on *Milo and *Cicero. But in 50 he was expelled from the senate by Clodius' brother, the censor Ap. *Claudius Pulcher. He joined *Caesar in the Civil War and held the praetorship of 47, but misconduct in his African provincial command led to a prosecution for extortion (45) which was quashed by Caesar but forced him to retire from politics. He now devoted himself to the writing of history: two monographs (which survive) on the war against *Jugurtha and the conspiracy of *Catiline, and a largely lost coverage of the years after 78. The historical value of the narrative is vitiated by political bias, excessive schematization, and tendentious moralizing. But his importance in Roman historiography is secured by his pioneering of the monograph form and by an unorthodox literary style which exerted a wide influence, particularly on *Tacitus.

BIBL. Earl, *The Political Thought of Sallust* (1961); Syme, *Sallust* (1964).

Sallustius Crispus (died AD 21) Counsellor of Augustus.

Like *Maecenas, Gaius Sallustius Crispus chose to serve *Augustus without becoming a senator, but surpassed most senators in his influence, especially after the eclipse of Maecenas; it was never as great under *Tiberius. In AD 14 he was responsible for the killing of *Agrippa Postumus. The Elder *Pliny reveals that part of his wealth came from metal-workings in the Alps, and like Maecenas he was a patron of poets, including *Horace and *Crinagoras.

BIBL. Tac. *Ann.* iii. 30; *Anthologia Palatina*, xvi; Horace, *Odes*, ii. 2.

Sallustius Passienus Crispus Consul AD 27 and 44.

Adopted son of *Sallustius Crispus, Gaius Sallustius Passienus Crispus was intimately connected with the imperial family (he married first *Nero's aunt Domitia, then his mother *Agrippina—his heir, and widely supposed to be his murderer). He was rich and obsequious, and was noted for his forensic oratory.

BIBL. Thomae *PIR add.*, p. 53.

Salonina Empress AD 254–68.

Wife of the Emperor *Gallienus, Cornelia Salonina Chrysogone was probably a Greek (from Bithynia?). She should probably not be identified with Pipa, Gallienus' concubine *c.* 254. Salonina was apparently a women of some erudition, and she and Gallienus were members of *Plotinus' circle.

BIBL. *PLRE* i, Salonina; *PIR* C 1499.

Saloninus Caesar *c.* AD 258–60, Augustus 260.

Younger son of the Emperor *Gallienus, Publius Licinius Cornelius Saloninus Valerianus was appointed nominal commander on the Rhine when Gallienus had to fight in Pannonia. *Postumus, Gallienus' chief general on the Rhine, besieged Cologne *c.* 260, murdered Saloninus, and was proclaimed emperor.

BIBL. *PIR* L 183; *CAH* xii; Walser and Pekary, *Krise*; *ANRW* ii. 2.

Salutius Praetorian prefect AD 361–7.

A Gaul of high culture, Saturninius Secundus Salutius was *Julian's praetorian prefect of the East, and, honoured by all for his fairness and integrity, continued in office for four more years, having declined the offer of the throne after Julian's death in Persia (363). He first met Julian when, after holding several offices, he was assigned as an adviser to the new Caesar in Gaul, and quickly became a close friend. *Constantius II recalled him, out of ill-will to Julian, who wrote a speech to console himself (*Or.* viii). A pious pagan who won praise from Christians for his impartiality in religious matters, he was a moderating influence on Julian.

BIBL. *PLRE* i, Secundus 3.

Salvian of Marseilles Gallic priest and writer, 5th century AD.

An observer of contemporary social evils and of
the effects of barbarian invasions on Gaul, Salvian
provides a unique insight into the internal
problems of the Roman Empire. Born in the north-
east, he moved south to the famous monastery at
Lérins (an island off Cannes), where he tutored the
sons of Eucherius, bishop of Lyons, and later
became a priest at Marseilles. A prolific author, his
main surviving works, *To the Church* and *On the
Governance of God*, attack the wealth and
corruption of the Church and of society, and justify
the workings of divine providence in the context of
the barbarian invasions.

BIBL. Gennadius of Marseilles, *On Famous Men*
(*De viris illustribus*), 68; Salvien de Marseille,
Oeuvres, SC 176 (1971) and 200 (1975); M.
Pellegrino, *Salviano di Marsiglia* (1940).

Saoterus Imperial courtier, late 2nd century AD.

Of Bithynian origin, Saoterus was chamberlain
and favourite of *Commodus, over whom he
exercised great influence. He appeared with the
emperor in his German triumph of 180. He was
murdered in 182 through the intrigues of
*Tarutienus Paternus and *Cleander.

BIBL. Grosso, *Lotta*.

Sapor: see **Shapur**

Saturninus Tribune of the plebs 103 and 100 BC.

As a young quaestor in charge of the grain
supply at a time of rising prices (104 BC), Lucius
Apuleius Saturninus was replaced in his duties by
the *princeps senatus*, M. Aemilius *Scaurus.
Embittered by this humiliation he turned his
considerable talents to the popular cause, and
delivered the most effective challenge to the
senatorial establishment since Gaius *Gracchus. His
success was largely determined by his co-operation
with the highly influential but politically
ineffective *Marius. In his two tribunates (103 and
100) Saturninus carried agrarian laws providing
land for Marius' veterans of the African and
German wars. In return he secured the assistance of
these veterans in passing more controversial,
popular legislation by organized violence. This
legislation included a law establishing *maiestas*
(treason) as a criminal charge and a law providing
for the subsidized distribution of corn to the
people.

In foreign affairs Saturninus may have inspired
the so-called Piracy Law (*c*. 100 BC), which
consolidated M. *Antonius' command against the
pirates; and his insulting treatment of *Mithridates'
ambassadors in 101 probably reflects an attempt to
stir up popular patriotic sentiment against
Mithridates' noble patrons in the senate. By this
time Saturninus' personal influence was becoming
considerable, as he grew increasingly independent
of Marius and vastly extended the colonization

programme. He stood again for the tribunate of 99,
but Marius took advantage of the violence
surrounding the consular candidacy of Saturninus'
principal associate, C. *Glaucia, to act on behalf of
the senatorial establishment against both of them.
They were subsequently killed in prison.

BIBL. Lintott, *Violence*; Gruen, *Politics*.

Saturninus, Gaius Sentius Consul 19 BC.

As consul in *Augustus' absence during the
period of popular discontent fomented by M.
*Egnatius Rufus, Sentius had responsibilities which
were becoming rare for holders of that office. Later
he governed Africa and Syria, and as legate of
*Tiberius in Germany won triumphal insignia. He
probably died before Augustus.

BIBL. Dio, liv. 10; Syme, *Rom. Rev.*, 371, etc; *RP*
45.

Saturninus, Gnaeus Sentius Consul AD 41.

Sentius was distinguished mainly for the zeal
with which he, like Q. Pomponius Secundus (see P.
*Pomponius Secundus), supported the abolition of
the principate after the death of *Gaius. He seems
also to have played a leading role in *Claudius'
British expedition of AD 43.

BIBL. Josephus, *Jewish Antiquities*, xix. 166–85.

Saturninus, Lucius Antonius Rebel AD 89.

Saturninus, governor of Germania Superior, and
his two legions revolted in January AD 89, but were
quickly crushed by *Domitian's decisive action and
the loyalty of *Lappius Maximus in Germania
Inferior. No accomplices are certainly known, and
the repercussions, which included military reforms,
were limited to Germany.

BIBL. Syme, *JRS* 1978; *CAH* xi. 172.

Saturninus, Lucius Volusius Consul AD 3, urban
prefect.

Volusius was urban prefect from AD 42 until his
death at 93 in AD 56: *Tacitus notes with
astonishment that he survived the intimacy of so
many emperors, and he was much respected, for
his uprightness among other things.

BIBL. Tacitus, *Annals*, xii. 30.

Saturninus Dogmatius Praetorian prefect AD
334/5.

The career of Gaius Caelius Saturninus Dogmatius,
a trusted servant of *Constantine who achieved
senatorial rank, is known from the inscription of
the statue erected in his honour at Rome. He held
seven offices at court in succession, before
becoming a deputy praetorian prefect, and
ultimately praetorian prefect.

BIBL. *PLRE* i, Saturninus 9.

Scaevola, Mucius

Gaius Mucius Cordus Scaevola allegedly

attempted to assassinate *Porsenna but, when arrested, won the latter's admiration by his courage. The legend perhaps originated as an aetiological explanation of the 'Mucian Meadows' (supposedly given to him), with his defiant burning of his right hand added subsequently to explain the *cognomen* Scaevola (interpreted as 'left-handed') of later Mucii.

BIBL. PW xvi. 416 ff.; Ogilvie, *Livy*, 262 ff.; E. Gjerstad, *Opuscula Romana* vii (1969) 149 ff.

Scaevola, Quintus Mucius Consul 95 BC.

An eminent orator and jurist Scaevola became a model of good provincial government for his conduct in Asia in the 90s. It was probably after his consulship with Lucius *Crassus in 95 that Scaevola was appointed to a special proconsular command in Asia with the senior ex-consul, P. *Rutilius Rufus, as his legate. Their task was not military but the reform of provincial administration and particularly of abuses associated with the *publicani*, with a view to improving Rome's distinctly tarnished image in the province. But even after their success, which was universally acknowledged, much ammunition remained for *Mithridates' anti-Roman propaganda in 88. Scaevola was extravagantly honoured in Asia as a second founder of the province, and received cult-worship. He survived *Cinna's regime until 82, when he met a violent death. As a jurist (who taught *Cicero), he composed the first systematic treatise on the civil law at Rome, which exercised a wide and prolonged influence.

BIBL. Magie, *Roman Rule in Asia Minor*; Badian, *Studies in Greek and Roman History*.

Scaurus, Marcus Aemilius Consul 115 BC.

A conservative senator of immense influence in the period between 120 and 90 BC, Scaurus was originally a protégé of the *Metelli, but rose to high political office and ultimately the leadership of their faction. In his consulship (115) he secured a triumph for victories in Liguria and was, surprisingly, appointed *princeps senatus* by the censors, in circumstances which are unclear. From 117 he was a consistent opponent of *Jugurtha's partisans in the senate, and in 112 led an embassy to Numidia which frightened Jugurtha but failed to stop his aggression. When war was declared in the following year, Scaurus served as legate in Africa. His anti-Jugurtha record enabled him to swim with the popular tide and secure appointment as a chairman of the *quaestio* of *Mamilius in 109, the year in which he also became censor. His true conservative colours were shown in 100, when he proposed the emergency senatorial decree which empowered *Marius, as consul, to use force against *Saturninus and his supporters. Shortly before his death he gave some initial backing to M. Livius *Drusus (2) in his tribunate (91), but probably

closed ranks with the senatorial establishment over the issue of Italian enfranchisement.

BIBL. Badian, *Studies*; Gruen, *Politics*.

Scipio, Publius Cornelius Consul 218 BC and Scipio Calvus, Gnaeus Cornelius Consul 222 BC.

When Rome declared war on Carthage in 218, the consul P. Scipio was dispatched (with his brother Gnaeus as legate) to meet *Hannibal in Spain. Hannibal slipped past his army in southern France, causing Publius to split his army and return to meet defeat at Hannibal's hands at the Ticinus and the Trebia. In 217 as proconsul he reached Spain, where Gnaeus had already fought a successful campaign. The two brothers worked to undermine Carthaginian influence in Spain and to win sympathy and support for Rome among the Spaniards; they extended Roman control over the east coast of Spain and captured Saguntum (c. 212); and above all they prevented *Hasdrubal from joining Hannibal in Italy by their victory near Ibera in 215. However, they were outnumbered by the Punic forces in Spain, and were both separately defeated and killed in 211.

BIBL. Lazenby, *Hannibal*.

Scipio Aemilianus Consul 147 and 134 BC.

An important military and political leader of the second century BC, Publius Cornelius Scipio Aemilianus was born c. 185 BC the natural son of Aemilius *Paullus (2), under whom he served in Macedonia (168). By this time, however, he had been adopted into the Cornelian *gens* by the elder son of *Scipio Africanus. The combined influence which he inherited from Paullus and Africanus goes far to explain his later political pre-eminence. To his admirer and close friend the historian *Polybius, the young Scipio stood out as a paragon of manly virtues amid a generation corrupted by the influx of luxury and Hellenism. But Scipio coupled a profound regard for traditional Roman austerity with a keen intellectual interest in Greek culture. The so-called 'Scipionic circle' was a loose grouping of like-minded political associates and their literary protégés (see *Laelius, *Terence, *Lucilius, *Panaetius).

As a junior senator in 151 Scipio relieved a desperate crisis of military recruitment by volunteering to serve in Spain and encouraging others to follow his example. A distinguished military record in Spain and Africa led to his irregular election to the consulship of 147 (for which he was qualified neither by age nor rank), and the command of the third war against Carthage. By the next year he had ended the war with the brutal destruction of Carthage. Scipio became censor in 142, but his plan to conduct an old-fashioned moral purge was frustrated by his more liberal colleague, L. *Mummius. Probably in 140 he led an important and wide-ranging embassy to the

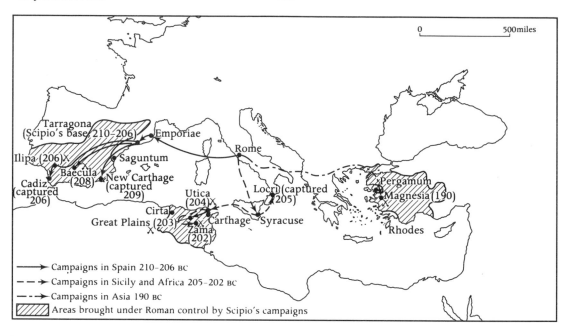

Campaigns in Spain 210-206 BC
Campaigns in Sicily and Africa 205-202 BC
Campaigns in Asia 190 BC
Areas brought under Roman control by Scipio's campaigns

East, which seems to have involved investigating the affairs of many of Rome's client states in the area. In 134 the constitutional rules were once again bent to allow Scipio's election to a second consulship. This time his military task was the termination of the embarrassingly long and costly Numantine War in Spain. He duly accomplished this by the capture and destruction of Numantia in 133 BC.

The absence of the politically influential Scipio may have determined the timing of Tiberius *Gracchus' agrarian legislation. On his return to Rome to a second triumph, Scipio's natural conservatism overcame any family sentiment towards his wife's late brother. He condemned his activities, approved of his lynching, and worked towards the undoing of his legislation. Scipio's once considerable popularity now sank to a low ebb, and in 129 he died suddenly in somewhat mysterious circumstances.

BIBL. Astin, *Scipio Aemilianus* (1967).

Scipio Africanus Consul 205 and 194 BC.

The conqueror of Spain, Africa, and Asia Minor, Publius Cornelius Scipio Africanus stands out more than any other individual as the architect of Rome's world supremacy. His great popularity with the people and proven military abilities elevated him in 210 BC to an extraordinary and quite unprecedented proconsular command in Spain, although he was only 26 and a private citizen. By 206 he had driven the Carthaginians out of Spain and brought it permanently under Roman control. The years in Spain saw the emergence of Scipio the great military genius and charismatic leader. He began to train his army to the degree of

The Career of Scipio Africanus

professionalism which would ultimately allow him to out-general *Hannibal, and which more immediately led to his two brilliant victories over Carthaginian armies at Baecula (208) and Ilipa (206). His magnetic personality and diplomatic skill secured the co-operation of native chieftains, many of whom saluted him as a king. This co-operation was vital for winning the war in Spain, and he benefited greatly from the contacts already established by his father P. Cornelius *Scipio in the years before 211 BC. He also won the devoted loyalty of his soldiers, among whom the legend arose that he was divinely assisted, especially after an apparently miraculous tidal ebb which helped him to capture New Carthage (209).

Returning to Rome a hero, Scipio was elected consul for 205, and proceeded to implement his ambitious strategy for finishing the war by the outright defeat of Carthage in Africa. Here he clashed with the conservative thinking of the senate, articulated by *Fabius Cunctator, that Hannibal should first be defeated in Italy. But, by threatening to bypass the senate and appeal to the people, he secured Africa as his sphere of operations. Further senatorial obstruction prevented Scipio from levying troops, but his prestige and glamorous image attracted an adequate number of volunteers for the African campaign. He spent a year in Sicily training his new army, and shocked traditional Roman opinion by wearing Greek dress and openly adopting Greek cultural pursuits. After narrowly surviving the *Pleminius scandal, he crossed to Africa in 204 where he vindicated his strategy by a series of victories which drew Hannibal back from Italy (203). Having secured valuable cavalry assistance from *Masinissa, he inflicted on the hitherto invincible Hannibal a defeat (at Zama in 202 BC) which decided the war. Scipio granted peace terms, which the senate later ratified, and returned to Italy to a splendid triumph, taking the surname Africanus for his great victory. In 199, when he reached the censorship, which was the apex of a Roman public career, he was still only 37 years old. His youth and numerous other parallels (some no doubt consciously cultivated) led to inevitable comparisons with Alexander.

In his second consulship (194) and with his eye on a possible command against *Antiochus III, Scipio vigorously but unsuccessfully opposed *Flamininus' policy of evacuating Greece. But in 190 he led the first Roman army into Asia, nominally as the legate of his brother L. *Scipio Asiagenus. En route he established a close friendship with *Philip V (now a vital Roman ally), and scored further diplomatic successes in Asia. He insisted on Antiochus' complete withdrawal from Asia Minor, and granted peace on those terms after the crucial battle of Magnesia. (The effective command at Magnesia was held neither by Scipio, who was ill, nor by his brother, but by the little acknowledged Gnaeus Domitius Ahenobarbus.)

Scipio had reached a greatness never previously attained by a Roman and not subsequently attained until *Pompey and *Caesar. His career had revealed several dangerous shifts away from traditional Roman practice towards the cult of personality and Hellenistic kingship. Consequently his political opponents closed ranks against him in the 180s, their attack proceeding through the attempted impeachment of L. Scipio for peculation in Asia. In a spirited and characteristic counter-attack Africanus tore up the relevant accounts before the people, while he reminded them of their obligations to him as their saviour. But he was later forced to retire into private life before his death in 183.

BIBL. Toynbee, *Hannibal's Legacy*, ii (see index); Walbank, *PCPS* 1967, 54 ff.; Scullard, *Scipio Africanus: Soldier and Politician* (1970).

Scipio Asiagenus Consul 190 BC.

Of meagre abilities, Lucius Cornelius Scipio Asiagenus owed his advancement to his elder brother *Scipio Africanus, whose fortunes his career followed. He received the consular command against *Antiochus III in 190 BC on the understanding that Africanus would serve as legate and take effective command. He led the first Roman army into Asia, and won a triumph and the surname Asiagenes for the decisive victory over Antiochus at Magnesia. In the 180s the attack on Africanus' position proceeded through the unfortunate Lucius: he was impeached in 187 for

Denarius (101 BC) showing Jupiter in chariot, recalling L. Scipio Asiagenus' triumph over *Antiochus III.

peculation in Asia and publicly humiliated by *Cato as censor in 184.

BIBL. Scullard, *Politics*.

Scipio Nasica Consul 191 BC.

The son of *Scipio Calvus (see *Scipio, Publius), Publius Cornelius Scipio Nasica was chosen in 204 BC, as the noblest and morally best of the Romans, to receive the sacred relic of the Asian Magna Mater onto Roman soil. The rest of his career did not quite live up to this auspicious beginning, although he reached the consulship and won a triumph in 191. He founded Aquileia in 181.

BIBL. Scullard, *Politics*, index.

Scipio Nasica Corculum Consul 162 and 155 BC.

The son of *Scipio Nasica, Publius Cornelius Scipio Nasica Corculum dominated Roman politics in the mid-second century BC, acquiring a reputation for learning and moral integrity. As a military tribune in 168 he played an important role in the victory at Pydna, his narrative of which was used as a source by *Plutarch. His election to the consulship of 162 was declared technically invalid; but this did not prevent him reaching the censorship (159) and a second consulship, in which he gained a triumph over the Dalmatians (155). He was *princeps senatus* from 147 until his death (*c*. 141). Like *Cato the Elder he opposed the growth of luxury and erosion of traditional morality at Rome; but in the late 150s he led the senatorial opposition against Cato's strident demands for the annihilation of Carthage, basing his case on the lack of a justifiable pretext and Rome's need to maintain an external enemy as a moral stimulus.

BIBL. Astin, *Scipio Aemil.*

Scipio Nasica Serapio Consul 138 BC.

The son of *Scipio Nasica Corculum, Publius Cornelius Scipio Nasica Serapio achieved notoriety in 133 BC, when as a senior senator and *pontifex maximus* he led the senatorial opposition to Tiberius *Gracchus' unconstitutional activities. On failing to persuade the consul to suppress Gracchus by force, he called on the other senators to join him, and with their clients they attacked and killed

Gracchus and his supporters. Nasica's action was regarded by conservatives as justifiable tyrannicide. But popular resentment forced him to leave Rome on an embassy to Pergamum within the year. He died there.

BIBL. Astin, *Scipio Aemil.*

Scribonianus Conspirator AD 42.

Lucius Arruntius Camillus Scribonianus' original family, the Furii, gave him more right to pretension than his adoptive one. This explains why Annius *Vinicianus chose him as *Claudius' successor in the attempted uprising of AD 42, when Scribonianus was governor of Dalmatia. The army remained loyal and a common soldier called Volaginius killed the pretender.

BIBL. *PIR* A 1140; Dio, lx. 15–16.

Scribonius Libo Drusus Conspirator AD 15.

Marcus Scribonius Libo Drusus was a young man of high birth and an equally high degree of stupidity, according to *Seneca. It was the family connections (including *Augustus' first wife Scribonia) which made an ill-considered plot against *Tiberius in AD 15 a serious matter. In 16 he was convicted of treason and committed suicide.

BIBL. Tac. *Ann.* ii. 27–32; Levick, *Tiberius*, ch. xi.

Sebastianus Master of the Infantry AD 378.

Sebastianus was a late-Roman professional soldier whose heretical beliefs (he was a *Manichee) did not affect his career. In Egypt (356–8) he gave military support to the *Arian bishop *George against the orthodox, by order of *Constantius II. He served the pagan *Julian in Mesopotamia (363), and the orthodox *Valentinian I across the Rhine (368) and Danube (375). By 375 he was popular with the troops, with a reputation for integrity. In 378 he returned to the eastern army as its commander-in-chief. After successfully directing guerrilla warfare against the Goths, he advised the Arian *Valens to risk a pitched battle, but lost his life in the disaster which ensued (August 378).

BIBL. *PLRE* i, Sebastianus 2.

Sejanus Praetorian prefect AD 14–31.

Lucius Aelius Seianus was the son of the equestrian Lucius Seius Strabo, from Volsinii, of better (though disputed) connections on his mother's side, and raised in standing by adoption. In AD 14 he was made praetorian prefect, at first jointly with his father, but later alone, and acquired vast influence with *Tiberius, which he used with sinister effect until his fall, especially when he had persuaded Tiberius to leave Rome for Capri. He improved his position by encouraging the emperor's distrust of his family, particularly *Drusus Julius Caesar his son and the family of *Germanicus, with dire results for them, and by

currying favour with the mob in Rome, it seems. But although he reached the consulate (AD 31) he never attained the dynastic marriage (with Livilla) which would have assured his position, for he was of too humble a background to hope for a role greater than that of an *Agrippa, whose sons might aim at adoption and the succession. Becoming desperate, he planned a conspiracy which was revealed by *Antonia to Tiberius, who, it proved, retained the authority to overthrow his minister. Sejanus was condemned to death and executed in 31, and this successful trial of strength did much to strengthen the principate as an institution.

BIBL. *PIR* A 255; Bird, *Latomus.* 1969, 61; Syme, *Hermes*, lxxxiv = *RP* 22.

Seneca (died AD 65) Philosopher and politician.

The political dealings of Lucius Annaeus Seneca the Younger are of rather more importance than his writings. He studied rhetoric, as was natural enough, considering his father's fame (see *Seneca the Elder), and philosophy, which was less common, and embarked on a senatorial career. His name had been made before *Gaius' reign, but in AD 41 he was exiled to Corsica for supposed adultery with Julia Livilla. *Agrippina (the Younger) had him recalled in 49 and he, like *Burrus, became tutor to *Nero, and on his accession one of his principal advisers. In this role his Spanish background was probably no advantage. Nero's increasing independence and waywardness and the death of Burrus greatly reduced Seneca's power, and he considered retirement. Nero permitted this, and Seneca enjoyed three years of leisure before he was implicated (perhaps unjustly) in the *Pisonian conspiracy of 65 and committed suicide with dignity. The relations between Seneca's philosophical views and his way of life, and the effect of his advice on the character of Nero's early years, have always excited much controversy, so piquant is the contrast between the philosophy of the minister and the debauchery of the prince. Seneca in general excites curiosity more than he compels admiration.

WORKS. He was an immensely prolific writer: the prose works which survive complete fill over a thousand closely printed pages: in addition, nine tragedies are extant. We have: (1) 12 dialogues: i *On Providence*; ii *On the Constancy of the Philosopher*; iii–v *On Anger*; vi *Consolation to Marcia*; vii *On the Happy Life*; viii *On Leisure*; ix *On Spiritual Tranquillity*; x *On the Brevity of Life*; xi and xii consolations to the imperial freedman Polybius and to Helvia. Written between AD 37 and 41. (2) *On Clemency*: 1½ books out of 3 survive; 55/6. (3) *On Benefits*: 7 books; after 56. (4) *Moral Epistles*: To Lucilius Junior; 124 *Epistulae morales* in 20 books; there were once more. Dramatic date 63/4 (?); publication 64/5. (5) *Natural Questions*: 7

books; datable allusions 62–4. (6) *Apocolocyntosis*: late 54. (7) Tragedies: *Hercules* (*Furens*), *Troades*, *Phoenissae*, *Medea*, *Phaedra*, *Oedipus*, *Agamemnon*, *Thyestes*, *Hercules Oetaeus*. The *Octavia* is not by Seneca: it is the only surviving *praetexta*. The tragedies are thought to belong to the period 49–62.

The range is clearly prodigious; apart from the vigorously argued and arguably hypocritical expositions of Stoic dogma, we should note (5) a survey of meteorology, seismology and hydrography; (7) tragedies written not for the stage but for recitation, revelling in extravagantly ensanguined detail (the *Thyestes* is recommended) and, perhaps most interesting, (6): Seneca wrote both the eulogy delivered by Nero upon *Claudius and the *Apocolocyntosis*, very shortly after, a parodic account of Claudius' deification; though the title means 'Pumpkinification' (probably), the work contains no such metamorphosis; a venomous outburst of personal and political relief in the form of a Menippean Satire.

The Emperor Gaius described Seneca's style as 'sand without lime' (i.e. dud concrete, Suet. *Calig.* 53.2); *Quintilian, the Elder *Pliny, *Tacitus, and *Fronto are not significantly politer; Kettel, president of Trinity, Oxford at the height of the Senecan revival, 'was wont to say that Seneca writes as a Boare does pisse, *scilicet* by jirkes' (Aubrey). His pointed, mannered, affected, antithetic style does not generally increase in popularity.

BIBL. Griffin, *Seneca: a Philosopher in Politics* (1976); Tarrant, *HSCP* 1978, 213 ff. (tragedies); Coffey, *Satire*, 165 ff. (Apocolocyntosis); for style, see most conveniently, *Select Letters*, ed. Summers (1913).

Seneca the Elder (c. 55 BC–AD 40) Writer on rhetoric.

A native of Cordova, Lucius Annaeus Seneca was an oddly obscure figure: the author of lost histories, but extremely important as the collector of ten books of *Controversiae* and seven *Suasoriae*. These surveys of Roman declamation he undertook from memory in old age at the request of his sons Novatus *Gallio, *Seneca the Younger, and Mela (father of *Lucan). The *Controversiae* are partially complete; five books survive in excerpts. The prefaces survey the work of individual orators; their epigrams, analyses (*divisiones*), and lines of approach (*colores*) on several given *controversiae* follow. The *Suasoriae* were undertaken later and survive yet more incompletely: only epigrams and *divisiones* survive, along with a mass of engaging anecdotes. Granted the essential lunacy, in our eyes, of the declamatory training, these two collections are a towering monument to perverse ingenuity and misapplied wit.

BIBL. See exceptional Loeb ed. by Winterbottom; Bonner, *Roman Declamation* (1949).

Sertorius Partisan of Marius, praetor 83 BC.

Quintus Sertorius distinguished himself as an officer under *Marius in the German wars, and attached himself to the Marian cause. He rose under *Cinna's regime in the 80s to reach the praetorship in 83 BC, and left for his Spanish province after *Sulla's invasion of Italy in that year. In 81 he was temporarily dislodged from Spain by a Sullan proconsul, but re-established himself the following year with native support. His military ability and powers of leadership over Romans and natives alike enabled him to control most of the peninsula for some years. He defeated a succession of generals sent against him by the Sullan establishment, including *Metellus Pius and *Pompey; but, after the latter had received reinforcements in 74, Sertorius was inexorably worn down. The counter-State which he organized along Roman lines was regarded as a continuation of the legitimate Roman government overthrown by Sulla: it provided a base for Marian exiles and the supporters of *Lepidus' (2) rebellion of 78. Prominent among the latter was M. Perperna Veiento, who eventually became resentful of Sertorius' authority and assassinated him (c. 72). Before his death Sertorius was certainly losing the war, and an increasing cruelty in his conduct lost him popularity. He had also begun to co-operate loosely with other enemies of the Roman government, namely *Mithridates and the pirates. Under Perperna's leadership Sertorius' rebellion rapidly collapsed.

BIBL. Plutarch, *Life of Sertorius*; Schulten, *Sertorius* (1926); Gabba, *Republican Rome, the Army and the Allies* (1976) 103–15.

Servianus, Julius Consul AD 90, 102, and 134.

Born c. AD 47 and probably of Spanish origin, Lucius Julius Ursus Servianus was married to *Hadrian's sister, Domitia Paulina. One of a powerful group of senators surrounding *Trajan and Hadrian, he was governor of Germania Inferior in 98, and went on to govern Pannonia and to serve with distinction in Trajan's Dacian Wars. He was a correspondent, friend, and patron of *Pliny the Younger. His third consulship shows great distinction but in 136, in his ninetieth year, he was forced by Hadrian to commit suicide, lest he should survive the emperor—he was suspected of harbouring imperial ambitions either for himself or for his grandson, Lucius *Pedanius Fuscus. As he prepared for his death he is said to have prayed that Hadrian might long for death and be unable to die.

BIBL. *PIR* I 631; Syme, *Tacitus*; Sherwin-White, *The Letters of Pliny*.

Servilia (1st century BC).

Granddaughter of Servilius *Caepio, Servilia was an ambitious noblewoman who wielded considerable political influence, especially through her stepbrother *Cato (Uticensis) and her son *Brutus. However, in 49 BC she was unable to prevent them both joining *Pompey, whom she hated as the slayer of her first husband (M. Junius Brutus). An early liaison with *Caesar gave rise to the chronologically implausible rumour that Brutus was his child.

BIBL. Syme, *Rom. Rev.*

Servilius Vatia Isauricus, Publius Consul 79 BC.

A partisan of *Sulla, Servilius reached the consulship of 79 BC and held a long proconsular command in Cilicia against the pirates. He achieved notable successes, particularly against the Isaurians, from whom he took his surname. Acclaimed *imperator*, he returned to a triumph at Rome in 74. He survived as a respected elder statesman for a further thirty years, holding the censorship in 55 and voicing moderately conservative opinions.

BIBL. Magie, *Asia Minor*; Gruen, *Republic*.

Servius Grammarian, early 5th century AD.

Author of the most important extant commentary on *Virgil, Servius was too young, according to *Macrobius, to have taken part in a learned discussion in 384; none the less he is anachronistically portrayed as one of the interlocutors in the *Saturnalia* as a diffident and extremely learned young man. Accordingly the monumental commentary, the work of a mature man, was probably written after 410. It exists in two forms, a simple one and a version augmented with the so-called *scholia Danielina*, and gives exceedingly valuable information both on the text of Virgil, and the state of Late Antique scholarship.

BIBL. E. Thomas, *Scoliastes de Virgile: Essai sur Servius et son commentaire sur Virgile* (1880).

Servius Tullius King of Rome, 6th century BC (?).

Servius Tullius was the sixth king of Rome (conventional dates: 578–535 BC). Despite his suspect identification by the Emperor *Claudius with Mastarna, an associate of Caeles *Vibenna, and Roman stories of his servile origins (derived from his *praenomen*), the real basis and political tenor of his rule are purely conjectural. The tribal system and centuriate organization, ascribed to him, may date from this period in a rudimentary form, reflecting, respectively, Rome's urban and territorial development and adoption of hoplite tactics. His establishment of the Aventine shrine of Diana as a Latin cult centre would also mirror Rome's growing importance, and archaeological finds support a sixth-century date for his temples of Fortuna and Mater Matuta (though his fortificatory wall is controversial). It is uncertain that all this was the work of a single king.

BIBL. PW vii A. 804 ff.; R. T. Ridley, *Klio* lvii (1975) 147 ff.; M. Pallottino, *CR* 1977, 216 ff.

St Severinus Monk in Noricum *c.* AD 455–82.

The *Life* of Severinus by his disciple, Eugippius, is the major source for the last years of Roman power in Noricum, and shows its hero engaged in the preservation of towns from famine and assault and in healing miracles benefiting Romans and the occupying Rugi alike. His cult was carried to Italy when Noricum was formally evacuated in 488.

BIBL. Eugippius, *Vita S. Severini*, MGH AA I. 2; L. Bieler (trans.), *The Life of St Severin* (1965); G. Alföldi, *Noricum*, (trans. A. Birley, 1974), ch. xii.

Severus, Septimius Emperor AD 193–211.

Lucius Septimius Severus was born in 145 at Lepcis Magna in North Africa and came to Rome in the early 160s, where he began his official career (the details of which are obscure). Always superstitious, he relied heavily on astrology, and his autobiography recorded numerous episodes and dreams which led him to believe he would one day become emperor. A small man but physically strong, he is said to have spoken little and with an African accent, but to have had many ideas. He rewarded friends lavishly and treated enemies harshly. In 169 he was elected quaestor at Rome, and served as provincial quaestor in Sardinia in 171. In 173 his kinsman, Gaius Septimius Severus, proconsul of Africa, chose Septimius as one of his three legates. At the age of 30 he returned to Lepcis and married Paccia Marciana, who died childless several years later. In 174 Severus was tribune of the plebs, and praetor in 177. In 180 he was appointed a legionary commander in Syria, but was dismissed by *Commodus in 182. In 184 he became governor of Gallia Lugdunensis, and he married *Julia Domna, a member of a prominent priestly family in Emesa, in 187. In 188 his son *Caracalla was born and in 189 *Geta. That year Severus was governor of Sicily, and became consul in 190. In 191 he was appointed governor of Pannonia, and his brother Geta was made governor of Moesia Inferior. Following the assassination of Commodus in 192, *Pertinax became emperor, but survived for only a few months before being murdered by the praetorian guard. He was succeeded by *Didius Julianus whose reign was also brief. Septimius was proclaimed emperor by his troops following the death of Pertinax, and he swore to avenge his predecessor's death, even adding Pertinax's name to his own. Sensing a threat in *Clodius Albinus, who had distant connections with Didius Julianus and who controlled the British legions, Septimus offered Albinus the title of Caesar, which he accepted. Meanwhile *Pescennius Niger had been proclaimed emperor by the eastern legions. Septimius marched on Italy meeting little resistance, and, after a large proportion of the senate had defected to him, Julianus was put to death. The praetorians were disbanded because they had murdered Pertinax.

Above: Basilica of Septimius Severus (c. AD 205), Lepcis Magna. View of interior with apse.

Severan Basilica, Lepcis Magna, detail: pilasters decorated with peopled scrolls flanking apse.

Severus' next major concern was Niger, and, after a series of successful campaigns in Asia Minor by his generals, Niger was finally defeated and killed at Antioch in 194. Septimius severely punished those cities and provinces disloyal to him. Early in 195, he began an invasion of Mesopotamia, where he subdued Osrhoeni, Adiabeni, and Scenite Arabs. In this year he also proclaimed himself the son of *Marcus Aurelius, and Albinus was declared a public enemy.

Septimius returned to Rome from the East, and in 196 set out for Lyons to deal with Albinus. After a fierce battle Albinus' troops were routed, and Albinus committed suicide. Severus then reorganized the north-western provinces and returned to Rome, where he took reprisals against those senators who had sided with Albinus. Caracalla was appointed emperor designate c. 197. In 198–9 Severus waged a successful campaign against the Parthians and then visited Egypt, where he engaged in major administrative reform. He then visited Syria, and returned to Rome in 203 to celebrate his ten-year jubilee, erecting a magnificent triumphal arch. He remained in Rome until 207, celebrating the Secular Games in 204. In 205 the all-powerful praetorian prefect *Plautianus fell, victim of a plot by Caracalla. In 207 Severus mounted an expedition to Britain, taking his wife and two sons with him. He remained in Britain

Contemporary portraits of Septimius Severus and his family (*Geta defaced): painted wooden roundel from Egypt. Berlin, Staatsbibliothek.

until his death in 211 and campaigned successfully in the north, perhaps wishing to extend Roman control over the whole island. In 209, worried by the mental instability of Caracalla, he had Geta created Augustus. Ill health led Septimius to return to York, and a second revolt by the Maeatae and Caledonians necessitated another campaign, this time led by Caracalla. His last advice to his sons as he lay dying in 211 was: 'Do not disagree among

yourselves, give money to the soldiers, and despise everyone else.' His uncertain temper, relentless capacity for hard work, and expansionist frontier policies make him a difficult figure to assess fairly. To some he was a ruthless autocrat, to others an efficient if cold ruler coping with the realities of his time.

BIBL. Birley, *Severus*; *ANRW* ii. 2.

Severus Alexander (Marcus Julius Gessius Alexianus Bassianus, Marcus Aurelius Severus Alexander) Emperor AD 222–35.

Born *c*. 209, Severus Alexander was the son of *Julia Mammaea and Gessius Marcianus, and grandson of *Julia Maesa (sister of *Julia Domna). As a result of the machinations of Julia Maesa he was formally adopted by his cousin *Elagabalus in 221, as the latter's son and heir, and his name was changed to Marcus Aurelius Severus Alexander. Like Elagabalus he was passed off as a bastard son of *Caracalla. Alexander became emperor after an irate soldiery assassinated Elagabalus in 222, when they learned that he had attempted to murder his young cousin. His reign was considerably less colourful and less dissolute than that of Elagabalus, and initially all went well. *Ulpian was appointed praetorian prefect, but was murdered *c*. 223/4. In 225 Alexander married *Barbia Orbiana, but she was sent into exile in 227 after her father's alleged

Audience hall of the Sassanian kings, Ctesiphon, Iraq.

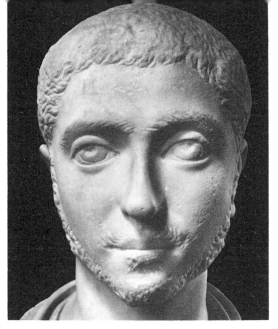

Portrait bust of the Emperor Severus Alexander. Rome, Capitoline Museum.

Shapur I triumphs over *Valerian on a vast cliff-face at Naqsh-i Rustam, near Persepolis, S.W. Persia.

attempt at revolution. Danger began to threaten on the eastern frontier with the collapse of the Parthian empire and the emergence of the Sassanians, under the leadership of Ardashir I. In 230 Ardashir invaded Roman Mesopotamia and menaced Syria. Negotiations failed, and in 231 Alexander set out on campaign, achieving moderate success in 232, when Ardashir was obliged to withdraw. Unrest on the Rhine led to Alexander's return to Rome in 233 and his departure for the German frontier in 234. In 235 Alexander's preference for negotiation rather than fighting so angered his troops that they murdered him, thereby bringing the Severan dynasty to an end.
  BIBL. *PIR* A 1610, I 342; Birley, *Severus*.

Severus the Tetrarch Emperor AD 305–7.
  Those who thought him a drunken boor were surprised when Severus, an officer in the imperial guard, was appointed Caesar to rule the western Mediterranean on the abdication of *Diocletian and *Maximian. The following year *Maxentius was proclaimed emperor by troops at Rome; Severus was captured after failing to crush this revolt. When his old friend *Galerius, by now the senior active Augustus, marched against Maxentius, the usurper had Severus executed.
  BIBL. *PLRE* i, Severus 30.

Severus, Sextus Julius Consul AD 127.
  Of equestrian origin, from Dalmatia, Sextus Julius Severus held governorships in Dacia, Moesia, and Britain under *Hadrian. He was taken from Britain to conduct the Second Jewish War, as Hadrian's best general, and he became the first governor of Syria Palaestina (formerly Judaea). He

was awarded triumphal decorations for his success in Judaea.
  BIBL. *PIR* I 576; Birley, *Fasti* (forthcoming).

Shapur (Sapor) I King of Persia AD 241–72.
  The second Sassanian king, Shapur waged a number of extremely successful campaigns against Rome in 241–4 and the 250s, when he attacked Armenia and later Syria and Mesopotamia.

Silver coin of Shapur I.

*Valerian was unable to stem his advance, and in 259 was defeated and personally captured by Shapur, an unprecedented disaster for Rome, which Shapur celebrated by depicting the scene in a monumental relief sculpture and an inscription recording his exploits. Shapur continued to ravage the East until defeated by *Odaenath, the ruler of Palmyra.
  BIBL. *PLRE* i, Sapor I; Walser and Pekary, *Krise*; *ANRW* ii. 2.

Shapur (Sapor) II King of Persia AD 309/10–379.
  Grandson of *Narses and son of Hormisdas II,

Persian king hunting wild boar. Sassanian silver dish (4th century AD). Washington, Freer Gallery.

Shapur II, thorn in the side of Rome, was made king by the nobles when very young, after the overthrow of his brother Adanarses. His brother *Hormisdas fled to the Romans in 324. During his long minority there was peace with Rome, but war broke out in 336 over that centuries-old bone of contention, the suzerainty of Armenia, and for the rest of his reign there was war nearly every campaigning season, with neither side gaining the upper hand permanently. Shapur's immediate objectives were the recovery of Roman Mesopotamia, won by *Galerius, and of Armenia. Highlights included the three vain sieges of Nisibis by the Persians (338, 346, and 350); the bloody but indecisive battle of Singara in 348; the Persian storming of Amida in 359, of which *Ammianus has left a thrilling eyewitness account; and the Persian expedition of *Julian (q.v.) in 363.

BIBL. *PLRE* i, Sapor II.

Sidonius Apollinaris (born AD 432) Poet and letter writer.

Born at Lyons in November 432 Gaius Solius Apollinaris Sidonius, a member of the senatorial order by birth, received a good classical education (c. 452), published some poetry (now lost) in his youth, and married Papianilla, daughter of Eparchius *Avitus, the man destined to become emperor in 456. Sidonius himself composed and delivered the panegyric on his father-in-law's accession, and was honoured as a poet with a statue in the Forum of Trajan. Sidonius' poetry is artificial, and carries the mannerisms of *Claudian to an extreme, but his nine books of letters are extremely interesting, and illuminate the social,

political, artistic, literary, and religious history of their time far better than those of *Symmachus did. They include a description of Theoderic (*Ep.* i. 2.) and one of Sidonius' own villa (*Ep.* ii. 2.). Unfortunately the letters are silent from 456–9: probably a reflection of the death of Avitus after his defeat at the battle of Placentia. Sidonius' second panegyric—on *Majorian—is, however, extant. He was Count of Auvergne in 461, resigned the office after a year, and went into retirement until 468, when yet a third panegyric, this time on *Anthemius, gained him the prestigious prefecture of Rome.

Sidonius returned to Auvergne in 469, published the remainder of his poetry, and was elected bishop of Clermont (such sudden elevations from lay to episcopal status being not uncommon at the time). He had no great theological expertise, and doubted his worthiness for such high office, but this did not prevent him from performing all the functions of a bishop, among them the arbitration of civil cases. In the terrible period 471–4 he sustained the attacks of the Goths under *Euric, and, when Clermont capitulated in 474, was exiled for two years to Carcassonne. Finally, after supplicating Euric, he returned to Clermont as bishop. Though no more than 45 at the time, he was already a broken man, and died on 21 August 480/90; he was canonized soon after.

BIBL. C. E. Stevens, *Sidonius Apollinaris and his Age* (1933).

Silanus, Lucius Junius Praetor AD 48.

While still young, Silanus was betrothed to *Claudius' daughter *Octavia (2), a match which he probably owed to his descent from *Augustus. He accompanied Claudius to Britain in AD 43 and received further honours; but in 48 fell foul of the emperor, was accused of incest, and deprived of his praetorship and senatorial rank. He killed himself on the wedding-day of Claudius and *Agrippina in 49.

BIBL. *PIR* I 829.

Silius Italicus (c. AD 35–100) Epic poet, consul AD 68.

A distinguished orator and known to *Pliny the Younger and *Martial, Tiberius Catius Asconius Silius Italicus was consul in 68 and proconsul of Asia c. 77. He composed a *Punica* in 17 books and over 12,000 lines: thus his theme was, like *Lucan's, historical (he followed *Livy's account of the Second Punic War closely), but his treatment was in close imitation of *Virgil, whose tomb he restored. Pliny comments, 'more care than talent' (*Ep.* III. vii. 5.), but Silius deserves credit for his rejection of the worst excesses of silver Latin rhetoric and for his often shrewd and effective reworking of Virgilian material.

BIBL. von Albrecht, *Silius Italicus* (1964).

Silvanus Usurper AD 355.

An army officer of Frankish descent, Silvanus deserted *Magnentius for the legitimate emperor *Constantius II before the battle of Mursa in 351. Made Master of the Infantry (352/3) and sent to Gaul to repel barbarian incursions, he found in 355 that he was being traduced before Constantius by enemies at court, by means of a forged letter. In an attempt to save his life, he had himself acclaimed emperor at Cologne, but Constantius, learning the truth too late, sent *Ursicinus to suppress him. He was assassinated by his own soldiers in the palace chapel where he was about to attend Christian worship.

BIBL. *PLRE* i, Silvanus 2.

St Simeon Stylites *c*. AD 390–459 Pillar-saint.

Simeon was a Syrian monk who pioneered a novel form of ascetic withdrawal, by spending his days at the top of a column. Pilgrims came from all over the Mediterranean to the base of his perch at Telanissos, where remains of the church and monastery which grew up around the saint's column are still to be seen.

BIBL. H. Delehaye, *Les Saints stylites* (1923).

Sisenna, Lucius Cornelius Historian, praetor 78 BC.

The colourful narrator of the Social and civil wars, Sisenna was a highly idiosyncratic stylist, who managed to combine innovation and archaism. If it was indeed he who translated Aristides' *Milesiaca* (see *Petronius), then he is also of importance as a proto-pornographer.

BIBL. *HRR* i. 276 ff.

Right: Stylite tempted by the Devil: side of a 6th-century silver reliquary from Syria. Paris, Louvre.

Below: 5th-century AD pilgrimage centre of St Simeon, Qala'at Seman, near Antioch (Syria).

Socrates (born *c.* AD 380) Church historian.

Socrates, a lawyer at Constantinople, continued the work of *Eusebius of Caesarea, by writing a history of the Church in seven books, covering the period from 305 to 439. He revised his history when he gained access to the writings of *Athanasius, and it is this second edition which survives. He also had access to a valuable collection of Church council documents. His narrative is on the whole unpartisan, and shows little interest in theological issues.

BIBL. J. Quasten, *Patrology* iii, 532–4.

Sopater Neoplatonist philosopher, early 4th century AD.

Native of Apamea in Syria and pupil (like *Aedesius) of *Iamblichus, Sopater was the leading Neoplatonist after his death. Despite his paganism, he became a close friend and adviser of *Constantine at Constantinople, seated at his right hand in public, and allegedly told him that expiation for the murder of *Crispus was impossible. He was executed at the instigation of the jealous prefect *Ablabius (q.v.), accused of fettering the winds and causing a corn shortage.

BIBL. *PLRE* i, Sopater 1; Piganiol, *Empire chr.*, 54, 57.

Sosius Senecio Consul AD 99 and 107.

Quintus Sosius Senecio was a friend of *Pliny the Younger; *Plutarch dedicated several of his *Lives* to him. He was well-connected and a close associate of *Trajan, prominent during his reign. Further details remain obscure, though he is clearly a man of the stature of Cornelius *Palma or Licinius *Sura.

BIBL. Syme, *Tacitus*, 53.

Sozomen Church historian, early 5th century AD.

Sozomen, a lawyer at Constantinople, continued the work of *Eusebius of Caesarea by writing a history of the Church in nine books, covering the period from 324 to 439 (the end of the last book, from *c.* 421, is lost). He was heavily dependent on his contemporary *Socrates, but had access to excellent sources not available to him, e.g. the 'western' narrative of *Olympiodorus of Thebes.

BIBL. J. Quasten, *Patrology* iii, 534–6.

Spartacus Leader of slave revolt 74–71 BC.

A Thracian slave gladiator, Spartacus escaped from Capua in 74 BC and led a slave revolt which quickly spread through southern Italy and assumed massive proportions. Spartacus' huge and ably commanded army created a serious military emergency, particularly when the rebels decided to enrich themselves with Italian plunder rather than escape to the north. He defeated a succession of Roman commanders including both the consuls of 72, but he was eventually defeated and the rebellion crushed by a large force under *Crassus.

A heroic figure, he was idealized in his lifetime and by posterity.

BIBL. Rice Holmes, *The Roman Republic* (1923) i. 386 ff.; Brunt, *Italian Manpower*, 287 ff.

Statilius Taurus Consul 37 and 25 BC.

For a *novus homo* a second consulship and a triumph (from Africa, 33 BC) were dizzy heights to reach at this period. Titus Statilius Taurus had done so by useful support of Octavian in Dalmatia and at Actium. His generalship in north-west Spain also considerably advanced *Augustus' pacification of the area. He is also known for the amphitheatre he built at Rome, the only one of any permanence before the Colosseum. In 16 BC, during Augustus' absence in Gaul, he was put in charge of affairs at Rome and, though elderly, did rather better than *Messalla Corvinus had done in a similar position in 26. He was the founder of a distinguished family from which came four later consuls and *Nero's third wife Statilia *Messalina.

BIBL. Syme, *Rom. Rev.*

Statius (AD 40/45–*c.* 96) Poet.

The son of a successful Neapolitan schoolmaster (*Silv.* v. 3) and himself victorious with a panegyric in one of the contests established by *Domitian, Publius Papinius Statius was a well-connected and well-established writer, whose surviving works are: (1) *Thebaid*, published *c.* AD 91: twelve books of hexameters on the conflict between Eteocles and Polynices. Statius strives after the bizarre, the pathetic, and the rhetorically effective in an epic variously characterized as 'baroque' or 'mannerist' by its admirers. (2) *Achilleid*: the second book was left unfinished at the poet's death. (3) *Silvae*: five books in varied metres, with prose prefaces, composed between 92 and the poet's death. This collection of 32 poems, on widely varied subjects, takes occasional and court poetry to a very high level. Readers who survive Statius' obsequiousness will find that he shows extreme ingenuity, allusive learning, and descriptive skill.

BIBL. *Achilleid*, ed. Dilke (1964); *Thebaid* x, ed. Williams (1972); Gossage in *Neronians and Flavians* i, ed. Dudley (1972) 184 ff.; D. Vessey, *Statius and the Thebaid* (1973), also on the *Silvae*.

Statius Priscus Consul AD 159.

Of equestrian origin, Marcus Statius Priscus was an important general in the reign of *Marcus Aurelius, and governor in Dacia, Moesia, Britain (161/2), and Cappadocia. In 163 during the Parthian War he won a victory in Armenia for which Lucius *Verus took the title of Armeniacus.

BIBL. Birley, *Marcus*; id., *Fasti* (forthcoming).

Stilicho Master of the Soldiers AD 394–408.

Flavius Stilicho, half-Vandal by birth, virtually ruled the western Empire as regent for *Honorius.

He had been promoted by Honorius' father
*Theodosius I, whose niece Serena he married *c.*
384; he later strengthened this connection by
marrying his daughter to Honorius. After
Theodosius' victory over *Eugenius at the Frigidus
(394), Stilicho became commander-in-chief; after
his patron's death, he claimed to have been
designated guardian not only of Honorius but also
of his elder brother *Arcadius. This claim divided
the two imperial courts, and at one point (397)
Stilicho was declared a public enemy at
Constantinople. He twice attempted to make good
his claim, by intervening (ineffectively) against
*Alaric and his Visigoths in Greece (397), and later
(407) by reaching an agreement with Alaric to
annex eastern Illyricum. The latter plan was
diverted by news of the invasions of Gaul and the
usurpation of *Constantine (q.v. III), and the senate
was forced by Stilicho to pay off Alaric, who was
now menacing Italy. This gave Stilicho's opponents
at court the opportunity of circulating allegations
of treason; in 408 troops mutinied against Stilicho's
officers, and Stilicho himself was arrested and
executed (22 August 408). His co-operation with
Alaric in later years branded him as a traitor in the
eyes of many, but he had defeated the Gothic
invasion of Italy in 401–2, and his subsequent
readiness to negotiate postponed the disasters in
Italy which soon followed his death.

BIBL. *PLRE* i, Stilicho; Matthews, *Aristocracies*,
ch. 10.

Stolo, Gaius Licinius Tribune of the plebs 376–
367 BC.

In 376 BC Licinius and Lucius Sextius proposed:
(1) the repayment of the capital alone of all debts
over three years; (2) the limitation of individual
holdings of public land to 500 *iugera* (about 350
acres); (3) the restoration of the consulship, with
one consul regularly plebeian. After prolonged
patrician resistance these bills were finally passed
in 367. The developed narrative of these events
contains much spurious elaboration (e.g., the five-
year 'anarchy') but, although these plebiscites
would strictly have no legal force and their terms
may be anachronistic, Licinius' agitation must have
some basis in fact. Some sources make him the first
plebeian Master of the Horse (368 BC), he was
variously identified with the consul of 364 or 361,
and was supposedly condemned for violating his
own land law (357).

BIBL. PW xiii. 464 ff.; K. von Fritz, *Historia* i
(1950) 3 ff.

Strabo (born *c.* 64 BC, settled in Rome 29 BC)
Geographer.

A native of Amaseia in Pontus, Strabo came from

Stilicho: right panel of ivory diptych, *c.* AD 400.
Monza, Cathedral Treasury.

a distinguished local family that supported first *Mithridates, then *Lucullus. He studied in Rome c. 44–35, and travelled, though selectively, 'from the Euxine to Ethiopia, from Armenia to Etruria' (II. v. 11); Ethiopia and Arabia Felix he visited with his patron Aelius Gallus, prefect of Egypt. He wrote *Historical Memoranda* in 47 books, from the end of *Polybius to (?) the fall of Alexandria to *Octavian, and notably 17 books (which survive) of geography (in which he includes much history, legend, antiquities, and ethnography), with explicit awareness of their potential utility to public men.

BIBL. Bowersock, *Augustus and the Greek World* (1965) 123 ff.; *FGH*. 90.

Suetonius (born c. AD 70) Biographer and encyclopedist.

Gaius Suetonius Tranquillus was born possibly at Hippo Regius in North Africa; of equestrian status, he worked as a *grammaticus*, then turned to the public service, and was in due course appointed to a series of posts with special responsibility for imperial libraries and correspondence. He was sacked in 121/2, with the praetorian prefect Septicius Clarus, allegedly for improperly free conduct towards *Hadrian's wife, *Sabina (also, perhaps, a reaction against the torrid minutiae of the lives of *Caesar and *Augustus). The result was that Suetonius was debarred from further access to the imperial archives, and the use of evidence such as Augustus' correspondence (in the lives of Augustus, *Horace and *Virgil, *Tiberius) was thenceforward denied him—as was the means of correcting *Tacitus' narrative, which he had previously not been slow to do.

WORKS. *On Famous Men*, a large collection of literary biographies, of very summary form; we have rather over half of the *Grammarians and Rhetoricians*, and, in less-than-Suetonian form, the lives of *Terence, Virgil, Horace, *Persius, and *Lucan (and some of the Elder *Pliny, classed as an orator). These works blend invaluable fact and pernicious misinformation inextricably. Suetonius also wrote widely on Roman antiquities, on natural sciences, and on grammar. Of the latter category, we have substantial excerpts in Greek of his works on Greek games and on curses. But his chief work is the *Lives of the Caesars* (correct title doubtful), 12 lives running from Julius Caesar to *Domitian, of which only the opening to the first is lost. The work has its vices, a trying and inexpert style, a sometimes pedantic thematic arrangement of anecdotes, and especially a boundless credulity, particularly when a story redounds to his victim's discredit. On the other hand, he is intimate, hugely entertaining, lively, gossipy, lubricious—and vastly influential upon both Einhard's *Life of Charlemagne* and our own conceptions of the early emperors' personalities.

BIBL. Townend in *Latin Biography*, ed. Dorey

(1967) 79 ff.; Works on games and curses, ed. Taillardat (1967).

Suetonius Paulinus Consul AD 42 and 66, general.

By AD 69 Gaius Suetonius Paulinus was the oldest ex-consul alive, and was also considered the greatest military expert. This reputation he had won in Mauretania in AD 42, and above all in Britain (58–60), where his success was marred by *Boudicca's revolt, which he nevertheless crushed successfully. He was a conscious rival of *Corbulo for military success. In the Civil War of 69 he fought for *Otho, but managed not to fall foul of *Vitellius.

BIBL. Tac. *Ann*. xiv. 29–39; *Hist*. ii. 32–3.

Silver coin (*denarius*) with posthumous portrait of Sulla (54 BC).

Sulla Consul 88 and 80; dictator 82–79 BC.

The career of Lucius Cornelius Sulla, an unorthodox and enigmatic figure who made much of his surname Felix ('lucky'), accelerated the downfall of the aristocratic republican constitution which he sought to uphold. Born in 138 BC of an obscure patrician family, he saw military service under *Marius in Africa (where he took some credit for capturing *Jugurtha) and in Gaul. As propraetor in Cilicia in 92 he conducted the first negotiations between Rome and Parthia, and made a striking display of Roman superiority by seating himself between the Parthian envoy and a Roman client prince. As legate in the Social War (90–89) he was the most successful Roman commander in south Italy; for this he was rewarded with the consulship of 88 and was allotted the coveted command against *Mithridates, who in that year invaded the Roman province of Asia. His command was transferred to Marius by a law of Publius *Sulpicius Rufus, and Sulla was forced to leave Rome in the ensuing violence. Like *Pompeius Strabo he had emerged from the Social War at the head of an army loyally devoted to him after two years' fighting. He now took the unprecedented step of appealing to that army to march with him against the legitimate government in Rome. The men were attracted to follow him by the prospect of booty in the Mithridatic War, and by the ultimate prospect of land allotments; the upper-class and naturally conservative officers refused, with the single exception of *Lucullus. Sulla took control of the city by force, killing Sulpicius and forcing Marius to flee. He annulled Sulpicius' laws and passed a largely reactionary body of legislation, which he obliged the new consuls L. *Cinna and Gnaeus Octavius to swear to observe, before departing to fight Mithridates in 87.

By 86 Sulla had captured Athens and driven Mithridates from Greece; he now turned towards Asia. But he no longer had any official authority: his command had been transferred to the consul of 86, L. Valerius Flaccus, who proceeded to Asia. Flaccus' murderer and successor, C. *Fimbria, made notable advances there and nearly captured Mithridates. But Sulla refused to co-operate or to hand over his command, and allowed Mithridates to go free. He then quickly made peace with Mithridates at Dardanus (85) on the basis of the pre-war *status quo*; this sell-out to Rome's most formidable foreign enemy gave Sulla a free hand to eliminate Fimbria, but it required a lot of explaining in his memoirs, a literary document which he entrusted to Lucullus for publication and which colours the surviving historical tradition of the period.

Sulla made numerous arrangements on his personal authority in Greece and Asia, principally to reward or punish states (and individuals) for their recent loyalty or lack of it. His personal influence became immense, and he was extravagantly honoured on a scale unparalleled since *Flamininus. He also accumulated huge sums in booty and arrears of tribute with which to strengthen his personal position against the government in Rome. After Cinna's death in 84 Sulla proceeded to an armed invasion of Italy and his second forcible seizure of power at Rome. Landing at Brindisi in 83 he received valuable military assistance from *Pompey, *Metellus Pius, and *Crassus. By 82 he had overcome all resistance under *Norbanus, *Carbo, and the younger Marius, and was installed at Rome as dictator to revise the constitution, a position which he resigned before his death in 78 and possibly before his second consulship (80). His eastern settlement was ratified, and a wide-ranging series of constitutional reforms was introduced, which aimed to improve administrative efficiency and to guarantee the ascendancy of the senatorial establishment. By suppressing the powers of tribunes Sulla sought to turn the clock back to the pre-Gracchan age. His revolutionary and unconstitutional methods were professedly used on behalf of the traditional regime and not in the pursuit of personal power, but they inevitably set an example to later ambitious dynasts.

BIBL. Plutarch, *Life of Sulla*; Balsdon, *JRS* xli (1951) 1 ff.; Badian, *Lucius Sulla: the Deadly Reformer* (1970).

Sulpicia Poetess.

Sulpicia was the authoress, not securely identified, of six elegies to one Cerinthus in book iii of the corpus of *Tibullus' poems. 'Her work is of interest only because the author is female.'

BIBL. Pomeroy, *Goddesses, Whores, Wives and Slaves* (1975) 173.

Sulpicianus, Flavius Urban prefect AD 193.

A distinguished senator who held a consulship and the governorship of Asia, Titus Flavius Sulpicianus was the father-in-law of the Emperor *Pertinax, and succeeded him as urban prefect. When Pertinax was killed on 28 March 193 Sulpicianus attempted to have himself proclaimed emperor by the praetorian guard. This ended in an 'auction', in which he and *Didius Julianus bid against each other in trying to buy the support of the guard; Sulpicianus lost. In 197 he was put to death by Septimius *Severus on the ground that he was a supporter of *Clodius Albinus.

BIBL. Grosso, *Lotta*; Birley, *Severus*; PIR F 373.

Sulpicius Rufus, Publius Tribune of the plebs 88 BC.

Like his political associate *Drusus (2), Sulpicius was an ambitious young noble who used increasingly demagogic methods as tribune in a crucial year (88 BC). His legislation providing for the equitable registration of new Italian citizens was carried by force with the support of *Marius, to whom Sulpicius had transferred the consul *Sulla's command against *Mithridates. This provoked Sulla's first march on Rome in which Sulpicius was killed.

BIBL. Badian, *Historia* xviii (1969) 481 ff.

Sulpicius Rufus, Servius Consul 51 BC.

A distinguished friend and correspondent of *Cicero (Cic., *Fam.* iv. 1-6, 12), Sulpicius was a notable jurist and a respected rather than influential figure in politics. Cautiously neutral, he opposed as consul his colleague's provocative anti-Caesarism, and took no part in the ensuing Civil War. Early in 43 BC he died of old age returning from a senatorial embassy to the recalcitrant proconsul, *Antony. Eulogizing him in the *Ninth Philippic*, Cicero represented his death as a patriotic act of martyrdom, and procured for him a statue in the Forum, an honour traditionally reserved for ambassadors killed on duty.

BIBL. *ORF* 376 ff.; Cicero, *Phil.* ix. *passim*.

Sulpicius Severus (c. AD 360–c. 420) Christian biographer.

Sulpicius Severus was a well-connected barrister of Aquitaine, who in c. 392 renounced the world like his friend St *Paulinus of Nola. He became a disciple of St *Martin, whose *Life* he wrote (c. 397, with later additions); he was critical of the clergy who would not accept Martin's miracles and monasticism, and gave a sympathetic account of the usurper *Maximus. The *Life*, though credulous, drew on first-hand testimony, and became a model for later saints' lives.

BIBL. *ODCC* Sulpicius Severus.

Sura, Licinius Consul AD 97, 102, and 107.

Although a successful orator and a companion of *Trajan in the Dacian War, Lucius Licinius Sura seems to have owed his second and third consulships largely to personal friendship with that emperor. Perhaps his most influential act was to recommend *Hadrian to Trajan. He died in 108.

BIBL. *PIR* L 253; Syme, *Tacitus*, ch. xix.

St Symeon: see **St Simeon**

Symmachus (*c.* AD 340–*c.* 402) Man of letters.

Quintus Aurelius Symmachus, despite his name an aristocrat of the highest birth, was a spokesman of the Roman senate from the 360s until his death, and was regarded by his contemporaries as an outstanding orator and prose stylist. Panegyrics of *Valentinian I and *Gratian (369–70) delivered on the senate's behalf at court, where he met *Ausonius, were rewarded by the governorship of Africa (373). In the 'thaw' which followed Valentinian's death (375), Symmachus enjoyed close relations with influential persons at court, but held only the traditional offices of his class: the urban prefecture (384) and, in spite of having praised the usurper *Maximus, the consulship of 391. His official correspondence as prefect survives, and is the major source of information about the duties of an officer who was chairman of the senate, judge of appeal for Rome and southern Italy, and responsible for food and public order in Rome.

Symmachus was a moderate pagan, unlike his friend Nicomachus *Flavianus, and did not over-commit himself; his appeal as prefect for the restoration of the altar of Victory to the senate house was successfully opposed by his kinsman St *Ambrose, but was preserved as a model of eloquence. Fragments also survive of speeches in the 'rich and florid' style of *Pliny's *Panegyric*. Symmachus' correspondence (over 900 letters survive) was published in ten books, like Pliny's; it was addressed to a wide circle drawn not only from 'the better part of the human race' (his fellow-senators), but also from *arriviste* officials and generals, who were taught the rules of a 'friendship' which ignored contemporary social, political, and religious conflicts. They are thus a major social document, but, being carefully composed in an opaque 'literary' Latin, and where possible ignoring external events, they can be tiresome reading.

Symmachus was a senator of only 'moderate'

Symmachi leaf of the Nicomachi and Symmachi ivory diptych, *c.* AD 400: priestess of Bacchus sacrificing to Jupiter. London, Victoria and Albert Museum.

means, but none the less owned estates in Sicily and Africa, as well as some twenty properties in Rome and southern Italy, which enabled him to conform to the lavish standards expected of his class; he spent 2,000 lb. of gold on his son's praetorian games (*c.* 400), a sum equivalent to the five-year bonus of 28,800 private soldiers.

BIBL. J. F. Matthews, *Western Aristocracies*.

Synesius of Cyrene (*c.* AD 370–413) Bishop, poet, and writer.

The life and character of Synesius are amply documented by his many letters. He was born *c.* 370 in Cyrene of a noble family, studied philosophy and mathematics under *Hypatia at Alexandria, and lived the life of a country gentleman, involved in his favourite pursuits of reading and hunting, until he was sent by his countrymen as an ambassador to Constantinople (399–401). There he wrote a treatise on kingship and a political allegory, the *Egyptian Tale*. He returned to Pentapolis and married a Christian woman in 403. He had three children by her, and had to give her up, after considerable mental anguish, upon his election as bishop. He hesitated for six months before accepting the episcopate of Ptolemais in 410/11 at the hands of *Theophilus of Alexandria (*Ep.* 105). Like *Sidonius, to whose life his own bears certain similarities, Synesius was probably selected as bishop for his ambassadorial and organizational skills and general rhetorical culture rather than for his specifically religious qualifications. In Synesius one finds an interesting blend of the Christian and the pagan, characteristic of the contemporary climate at Alexandria: he found his priestly role 'not a departure from, but a return to, philosophy' and his eloquent hymns contain little specifically Christian terminology. Instead they are imbued with the language of the *Chaldaean Oracles* (see *Julian the Theurgist). Among Synesius' remaining writings are a treatise on dreams, *In Praise of Baldness*, and the *Dion* (405), a plea for Greek culture. Unfortunately his *Cynegetics*, a work on hunting, is now lost. Synesius was ailing towards the end of his life, and he must have died before March 415, since his letters show no knowledge of the murder of his beloved mentor Hypatia.

BIBL. C. Lacombrade, *Synésius de Cyrène, Hellène et Chrétien* (1951); H-I. Marrou, 'Synesius of Cyrene and Alexandrian Neoplatonism', in *Conflict*, ed. Momigliano.

Syphax Numidian chieftain, floruit *c.* 205 BC.

After his wavering between Rome and Carthage, Syphax's marriage to the Carthaginian Sophonisba induced him to support the latter when *Scipio Africanus invaded Africa. He was defeated and captured in 203 by Scipio's legate, Laelius, and *Masinissa. Sophonisba poisoned herself, but Syphax died later in Italy, perhaps before Scipio's triumph.

BIBL. Lazenby, *Hannibal*.

Tacfarinas African rebel AD 17–24.

A former Numidian auxiliary, Tacfarinas became a robber chief and encouraged rebellion in the African province. He was three times defeated by Roman generals, who won triumphal insignia in

doing so, but was not crushed. In 24 Cornelius *Dolabella defeated him a fourth time, and he was killed in battle.

BIBL. Tacitus, *Annals,* iv. 23–6; *RP* 16.

Tacitus (born AD 56/7) Historian.

Publius Cornelius Tacitus was possibly a native of Gallia Narbonensis. He obtained senatorial rank under *Vespasian, married *Agricola's daughter in 77, was quaestor in 81/2, praetor in 88, and suffect consul in 97. He delivered, as Rome's leading orator, the funeral laudation on *Verginius Rufus (97 (?)), prosecuted Marius Priscus with the Younger *Pliny (99–100), served as proconsul of Asia (112/3), and died under *Hadrian. In *Agricola* 1 ff. and 44 ff. and *Histories* i. 1 he describes movingly and trenchantly the difficulties of maintaining political and intellectual integrity under *Domitian's tyranny.

WORKS. *Dialogue on Orators* (the dramatic date is the mid-70s, but it is now generally agreed that the date of composition is *c.* 100–5). The text is incomplete; it contains Tacitus' analysis of the decline of oratory and its causes: notably the dependence of great oratory upon the institutions and life of a free republic (e.g. ch. 36). (2) *Germania* or *On the Origin and Country of the Germans*. A historical and ethnographic monograph (AD 98), heavily dependent upon (for example) *Posidonius, *Livy (civ), and the Elder *Pliny. Tacitus sensed in the Germans a threat to the Roman Empire, not least because of their strong sense of *libertas* (freedom, absent at Rome) and their abundant *virtus* (guts). (3) *Agricola* (*On the Life of Julius Agricola*) (AD 98). A biography of his late father-in-law, with a flavour of panegyric and of funeral laudation, sharing also in the character of a historical monograph (like *Sallust's, *Catiline* and *Jugurtha*), not least on account of its historical and geographical excursuses. Tacitus is concerned to show how it was possible to survive under a bad emperor such as Domitian, not in futile opposition (such as that of *Helvidius Priscus), but in continuing and valuable service to the State (his own, by implication, and Agricola's). (4) *Histories* (on which Tacitus was working in 106–7), covering AD 69–96, possibly in 14 books, of which four and part of a fifth survive. (5) *Annals* (on which Tacitus was certainly active *c.* 116–18), in 16 books, covering AD 14–68. There survive books 1–6 (with the exception of most of 5) and 11–16 (less the opening of 11 and the close of 16).

Tacitus is a writer of daunting and dominating brilliance. We are left wondering at his colour, drama, pathos, and epigrams, we are inescapably influenced by the bias he disingenuously disavows, we may be repelled by his pessimism, and our view of early imperial history is often conditioned by what Tacitus sees fit to include or to omit. No other Roman author continues so to control today's view of the events he narrates, though research is slowly uncovering the immensely complex and subtle techniques he employs.

BIBL. Syme, *Tacitus* (1958); Goodyear, *GRNSC* iv (1970) (excellent). Rhetoric: Kennedy, *Rhetoric*, 515 ff.; Williams, *Change and Decline*, 26 ff.; Germany: Norden, *Die germ. Urgeschichte* (1920), and *Alt-Germanien* (1934); *Agricola*, ed. Ogilvie and Richmond (1967); *Histories*, ed. Heubner (1963–); *Annals*, ed. E. Koestermann (1963–8).

Tacitus (2) Emperor AD 275–6.

Marcus Claudius Tacitus was nominated by the senate as emperor at the request of the army, after the death of *Aurelian late in 275. An elderly senator, the details of whose early career are unknown, he made his brother Marcus Annius Florianus praetorian prefect. Florian became emperor in 276, after Tacitus had either died or been killed by the troops after a reign of only six months. Florian survived another three months before suffering the same fate.

BIBL. *CAH* xii; Syme, *Emperors and Biography*; *PIR* C 1036.

Tanaquil

Tanaquil reputedly spurred the ambitions of her husband *Tarquinius Priscus and engineered the accession of *Servius Tullius. Although her name may be authentic, her portrait (including her celebrated divinatory skills) reflects popular and literary elaboration, not an enhanced female status in Etruscan society.

Relief from Basilica Aemilia (Augustan period): the death of Tarpeia (right). Cast in Forum Romanum.

BIBL. PW iv A. 2172 f.; Ogilvie, *Livy*, 143 f.; A. Momigliano, *Quarto Contributo*, 456 ff.

Tarpeia

In the usual version (an aetiology of the Tarpeian Rock) Tarpeia betrayed the Capitol to Titus *Tatius for the ornaments on the Sabines' left arms: Tatius had her crushed by their shields. L. Calpurnius *Piso Frugi turned her into a heroine who was attempting to disarm the Sabines.

BIBL. Ogilvie, *Livy*, 74 f.; J. Poucet, *Recherches sur la légende sabine* (1967) 113 ff.; J. Beaujeu, *L'Information littéraire* xxi (1969) 163 ff.

Tarquinius Priscus, Lucius
Tarquinius Superbus, Lucius Kings of Rome 7th (?)–6th centuries BC.

The Tarquins were conventionally the fifth (616–579 BC) and seventh (534–510) kings, but their reigns are so thoroughly confused that tradition evidently offered no reliable detailed differentiation between them. That the family (perhaps from Caere rather than Tarquinia) ruled twice is credible, but their chronology and the details of their accessions are unreliable. Whether either was dependent on outside support is unknown, although a Gnaeus Tarquinius from Rome was apparently involved, with other Etruscan associates, in Vulcentan affairs (see Aulus and Caeles *Vibenna). Later sources ascribed to one or both kings measures which (whoever their author) certainly reflect Rome's development as a city-state under Etruscan influence in the sixth century BC: the drainage and organization of the Forum, the Circus and games, the (re-modelled) triumph, the *fasces* and other insignia, the Capitoline temple, and Sibylline books.

Both kings are also attributed a significant part in Rome's external conquests, notably Superbus who establishes Roman hegemony in Latium. Priscus' portrayal is largely favourable but Superbus, supposedly his son or grandson, has acquired the characteristics of a Greek tyrant, to justify his expulsion by L. Junius *Brutus.

BIBL. PW iv A. 2348 ff.; Ogilvie, *Livy*, 145 f., etc.; E. Gjerstad, *Early Rome* (1953–73) (chronology controversial).

Tarutienus Paternus Praetorian prefect AD 180–2.

A lawyer and writer on military law and tactics, Publius Tarutienus Paternus was secretary for Latin correspondence under *Marcus Aurelius, and was entrusted with a diplomatic mission to the Cotini in Marcus' first German War. He held an important command in the second German War. He was removed from his praetorian prefecture by Tigidius *Perennis and given the honorary rank of ex-consul, but was soon implicated in an alleged plot against *Commodus and executed.

BIBL. Birley, *Marcus*; Grosso, *Lotta*; Howe, *Pretorian Prefect*.

Tatian Christian theologian, 2nd century AD.

An Assyrian, educated in Greek rhetoric and philosophy, Tatian became a Christian (*c.* 150/65) and was a pupil of *Justin Martyr. During a visit to the East (*c.* 170) he founded the sect of Encratites. He wrote an *Address to the Greeks*, a defence of Christianity and a polemical attack on Greek culture and civilization, and a work called the *Diatessaron*, a history of the life of Christ from the evidence of the Gospels.

BIBL. M. Elze, *Tatian und seine Theologie* (1960).

Tatianus Praetorian prefect AD 388–92.

Flavius Eutolmius Tatianus was a Lycian barrister who, after governing a series of eastern provinces, retired in 380 after six years at court as a minister of finance. In spite of being a pagan and an easterner, he was recalled in 388 to succeed *Cynegius as praetorian prefect (and was consul in 391) during the absence of *Theodosius I in the West. A large number of surviving laws attest his activity, especially in the sphere of finance; he also attempted to restrict the privileges of clergy and monks. His son Proculus became urban prefect of Constantinople, and in 390, to celebrate the overthrow of the usurper *Maximus, erected the Obelisk of Theodosius in the Circus, where it is still standing today. When the court returned, however, Tatianus was supplanted by the Master of the Offices *Rufinus, who made him witness the execution of Proculus. Tatianus himself was formally disgraced, and so was his native province of Lycia, though they were rehabilitated after the death of Rufinus.

BIBL. *PLRE* i, Tatianus 5, Proculus 6.

Obelisk of Theodosius, Istanbul: erected in 32 days by Tatianus' son on a carved stone plinth (see *Theodosius I).

Silver coin (*denarius*) of L. Titurius Sabinus (89 BC) showing head of Titus Tatius.

Tatius, Titus

The reputed king of Cures who campaigned against *Romulus after the seizure of the Sabine women and then ruled Rome with him, Tatius symbolizes the legend of an early Sabine presence at Rome. He supposedly instituted 'Sabine' cults, the Titian brotherhood (an obscure priesthood), and an early tribe, the Tities (which perhaps suggested his name).

BIBL. PW iv A. 2471 ff.; Ogilvie, *Livy*, 72; J. Poucet, *ANRW* I. i (1972) 48 ff.

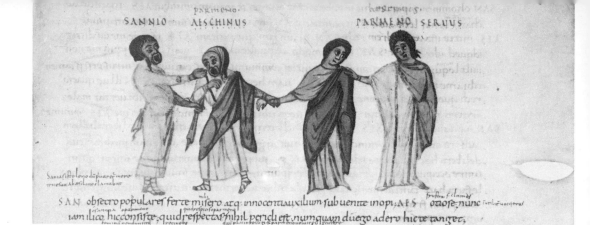

SANNIO   AESCHINVS   PARMENO   SERVVS

SAN obfecro populares ferte mifero arq: innocenti auxilium fub uenite inopi. AES otiofe. nunc iam ilico hic confifte. quid refpectaf nihil periclu eft. numquam dum ego adero hic te tanget.

Terence (195/185–159 BC) Comic dramatist.

Publius Terentius Afer was an African, who reached Rome as a slave, but came to enjoy the friendship—which brought him envious criticism—and support of (e.g.) *Laelius and *Scipio Aemilianus. He produced only six plays, all between 166 and 160 BC; the *Hecyra* appeared three times, twice unsuccessfully. Only one play, the *Eunuchus*, his most Plautine in its boisterousness, enjoyed real popular success. But his fidelity to Menander's manner (if not always to his plots), his highly complex intrigues, subtle studies of emotional, familial, and even educational issues (notably in the *Adelphi* (*The Brothers*)), immensely elegant verbal characterization, chaste and sober use of language, polemical and self-justificatory prologues, devotion to comic irony as his chief form of humour and abandonment of much of the element of music and song so important to *Plautus were all likely to cost him popular favour.
See Plautus, *Luscius Lanuvinus.

Tertullian (born c. AD 170 (?)) Christian controversialist.

Quintus Septimius Florens Tertullianus was born in or near Carthage (the traditional date is c. 160 but it might have been a decade after that), but little reliable biographical detail survives. Although he remained a layman, he was the first significant Latin Churchman, a prolific writer who exercised a profound influence on the development of Christianity in the West. He was converted to Christianity probably c. 195/7, and began to write a series of moral and ethical works for his fellow-Christians, including a treatise in 5 books against *Marcion. His *Apology* is a powerful defence of Christianity against charges that were popularly levelled at it. By 210 he had become dissatisfied with the mainstream of Christian thought and activity, and he joined the ecstatic and prophetic sect of the *Montanists, who held extreme views on the polarity between Christianity and the pagan world. He continued to write vigorous propaganda, including a letter to the proconsul of Asia, Scapula, in 212 protesting about the repression of Christianity. His erudition and rhetorical skill

Terence, *Adelphi* (9th-century MS). Rome, Vatican Library.

invite comparison with writers of the Second Sophistic (e.g. his fellow African, *Apuleius). He writes with compressed energy and idiosyncratic violence; passionate conviction gives force and purpose to rhetorical expertise. His literary activity (over 30 works survive) is probably to be dated between c. 196 and 212, and there is no certain evidence that he lived much beyond 212. The notion that in his later life he broke with the Montanists and founded his own sect, called the Tertullianistae, is also based on dubious evidence.

BIBL. T. D. Barnes, *Tertullian* (1971); H. Chadwick, *The Early Church*; *Corpus Christianorum, Series Latina* (1954).

Coins of Tetricus I (left, gold) and Tetricus II (right, bronze, wearing radiate crown).

Tetricus Emperor in Gaul AD 270–3.

Of noble birth, Gaius Pius Esuvius Tetricus was proclaimed emperor by the Gallic army in 270, having previously served as governor of Aquitania. He created his young son Gaius Pius Tetricus Caesar and then Augustus. Tetricus' reign was troubled by barbarian invasions and the insubordination of his troops. He submitted to *Aurelian c. 273/4, saving his own life and that of his son, and apparently died peacefully many years later. With his surrender the independent Gallic empire came to an end.

BIBL. *PLRE* i, Tetricus 1, 2; *ANRW* ii. 2.

Themistius (c. AD 317–88/9) Court philosopher.

A native of Constantinople, Themistius was the

son of a philosopher from Asia Minor, and early established himself as an expert on Aristotle (of whose studies he promoted a revival), and as a leading teacher of philosophy. He attracted imperial notice with a speech *On Clemency* delivered at Ankara in 350 before *Constantius II (*Or.* i). This praises the emperor while laying before him the ideals of good government, and set the pattern for his panegyrics of emperors down to *Theodosius I (*Or.* i–xix; that on *Julian is lost). He was made a senator of Constantinople (355), and then proconsul of the city (358–9), and was given the important task of recruiting new senators for Constantinople, whose senate was now given parity with that of Rome. On Julian's accession (361) Themistius wrote to him about the duties of a philosopher-king, praising the life of action above that of contemplation—a significant reversal of the Platonic position; Julian's reply is extant. Themistius' moderate paganism was no bar to the favour of three more Christian emperors after Constantius: *Jovian, *Valens, and even Theodosius I. Theodosius made him tutor to *Arcadius, and urban prefect of Constantinople (384). He also served on ten embassies. Like his friend and correspondent *Libanius, his career shows the influence of leading members of the pagan literary establishment under the Christian Empire.

In addition to political discourses, Themistius wrote private speeches, including a funeral oration on his father (*Or.* xx). His works on Aristotle are probably to be dated to c. 345 when he opened his school in Constantinople. Those that remain are interpretations of the *Posterior Analytics*, the *De anima*, and the *Physics* in Greek, and Hebrew versions of the works on *De caelo* and the *Metaphysics*, all of which show no particular originality, and virtually no Neoplatonic influence, but none the less provide intelligent comments and paraphrases.

BIBL. *PLRE* i, Themistius 1; H. Bouchéry,

Themistius in Libanius' Brieven (1936); Bowder, *Constantine and Julian*, 85–8, 113, 212.

Theodoret Bishop of Cyrrhus (Syria) AD 423–c. 466.

Theodoret, a follower of *Nestorius, defended the 'Antiochene' separation of the two (divine and human) natures of Christ. This brought him into conflict with the bishops of Alexandria, *Cyril and Dioscurus, and he was deposed by the 'Robber' synod at Ephesus (449); at the cost of condemning Nestorius, he was rehabilitated at Chalcedon (451). His writings include the *Cure of Pagan Ills* (a defence of Christianity against paganism), the *Religious History* (a collection of lives of Syrian monks), and a *Church History* of the period from 323 to 428.

BIBL. J. Quasten, *Patrology* iii, 536–54.

Theodoric I King of the Visigoths AD 418–51.

As king of the Visigothic kingdom in Aquitaine, Theodoric pursued a policy of qualified co-operation with some Roman officials but responded aggressively to the hostile policy of *Aëtius, perhaps with the aim of winning the Mediterranean coast of southern Gaul. Treaties were made in 430, after the repulse of the Goths from Arles (427) and after Litorius' defeat at Toulouse (439), the latter through the mediation of *Avitus. In 451 Aëtius was allied with the Goths against the Huns and won a decisive victory at the Catalaunian Plains. Theodoric, however, died in the battle, and was succeeded by his son, Thorismund.

BIBL. Sidonius Apollinaris, *Poem* VII; Jordanes, *Gothic History*, 176–7, 184–217; Gallic *Chronicles*.

Theodorus Bishop of Aquileia AD 308–c. 320.

Bishop of the important city of Aquileia at the

Basilica of Theodorus, Aquileia: Jonah and the Whale, Jonah under gourd-tree (4th-cent. AD mosaic pavement).

Obelisk of Theodosius, Istanbul: base (see *Tatianus) showing emperor and court presiding at circus games.

time of the Peace of the Church (313), Theodorus built a large double basilica, floored with (surviving) beautiful figured mosaics, uniting decorative themes with Christian symbolism.

BIBL. Brusin and Zovatto, *Monumenti paleocristiani di Aquileia e di Grado* (1957) 17–140; Bowder, *Constantine and Julian*, 133–4.

Theodosius I Emperor AD 379–95.

Theodosius 'the Great'—to distinguish him from his incompetent sons *Arcadius and *Honorius, and his equally incompetent grandsons *Theodosius II and *Valentinian III, but also because he was a devout Catholic who persecuted minority Christian sects and pagans—was an able general who won civil wars. He was the son of Count *Theodosius, like him a Spaniard (born *c.* 346), who in 374 as a frontier general on the middle Danube defeated Sarmatian raiders. His father's execution forced him into retirement, but after the death of *Valens (August 378) he was recalled by *Gratian and soon (19 January 379) made eastern emperor.

After inconclusive campaigning, Theodosius allowed the Goths to settle in the Empire under their own leaders, in return for military contingents (October 382). They remained a potential menace, but Theodosius had little choice. He secured the eastern frontier (*c.* 386) by partitioning Armenia with Persia. When Gratian was killed (August 383), Theodosius recognized *Maximus (his own kinsman) *de facto*; but when Maximus invaded Italy, he overthrew him in a lightning campaign (388). He remained in Italy until 391, where he came under the influence of St *Ambrose; thus in 390, after ordering a massacre at Thessalonica in which 7,000 people died, he was excommunicated by Ambrose until he offered public penance. Theodosius had to intervene once more, when *Eugenius usurped the western Empire (392). A few months after his defeat of the western army on the borders of Italy (September 394), Theodosius died at Milan (17 January 395), leaving the Empire to be divided between his two sons—or rather their mutually hostile courts.

Theodosius filled his court with Catholic westerners like himself, and was baptized soon after his accession; he quickly reversed Valens' *Arianism, and in May 381 summoned an ecumenical council at Constantinople which affirmed the Nicene Creed. Numerous laws followed against heretics. The praetorian prefect *Cynegius encouraged the (illegal) demolition of pagan temples in Syria and Egypt; after his death (388) there was a relaxation, but in 391 at Milan,

Land walls of Constantinople, built under Theodosius II by the prefect *Anthemius (early 5th century AD).

and thus probably prompted by Ambrose, Theodosius prohibited all pagan sacrifice.

BIBL. J. F. Matthews, *Western Aristocracies*.

Gold coin (*solidus*) of the Emperor Theodosius II.

Theodosius II Eastern emperor AD 408–50.

Theodosius (born 10 April 401) was the only son of *Arcadius, whom he succeeded in 408. Throughout his long reign, while others competed for political influence, Theodosius pursued a life of piety and learning, reflected in his organization of the 'university' at Constantinople (425) and in his instigation of the collection of imperial legislation which bears his name, the *Theodosian Code* (429–38). The 'cold war' with the West was ended, armies being sent in its defence against *Alaric, the usurper John, and the Vandals; the *rapprochement* was symbolized by the marriage of Theodosius' daughter Eudoxia to the western emperor *Valentinian III in 437. The second half of the reign was dominated by the threat of the Huns; from *c.* 430, and particularly during the supremacy of *Attila in the 440s, Constantinople kept trying to check the Huns by diplomatic means. Theodosius was a passive observer of the theological controversies of his reign; he acquiesced in the condemnation of *Nestorius (his own appointee to the see of Constantinople) by the council which he summoned to Ephesus in 431. He died after a fall from his horse, on 28 July 450.

BIBL. PW Supp. xiii. 961–1044.

Theodosius, Count Master of the Cavalry AD 368–75/6.

Brutal but effective general of *Valentinian I, Spanish by origin, Flavius Theodosius was the father of *Theodosius I. After campaigning successfully in Britain (367–8), he was promoted commander-in-chief with Valentinian on the Rhine. In *c.* 373 he was sent to Mauretania with a small force to suppress an uprising (see *Gildo), in which he succeeded by long marches and savage reprisals. He was executed at Carthage shortly afterwards, in obscure circumstances, perhaps because it was feared (by *Merobaudes (1) ?) that he would seize power in the confusion which followed Valentinian's death (November 375). His memory was rehabilitated after his son's accession.

BIBL. PLRE i, Theodosius 3.

Theophanes (died after 44 BC) Historian.

A native of Mitylene, Theophanes was the friend and adviser of *Pompey, even down to the flight to Egypt in 48 BC. He recorded in his histories Pompey's campaigns in the eastern Mediterranean, and was posthumously deified by the grateful Mitylenaeans.

BIBL. *FGH* 188.

Theophilus Bishop of Alexandria AD 385–412.

It was said of Theophilus that Egypt prefers a Pharaoh to Moses. Pagans were dismayed by his destruction of one of their greatest shrines, the Serapeum at Alexandria (391). After being a defender of *Origen's teaching, he turned against it and expelled its adherents from Egypt in 400. When they took refuge at Constantinople, Theophilus asserted the primacy of his own see by packing the council at Constantinople (403) which deposed the bishop of the capital, St *John Chrysostom.

BIBL. *ODCC* Theophilus.

Theotecnus (died AD 313) Governor and persecutor.

During *Maximin Daia's reign (*c.* 309–13) Theotecnus rose from civic office at Antioch to a provincial governorship. He showed considerable virtuosity in orchestrating opposition to the Christians, and an oracle of Zeus Friend of Men which he set up at Antioch gave a resonance of divine authority to the policy of persecution. After the defeat of his imperial patron, the Christians wreaked their revenge by torturing Theotecnus to death.

BIBL. *PLRE* i, Theotecnus 2.

Thrasea Paetus Stoic dissenter, consul AD 56.

Publius Clodius Thrasea Paetus was the most influential figure among those who chose to publicize their disagreement with the early principate, and, not untypically, was from a north

The Family Connections of Thrasea Paetus

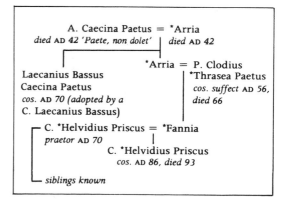

Italian background (Padua): *Tacitus considered that the shock to small-town morality occasioned by life at Rome was responsible for the uncompromising attitudes of men like these. Thrasea's independent attitude in the senate (though often on uncontroversial issues) eventually set *Nero against him; his absence on occasions for demonstrating loyalty became increasingly marked; in AD 66 he was condemned and given the luxury of killing himself. He was a friend of *Persius and *Vespasian, an associate of *Demetrius the Cynic, and son-in-law of Caecina Paetus and *Arria, a biographer of *Cato Uticensis, and the subject of a biography. His influence was particularly potent when *Domitian's reign generated similar pressures and sympathies among the survivors and descendants of this circle; it is from this that Tacitus' interest derives.

BIBL. Tac. *Ann.* xv. 23, xvi. 21, 22, 24–9, 33–5; *Hist.* v. 6–8.

Tiberianus Poet, 3rd–4th century AD.

Little remains of the work of Tiberianus, whose date is very uncertain, but a fine description of a natural paradise, a fragment on avarice, and a very interesting *Hymn to the Creator* which shows distinct Orphic influence. He may well be the author of the *Pervigilium Veneris* (*Vigil of Venus*), (see forthcoming article by A. Cameron).

BIBL. H. Lewy, *HTR* xxxix (1946) 243; T. Agozzini, *Dignam Dis. à G. Vallot* (1972) 169–210.

Tiberius (42 BC–AD 37) Emperor AD 14–37.

Tiberius Claudius Nero (consul 50 BC) married *Livia Drusilla, who bore him two sons. The elder,

Emperor Tiberius, portrait. Naples, Museo Nazionale.

'Tribute penny' with 'image and superscription' of Tiberius, to 'render unto Caesar . . .' (Matt. 18:28).

of the same name as his father, succeeded him as head of the highly aristocratic Claudian family on his death in 33 or 32 BC. His aristocratic mother's second marriage to Octavian involved him closely in the affairs of the ruling family, and he was married to Vipsania Agrippina, the daughter of his step-father's great marshal M. *Agrippa. After his second marriage, to *Augustus' own daughter *Julia (2) (which ended in disgrace), he was moved to tears by the mere sight of his first wife, whom he had been compelled to divorce in 12 BC.

In the East in 20 BC, in Pannonia 12–9 BC, and in Germany 9–7 BC and AD 4–6 he was the untiring agent of Roman imperialism, although the incomplete accounts of these wars that we possess naturally assign to the commander-in-chief some of the glory won by his elder subordinates. He did, however, prove himself a most competent general. After Agrippa's death he was the eldest close male relative of Augustus, and therefore of great importance until the increasing maturity of Agrippa's children Gaius and Lucius *Caesar made his position intolerable. Finding the tensions and problems excessive, Tiberius withdrew to Rhodes (as he was to do later to Capri) in 6 BC, even though that very year his position had been ostensibly improved by the grant of the tribunician power. Augustus seems not to have been fond of Tiberius —Livia was presumably his strongest backer—and when the deaths of Gaius and Lucius made it essential to recall Tiberius from his literary and philosophical retreat, Augustus does not seem to have been whole-hearted about it. Tiberius was adopted in AD 4 and his tribunician power renewed, and in AD 13 he was given proconsular *imperium* like that of Augustus himself. He had been forced by the crisis of the Pannonian revolt and the disaster of *Varus to spend these years restoring the conquests he had himself earlier made for Rome.

In AD 14, on the death of Augustus, Tiberius had the appallingly hard task of being first successor to the institution Augustus had created. He did not do very well. An awkward and embarrassing debate in the senate foreshadowed the failure to communicate or make clear their mutual roles,

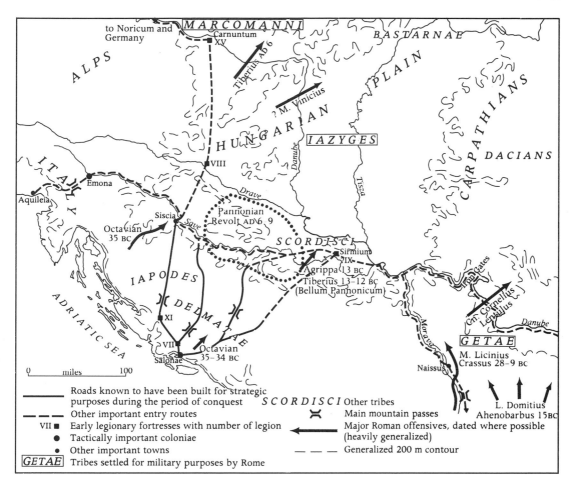

The Conquest of the Middle Danube

which spoiled relations between emperor and senate throughout the reign. The main product of this failure was a series of accusations and trials for treason (*maiestas*). Tiberius had not been able to build up the personal position which the length of his reign had given Augustus; he had to depend on informers since he had few friends; naturally cold and aloof, he had spent so long away from Rome that its politics were uncongenial and unfamiliar; the loyalty and habits of the Augustan principate died with their creator, and Tiberius inherited only precedents and powers. Moreover, as heir to the great traditions of the Claudii, he was, we may imagine, less keen than Augustus to reduce the chances of senators' achieving prominence in the State by their own efforts. It is not surprising that he let many of these questions slip, giving power to his praetorian prefect, and in the end escaping altogether to Capri in AD 29 never to return.

The grim story of old friends betrayed and relatives condemned, amply narrated by *Tacitus, is the outcome of these difficulties: the suspicions of the ageing emperor, fostered by the power-seeking prefect *Sejanus, resulted in the destruction of nearly all the family of *Germanicus, and only its least worthy representative was spared to be Tiberius' successor. Because of his lukewarm attitude to the Augustan system—though he was careful to alter no important Augustan precedent—his reign was administratively quiet. Provincial governors were allowed enormous tenures—but might be kept at Rome for security. Domestic thrift reached such a pitch that there was a shortage of coined money in the provinces. No expensive wars (after Germanicus' death, at least), no expensive buildings; but by the successful crushing of Sejanus even from Capri, Tiberius demonstrated that both he and the system were vigorous. The passive and unpopular regime survived until Tiberius' (probably natural) death in AD 37.

Tiberius was reserved, cold, introverted, and proud, well-built, healthy, cultured, and scholarly in a pedantic way. In his character thrift, firmness, and Stoic morality (he was unreligious) were said to have given way to meanness, cruelty, and

debauchery. It seems that at any rate he became
hard and bitter and sour, with unpleasant
consequences, especially for those at Rome.

BIBL. B. Levick, *Tiberius the Politician*; R. Seager,
Tiberius.

Tiberius Julius Alexander Praetorian prefect *c.*
AD 70.

Ti. Julius Alexander was an Alexandrian Jew by
birth: *Philo was his uncle. His distinguished
equestrian career included the governorship of
Judaea, where he was active in extirpating
dissidents, and a post under *Corbulo in Armenia
from AD 63. In 66 he was made prefect of Egypt,
where he again had to quell disturbances; an
important edict concerning the administration of
the province, issued by him under *Galba, survives.
Support of *Vespasian and help in the Jewish War
—though he attempted to dissuade *Titus from the
destruction of the Temple—was rewarded with the
praetorian prefecture, the climax of his career.

BIBL. E. G. Turner, *JRS* 1954.

Tibullus (*c.* 54–19 BC) Elegiac poet.

Albius Tibullus was of uncertain origin, but
apparently of sufficient standing to have suffered
in the property confiscations of the civil wars (I. i.
41 f.). A friend of *Horace (*Epistles*, i. 4, *Odes* i. 33)
and known to *Ovid (*Tristia* I. x. 51), he belonged
to the circle of poets round M. Valerius *Messalla,
whom he may have followed on campaign in Gaul.
He wrote two books of elegies (the first *c.* 26 BC);
for book iii, see *Lygdamus and *Sulpicia. The first
book interweaves homosexual (Marathus) and
heterosexual (Delia) themes, the second sings of
Nemesis (female). Tibullus additionally
commemorated his patron, his patron's son, and the
blessings of peace. By comparison with either
*Propertius or Ovid, Tibullus appears cool, arid,
and even dull, but a 'dry and elegant' (*Quintilian,
x. i. 93) talent and a wry exploitation of the
conventions of elegy and bucolic are to be
discerned.

BIBL. Ed. K. F. Smith (1913); D. Bright, *Haec mihi
fingebam* (1978); Gotoff, *HSCP*, 1974, 231 ff.
F. Cairns, *Tibullus*, (1979).

Tigellinus Praetorian prefect AD 62–8.

Even allowing for a bad press, the background of
Gaius (S)ofonius Tigellinus was shady: 'obscure
parentage and corrupt childhood', says *Tacitus.
We hear later of adultery with princesses, a period
making money from fish (or baking) in Greece,
several suspicious inheritances, and horse-breeding
in Apulia which brought him to *Nero's attention.
Sharing the emperor's indecent interests helped
him to prefectures first of the Watch, then of the
praetorians after *Burrus, in which part he
persevered with cruelty and lechery, rising higher
in the imperial esteem after *Piso's conspiracy.

*Vinius' influence saved him from popular hatred
under *Galba, but he was compelled to suicide by
*Otho.

BIBL. Griffin, *Seneca*, 448; T. K. Roper, *Historia*
1979.

Silver coin ot Tigranes I, possibly struck at Antioch
(*c.* 80–70 BC).

Tigranes I King of Armenia, floruit 90–60 BC.

Originally a Parthian candidate for the Armenian
throne, Tigranes massively expanded his small
kingdom partly at Parthia's expense but mainly by
mopping up the remains of the disintegrating
Seleucid kingdom (83 BC). An alliance with
*Mithridates of Pontus drew him into conflict with
Rome (69 BC), and he was defeated successively by
*Lucullus and *Pompey. The latter dismembered
Tigranes' short-lived empire, but allowed him to
retain Armenia as a Roman client.

BIBL. Magie, *Asia Minor*.

Tigranes V King of Armenia AD 60–2.

Descended from the *Herods of Judaea and the
family of Archelaus of Cappadocia, Tigranes was a
hostage at Rome for many years, and not very
successfully imposed on Armenia by *Nero in AD
60.
See also *Tiridates.

BIBL. Tacitus, *Annals*, xv. 1–6.

Timaeus (mid-4th–mid-3rd century BC) Historian.

Timaeus was the son of the ruler of Taormina in
Sicily. His histories in 38 or more books covered
events 'in Italy, Sicily, and Libya'; they survive in
copious fragments and their influence is widely
detectable (e.g. on *Lycophron); enthusiasm,
curiosity, and zeal for research are at times marred
by a love of the improbable and a lack of critical
acumen. Both in the *Histories* and in his account of
*Pyrrhus he was concerned with Rome: he knows
something of her Trojan foundation legend, and
refers to the monuments both of Rome and of
Lavinium.

BIBL. *FGH* 566 F 59 ff.; Momigliano, *Ancient and
Modern Historiography*, 46 ff.

Timagenes Historian (reached Rome 55 BC).

A native of Alexandria, Timagenes was freed
from slavery by *Sulla's son. He was the author of

the apparently very anti-Roman *On Kings*, much of which appears to have been preserved in *Trogus. A highly contentious figure: *Augustus drove him from his house for repeated insolence, whereat he ostentatiously burned his history of the emperor and took up with *Asinius Pollio, to whom Augustus commented 'you feed wild beasts' (Seneca, *De ira*, iii. 23).

BIBL. *FGH* 88.

Timesitheus Praetorian prefect AD 241–3.

Gaius Furius Sabinus Aquila Timesitheus had a long and distinguished career specializing in finance. In 241 he became *Gordian III's praetorian prefect, and his daughter *Tranquillina married Gordian. A capable administrator, of controlled ambition, he also demonstrated outstanding military competence. During his years in power he strengthened the African frontier and, in 242, began a campaign with Gordian against the Persians. In 243 he freed Syria, retook Carrhae, and secured the whole of Mesopotamia, but unfortunately succumbed to a fatal illness that same year.

BIBL. *CAH* xii; *PIR* F 581.

Gold coins (staters) of British Kings: Tincommius (left), Verica (centre), and Tasciovanus (right).

Tincommius British king, *c.* 25 BC–before AD 7.

Tincommius succeeded *Commius (king at the time of *Caesar's invasion) as king of the Belgae in southern Britain. *Augustus, after abandoning the idea of conquest, arranged diplomatic ties which were aimed, perhaps, at containing the influence of the Catuvellauni under Tasciovanus (a ruler known only from coins). At some stage, like Dubnovellaunus of the Trinovantes, he found it expedient to flee to Rome. He was succeeded by his brothers Eppillus and Verica (who abandoned his kingdom before *Claudius' invasion in AD 43).

BIBL. Frere, *Britannia* ch. iv.

Tiridates Name of several members of the Arsacid royal family of Parthia.

The best known Tiridates is the brother of

*Vologeses I who towards the end of *Claudius' reign was Parthian candidate for the Armenian throne, which he intermittently held. He was defeated by *Corbulo, but later, after the Roman defeat under Caesennius *Paetus, came to an agreement with *Nero, ratified at Rome in AD 66 with great pomp, which secured his rule.

See also *Tigranes V

BIBL. Tacitus, *Annals*, xii–xv.

Tiridates III First Christian king of Armenia *c.* AD 287–318/330 (?).

Consistent Roman support enabled Tiridates to withstand Persian interference; his position was assured by the crushing victory of *Galerius over *Narses in 298. Mighty signs performed by *Gregory the Illuminator in the king's own palace convinced Tiridates that he should impose Christianity on his people and destroy their ancient national shrines. These events were so traumatic that the king's conversion came to form the national myth of Christian Armenia.

BIBL. M.-L. Chaumont, *Recherches sur l'histoire de l'Arménie* (1969).

Tiro, Marcus Tullius (103–4 BC) Secretary to Cicero.

A slave of *Cicero's family, freed in 53 BC, Tiro was the orator's lifelong companion and close friend. He assisted him in the preparation and publication of his works, and continued to do so after his master's murder. He was also distinguished as a librarian and as the inventor of a system of shorthand; his name is given to an extant collection of ancient abbreviations.

Titus (AD 41–81) Emperor AD 79–81.

Elder son of *Vespasian, perhaps because of *Claudius' approval of his father's military prowess in Britain Titus had the honour of being educated with *Britannicus, and became a firm friend of the boy. He distinguished himself as a military tribune in Britain and Germany, and was appointed commander of one of the legions under his father in Judaea, where he showed conspicuous gallantry, and took over the direction of the war when his father was proclaimed emperor in 69.

He shared the imperial power throughout Vespasian's reign, despite hints that he had been considered as a candidate for sole emperor in 69, and held seven consulships, and—an innovation—the command of the praetorian guard. In maintaining security (for Vespasian's reign, if conscientious and efficient, was not untroubled) he showed an arrogance that could be described as ruthlessness. In his private life he was not entirely above suspicion—his affair with *Berenice, who was considerably older than he, was much criticized—and he possessed an extraordinary and rather sinister talent for forging handwriting. But

Arch of Titus (c. AD 81/90), Forum Romanum.

none of these things, nor the disasters of fire at Rome and the eruption of Vesuvius, diminished the favourable reputation he enjoyed during his reign and thereafter. It might have been different had he ruled for longer. However, several of the anecdotes recorded of him reveal some preoccupation with morality: the most enigmatic, perhaps, being his observation on his death-bed that he only regretted one thing that he had done in his life. Whatever it was, his generosity and good sense in the face of irritation and conspiracy, especially from his brother *Domitian, and some useful measures,

Coin type of the Emperor Titus.

above all against informers, quite outweigh it.
BIBL. *CAH* xi. 1.

Torquatus, Titus Manlius Imperiosus Consul 347, 344, and 340 BC.

Torquatus reputedly derived his *cognomen* from the torque of a Gallic warrior whom he slew as a young man in single combat. In 340 BC he allegedly defeated the Latins and their allies near Capua through the *devotio* of his colleague P. *Decius Mus (1) (*Diodorus apparently records only a second victory, attributed to Manlius alone by *Livy, 'near Trifanum', but Livy's two battles may be an unconscious duplicate); the proverbial 'Manlian orders' supposedly derived from Manlius' execution of his son for defying instructions by fighting in single combat. His dictatorships (353, 349, and 320) are all suspect.
BIBL. PW xiv. 1179 ff.; R. G. M. Nisbet, *CQ* N.S. xix (1959) 73 f.; Salmon, *Samnium* 207 f.

Traianus, Marcus Ulpius Consul AD 69/70.

Father of the Emperor *Trajan, Ulpius Traianus commanded a legion in the Jewish War, and was rewarded for his support, significantly soon after *Vespasian's accession, with the consulship and then governorship of Syria, very likely with wider responsibility for the reorganization of the eastern frontier. Here he earned triumphal insignia.
BIBL. Syme, *Tacitus*, 31; Bowersock, *JRS* 1973; *OCD*.

Trajan Emperor AD 97–117.

The Ulpii were an Umbrian family settled in Baetica (Spain). Marcus Ulpius Traianus' homonymous father (q.v.) was their first senatorial member, and he was able to use the distinction and rank attained by his father as a foundation for his own career. His reputation was first boosted by his prompt service to *Domitian in 89 against Antonius *Saturninus, when Trajan was commanding a legion in Spain. The prosperity and advantages which followed, including the consulship in 91, are hidden in obscurity, because those to whom we owe most of our information did not consider it admirable to win the favour of such an emperor as Domitian.

*Nerva made him governor of Germania Superior and after the crisis of 96 and the threat from the praetorian guard, adopted him as heir. Although Trajan was clearly active and able, distinguished by his father's achievements and Domitian's favour, but not deeply implicated in the less respectable associations of the previous reign, this move is not easily explained, and it is quite possible, as some ancient accounts suggest, that suggestion on the part of Trajan or his friends and the tacit threat of force combined with the difficulties of the time to persuade Nerva to take this step. Trajan's reluctance to return to Rome after Nerva's death,

Trajan's Column, Rome (details): Trajan with an aide (left), and addressing his troops (right).

his speedy preparations for aggressive foreign war, and his effective dealing with the praetorians all suggest that the situation in 97 was, for whatever reason, more insecure than our sources suggest.

The aggression took the form of punitive wars against Decebalus and the Dacians, whom Domitian had never decisively settled. The first war was quickly over, but Decebalus broke faith and a second war ended with his suicide and the conversion of Dacia into a Roman province; mineral wealth and frontier security were the pretexts. In 114 he achieved similar successes in Mesopotamia and reduced that and Assyria to provinces, but the area proved too difficult to rule in this way, and by the time he died (in Cilicia) widespread revolts in Assyria, which were only put down with difficulty, and the threat of trouble in Judaea and Syria led him to revert to the client king system for Parthia.

Trajan managed to acquire the sobriquet *optimus princeps*, and strove to represent the ideal emperor as imagined by many of those senators who had disagreed with and suffered under earlier rulers. Respect for the senate and increased use of senatorial talent to manage schemes like that of the *alimenta* (a poor-relief system for Italy) or to deal with problems like those which *Pliny the Younger was required to solve in Bithynia improved relations with that body, and the men whom he promoted, *Sosius Senecio, Licinius *Sura, or Cornelius *Palma, were given no greater honours than such stalwarts of the senate as Vestricius Spurinna, *Frontinus, and *Verginius Rufus. At the same time he devoted much energy to administrative changes, and vast sums of money to building projects such as his Forum (and Column) and Baths in Rome. His wife *Plotina shared in his good reputation, and the fact that he was himself adopted, and adopted an heir—*Hadrian—

endeared him to those who believed in succession by merit rather than birth. His opponents could find only drink and homosexuality to upbraid him with, but he was excessive in neither. His reputation has perhaps been gilded, but he remains an example of a competent and conscientious ruler.

BIBL. Syme, *Tacitus*, chs. ii. iv, xix; 'Life of Trajan' in Penguin *Historia Augusta*, (Birley).

Tranquillina Empress AD 241–4.

Sabinia Furia Tranquillina was the daughter of *Timesitheus, *Gordian III's praetorian prefect, and married Gordian in 241. Her fate after Gordian's death is unknown.

BIBL. PW Furius 98; *PIR* F 587.

Trebonianus Gallus Emperor AD 251–253/4.

Gaius Vibius Trebonianus Gallus served as

Portrait of the Emperor Trebonianus Gallus (terracotta). Florence, Museo Archeologico.

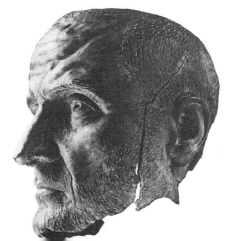

general under Trajan *Decius, and was responsible
for restraining the inroads of the Goths who had
devastated Thrace *c.* 248–51. After Decius fell in
251 he was proclaimed emperor, made peace with
the Goths, and returned to Rome, where he ruled
jointly with *Hostilian (Decius' son) as Augustus
and his own son *Volusian as Caesar. Gallus' reign
was troubled as Gothic invasions recurred in 252–3,
the situation on the eastern frontier deteriorated,
and the Roman world was devastated by plague. In
253 he began a persecution of the Christians, and
he and Volusian died in northern Italy that year,
fighting *Aemilian.
    BIBL. PW Vibius 58; *ANRW* ii. 2.

Triphiodorus Poet, 5th century AD.
    Probably born in Panopolis, Triphiodorus was a
mediocre poet who wrote an *Odyssey
Leipogrammatos* (now lost) and a short *Capture of
Ilium*. He is probably prior to *Nonnus.
    BIBL. A. Cameron, *Claudian*, Appendix D, 478 ff.

Trogus, Pompeius Historian, Augustan era.
    From Gallia Narbonensis (see XLIII. v. 11), Trogus
was the author of *Philippic Histories*, a 'universal
history' in 44 books which concentrates, probably
under the influence of *Timagenes, not on Rome
but on the history, partly in geographical and
partly in chronological sequence, of the other
Mediterranean empires, notably Macedon and
Parthia. The work survives only through its
contents-tables and in an epitome by Justin
(Marcus Junian(i)us Justinus, dating from the
third century AD (?)).

Tullus Hostilius King of Rome, 7th century BC (?).
    The third king of Rome (conventional dates:
672–641 BC), Tullus' re-awakening of Rome's
military ambitions and institution of associated
rituals (including the fetial procedures) were
probably suggested by his name (Latin *hostis*
means 'enemy'): his campaigns, including the
conquest of Alba Longa, reflect only later
conceptions of Rome's early expansion. He also
reputedly constructed the senate house (*curia
Hostilia*) and neighbouring Comitium.
    BIBL. PW vii A. 1340 ff.; Ogilvie, *Livy*, 105 f.

Turbo, Marcius Praetorian prefect from AD 119.
    From Dalmatia, Quintus Marcius Turbo rose
through the ranks (acquiring the friendship of
*Hadrian) and gained equestrian status. He
commanded the fleet at Misenum in 114, then
crushed the Jewish revolt in Egypt and Cyrene,
suppressed an insurrection in Mauretania, and
reorganized the province of Dacia before his
appointment as praetorian prefect. In 136 he was
forced by Hadrian to commit suicide.
    BIBL. R. Syme, *JRS* 52 (1962); id., *Tacitus*;
Pflaum, *Carrières*, no. 94.

Turranius, Gaius Prefect of the corn supply AD
14–*c.* 48.
    In AD 48, at nearly 100 years of age and after 34
years in the job, Turranius was still prefect of the
corn supply: *Gaius had tried to relieve him of the
office but he found he could not live without it. It
seems possible that he was the Turranius who was
prefect of Egypt under *Augustus, and a splendid
example of an equestrian administrator.
    BIBL. Tacitus, *Annals*, i. 7, xi. 31.

Ulfila (*c.* AD 311–83) Bishop of the Goths.
    Descendant of a Cappadocian Christian captured
by the Visigoths in the third century, Ulfila was
born and brought up among the Goths, returning
to the Empire in the 330s. He studied in
Constantinople and Asia Minor before being
consecrated bishop of the Goths by the Arian
*Eusebius of Constantinople (ex-Nicomedia) *c.* 341,
and beginning his mission to the Goths. Driven out
by a persecution in 348, he and his followers took
refuge in Thrace, later ministering to the Goths
settled in the Empire. He translated the Bible into
Gothic, for which he invented a script derived
from Greek and Roman letters and runes.
    BIBL. E. A. Thompson, *The Visigoths in the Time
of Ulfila* (1966); *Die gotische Bibel*, ed. Streitberg
(5th ed., 1965).

Ulpian (died AD 228) Jurist, praetorian prefect.
    Born in Tyre, Domitius Ulpianus became a

Ulfila's Gothic Bible: Codex Argenteus (silver ink on
purple vellum, 4th cent.). Uppsala, Universitetsbibl.

famous jurist, most of whose works were probably written during the sole reign of *Caracalla (212–17). He was apparently banished by *Elagabalus, but became *Severus Alexander's secretary for petitions c. 222, and was subsequently prefect of the corn supply and praetorian prefect. He was murdered by the praetorian guard in 228. His legal writings were extensive and formed the basis of the Roman Law codified in the late Empire.

BIBL. Kleine Pauly, Ulpian; Birley, *Severus*; *ANRW* 15.

Ummidius Quadratus Consul II under Claudius.

The career of Gaius Ummidius Durmius Quadratus was a very successful one, with steady promotion during the reign of *Tiberius culminating in a second consulship under *Claudius and a long and successful governorship of Syria, where he did not see eye to eye with *Corbulo. He died there in harness by AD 60, a good example of a man who succeeded despite the political turmoil of the times.

BIBL. Tacitus, *Annals*, xii. 45–51, xiii. 8–9; *RP* 51.

Uranius Antoninus Usurper AD 248–53/4.

Lucius Julius Aurelius Sulpicius Uranius Antoninus was a Syrian usurper who rose against harsh tax exactions imposed by Gaius Julius Priscus, *Philip I's brother. He survived until 253/4.

BIBL. *CAH* xii; *PIR* A 195.

Ursacius and **Valens** Arian bishops, mid-4th century AD.

Ursacius, bishop of Singidunum (Belgrade) (floruit c. 335–71), and Valens, bishop of Mursa, were pupils of *Arius and enemies of *Athanasius. They took up a moderate Arian position and became spiritual advisers to *Constantius II after the death of *Eusebius of Nicomedia and Constantinople (c. 341). They followed Constantius' changes of policy, retracting in 347 their charges against Athanasius, and repudiating their palinode after the death of the orthodox emperor *Constans (350), and continued to support Constantius' struggle for the establishment of Arianism.

BIBL. *ODCC* Valens.

Ursicinus Master of the Cavalry AD 349–59.

Ursicinus owes his fame to the fact that the historian *Ammianus (q.v.) served on his staff and has left a somewhat partial account of a man he admired. A competent soldier who had served under *Constantine, Ursicinus was appointed Master of the Cavalry by *Constantius II in 349 and sent to the East. In 354 he was summoned from Nisibis by *Gallus Caesar to preside at treason trials—Ammianus blames Gallus for the injustice and cruelty perpetrated. He was then recalled to court, and in 355 sent to Cologne to suppress

*Silvanus. In 357 he was sent back to the East, and in 359 appointed Master of the Infantry, but was unable to relieve Amida during the Persian siege because of the inaction of his successor as Master of the Cavalry. He was blamed for the fall of Amida and dismissed in 360.

BIBL. *PLRE* i, Ursicinus 2; Thompson, *Ammianus*, ch. 3.

Ursulus Count of the Sacred Largesses AD 355–61.

*Constantius II's chief treasurer, who released money for *Julian's use as Caesar in Gaul, Ursulus earned the hate of the military by his remark in 360 over the ruins of Amida: 'See with what courage the cities are defended by the soldiery, for whose high pay the resources of the Empire are exhausted!' *Arbitio and his fellow generals on the Commission of Chalcedon under Julian (361) took their revenge and executed him. 'Justice herself wept', says *Ammianus, 'for the death of this upright man.'

BIBL. *PLRE* i, Ursulus 1.

Silver coin (*antoninianus*) of the boy Vaballath portrayed as a man.

Vaballath King of Palmyra AD 266–72.

Son of *Odaenath and *Zenobia, Lucius Julius Aurelius Septimius Vaballathus Athenodorus apparently succeeded to his father's titles after the latter's murder, although his mother held effective power. He styled himself Augustus c. 272, but was defeated and deposed by *Aurelian in that year.

BIBL. *PLRE* i, Athenodorus 2; *CAH* xii.

Vadomar Roman general, AD 360s.

Vadomar was the king of a restless Alamannic tribe in the Black Forest until he was kidnapped by order of the Emperor *Julian (361). After Julian's death he helped suppress the usurpation of Julian's cousin *Procopius, and served the Emperor *Valens as a general on the eastern frontier.

BIBL. *PLRE* i, Vadomarius.

Valens Eastern emperor AD 364–78.

Valens usually gets the blame for the disaster of Adrianople from which the Roman army never recovered. He was the younger brother of *Valentinian I, who made him eastern emperor. He was a Pannonian like his brother, but lacked his military ability and forceful personality. A civil war against the usurper *Procopius (365–6) left him insecure. Unlike his brother, he was a baptized *Arian and half-heartedly persecuted eastern Catholics (see *Basil). His principal achievement was to reduce taxation by careful economy. Through his generals (*Victor and others), he imposed a favourable peace on the Goths (369) and intervened successfully in Armenia (from 371), but unwisely allowed the Goths to cross the Danube when they sought refuge from the Huns (376). When they rebelled, Valens mobilized and on *Sebastianus' advice fought a pitched battle before western reinforcements could arrive. He was overwhelmed and killed with two-thirds of his army (9 August 378).

BIBL. *PLRE* i, Valens 8.

Valens, bishop of Mursa: see **Ursacius**

Valens, Fabius Consul AD 69.

As commander of a legion in Germania Inferior, Fabius encouraged *Vitellius to march against *Galba. He and A. *Caecina were the main Vitellian generals, and he led the fighting against *Otho and organized Vitellian activity in Rome after the victory of Bedriacum. Although *Tacitus praises his intelligence, it seems that it was inertia as well as illness that impeded his resistance to the supporters of *Vespasian: he was captured and killed.

BIBL. Tacitus, *Histories*, i. 62; *OCD*.

Valentinian I Emperor AD 364–75.

Valentinian has been called the last truly great Roman emperor; he was certainly the last successful western emperor. His father was a muscular Pannonian peasant who rose to be a general. Flavius Valentinianus (born 321) received some education before becoming a cavalry officer; he was unjustly dismissed (357–63), but recalled by *Jovian to command a Guards regiment, and elected emperor (25 February 364) when Jovian died. A

Coin type of the Emperor Valentinian I.

month later he proclaimed his younger brother *Valens as his colleague, and that summer divided the Empire, taking the West for himself. He made frontier defence his priority. Alamannic invaders of Gaul (365–6) were destroyed, and their homeland in southern Germany devastated; fortifications from Switzerland to the North Sea were reconstructed for the last time, and army strength increased. An invasion of Britain (367–8), and in Africa a Moorish uprising (373–5), were suppressed by Count *Theodosius. In 375 Valentinian had to leave Gaul to conduct reprisals against invaders of Pannonia; while berating a delegation of those responsible, he suffered an apoplectic stroke and died (17 November).

Although given to such fits of rage, Valentinian was a conscientious administrator (justifiably) suspicious of his agents, who tried with limited success to control abuses and over-taxation; his failure to supervise Petronius *Probus was a disaster. Relations with the senatorial aristocracy were strained: court office went to bureaucrats, consulships to the commanders-in-chief, and even frontier generals were allowed to gain senatorial rank; *Maximinus executed senators at Rome for sexual misdemeanours or the use of poison or magic. Valentinian, although a Catholic, pursued a

Aqueduct of Valens, Constantinople (Istanbul), late 4th century AD.

religious policy almost unique then and later: he
tolerated pagans and most heretics, and intervened
in Church politics only to maintain public order.

BIBL. J. F. Matthews, *Western Aristocracies*.

Valentinian II Western emperor AD 375–92.

Flavius Valentinianus was the younger son of
*Valentinian I by his second wife *Justina, born in
371. At the age of four he was proclaimed emperor
by *Merobaudes (1), to forestall any coup after his
father's sudden death (17 November 375). He
remained a puppet-emperor all his life, at first in
Illyricum under *Gratian's protection (until 383),
and then at Milan; real power was exercised by
Justina. Expelled by the usurper *Maximus (387),
he was restored next year by *Theodosius I, but
left under the tutelage of *Arbogast, with whom he
quarrelled. His mysterious death (15 May 392) may
well have been suicide.

BIBL. *PLRE* i, Valentinianus 8.

Valentinian III Western emperor AD 425–55.

Valentinian owed his throne to his cousin
*Theodosius II, the eastern emperor, whose army
installed him at Rome on 23 October 425 at the age
of six. At first his mother, Galla *Placidia, was
regent, but after 433 her influence yielded to that
of the commander-in-chief *Aëtius. Despite the
intervention of two eastern armies, Valentinian was
forced to concede the Vandals' settlement in Africa
(442). In 449 the treachery of his sister *Honoria
brought *Attila and the Huns down upon the
western Empire: despite Aëtius' victory near
Troyes, they invaded Italy in 452. These disasters
enabled Aëtius' enemies to persuade the emperor to
free himself from him—and Valentinian in person
assassinated his general (454). Soon afterwards (16
March 455), he was himself murdered in revenge
by two of Aëtius' bodyguards.

BIBL. Oost, *Galla Placidia*, chs. 6–8.

Valeria Empress AD 293–311.

Daughter of *Diocletian (284–305), Galeria
Valeria was married to the Caesar *Galerius (293–
311), in order to establish dynastic unity within the
newly-formed Tetrarchy. When her father and
husband inaugurated the Great Persecution she and
her mother Prisca were among the first to sacrifice.
She was eventually beheaded (315 ?) by *Licinius,
the old comrade-in-arms to whose care Galerius had
commended her as he lay dying, but whose wrath
she had incurred by fleeing instead to the
protection of *Maximin Daia, who exiled her when
she refused to marry him. Prisca accompanied her
throughout, and died with her daughter after
Maximin's defeat.

BIBL. *PLRE* i, Valeria.

Valerian Emperor AD 253–60.

Publius Licinius Valerianus was born *c.* 190.

Little is known of his early career, but he was
probably consul suffect before 238. In 253 he held
a military command in Raetia, and was proclaimed
emperor by the troops. He marched on Rome,
where he made his son *Gallienus co-emperor and
his chief general. He began a persecution of the
Christians, but his main energies were concentrated
on the eastern frontier, where he tried vainly to
stem the Sassanian advance under *Shapur I. Dura
Europos and Antioch had fallen in 256. Valerian
was captured by the Persians in 260 and subjected
to severe personal humiliation: Shapur used him as

Portrait statue of the Emperor Valentinian II, from
Aphrodisias (Turkey). Istanbul, Archeological Museum.

a footstool when mounting his horse, and finally put him to death. His skin was flayed and presented as an object-lesson to Roman envoys seeking to negotiate.

BIBL. Kleine Pauly, Valerianus I; L. de Blois, *Talanta* 1975; *PIR* L 258.

Valerianus Caesar c. AD 253/7–258.

Elder son of the Emperor *Gallienus, Publius Licinius Cornelius Valerianus was made Caesar sometime during the joint reign with *Valerian, 253–8. He died c. 258, probably in Illyricum.

BIBL. *PIR* L 184; *ANRW* ii. 2.

Valerius Antias Historian (active after 80 BC).

Valerius Antias 'marks the nadir of historiography' (Badian). His scale, simplicity, and plausibility unfortunately recommended him to *Livy as a major source.

BIBL. *HRR* i. 238 ff.; Ogilvie, *Livy*, i–v, 12 ff.; Badian, in *Latin Historians*, ed. Dorey (1966).

Valerius Asiaticus Consul before AD 41, and in 46.

From Vienne in Gallia Narbonensis, Decimus Valerius Asiaticus cultivated *Antonia and was intimate with *Gaius. He was a man of great wealth with a taste for gardens and athletics. A principal actor in the conspiracy against *Gaius and a companion of *Claudius in Britain, he was honoured with a second consulship—but was then condemned for treason in 47, perhaps through *Messallina, and forced to suicide. Next year in a speech Claudius refused to mention 'the foul name of that bandit'.

BIBL. Smallwood, *Documents*, no. 369 col II l. 15.

Valerius Corvus, Marcus Consul 348, 346, 343, 335, 300 (?), and 299 (?) BC.

Valerius' *cognomen* ('raven') supposedly commemorated a bird which assisted him in defeating a Gaul in single combat (349 BC). He reputedly captured Satricum (346), won victories in Campania (343), took Cales (335), and intervened against the Marsi and Etruscans (as dictator 302/1) and against the Aequi (300). His alleged ending of a mutiny as dictator in 342 is probably Valerian fabrication (see C. *Marcius Rutilus). He passed the only authentic Valerian law upholding the right of appeal against summary execution (300 BC), although some scholars attribute his last two consulships and second dictatorship (302/1) to his son.

BIBL. PW vii A. 2414 ff.; Salmon, *Samnium* 196 ff.; Harris, *REU* 63 ff.; A. W. Lintott, *ANRW* i. 2 (1972) 226 ff.

Valerius Flaccus (died c. AD 95) Epic poet.

The *Argonautica* of Gaius Valerius Flaccus Setinus Balbus, begun 15 or 20 years before his death, were never finished: seven books and an incomplete eighth survive. *Quintilian comments unenthusiastically (x. i. 90) 'in Valerius we have lately lost much'. Garson makes a determined attempt to establish the poem's merits.

BIBL. Garson, *CQ* 1963, 1964, 1965, and 1969.

Valerius Maximianus Consul AD 184/5.

Of equestrian origin, Marcus Valerius Maximianus had a long and distinguished military career in the reign of *Marcus Aurelius, winning decorations in the Parthian War (162–6), and in the German Wars for slaying the chief of the Naristi. He was one of the officers chosen to accompany Marcus on the expedition to quell the revolt of *Avidius Cassius. After procuratorships in the Moesian provinces and in Dacia, he was adlected into the senate, and held a legateship before becoming consul.

BIBL. Pflaum, *Carrières*, no. 181bis; Birley, *Marcus*.

Valerius Maximus Compiler, 1st century AD.

Valerius Maximus was a collector of moral examples. His work, begun after he followed his patron Sextus Pompeius (consul AD 14) to Asia (AD 27), and finished after AD 31 (fall of *Sejanus), was dedicated to *Tiberius. The nine books of *Memorable Words and Deeds* are roughly arranged by moral themes, under 95 headings, further subdivided into 'Roman' and 'foreign' examples, for the orator's use. Highly popular in the Middle Ages, the work, written in a tediously rhetorical manner, is altogether derivative and often grossly inaccurate.

BIBL. Carney, *Rh. Mus.* 1962, 289 ff.; *RAC* s.v. *exemplum*; Carter in *Empire and Aftermath*, ed. Dorey (1975) 26 ff.

Valerius Poplicola, Publius Consul 509 (fiction), 508, 507 (?), and 504 BC.

Through family propaganda Poplicola became the hero of the newly-established Republic, and was ascribed important constitutional innovations, including a fictitious populist law of appeal (note his *cognomen*, Poplicola, misinterpreted as 'the people's friend', and see M. *Valerius Corvus). If his last three consulships are authentic (some sources omit that of 507 BC), he was presumably deeply involved in the aristocracy's fight for independence and power, but further precision is impossible. That a fifth-century Satrican inscription refers to him is most uncertain.

BIBL. PW viii A. 180 ff.; Ogilvie, *Livy*, 224, etc.; C. M. Stibbe, *Archeologia Laziale* i (1978) 56 ff.

Valerius Poplicola Potitus, Lucius Consul 449 BC.

After the supposed overthrow of the (fictitious) Second Decemvirate, Valerius and Marcus Horatius Barbatus completed the compilation and publication of the Twelve Tables (*Diodorus), or passed popular laws making plebiscites binding on the State, forbidding the appointment of magistrates not subject to appeal, and officially safeguarding the persons of plebeian officers (*Livy, etc.): these bills are probably fiction.

BIBL. PW viii. 2328 ff., viii A. 188f.; Ogilvie, *Livy*, 497 ff.

Varius Rufus Poet, Augustan era.

Lucius Varius Rufus was a friend of *Virgil and *Horace, who admired his poetry, and the author of *On Death* (an Epicurean (?) poem, like *Lucretius'); a tragedy, *Thyestes*, performed in 29 BC at the Actian Games, which earned him a million sesterces; and an epic in honour of *Augustus. After Virgil's death, he and Plotius Tucca edited the *Aeneid* on Augustus' orders.

BIBL. Hollis, *CQ* 1977, 187 ff.

Varro (116–27 BC) Soldier and polymath.

Marcus Terentius Varro was born at Reate (Rieti) or possibly Rome. He reached the rank of praetor, and served in Dalmatia, and also with *Pompey in Spain and against the pirates, being awarded the *corona rostrata* ('beaked crown') for bravery. He campaigned catastrophically against *Caesar in Spain and in the Balkans, but was later reconciled and was commissioned to collect a great library. In 43 he was proscribed, but escaped with some loss to his huge property and library. He was a notoriously difficult individual, but by universal consent the most learned Roman of his day.

Of his colossal literary output, which reveals Platonic, Stoic, and Pythagorean influences, only the *Res rusticae*, a work of his old age on agriculture, in three books, survives complete, along with six mutilated books out of the original 25 of the *On the Latin Language*, which display a passion for etymology and for social history. He wrote explicitly, at speed, with limited concern for organization, and with scant regard for stylistic and grammatical niceties. The *Res rusticae*, however, is often wryly entertaining and can, in small doses, prove highly readable. Varro wrote in all some 620 books; the total number of separate works (of which an incomplete catalogue survives) is considerably smaller. Copious fragments survive, notably of the *Res divinae* (*On Religion*), preserved in St *Augustine's *City of God*, and the pursuit of Varronian influence on later works has exercised scholars for generations. The output ranges from Menippean satires in prosimetrum to literary history (many of our facts on the life of early Roman authors we owe ultimately to Varro), and from portraiture (the *Imagines*, 700 portraits in colour, which influenced both *Virgil's Parade of Heroes (*Aen.* vi) and the statues of *Augustus' Forum), to constitutional practice (he compiled a handbook to assist Pompey) and to the 9 books of *Disciplinae* (Grammar, Dialectic, Rhetoric, Geometry, Arithmetic, Astronomy, Music, Medicine, and Architecture). But the 41 books of *Antiquitates* (25 books on human affairs, then the 16 on religion, dedicated to Caesar) were his masterpiece.

BIBL. Fragments: *GRF* 183 ff.; the editions of the non-grammatical fragments are widely scattered; *Res divinae*, ed. Cardanus, 1974. See J. E. Skydsgaard, *Varro the Scholar* (1968); G. Boissier, *Étude sur Varron* (1861) is still preferable to F. della Corte, *Varrone* (1954).

Varro, Gaius Terentius Consul 216 BC.

A *novus homo*, Varro's election to the consulship reflected popular discontent with *Fabius Cunctator's cautious policy. He commanded at Cannae, and escaped with a small remnant of Rome's army. At Rome the senate thanked him for 'not despairing of the Republic', and extended his command. This belies the aristocratic tradition (preserved by *Livy) that he was a second *Flaminius—a popular demagogue of humble origin, who was personally responsible for the Cannae disaster—and that the senate vigorously opposed both his election and his strategy. In fact he and his colleague *Paullus (1) were both executing the senate's strategy.

BIBL. Scullard, *Politics*; Walbank, *HCP* i. 435 ff.

Varus Governor of Germany AD 9.

Publius Quinctilius Varus was of decayed patrician stock exalted by marriage connections with *Augustus. In Syria he averted trouble after the death of *Herod the Great, but his talents were more administrative than warlike, and it was probably for that reason that he was entrusted with the conversion of Germany into a more settled province. This proved premature: Varus was betrayed by *Arminius and ambushed among swamps and forests. His three legions were completely destroyed, and he committed suicide. The disaster was made the excuse for ending Roman expansion in north Germany for ever.

BIBL. Wells, *The German Policy of Augustus* (1965); Syme, *Rom. Rev.*, ch. 28.

Vatinius, Publius Consul 47 BC.

As tribune in 59 BC Vatinius became prominent as an agent of the triumvirs, and secured the passage of laws on their behalf which the senate opposed, notably the ratification of *Pompey's arrangements in Asia and the conferment of a five-year proconsular command on *Caesar (in Cisalpine Gaul and Illyricum). After his praetorship (55) he was defended on a charge of bribery by *Cicero, who was forced by the triumvirs to retract his former hostility. Vatinius served Caesar as legate in Gaul and in the Civil War, and was rewarded with a brief consulship late in 47. He achieved military successes as proconsul in Illyricum, but after Caesar's death (44 BC) he could not prevent his legions deserting to *Brutus. He triumphed in 42.

BIBL. Pocock, *Commentary on Cicero, In Vatinium* (1926) 29–45.

Vedius Pollio, Publius (died 19 BC) Minister of Augustus.

Syme conjectures that the man whom *Cicero encountered in Cilicia with a baboon and a troop of wild asses (and disliked intensely) is the same as the notorious equestrian who fed slaves to the lampreys in his Campanian villa. He seems to have been an important minister of *Augustus, and is also found in literary circles.

BIBL. Syme, *JRS* 1961 = *RP* 39.

Vegetius Military writer AD 383/92.

Flavius Vegetius Renatus in his surviving *Military Digest* advocates a return to the classic Legion, whose training and organization is described from a variety of (lost) sources of different dates. The author, who may have been a finance minister of *Theodosius I, writes as an amateur.

BIBL. *PLRE* i, Renatus.

Veiento, Fabricius Consul II AD 80, III 83 (?).

Exiled for libel and sale of public office in AD 62, Aulus Didius Gallus Fabricius Veiento returned to Rome under the Flavians, to whom he gave his services on a scale eloquently attested by his three consulships. He remained influential under *Nerva, although criticism of him became more overt: it was generally agreed that his influence was sinister.

BIBL. Juvenal, *Satires*, iv. 113 ff.; G. Houston, *AJP* 1970; *PIR* F 91.

Velleius Paterculus Historian, floruit under Tiberius.

Actively involved in Roman military and public life from 2 BC, Gaius Velleius Paterculus was ultimately promoted from equestrian to senatorial rank and acknowledged as an aide (*adiutor*) by *Tiberius himself. His rapidly composed history he dedicated in AD 30 to Marcus Vinicius, consul in that year. This work, a 'universal history' in two books, survives—with a gap between the rape of the Sabine maidens and 171 BC (i. 9). Velleius' extreme concision, in contrast to (for example) *Trogus, arises from a conscious pursuit of speed and brevity; his work is indeed intended as a summary, to show all history, and especially Roman, as building up to the perfect climax of Tiberius' rule, with liberal use of the traditional manner and techniques of panegyric, whereas on *Sejanus he is constrained to deploy ingeniously but unenthusiastically the techniques of defensive rhetoric.

BIBL. Woodman, *CQ* 1975, 272 ff, and in *Empire and Aftermath*, ed. Dorey (1975) 1 ff; Sumner, *HSCP* 1970, 257 ff.

Ventidius, Publius Consul 43 BC.

A leading general of the late Republic of refreshingly humble origin (reputedly a muleteer but probably a lesser *publicanus*), Ventidius' career was advanced by *Caesar and *Antony and symbolized the demise of Rome's restricted governing oligarchy. He became praetor in 43 BC, and assumed the consulship vacated by *Octavian later in the year. He was greeted with the inevitable Roman snobbery, but proceeded to establish a formidable military reputation. As proconsul under Antony in the East he won a series of crushing victories over the invading Parthians (39–38) before being superseded by a jealous Antony. His memorable triumph in 38 was the first over the Parthians, and he was later honoured with a public funeral.

BIBL. Syme, *Rom. Rev.*

Veranius, Quintus Consul AD 49.

Veranius was the first governor of Lycia (AD 43–8). An inscription records his success at reducing and pacifying rebel strongholds. *Claudius advanced his career thereafter. *Nero put him in charge of Britain in AD 58, but he died within the year.

BIBL. A. E. Gordon, *California Studies*, v (1952) 231.

Silver coin (*denarius*) of *c.* 48 BC showing Vercingetorix(?) with chained neck.

Vercingetorix Gallic chieftain, died 46 BC.

A young Arvernian noble, Vercingetorix became *Caesar's most formidable opponent in the Gallic Wars when he raised a widespread revolt throughout Gaul (52 BC). He won a series of victories before eventually being forced to retreat to a fortified position at Alesia. Here, after a massive siege, Caesar destroyed Vercingetorix' forces; the chieftain graced Caesar's triumph in 46.

BIBL. Caesar, *De Bello Gallico*, vii.

Vergil: see **Virgil**

Verginia

Verginia was killed by her father to protect her chastity against the lust of Ap. *Claudius Crassus Inrigillensis. The story, resembling that of *Lucretia, may originally have been anonymous: the name Verginia was added because it suggested the Latin *virgo* ('maiden').

BIBL. PW viii A. 1530 ff.; Ogilvie, *Livy*, 476 ff.; A. Watson, *Rome of the Twelve Tables* (1975) 168 f.

Verginius Rufus (AD 14–97) Consul AD 63, 69, and 97.

Lucius Verginius Rufus' hour of glory came when, as governor of Germania Superior in 68, he marched to defeat *Vindex at Besançon but resisted the temptation to push his own claims to the throne (in fact his origins made him a much weaker candidate than *Galba). *Otho favoured him as Galba had not, and he survived the reign of *Vitellius (with at least one narrow escape). Later he was a friend and patron of the Younger *Pliny, and was selected by *Nerva as a suitable ornament to his reign: he was given a third consulship, but injured himself fatally while delivering a speech of thanks to the emperor. *Tacitus gave his funeral address.

BIBL. Pliny, *Letters*, ii. 1, vi. 10, ix. 19.

Verres Praetor 74 BC.

As a young quaestor in *Carbo's army Gaius Verres defected to *Sulla in 83 BC, and subsequently rose in the post-Sullan establishment to become praetor (74). For three years, as propraetor in Sicily (73–71), he systematically squeezed the province for his personal enrichment, and became a notorious paradigm of the corrupt and oppressive provincial governor. His conduct was excessive but not atypical, and he expected to survive prosecution in the Roman extortion court with the help of powerful friends (the *Metelli and Q. *Hortensius) and extensive bribery. But at his trial in 70 he was overcome by the formidable political influence of the consul *Pompey (whose Sicilian clients he had offended) and by the legal talents of the prosecuting counsel, *Cicero, whose *Verrine Orations* have survived to mark Verres as a great villain of history.

BIBL. Cowles, *Gaius Verres: An Historical Study* (1917).

Verus, Lucius Emperor AD 161–9.

The son of Lucius *Aelius Caesar, Lucius Aelius Aurelius Commodus was born in 130. When *Hadrian adopted *Antoninus Pius as his successor, he in turn was made to adopt Lucius Aelius Commodus, renamed Lucius Verus. Lucius was at first betrothed to *Faustina II, Antoninus' daughter, but this betrothal was dissolved immediately after Hadrian's death. During the reign of Antoninus he shared in the education given to *Marcus Aurelius (he also appears as writer and recipient in the letters of *Fronto), though apparently taking a back seat. He participated with Marcus in the emperor's

Portrait bust of the Emperor Lucius Verus.

counsels. He is said to have enjoyed life's pleasures, having a particular fondness for sports and gladiatorial spectacles. He became consul for the first time in 154, and for the second time (with Marcus) in 161. When Antoninus Pius died (7 March 161), Lucius became joint emperor with Marcus, on the latter's insistence, although he was ten years younger. He was soon betrothed to Marcus' second daughter, *Lucilla, whom he married c. 164. In the spring of 162 he went to the East to deal with the Parthian threat, and remained there until it was dissipated by victories in 165–6. He returned to Rome in 166 but set off again for the north with Marcus in 168, spending the winter at Aquileia. Early in 169, on his way to the northern frontier, he had a stroke and died near Altinum.

BIBL. Birley, *Marcus*; T. D. Barnes, *JRS* 57 (1967); *PIR* C 606.

Vespasian (AD 9–79) Emperor AD 69–79.

In the Sabine town of Reate the Flavii were of some importance; like others of their class they seem to have devoted themselves to careers in such fields as the army or the collection of taxes; they were solid, shrewd, and respectable. The two brothers Titus Flavius *Sabinus and Titus Flavius Vespasianus rose through the patronage of *Narcissus and won honours in the British invasion of AD 43, when Vespasian was responsible for the campaign which reduced most of southern Britain

Bronze coin of *Titus depicting Colosseum (Flavian Amphitheatre) begun by Vespasian.

and the Isle of Wight. Sabinus shared his brother's reputation for decency and fairness, and his death in 69 was to be a loss to the family. Vespasian found *Agrippina's hostility to those who owed their position to Narcissus, a disadvantage, and compounded his disgrace by falling asleep while *Nero recited. None the less, in 66 he was given the command of three legions in the Jewish War, which provided his springboard to power. The events of AD 69 showed that neither high birth nor prominence in the senate was required of an emperor: it was far more important that he should know the army. Vespasian had this qualification as well as the glory of his successful campaigns and the promise of a secure succession implicit in the existence of two adult sons, *Titus and *Domitian. Loyal supporters, especially *Mucianus, and the strategic importance of his command further assisted his success.

The troubles which had caused the Civil War had been directed at Nero, and not at the principate

Portrait bust of the Emperor Vespasian.

as a system. Constitutional creativity was not required of Vespasian, only the careful exercise of sound administrative principles, a task for which he was well suited. The hatred of Nero and the ravages of war had carried off many of the older nobility and this meant that a new order could be created to serve the new dynasty. Former friends and relatives, and subordinates or men of talent, were increasingly encouraged by the subtle system of promotion and status which was now formed out of the old *cursus honorum*; so a supply of administrators, as well as a new ruling class, was provided. Titus and Mucianus were particularly prominent, but men whose service as prosecutors had already commended them to Nero (for example, *Eprius Marcellus or *Vibius Crispus) and commanders to whom armies could be entrusted for campaigns which would distract them from disobedience, also benefited. There was much continuity—so much so that those who had made a name by their stand against Nero found Vespasian little better constitutionally; *Helvidius Priscus was the most illustrious victim of the new regime, though there were also less highly motivated and equally unsuccessful attempts at opposition.

Vespasian, a sound, fair, just administrator, with his concern for boundaries and revenues and his perhaps conscious imitation of the rule of Claudius (e.g. in becoming censor), seems a good emperor, especially when the sense of humour recorded by *Suetonius is considered: imperial jokes make pleasanter reading than imperial perversions. But his rule was hard, and he was undoubtedly an uncompromising and firm individual, which is why he succeeded so well in overcoming the difficulties he found on his accession.

BIBL. *CAH* xi. 1.

Bronze coin of Vetranio with emperor and Victory, and legend commemorating *Constantine's vision.

Vetranio Usurper AD 350–1.

On *Magnentius' usurpation in the West in 350, Vetranio, aged Master of the Infantry, was persuaded by the princess *Constantina to have himself proclaimed emperor by the troops in Illyricum, to block Magnentius' progress eastwards. This was certainly done with the connivance of *Constantius II, who next year met Vetranio at

Naissus for a set-piece abdication scene; Vetranio
retired to Bithynia on a good state pension. The
coins he issued, with the legend HOC SIGNO
VICTOR ERIS, form the first independent witness
to *Constantine's famous vision.

BIBL. *PLRE* i, Vetranio 1; Bowder, *Constantine
and Julian*, 46–7, 92.

Vettius Valens Astrologer, 2nd century AD.

Nothing is known of the life of Vettius Valens of
Antioch who wrote a detailed Greek astrological
handbook, the *Anthology*, between 152 and 162.

BIBL. O. Neugebauer, *HTR* xlvii (1954) 65 ff.

Vibenna, Aulus and Caeles

Legendary brothers from Vulci, the Vibennae
appear on the François tomb paintings (*c.* 300 BC
(?)) in a heroic episode from Vulcentan history,
where their associates include Mastarna (sometimes
identified with *Servius Tullius), their opponents,
a Gnaeus Tarquinius from Rome. Roman historians
made Caeles the eponym of the Caelian hill (at
various dates within the regal period): this may
indicate his intervention at Rome (in the sixth
century?), but any reconstruction is highly
conjectural (so, too, the attribution of a sixth-
century Veientan dedication to our Aulus Vibenna).
The aetiological legend of the Capitol (the discovery
of the 'head (*caput*) of Olus (Aulus)') prompted
explanations that Aulus was buried there.

BIBL. Alföldi, *Early Rome and the Latins*, 212 ff.;
R. T. Ridley, *Klio* lvii (1975) 162 ff.

Vibius Crispus Consul under Nero, Vespasian, and
Domitian.

Oratorical ability compensated for Quintus
Vibius Crispus' humble origins, and the
determination to prosecute, which led him to
accuse even his brother, bought him friendship
with *Nero, *Vitellius, *Vespasian, and *Domitian,
and three consulships. Though hated in the senate,
he is said by some to have been a congenial and
mild-mannered man.

BIBL. Syme, *Tacitus*, 4–5, 100–1.

Victor Master of the Cavalry AD 363–*c.* 379.

Victor (consul 369) was commander-in-chief
throughout the reign of *Valens, having been
appointed to this rank by *Jovian. He had already
been a senior officer under *Constantius II and
*Julian. He negotiated with the Goths (366/7 and
369) and the Persians (377); he was a careful
general, who advised Valens to wait for western
help before fighting the Goths (378), and survived
the ensuing disaster. Despite his name, he was a
Sarmatian from across the Danube, and married an
Arab queen's daughter (see *Mavia). He was a
devout Catholic, and received letters from St *Basil
and St *Gregory of Nazianzus.

BIBL. *PLRE* i, Victor 4.

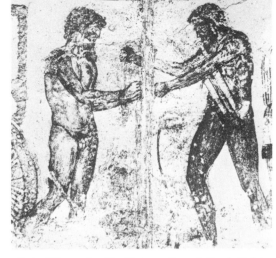

Caeles Vibenna freed by Mastarna. François Tomb, Vulci.

Victor of Vita Writer and bishop, mid-5th century
AD.

Priest at Carthage and later bishop of Byzacena in
North Africa, Victor wrote (480/90) a *History of the
Persecution of the Province of Africa*, which paints a
black picture of orthodox life under the *Arian
Vandals *Geiseric and Huneric.

BIBL. C. Courtois, *Victor de Vita et son oeuvre*
(1954).

Victor, Aurelius Historian AD 360.

Sextus Aurelius Victor was the author of the
(surviving) *Caesars*, published in AD 360, a
connected series of accounts, pithy and moralizing,
of imperial reigns from *Tiberius to *Constantius II.
By his own account he was an African of humble
origin who bettered himself by studying literature.
Soon after publication he was honoured by *Julian
with a public statue and a provincial governorship.
He was urban prefect of Rome *c.* 389.

BIBL. *PLRE* i, Victor 13.

Silvered bronze coin (*antoninianus*) of Victorinus.

Victorinus Emperor in Gaul AD 268–70.

Marcus Piavonius Victorinus apparently held a
joint consulship with *Postumus in 267, and

became emperor following his death and the ephemeral reign of *Marius. Little is known about his rule other than the fact that he successfully besieged the mutinous city of Autun. He reigned for two years before being murdered at Cologne.

BIBL. *PLRE* i, Victorinus 12; *ANRW* ii. 2.

Victorinus, Marius Philosopher and professor of rhetoric, 4th century AD.

Gaius Marius Victorinus, an African pagan born late in the third century, taught rhetoric at Rome under *Constantius. He was a many-talented man who composed grammatical and logical textbooks, translations of Aristotle and *Porphyry, and, after his spectacular conversion to Christianity (356) in his old age, theological tractates (the *Against Arius*), hymns, and commentaries on the Pauline epistles.

BIBL. P. Hadot, *Marius Victorinus* (1971).

Vigilantius Reformer *c*. AD 400.

Vigilantius' teaching, which is known only from its refutation by St *Jerome, seems to anticipate ideas of the Reformation. According to Jerome ('he calls us ashmongers and idolators who pay homage to dead men's bones'), he attacked the cult of martyrs, vigils, and the ascetic practices of fasting and virginity. He was overwhelmed in an abusive pamphlet (406).

BIBL. W. S. Gilly, *Vigilantius and His Times* (1844); Kelly, *Jerome*.

Vindex Rebel in Gaul AD 68.

Of senatorial background, though descended from the Gallic nobility, Gaius Julius Vindex led the leaders of the Gallic tribes against *Nero in AD 68. He encouraged *Galba to take the lead, and minted coins with legends such as 'The Well-being of the Human Race' and 'Freedom'. Nero was slow to react, but Vindex was defeated at Besançon by *Verginius Rufus, and committed suicide.

BIBL. Brunt, *Latomus* 1959.

Vinicianus, Annius (died AD 66) Conspirator under Gaius and Nero.

In AD 32 Vinicianus narrowly escaped trial for treason. He took part in the successful plot to murder *Gaius in 41, and was considered a possible successor to him. In 66 he helped persuade *Scribonianus to revolt, and killed himself when the plan failed.

BIBL. Josephus, *AJ* xix. 251–2; Swan, *AJP* 1970, 149.

Vinicius, Marcus Augustan general.

A *novus homo*, consul 19 BC Vinicius was *Agrippa's colleague in the early stages of the Pannonian War of 13 BC, and in AD 1 was successful in Germany, winning triumphal insignia. He is probably the man referred to in a fragmentary inscription as leading an expedition beyond the

Danube between 9 BC and AD 6, and is known as a dining and dicing companion of *Augustus.

BIBL. Syme, *Danubian Papers* (1971) no. 2.

Vinius, Titus Partisan of Galba AD 68–9.

Vinius' unsavoury early record included the seduction of a commander's wife in the commander's own headquarters and the theft of a cup from *Claudius' dinner-table. He was responsible for persuading *Galba to join *Vindex, and became his principal adviser. Although probably aware of *Otho's plans, when the *coup* took place he was killed in front of the temple of *Caesar in the Roman Forum.

BIBL. Tacitus, *Histories*, i. 6, 32–4.

Virgil (70–19 BC) Pastoral, didactic, and epic poet.

Born near Mantua and educated at Cremona, Milan, and Rome, where he seems to have studied with *Parthenius, Publius Vergilius Maro became a pupil of the Epicurean Siro at Naples. It is possible that in the land-confiscations of 40 BC, his family's property was affected, but, if so, powerful friends (e.g. Cornelius *Gallus (*Ecl*. x. 2), *Asinius Pollio (*Ecl*. iv. 12)) secured its return. By 38, he was acquainted with *Horace, *Varius, and *Maecenas (Horace, *Satires* i. 5, i. 6). In 29 he read the completed *Georgics* to Octavian on his return from the East. For the last ten years of his life he was under heavy pressure to complete a widely-awaited masterpiece, the *Aeneid* (see *Propertius ii. 34). In

Dido and Aeneas in the cave (*Aeneid* iv): Virgilius Romanus, *c*. AD 500. Rome, Vatican Library.

23, he read books ii, iv, and vi (?) of the *Aeneid* to the imperial family, but died four years later, before it could receive all finishing touches. The poem was published, possibly despite his wishes, by Varius and Tucca.

WORKS. 1. *Bucolics* (*Eclogues*, improperly), that is 'poems about oxherds' after the third-century BC Syracusan pastoral poet Theocritus: a collection of ten hexameter poems, probably written between 42 and 38, though certainly not in the published order, which is the product of elaborate design. Within the pastoral form, and at times exquisitely and frustratingly disguised behind melodious poetry and an enchanted portrayal of an idealized landscape, there stands a wide range of serious and important themes: the passions of love (x), literary criticism (vi), the horrors of civil war in Italy (i, ix), the death of *Caesar (perhaps: v), and hopes for the future expressed through the birth of a miraculous child (iv), as yet unidentified and perhaps not conceived historically, whose association with both *Augustus and *Jesus Christ misled centuries of readers.

2. Four *Georgics* ('Poems about farming'), in hexameters and finished by 29. There is no reason to suppose that Virgil began work on them before 36, following the 'un-soft orders' (*haud mollia iussa*) of Maecenas (iii. 41). But these poems, which owe much to Hellenistic didactic, to *Lucretius (ii. 490 ff., a moving tribute) and to the *Res rusticae* of *Varro are certainly not 'court poetry', 'command poetry' or, for all their idealization of Italy (ii. 136 ff.) and praise of Octavian, (ii. 170 ff., iv. 560 ff.) propaganda in comprehensible form. Their ostensible themes are (i) arable farming (ii) viticulture (iii) stock-farming and (iv) apiculture. But, for all that the agricultural information conveyed is not infrequently correct, these poems are not a handbook for farmers, who would have found them obscure, incomplete, and unsystematic. Nor are they compatible with what is known of agricultural conditions in contemporary Italy. The reader will rather find profound enthusiasm for hard work, a deep love of the countryside, brilliant descriptive powers, and an extreme sense of pathos, notably in the Aristaeus-epyllion, which encloses the story of Orpheus and Eurydice and bafflingly concludes *Georgic* iv.

3. *Aeneid*. In Virgil's mind as early as *Eclogue* iv and adumbrated in some detail in *Georgic* iii. 10 ff. Superficially, the poem contains the narrative of Aeneas' flight from Troy to found a new city in Italy: in (i) he is already *en route* and reaches Carthage; there, entertained by Queen Dido he narrates (ii–iii), in imitation of Odysseus' narrative in *Odyssey* ix–xii, the fall of Troy and his travels. In (iv) Dido and Aeneas fall in love, but Aeneas flees, reviled, on divine orders. In (v) he celebrates funeral games for his father, and in (vi) reaches Italy, enters the Underworld at Cumae near Naples,

The Trojans arrive in Carthage (*Aeneid* i.586–90): page from the Vatican Virgil, *c.* AD 400. Rome, Vatican Library.

and is told by his father of Rome's future destiny. In (vii) he reaches Latium, but the goddess Juno prevents his fated remarriage to the princess Lavinia, and rouses the local tribes to war under the leadership of Lavinia's thwarted suitor Turnus. Aeneas, however, acquires allies and heavenly armour (viii), and after prolonged warfare sacrifices in Pallas' memory (slaughters, say hostile critics) Turnus (ix–xii). The poem is immensely complex, drawing on a minute study of Homer, Greek tragedy, Apollonius Rhodius' *Argonautica*, *Ennius, Roman tragedy, and even Varro's antiquarian works. Sound, imagery, and language are rich and varied, conveying at times a sense of bafflement to the honest reader; in (iv), (vi), and (xii) particularly the moral and theological issues have defied all attempts at solution. There is in the poem an element of majestic patriotism (notably Jupiter's prophecy in (i), Anchises' speech to Aeneas in (vi), and the shield in (viii), linking Roman and heroic past in a grandiose continuum, reminiscent of the works of *Naevius and Ennius. On the other hand, the disappearance of Aeneas' first wife Creusa in (ii), and the deaths of Dido, Anchises, and Turnus, as of the young heroes Nisus and Euryalus (ix) and Lausus and Pallas (x), suffuse the poem with an inescapable sense of gloom and loss.

BIBL. *Bucolics*, ed. Coleman (1977); L. P. Wilkinson, *The Georgics of Virgil* (1969); W. A Camps, *An Introduction to Virgil's Aeneid* (1969). The poems of the *Appendix Vergiliana* are not by

Mosaic with scenes from Virgil's *Aeneid* (iv): mid-4th cent. AD, from Low Ham, Somerset. Taunton, Castle Mus.

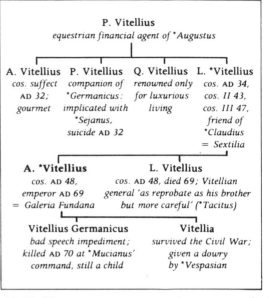

The Vitellii

Virgil—or rather, it cannot be proved that Virgil is not the author of *Catalepton* 5 and 8; the remainder of the collection consists of occasionally attractive minor verse of the century after Virgil's death.

Viriathus Lusitanian chieftain, died 138 BC.

Viriathus survived a treacherous massacre by Servius Sulpicius Galba in 150 BC to become Lusitanian military leader, and inflict successive defeats on Roman commanders from 147 to 139. But Roman treachery repudiated the peace treaty he obtained in 140, and finally procured his assassination in 138. With his death Lusitanian resistance collapsed.

BIBL. Simon, *Roms Kriege in Spanien* (1962).

Vitellius (AD 15–69) Emperor AD 69.

Although of recent importance, the Vitellii acquired vast influence under *Gaius and *Claudius through the popularity L. *Vitellius enjoyed with those emperors. Aulus Vitellius had a number of posts in which he showed his capacity for vice and dishonesty. T. *Vinius and A. *Caecina Alienus persuaded him to try to oust *Galba with the help of the Rhine armies which he was commanding in 69, but, by the time Vitellius reached Italy, *Otho was his opponent: the victory was easily won. As emperor he abandoned himself to gluttony, and failed to deal adequately with the armies which had elevated him. The spectacular advances of the

Flavians made him think of coming to terms, but the loyalty of the Roman mob made him change his mind, and instead he condemned Rome to the horrors of warfare, in the course of which the Capitol was burnt to the ground. The Flavian troops under Antonius *Primus were successful, but at a great cost, including the loss of *Vespasian's brother *Sabinus. Vitellius was put to death by the Flavian troops.

BIBL. Tacitus, *Histories*.

Vitellius, Lucius Consul AD 34, 43, and 47.

Vitellius cultivated *Antonia from an early age, and so became a friend of *Claudius. His conduct of eastern affairs from 35–7 as governor of Syria was energetic and effective; it was he who dismissed *Pontius Pilate. *Tacitus considered his obsequious flattery of *Gaius and his undignified overfamiliarity with Claudius a come-down after this, but he remained a man of great importance throughout the latter's reign, sharing two consulates and the censorship of 47 with the emperor. He was so able a politician that he was the friend equally of *Messalina and *Agrippina (the Younger). He died in 51 leaving two sons, one of whom became the short-lived emperor *Vitellius (see stemma).

BIBL. Suetonius, *Vitellius*, 2–3; Tac. *Ann*. xi. 2–4, 33–5; xii. 4–5.

Vitruvius Augustan architect.

Under *Augustus Vitruvius was a prominent architect and engineer, whose textbook of architecture, which is based on Hellenistic principles, has always been highly influential. Although he dedicated his work to Augustus, it is

Portrait of the Emperor Vitellius. Florence, Uffizi.

striking that no building of Augustan Rome is mentioned, and his treatment ignores contemporary developments in architecture. Topics covered by *On Architecture* include: town-planning, proportion, building materials and methods, public and domestic buildings, decorative pavements and plaster-work, and water-supplies.

Vologeses I King of Parthia AD 51/2–79/80.

A strong ruler, Vologeses was responsible for the more determined—but not blind—opposition to Rome which characterized the mid-first century AD. His great adversary was *Corbulo, but the struggle was indecisive and the settlement of 66 was favourable to Parthia. Vologeses offered assistance to *Vespasian in 69, though his relations with Rome remained ambiguous. See also *Tiridates.

BIBL. *PIR* V 629.

Volusianus Caesar AD 251, Augustus 253.

The son of *Trebonianus Gallus, Gaius Vibius Afinius Gallus Veldumnianus Volusianus was created Caesar in 251, married *Hostilian's sister, and became Augustus c. 253. He perished in northern Italy with Gallus, fighting *Aemilian.

BIBL. PW viii A. 2. Vibius 58, 65; *ANRW* ii. 2.

Vulso, Gnaeus Manlius Consul 189 BC.

Succeeding *Scipio Asiagenus in the Asian command in 189 BC, Manlius accomplished the task of pacifying the troublesome Galatians of central Anatolia, acquiring a massive quantity of accumulated booty. This he increased by the systematic holding to ransom of neutral States, demanding a money price for Roman friendship. Much of this booty and many men were lost on his return march through Thrace, but on reaching Rome he still had enough to allow the treasury to repay the tribute it had received during the *Hannibalic War. He was blamed for starting the flow of Greek luxury goods into Italy and for the adverse moral consequence of this. His request for a triumph in 187 was strongly opposed on the grounds that his Asian campaign was 'private brigandage' rather than a series of just wars; his request was eventually granted.

BIBL. Scullard, *Politics*; Toynbee, *Hannibal's Legacy*, 626 ff.

Xanthippus Spartan soldier c. 255 BC.

A Spartan mercenary commander employed by Carthage, Xanthippus' shrewd tactical use of war elephants was responsible for the overwhelming defeat of *Regulus' army in Africa in 255 BC. After this he is not heard of again.

BIBL. Walbank, *HCP* i. 91 ff.

Silvered bronze coin (*antoninianus*) of Zenobia.

Zenobia Queen of Palmyra c. AD 266–73.

Wife of *Odaenath, Septimia Zenobia ruled Palmyra after his death through her young son *Vaballath. An ambitious woman, she decided to extend her power, and, although a nominal ally of Rome, she moved into Egypt and occupied a large section of Asia Minor in 269–70. Initially *Aurelian did nothing, but when Zenobia had Vaballath proclaimed Augustus in 271 he marched against her. He quickly recovered Asia Minor and Egypt, defeating the Palmyrene general Zabdas first at Antioch and later at Emesa. Aurelian then besieged Palmyra, and after its surrender tried Zenobia and her councillors. She was taken back to Rome and exhibited in Aurelian's triumphal procession in 272; she was granted a pension, and lived on into old age in the city.

BIBL. *PLRE* i, Zenobia; *CAH* xii; Pekary and Walser, *Krise*.

Index of Persons mentioned but without an entry

Glossary

adlection (*adlectio*): the entering of a man's name on the roll of the senate (q.v.), whereby he became a senator without first holding a magistracy; also sometimes used to promote someone within the senate (e.g. adlection among the ex-consuls (see consular)). Sparingly used in the Republic and by the first emperors, it became a normal power of the emperor.

advocate of the imperial treasury (*advocatus (or patronus) fisci*): crown counsel, a position held by the senior barrister at each bar.

aedile: a middle-ranking magistracy with important administrative duties, including the organization of public games (transferred by *Augustus to the praetors (q.v.)). The curule aediles, originally patricians (q.v.), ranked higher.

aetiology: explanation of the origin of a custom, institution, etc. often based on the supposed etymology of its name.

Alexandrian: of Alexandria, a notable centre in the Hellenistic period for libraries and book-production, hence for the writing of learned poetry.

annales maximi: formal chronological arrangement, in 80 books, of official events of Roman history from the time of the kings to *c.* 130/115 BC.

annalist: Roman historian writing in the tradition of the *annales maximi* (q.v.).

arithmology: Pythagorean pseudo-scientific speculation on the mystical significance of numbers.

Asianism: term first used by *Cicero to describe the oratory of *Hortensius; artificial, ornate, and bombastic prose style. See also Atticism.

Atticism: purist movement which sought to imitate the diction and manner of classical Attic prose, in opposition to Asianism (q.v.).

augur: see priestly colleges.

augury: divination of the future by the observation of sacred birds.

Augusta: honorific title bestowed on an empress or other important lady of the imperial family.

Augustus: title given to the emperor, or senior emperor(s), while 'Caesar' was given to a junior emperor or heir apparent.

Boukoloi: literally 'herdsmen' the name attached to a popular rising in AD 172–3 in the Delta in Egypt.

Bucolica: pastoral poems, literally 'about cow-herding'.

Caesar: junior emperor; see also Augustus.

Campus Martius (the 'Field of Mars'): large open space in Rome used in earliest times for military exercises; it continued in use as a place for public assemblies, and contained numerous public buildings. It took its name from the altar of Mars that stood there.

celestial harmony: ancient theory, of Pythagorean origin, that the planetary spheres produce music as they revolve because of the differential speeds of their rotation.

censor: a powerful magistracy to which two ex-consuls (q.v.) were normally elected every five years. Among their general duties of economic administration were the supervision of the census and the leasing of public contracts (see *publicani*). Their great prestige derived from their power to revise the roll of senators (q.v.) and equestrians (q.v.). (See especially *Cato the Elder.) The office disappeared under the Empire, with the emperors fulfilling censorial functions themselves, or delegating them to officials. *Constantine used 'censor' as an honorific title for Fl. *Dalmatius.

centuriate assembly (*comitia centuriata*): a legislative and electoral assembly of the Roman people, who were distributed among centuries grouped into five classes. The form of the assembly originated in the centuriate organization adopted for the Roman army at the introduction of hoplite (heavily-armed soldier) tactics, perhaps in the sixth century BC, and its developed form was heavily weighted in favour of the wealthier and older citizens.

chamberlain: see Grand Chamberlain.

cheiromancy: palmistry.

clausula: one of a set series of metrical phrase endings used in Latin artistic prose.

clientela: the collective term for a body of clients, i.e. the persons or communities standing in a position of quasi-legal dependence on a patron, involving ties of mutual obligation.

codex: a manuscript in modern book-format, as opposed to a scroll.

cognomen: see Introduction, page 10.

colony: agrarian foundation of Roman settlers in outlying territory, usually located strategically as a garrison.

Comitium: an area north of the Forum used for meetings and assemblies of the people.

commander-in-chief: see Master of the Cavalry, etc.

commentarium: a continuous prose commentary on a given text.

commissioner of the corn supply (*curator annonae*): the Augustan and earlier senatorial (q.v.) equivalent of the later, equestrian prefect of the corn supply (q.v.).

consul: the highest-ranking regularly elected magistrate in republican Rome; two were elected annually to perform the supreme executive functions of State, the most important of which was command of the legions. Under the Empire, the office became largely honorific. The *consules ordinarii* continued to give their names to the year, while several pairs of suffect consuls were appointed each year, as the consulship was, in the *cursus honorum* (q.v.), the qualifying stage for the higher governorships. *Constantine reformed the consulship, which became again the peak of a man's career, though it remained merely decorative, and involved the giving of costly games.

consular (*consularis*): an ex-consul (see above) or person deemed to have held the consulship; in the later Empire, the title of certain provincial governors.

consular insignia (*ornamenta consularia*): the insignia of the consulship (see above), given by the emperor as an honour to someone who had not been consul; they conferred consular status without actual promotion in the person's career (contrast adlection (q.v.)).

controversia: rhetorical exercise in judicial declamation in which one or more laws are cited, and the orator must defend a given position.

Count (*comes*): originally a title given to important members of the emperor's retinue ('companions'); *Constantine made it an officially granted rank, divided into three grades, and it soon became part of the designation of certain high officials (see, for example, Count of the Sacred Largesses) and army commanders (see Count of Africa). It was also granted as a mere honour. It continued to be used in the barbarian kingdoms of the West.

Count of Africa (*comes Africae*): commander of the army in North Africa (later Empire).

Count of Auvergne (*comes civitatis Arvernorum*): major urban defensive military post with responsibility for modern Clermont-Ferrand and its territory (fifth century AD).

Count of the Domestics (*comes domesticorum*): commander of the corps of officer cadets (*domestici*).

Count of the Sacred Largesses (*comes sacrarum largitionum*): one of the chief financial officials of the later Empire, responsible chiefly for mints and precious metal mines, for taxation in money, and for paying the army and civil service.

cursus honorum: the sequence in which magistracies could be held at Rome, dictated originally by custom but increasingly by legislation. In ascending order, the basic (senatorial—see senate) *cursus* was: quaestor, aedile, praetor, consul (qq.v.). Under the early Empire a *cursus* for equestrians (q.v.) also developed.

Cynegetica: works on hunting.

Cynicism: a primarily ethical philosophical movement founded by Diogenes ὁ κυνικος ('the dog') in the late fourth century BC, and continued by such followers as Bion, Menippus, Teles, and, in the later period, *Demetrius the Cynic, *Dio Chrysostom, and Peregrinus Proteus (see A. *Gellius). It emphasized poverty, self-sufficiency, free speech, and the flouting of traditional values.

Decemvirate: two successive boards (451, 450 BC) of ten men appointed to compile the Twelve Tables (q.v.); the second of these boards is probably fabrication.

declamatio: rhetorical exercise in forensic speaking—on a historical or mythological theme.

devotio: a ritual by which a general vowed himself and the enemy to the gods.

diatribe: popular ethical lecture composed of commonplace arguments. The form originated among the Stoic (q.v.) and Cynic (q.v.) philosophers of Greece.

dictator: a magistrate appointed by a consul (q.v.) to be in supreme charge of the Roman State for a maximum of six months, originally to meet a military crisis, later for religious or political functions. The term of office was extended for *Sulla and Julius *Caesar.

didactic: written with the intention to teach, usually by imparting specific scientific information. e.g. Aratus, *Phaenomena*;

*Lucretius, *De rerum natura*.

duoviri (perduellionis): a two-man judicial commission, probably specially appointed to investigate cases of treason.

elegiacs: verse composed in a series of couplets consisting of one hexameter (q.v.) followed by one pentameter.

elogium: rhetorical set piece in praise of a given thing or person.

epic: a long narrative hexameter (q.v.) poem, usually on a heroic subject.

Epicureanism: philosophical school founded by Epicurus in the late fourth century BC. Its teachings advocated a life of extreme simplicity, indifference to external circumstances, and pursuit of 'pleasure' (defined as the absence of pain). Most important was this strictly materialist philosophy's adherence to its version of Democritus' atomic theory, and its rejection of the fear of divine intervention in human affairs. The most striking exposition of Epicureanism is found in *Lucretius' didactic (q.v.) poem, *De rerum natura*.

epigrams: short, pithy poems.

epitome: a *breviarium* or condensed version of a given text.

epode: term applied to poems of *Horace in diverse metrical units.

epyllion: miniature epic often containing a secondary narrative of significant thematic relationship—characteristic of the neoteric (q.v.) poets.

equestrians (*equites*): originally those who could afford to serve as cavalry in the Roman army; later the name of the census property-group below that of senators (see senate). It comprised the non-senatorial aristocracy and landed gentry.

extortion (*de repetundis*): action held in the 'extortion' court for the restitution of property illegally seized from provincials by Roman magistrates. This was a major arena for political trials in the late Republic.

fabulae: plays; *praetexta*: technical term for a Latin play on a Roman subject—from the purple-edged garment worn by chief characters; *palliata*: adaptation of Greek comedy; *togata*: native Roman form of comedy.

fasces: a bundle of rods symbolizing, particularly, the coercive power of the magistrates.

fetial procedures: early formal procedures for the declaration of war and the conclusion of treaties.

galliambics: rare Ionic metre used by *Catullus in poem 63. $\cup\cup \mid -\cup-\cup \mid --\cup\cup \mid -\cup\cup\cup\cup \mid -$

gens: see Introduction, page 10.

Gigantomachy: an epic battle of gods and giants.

Gnosticism: Gnostics believed that spiritual redemption was achieved through the revealed knowledge of God, to which they claimed superior access. See *Basilides, (*Marcion), *Irenaeus; cf. also *Mani, *Montanus.

governor-general (*vicarius*): in the provincial administration system as reorganized by *Diocletian, a deputy of the praetorian prefect (q.v.), supervising the administration of a group of provinces (a (secular) diocese) under their provincial governors.

grammaticus: professional school-teacher paid to teach literature.

Grand Chamberlain (*praepositus sacri cubiculi*): a eunuch, head of the eunuch staff (*cubicularii*) of the Sacred Bedchamber in the later Empire. Intimacy with the emperor and control of access to him led to great influence and wealth. See especially *Eusebius, *Eutropius (2). Simple chamberlains (*a cubiculo*) are also found in the middle Empire, e.g. *Cleander, *Saoterus.

Great Persecution: the last persecution of the Christians by Roman emperors, AD 303–13 (see *Diocletian, *Galerius, *Maximin Daia, *Martyrs).

Hellenistic: of the era of Alexander the Great and his successors.

hexameter: the most popular metre of Antiquity, the metre of epic (q.v.); a six-foot line which followed the schema:
$$-\cup\cup \mid -\cup\cup \mid -\cup\cup \mid -\cup\cup \mid -\cup\cup \mid --$$

iambi: poetry using iambic feet $\cup-\cup-$, notably the *senarius* (q.v.).

ictus: the stress accent on a given word.

imperator ('commander'): a form of acclamation given to a victorious general by his troops under the Republic, and taken over by emperors as an honorific *praenomen* (q.v.)—hence the title 'emperor'.

imperium: the executive power vested in the more senior Roman magistrates, especially consuls and praetors (qq.v.). *Augustus assumed proconsular (q.v.) *imperium* as the main legal basis of his power as emperor.

IVviri (i.e. *quattuorviri*) consulares: a board of four ex-consuls (q.v.) with judicial authority, each responsible for one area of Italy; set up by *Hadrian (q.v.), abolished by *Antoninus Pius, and re-established by *Marcus Aurelius.

Latin festival: an annual religious festival common to all the peoples of Latium, celebrated on the Alban Mount.

legate (*legatus*): a person appointed to a specific task, (1) by the senate (q.v.) as envoy; or (2) by a magistrate as envoy or staff officer.

locus amoenus: one of the set pieces of poetic and rhetorical description: the description of a natural paradise.

magister memoriae: head of one of the imperial bureaux (middle and later Empire), concerned with drafting replies to petitions; chief legal adviser to the emperor until *Constantine made the office subordinate to the Master of the Offices (q.v.).

Master of Horse (*magister equitum*): a republican magistrate appointed by the dictator (q.v.) as his subordinate; originally commander of the cavalry.

Master of the Cavalry (*magister equitum*)

Master of the Infantry (*magister peditum*)

Master of the Soldiers (*magister militum*) (or Master of Both Arms (*magister utriusque militiae*)): *Constantine created two commanders-in-chief (of Cavalry and Infantry); the number was increased in later reigns, some Masters (of Cavalry, Soldiers, or Both Arms) commanding regional armies, while a pair of Masters (of Cavalry and Infantry, or in the East, from the reign of *Theodosius, of Soldiers or Both Arms) continued to command the armies immediately attached to the emperor. The term 'commander-in-chief' is reserved for the holder of one of these offices.

Master of the Offices (*magister officiorum*): court official instituted by *Constantine with a wide range of responsibilities, including the mounted guards (*scholae*), bureaux (correspondence, petitions—see *magister memoriae*—etc.), imperial audiences, *agentes in rebus* (see State agent) and (from the 390s) the arms factories.

Master of the Soldiers: see Master of the Cavalry, etc.

Menippean Satire: a satirical diatribe in prosimetric form (see *satura*, diatribe, *prosimetrum*).

military tribune (*tribunus militum*): an officer attached to a legion.

military tribune with consular power (*tribunus militum consulari potestate*): boards of three, four, or six such magistrates replaced the consuls as the chief annual magistrates of the Roman State with increasing frequency over the period 444–367 BC.

mime: popular theatrical piece in 'low' or parodic style.

Neoplatonists (Neoplatonism): late Platonic philosophers beginning with *Plotinus (q.v.), e.g. *Porphyry, *Iamblichus, *Proclus.

neoteric: term used by *Cicero of a coterie of young poets much influenced by Alexandrian (q.v.) themes and techniques, e.g. *Catullus, *Calvus, C. Helvius *Cinna, Cornelius *Nepos.

nomen: see Introduction, page 10.

notary: State secretary, one of a body which, in the later Empire, kept the minutes of the privy council (consistory). Under certain emperors (especially *Constantius II) they were very influential, and used for confidential missions. *Julian drastically reduced their numbers, but they multiplied again after his reign.

novus homo: a newcomer to high office: the first man in his family to reach the senate (q.v.) or, more specifically, the consulship (see consul). The most famous *novus homo* was *Cicero.

Odyssey Leipogrammatos: the *Odyssey* rewritten as an exercise in poetic ingenuity, omitting a different letter of the alphabet throughout each book.

optimates: a strongly conservative coalition of aristocratic interests, which periodically closed ranks to defend the traditional supremacy of the senatorial (see senate) establishment against challenges from *popularis* (q.v.) leaders and military dynasts in the late Republic.

Orphism: the doctrine of an ancient Greek mystical sect which purported to follow the teachings of the legendary Orpheus, known entirely from heterogeneous fragments.

ovatio: a minor and less prestigious form of triumph (q.v.), granted to successful commanders who did not qualify for a full triumph.

palimpsest: a manuscript containing two or more different texts, one written between or over the lines of the other.

panegyric: speech in praise of a notable person.

patria: a work on the origin and founding of a city.

patricians: members of the early hereditary aristocracy at Rome; they had lost most of their political privileges by the early third century BC. Certain emperors, notably *Augustus and *Claudius, created new patricians in virtue of their censorial (see censor) powers. The name 'patrician' (*patricius*) was revived by *Constantine as an honorific title (see, for example, Julius *Constantius, *Datianus), and, in the fifth century AD, became the regular title conferred on the commander-in-chief (q.v.) (e.g. *Orestes). See also plebeians.

plebeians: originally the mass of the common people outside the patrician (q.v.) aristocracy. Later the powerful plebeian families dominated an enlarged aristocracy, and the term lost any socio-economic significance.

plebiscite: bill passed by the plebeian (q.v.) assembly.

pontifex maximus: the head of the college of *pontifices* (see priestly colleges) and the most influential of the priestly offices at Rome, with general oversight of the State cult and religious matters. Julius *Caesar was elected *pontifex maximus*, and the office was held by every emperor from *Augustus to *Gratian and *Theodosius I, who repudiated it in AD 379 as inconsistent with their character as Christian emperors.

populares: generic term for the political leaders of the late Republic who challenged the entrenched position of the senate (q.v.) and sought advancement by popular means, especially by the use of the tribunate of the plebs (q.v.).

praenomen: see Introduction, page 10.

praetexta: see *fabulae*.

praetor: a senior magistrate possessing a lesser *imperium* (q.v.) than the consul (q.v.). The number of praetors was progressively increased to accommodate the escalating administrative burden of the expanding Roman Empire. They had important judicial functions. The office declined in importance under the Empire (being chiefly a qualification for second-rank governorships and commands), and was eventually reduced to an honorary appointment involving the giving of expensive games (see aediles).

praetorian guard, praetorians: a corps of troops stationed at Rome, created by *Augustus in 27 BC to form the imperial bodyguard and household troops, and disbanded in AD 312 by *Constantine. The praetorians originally comprised nine cohorts 500 strong, and were armed like legionaries. The power of their commanding officer, the praetorian prefect (q.v.), and their role in the making of emperors became notorious.

praetorian prefect (*praefectus praetorio*): originally the commander of the praetorian guard (q.v.), of equestrian (q.v.) rank, the praetorian prefect rapidly became the emperor's second in command, with a wide variety of civil and military functions. The growth of important judicial functions in the second century led to the position being held in the early third by leading jurists (e.g. *Papinian, *Ulpian). In the mid-third century the office proved a menace to the security of the throne, and from the Tetrarchy (q.v.) onwards, was regularly divided, at first on a personal and subsequently on a territorial basis, with three or four prefectures (the Gauls with Britain and Spain, Italy and Africa and Illyricum (the latter sometimes separate), and the East). *Constantine detached the military functions, which went to the Masters of the Soldiers (q.v.).

prefect of the corn supply (*praefectus annonae*): the official (originally of equestrian (q.v.) rank) responsible for the corn and bread supply at Rome. In the later Empire there was also a prefect at Constantinople and in the 'granary' regions of North Africa and Egypt. See also commissioner of the corn supply.

prefect of Egypt (*praefectus Aegypti*): governor of Egypt, of equestrian (q.v.) rank (established by *Augustus; see Cornelius *Gallus).

prefect of the Watch (*praefectus vigilum*): equestrian (q.v.) commander of the fire brigade established by *Augustus. The *vigiles* were also used for military purposes in an emergency. The post acquired some judicial functions, and was held by distinguished jurists in the third century (see also praetorian prefect).

presbyter: Christian priest (literally 'elder').

priestly colleges: official bodies consisting of men holding certain priesthoods (secular offices involving the conduct of ritual). The two most important were the *pontifices* (see *pontifex maximus*) and the *augures* (see augury). Under

the Republic these were elective offices of great political importance, while under the Empire the holders were appointed by the emperor, and the importance of the position was essentially social.

princeps senatus: the most senior member of the senate (q.v.), usually the senior ex-censor (q.v.), who was entitled to speak first in all senatorial discussions.

proconsul: a man holding the same *imperium* (q.v.) as a consul (q.v.) but outranked by a consul and invariably limited to a defined province outside Italy; hence a provincial governor. Proconsuls were usually ex-consuls or ex-praetors (q.v.) with prolonged commands. Under the Empire the title was restricted to the governors of senatorial (see senate) provinces, of which the most important were Asia and Africa Proconsularis.

Proculian school: see Sabinian school.

propraetor: a man holding the same *imperium* (q.v.) as an elected praetor (q.v.), usually within a defined province: often an ex-praetor with a prolonged command.

proscription: the outlawing of political opponents by virtue of specially conferred powers; used as a partisan device by *Sulla as dictator (q.v.) in 81 BC, and by the Second Triumvirate (q.v.) in 43 BC.

prosimetrum: a work in alternating verse and prose.

publicani: members of private companies who bought contracts for the performance of public services for which no State machinery was available (especially under the late Republic). The most important of these services was provincial revenue collection.

Pythagoreanism: philosophical school founded by the Samian Pythagoras in Croton in the sixth century BC; notable for its practice of silence, ascetic abstention from various foods, and belief in the transmigration of souls. Its most important and far-reaching contributions were mathematics, arithmology (q.v.), music, and philosophical astronomy.

quaestor: the most junior republican magistracy, tenure of which came to be the necessary qualification for membership of the senate (q.v.).

quantity: the nature and length of a syllable: long or short.

Rostra: a platform from which to address the people assembled in the Comitium (q.v.). It was decorated early on with the prows (*rostra*) of captured ships.

Sabinian school: one of the schools of Roman jurisprudence in the early Empire, named after Masurius Sabinus (first half of the first century AD), the other being the Proculian school, named after the jurist *Proculus of the same period. Little is known of the difference between them. See *Javolenus Priscus, Salvius *Julianus

(Sabinians), *Nerva (grandfather of the emperor), *Pegasus, *Neratius Priscus (Proculians).

satura: literally a 'hodge-podge' or medley; early Latin diatribe (q.v.) which developed into satire proper under *Lucilius.

Saturnian: early alliterative native Latin verse with a six-stress line.

scholarch: philosopher in charge of one of the major schools—usually with reference to the Neoplatonic (q.v.) succession at Athens and Alexandria.

scholia: commentary, often in the margin, on a set text.

Second Sophistic: *Philostratus' phrase for the colourful revival of rhetoric in the second century AD. See *Alexander Peloplaton, *Apuleius, Aelius *Aristides, *Favorinus, *Fronto, *Galen, *Herodes Atticus, *Lucian, *Maximus of Tyre, Philostratus.

secretary for correspondence (*ab epistulis*): one of the important secretaries in the imperial palace in the early and middle Empire, responsible for answering official letters. Later the office was split, with a secretary for Latin correspondence and a secretary for Greek correspondence. The office was originally held by imperial freedmen, but *Hadrian made it an exclusively equestrian (q.v.) appointment.

secretary for finance (*a rationibus*): the imperial secretary responsible for keeping accounts and for financial matters. Like the other important secretaryships (qq.v.), the post was originally held by a freedman, but from *Hadrian's time exclusively by equestrians (q.v.).

secretary for Greek correspondence (*ab epistulis Graecis*)

secretary for Latin correspondence (*ab epistulis Latinis*)
see secretary for correspondence.

secretary for petitions (*a libellis*): one of the important secretaries in the imperial palace in the early and middle Empire, concerned with drafting replies to petitions from cities or individuals. Originally held by imperial freedmen, the post became exclusively equestrian (q.v.) from the time of *Hadrian.

secretary for petitions and legal suits (*a libellis et cognitionibus*): an imperial secretary who combined the duties of the secretary for petitions (q.v.) with the administration of legal cases.

Secular Games (*ludi saeculares*): sacrifices and games held in the theatre and circus (race-course) on the order of the Sibylline Books (q.v.) to mark the beginning and end of a *saeculum*, regarded as the longest span of human life. Perhaps first celebrated in 348 BC, then in 249 BC and in 146 BC, they were omitted in the confusion following *Caesar's death, and were revived by *Augustus in 17 BC (for which *Horace wrote the *Carmen saeculare*), after which there were two conflicting

reckonings based on 100 and 110 years respectively. Thus *Claudius celebrated them in AD 47, *Domitian in AD 88, Septimius *Severus in AD 204, and *Philip the Arab in AD 248, the thousandth anniversary of Rome and last occasion of their celebration.

senarii: six-foot iambic (q.v.) lines.

senate: an advisory body of ex-magistrates, which progressively usurped executive powers and became the principal administrative organ of republican government. The conflict between senate and emperor and the changes in senatorial function and membership are some of the best-documented developments of the early Empire. The senatorial aristocracy was always the highest class of the Roman State, even in its last days.

Seven Liberal Arts: loose classification of disciplines comprising ancient encyclopedic knowledge. Originally nine (*Varro): Grammar (i.e. literature), Rhetoric, Dialectic, Music, Arithmetic, Geometry, Astronomy, Medicine, and Architecture; the last two were removed in the later period (c. AD 470), and a canon of seven was established.

Sibylline Books: a collection of Greek prophecies consulted by order of the senate, and responsible for the introduction of several Greek rituals and deities, allegedly from the time of *Tarquinius Priscus. See also Secular Games.

sophist: a professional rhetorician-cum-philosopher.

spolia opima: 'spoils of honour' were dedicated to Jupiter Feretrius by a Roman consul (q.v.) who killed an enemy leader on the battlefield, a feat recorded only twice in the history of the Republic (the attribution to *Romulus is unhistorical). See M. Claudius *Marcellus, M. Licinius *Crassus.

State agent (*agens in rebus*): one of a body of imperial couriers and inspectors of the public post, established by *Constantine. Like the more important notaries (q.v.), they were used (especially by *Constantius II) for confidential missions. Reduced in number by *Julian, they multiplied again after his reign.

stemma(ta): family tree(s).

Stoicism: founded by Zeno of Citium in the third century BC, this school was systematized by Chrysippus and became the representative philosophy of the Graeco-Roman world. Belief in divine providence, and a *logos* (rational principle) embodied in the element fire which impregnated the universe lay at the centre of the philosophy. Virtue, equated with knowledge, was the highest good. Notable exponents include *Epictetus, *Panaetius, *Posidonius, and *Marcus Aurelius.

suasoria: rhetorical exercise where advice is given for or against a given issue.

symposium: ancient literary form consisting of philosophical or literary discussion by a number of speakers at a dinner party.

Tetrarchy: the sytem of government devised by *Diocletian (AD 284–305), intended to have two Augusti (of which only the senior could legislate) and two Caesars (qq.v.); it finally disintegrated in 313.

theurgy: magical mystic art which sought to establish union with the gods through the animation of sacred images and various purificatory rituals.

tribune of the plebs (*tribunus plebi(s)*): important magistracy with extensive powers of veto, conferred by the plebeians (q.v.). The tribunes originally protected plebeian interests against the privileged aristocracy, but subsequently the office lost its radical flavour, until the *Gracchi rediscovered its potential as an instrument of reform. As a gesture towards the people of Rome, *Augustus and succeeding emperors held tribunician power (*tribunicia potestas*), while the importance of the actual office dwindled.

tribute: until 167 BC the direct tax paid by Roman citizens in Italy, assessed and collected by tribes; subsequently it was levied only in the external provinces.

triumph: ritual procession by a victorious Roman general into the city of Rome; it conferred considerable prestige and was keenly sought after by republican magistrates, thus encouraging them to exercise overseas commands with belligerence and brutality. See also *ovatio*, triumphal insignia.

triumphal insignia (*ornamenta triumphalia*): under the Empire the holding of a triumph (q.v.) was reserved for the emperor and his family, private citizens being given merely honorific insignia (e.g. the crown of bay).

triumvirate: generally, a board of three men, appointed for a specific purpose; in particular, the commission of *Antony, *Lepidus, and *Octavian (see *Augustus) with extraordinary powers to 'restore the Republic' in 43 BC (Second Triumvirate). By analogy the term is applied to the informal dynastic coalition between *Pompey, *Crassus, and *Caesar in 59 BC ('First Triumvirate').

Twelve Tables: a compilation of chiefly private law, executed and publicly displayed by the Decemvirates (q.v.) in 451–450 BC.

urban prefect (*praefectus urbi*): a civil official of senatorial (see senate) rank at Rome, who acted as the emperor's deputy (the office was instituted by *Augustus), was particularly concerned with the maintenance of public order, and rapidly acquired important judicial functions. From AD 359 there was also an urban prefect of Constantinople.

vicarius: see governor-general.

water-board (*cura aquarum*), **water-commissioner** (*curator aquarum*): a water-board, composed of (originally) three commissioners, was set up by *Augustus in 11 BC to administer the water-supply and aqueducts of Rome. See also *Frontinus.

Bibliography

General Abbreviations

c.   circa
cos(s).   consul(s)
ed.   edited by, edition
N.S.   New Series
pl(s).   plate(s)
q.v., qq.v.   *quod vide, quae vide*
s.v.   *sub voce*
trans.   translated by

Abbreviated Titles of Books, Periodicals, etc.

AJP   American Journal of Philology
*ANRW   Aufstieg und Niedergang der römischen
    Welt*, ed. W. Haase
Astin, *Scipio Aemil.*   A. E. Astin, *Scipio Aemilianus*
    (1967)
Badian, *Clientelae*   E. Badian, *Foreign Clientelae
    264–70 BC* (1958)
Badian, *Studies*   E. Badian, *Studies in Greek and
    Roman History* (1964)
Balsdon, *Gaius*   J. P. V. D. Balsdon, *The Emperor
    Gaius (Caligula)* (1934)
B.A.R.   British Archaeological Reports
Bernstein, *Gracchus*   A. E. Bernstein, *Tiberius
    Sempronius Gracchus: Tradition and Apostasy*
    (1978)
BICS   Bulletin of the Institute of Classical Studies
Birley, *Fasti*   A. R. Birley, *The Fasti of Roman
    Britain* (forthcoming)
Birley, *Marcus*   A. R. Birley, *Marcus Aurelius*
    (1966)
Birley, *Severus*   A. R. Birley, *Septimius Severus*
    (1971)
Bowder, *Constantine and Julian*   Diana Bowder,
    The Age of Constantine and Julian (1978)
Bowersock, *Sophists*   G. W. Bowersock, *Greek
    Sophists in the Roman Empire* (1969)

Briscoe, *Livy*   J. Briscoe, *Commentary on Livy
    Books 31–33* (1973)
Brown, *Religion and Society*   Peter Brown,
    Religion and Society in the Age of St. Augustine
    (1972)
Bury, *Later Empire*   J. B. Bury, *History of the Later
    Roman Empire from the Death of Theodosius I to
    the Death of Justinian* (1923)
CAH   The Cambridge Ancient History (1st ed.,
    1923–39; 2nd ed., 1961–)
A. Cameron, *Claudian*   A. D. E. Cameron,
    *Claudian: Poetry and Propaganda at the Court of
    Honorius* (1970)
Chadwick, *The Early Church*   H. Chadwick, *The
    Early Church* (Pelican, 1967)
Chastagnol, *Fastes*   A. Chastagnol, *Les fastes de la
    préfecture de Rome au Bas-Empire* (1962)
CIL   Corpus Inscriptionum Latinarum (1863–)
Coffey, *Satire*   M. Coffey, *Roman Satire* (1976)
C. Phil.   Classical Philology
CQ   Classical Quarterly
*CR Acad.Inscr./CRAI   Comptes rendus de
    l'Académie des Inscriptions et Belles-lettres*
Crawford, *RRC*   M. H. Crawford, *Roman
    Republican Coinage* (1974)
CRF   O. Ribbeck, *Comicorum Romanorum
    Fragmenta* (1898)
CSEL   Corpus Scriptorum Ecclesiasticorum
    Latinorum
Diz. Epigr.   E. de Ruggiero, *Dizionario epigrafico di
    antichità romana* (1886–)
Ehrenburg and Jones, *Documents   Documents
    Illustrating the Reigns of Augustus and Tiberius*,
    ed. V. Ehrenburg and A. H. M. Jones (2nd ed.
    (amended), 1976)
Ep.   Epistulae
Errington, *Dawn of Empire*   R. M. Errington,
    Dawn of Empire (1971)
FGH   F. Jacoby, *Die Fragmente der griechischen
    Historiker* (1923–)

FPL W. Morel, *Fragmenta Poetarum Latinorum epicorum et lyricorum . . .* (1927)

Frend, *Martyrdom and Persecution* W. H. C. Frend, *Martyrdom and Persecution in the Early Church* (1965)

Frere, *Britannia* S. S. Frere, *Britannia* (2nd ed., 1978)

GRBS *Greek, Roman, and Byzantine Studies*

GRF H. Funaioli, *Grammaticae Romanae Fragmenta* (1907)

Griffin, *Seneca* M. T. Griffin, *Seneca: A Philosopher in Politics* (1976)

GRNSC *Greece and Rome, New Surveys in the Classics* (series, Clarendon Press, Oxford): G. W. Williams, *Horace* (1972) (no. 6); G. W. Williams, *Livy* (1974) (no. 8); E. J. Kenney, *Lucretius* (1977) (no. 11)

Grosso, *Lotta* F. Grosso, *La lotta politica al tempo di Commodo* (1964)

Gruen, *Politics* E. S. Gruen, *Roman Politics and the Criminal Courts, 148–78 BC* (1968)

Gruen, *Republic* E. S. Gruen, *The Last Generation of the Roman Republic* (1974)

HAC *Historia Augusta Colloquia*

Harris, *REU* W. V. Harris, *Rome in Etruria and Umbria* (1971)

Hist. eccl. *Historia ecclesiastica*

Howe, *Pretorian Prefect* L. L. Howe, *The Pretorian Prefect from Commodus to Diocletian* (1942)

HRR H. Peter, *Historicorum Romanorum Reliquiae* (1914, 1906)

HSCP *Harvard Studies in Classical Philology*

HTR *Harvard Theological Review*

ILS H. Dessau, *Inscriptiones Latinae Selectae* (1892–1916)

Jolowicz, *Roman Law* H. F. Jolowicz, *A Historical Introduction to the Study of Roman Law* (2nd ed., 1954)

Jones, *Constantine* A. H. M. Jones, *Constantine and the Conversion of Europe* (2nd ed., 1972)

Jones, *LRE* A. H. M. Jones, *The Later Roman Empire, 284–602* (1964)

Josephus, *AJ* Josephus, *Antiquitates Judaicae*

JRS *Journal of Roman Studies*

JTS *Journal of Theological Studies*

Kelly, *Jerome* J. N. D. Kelly, *Jerome* (1975)

Kennedy, *Rhetoric* G. Kennedy, *The Art of Rhetoric in the Roman World* (1972)

Kl. Pauly *Der kleine Pauly* (1964–)

Lazenby, *Hannibal* J. F. Lazenby, *Hannibal's War* (1978)

Levick, *Tiberius* B. Levick, *Tiberius the Politician* (1976)

Lintott, *Violence* A. W. Lintott, *Violence in Republican Rome* (1968)

Loeb Loeb Classical Library (texts with English translation)

MacMullen, *Enemies* R. MacMullen, *Enemies of the Roman Order* (1967)

Magie, *Asia Minor* D. Magie, *Roman Rule in Asia Minor* (1950)

Matthews, *Aristocracies* J. F. Matthews, *Western Aristocracies and Imperial Court* (1975)

MGH Monumenta Germaniae Historica

MGH, AA Auctores Antiquissimi

Migne, *PG* Migne, *Patrologiae Cursus, series Graeca*

Migne, *PL* Migne, *Patrologiae Cursus, series Latina*

Millar, *Dio* F. Millar, *A Study of Cassius Dio* (1964)

ed. Momigliano, *Conflict* *The Conflict between Paganism and Christianity in the Fourth Century*, ed. A. Momigliano (1963)

Momigliano, *Ancient and Modern Historiography* A. Momigliano, *Essays in Ancient and Modern Historiography* (1977)

Nash, *Pict. Dict.* E. Nash, *Pictorial Dictionary of Ancient Rome* (1961–2)

Nov. Val. *Novellae Valentiniani* (with *Theodosian Code*)

OCD *The Oxford Classical Dictionary* (2nd ed., 1970)

O.C.T. Oxford Classical Texts

ODCC *The Oxford Dictionary of the Christian Church*, ed. F. L. Cross (2nd ed., 1974)

Ogilvie, *Livy* R. M. Ogilvie, *A Commentary on Livy Books 1–5* (1975)

Oost, *Galla Placidia* S. I. Oost, *Galla Placidia Augusta* (1968)

Or. *Orationes*

ORF H. Malcovati, *Oratorum Romanorum Fragmenta* (2nd ed., 1955)

PBSR *Papers of the British School at Rome*

PCPS *Proceedings of the Cambridge Philological Society*

Pflaum, *Carrières* H.-G. Pflaum, *Les carrières procuratoriennes équestres sous le Haut-Empire romain* (1960)

PG see Migne

Piganiol, *Empire chr.* A. Piganiol, *L'Empire chrétien* (2nd ed., 1972)

PIR *Prosopographia Imperii Romani Saeculi I, II, III* (1st ed., by Klebs and Dessau, 1897–8 (still to be consulted for the later letters of the alphabet); 2nd ed., by Groag and Stein, 1933– (for the earlier letters of the alphabet, in progress))

PL see Migne

PLRE A. H. M. Jones, J. R. Martindale, and J. Morris, *The Prosopography of the Later Roman Empire*, volume i, A.D. 260–395 (1971)

praef. *praefatio* (preface)

PW A. Pauly, G. Wissowa, and W. Kroll, *Real-Encyclopädie der klassischen Altertumswissenschaft* (1893–)

RAC *Reallexikon für Antike und Christentum* (1941–)

REL *Revue des Études Latines*

Rh. Mus. *Rheinisches Museum für Philologie*

RIC *The Roman Imperial Coinage*, ed. Mattingly, Sydenham, etc. (1923–)

Röm. Mitt.   *Mitteilungen des deutschen archäologischen Instituts, Römische Abteilung*

Russell and Winterbottom, *Lit. Crit.*   D. A. Russell and M. Winterbottom, *Ancient Literary Criticism* (1972)

Salmon, *Samnium*   E. T. Salmon, *Samnium and the Samnites* (1967)

SC   Sources chrétiennes

Scullard, *Politics*   H. H. Scullard, *Roman Politics 220–150 BC* (2nd ed., 1973)

Seager, *Pompey*   R. Seager, *Pompey: A Political Biography* (1979)

Sherwin-White, *The Letters of Pliny*   A. N. Sherwin-White, *The Letters of Pliny: A Historical and Social Commentary* (1966)

Smallwood, *Documents*   E. M. Smallwood, *Documents Illustrating the Principates of Gaius, Claudius, and Nero* (1967)

Stein, *Bas-Empire*   E. Stein, *Histoire du Bas-Empire*, trans. J.-R. Palanque (1928)

Stroheker, *Adel*   K. F. Stroheker, *Die senatorische Adel im spätantiken Gallien* (1948)

Syme, *Emperors and Biography*   R. Syme, *Emperors and Biography* (1971)

Syme, *Rom. Rev.*   R. Syme, *The Roman Revolution* (1939, 1952)

Syme, *RP*   R. Syme, *Roman Papers* (1979)

Syme, *Sallust*   R. Syme, *Sallust* (1964)

Syme, *Tacitus*   R. Syme, *Tacitus* (1958)

Tac.   Tacitus

Tac. *Agr.*   Tacitus, *Agricola*

Tac. *Ann.*   Tacitus, *Annals*

Tac. *Hist.*   Tacitus, *Histories*

TAPA   *Transactions of the American Philological Association*

Taylor, *Party Politics*   L. R. Taylor, *Party Politics in the Age of Caesar* (1949)

Thomae *PIR* add.   Benedictus Thomae addendum to *PIR* (q.v.)

Thompson, *Ammianus*   E. A. Thompson, *The Historical Work of Ammianus Marcellinus* (1947)

Toynbee, *Hannibal's Legacy*   A. J. Toynbee, *Hannibal's Legacy* (1965)

TRF   O. Ribbeck, *Tragicorum Romanorum Fragmenta* (1897–8, 1962)

Walbank, *HCP*   F. W. Walbank, *A Historical Commentary on Polybius* (1957–79)

Walser and Pekáry, *Krise*   G. Walser and T. Pekáry, *Die Krise des römischen Reiches* (1962)

Will, *Hist. pol.*   E. Will, *Histoire politique du monde hellénistique* (1967)

ZPE   *Zeitschrift für Papyrologie und Epigraphik*

Suggestions for Further Reading

Detailed bibliographical references are to be found at the foot of individual entries consulted; in addition, the above list of abbreviations contains all the works frequently cited. For those in search of general reading matter on various parts of the Roman period, the following books (many of them obtainable in paperback editions) are recommended:

R. M. Ogilvie, *Early Rome and the Etruscans* (1976)

M. H. Crawford, *The Roman Republic* (1978)

R. M. Errington, *The Dawn of Empire: Rome's Rise to World Power* (1971)

H. H. Scullard, *From the Gracchi to Nero, 133 BC to AD 68* (4th ed., 1976)

R. Syme, *The Roman Revolution* (1939, 1952)

E. T. Salmon, *A History of the Roman World from 30 BC to AD 138* (1944)

R. Syme, *Tacitus* (1958)

A. Garzetti, *From Tiberius to the Antonines: A History of the Roman Empire, AD 14–192* (1974)

P. Petit, *Pax Romana* (1976)

H. M. D. Parker, *A History of the Roman World from AD 138 to 337* (2nd ed., 1958)

R. MacMullen, *The Roman Government's Response to Crisis AD 235–337* (1976)

A. H. M. Jones, *The Later Roman Empire, 284–602* (1964)

A. H. M. Jones, *The Decline of the Ancient World* (1966) (an abridgement of the above)

Peter Brown, *The World of Late Antiquity* (1971)

Diana Bowder, *The Age of Constantine and Julian* (1978)

J. F. Matthews, *Western Aristocracies and Imperial Court* (1975)

Maps and Stemmata

The following will be found in the Dictionary, accompanying the entry indicated by an asterisk:

TRANSPADANE
GAUL

C I S A L P I N E   G A U L

CISALPINE

LIGURIA

Po
Ticinus
Piacenza
Bobbio
Trebia
Bedriacum
Verona
Padua
Aquileia

Modena
VIA AEMILIA
Po
Ravenna

Lucca
Arno
Sarsina
Rubicon
Rimini
Pesaro
Metaurus

Volterra
Clusium
Lake Trasimene
Perugia
Assisi
UMBRIA
Sentinum

ELBA
PLANASIA

ETRURIA
Volsinii

Vulci

Tarquinii
Falerii
Sutrium
Nep(e)te
Caere
Veii
Cures
VIA FLAMINIA
Reate

PICENUM
Ausculum

Tivoli
Rome
Praeneste
Ostia
Tusculum
Aricia
Lavinium
Satricum
Antium
LATIUM
AEQUI
MARSI
Corfinium
Sulmo
HERNICI
VOLSCI
Privernum
VIA APPIA
AURUNCI
Suessa Aurunca
Cales
Capua
Beneventum
CAMPANIA
SAMNIUM
Luceria
APULIA
Ausculum
Cannae
Venusia
Nola
Caudine Forks
Cumae
Baiae
Misenum
Naples
Nuceria
VIA APPIA
Sorrento
CAPRI

LUCANIA
Brindisi
Tarentum
Heraclea
Rudiae

Thurii

BRUTTIUM

ROME AND ITALY

0 ———————— 100 miles

AEGATES
INSULAE
Drepana
Palermo
LIPARA
Mylae
Naulochus
Messina
Locri

SICILY
Taormina
Agyrium

Syracuse

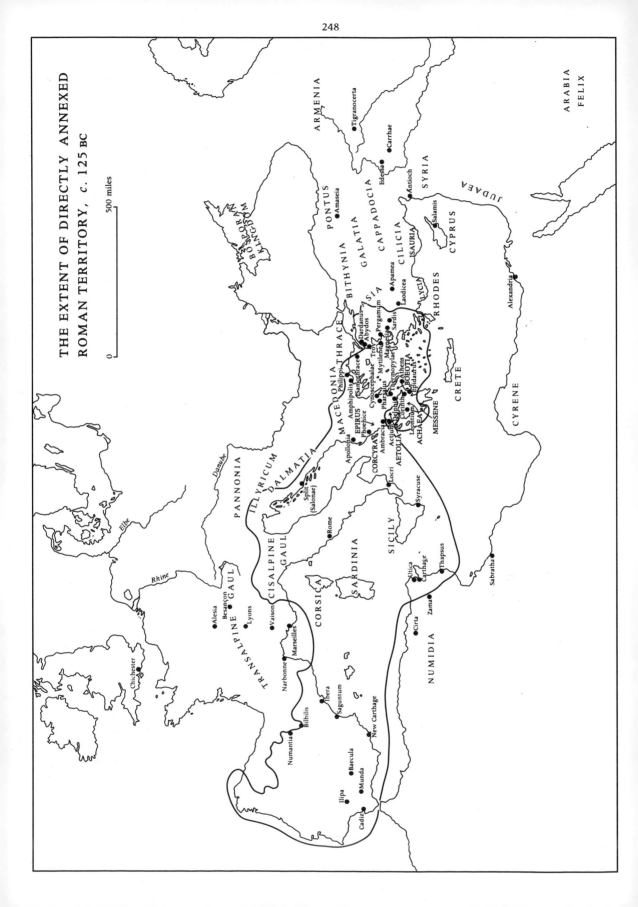

THE EXTENT OF DIRECTLY ANNEXED
ROMAN TERRITORY, c. 125 BC

0   500 miles

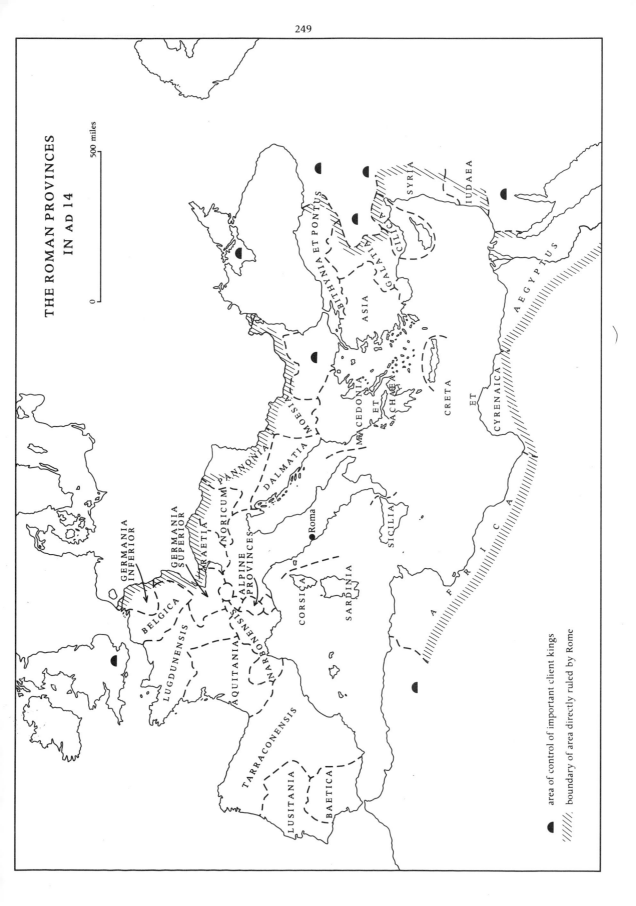

THE ROMAN PROVINCES
IN AD 14

500 miles

0

GERMANIA
INFERIOR

GERMANIA
SUPERIOR

RAETIA

NORICUM

ALPINE
PROVINCES

BELGICA

LUGDUNENSIS

AQUITANIA

NARBONENSIS

TARRACONENSIS

LUSITANIA

BAETICA

CORSICA

SARDINIA

SICILIA

Roma

PANNONIA

DALMATIA

MOESIA

MACEDONIA
ET
ACHAEA

CRETA
ET
CYRENAICA

BITHYNIA ET PONTUS

GALATIA

ASIA

CILICIA

SYRIA

IUDAEA

AEGYPTUS

A F R I C A

area of control of important client kings

boundary of area directly ruled by Rome

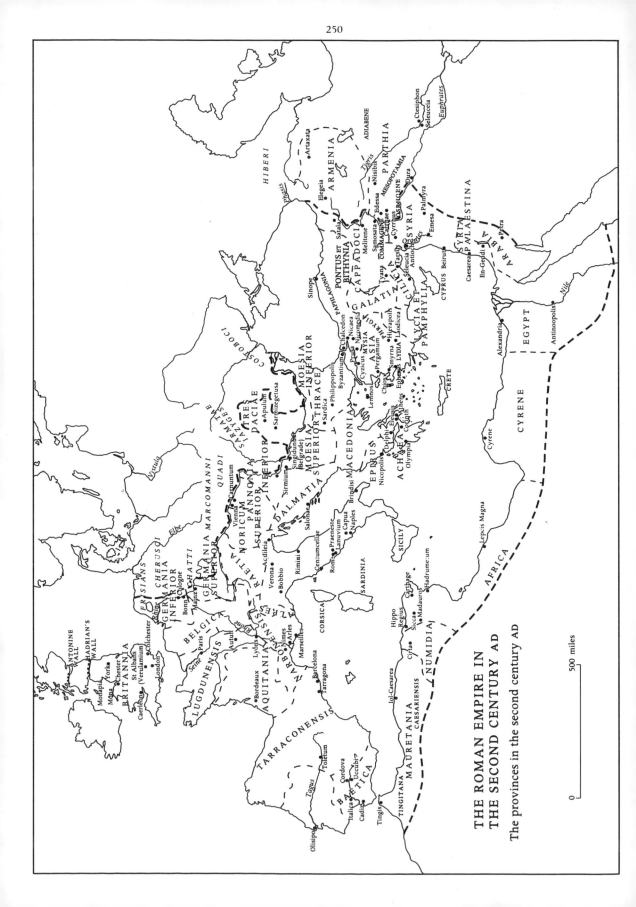

THE ROMAN EMPIRE IN
THE SECOND CENTURY AD

The provinces in the second century AD

500 miles

0

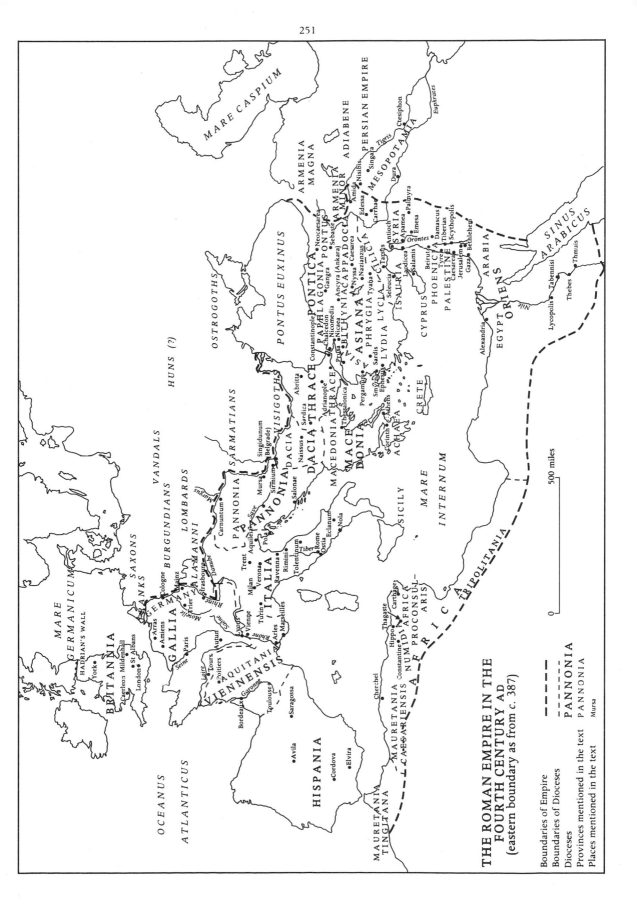

THE ROMAN EMPIRE IN THE FOURTH CENTURY AD
(eastern boundary as from c. 387)

Boundaries of Empire
Boundaries of Dioceses
Dioceses · **PANNONIA**
Provinces mentioned in the text · PANNONIA
Places mentioned in the text · Mursa

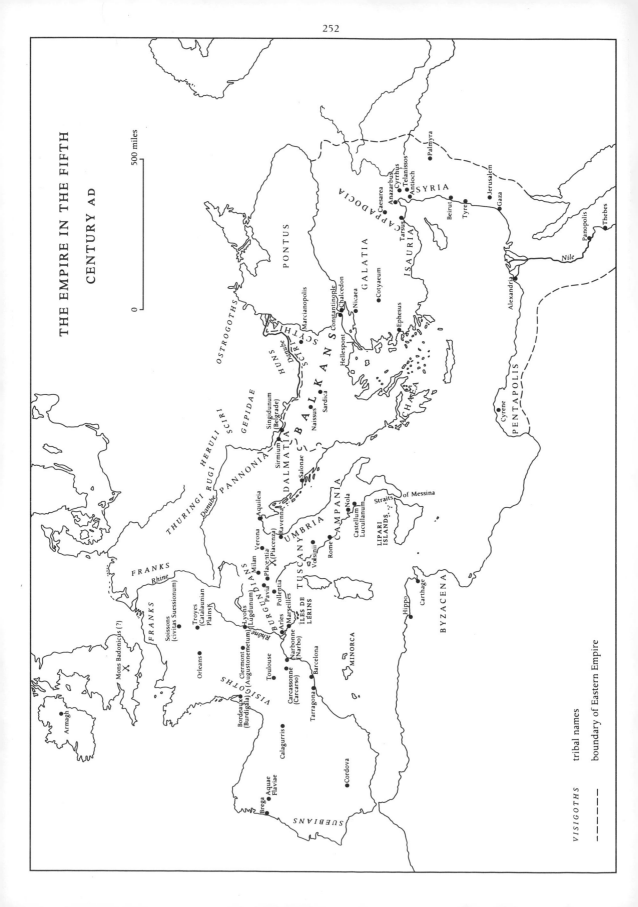

THE EMPIRE IN THE FIFTH CENTURY AD

500 miles

0

tribal names VISIGOTHS

- - - - - boundary of Eastern Empire

PONTUS

OSTROGOTHS

SCYTHIA

HUNS

SCIRI

Danube

GALATIA

CAPPADOCIA

ISAURIA

SYRIA

Anazarbus
Caesarea
Cyrrhus
Telanissos
Antioch
Tarsus

Palmyra

Beirut
Tyre
Jerusalem
Gaza

Nile

Panopolis
Thebes

Alexandria

Marcianopolis
Constantinople
Chalcedon
Nicaea
Cotyaeum

Ephesus

Hellespont

ACHAEA

Cyrene

PENTAPOLIS

BALKANS

Singidunum (Belgrade)
Sirmium
Salonae
Naissus
Sardica

GEPIDAE

HERULI

SCIRI

RUGI

THURINGI

PANNONIA

Danube

DALMATIA

Aquileia
Verona
Milan
Pavia
Placentia (Piacenza)
Ravenna
Pollentia

UMBRIA

TUSCANY

CAMPANIA

Nola
Castellum
Lucullanum
Rome
Volsinii

Straits of Messina

LIPARI
ISLANDS

FRANKS

Rhine

FRANKS

Mons Badonicus (?)

Soissons (civitas Suessionum)
Troyes
Catalaunian
Plains
Orleans

Clermont
Lyons (Lugdunum)
BURGUNDIANS
Arles
Marseilles
ÎLES DE
LÉRINS
Narbonne (Narbo)

VISIGOTHS

Toulouse
Carcassonne (Carcaso)
Bordeaux (Burdigala)
Barcelona
Tarragona

MINORCA

Calagurris

Cordova

Armagh

Brega
Aquae
Flaviae

SUEBIANS

Hippo

Carthage

BYZACENA

253

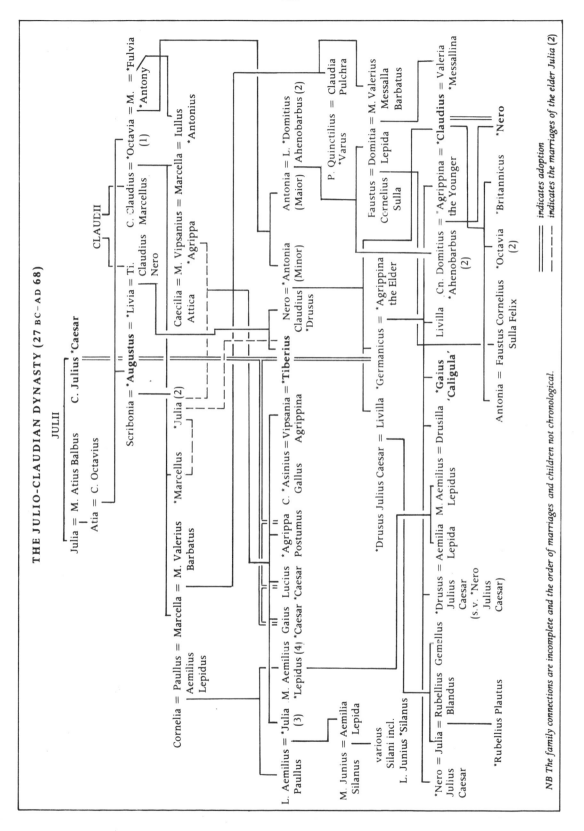

THE JULIO-CLAUDIAN DYNASTY (27 BC–AD 68)

NB The family connections are incomplete and the order of marriages and children not chronological.

indicates adoption
indicates the marriages of the elder Julia (2)

254

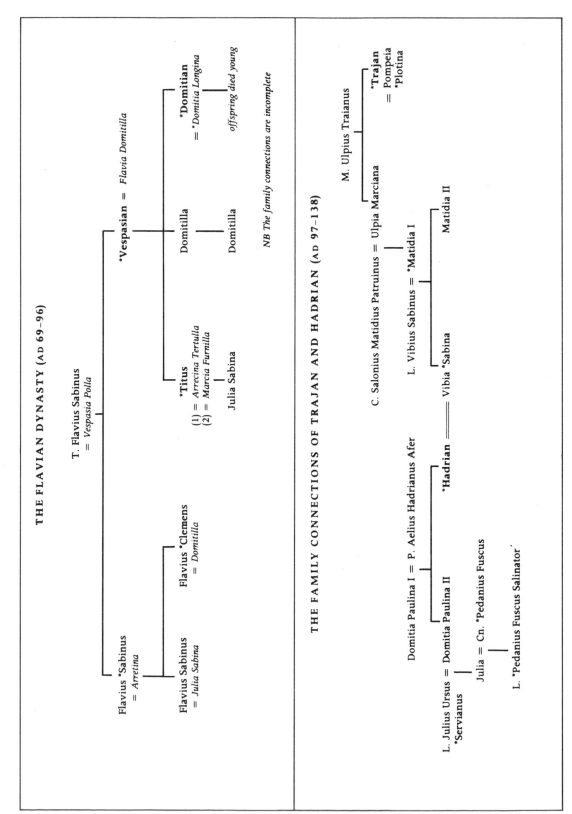

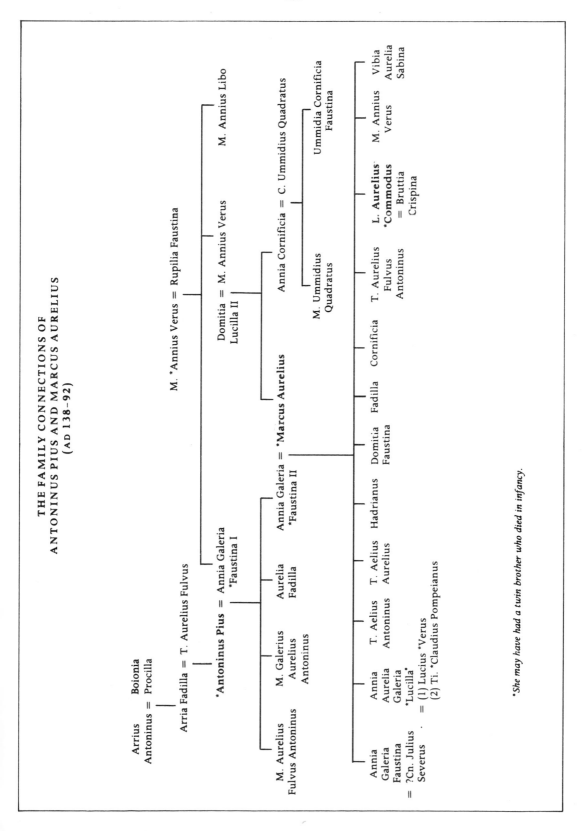

THE FAMILY CONNECTIONS OF
ANTONINUS PIUS AND MARCUS AURELIUS
(AD 138–92)

*She may have had a twin brother who died in infancy.

256

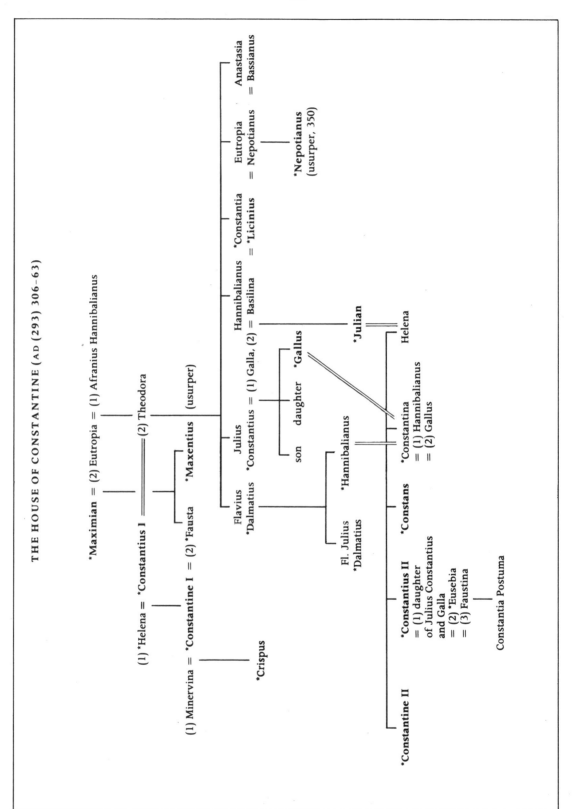

THE HOUSE OF CONSTANTINE (AD (293) 306–63)